South Carolina Women

South Carolina Women

THEIR LIVES AND TIMES

Volume 3

EDITED BY

Marjorie Julian Spruill, Valinda W. Littlefield,

and Joan Marie Johnson

The University of Georgia Press   *Athens and London*

© 2012 by the University of Georgia Press

Athens, Georgia 30602

www.ugapress.org

All rights reserved

Set in Minion by Graphic Composition, Inc.

Printed digitally in the United States of America

The Library of Congress has catalogued the first volume of this book as follows:

South Carolina women : their lives and times /

edited by Marjorie Julian Spruill,

Valinda W. Littlefield,

and Joan Marie Johnson.

p. cm.

Includes bibliographical references and index.

ISBN-13: 978-0-8203-2935-2 (hardcover : alk. paper)

ISBN-10: 0-8203-2935-5 (hardcover : alk. paper)

ISBN-13: 978-0-8203-2936-9 (pbk. : alk. paper)

ISBN-10: 0-8203-2936-3 (pbk. : alk. paper)

1. Women—South Carolina—Biography.

2. South Carolina—Biography.

I. Spruill, Marjorie Julian, 1951–

II. Littlefield, Valinda W., 1953–

III. Johnson, Joan Marie.

CT3262.S65S68 2009

975.7′043082—dc22

[B]   200850102

Volume 3 ISBN-13: 978-0-8203-4214-6 (hardcover : alk. paper)

ISBN-10: 0-8203-4214-9 (hardcover : alk. paper)

ISBN-13: 978-0-8203-4215-3 (pbk. : alk. paper)

ISBN-10: 0-8203-4215-7 (pbk. : alk. paper)

British Library Cataloging-in-Publication Data available

To our children:

Scott Spruill Wheeler
Jesse Spruill Wheeler

Quentin Lemont Whitted

Darci Nicole Johnson
Sophie Danielle Johnson
Elise Corinne Johnson

And to the memory of
Harriet Keyserling
1922–2010
and
Constance Ashton Myers
1926–2012

Contents

Contents

Preface

The three volumes of *South Carolina Women: Their Lives and Times* highlight the long and fascinating history of the women of the Palmetto State, women whose stories have often been told as well as women whose lives warrant far more attention than they have received. The collection of essays is designed to enrich our understanding of the history of South Carolina and the nation as we examine the lives and times of the dozens of women whose stories appear within. The essays are intended to be of interest to a wide audience as well as useful to scholars at every level. For that reason we have chosen a "life and times" approach, through which the lives of individual women are explored within the context of time and place.

As editors we have not attempted to be inclusive: there are countless notable women in the history of the Palmetto State. Readers seeking information on these women should refer to *The South Carolina Encyclopedia*, edited by Walter B. Edgar.[1]

We do seek, however, to be representative, to include in these pages accounts of women from the Carolina Lowcountry, the Midlands, and Upstate; from all social classes; and from the many racial, ethnic, and religious groups that have made the history of South Carolina so full and rich. The women featured in the three volumes range from the well known to the largely forgotten and were involved in many different occupations. They include, among others, a Native American queen, a Catholic mother superior, an entrepreneurial farmwife, a NASCAR driver, and a Supreme Court justice. There are enslaved women and slave mistresses, free black women and poor white women, black and white civil rights activists. Some of these women are quite famous, having earned distinction in a wide variety of areas. Many were pathbreakers for their sex. Others led quiet, even ordinary lives, serving their families and society in ways that were fairly typical and that rendered their stories quite obscure though no less meaningful. Most lived in an era when prevailing customs dictated that women were not to play public roles or to engage significantly in activities beyond home and family, a time when a respectable woman's name appeared in the papers only in the announcement of her engagement or in her obituary. A proper woman, it was said, did not seek the limelight.

Thus we have the saying "well-behaved women seldom make history," which is true all too often—although not always—in South Carolina.[2] Most of these women were "well behaved" and well respected even in their times, though some created considerable controversy—a few to the point that they felt they needed to leave the state. For the most part, however, those who were social critics and who sought to reform their society seemed to navigate South Carolina and southern culture—with all its restrictions on the lives of women—in such a way that they lived comfortably or at least quietly among fellow South Carolinians—even as they fostered change through their ideas and actions. For some, the ability to so navigate was the key to their success. This was of course easiest to do if a woman was from the white elite, protected by racial and class privilege and influential relations. The South Carolina women who were reformers and African American had the most to protest and the least protection but still won great admiration in many circles and, at least in the late twentieth century, managed to prevail.

As we began the task of collecting essays for this project, we anticipated publishing only one volume. As we learned, however, of more and more women whose stories we wanted to tell and found more and more talented scholars interested in writing about them, the project soon grew to three volumes. And still, there are countless South Carolina women whose stories are also compelling and enlightening and awaiting the attention of future scholars.

The history of women in South Carolina has grown along with the field of women's history. Early books on southern women, including Julia Cherry Spruill's *Women's Life and Work in the Southern Colonies* (1938), did not focus on South Carolina in particular but included them.[3] This was also true of the work of pioneering historian Mary Elizabeth Massey, who spent much of her distinguished career at South Carolina's Winthrop College and whose work, especially *Bonnet Brigades: American Women and the Civil War* (1966), was an enormous contribution.[4] South Carolina women also appeared prominently in Anne Firor Scott's *The Southern Lady: From Pedestal to Politics, 1830–1930* (1970), which established southern women's history as a field.[5] This book was particularly important given the fact that the outpouring of scholarship on American women that accompanied the success of the modern women's movement focused principally on women in the Northeast with its highly influential regional culture, the area where the women's movement originated and was most successful and where many of the scholars in the emerging field of women's history lived and worked.

Just as much of the early work in women's history focused on elite white women, so too did the work on South Carolina women. Women of the planter class received considerable attention as did the middle- and upper-class white women who were most prevalent in the campaign for women's rights. The publication of Gerda Lerner's award-winning biography, *The Grimké Sisters from South Carolina: Rebels against Authority* (1967), about two extraordinary women who were born to an elite white slaveholding family but were among the earliest leaders of both the antislavery movement and the women's movement in America, directed attention to the South and especially to the Palmetto State.[6] C. Vann Woodward's edition of the Civil War diary of South Carolinian Mary Chesnut (1981), for which he won the Pulitzer Prize, Elisabeth Showalter Muhlenfeld's biography of Chesnut (1981), and later, Thavolia Glymph's award-winning essay "African-American Women in the Literary Imagination of Mary Boykin Chesnut" (2000) also brought South Carolina women into the public eye.[7] South Carolina women who participated in the campaign for woman suffrage also attracted early attention, beginning with A. Elizabeth Taylor's articles on the movement in the state published in the 1970s, and continuing with important work by Barbara Bellows, Sidney Bland, and others.[8]

From these important beginnings, women's history, including the history of women in South Carolina, has broadened as it has flourished. The last fifteen years have produced an impressive array of scholarship on a diversity of women and subjects. We now know more about South Carolina plantation mistresses and even poor white women. Cara Anzilotti, Barbara Bellows, and Jane H. Pease and William H. Pease have examined the lives of slaveholding women, while Stephanie McCurry's important work has provided valuable insights regarding gender and the state's yeoman class.[9]

We also know much more about the African American women whose labors supported the plantation mistresses and who were largely excluded from the suffrage movement. The outpouring of new scholarship on black women in South Carolina is as welcome as it is overdue; after all South Carolina long had a black majority and continues to have one of the highest concentrations of African Americans in the United States. Marli Weiner, Cynthia Kennedy, Emily West, and Julie Saville unearthed important details of slave women's lives, labors, and loves. Thavolia Glymph has examined the relationship between white women slaveholders and enslaved African American women, revealing much about each group as well as about the institution of slavery and its aftermath. Amrita Myers turned our attention to the free African American women of Charleston. Leslie Schwalm traced how African American women transformed their lives after the Civil War, defining freedom for themselves in work and family life during Reconstruction.[10] Joan Marie Johnson helped us to understand how middle-class African American clubwomen fought segregation and established social services for their community at the beginning of the twentieth century, while Voloria Kibibi Mack examined the relations between clubwomen and working women in her book on class relations among African American women in Orangeburg.[11] Significant work has also been produced about outstanding professional women, including, for example, the work of Darlene Clark Hine on Dr. Matilda Evans.[12]

Racial identification was essential in both the slave South and the segregated South and played a crucial role in the lives of all South Carolina women. In a state where proslavery defenders dominated antebellum political life, where an African American majority was violently disfranchised and subjected to Jim Crow and economic deprivation, and where whites were so determined to avoid school integration that they voted to remove responsibility for public education from the state constitution as a potential means of avoiding it, choices for black women were quite limited. Yet the large urban population in Charleston, which included a substantial number of both slaves and free African Americans, made it possible for some black women to create financial independence for themselves. Neither the imposition of segregation nor the violence of lynching stopped South Carolina's black clubwomen and professionals from seeking to improve African American living conditions and challenging the state to provide more substantial resources in education and health.

White women, too, were constrained by the system, and slaveholding mistresses rarely opposed slavery even if they complained privately about its injustice or inconveniences to them. The extraordinary Grimké sisters, who left Charleston and became abolitionists, lived out their lives in exile in the North. Even those women who were sometimes considered outsiders because of their religion, like the Quaker Mary Fisher or the Catholic mother superior Ellen Lynch, did not renounce slavery. White suffragists, including Eulalie Salley and Emma Dunovant, fought for their own enfranchisement while accepting the disfranchisement of African Americans: like most white suffrage leaders in the region, they either favored disfranchisement or knew their cause would be doomed if they allied it with the cause of black suffrage.

Yet by the 1930s and 1940s, conditions in the state had changed to the point that several white women were willing and able to challenge racial oppression in several different ways. Two such women were Hilla Sheriff, a white public health professional who sought to empower and educate black midwives, and Wil Lou Gray, who extended her adult education program to reach African Americans. The white women were often inspired by African American women, including some who had been toiling quietly to raise money and improve conditions, and some who were already active in the early phase of the modern civil rights movement, including Modjeska Simkins and Septima Clark. The citizenship schools Clark developed and the schoolteacher equalization salary movement in which Simkins was a leader were part of what recent scholars have called the "long civil rights movement." One of the earliest white women of South Carolina to work along with African American leaders to end segregation was Alice Buck Norwood Spearman Wright, executive director of the biracial South Carolina Council on Human Relations from 1954 to 1967, a woman deeply committed to advancing civil rights for African Americans.

This collection also emphasizes that many women, even in this most conservative of states with its strong emphasis on traditional gender roles, took on very public roles. From the Lady of Cofitachequi, a Native American woman of considerable political power in the 1500s, to Jean Toal, the current state supreme court chief justice, women in South Carolina have a long tradition of influencing local and national affairs. During times of war, women, including Rebecca Motte of Revolutionary War fame, Lucy Pickens and Mary Chesnut of the Civil War era, and the Delk sisters, Julia and Alice, who worked in the Charleston Navy Yard during World War II, demonstrated the ability of women on the home front not only to follow political developments but also to affect them through their willingness to work and sacrifice for a cause.

When social reformers in the late nineteenth and early twentieth century began to make public speeches, lobby legislatures, and advocate woman suffrage, they were careful to disarm critics with their manners and charm. African American reformers in particular had to maintain a reputation of virtue and refinement owing to the negative stereotypes of African American women's character. Given the importance South Carolinians attached to family, women like the Poppenheims, the Pollitzers, Susan Frost, and Marion Birnie Wilkinson legitimized some of their activism simply by the power of who they were. This attention to character, deportment, and family name continued to serve white women who broke with convention and advocated for African Americans in the 1940s and 1950s. Women without wealth or high social status, however, also broke barriers, including Polly Woodham, a leader among farmers, and Louise Smith, who was a female pioneer in the unlikely field of NASCAR racing.

Women in politics, especially those who wished to run for office, faced particular challenges in South Carolina, where many equated leadership with maleness, saw the aggressiveness and confidence politics called for and a willingness to be in the limelight as unladylike, and expected women to remain in a supporting role. Mary Gordon Ellis, the first female state senator, received little recognition during her lifetime. Since the 1970s, women who broke barriers have received a bit more support and appreciation, though not enough to encourage large numbers to seek political leadership in the state.

As South Carolina entered the twenty-first century, it continued to trail the other fifty states in the numbers of women who had won statewide elective office. Only one woman, Nancy Stevenson, had been elected as lieutenant governor (serving 1979–82) and none as governor. That Jean Hoefer Toal had been appointed as the chief justice of the South Carolina Supreme Court was for women of the state a point of pride. Then, in 2009, a second woman, Justice Kaye G. Hearn, was appointed to the state supreme court. And in 2010, Nikki Haley, a state legislator from Lexington, surprised many in the state and nation by capturing the Republican nomination for governor and then winning the general election. Her victory was hailed as a particularly dramatic departure from the politics of South Carolina's past as she was not only a woman and a mother of two small children but also of Indian descent—the daughter of Sikhs (she was born Nimrata Randhawa) who emigrated to the United States from the Indian state of Punjab in 1963. Many South Carolina women hope that Haley's election will inspire other women in the state to seek elective office.

The essays in this three-volume collection help us to understand the ways that South Carolina women have been similar to and different from other women in the South and indeed the nation. They allow us to understand the complex roles that gender played in the lives of women from many different backgrounds and ethnicities as well as the varying contributions and experiences of women in the history of the Palmetto State.

As we complete the last volume of this three-volume anthology, we realize that there are so many wonderful stories left untold. Therefore we hope that these three volumes will not only inform and inspire but also encourage further research and writing about the lives and times of South Carolina women.

Marjorie Julian Spruill
Valinda W. Littlefield
Joan Marie Johnson

NOTES

1. Walter B. Edgar, ed. *The South Carolina Encyclopedia* (Columbia: University of South Carolina Press, 2006).

2. This phrase was coined by historian Laurel Thatcher Ulrich in a scholarly essay and then be-

gan to appear on countless T-shirts, bumper stickers, mugs, and so forth. As a result Ulrich decided to write a book about the phrase and its meaning (*Well-Behaved Women Seldom Make History* [New York: Knopf, 2007]).

3. Julia Cherry Spruill, *Women's Life and Work in the Southern Colonies* (Raleigh: University of North Carolina Press, 1938; rpt., New York: Norton, 1998).

4. Mary Elizabeth Massey, *The Bonnet Brigade: American Women and the Civil War* (New York: Knopf, 1966). See essay by Constance Ashton Myers on Massey in this volume, 135–53.

5. Anne Firor Scott, *The Southern Lady: From Pedestal to Politics, 1830–1930* (1970; rpt., Charlottesville: University Press of Virginia, 1995).

6. Gerda Lerner, *The Grimké Sisters from South Carolina: Rebels Against Slavery* (1967; rpt., Chapel Hill: University of North Carolina Press, 2004).

7. *Mary Chesnut's Civil War*, ed. C. Vann Woodward (New Haven, Conn.: Yale University Press, 1981); Elisabeth Muhlenfeld, *Mary Boykin Chesnut: A Biography* (Baton Rouge: Louisiana State University Press, 1981). See also Mary Boykin Chesnut, *The Private Mary Chesnut: The Unpublished Civil War Diaries*, ed. C. Vann Woodward and Elisabeth Muhlenfeld (New York: Oxford University Press, 1984), and Thavolia Glymph, "African American Women in the Literary Imagination of Mary Boykin Chesnut," in *Slavery, Secession, and Southern History*, ed. Louis Ferleger and Robert Paquette (Charlottesville: University Press of Virginia, 2000).

8. A. Elizabeth Taylor, "South Carolina and the Enfranchisement of Women: The Early Years," *South Carolina Historical Society Magazine* 77, no. 2 (1976): 115–26; A. Elizabeth Taylor, "South Carolina and the Enfranchisement of Women: The Later Years," *South Carolina Historical Magazine* 80, no. 4 (1979): 298–309; Barbara Bellows Ulmer, "Virginia Durant Young: New South Suffragist" (master's thesis, University of South Carolina, 1979); Sidney R. Bland, "Fighting the Odds: Militant Suffragists in South Carolina," *South Carolina Historical Magazine* 82, no. 1 (1981): 32–43; Sidney R. Bland, *Preserving Charleston's Past, Shaping its Future: The Life and Times of Susan Pringle Frost* (Columbia: University of South Carolina Press, 1999).

9. Cara Anzilotti, *In the Affairs of the World: Women, Patriarchy and Power in Colonial South Carolina* (Westport, Conn.: Greenwood Press, 2002); Barbara Bellows, *Benevolence among Slaveholders: Assisting the Poor in Charleston* (Baton Rouge: Louisiana State University Press, 1993); Jane H. Pease and William H. Pease, *Ladies, Women, and Wenches: Choice and Constraint in Antebellum Charleston and Boston* (Chapel Hill: University of North Carolina, 1990); Stephanie McCurry, *Masters of Small Worlds: Yeoman Households, Gender Relations, and the Political Culture of the Antebellum South Carolina Low Country* (New York: Oxford University Press, 1995).

10. Marli F. Weiner, *Mistresses and Slaves: Plantation Women in South Carolina, 1830–1880* (Urbana: University of Illinois Press, 1998); Cynthia M. Kennedy, *Braided Relations, Entwined Lives: The Women of Charleston's Urban Slavery Society* (Bloomington: Indiana University Press, 2005); Emily West, *Chains of Love: Slave Couples in Antebellum South Carolina* (Urbana: University of Illinois Press, 2004); Julie Saville, *The Work of Reconstruction: From Slave to Wage Laborer in South Carolina 1860–1870* (New York: Cambridge University Press, 1996); Leslie A. Schwalm, *A Hard Fight for We: Women's Transition from Slavery to Freedom in South Carolina* (Urbana: University of Illinois Press, 1997); Thavolia Glymph, *Out of the House of Bondage: The Transformation of the Plantation Household* (New York: Cambridge University Press, 2008); Amrita Chakrabarti Myers, *Forging Freedom: Black Women and the Pursuit of Liberty in Antebellum Charleston* (Chapel Hill: University of North Carolina Press, 2011).

11. Joan Marie Johnson, "'How Would I Live without Loulie?' Mary and Louisa Poppenheim,

Activist Sisters in Turn-of-the-Century South Carolina," *Journal of Family History* 28, no. 4 (2003): 561–77; Joan Marie Johnson, *Southern Ladies, New Women: Race, Region and Clubwomen in South Carolina, 1890–1930* (Gainesville: University Press of Florida, 2004); Voloria Kibibi Mack, *Parlor Ladies and Ebony Drudges: African American Women, Class, and Work in a South Carolina Community* (Knoxville: University of Tennessee Press, 1999).

12. Darlene Clark Hine, "The Corporeal and Ocular Veil: Dr. Matilda A. Evans (1872–1935) and the Complexity of Southern History," *Journal of Southern History* 70, no. 1 (2004): 3–34. See essay by Hine on Evans in *South Carolina Women: Their Lives and Times*, vol. 2.

Acknowledgments

No book, but especially no three-volume anthology like this, is possible without a great deal of support. We would like to thank several people who were particularly helpful in selecting the subjects and essayists, including Walter Edgar, director of the Institute for Southern Studies at the University of South Carolina and editor of *The South Carolina Encyclopedia*, and Amy Thompson McCandless, dean of the Graduate School and associate provost for research at the College of Charleston and an associate editor for the section on women in the *Encyclopedia of South Carolina*. Robin Copp, Henry Fulmer, and Allen Stokes of the South Caroliniana Library also provided valuable suggestions as well as other forms of assistance, as did the *SCLC*'s Beth Bilderback, who helped us locate illustrations, and Nicholas Meriwether who helped us with oral histories. Herb Hartsook and Lori Schwartz of the South Carolina Political Collections also helped us a great deal. Elease Slaughter, African American Studies' graduate assistant, committed considerable time and effort during the final compilation stage of this volume. We are forever grateful to all of them.

We would like to thank several administrators at the University of South Carolina who have been generous with support at crucial junctures: Lawrence Glickman, History Department chair; Lacy Ford, former History Department chair and vice provost; Mary Anne Fitzpatrick, dean of the College of Arts and Sciences; and Harris Pastides, president.

It has been a pleasure working with the University of Georgia Press. We are especially grateful to Nancy Grayson, associate director and editor in chief, whose support for this anthology and the series of which it is a part has made this project possible. We are also thankful for the help provided by others at the press: Nicole Mitchell, Courtney Denney, Regan Huff, Derek Krissoff, John McLeod, David E. Des Jardines, Pat Allen, Samantha Knoll, Jon Davies, and Beth Sneed. Finally, we thank MJ Devaney for her meticulous copyediting and Robert Ellis for his skillful indexing.

As we indicated in the dedications to the two previous volumes, we are grateful to our mothers, Edna Whitley Spruill, Bessie M. Pearley, and Dorothy Infosino, for inspiring us, and to our husbands, Don H. Doyle, Dan Littlefield, and Don Johnson, for their encouragement. This volume is dedicated to our children Scott Spruill Wheeler and Jessie Spruill Wheeler; Quentin Lemont Whitted; Darci Nicole Johnson, Sophie Danielle Johnson, and Elise Corinne Johnson, and to the memory of Harriet Keyserling and Constance Ashton Myers.

As we complete the final volume of the anthology, we cannot help but think back to the meeting seven years ago when the three of us and Nancy Grayson met around Marjorie's dining room table and began planning this ambitious project. Three volumes, forty-seven essays, and 1082 pages later, *South Carolina Women: Their Lives and Times* is a reality. We continue to believe in its importance and are gratified by the response to it thus far. We have enjoyed working with one another as well as with the authors of the essays. We appreciate their talents, diligence, and patience.

Finally, we thank the South Carolina women whose lives inspired the essays, those who have passed away and those who are very much alive and with whom we look forward to celebrating.

Marjorie Julian Spruill
Valinda W. Littlefield
Joan Marie Johnson
January 2012

South Carolina Women

Introduction

MARJORIE JULIAN SPRUILL, VALINDA W. LITTLEFIELD,

AND JOAN MARIE JOHNSON

The period from 1920, when women won the right to vote, to the end of the twentieth century was a transformative era for women in American society. Dramatic events, including a major depression and a second world war, ushered in important social, economic, and political changes. In addition, through the civil rights movement and the women's rights movement, numerous Americans demanded and won still more changes, including significant reforms that created new opportunities for women. All of these developments had a significant impact on the lives and times of the South Carolina women profiled in this volume.

Volume 3 presents the stories of a diverse group of South Carolina women, black and white, from elite as well as humble origins. The women also represent a variety of religious backgrounds and political persuasions—liberal, moderate, and conservative—and the ever-widening array of activities and occupations in which twentieth-century South Carolina women were engaged. Their stories reflect many important developments in the history of their state, including remarkable changes that the women portrayed in these essays helped to bring about such as improvements in educational opportunities and living conditions for South Carolinians, long-overdue changes in race relations, and enhancement of the status of women, who found new opportunities for employment and participation in politics and government.

Progress came slowly and gradually and was dearly bought: in the period from 1920 to 2000, long-held assumptions about race and class and gender that shaped the lives of South Carolinians in the past continued to have a strong hold. Often, and not by coincidence, the most powerful people in the state were also those most hostile to change. As in the past, South Carolina women promoting reform, whether on behalf of others or for themselves, had to proceed carefully to convince or compel others to make changes. Looking back from the vantage point of today their actions at times appear cautious and measured. However, they were working within a social and political climate in which demanding more drastic changes could well have cost them their positions and thus the ability to bring about any change at all.

The South Carolina women discussed in this volume had far more opportunities for education than those whose stories appeared in the first two volumes. Some came from families that could easily afford to send their daughters to college. Others managed to become educated against great odds. Many received undergraduate degrees from colleges near home in South Carolina or other southern states. Some followed their undergraduate studies with graduate or professional studies, earning advanced degrees, including the JD, MA, MLS, MSW, MD, and the PhD. African American women often had to attend graduate school out of state. Although the University of South Carolina had briefly admitted black students during Reconstruction, it did not admit African Americans from 1880 until 1963. Armed with academic credentials, women increasingly began to enter professions in which they had been underrepresented for decades.

Like the women in volumes 1 and 2, the women appearing in volume 3 of *South Carolina Women* faced obstacles resulting from traditional ideas about gender. The traditional assumption that women belonged mainly in the domestic sphere was challenged but remained strong throughout most of the twentieth century, and the women who joined the labor force, especially those who entered careers unusual for women or ventured into the political arena, benefited greatly from the support of family and friends. Strong friendships with other women and supportive husbands were often vital elements of their success. The controversial nature of their activism led some of these women to have strained relations with family members or to lose friends.

Whenever possible these women promoted change without provoking controversy. They were well aware that they were operating within a social system with well-defined and traditional expectations about women's conduct and appearance. From the state's first woman senator, who in the 1920s insisted on wearing a hat in the legislature (where, in keeping with southern male traditions, men were prohibited from wearing them), to the advocates of the Equal Rights Amendment (ERA), who in the 1970s were adamant that women lobbying legislators wear dresses or skirts, the South Carolina women discussed in this volume believed it to be important to remain "ladylike" even as they redefined gender roles.

And they did indeed bring about important changes. Some of the earliest work done by these women focused on enhancing educational opportunities and improving living conditions in the state. In the 1920s and 1930s South Carolina women, black and white, made major contributions in each of these areas in a period marked by segregation and disfranchisement, growing economic challenges, inadequate state funding for education and public health especially for blacks, and high rates of illiteracy and infant and maternal mortality. Indeed throughout the rest of the century, the South Carolina women whose stories are told in volume 3 brought improved education and health to their state as teachers, educational administrators, health providers, social workers, leaders of voluntary associations, political activists, and elected officials.

Whereas earlier in the century, white and black women reformers worked separately, each addressing the needs of their own racial group, increasingly some white women began to try to improve educational, health, and other opportunities for African Americans and to work together with black women to create dialogues between whites and blacks and confront racial injustice. They did so through interracial organizations such as the Commission on Interracial Cooperation and the South Carolina Committee on Human Relations and through the difficult and slow process of integrating formerly all-white associations, including the League of Women Voters (LWV). While most of the white women whose stories are told in this volume did not end up as active supporters of direct action protests in the civil rights movement of the late 1950s and early 1960s, they were still strong voices for change at a time when few white South Carolinians were speaking out on race issues.

Thus one of the most striking revelations that the essays in this volume of *South Carolina Women: Their Lives and Times* provide is the breadth of interracial work being done by women in the state from the late 1920s through the 1950s. These decades have received more attention from scholars in recent years as several leading historians have urged us to reconsider our understanding of the modern civil rights movement, to think of it not only as the decade between the U.S. Supreme Court decision *Brown v. Board of Education* in 1954 and adoption of the Voting Rights Act of 1965 but also as a "long civil rights movement" that encompasses the decades preceding *Brown* and those following the landmark federal legislation. In South Carolina this wider angle leads to greater understanding of the role women played in the gradual and often halting process of improving race relations in the state.

Not surprisingly, these pioneering white women were at times condescending and limited in their vision. Many did not advocate desegregation but rather tried to improve conditions within the system. The African American women who are the subjects of essays in this volume often found it frustrating to work with them as well as with other whites who seemed to be on their side but also appeared overly cautious. Indeed these stories of South Carolina women illuminate the problems and achievements of the early civil rights movement. By the 1960s, both black and white activists confronted segregation more directly and unambiguously called for racial equality.

The essays about the women herein who supported themselves financially through paid positions in activist organizations also call attention to changing career opportunities and paths for women in South Carolina. Throughout the early twentieth century, there were relatively few careers open to women, and many who worked for wages went into teaching. However, the women discussed here often carved out their own opportunities and made contributions in many fields, including as doctors—a trend that would only grow through the rest of the twentieth century. Historians have long associated women's service during World War II with a significant increase in the number and proportion of working women, particularly married women and women with children. The experiences of the South Carolina women who were employed in the Charleston Navy Yard illuminate the opportunities as well as the difficulties women workers experienced during World War II. Despite the still widespread stereotypes of American women of the 1950s as suburban housewives and stay-at-home mothers, historians have shown that in reality the number of women in the paid labor force remained as high in the 1950s as it had been during the war and began to grow significantly in the decades following. Gradually they gained access to new and more lucrative types of employment.

Several of the women featured in this volume were among the pioneers who broke barriers and entered fields traditionally dominated by men, including stock car racing. They also include a college professor and scholar who became president of her highly conservative professional association, a union organizer who worked to place women in nontraditional jobs, and owners of a variety of businesses. One was a self-described "farmwife" who opened a horseback riding school, a cosmetics business, and a ladies' apparel store. Some women started businesses with other women, such as the state's first all-woman public relations and political consulting firm, an all-woman law firm, and a feminist bookstore. Others were employed by the state government. African American women broke occupational barriers related to both gender and race. One was a banker as well as a civil rights advocate employed by the NAACP. Another ran a millinery shop that employed four other African American women before she created a library for blacks in Charleston. A basket maker went from farm worker to artist and entrepreneur, adapting the traditional forms of Lowcountry baskets and inventing new ones. The diversity of experience of these South Carolina women underscores the breadth of new employment opportunities that were opening to women and that women were opening for themselves all over the nation.

Women also sought new political opportunities in the twentieth century. South Carolina women received the right to vote in 1920 by means of a federal amendment, though suffragists in the state could not persuade the legislature to ratify it. However, right away women began to seek additional means of exercising influence, including running for office. It has been no small task for women to overcome cultural barriers to women's participation in politics enough to be elected to office. Thus it is surprising that the first woman to be elected to the state senate (1928)—like our current governor—was a married woman with young children; this was highly unusual in that era when women officeholders were so often propelled into office by the deaths of husbands that politics was sometimes called "a widow's game." Another legislator profiled in this volume who ran for office for the first time when she was in her fifties went on to become one of the most effective legislators in the state in the twentieth century. Women also broke new ground in state politics in other ways: one was co-owner of a public relations firm specializing in political campaigns and the key strategist behind many leading politicians of the state, both Democrats and Republicans.

In the last decades of the twentieth century opportunities for women in employment and politics expanded dramatically in part as a result of the women's rights movement. New federal legislation was adopted that prohibited gender discrimination and gave unprecedented rights to American women regarding employment and education. However, it would take considerable pressure from women's organizations before American women received the full benefits of these reforms. Nowhere was that more true than in South Carolina. Women's rights advocates in the state organized to demand compliance and won important victories, some of them through the courts. Their successes resulted in greater pay equity and admission to more professions, including law and medicine. South Carolina women had made dramatic progress in these fields by the end of the century.

South Carolina women who fought for women's rights were not always successful. The essays in this volume describe defeats, including a failed campaign to gain the right for women to serve on juries. Most notable was the protracted struggle between 1972 and 1982 for ratification of the ERA, which fell three states short of the number required for it to be added to the U.S. Constitution. Some of the South Carolina women discussed in this volume were leaders of the pro-ERA forces and were dismayed at the failure of their ratification campaign. However, they were still highly effective champions of the women's rights movement and helped bring about many other changes that enhanced the status of women in the state. In addition to obtaining greater opportunities in employment and education, they also pushed lawmakers to reform laws and policies regarding rape and domestic violence. Their influence—and that of the many other advocates for women's rights in South Carolina in the 1970s—is still felt today.

Volume 3 begins with several essays examining the efforts of African American and white women, who in the 1920s through the 1950s made small but significant attempts to work together to improve social and economic conditions for black South Carolinians. In the first essay, historian Valinda W. Littlefield discusses two African American teachers, Ruby Forsythe and Fannie Phelps Adams. As Littlefield points out, economic necessity compelled large numbers of African American women to work outside their homes. Both race and gender kept most of them in traditionally female occupations, in fields, factories, and in the homes of others. Of the positions open to them, working in the schoolhouse was, perhaps, the most desirable. African American teachers, including Forsythe and Adams, used their positions to create better lives for themselves and their communities. Moreover, Forsythe's and Adams's stories demonstrate how women teachers conceived of their work as essential to fighting racial oppression. They were part of the vanguard whose work created the foundation for a modern civil rights movement. Their teaching strategies played a major role in fostering the emergence of a larger arena of protest. Littlefield argues that instilling knowledge, dignity and self-awareness against mental and spiritual boundaries imposed by a Jim Crow system was a prerequisite for any form of collective and political activism.

The schools in which Forsythe and Adams taught received little support from the state government, which disproportionately funded white schools and neglected black education. South Carolina's first female state legislator, Mary Gordon Ellis, was a rare white politician who was willing to risk her political career to obtain better educational opportunities for black children. As described by political scientist Carol Botsch, Ellis was elected to the state senate in 1928, only eight years after women received the right to vote. She first exhibited an interest in politics as a child, sneaking into the county courthouse to listen to cases being tried there. After receiving her college degree at Winthrop, Ellis taught public school in Jasper County. Appalled by the deficiencies of the local school system, she sent her own children to Savannah for their education. Believing that schools that were not good enough for her children were not good enough for other children, she ran for county school superintendent in 1924. In this position she consolidated schools and won funding from the Rosenwald Fund to build additional schools for African American children. When she tried to obtain buses for black children, her position as the elected superintendent was abolished and replaced with an appointed position: she was therefore fired. In response, Ellis ran for state senate—and won—against the representative who had engineered her dismissal. In that position she continued to work to improve education, especially for African Americans. According to Botsch, she was motivated by a sense of fairness and independence and was very effective. That she projected a traditionally feminine image—in the senate she gave few speeches and insisted on wearing a hat—helped her work with male colleagues.

Soon after Ellis challenged the injustices of segregation in the school system, Wil Lou Gray and Julia Peterkin also challenged what historian Mary Mac Ogden calls "the dominant regional narrative of black racial inferiority." Wil Lou Gray was a white educator and social reformer who tried to eradicate illiteracy among black and white adults, while Julia Peterkin was a white novelist who portrayed African Americans sympathetically in her books. While neither confronted segregation itself, each pushed white South Carolinians to rethink some of their assumptions about black life. Both came from prosperous families in the town of Laurens and were educated at South Carolina colleges, Peterkin at Converse College and Gray at Columbia College. Their lives diverged when Peterkin married and became mistress of a large former plantation in the southern part of the state. In her novel *Scarlet Sister Mary*, for which she was awarded the 1929 Pulitzer Prize, Peterkin featured a black female heroine who survives hardships through her tenacity and wisdom. Though her work has been criticized for racial stereotyping, at the time Peterkin was praised for capturing the reality of black life in South Carolina in that era. Gray, as supervisor of adult education in South Carolina, ran summer "opportunity schools" for adults. In 1931, she conducted an experiment in which she ran simultaneous schools, one for whites at Clemson and one for blacks at Seneca, aiming to determine if there was a difference in learning abilities between whites and blacks when given equal opportunity. The results showed that blacks were just as capable of learning as whites, helping her gain the funding she required to continue to offer adult education opportunities to blacks throughout the state.

From the 1930s through the 1940s physician Hilla Sheriff, born in Pickens County, South Carolina, addressed another problem confronting impoverished and segregated African Americans, the need for better health care, particularly in regard to childbirth. Faced with state officials averse to funding facilities for African Americans and hospitals unwilling to serve them, Sheriff, who headed the state board of health's Division of Maternal and Child Health, sought an alternative means of delivering better care to them within South Carolina's segregated society. She decided to focus on training African American midwives. Historian Patricia Evridge Hill contends that the program Sheriff created may have been at odds with her other efforts to modernize medicine in the state, but she made a pragmatic choice that resulted in better health-care delivery to many rural African Americans. Sheriff worked closely with several African American midwives who designed and directed much of the training. She treated them with respect: she symbolically took down a curtain separating black midwives from white public health nurses at the sessions and provided opportunities for all of the participants to interact over meals, challenging segregation at least in this setting.

World War II had a transformative effect on women throughout the nation, including Julia and Alice Delk. As the nation turned to women workers during the war, the Delks seized the opportunity to escape from the limitations of life in rural South Carolina and to earn higher wages. They moved from Orangeburg to Charleston, where they worked as welders, motivated not only by better pay and more excitement but also by their sense of patriotic duty. Their story illustrates how hard American women worked in these unaccustomed and often dangerous tasks, well aware of the importance of their work to the success of the war effort. The nation turned to women to provide labor for "the duration" but then turned them out of those jobs after the war, despite a record of successful performance on the job. But the work of these women, symbolized by the iconic "Rosie the Riveter," had shown the nation and the women themselves that women could do "men's work." Historian Fritz P. Hamer recounts how the experience opened new worlds to women, many of whom would soon return to the workforce.

Louise Smith also entered defense work during World War II, briefly leaving South Carolina to work in an airplane factory on the West Coast. Shortly after her return home to Greenville, she drove in her first stock car race, fell in love with the speed and the excitement, and began to pursue a career as a driver. A fearless competitor, Smith was also a hard drinker off the course and was involved in several of the fights that often broke out among racers. Although many male drivers did not want to compete against her, she won them over with her driving ability and her daring. In 1956 she abruptly quit racing due to a call from a preacher who convinced her to abandon her wild ways and dedicate herself to charity and church. In 1971 she was drawn back into racing, though this time as a sponsor. Smith's highest honor was her induction into the International Motorsports Hall of Fame, the first woman ever to be selected. Historian Suzanne Wise argues that Smith succeeded in the male-dominated world of racing because she did not position herself as a woman but rather broke barriers on the strength of her talent and her will to succeed in the sport.

Mary Blackwell Baker also worked in a male-dominated field: labor organizing. Born to textile workers in Aiken County, she worked in a dye plant for two years before launching a small restaurant with her husband that catered to mill workers. When they closed the restaurant, Mary took a job with a unionized food service contractor and found her life's calling in the labor movement. She served as secretary-treasurer, bookkeeper, and/or delegate to five different unions and helped organize and place workers at many different plants in and around Aiken County. Historian Constance Ashton Myers argues that Baker's fierce dedication to unions was forged in her youth when her parents and other workers were locked out of the Warrenville mill and Baker witnessed the crucial impact that unions had on the daily life and the survival of her family and community. Her passion for justice also led her to work against both racial and gender oppression. She later took a job with the National Urban League assisting African Americans with employment placement and worked with the National Organization for Women (NOW) to help place women in industrial jobs such as welding. Her loyalty to the union and to the Catholic Church in a community where neither was popular demonstrated her willingness to work for what she believed in despite local opposition.

Susie Dart Butler and Ethel Martin Bolden also linked their desire for justice with their work for better employment opportunities. They sought to provide improved library services to African Americans in Charleston and Columbia and, in the process, secured for themselves professional opportunities. Historian Georgette Mayo points out that limited options for black teachers in Charleston compelled Butler to open a millinery business and a private school. When a student approached her asking for books to read and a space to read them in, Butler was inspired to embark on a new career as a librarian. She soon opened a reading room in her father's former school, which, through Butler's work with the Charleston Interracial Commission, eventually became the black branch of the Charleston public library. Like Butler, Ethel Bolden, a graduate of Johnson C. Smith College in Charlotte, understood that libraries provided educational benefits crucial to race uplift. As an elementary school teacher she assisted in opening the first library in a black elementary school in Columbia. Pushed to obtain a library science degree, Bolden had no choice but to move to Atlanta for two years, as there was no accredited program for African

Americans in South Carolina. Ultimately, she helped to desegregate Columbia's public schools, working as a librarian at the formerly all-white Dreher High School: notably, at that time the school would hire an African American in a position such as a librarian but not as a teacher. Bolden also served dozens of civic, church, and corporate boards and worked through interracial associations to ease tensions associated with integration in Columbia. Butler and Bolden demonstrated the myriad ways in which African American women sought to improve education for African Americans, break racial barriers to professional jobs, and foster interracial dialogue.

Harriet Porcher Stoney Simons, from an elite white Charleston family, first became interested in interracial cooperation in the 1930s through her work on the Urban League Survey Committee, which surveyed housing and education conditions for African Americans. She also started a birth control clinic in Charleston that served both black and white clients. She then helped revive the League of Women Voters of South Carolina (LWVSC), over which she presided during several controversial episodes related to race issues in the late 1940s and 1950s. With Simons as president, the organization campaigned against a state amendment that gave South Carolina the option to close public schools rather than desegregate, and she fought unsuccessfully for women to be allowed to serve on juries, a goal attained by South Carolina women in 1969. She also presided over the initial steps toward integrating the league itself. Historian Jennifer E. Black describes Simons as a dedicated community servant trying to improve conditions and promote justice in her state in an era marked by heightened racial tensions. Simons was a talented leader, relatively progressive for her times, who tried to promote change without arousing opposition that would prevent her and the LWVSC from continuing to function. Black concludes that Simons achieved much through her pragmatic approach. The challenges Simons faced while trying to improve her city and state, promote better race relations, and expand women's rights reflected those frequently encountered by southern women reformers that imposed limits to what they could accomplish.

Alice Spearman Wright demonstrated that a more daring and uncompromising approach to civil rights was possible for white women, though she too faced strong opposition. According to historian Marcia G. Synnott, Wright was willing to forge relationships with African American leaders including Ella Baker and others who were considered far more radical than the elite black women of Charleston with whom Simons worked. While at Converse College, Wright had joined the interracial committee of the YWCA. As executive director of the biracial South Carolina Council on Human Relations from 1954 to 1967, she forged connections among national, state, and local civil rights activists, between white and black supporters of the movement, and between the council and white politicians and businessmen. She also mentored college students and helped prepare the way for desegregation at Clemson and the University of South Carolina. Typically wearing a hat and gloves, Wright may have appeared to be an unlikely radical, but she astonished many South Carolinians when she introduced Martin Luther King Jr. at a rally in the state. Like Mary Gordon Ellis, Wil Lou Gray, Hilla Sheriff, Harriet Simons, and others, Wright worked with African Americans to improve conditions for the race; unlike the others, Wright was willing to confront segregation directly and to support direct action civil rights protests in the mid-1960s.

Among the African American civil rights activists with whom Alice Spearman Wright worked were two nationally known women, Modjeska Simkins and Septima Clark. Born in Columbia and educated at Benedict College, Simkins began working for the South Carolina Tuberculosis Association, but her membership in the NAACP and her efforts to improve African American health care were deemed too extreme, and she was fired in 1942. Ironically, this allowed Simkins more time to work with the NAACP, and, as historian Cherisse Jones-Branch makes clear, Simkins became one of the most important leaders of the civil rights movement in South Carolina. She raised funds and provided support for three crucial legal battles: the teacher pay equalization campaign; the challenge to the white primaries and the all-white Democratic Party in the state; and *Briggs v. Elliot*, a school segregation case which became part of the *Brown v. Board of Education* decision. Realizing the economic repercussions for African Americans who registered to vote and sent their children to integrated schools, Simkins solicited donations and worked with her brother, the president of the Victory Savings Bank, to secure loans and other assistance for civil rights activists. Ultimately purged from the NAACP in 1957 because of her ties to organizations and individuals linked to communism, Simkins continued her activism in the 1960s and 1970s through the Richland County Citizens Committee, becoming an early advocate of environmental causes. Well aware of historic patterns of discrimination against women as well as African Americans, she also supported equal rights for women.

Like Simkins, Septima Clark also came to the civil rights movement in part through her focus on education issues, including a campaign demanding that black teachers be hired in black schools in Charleston and a statewide teacher pay equalization campaign. Historian Katherine Mellen Charron argues that it was as a teacher that Clark learned to adapt education to the needs of students, especially adult students, a technique that would later guide her in creating a key program of the civil rights movement, Citizenship Schools. Once Clark came to the decision to work for full integration of African Americans, she attended the Highlander Folk School in Tennessee. There the staff prepared individuals who would lead the movement for integration, teaching them to empower ordinary people to define their needs and develop programs to meet them. Like Simkins, Clark was fired from her job because of her membership in the NAACP. Like Simkins, it only spurred her on to more activism; she took a job with Highlander, where she designed the Citizenship School program that employed black women to teach other blacks to read, based on the idea that political literacy had to start with actual literacy. Ultimately, the program was transferred to the Southern Christian Leadership Conference (SCLC), where Clark worked until 1970. The Citizenship Schools proved to be a crucial element in SCLC and other civil rights organizations' programs for training African Americans for registering to vote and challenging segregation.

While the civil rights movement was heating up in South Carolina, Mary Elizabeth Massey was fighting her own battles for inclusion—in her case, as a white woman in academia. After earning her PhD in history under Fletcher M. Greene at the University of North Carolina, Massey became a beloved professor at Winthrop University, teaching there from 1950 to 1974. Like other women academics of her time, Massey did not so much choose Winthrop as the small women's college chose her: as historian Constance Ashton Myers points out, Massey and her female colleagues did not receive offers from more prestigious research universities. But Massey was dedicated to her research and her profession and was active for many years in the Southern Historical Association (SHA), culminating with her becoming the association's third female president in 1972. Massey distanced herself from the more activist women she referred to as "the women's lib group" in the SHA and other historical associations. However she made a statement regarding her own feminist beliefs by delivering her presidential address on the life of Gertrude Thomas, a Georgia woman who lived through the Civil War and afterward overcame traditional gender limitations and became active in women's organizations, including the woman suffrage movement. Massey owed much of her success in the SHA to the quality of her scholarship which gained her great respect. Her most important contribution to the field was introducing historians to women's history and social history (the history of ordinary individuals) through her work, including her book *Ersatz in the Confederacy*, which argued that as male politicians and military leaders led the effort on the battlefields, women had to improvise on the home front in order to survive the deprivations of war.

It might be argued that the enterprising Polly Woodham was a twentieth-century version of the resourceful southern women of the nineteenth century that Massey often wrote about. According to historian Melissa Walker, Wood-ham, a Converse graduate, represented a new kind of farmwife who put her education to work as she established several small businesses, worked on behalf of farmers, and fulfilled her traditional domestic duties. In the 1940s and 1950s farming changed dramatically across the South as technological advancements allowed farmers to increase production and expand their operations at the same time that thousands of sharecroppers left the land. These changes meant that in the second half of the twentieth century, farm women's subsistence farming and egg and dairy production became less important, and farmwives often began to take "off-farm jobs" to help the family economy. In order to assist her family and follow her interests, Woodham taught school for several years, established a horse-breeding operation and riding academy, sold cosmetics, and opened a retail clothes store for women. In the 1970s she became involved in a new or-ganization, Women Involved in Farm Economics (WIFE), even testifying before Congress about conditions for farmers. The mix of Woodham's off-farm entre-preneurial jobs and her political activism on behalf of farmers illustrates the impact of changes in agriculture on women and families as it tells one woman's story about trying to save the family farm.

Like Polly Woodham, the farmer, entrepreneur, and artist Mary Jane Mani-gault also found her calling outside the fields. Born in 1913 near Charleston on land owned and farmed by African Americans who obtained it at the end of the Civil War, Manigault grew up picking crops and constructing coiled bas-kets, a tradition brought from Africa. She soon left the farm to make her way in Charleston, where she initially worked in a peanut factory. After marrying, she again worked the fields and made baskets until she got a job managing work crews at Boone Hall Plantation. She worked there until her children were grown. In 1962, she opened a basket stand on the highway outside Charleston, and her artistic ability and expression flourished. Her highly prized baskets in-fluenced other basket makers. Anthropologist Kate Porter Young shows how Manigault actively sought to expand the public's understanding and apprecia-tion of the craft and the tradition behind these beautiful baskets, originally used in processing rice in Africa.

By the time these entrepreneurial women were developing their businesses, Lottie "Dolly" Hamby was using her business acumen to build a leading public relations firm in Columbia that also gave her the opportunity to wield consider-able influence on South Carolina in a transitional era. After earning a master's degree in French from the University of South Carolina, Hamby worked in an ad-vertising agency before she and two associates established their own all-woman firm, Bradley, Graham, and Hamby. Ultimately she became the guiding force in political marketing campaigns run by her firm, beginning with the presidential campaign of Dwight D. Eisenhower in South Carolina. Hamby helped shape the responses of white political leaders to changing race relations, encouraged moderation, and worked with both Democratic and Republican candidates— guiding Republicans toward the success that made South Carolina a two-party state. Hamby steered her clients away from blatantly racist language and appeals. She recommended that they appeal to conservatives who opposed "big government" by calling for states' rights and local decision making rather than directly denouncing entitlement programs and civil rights legislation. Hamby warned that portraying themselves as extreme segregationists could cause them to lose the votes of moderate white voters as well as of African Americans who after 1965 constituted an increasingly significant block of voters in the state. Historian John W. White argues that Hamby's political sense was acute and candidates who refused to listen lost. Though she preferred to work behind the scenes, Hamby and her firm were well regarded by political leaders and envied by their competitors. She paved the way for women in a field new to women even as she had a tremendous impact on South Carolina and national political history.

Harriet Keyserling exerted political influence more directly than Hamby. As historian Page Putnam Miller tells us, Keyserling served as a state legislator for sixteen years, from 1976 to 1992. Born in New York and educated at Barnard College, Keyserling married a South Carolina doctor, moved to Beaufort in the 1940s, and remained there for the rest of her long life. Introduced to politics through her experiences supporting the arts and establishing a local chapter of the LWV, Keyserling first ran for county council in 1974. Two years later she won a seat in the state legislature where she was one of 10 women out of 124 members. There she became known as an advocate for advancing the arts and improving public education and the environment. She became active in the National Conference of State Legislatures (NCSL) and served as cochair of the organization's Women's Legislative Network. As a member of the NCSL's energy and arts committees she garnered ideas that became essential to her legislative agenda. Despite accusations that she was "un-American" and unconcerned about national defense, she worked to raise awareness of the dangers of South Carolina becoming a major dumping ground for the nation's nuclear waste, shrewdly presenting this as a states' rights issue as well as a health issue. She was widely regarded as one of the most capable and influential legislators in twentieth-century South Carolina. Ironically, Keyserling, a Democrat, had long encouraged women to run for office, but in 2010 opposed Nikki Haley, a Republican, in her race with Vince Sheheen to become governor, creating and leading "Women for Sheheen." Keyserling believed that Haley's policies were detrimental to many of the causes she had championed in her career. She died a month after Haley's election.

As women became more politically active, it was increasingly clear that not all women thought or voted the same way or supported the same policies. In the 1970s, women were divided in their response to the women's movement. Among the many South Carolina women who supported it were the five Columbia women whose stories are told here by historian Marjorie Julian Spruill. Through long-standing women's organizations, including the LWV and the National Organization for Women (NOW) in Columbia, a new organization founded specifically to support feminist goals, they worked to promote equal rights for women in the Palmetto State. While still a student at the University of South Carolina 's law school, Victoria Eslinger led the way: after being denied a lucrative job enjoyed by many a male law student as a page in the state legislature because of her sex, she sued the state and won. With Mary Heriot, a former army nurse who had served in the South Pacific and was indignant at the widespread employment discrimination against women in South Carolina, Eslinger founded a Columbia chapter of NOW in 1972. Eunice "Tootsie" Holland was also a founding member of NOW who went on to become a leader in the state NOW and a member of its national board. Lutricia "Pat" Callair, also a state and national NOW leader, had been involved in the NAACP and the Congress for Racial Equality (CORE) and found them both to be too male dominated. She became the most prominent African American feminist in the state. Keller Bumgardner Barron, a state and national leader in the LWV, was also a prominent women's rights advocate in South Carolina.

All of these women worked together in support of the ERA; like ERA supporters across the nation, they believed that the amendment would benefit women by making unconstitutional any legislation that discriminated on the basis of sex. However, many women in the state opposed the amendment; they maintained that it would deprive women of privileges, including the right to be supported by their husbands. The opposition of conservative women and that of powerful conservatives within state government led to the defeat of the amendment in South Carolina. Though they lost the fight over the ERA, in many other respects Palmetto State feminists were quite successful. In particular, they invoked federal laws calling for equal opportunities in employment to get newspapers to end their policy of gender-segregated want ads, cited Title IX (banning gender discrimination in education) to get officials at the University of South Carolina to give equal rights and privileges to its female students, notably in regard to sports, and pressed the state government to end discrimination against women in employment. They also worked to prevent unwanted pregnancies and to enable women to have more control over their reproductive lives. In addition, they demanded changes in laws regarding rape and violence against women and founded programs to help the victims as well as to prosecute such crimes more effectively and to prevent domestic violence.

Among those working for women's rights in South Carolina was a young lawyer named Jean Hoefer Toal, a native of Columbia and a graduate of Agnes Scott College and the University of South Carolina School of Law. Toal was Victoria Eslinger's attorney in her suit against the state after having been denied the job as a page in the state senate. Toal was joined on the appeal by another young woman lawyer, Ruth Bader Ginsberg, then with the Center for Study of Women and later the second woman to serve on the U.S. Supreme Court. Encouraged to run for a seat in the state house of representatives by the National Women's Political Caucus, Jean Toal followed its advice in 1974 and was elected. There she worked hard but in vain for ratification of the ERA. During the ERA fight, like Eslinger, Heriot, and Callair, she debated the leader of the national anti-ERA forces, Phyllis Schlafly. Unlike many in the women's rights movement, Toal, a Catholic, was opposed to abortion. Toal impressed many with her keen intellect, strong work ethic, and ability to work with others, even in the "old boy's club" atmosphere of the South Carolina legislature. Many were also impressed that she loved both football and making "scratch biscuits." Toal was elected to the Supreme Court of South Carolina, taking office in 1988. In 1999 the state legislature elected her as chief justice of the state supreme court. Toal's story, told by W. Lewis Burke, a professor at the University of South Carolina School of Law, and by Bakari T. Sellers, a University of South Carolina law graduate and a member of the state legislature, is situated within a long history of women's advancement in the legal profession in the state. Her selection as chief justice was celebrated by women of the state, particularly by those in her profession, who gathered on the steps of the supreme court on March 23, 2000, the day Toal was sworn in.

The photograph on the cover of volume 3 was taken on that day. It shows Chief Justice Toal surrounded by members of the South Carolina Women Lawyers Association, holding the traditional congratulatory bouquet of roses in one hand while giving a feminist celebratory salute with the other hand, and it speaks volumes. That moment of celebration at the end of one century and the beginning of another suggests the combined influence of tradition and modernity in the lives of South Carolina women. For many South Carolina women, including Chief Justice Toal, embracing their feminine as well as feminist side has allowed them to make their mark on South Carolina and, indeed, the nation.

Ruby Forsythe and Fannie Phelps Adams

Teaching for Confrontation during Jim Crow

VALINDA W. LITTLEFIELD

❀ ❀ ❀

African American children growing up in the Jim Crow South encountered white supremacist messages of black inferiority as they crowded into inadequate school buildings and read from secondhand books. But despite these gross inequalities, on a daily basis southern African American teachers taught their students how to resist that racist ideology. Teachers instilled in students a positive yet responsible view about one's place in the world that allowed them to think beyond the narrow boundaries of the color line. Teachers helped African American students to believe they were intelligent individuals with a rich history and heritage as they learned the value of respectability, racial uplift, and community service. By pointing out unequal power structures within the Jim Crow system, teachers both directly and indirectly motivated students to challenge an oppressive system. Ruby Middleton Forsythe (1905–92), known as "Miss Ruby," a teacher in the Charleston County public schools and at a Christian school on Pawleys Island for more than seven decades, and Fannie Phelps Adams (1917–), who taught in Columbia from the 1930s until she retired in 1979, well represent those teachers whose efforts provided an important front on the assault on Jim Crow. Forsythe and Adams demonstrate the importance of the schoolhouse to the modern civil rights movement.[1]

Many southern whites recognized the potential for African American teachers to challenge the Jim Crow system. Benjamin Tillman, governor of South Carolina from 1890 to 1894, argued against the "over education" of African Americans. Tillman believed that education was potentially dangerous in that it could lead to African American discontent and pose an economic threat to

RUBY FORSYTHE

Courtesy of Burns Forsythe.

FANNIE PHELPS ADAMS
Courtesy of Fannie Phelps Adams.

Jim Crow. Continuing the work of Tillman, Coleman Blease, governor of South Carolina from 1911 to 1914, followed his mentor's practice of curtailing African American access to education. Blease opposed state support for black colleges and targeted white teachers at black colleges. Angry that white women were teaching at Benedict College, a private school for African Americans in Columbia, South Carolina, in 1914 Governor Blease attempted to ban whites from teaching in black schools anywhere in the state, private or public. But a white Charleston County legislative delegate objected, observing that "it has been found necessary for the preservation of communities where negroes outnumber the whites, to teach the negroes from the very beginning that they are inferior to whites[;] . . . if we should turn the teaching of Negroes over to Yankee-educated negroes, nobody could predict the result."[2] Prior to 1920, white teachers staffed all public schools—black and white—in the city of Charleston, South Carolina. Well into the 1940s, much of the state consisted of communities with a substantial African American population. Of the forty-five counties in South Carolina in 1950, twenty-one had a black population of 50 to 80 percent and fifteen counties had a 30 to 49 percent black population. That blacks educated by northern whites would defy white supremacy was a real concern for many white southerners.[3]

As the careers of Forsythe and Adams illustrate, white southerners had more to fear than just "Yankee-educated negroes." Forsythe, Adams, and other African American women teachers born and educated in the South did not have to rely on northerners to show them the importance of teaching black children to resist oppression. They understood that the underpinning of Jim Crow was the racist education system and worked daily against it. In Charleston, black teachers challenged the city's refusal to hire them into teaching positions with a massive petition campaign, as Charlestonian Septima Clark recalled in her memoir, *Echo in My Soul*. In 1919 African Americans demanded that black teachers be allowed to teach in black schools in Charleston. Clark considered her work gathering signatures for the petition to be her introduction to a career in civil rights. Although Tillman had declared that ten thousand signatures would never be obtained, Clark and others proved him wrong. In 1920, African American teachers were teaching in the public schools of Charleston and by 1921, African American principals were being hired.[4] The "white community didn't want blacks to be educated out of their place," stated Forsythe.[5] Yet educate students out of their place is exactly what Forsythe, Adams, and others did.

Ruby Middleton Forsythe was born in Charleston, South Carolina, on June 27, 1905. She was the daughter of Lewis Burns Middleton, a brick mason and plasterer, and Marthenia Brown Middleton, a domestic who washed and ironed the local white nurses' and doctors' uniforms at her home. Ruby Middleton attended a private elementary school in the home of Miss Sever Montgomery, one of several private schools in the city of Charleston that provided education up to the eighth grade. Parents like the Middletons sacrificed in order to send their children to such schools; they did not want to send them to the city public schools because those schools only hired white teachers. Middleton remembered the white teachers she had during a brief attendance at a Charleston public school as "mean." Her mother felt that Middleton would not learn in a school run by whites because her daughter was a "bit obstinate."[6] When Middleton reached the seventh grade, she entered Avery Institute, a private high school for blacks. She graduated from Avery in 1921 with a licensed instructor degree and taught in several schools in the Charleston County area for the next fifteen years.[7] In 1928, she married William Essex Forsythe, an Episcopalian minister at Faith Memorial Church and principal of the church school on Pawleys Island.[8]

Fannie Phelps Adams, daughter of Mary and James Phelps, was born on June 27, 1917, the eighth of ten children. She grew up in the community of Wheeler Hill in Columbia, South Carolina. When she was four years old and her mother was pregnant with her tenth child, Phelps's father died. Her mother washed, ironed, and sewed for a living. When Phelps's oldest brother and his wife died within eleven months of each other, her mother moved their four children in with the Phelps family. Phelps remembered a crowded but love-filled house and that she slept with her mother until she went to college.[9]

Phelps graduated from the only high school for African Americans in Columbia, Booker T. Washington High School, in 1934. She earned a bachelor of arts from Allen University in 1938 and a master's from South Carolina State University in 1953. She married David King Adams Jr. on December 27, 1947. Adams taught third grade at Booker T. Washington Heights Elementary School in Columbia (renamed Sarah Nance Elementary and now called Watkins-Nance Elementary) until 1943. She then taught English and social studies at Booker T. Washington High School. Adams later served as guidance counselor, assistant principal, and acting principal until the school closed in 1974. She then served as assistant principal at the by-then integrated A. C. Flora High School until her retirement in 1979.[10]

Forsythe and Adams faced similar personal and professional issues during their teaching careers. Both Forsythe and Adams continued to teach after marriage. The Forsythes had a commuter marriage for almost ten years owing to family obligations: William stayed on Pawleys Island, while Ruby lived in Charleston. In addition, Forsythe felt responsible for providing support for her elderly parents. She stated, "If my husband wanted me, and if he wanted that arrangement, then that was fine. If he didn't want that, then he had to go on about his business."[11] Although Forsythe was committed to her marriage, her husband was free to leave if he did not understand her obligation to take care of her parents. In 1938 Forsythe finally joined her husband on Pawleys Island and began teaching with him at Holy Cross Faith Memorial School, where she taught until retirement. After growing up and living in Charleston, she found it hard to adjust to the rural isolation of Pawleys Island. She "cried for one solid month" after arriving and described her early days living there as "awful." She began teaching first grade and later taught grades one through four and eventually grew to love the place and its people. Forsythe taught at the school for forty-three years.

Fannie Adams met her husband, David, at Allen University, where both were students. Unlike the Forsythes' marriage, the Adamses' marriage was not a commuter one. However, both women's ideas about marriage were similar. They believed that a woman's career and happiness were as important as a man's and that marriage should not interfere with their obligation to their parents. David became so frustrated with his future wife over setting a wedding date that he finally gave her an ultimatum. Their marriage in 1947 occurred after they had dated for almost ten years. Adams recalled that she delayed the wedding in part because of her desire to assist her family, especially her mother. Adams considered herself "blessed for having a mother who was a very dedicated mother." She did not take a scholarship to go to college out of state but instead attended Allen so that she could continue to help with her mother's financial and domestic burdens. She took a heavier course load many semesters in order to graduate early. She completed her course work at Allen in three and a half years. Working with students brought Adams happiness, and she often worked long hours. David understood her devotion to her mother as well as her love for teaching. Adams remembered her husband coming to the school sometimes at 11 or 11:30 at night to get her. She said, "He would knock on my window and I would come out and get in the car. He understood how important my job was to me."[12]

Forsythe and Adams shared a dedication to teaching born in part of their own educational experiences. They were among a minority of black students in South Carolina who attended such schools as Avery and Booker T. Washington, two of a limited number of high schools for blacks in the state. The schools were well respected by both the African American and white communities for their excellent academic standards and the achievements of their graduates. Charleston's public school system allowed students who attended Avery's teacher education program access to teaching appointments without having to take an annual examination. The second public school built for African Americans in Columbia, Booker T. Washington served as the city's only black high school from 1918 to 1948. In 1933, both Booker T. Washington and Avery became regionally accredited by the Southern Association of Colleges and Schools (SACS). By 1931, only twenty high schools in the south for African Americans were fully accredited by SACS.[13]

Most African American children around the state had a more difficult time obtaining a high school education than Forsythe and Adams did. Like most of the South Carolina Sea Islands, Pawleys was predominantly black, isolated, and impoverished. Holy Cross Faith Memorial School, a private school founded by white missionaries in 1903, was the only educational institution on the island. However, the school was in term for nine months of the year and offered academic courses such as Latin and algebra through the tenth grade. In order to attend the eleventh grade, students had to go by boat to Georgetown, South Carolina.

Because there were a limited number of schools like Booker T. Washington High School, Avery Institute and Holy Cross Faith Memorial School that offered a high school education or at least some high school classes, most black South Carolina students had to travel long distances for a high school education. There were even whole counties across South Carolina that lacked a public high school for African Americans. For example, in 1927 Aiken County had eight accredited high schools for whites but no public high schools for blacks. Two private schools, Schofield in Aiken and Bettis Academy in Edgefield, provided the only access to a high school education for African Americans in the county.[14]

Obtaining an education beyond elementary school often meant that students had to board with relatives or community members who lived close to high schools. Others made a daily trip, sometimes traveling miles, to secure an education. The parents of Minnie Kennedy, for example, sent her and three sisters by ferry each Monday from Hobcaw Barony to Georgetown to stay with their grandmother during the week. Their local school, Strawberry School, only went to the fourth grade. Kennedy's parents scraped together enough money to purchase a house in Georgetown for the specific purpose of providing additional education for their children. A grandmother moved from Hobcaw Barony to the house in Georgetown to care for the children while their parents remained behind to work. In Georgetown, the girls attended Howard School, the only school for blacks that offered an education through the tenth grade at the time in the Georgetown area. Kennedy graduated from Howard in 1926.[15]

Most African American parents were unable to purchase another house; the children of these generally boarded with community members or relatives. Black teachers in Charleston often arranged housing for Sea Island children so that they might obtain education beyond elementary school. Alice LaSaine, a Jeanes teacher in Charleston, and her friend and fellow teacher Albertha Johnston Murray often housed students from Johns Island. Murray's daughter, Hazel Stewart, and another Charleston resident, Lela Potts-Campbell, both remember their parents providing housing for students as late as the 1950s.[16] Adams also recalled that students from surrounding counties attended Booker T. Washington in Columbia. Students from communities in Blythewood, Gadsden, Eastover and Hopkins, some twenty to thirty-five miles away, came in horse-driven buggies, walked, or carpooled. Others rented rooms with African American families.[17]

Across the South, even when black children could access a school, the school was likely to be overcrowded. Unequal funding for African American schools often resulted in a high student-to-teacher ratio and overcrowding compared to white schools. The public schools in Charleston, where Forsythe grew up and taught during the first fifteen years of her teaching career, were typical. At the George Lamb Buist School the average student-to-teacher ratio in 1921 was fifty-seven to one compared to thirty-nine to one in white schools in Charleston. The school board spent only 25 percent of its budget on black schools, an inequity it justified by arguing that whites paid the majority of taxes and therefore deserved the majority of the funding. Because the city refused to build additional schools for black children, black schools had to hold double sessions or ask students to attend part time in order to accommodate enrollment. In 1940, the outgoing school board chairman, M. Rutledge Rivers, stated that "the present congested condition of the negro schools is . . . a disgrace to us and a potential factor for breeding unhealthy conditions in our City; in some of our negro schools the situation of the pupils may be compared to the enforced proximity of sardines in their cans."[18]

Conditions for African Americans in Columbia were only marginally better than in the rest of the state. Between 1883 and 1915, Howard School, erected in the capital in 1867, was the only public school for African Americans in the city. A 1916 report entitled "Negro Education: A Study of the Private and Higher Schools for Colored People in the United States" noted that "the plant consists of a large city lot and two frame buildings. The elementary classrooms are crowded."[19] Booker T. Washington School was finally built in 1916 to accommodate the growing elementary school population, becoming a high school in 1924. Funding from the federal government, through the Works Projects Administration and the Public Works Administration, and from private foundations such as the General Education Board spurred more funding from county and state officials.[20]

In addition to overcrowded classrooms and schools, sporadic attendance by students who provided a labor source for agricultural and domestic jobs, short school terms, and lack of sufficient physical space in black schools made it harder for students to learn and they often repeated grades. Most southern schools during the first half of the twentieth century did not have age restrictions, and so it was not unusual to find children as young as three or young adults as old as twenty attending school. Charlestonian Mamie Fields recalled that at age three, she got tired of sitting at home and took her potty to the school. When Cecelia McGee in Aiken, South Carolina, started school at six years old, her four-year-old sister started school with her because her sister wanted to attend school and her mother stipulated that if the four-year-old could not attend school, neither could the six-year-old.[21] A step system, with students repeating first grade two to three times before being advanced to second grade, and attendance by children not yet of school age contributed to the problem of overcrowding well into the late 1940s. Adams, a product of the step system, started school at age five in 1922, attending Booker T. Washington School for first grade and then advanced to first grade before joining the second grade and continuing through high school.[22]

In the end, African American teachers faced dismal circumstances but eager learners in black schools in Columbia, Charleston, and across the state. White state and local officials denied adequate funding and refused to build new schools for black children. In 1911, only 12.8 percent of every dollar spent for public school property in South Carolina went to black schools. In 1936, 12.2 percent went to black schools. By 1925, there were 261 high schools for white students and 15 for black students, although the black school population was larger than the white student population. The disparity in funding and obstacles they faced were not enough to discourage black students, and they outnumbered white students in South Carolina from 1911 to 1923 both in enrollment and average daily attendance. Black families clearly understood the importance of education, made even more valuable because of the presence of black teachers.[23]

Although filled with obstacles, teaching provided Forsythe and Adams the opportunity to improve the lives of many African Americans. Within a segregated school system, Forsythe and Adams motivated students and provided the tools blacks needed in preparation for dismantling an unjust system. They did so by instilling positive attitudes in students, providing encouragement, and demanding results. Teachers like Forsythe and Adams taught the value of cooperation and responsibility to the larger community as well as to individual students, in part through their own daily behavior. Florence Linnen, of Georgetown, South Carolina, remembered that her high school teacher and principal, Maudest K. Squires, alerted the community whenever there was an educational or health issue they needed to know about. Squires contacted black leaders such as ministers and business owners, who would then disseminate the information to ensure that the entire community was aware of any relevant issues or meetings. Linnen's teachers also encouraged students to share what little they had. If a student needed paper and another student had paper, it was expected that the one with paper would share.[24] Ruby Forsythe also encouraged a sense of responsibility in the community by pushing her fast learners so that they could help teach the class. This allowed her more time with students who needed additional help. These lessons showed students the importance of sharing, cooperation, and unity.[25] Teachers also stressed responsibility by requiring students to memorize short quotations, such as "If a task is once begun, never leave it until it is done; be the labor great or small, do it well or not at all," remembers former Aiken, South Carolina, teacher Cecelia McGhee.[26]

Forsythe felt that "at an early age teachers must build self-esteem, a bit of independence, dependability, and a desire not to be the tail end all the time." Students should be taught "not to be dependent on somebody else." Forsythe believed that students "have it within them and can do it if they only try." She taught them these lessons by providing encouragement to each child and by being an astute observer of her students' behavior. In motivating her students to improve, she told them "you need to do a little better tomorrow than today." She thought the role of teachers in motivating students was to always "make them feel that they can do better" and that "this must be done daily."[27]

The margins of Forsythe's lesson plans provide a window into her techniques for getting students to reach their potential. For example, throughout October 1922, she paid particular attention to four of her students, Lillian, Harry, Inez, and Lewis. On October 16, she wrote, "Work on Harry H. He is a bit doubtful." On October 17, she entered, "Ask Lillian and Harry questions on our reading especially and try to get Inez not to *drag* her words so much." By October 18 she had noted, "Harry did well today, Lillian read well, Inez still drags." Students worked on arithmetic problems on October 23, and Forsythe noted that "Harry H. is a bit timid about his work." Her goal was to "try and get the children who are timid or do not understand so well to see where their trouble lies and drill on words, seven, eleven, and twelve." By October 24, Forsythe was still paying special attention to Harry and Lillian and had added Lewis to the group. They showed effort and progress. On October 27, she wrote that "Harry did better and that Lillian is doing better in writing. Each pronounced words clearly except Lewis. He is trying to do better." Still concerned about Lewis, in the next entry Forsythe wrote, "Teach spelling pronunciation and sound of words. Have Lewis give me the sound of hard, lard, card."[28]

The teaching techniques used by Forsythe worked. Frank Wineglass, a Pawleys Island resident, took his son from another school and enrolled him in Holy Cross because the students were "well disciplined, walked and talked differently." He wanted this kind of environment for his son, who was having difficulties in school. Within a short time, Forsythe had his son running home excited to show his dad how "Miss Ruby" had taught him to read. Wineglass said that the most important lesson his son learned was that "Miss Ruby was not going to give up on him."[29] Margaret Forbes Gant, former chairman of the board of Holy Cross School, explained that "Miss Ruby instilled good work habits, respect for others, and an interest in learning" and that they learned self-respect, a belief in success, and a work ethic. When Holy Cross students left the one-room school for a more modern school, "the principals could always pick out Miss Ruby's kids."[30] These traits instilled in African Americans the confidence needed to challenge white supremacy. For example, Waymon Stover, a former student in an all-black Camden, South Carolina, school noted that "within my first two years of school, teachers made it known that we were at a disadvantage; whites had buses, blacks did not. Teachers pointed these things out and talked about better facilities of whites while simultaneously encouraging students to intellectually prepare for a better day and to overcome those disadvantages."[31]

Forsythe more directly agitated against inequities by encouraging African Americans to organize or join organizations supporting equity issues. As late as 1989, Forsythe told Pawleys Island residents to "join the NAACP," lamenting "there's no justice yet." She noted that two-thirds of Pawleys Island property once belonged to blacks and that when the state decided to build a bridge and a highway, it effectively just took the land by not compensating blacks fairly. The state gave a black man only $2,000 for his twenty-eight acres, yet paid the "diocese a fair price for cutting through their land." She commented that if whites wanted the land and blacks would not sell, whites simply raised the taxes.[32]

Forsythe and Adams were inspirational and effective teachers because they drew from their own experiences. They and their colleagues were trained in black institutions themselves, and they passed their memories from generation to generation.

Childhood and adult experiences shaped the lessons teachers taught. For example, Forsythe's mother washed her only school dress each night and ironed it the next morning. In addition, her parents sacrificed to send her to a private school. Adams's mother also washed clothes for families and provided for fourteen children. Such experiences taught Forsythe and Adams to appreciate progress and to value hard work. One of Forsythe's favorite sayings was "Easy come, easy go," by which she meant nothing of value could be achieved without hard work. Adams reminded her students that "no one can tell me about being poor"; she did not want them to allow their poverty to hold them back.[33] Combating a Jim Crow system required sustained efforts, and Forsythe and Adams, along with others, provided a daily education in sustainability for their students.

Adams believed "people are watching you when you don't know it," and lived accordingly, working hard and doing the right thing day after day. She argued that if she could succeed, so could her students, and she felt she needed to reinforce positive and responsible attitudes by example. Warren Bolton, a senior editor at *The State*, described Adams as "frank, to the point and [she] didn't take any mess. We knew where we stood with her and what she expected of us. Most of all, she was every child's greatest cheerleader. She constantly encouraged us to work hard to reach our potential."[34]

Shaped by their childhood experiences, educational experiences, and community, Forsythe and Adams demanded the best from their students. Failure to adhere to these demands often meant corporal punishment. Historian James Anderson wrote that every teacher in his Alabama school had a strap or other instrument that teachers used to punish students for what they considered bad behavior. Bad behavior could range from forgetting homework or talking to disobeying direct orders.[35]

Forsythe believed in consistency and demanded that her students do their homework regularly, a requirement that one of her former students, Carolyn Wallace, noted was reinforced with the threat of corporal punishment. Wallace remembered that it was impossible for students to shirk their duties— "no homework," and you were "introduced to Mr. Strap," she recalled. Another possible punishment for missing homework was having to skip recess. Given that school lasted from 7:30 a.m. to 4:30 p.m., children learned quickly to always bring their homework.[36] Forsythe informed parents of her practices when they registered their children. "I tell them I use whatever method of discipline that will bring success. I let them know I'm going to spank their child if they need to be spanked. I will talk to them two or three times." She explained that obedience is the first thing you have to teach children, then honesty and responsibility. Children must be responsible for their work themselves. "I show them what I use. I am not going to kill them, but I am going to put it on them enough to be felt. If you don't want that, this is not the place," she noted. For the small children, she used a leather strap and a paddle one of the boys made; for larger children, she used a black automobile fan belt. She administered a dose of horseradish for talking after being told to stop and a Listerine, peroxide, and Tabasco sauce mixture for bad language.[37]

Harsh as such punishment may seem in the twenty-first century, their students were living in a Jim Crow environment, where racism often meant African Americans experienced humiliation, provocations, and possibly even maiming and death for the least infraction against a white person. Many African Americans felt that discipline necessary to survive in such an environment; its absence could mean harm or death. It took discipline not to respond with violence when called "nigger" or when spat on or humiliated in the thousand of ways African Americans were in the Jim Crow South. Black children were taught early on not to share information with whites. Adults knew that whites might behave kindly in order to get information or that they might provoke young blacks in order to incite reactions that would lead to violence. Discipline was required to avoid divulging information or reacting to provocation. In African American communities the adage was "Better to be whipped by someone who loves than killed by someone who hates you."[38] Hence, punishment was used to encourage learning, and "proper" behavior was related to the need to hold one's tongue before whites. Such actions may seem contradictory given that African American teachers were teaching students to confront a Jim Crow system. However, African American teachers were also aware that in order to dismantle a racist society, one needed to be alive. Often, the timing of confrontations during Jim Crow was as important as the confrontation itself. They hoped that they both instilled children with the confidence to resist internalizing messages of black inferiority and taught them the skills necessary to challenge their oppression in an organized fashion.

Even as they administered corporal punishment and taught discipline, generations of African American schoolteachers also taught students that they were loved and the intellectual equals of any race. "Teachers had your best interest at heart and wanted you to succeed and they took intimate interest in you," said Waymon Stover. He remembered that his first-grade teacher, Helen McLeod, kept safety pins and extra clothing for children. She would alter "too large clothing" on children or supply them with clothing so they would not be ashamed of their appearance. His English teacher, T. E. McLester, secured summer jobs in Rhode Island for students so that they could help pay their college tuition.

A Jim Crow system created more problems than solutions for whites anxious to control blacks through teachers who shaped the minds of the youth. For instance, a segregated school system often left day-to-day decisions about what was taught in the classroom in the hands of African Americans. It was almost impossible for a minority white population in a rural South that had a substantial number of counties with a large African American population to closely monitor blacks.

In addition, white arrogance and paternalism allowed most whites to believe that blacks behaved in the way whites wanted them to and believed what whites wanted them to. African American teachers proved to be more influential in shaping the minds of black youth than the racist messages of inferiority inherent in the Jim Crow system. Moreover, whites refused to see African American intellectual traditions and activism. Their arrogance limited the accuracy of their understanding of the potential of African Americans. Most southern whites thought they had intimate knowledge of black aspirations or lack thereof and that surely their southern blacks would not demand such things as equal rights.

Like their ancestors in the nineteenth century, they did not understand their southern black sisters and brothers. Generations of whites inaccurately thought only northern whites or "outsiders" were the potential threat to a carefully crafted Jim Crow social order. Yet within financially starved schools, a revolution fermented under southern white noses. Bright and intelligent students, taught by teachers with few resources that they were equal and deserving of an equal opportunity, challenged a system decades in the making and thought to be impenetrable.

Serving as role models who expected themselves and others to reach their highest potential, Forsythe, Adams and other teachers influenced future generations. The lessons they taught could encourage direct confrontation against the oppressor or against the system. Teachers, like many others in the long civil rights movement, often picked their battles and their times of entry into the fight for equality. Instilling dignity and self-awareness worked against mental and spiritual boundaries imposed by Jim Crow and were prerequisite to any form of collective action or political activism. The main objectives of Forsythe and Adams were to motivate students to succeed, to get them to understand that they were part of a larger world, to develop in them independence and self-sufficiency, and to challenge them to counter a Jim Crow world that called for their dependency and subordination.

Forsythe and Adams were part of the struggle for equality collectively in their teaching careers for a total of 110 years. Forsythe retired in 1991 and died in Mt. Pleasant, South Carolina, on May 29, 1992, having taught for seventy-one years. Miss Ruby's Kids, an early literacy program for families in Georgetown County, South Carolina, founded in 2003, continues her social justice efforts by providing children ages two and three and their families two years of home visits to prepare them for success in school.[39]

Adams taught for forty years, and even after her retirement she continued to be a role model. Adams embraced community activism with the same zeal she had demonstrated in her teaching, showing students that supporting and improving one's community is essential for progress and success. In the late 1970s she was directly involved with programs and campaigns that resulted in the election of the first three black members to the Richland School District One Board of Commissioners, resulting in a racially mixed board for the first time in its ninety-six-year history.

Adams is a lifetime member of St. James AME Church and serves as a trustee, assistant class leader, and member of the church school and Bible study groups, and she was the church's "1975 Mother of the Year." She has received numerous other awards, including the Human Relations Award from the Richland County Education Association, the South Carolina Education Association, and the National Education Association. She was a 1996 inductee into the South Carolina Black Hall of Fame and a 2008 inductee into the Richland One Hall of Fame. In 2008, the University of South Carolina Education Museum pavilion unveiled a commemorative bench in her honor. In 2010 Adams was an inductee into Bell South's South Carolina African American history calendar. Adams is a founder of the Palmetto Cemetery Association and served as a director of the Wheeler Hill Neighborhood Association. She is a member of the NAACP, the Columbia Branch of the National Association of University Women, Zeta Phi Beta Sorority, and the University of South Carolina President's Community Advisory Committee. She is a former board member of Palmetto Richland Hospital and a charter member of the Palmetto Richland Children's Hospital.

At the age of ninety-five, Adams is still creating her legacy to future generations by serving as a community activist and humanitarian. In addition to staying active in many organizations, she shares her experiences with future educators and gives back to the community by serving as a volunteer with the Retired Senior Volunteer Food Co-Op Program. She "bags groceries for the elderly," but in one small concession to her age, allows her daughter to lift the bags.

NOTES

1. The most thorough account of southern black education is James D. Anderson's *The Education of Blacks in the South, 1860–1935* (Chapel Hill: University of North Carolina Press, 1988). Several valuable new studies contribute to the historiography by addressing roles of teachers. Ronald Butchart's *Freed People: A Comprehensive Quantitative Study of the Origins of Black Education in Freedom* (Chapel Hill: University of North Carolina Press, 2010) and Heather Williams's *Self-Taught: African American Education in Slavery and Freedom* (Chapel Hill: University of North Carolina Press, 2005) examine African Americans' quest for literacy. Williams's work is devoted to both pre- and postslavery; Butchart focuses on freedmen teachers from 1861 to 1876. Historians arguing for the importance of teachers in renegotiating "southern traditions" include Katherine Charron's *Freedom's Teacher: The Life of Septima Clark* (Chapel Hill: University of North Carolina Press, 2009), which uses Clark's experiences as a teacher to examine her role in the modern civil rights movement; Ann Short Chirhart's *Torches of Light: Georgia Teachers and the Coming of the Modern South* (Athens: University of Georgia Press, 2005), a study of the role of black and white

teachers as mediators between the Old and New South; Sonya Ramsey's *Reading, Writing, and Segregation: A Century of Black Women Teachers in Nashville* (Urbana: University of Illinois Press, 2008), which argues in a chapter dealing with the 1940s that teachers "continued to teach, although they did so quietly, that equality is the true foundation of democracy"; Chris Span's *From Cotton Field to Schoolhouse: African American Education in Mississippi, 1862–1875* (Chapel Hill, University of North Carolina Press, 2009), which looks at postwar education and notes that African Americans envisioned it as a means to full citizenship; and Vanessa Siddle Walker's *Hello Professor: A Black Principal and Professional Leadership in the Segregated South* (Chapel Hill: University of North Carolina Press, 2009), which examines the role of principals during the 1950s and 1960s in supporting black resistance to a Jim Crow system.

2. Edmund L. Drago, *Initiative, Paternalism, and Race Relations: Charleston's Avery Normal Institute* (Athens: University of Georgia Press, 1990), 118, 127.

3. Walter Edgar, *South Carolina: A History* (Columbia: University of South Carolina Press, 1998), 526; See also George Rogers and James Taylor, *A South Carolina Chronology, 1497–1992* (Columbia: University of South Carolina Press, 1994). South Carolina had a majority African American population until 1930.

4. African Americans were allowed to teach in Charleston county schools but not in city schools (Septima Poinsette Clark with LeGette Blythe, *Echo in My Soul* [New York: E.P. Dutton, 1962], 60–61).

5. Michelle Foster, *Black Teachers on Teaching* (New York: New Press, 1998), 27.

6. Ibid., 24, 25. Drago discusses a number of private schools, including Miss Montgomery's, many of them taught by former Avery students. Since black teachers could not teach in Charleston's public schools, they often opened these private schools and enrolled forty-five to fifty students from grades one to eight (*Initiative, Paternalism, and Race Relations*, 124).

7. Foster, *Black Teachers*, 25; William Hine, "Forsythe, Ruby Middleton (1905–1992)," in *Black Women in America: An Historical Encyclopedia*, ed. Darlene Clark Hine et. al. (New York: Carlson Publishing, 1993), 441–42.

8. In 1929 they had a son, Burns Minard Forsythe. They were also responsible for an eleven-year-old niece, Susie L. Small (1930 U.S. federal census, Charleston, S.C., roll 2190, page 3A, enumeration district 41, image 311.0).

9. Fannie Phelps Adams, interview by author, June 2, 2009.

10. David attended Allen University, served in World War II, and worked at Veterans' Hospital in Columbia, South Carolina. They had one child, Mary Suzette (Adams, interview by author, June 2, 2009). Biographical information can also be found in the National Association of University Women, Columbia Branch, annual scholarship luncheon brochure, April 25, 2009.

11. Foster, *Black Teachers*, 27.

12. Ibid., 28.

13. Anthony L. Edwards, "Booker T. Washington High School (1916–1974): Voices of Remembrance" (PhD diss., University of South Carolina, 1994) 93. See also William H. Brown and William A. Robinson, *Serving Negro Schools: A Report on the Secondary School Study in Purposes, Working Techniques and Findings* (Atlanta: Secondary School Study of the Association of Colleges and Secondary Schools for Negroes, 1946).

14. Schofield School, founded in 1868 by Martha Schofield, offered academic courses such as Latin and Algebra as well as blacksmithing, carpentry and cooking, and sewing. Schofield received some public funding from the state by 1938 to assist with its high school preparation of African

Americans, and after integration in the 1960s, it became a middle school. Bettis, founded in 1882 by Reverend Alexander Bettis, remained a private school until it closed in 1950. It offered training in religious instruction, literacy, mechanical and agricultural arts, and home economics. See James O. Farmer, "Aiken" in *South Carolina Encyclopedia*, 11, Bettis Academy, *Bulletin of Information*, 1951, and Louise Allen, "Bettis Academy," in *South Carolina Encyclopedia*, 71. For a biographical account of Martha Schofield, see Katherine Smedley, *Martha Schofield and the Re-education of the South* (Lewiston, N.Y.: Edwin Mellen Press, 1987). See also Louise Allen, "Martha Schofield," in *South Carolina Encyclopedia*, 846–47.

15. Minnie Kennedy, interview by author, December 19, 2001. Howard would later offer eleventh grade and by 1949 had added twelfth grade (Georgetown County Library records, Georgetown, S.C.).

16. Kennedy, interview by author, December 19, 2001; Hazel Stewart, interview by author, May 23, 2008; Lela Potts-Campbell, interview by author, April 23, 2008.

17. Adams, interview by author, June 2, 2009; Edwards, "Booker T. Washington High School," 109.

18. Drago, *Initiative, Paternalism, and Race Relations*, 180.

19. Edwards, "Booker T. Washington High School," 82.

20. Ibid., 87–88.

21. Commission on Interracial Cooperation, *The South—Child Rich, Dollar Poor* (Atlanta, Ga.: Commission on Interracial Cooperation, 1942), 11; Cecelia McGhee, interview by author, July 13, 2005. Parents sent their underage children to school for a number of reasons, including lack of access to child care. Teachers also took their underage children to school. Mary Pauline took her adopted niece, Pauli Murray, to school with her and placed her in a classroom with another teacher at one point. See Pauli Murray, *Proud Shoes and Song in A Weary Throat* (Boston: Beacon Press, 1999). Historian James D. Anderson's mother sent him to school before he became of school age because he begged to go to school with his older brother (James Anderson, conversation with author, January 20, 1998). See Mamie Garvin Fields with Karen Fields, *Lemon Swamp and Other Places: A Carolina Memoir* (New York: Free Press, 1983), 41.

22. Adams, interview by author, June 2, 2009.

23. Edwards, "Booker T. Washington High School," 86–89. For an overview of southern high schools, see Anderson, *Black Education in the South*, chap. 6.

24. Florene Linnen, interview by author, December 17, 2001. Maudest Kelly Squires was born in 1903 in Georgetown, South Carolina. She became a teacher, a Jeanes teacher, and a principal. She retired in 1974 (Ramona La Roche, *Georgetown County, South Carolina* [Charleston: Arcadia Publishing, 2000], 74). For additional information on Squires, see Squires folder, Georgetown Library archives, Georgetown, S.C.

25. *Ruby Forsythe* (Georgetown, S.C.: Video South Productions, Rice Museum, 1993).

26. McGhee, interview by author, July 13, 2006.

27. *Ruby Forsythe.*

28. Forsythe, 1923 lesson plan, Rice Museum, Georgetown, S.C.

29. *Ruby Forsythe.*

30. Ibid.

31. Waymon Stover, interview by author, April 12, 2007.

32. Foster, *Black Teachers on Teaching*, 29.

33. *Ruby Forsythe.*

34. Warren Bolton, "Two Sisters, two Educators, Two Lives Dedicated to Service," *The State*, August 17, 2007.

35. Anderson, conversation with author, January 20, 1998.

36. *Ruby Forsythe*.

37. Ibid.

38. On Jim Crow, see Leon Litwack, *Trouble in Mind* (New York: Vintage, 1999); Glenda Gilmore, *Gender and Jim Crow* (Chapel Hill: University of North Carolina Press, 1996); and Benjamin Mays, *Born a Rebel* (Athens: University of Georgia Press, 2003).

39. Miss Ruby's Kids, www.missrubyskids.net.

Mary Gordon Ellis

The Politics of Race and Gender from Schoolhouse to Statehouse

CAROL SEARS BOTSCH

❊ ❊ ❊

In March 1995, more than sixty years after their mother's life was cut short by cancer, Mary Gordon Ellis's three children joined with members of the South Carolina Senate to honor the memory of the state's first woman senator. A controversial figure in the early 1900s who fought to provide educational opportunities for African American as well as white children, Ellis (1890–1934) had been virtually forgotten. But by the 1990s, both South Carolina and the nation had changed. The schoolhouse doors had opened to children of all races, although many inequities remained. Women were beginning to run for office and in some cases were winning. Politicians were courting the female vote. It was a time of progress, and officeholders were seeking opportunities to celebrate women in politics. Ellis's children had fought for years to have their mother recognized for her accomplishments but now they had the support of the South Carolina Governor's Commission on Women, headed by Mary Baskin Waters. Their combined efforts bore fruit in 1995 when her portrait was unveiled in the state senate chambers. Now an oil painting of Ellis, who died in her early forties, would join those of other South Carolina notables in the senate portrait gallery at the statehouse—the first portrait of a woman to be hung there. The state and its citizens would finally recognize the accomplishments of this pioneer who was in so many ways far ahead of her time.

Ellis's short life is even more remarkable when one considers that South Carolina's women had only had the right to vote for a few years in 1924 when she ran for office. Although some southern women campaigned for suffrage in the late nineteenth and early twentieth centuries, the dominant culture in the South

MARY GORDON ELLIS
Courtesy of Margaret E. Taylor.

did not encourage women to be politically active. South Carolina did not vote to ratify the Nineteenth Amendment to the U.S. Constitution in 1920 and only formally ratified it in 1969. A few American women had been elected to state level office as early as the 1890s. But these women lived in the western states of Utah and Colorado, and came from a very different culture.[1] As one historian noted, the South was a region that "had adopted a more rigid definition of the role of women than any other part of the country and had elevated that defini- tion to the position of a myth."[2] Southern women were supposed to be gentle, docile, and submissive to male authority. For most, marriage was their career. The home was their castle, at least in theory, but they were not supposed to play any significant political role in life outside the home. The reality, however, was that women had begun to assert themselves politically through women's clubs, the suffrage movement, and other social reforms, but political officeholding still seemed off limits to women.[3] In the early years of the twentieth century, few women ran for office and few were elected. In 1922 Kate Vixon Wofford knocked down South Carolina's "No women allowed" sign with her election as superintendent of education in Laurens County. Two years later Mary Gordon Ellis was elected to the state senate, although only a few women followed her into state level office during the remainder of the twentieth century.

Although some will remember Ellis because she was the state's first woman senator, she merits recognition for her work as an early civil rights activist. In the South of the 1920s, there were some well-meaning women and men, both black and white, who sought to improve relations between the races in a time of increasing racial tension.[4] In 1919 religious moderates joined together to form the South Carolina Commission on Interracial Cooperation. Their goal was not to end segregation or to change the social order in which blacks ranked below whites.[5] But this group and others like it sought better education, housing, and living conditions for African Americans in South Carolina and elsewhere in the South.[6] Ellis, a small-town woman, was not herself involved with any such for- mal organization, but she was a determined individual who recognized a wrong and sought to right it, regardless of the opposition she faced.

The future state senator was born on April 21, 1890, in Gourdin, a small town in Williamsburg County, South Carolina, located at the intersection of state roads 375 and 377. She was one of ten children, including seven girls, of Alexan- der McKnight Gordon, a farmer, and Mary Lee Gamble. When she was still quite young, the family moved to the county seat of Kingstree, a larger town about fifteen miles to the north. She was a determined girl with a bright, inquiring mind. Even as a child she was interested in the world of politics, traditionally the realm of men. "She had an interest in public affairs early on," recalled daughter

Margaret Ellis Taylor.[7] She would often sit outside the Williamsburg courthouse listening to the legal proceedings inside. Her eldest daughter, Elizabeth Ellis Roe Taylor, later recounted the story of how at the age of thirteen, her mother slipped away from their home in Kingstree, where she was supposed to be doing chores. After a search, Mary's father found her in the courthouse, curled up on a seat in the back, listening to the cases. "One little girl in all those men. Do you think she was destined to be like anybody else?" Elizabeth mused.[8]

In the early 1900s, with few careers open even to educated young women, many became teachers. Thus, after graduating from Kingstree High School in 1909, one of six girls in a class of seven students, Mary Gordon obtained a teaching job at Sutton's School, where she taught for a year. It was more the exception than the rule for teachers in country schools to have college degrees, but the Gordons were a family that had always valued education. Mary quickly realized that she would benefit from a college degree and made up her mind to attend Winthrop College, a woman's college in Rock Hill. South Carolina began to expand its public education system during the post–Civil War years, and Winthrop was founded in 1886 to prepare young women to teach in the state's public schools. Mary Gordon had to pay her own way, as her parents were unable to cover the costs. She applied for and received a scholarship to pay for her education. She worked in the dining hall, waiting on tables. Often sickly, she had to leave college for a year in 1912, at which point she took up a teaching position at Graves School in Rock Hill. The following year she returned to complete her degree.[9] In 1913 she graduated from Winthrop College with a bachelor of arts degree and a certificate that allowed her to teach in the South Carolina schools for life.[10] Two of her sisters later followed her to Winthrop to earn their own degrees and to become teachers.

Gordon's first job after college took her to Gillisonville School in Jasper County. She received a higher salary there than she could closer to home. She was paid $50 a month to teach, $15 more than she could earn teaching elsewhere.[11] She was also the first teacher in tiny Jasper County with a college degree.[12] There she met her future husband, Junius Gather Ellis, a farmer and turpentine operator who served as chairman of the board of directors of Gillisonville School. The two married in 1914, settling at Junius's family home of Stockholm, located between Gillisonville and Coosahawchee. In the years that followed, Ellis gave birth to three children, two girls, Mary Elizabeth (Beth) and Margaret Lee (Mickey), and a boy, Junius Gather Jr. (Jake).

Ellis was, in the words of daughter Margaret, "very independent and very capable for whatever she undertook."[13] A typical wife and mother, she took care of house and home, handling all the challenges of raising a family and doing whatever needed to be done. Her children remembered that she was "always busy at something."[14] She was not very good at spelling, perhaps because her mind moved so quickly, but she was better at math, taking care of the books for the family turpentine business, according to daughter Elizabeth.[15] She managed the family's finances well. "I don't remember anything being a financial burden," said Margaret.[16] She knew how to "butcher a hog, garden[,] . . . cook, and sew," Elizabeth remembered. "She was the one who ran the farm. My father was not a farmer," Margaret recounted.[17] As a young child, son Jake remembered coming home at night after accompanying his father as he supervised the milking of the trees for their juices. His mother, who would often be "canning or repairing broken fences," would not have forgotten about their dinner, he recalled. They would be greeted by the sight and smell of "steaming vegetables on the stove from the garden."[18] And in the summer, relatives and friends filled the house for parties.[19]

Margaret remembered her mother as "a very compassionate person" who would reach out to others in need. As often as possible she helped her nearby neighbors, a family with ten children beset by financial difficulties. "The neighbor on the other side, a tenant farmer, the father had died," recalled Margaret. There were "five children, the older son was plowing for fifteen cents a day and had to quit school" to help support his family. "She taught him and later he came to me and said 'Everything I am I owe to your mother.'"[20] Her caring concern for her immediate neighbors later translated to a caring concern for her entire community and her state when she served in public office.

Ellis expected her children to develop independence and a sense of responsibility as well. Although the family had household help, Ellis felt that one "couldn't be dependent on others waiting on you," recalled Margaret. Ellis wanted each of her children to be "a person who must think for yourself and do for yourself." Margaret recalled her mother's positive response to her attempt to bake a cake when she was very young: "If it failed, she wouldn't criticize." She believed you should "learn from your mistakes" and "go in and try again."[21] That determination was evident in her political career.

With encouragement from her husband, Junius, who hired a teacher to live on the family farm and tutor the three children, Mary continued to teach public school. This was unusual for married women with children who could afford to stay home. Ellis sometimes even took her small children with her to work. They drove the ten miles to Pine Tree School sometimes going through rough terrain on the country roads. "Through the sand beds and pine trees, if she met some obstacle . . . . she would cut out the stump rather than back away from it," recalled Elizabeth.[22]

In many respects, teaching in the South Carolina of the early 1900s must have been a challenge that involved more than just removing physical obstacles. As historian Walter Edgar has noted, "The state's public schools were under-funded and understaffed."[23] Many people were illiterate. Only about one-third of the eligible children attended school, and most for just a few months a year. Many communities had little support for compulsory education because children needed to work to contribute to the family's income. The state was reducing its contribution to public education, placing much of the burden on local communities.[24]

As bad as white schools were, black schools were even worse. Under the system of segregation, the state gave African American schools far less support than white schools. Black students, who typically spent even less time in school each year than white children, thus received little education. Black teachers were paid much less than their white counterparts. In 1911, at a time when about 55 percent of South Carolina's schoolchildren were African American, the average per capita expenditure for a white student was $12.62, while the average per capita expenditure for a black student was only $1.71.[25] State superintendent of education John E. Swearingen wrote in his annual report that "the negro schoolhouses are miserable beyond all description. They are usually without comfort, equipment, proper lighting, or sanitation. Nearly all the negroes of school age in the district are crowded into these miserable structures during the short term which the school runs."[26] In 1919, Joseph Brown Felton, the new state agent for Negro schools, traveled through the state to evaluate the black schools. In his annual report, he stated that "the furnishings of the school buildings for the colored children in South Carolina could not be worse. . . . [T]he children are required to sit on benches without backs and their feet unable to reach the floor. A more uncomfortable position could hardly be imagined."[27]

The schools in Jasper County were no better than schools elsewhere in the state. Appalled by the conditions, Ellis enlisted her sisters, who were students at Winthrop, to come and live with the family during the summer and tutor the local school children. They helped some children prepare for college. "One of the first people" that Ellis "helped get an education out of Jasper County ended up as head of the theological program at Duke," recalled Margaret. Another ended up in a prominent position at Clemson.[28]

Despite her efforts, the schools were not up to the standards Ellis had for her own children. She decided to send them to live with relatives in Savannah to continue their education there.[29] Elizabeth was sent to Savannah at age six, and Margaret followed two years later when she turned six. Although this permitted her to get a good education for her own children, Ellis was determined to help other children in Jasper County, and as a teacher, she had the firsthand experience to know what was needed. In 1924 she ran for school superintendent of Jasper County. When Ellis first announced her intention to run, many people thought that she was joking. The idea of a woman running for office was simply ludicrous in their minds.[30] Asked why she was running given that her own children were not in the local schools, she responded, "If they are not good enough for my children, they are not good enough for yours."[31] In the words of her family, Ellis "had strong convictions about certain things."[32] Once she made up her mind to do something, she would go ahead and do it. Ellis defeated two male candidates to become one of the first women elected to office in South Carolina. Although the election was over, her battles had really just begun.

During her term of office as school superintendent Ellis was diagnosed with uterine cancer. The indomitable Mrs. Ellis traveled on the train to Florence for radium treatments, determined to keep up with her responsibilities as an elected official. Part of her job was to manage the school system's finances, so she brought along an adding machine and ledgers in order to work as she traveled back and forth to the clinic. Her health gradually declined as the years went by.[33]

Despite her illness, Ellis continued her struggle for Jasper County's children. In her campaign to improve educational opportunities for other people's children, she did not hesitate to do what she thought was necessary. She immediately set about consolidating the county's schools, closing many small and inefficient schools, including some of the black schools. Many schools had just one teacher, so Ellis consolidated several dozen of these into just five schools. Furthermore, she made sure that a representative from each of the five sat on the county board of education. School officials, parents, and residents of each part of the county would be more likely to accept the school board's decisions as legitimate if "their school" had a voice in making those decisions. Tiny Gray's school, where Ellis had taught from 1915 to 1916, was one of the schools consolidated.

Ellis's children were proud of her accomplishments as county superintendent. In 1930, two years after Ellis was elected state senator, a reporter joined the family on an automobile trip to Jasper County. Before they arrived at the Ellis home, Elizabeth called out, "I want to show you Senator Mary G. Ellis' masterpiece!" She refused to say more, but after they went around a curve in the road, Elizabeth said, "There it is!" As recounted in the newspaper story, during her tenure as Jasper's superintendent of education, Ellis had replaced a one-room, one-teacher school with a consolidated high school that stood on the same spot. Elizabeth was quite proud of this building's structure, and the reporter agreed that it was truly a "masterpiece." In the words of the reporter, it was "one which any one would be proud to have as a living monument, for it was a handsome brick school building."[34]

Ellis was particularly concerned about the desperate needs of black children. She sought out funding from philanthropist Julius Rosenwald, a white, northern businessman who became interested in black education in the South after meeting African American educator Booker T. Washington in 1911. In 1917 Rosenwald set up a foundation to provide matching funds for the construction of black schools. Ellis obtained matching funds from Rosenwald to build four new schools. With her support and encouragement, the African American community held ice cream socials and other fundraisers to raise their share of the money. Throughout the South, black schools generally had old and damaged books and few supplies. Ellis tried to get better books for black students to use, books that were not missing any pages.[35] She demanded better teacher training, requiring that her teachers obtain A certificates. She even hired a new supervisor who had graduated from a black college to help oversee the black teachers, introducing her to the all-white school board as "*Mrs*. Miller."[36] Whites typically did not address blacks by their title.

By 1926 Ellis had provided bus transportation for the white students, although some residents were upset that they were paying the salary of a part-time driver. Undeterred, Ellis went even further: she called together the county board, saying "Gentlemen, I have done my homework." She noted that according to the census, twice as many blacks lived in the county as whites. She pointed out that "no society with one thousand white adults and four thousand black adults can survive unless all have equal educational opportunities." She then noted that no bus transportation was provided for black students. She demanded that the all-white board provide bus transportation for black students as well as whites, saying, "We are asking black children to walk several miles to school in all kinds of weather. They are ill clad, ill fed, and poverty stricken. We must look to our future and provide bus transportation for blacks." But with this request, Ellis had "gone too far" for many of the people of her community, and she lost public support, at least among the voting public.[37]

As an elected politician, Ellis was either brave or foolhardy to take such a risk in representing the disenfranchised. African Americans held no political power in the South of the 1920s. Almost all of them had lost the right to vote after the state adopted a new constitution in 1895; less than 5 percent were registered to vote in South Carolina although they made up about 60 percent of the population. Blacks were unable to get elected to office, and none served in the state legislature between 1902 and 1970. The successful candidate for office was always the winner of the whites-only Democratic primary.[38] Although some white, southern women were involved in interracial work in the 1920s through nonprofit organizations like the League of Women Voters, a politician, male or female, taking a public stand in favor of rights for blacks was unusual.[39]

Local whites complained to their state representative, a young lawyer named H. Klugh Purdy, and he asked Ellis to resign. Friends urged her not to do so, as she had been elected by the people of Jasper County, not by Purdy. "Make them kick you out," her friends advised. Ellis took Purdy's letter to his father-in-law, a local physician, who told her the same thing. She refused to resign. Meeting with Purdy, she declared, "You must take me for an idiot. I will not resign."[40] At Purdy's behest, the elected office of superintendent was abolished, and it became an appointed office controlled by the local legislators. Soon after, Ellis received a letter in the mail telling her that she was fired.[41] Not until 1958 would the office of superintendent of schools for Jasper County once again become an elected position, with the passage of a bill sponsored by Senator W. J. Ellis, Mary Gordon Ellis's brother-in-law.[42]

When Purdy filed for election to the state senate in 1928, Mary Ellis was quite literally not far behind. All that Purdy had succeeded in doing was making her angry enough to run against him. She went straight into the courthouse as soon as he had filed and filed for the seat herself. Purdy immediately decided that the best way to win was to encourage an additional candidate, a local bank president, to run. Since South Carolina required a runoff if no one received a majority of the votes, Purdy assumed that the two men would come in first and second and he would win in the runoff. But as political scientists have demonstrated, turnout ultimately decides the outcome of elections. Ellis worked hard to persuade voters that she should serve as their senator. Even her children helped during the campaign as best they could. Elizabeth, the eldest child at twelve, remembered attending stump meetings where politicians kissed babies and gave people sugar.[43] Margaret, who was only ten at the time, recalled going to just one stump meeting, in the community of Tillman. She remembered there was a man at the meeting who did not want her mother to be elected to the senate and who was calling her names. As they entered, the man "swallowed hard . . . and said well we have to take into consideration that she isn't well." Perhaps he was embarrassed, or perhaps he was disparaging her candidacy. There was a "lot of mudslinging," Margaret recalled.[44] But despite the heavy opposition of some citizens Ellis succeeded in the turnout battle, made it to the runoff with Purdy, and won the runoff by about 150 votes out of some 800 or so cast.[45]

After the formality of a general election in August 1928 Ellis became the first woman elected to the South Carolina Senate. No other woman served in that body for half a century until Elizabeth Patterson was elected in 1979. Indeed, no woman even served in the state house of representatives until 1945, when Harriet Frazier Johnson was elected in a special election. Ellis became one of only 153 women serving in state legislatures around the country in 1929. She was not the first in the South: Georgia and Alabama had sent women to their legislatures as early as 1922, and Mississippi elected a woman in 1923. But most of these women served in their state's house of representatives. Ellis was one of a select few who served in a state senate.[46]

In some respects Ellis was much like other women who have served in state legislatures over the years, focusing on issues that affected families and family life.[47] This was also true of the other southern women state legislators in the early twentieth century.[48] Ellis was interested in helping the poor, aiding women and children of all races, and making life better for the people of her community, especially through public education.[49] In the parlance of the twenty-first century, Ellis was a liberal on certain economic and social issues, supporting government action to give people a chance to reach their full potential. But like other middle-class southern women of her time, Ellis held what newspapers of the day described as "conservative" positions on a number of social issues. For example, she opposed divorce and favored "stricter marriage laws."[50] With the exception of a brief period between 1868 and 1878, divorce was not legal in South Carolina until 1949. She was a bit more liberal on the issue of horse racing, an issue that gained some national attention as states looked for ways to fill their coffers in the 1920s. Some states began to legalize racetrack betting in a climate more tolerant of gambling. Reporters asked Ellis how she felt about this. Citing her own love of horses, she said she was in favor of horse racing. She took a pragmatic view of legalized betting, arguing that it was inevitable, and that in Kentucky, where it was legal, it operated without a great number of problems.[51] Despite her endorsement, South Carolina did not legalize betting on horses.

In other respects Ellis differed from the typical female legislator and the typical southern woman of her day. There is no evidence that before her election, Ellis, living in a rural section of a rural state, had been involved in the swirling political battles over woman suffrage or temperance that served as a training ground for some women of her generation.[52] She was not, in the words of her children, a "militant." But although there is no evidence of her supporting women's rights in an organized movement, she did hold progressive views about women's roles. She did not believe educated women should necessarily confine themselves solely to their homes, and she favored women working if it was necessary for them to support themselves or their families.[53] Furthermore, Ellis respected her fellow citizens regardless of color and sought to give African

Americans as well as poor whites the opportunity to have a better life. As Margaret said, "She was for the rights of all the people."[54]

Nor did Ellis fit the typical demographic profile of a female state legislator of her time or of her children's and grandchildren's times, for that matter. Historically, many women have first gained office through the "widow's mandate," when they were elected or appointed to their deceased husband's seat.[55] Others were able to take advantage of name recognition because their father was a well-known political figure. But Ellis ran for and was elected to office on her own. Women also tended to wait until their children were older and they had fewer family responsibilities before seeking elective office.[56] Ellis, however, was fairly young, in her thirties, with a young family when she ran for both county and state level offices.

Having a supportive spouse was certainly critical for her success. "I take my hat off to my father," Margaret remarked. He "supported my mother in everything she did," driving her on the long trip to Columbia and taking care of the home front in her absence.[57] He was himself an educated man, a graduate of Richmond Business Academy in Savannah, Georgia. This may explain his understanding of the importance of what his wife was doing. Ellis's success, however, was primarily due to her own desire to make a difference. Having an issue—education—that she greatly cared about provided the motivation for a woman who, in the words of her son, "had [her] own mind" and "said what she believed."[58]

Introducing her as speaker for the annual meeting of the South Carolina Building and Loan Association in Columbia in 1930, Senator James Hammond remarked that "this good lady has shown that she can represent the county as a senator and still be the mother of her children." Ellis herself said in her speech that a woman's "first thought in life should be home," and speaking in general of families with working mothers, she noted that oftentimes "the children run wild because the mother is not home." But in the same speech, she told the bankers' wives who had joined their husbands in the audience to hear her speak that the state senate "is a mighty good place for a good many of you to try to go."[59] Like late twentieth-century female public figures, often judged by the media and the public on the color and length of their skirts, the stylishness of their hairdos, and even the quality of their chocolate chip cookies, Ellis was questioned about her cooking and homemaking skills. In a 1930 newspaper interview, Ellis assured a reporter that she had spent an enjoyable weekend caring for hearth and home. "I repotted my ferns and also put eggs under nine hens. So I was pretty busy. Besides this I spent one day at Allendale helping them in making out their 6-0-1 report. So I did not have as much spare time as I have in Columbia," Ellis stated.[60] The reporter also reassured the reader that the woman senator had excellent culinary skills, noting that "Senator Ellis can go into the kitchen and broil a steak to perfection, scramble eggs to the proper consistency, make good biscuit and coffee, a meal good enough to put before a king."[61]

Concerns rose immediately over how to handle the social niceties of being the first and only female in the South Carolina Senate. Ellis was somewhat of a curiosity to her fellow senators, although in time they came to see her as a collegial member of their body. Some people were concerned about whether it was appropriate for her to wear a hat during her swearing-in ceremony. (She did.) Elizabeth, who was twelve, remembered a "big debate at the time" over etiquette issues in an era when "many men weren't ready to accept them [women] in public office."[62] Male senators were confused over how to address Ellis after she was in office, some suggesting the term "Senatrix." Some opposed her wearing a hat in the senate chambers. In the end, she won the battle to keep the hat, and senators agreed to address her as "Mary G."[63]

Ellis was also a bit of a curiosity to the general public and to the media. A newspaper of the day described her as "a woman of striking personality. She is tall and handsome, with dark wavy hair and beautiful blue-gray eyes and has the determination and independent courage of her Scotch-Irish ancestors."[64] Another newspaper story reported that "she had the true southern intonation, 'her voice was low and sweet.'"[65] She was a woman who did not quite fit the expectations of what a genteel southern lady should be and yet managed to combine a professional life outside the home with the traditional role of wife and mother. "Mama was not all business. She was a mother and a wife," who enjoyed cooking, embroidery, and working on the family farm, said Elizabeth.[66] People wanted to know how she did it. Perhaps part of the answer is that underneath the exterior of that sweet low voice was a woman of steel, strong and determined, who didn't talk about what she was doing but instead, as Margaret put it, "just went about her business."[67]

Tip O'Neill, the late Speaker of the U.S. House of Representatives, is often quoted as having said "all politics is local." Like any good politician, Ellis came into office determined to work hard for her constituents and not to impose her personal agenda on her fellow legislators. She introduced or cosponsored many bills that would benefit the citizens of Jasper County. The first bill she introduced was not groundbreaking. Rather, it was a joint resolution, which could be seen as somewhat of a "housekeeping" measure, to pay $344 in fees that were due to the estate of the late county treasurer, J. S. Berg.[68] Subsequently she introduced bills to improve rural roads, to provide highway construction in Jasper County, and to provide bus transportation for county children.[69] According to one newspaper account, the only time she rose to make a speech was when the senate considered a bill that would provide state aid for buildings in Jasper County.[70] "Her concern for the welfare of the colored race in her county prompted this," reported the newspaper. Most of the bills she introduced dealt with local matters. For example, she sponsored tax relief for Jasper County residents after the Savannah River flooded in 1930. Ellis also supported a law that ensured that the Confederate Home in Columbia would admit sisters as well as wives of war veterans. Her efforts to revert the office of superintendent of education for Jasper County back to an elected position were unsuccessful, however.[71]

Ellis took an independent path during her term in the senate. She chose not to align herself with any factions in the legislature, gaining a reputation for honesty, although some wished she would wheel and deal. A newspaper of the day reported that "in casting her vote she does not swap, but carefully weighs in her own mind why the matter should go through or vice versa, then votes." In essence, she kept her colleagues guessing as to what position she would take.[72] Special interests found her unassailable.[73] Margaret recalled the legislators saying that "Mary G. can't be bought."[74] Elizabeth remembered her mother turned down a bribe from a group that wanted to buy her vote. Instead she did her homework and endeavored to get along well with her colleagues.[75] However, Ellis was at times highly critical of professional politicians, telling members of the Business and Professional Women's Club in Columbia that politicians should make decisions based on what is best for their constituents, not on what will help them to get reelected: "Selfishness and the fear of politicians that they will not be returned to office if they sponsor certain measures are responsible for the backwardness of South Carolina."[76] About a year after she came into office, Ellis described in a speech what she had learned from her colleagues. She said that they "are beginning to teach me to think, to dream and to talk about taxes all of the time."[77] Summing up her career after her death, a newspaper reported that she "served her county quietly and seldom made a speech."[78]

If Mary Gordon Ellis could be said to have had an agenda, it was improving education. South Carolina's 1895 constitution required separate schools for blacks and whites, but the state made no efforts to provide equal funding or to ensure that children would actually attend school. Although the Progressive Era was in full swing across the nation by the early 1900s, support for reforms, including reducing illiteracy, came slow to South Carolina. In a January 1911 speech, Governor Coleman Blease expressed his opposition to compulsory education. Following the election of Governor Richard Manning in 1914, the legislature provided more funding for education and passed a compulsory education law. The next governor, Robert Cooper, supported increasing taxes for education, but the state still ranked at the bottom nationally, and after farm prices dropped in 1921, many of Cooper's reforms went by the wayside.[79] Also, the women, mostly white, who provided much of the impetus for reform focused primarily on the needs of the white population. In 1924 the legislature passed the "6-0-1" Act to ensure that all of the white children in the state would be able to go to school for at least seven months a year and that there would be adequate financing. The state would cover the costs for six months and the district had to cover the costs for the remaining month. Some black students did benefit down the road. But although there were several good black high schools in the state, no black student had yet been awarded a state diploma when Ellis took her place as a state senator.[80]

In a February 1929 newspaper interview, Ellis explained that education was her primary interest, which she attributed to her service as superintendent of education for Jasper County. Laws requiring school attendance were poorly enforced in the state. She supported a proposal to make education compulsory for South Carolina's children so long as it was "adequately financed," expressing concern that not enough money was being provided to enforce existing law. Compulsory education was a "step in the right direction," and it would benefit the state economically.[81] But such proposals were no doubt controversial in a state where most whites did not believe that blacks were their equals, although change was in the air. A new and more assertive generation of black veterans had returned home after serving in World War I, and some had begun to agitate for civil rights through organizations like the NAACP. The Ku Klux Klan also became active across the South during this period and some African Americans were lynched. There had been race riots in Charleston and other American cities after the war. But regardless, the state's depressed economy made it difficult for state leaders to accomplish much during the 1920s and forced the legislature to take a creative approach to taxing to pay for highways and education.[82]

It was within this context that Ellis assumed office. Senate leaders appointed her to serve on the Education Committee owing to her special interest and her background in this area. She also served on a number of other senate committees, including Privileges and Elections, Retrenchments, Incorporations, and Penitentiary, Penal, and Charitable Institutions.[83]

By the time her term of office was drawing to a close, Ellis was gravely ill. She ran for reelection but was too sick to campaign, losing in a rematch with Purdy in 1932. Jake remembered that she was so sick during the 1932 campaign that it took every bit of her energy to get up each day and get dressed. Exhausted, she would go back to bed, unable to attend the stump meetings that were an integral part of campaigning.[84] But Purdy, in turn, was defeated in his next reelection bid in 1936 by a brother-in-law of Mary Ellis.

After her defeat she returned home to Kingstree to spend the final fifteen months of her life bedridden at the home of her sisters, Martha Gordon, a registered nurse, and Emma Gordon, a homemaker. These two sisters had not married and had stayed home and taken care of their father until he died in 1932.[85] Ellis had received some conflicting advice from the physicians she consulted, but in any case, medical science could do little to help her, except to give her medication for the pain as the end drew near.[86] The family was scattered, but saw Mary G. when they could. Junius, who had a business to run, remained at their home near Coosahawchee. Both daughters were still at school in Savannah, where Elizabeth was about to finish high school. Elizabeth began college during her mother's last year of life. Both Elizabeth and Margaret came on the weekends to visit, watching their mother's eyes light up as they recounted their week.[87]

Although unable even to attend her daughter Elizabeth's graduation from Savannah High School in 1933, Ellis was determined that her children would continue their education. Even Ellis's young son Jake understood. Staying at the Gordon home in Kingstree, he went to see a family friend one evening, a teacher who was tutoring him. He begged her to help him prepare for a test he was taking that evening, saying, "Mama is dying and she just has to know that I passed."[88]

Mary Gordon Ellis did not lose her concern for state politics in her last years of declining health. A newspaper reported that "long after her health failed, she continued active in county politics and friends said that her indomitable will power kept her alive through the eight years of her illness."[89] Her final act as a citizen was to cast her vote. Although she could not get up from bed to go to the polls, she voted absentee just one day before she died. A newspaper of the time reported that "Mrs. Ellis' voting on the day before her death was another evidence of her faithfulness to her political duties to the very end."[90] Ellis died on Sunday, September 9, 1934. Election officials received and counted her ballot the day after she died, on Monday. Even that involved some controversy, requiring a legal opinion in order for it to be counted. A lawyer who was consulted stated that since the ballot had not been challenged when it was placed with the other absentee ballots, it should be counted.[91]

Ellis was survived by her husband Junius, who never remarried, and their three children, ages seventeen, fifteen, and thirteen, as well as three brothers and five sisters. She was buried in Kingstree, in Williamsburg Cemetery.

Ellis died when her children were still young, but her legacy to them was to teach them how to grow into strong and independent adults with careers of their own. Like her mother, Elizabeth played a groundbreaking role in the education field. A longtime public school teacher in Greenville, she served on the state board of education from 1972 to 1976, the only woman on the board at that time.[92] Elizabeth was a "renegade" who invited the press to attend state school board meetings, where previously they had not been welcome. Elizabeth also believed that school board members, who visited districts around the state, should themselves "get a taste" of what the students experienced. When the school board visited Greenville, Elizabeth did not take them to a local restaurant for lunch. Rather, she invited them to come to one of the schools and eat a typical school lunch. She provided them with transportation to the school as well—on a school bus.[93]

Margaret had no interest in teaching and became a nurse. When the time came for her to attend college, she wanted to go north and attend Yale University in Connecticut, but her father was opposed. So Margaret went to work, and when she had earned enough money she went north to school on her own. She took the train to New York City, where a friend was a nursing instructor, and enrolled at school nearby in Hackensack, New Jersey, at "one of the best nursing schools around," she recalled. Although Margaret was not able to attend the school of her dreams, years later one of her two sons graduated from Yale University.[94]

It was inevitable that Jake, the youngest child, took his mother's death quite hard. His father's supervision and care could not substitute for his mother's presence as he grew into his teens. He was drafted into the military at the beginning of World War II, served in Europe and survived the Battle of the Bulge. Like many soldiers, he would not talk about his experiences there. By the time he returned home in 1945, his father had sold the turpentine business. Junius died a year later in 1946. After trying his hand at several occupations, Jake took a position with the postal service.[95]

In 1987 Winthrop College recognized Ellis as a distinguished alumnae at its one hundredth anniversary celebration. In conjunction with the celebration, the South Carolina General Assembly recognized Winthrop alumni who had served in the state legislature. Ellis's daughter, Elizabeth Taylor, herself a Winthrop graduate, attended, along with her siblings and their spouses.[96]

To Ellis's children, the recognition was long overdue. Long after her death, controversy still swirled around this pioneer. Ellis was barely mentioned in a history of the county published in the late 1940s.[97] A generation later many in Jasper County were still reluctant to acknowledge Ellis as one of their own. Ellis's son tried without success to have a historical marker put up in the town of Ridgeland, the county seat. Although the area's chamber of commerce agreed, the location that was selected did not meet with the children's approval.[98] In 1992 Jasper County Council asked the public to make suggestions for the name of a new building. Some people wanted the building named for a living local political figure. The Ellis children thought that their mother should be honored, and Jake Ellis proposed that the building be named for her. Despite the urging of her son and the support of the Ridgeland Town Council and the Jasper County School Board, the Jasper County Council refused to name the new building for Ellis.[99] Although she had lived in Jasper County most of her adult life, one council member stated that the reason the council declined to name the building after her was that she was not a county native.[100]

In 1993, at the behest of the Hardeeville Chamber of Commerce, Ellis was honored at the Jasper County Fair as one of the first three Jasper County citizens inducted into its new hall of fame.[101] Her photo was placed in the Hardeeville Chamber of Commerce hallway, along with those of the other inductees.[102] That was a first step toward county recognition of Ellis. Elizabeth Taylor appeared before the county council when it was discussing the naming of the county executive building in 1998, recounting all that "Mary G." had done for Jasper County and her role in providing school buses for African American children.[103] In April 1999, the Jasper County Council voted unanimously to name the county's executive office building for the woman who had wholeheartedly adopted the county as her own. Many county functions would be housed in the former church that was to become the Mary Gordon Ellis Executive Building.[104]

Gaining the support needed to allow a portrait of Ellis to be placed in the South Carolina Senate chambers was also extremely difficult.[105] In 1993 Mary Baskin Waters, director of the South Carolina Governor's Commission on Women, began a process with the consent of the commissioners that would culminate in the hanging of Mary Gordon Ellis's portrait in the chambers. Waters first met with Ellis's children to discuss the process of commissioning a portrait of their mother to be hung in the chambers. The family commissioned a portrait at its own expense. It was painted by Janet Fleming Smith, a Greenville portrait artist who has painted many other prominent people. She sat down with a picture the family gave her. Working from a grainy black and white newspaper photograph to paint a color portrait "was one of the most difficult things I've ever had to do," Smith recalled.[106] Ellis's two daughters worked with her, providing details about their mother's hair color and other information about her appearance.[107]

Several state representatives encouraged the children's efforts to get their mother's portrait hung in the senate chambers. But initially the efforts of family and supporters were not successful. One legislator contacted Governor Carroll Campbell, who was considering running for president and thus under some pressure to show his support for women. He responded positively. Lieutenant Governor Nick Theodore was preparing to run for governor and receptive to overtures. Both officials, in turn, contacted others.[108] In January 1994 Governor Campbell and Lieutenant Governor Theodore sent a letter to Verne Smith, chair of the Rules Committee. They requested that the committee approve the placement of a portrait of South Carolina's first woman senator. Mary Waters wrote the letter for them and then hand delivered it to Senator Verne Smith. Senator Smith then requested that she research whether Ellis was elected or appointed.

Waters attributes their eventual success to a combination of factors. Because Mary Ellis, her daughter Elizabeth, and two of the Gordon sisters were Winthrop graduates, the school put pressure on the legislature.[109] Furthermore, at the time, the state legislature had three powerful women senators, and the Commission on Women had been moved into the governor's office as a result of the Restructuring Act of 1993. Across the nation more women were running for political office, and many were winning their races. Women were elected in record numbers to Congress in 1992.[110] In this changing environment, politicians were becoming more receptive to efforts to honor women. Waters made sure that Mary Gordon Ellis, South Carolina's first woman senator, was recognized at every opportunity.[111]

In 1994 and 1995 Ellis was honored at the South Carolina Governor's Commission on Women's "Women of Achievement Awards Ceremonies." In 1995 "South Carolina Women: A Timeline," published by the South Carolina Department of Archives and History in conjunction with the South Carolina Governor's Commission on Women, recognized Ellis's pioneering role. As Waters noted, it had become harder and harder for the men who ran state government to "continue to make excuses for not allowing her portrait to be hung in the Senate Chambers."[112]

When the portrait was finished, Elizabeth brought it to Waters's office, where it sat for a year as she and the family and other supporters, including Waters and a Columbia women's organization, continued the battle to get the portrait hung. It was not easy: Margaret recalled one of the senators commenting, "Well, I'd like to have my portrait hanging there too!"[113] Supporters, including a Winthrop biographer, contacted the state ombudsman about getting a portrait placed in the senate chambers.[114]

At last the senate approved plans to hang the portrait and an unveiling ceremony was held on March 29, 1995. This was the one-hundred-year anniversary of the election of the first woman to a state senate seat, Martha Hughes Canon of Utah.[115] Thus, the ceremony was held in conjunction with the one hundredth year of women in the legislature celebration sponsored by the National Organization of Women in Legislatures and the South Carolina Women's Caucus. The ceremony was coordinated by Waters, together with Representative Rita

Allison, Representative Frank Cagianno, Senator Holly Cork, Senator Maggie Glover, and Senator Linda Short. Winthrop University was also a sponsor of the event. Jasper County officials subsequently placed a copy of the portrait in the main entranceway of the Mary Gordon Ellis Executive Building.[116]

At the unveiling of the portrait in the senate chambers, Governor David Beasley lauded Ellis's accomplishments, saying that "in every state there has been a Mary G. Ellis who paved the way. Government needs the experience of our mothers, our women, our sisters, our business leaders."[117] Ellis did more than simply pave the way for women, although she did show that women can succeed as agents of change. Many citizens would have ignored the poor conditions of the public schools and simply looked out for the best interests of their own children. Asked why Ellis, a middle-class, white southern woman of the early twentieth century would have cared about education for black children, a distant cousin responded simply, "She was a fine person from a fine family."[118] Ellis thought that all children should have the opportunity for a better life. She ran for office in order to make that dream come true.

Although many of her contemporaries would have disagreed with her, Ellis firmly believed that women should be actively involved in politics. Asked whether women could comfortably serve in such a public venue, she replied, "The atmosphere in the Senate is never embarrassing."[119] Mary Gordon Ellis believed that women could handle almost any problem that they were likely to face. She never hesitated to take on a challenge herself and in doing so made life immeasurably better for many South Carolinians. As she once said, "As for going into politics, why not? Women meet unpleasant situations in other facets of life, why not in politics?"[120]

NOTES

1. Lori Cox Han, *Women and American Politics: The Challenges of Political Leadership* (New York: McGraw-Hill, 2007), 95; Lynne E. Ford, "Women in South Carolina Politics," *Journal of Political Science* 24 (1996): 103; Anne Firor Scott, "After Suffrage: Southern Women in the Twenties," *Journal of Southern History* 30, no. 3 (1964): 299; Wilma Rule, "Why Are More Women State Legislators?" in *Women in Politics: Outsiders or Insiders?* 3rd ed., ed. Lois Duke Whitaker (Upper Saddle River, N.J.: Prentice-Hall, 1999), 193.

2. Scott, "After Suffrage," 299.

3. Ibid., 299–303.

4. Joan Marie Johnson, "The Shape of the Movement to Come: Women, Religion, Episcopalians, and the Interracial Movement in 1920s South Carolina," in *Warm Ashes: Issues in Southern History at the Dawn of the Twenty-First Century*, ed. Winfred B. Moore Jr., Kyle S. Sinisi, and David H. White Jr. (Columbia: University of South Carolina Press, 2003): 201–2; Carol S. Botsch, "South Carolina Council on Human Relations," African Americans in South Carolina: History, Politics, and Culture, http://www.usca.edu/aasc/scchr.htm (accessed July 21, 2011).

5. Johnson, "The Shape of the Movement to Come," 202.

6. Botsch, "South Carolina Council on Human Relations."

7. Margaret Taylor, telephone conversation with author, November 20, 2006.

8. Mark Bellune, "A Daughter's Memories," *Greenville News*, April 16, 1995.

9. Margaret Taylor, telephone conversation with author, November 20, 2006.

10. Ron Chepesiuk and Louise Pettus, "First Woman Senator Perplexed the Men," *Lancaster News*, March 19, 1986, B-8.

11. Elizabeth Ellis Taylor, interview, April 25, 1993, transcript, Mary Gordon Ellis Collection, South Caroliniana Library, University of South Carolina, Columbia (hereinafter cited as MGEC-SCL). The interviewer is unnamed in the transcript.

12. Margaret Taylor, telephone conversation with author, November 20, 2006.

13. Ibid.

14. Mary B. Waters, "Mary Gordon Ellis: First Woman Senator in the South Carolina Legislature, 1929–1931," unpublished paper, 12, MGEC-SCL.

15. Elizabeth Taylor, interview, April 25, 1993, MGEC-SCL.

16. Margaret Taylor, telephone conversation with author, November 20, 2006.

17. Ibid.

18. Waters, "Mary Gordon Ellis," 11, MGEC-SCL.

19. Ibid., 12.

20. Margaret Taylor, telephone conversation with author, November 20, 2006.

21. Ibid.

22. Alan Richard, "Trailblazer Ellis Never Let Stumps Block Her Path," undated clipping, MGEC-SCL.

23. Walter Edgar, *South Carolina: A History* (Columbia: University of South Carolina Press, 1998), 463.

24. Ibid., 463–64.

25. Bob Gorman and Lois Stickell, "Partners in Progress: Joseph B. Felton, the African American Community, and the Rosenwald School Program," *Carologue* 18, no. 3 (2002): 15.

26. Ibid., 15.

27. Ibid., 16.

28. Margaret Taylor, telephone conversation with author, November 20, 2006.

29. Louise Pettus and Ron Chepesiuk, "First Woman Senator Perplexed the Men," *Lancaster News*, March 19, 1986, B-8.

30. Laura Hemingway, "Women of South Carolina: Mary Gordon Ellis," undated clipping, MGEC-SCL.

31. Waters, "Mary Gordon Ellis," 5, MGEC-SCL.

32. Herb Bryant, "South Carolina's First Feminine State Legislator Propelled into Senate Race by Political Maneuver," *Charleston News and Courier*, March 2, 1958.

33. Richard, "Trailblazer Ellis Never Let Stumps Block Her Path," undated clipping, MGEC-SCL.

34. Carrie McCully Patrick, "Woman Senator Talks Politics," clipping dated 1930, MGEC-SCL.

35. Idella Bodie, "Mary Gordon Ellis," in *South Carolina Women* (Orangeburg, S.C.: Sandlapper Publishing, 1991), 96–98.

36. Richard, "Trailblazer Ellis Never Let Stumps Block Her Path," undated clipping, MGEC-SCL.

37. Elizabeth Taylor, interview, April 25, 1993, MGEC-SCL; Waters, "Mary Gordon Ellis," 6, MGEC-SCL.

38. Carol S. Botsch and Robert E. Botsch, "African Americans in South Carolina Politics," *Journal of Political Science* 24 (1996): 66–67.

39. Scott, "After Suffrage," 309.

40. Pat Berman, "The Road to Equal Rights," *The State*, August 26, 2000, D-3; Waters, "Mary Gordon Ellis," 6–7, MGEC-SCL.

41. Bodie, "Mary Gordon Ellis," 97; Elizabeth Taylor, interview, April 25, 1993, MGEC-SCL; Waters, "Mary Gordon Ellis," 7, MGEC-SCL.

42. Bryant, "South Carolina's First Feminine State Legislator Propelled into Senate Race by Political Maneuver."

43. Elizabeth Taylor, interview, April 25, 1993, MGEC-SCL.

44. Margaret Taylor, telephone conversation with author, November 20, 2006.

45. Waters, "Mary Gordon Ellis," 7–8, MGEC-SCL; Richard, "Trailblazer Ellis Never Let Stumps Block Her Path," undated clipping, MGEC-SCL; Bryant, "South Carolina's First Feminine State Legislator Propelled into Senate Race by Political Maneuver."

46. Emmy E. Werner, "Women in the State Legislatures," *Western Political Quarterly* 21, no. 1 (March 1968): 42; Joanne V. Hawks and Mary Carolyn Ellis, "Women Legislators in the Lower South: South Carolina, Georgia, Alabama, and Mississippi, 1922–1984," in *Women in the South: An Anthropological Perspective*, ed. Holly F. Mathews (Athens: University of Georgia Press, 1989), 111.

47. Han, *Women and American Politics*, 94.

48. Hawks and Ellis, "Women Legislators in the Lower South," 112.

49. Ford, "Women in South Carolina Politics," 114.

50. "Woman Senator Favors Education," undated clipping, MGEC-SCL.

51. Hemingway, "Women of South Carolina," undated clipping, MGEC-SCL.

52. Hawks and Ellis, "Women Legislators in the Lower South," 111.

53. "Woman Senator Favors Education," undated clipping, MGEC-SCL.

54. Margaret Taylor, telephone conversation with author, November 20, 2006.

55. Marcia Lynn Whicker, Malcolm Jewell, and Lois Lovelace Duke, "Women in Congress," in *Women in Politics: Outsiders or Insiders?* 2nd edition, ed. Lois Lovelace Duke (Upper Saddle River, N.J.: Prentice-Hall, 1996), 136; Marjorie Williams, "The 'Widow's Mandate,'" *Washington Post*, October 27, 2000, A-35; National Conference of State Legislatures, "Widow Succession in State Legislatures," *Capital Ideas*, April 26, 2006, http://www.ncsl.org/programs/press/2006/cit060426.htm (accessed July 21, 2011).

56. Lynne E. Ford, *Women and Politics: The Pursuit of Equality*, 2nd ed. (Boston: Houghton-Mifflin, 2006), 118; Han, *Women and American Politics*, 91, 94.

57. Margaret Taylor, telephone conversation with author, November 20, 2006.

58. Jake Ellis, interview, April 9, 1993, transcript, MGEC-SCL. The interviewer is unnamed in the transcript.

59. Michael Sponhour, "Educator Blazed Trails in Politics," *The State*, March 13, 1994, E-4.

60. Patrick, "Woman Senator Talks Politics," clipping dated 1930, MGEC-SCL.

61. Ibid.

62. Jim McAllister, untitled, *Greenville News*, January 12, 1979.

63. Ron Chepesiuk and Louise Pettus, "First Woman Senator Perplexed the Men," *Lancaster News*, March 19, 1986, B-8; Victor F. Long, "From Schoolhouse to Statehouse," *Savannah (Ga.) News-Press*, October 6, 1991, C-2.

64. "Mrs. Ellis State Senator Is Charming and Capable Woman," undated clipping, MGEC-SCL.

65. "Only Woman Ever Member of General Assembly Dies," undated clipping, MGEC-SCL.

66. Richard, "Trailblazer Ellis Never Let Stumps Block Her Path," undated clipping, MGEC-SCL.

67. Margaret Taylor, telephone conversation with author, November 20, 2006.

68. "Woman Senator Introduces Her First Bill in Senate," *The State*, February 1, 1929.

69. "Introduction of Bills," *Journal of the Senate*, 1929–31, MGEC-SCL.

70. Eleanor Winn Foxworth, "She Entered the Senate to Work for Education," *The State*, April 22, 1970, A-5.

71. Richard, "Trailblazer Ellis Never Let Stumps Block Her Path," undated clipping, MGEC-SCL.

72. Patrick, "Woman Senator Talks Politics" clipping dated 1930, MGEC-SCL.

73. Hemingway, "Women of South Carolina," undated clipping, MGEC-SCL.

74. Margaret Taylor, telephone conversation with author, November 20, 2006.

75. Elizabeth Taylor, interview, April 25, 1993, MGEC-SCL.

76. "Mrs. Ellis, State Senator," clipping dated September 9, 1934, MGEC-SCL.

77. Sponhour, "Educator Blazed Trails in Politics," E-4.

78. "Woman Senator of 1929–1934 Dies," undated clipping, MGEC-SCL.

79. Edgar, *South Carolina*, 448–53, 475–76, 481; Paul A. Horne Jr. and Patricia Klein, *South Carolina: The History of an American State* (Selma, Ala.: Clairmont Press, 2001), 382.

80. Edgar, *South Carolina*, 491; Horne and Klein, *South Carolina*, 382.

81. "Woman Senator's Interest Primarily in Education," clipping dated February 4, 1929, MGEC-SCL.

82. Edgar, *South Carolina*, 489; Horne and Klein, *South Carolina*, 390.

83. "Senate Groupings Made Yesterday," undated clipping, MGEC-SCL.

84. Waters, "Mary Gordon Ellis," 11, MGEC-SCL.

85. Margaret Taylor, telephone conversation with author, November 20, 2006.

86. Elizabeth Taylor, interview, April 25, 1993, MGEC-SCL.

87. Waters, "Mary Gordon Ellis," 13, MGEC-SCL.

88. Foxworth, "She Entered the Senate to Work for Education," A-5.

89. "A Legal Ballot May Be Cast by Dead Voter, Lawyer Says," undated clipping, MGEC-SCL.

90. Richard, "Trailblazer Ellis Never Let Stumps Block Her Path," undated clipping, MGEC-SCL.

91. Berman, "The Road to Equal Rights," D-3; "A Legal Ballot May Be Cast by Dead Voter," undated clipping, MGEC-SCL.

92. Richard, "Trailblazer Ellis Never Let Stumps Block Her Path," undated clipping, MGEC-SCL; Margaret Taylor, telephone conversation with author, November 30, 2006.

93. Margaret Taylor, telephone conversation with author, November 30, 2006.

94. Ibid.

95. Ibid.

96. "Winthrop Ceremony Honors Mother of Greer Resident," *Greer Citizen*, April 15, 1987, B-20.

97. Victor F. Long, "From Schoolhouse to Statehouse," *Savannah (Ga.) News-Press*, October 6, 1991, C-2.

98. Waters, "Mary Gordon Ellis," 14, MGEC-SCL.

99. Victor F. Long, "Jasper Seeking to Honor First Woman Senator," *Savannah (Ga.) News-Press*, April 4, 1992, C-1, C-4; "Tell Us What You Think," *Jasper County News*, May 5, 1992.

100. Victor F. Long, "State's First Woman Senator Due Honor," *The State*, May 26, 1994, A-16.

101. Brochure, Jasper County Fair, May 16, 1993.

102. Teresa H. Spires, "Hall of Fame to Honor Three Jasper Natives," *Southern Times*, May 14, 1993, 2.

103. William H. Whitten, "County Names Building for Woman Senator," *Jasper County Sun*, April 21, 1999, 1; William H. Whitten, telephone conversation with author, December 12, 2006; "The Women's Caucus Celebrates 'Female Firsts,'" *Beaufort Gazette*, undated clipping, MGEC-SCL.

104. Whitten, telephone conversation with author, December 12, 2006.

105. Long, "From Schoolhouse to Statehouse," C-2.

106. Janet Fleming Smith, telephone conversation with author, December 13, 2006.

107. Margaret Taylor, telephone conversation with author, November 20, 2006.

108. J. Verne Smith to Nick A. Theodore, January 17, 1994, MGEC-SCL; J. Verne Smith to Carrol A. Campbell Jr., January 17, 1994, MGEC-SCL.

109. Mary Baskin Waters to Marjorie Spruill, January 2011.

110. Center for American Woman and Politics, "Summary of Women Candidates for Selected Offices, 1970–2010 (Major Party Candidates)," http://www.cawp.rutgers.edu/fast_facts/elections/documents/can_histsum.pdf (accessed July 21, 2011). 1992 has also been dubbed the "Year of the Woman" by many observers (Women in Congress, "Assembling, Amplifying, and Ascending: Recent Trends Among Women in Congress 1997–2006," http://womenincongress.house.gov/historical-essays/essay.html?intID=5&intSectionID=26 [accessed July 21, 2011]).

111. Waters to Spruill, January 2011.

112. Ibid.

113. Waters, "Mary Gordon Ellis," 14, MGEC-SCL.

114. Winthrop College Alumni Association to Elizabeth Taylor, June 5, 1987, MGEC-SCL; Maebeth Bobb, Winthrop College, assistant to the president for institutional planning, to Elizabeth Taylor, June 8, 1987, MGEC-SCL.

115. "Senate Honors First Woman in Legislature," *The State*, March 30, 1995, B-4.

116. Whitten, telephone conversation with author, December 11, 2006.

117. "Senate Honors First Woman in Legislature," B-4.

118. Jean Carroll, telephone conversation with author, November 10, 2006.

119. "Portrait Unveiling Ceremony Program," March 29, 1995.

120. Ibid.

Julia Mood Peterkin and Wil Lou Gray

The Art and Science of Race Progress

MARY MAC OGDEN

❀ ❀ ❀

Though using two very different mediums—literature and social science—two white South Carolina women, Julia Mood Peterkin (1880–1961) and Wil Lou Gray (1883–1984), challenged regional conceptions of race through nationally recognized projects.[1] In 1929 Peterkin received the Pulitzer Prize for her novel *Scarlet Sister Mary* (1928). Though written partly in the Gullah dialect, the novel departed from the racial stereotypes commonly found in southern literature and presented a humane portrait of southern African American life.[2] Two years later, in 1931, Gray conducted an experiment to test the ability of adult illiterates to learn to read and write at two coeducational summer camps, one for whites at Clemson College and the other for blacks at nearby Seneca Institute. Gray's report on the experiment, referred to herein as the Seneca study, found little variance in the learning abilities of black and white adults and challenged the widespread idea of innate differences in the mental capacities of the two groups.

These two women offered positive portrayals of African Americans that had the potential to change white perceptions of race during an important transitional period in American history. They produced these influential works despite having come of age during the height of the Jim Crow era in the South, a time when eugenics, scientific racism, segregation, and racial violence were widely accepted and when a global economic crisis sorely tested democratic institutions and values in the United States. Fascist governments abroad promoted racial discrimination backed by some of the same scientific theories that bolstered Jim Crow laws and involuntary sterilization at home, practices

that reified the void between America's actions and democratic creed.[3] Against
this backdrop, Peterkin with her pen and Gray with her tests and measurements
promoted democracy and social justice by casting aside stigmas assigned collectively to black people and revealing the individual black person's experience
and humanity.[4] Peterkin stated it clearly: "It is absurd to place all Negroes in one
great social class, mark it 'colored' and make generalizations about its poverty,
ignorance, immorality. . . . Negro individuals differ in character and mentality
as widely as do people with lighter skin."[5] Gray agreed, declaring that "*illiteracy
in South Carolina is today chiefly a negro problem.* . . . If the state is to prosper
it must do so on the progress of the masses rather than the aristocratic few. . . .
It is the duty of the State to provide all its people with an elementary education
which makes for better living."[6]

Brought up in white, upper-class households in South Carolina, the two
women—who were friends—had been reared to accept prevailing gender,
class, and racial mores of their region. Yet Peterkin, with an artist's eye, and
Gray, with the analytical approach of a social scientist, each proffered a perspective on black life that defied the dominant regional narrative of black racial
inferiority. Regional progress on race relations depended on whites envisioning
black people as fully human with similar potential, and Peterkin and Gray were
instrumental in this process. Peterkin's *Scarlet Sister Mary* and Gray's Seneca
study offered audiences outside of the South virtual encounters with southern
black culture as proxies for the actual. As cultural texts, *Scarlet Sister Mary* and
the Seneca study conceptually linked a broad-based, literate audience with an
image of black life that was positive and fostered a progressive view of South
Carolina and its people.[7] When these projects are examined together, they demonstrate that the printed word is more than just a reflection of what a culture
believes or thinks it knows: it generates perceptions as well. Studying these two
South Carolina women and their work demonstrates how change came to the
South piecemeal and from different sources, always in the shadow of tradition
and often by indirect means.

Furthermore, Peterkin and Gray demonstrate the range of the long civil rights
movement. Historians have recently begun to uncover significant civil rights
activism in the decades before the 1950s, particularly among labor unions, the
NAACP, and the Communist Party. Peterkin and Gray reveal the significant role
that a handful of white women also played in these early decades as they devi-
ated from the racism that stifled the vast majority of white southerners.[8]

Little in Peterkin's and Gray's background and early professional work suggested the humanitarian and progressive turn that their later projects would
demonstrate or that race would play an important role in their careers. They

JULIA PETERKIN
Courtesy of South Caroliniana Library,
University of South Carolina, Columbia, S.C.

DR. WIL LOU GRAY

Originally from the Wil Lou Gray estate.

Courtesy of Mary Mac Ogden.

were friends and shared a common hometown, family ties, motherless child-
hoods, midlife career success, national acclaim at the age of forty-eight—and
even red hair. Although their personal and professional lives took them in very
different directions and each project was accomplished independently of the
other, the parallel experiences of these important women are unusual.

Peterkin and Gray both were born in Laurens, South Carolina, a town situated in the northwest section of the Upcountry with "inimitable charm" and
tree-lined streets shaded by magnolias, elm, and crepe myrtle.[9] Julia Mood
Peterkin was born on October 31, 1880, the youngest daughter of Julius Andrew
Mood and Alma Archer. Three years later, on August 29, 1883, Wil Lou Gray
entered the world, the sole daughter of William Lafayette Gray and Sarah Louise
Dial. Both Methodists, the Moods and Grays were respected families with roots
in the state that spanned four generations.

The friendship of their fathers connected Peterkin and Gray early in their
lives. As young men, Julius Mood and William Gray roomed together at Wofford College in Spartanburg, South Carolina, from which they graduated in
1875. While at Wofford, both men joined Kappa Alpha in 1872, a fraternity devoted to the ideals of Confederate hero Robert E. Lee—fidelity to God and
woman, fraternal love, and an unwavering relationship of trust, obedience, and
loyalty with others.[10] Gray returned to Laurens after graduation from Wofford
and in 1878 married Sarah Dial, the sister of Senator Nathaniel Barksdale Dial
(1919–24). Gray briefly practiced law, clerked at the South Carolina House of
Representatives from 1890 to 1892, became a merchant and farmer, and served
as a representative in the South Carolina General Assembly from 1922 to 1924.
After graduation Gray exhibited loyalty to his fraternity brother, when, in 1876,
Mood married Alma Archer against the wishes of her family. Gray offered him
a two-week honeymoon at his family home in Gray Court, and reportedly, the
stay was so pleasant Mood remained to tutor Gray's siblings and serve as headmaster at Dial's School.[11] Mood taught there for two years, then in nearby Barksdale where he built a large eight-room house that became known as the "Mood
House." During these years, in addition to teaching, Mood pursued a medical
degree under the direction of a local physician for a fee of $50, graduating from
the Medical College of Charleston in 1879. In 1881, Mood moved his family to
Sumter, where he became a prominent physician and newspaper editor and
eventually the mayor.[12] Both men died in 1936.

Like the friendship of their fathers, the premature deaths of their mothers
further connected the early lives of Julia Peterkin and Wil Lou Gray. In 1883
when Julia was two, Alma Mood died from tuberculosis after a long struggle
with the disease. As an adult, Peterkin reflected on her motherless childhood

in a letter to the twentieth-century satirist H. L. Mencken, who was a friend of hers, observing that motherless children received "precious little real loving" after their natural mother died.[13] Motherlessness is a common theme in Peterkin's fiction and especially significant in *Scarlet Sister Mary*, where Mary, the protagonist, is motherless but mother to numerous children and motherless grandchildren. Despite the loss of her mother, Peterkin recalled her childhood as a good one. In an autobiographical sketch, she wrote, "I knew I had many blessings. I was protected from discomfort and ugliness and fear. My days were pleasant. I had no reason to complain of the scheme of which I was a living part."[14]

As a young girl, Julia and her sister Laura lived with her maternal grandparents, while her eldest sister, Marian, lived with Julius and his second wife Janie Brogden, whom he married in 1883 shortly after the death of Alma Mood. As a result of these living arrangements, Julia was devoted to Laura and worked diligently as a college student to assure she would graduate with her sister. "My one ambition was to stay in my sister's classes, so we might finish college together, for I loved my sister more than anybody else in the whole world and could not bear to think she would leave me behind," recalled Peterkin.[15] Although the death of Alma Mood disrupted Peterkin's family cohesion, Julius Mood remained a central figure in Peterkin's life and a chief critic during her literary career. In a 1932 interview, Peterkin revealed that her family was not "elated over her work" and her father wished "she would write more ladylike stories."[16] Although recent scholarship has scrutinized Peterkin's relationship with her father, she loved her father and spoke of him affectionately in her correspondence.[17]

Like Peterkin's mother, Gray's mother died when she was young. Gray was eight in January 1892 when Sarah Gray died from tuberculosis after battling the disease for two years.[18] Sarah Gray was bedridden for much of her illness, and thus Gray took care not to "dirty her dress" around her mother.[19] After Sarah Gray's death, William Gray sent his children to live with an aunt ten miles from Laurens, visiting once a week on Sundays for three years.[20] In December 1895 William Gray remarried the family's former babysitter, Mary Dunklin, and in January 1896 he brought his children back home to live with him. At age twelve, Gray was one grade level behind her peers in school, a sign of the impact of death and displacement in her formative years.[21]

As young women, Julia Peterkin and Wil Lou Gray attended local women's colleges and were among the growing number of women—still a distinct minority, especially in the South—who benefited from higher education during the Progressive Era. In 1896, at sixteen, Peterkin finished her undergraduate degree at Converse College and completed a master's degree the following year. After graduation, she taught seven pupils in a rural school in Calhoun

County. Gray finished Columbia College in 1903 and, like Peterkin, taught in a one-room schoolhouse, Jones School, in the community of Ware Shoals. The following year she pursued graduate work at Winthrop College and in 1905 at Vanderbilt University. In 1908, she taught for a year at Martha Washington College in Abingdon, Virginia, and in 1911, she earned a master's of arts in political science from Columbia University. Perhaps achieving such a high level of education as well as spending time in the North opened Gray's mind to think differently about race. Both women received honorary doctorates from their alma maters, Peterkin in 1927 and Gray in 1978.[22]

After sharing such similar experiences during their youth, their paths diverged in 1903 when Peterkin married William George Peterkin, who farmed a large plantation in Fort Motte, a town in the southern part of the state. Upon her marriage, Julia became the mistress of Lang Syne, a farm that specialized in the production of cotton and asparagus that had once been the home of Civil War figure Louisa McCord. Approximately five hundred black people worked the farm.[23] "When I came to this plantation to live, my whole physical world changed," wrote Peterkin. "Here everyone was black except the few members of my own household. The current speech was different, the conventions were new and strange. Few of my old rules of living applied."[24] Peterkin was fascinated by the black people around her and admired their resiliency in light of poverty and hardships, observing in a self-reflective way that "they met what life sent with courage and grace. Why couldn't I do it as well as they could? What ailed me?"[25]

This setting inspired Peterkin's literary career, a career that began by chance, in midlife. Peterkin, an accomplished pianist, began piano lessons at Chicora College in Columbia to refine her technique.[26] Her instructor, Dr. Henry Bellamann, found her stories of life at Lang Syne fascinating, and he asked her to bring a sketch of life on the farm with her to each lesson. Bellamann, a well-connected musician, also wrote fiction, and with his encouragement Peterkin began the stories of southern life for which she became famous. Bellamann knew Carl Sandburg, H. L. Mencken, and Emily Clark, editor with James Branch Cabell of the *Reviewer* (1921–25), a magazine based in Richmond, Virginia, that showcased southern writers. Mencken's literary magazine *Smart Set* and Clark's *Reviewer* published Peterkin's stories, and in 1924, Alfred A. Knopf published her first collection of short stories, *Green Thursday*.[27] Through these connections, Peterkin entered the literary scene of the 1920s, and, over the subsequent decade, she won critical acclaim for *Green Thursday* (1924), *Bright Skin* (1927), *Black April* (1927), *Scarlet Sister Mary* (1928), and *Roll, Jordan, Roll* (1933).

"It seems to me that women are divided into two classes," wrote Peterkin, "those who are doing things and those who are not and that the most alive and most interesting ones are doing things—something for which they have respect."[28] With two O. Henry Awards, a Pulitzer, an honorary doctorate from Converse College, and critically acclaimed publications, Peterkin was most definitely doing things. However, by World War II, owing to family demands, Peterkin had quit writing and disappeared into obscurity, claiming, "I'm no longer a writer, nor have I ever been a literary person."[29] Years later, when the archivist at the South Caroliniana library wrote to ask for original manuscripts, Peterkin responded, "I've no papers left, no manuscripts. . . . All these somehow belong to another existence of mine."[30]

Peterkin was part of a broad artistic movement in the 1920s that centered literary focus on black life. After World War I, many Americans supported the idea of cultural assimilation, but some intellectuals criticized this idea as detrimental to the diversity that made America unique. Cultural pluralism countered the mythic potential of assimilation and emerged as the lifejacket for the individuality and ethnic expression that "created a whole more beautiful than the sum of its parts" in postwar America.[31] In the arts, white writers were "drunk with the exuberance of discovery" of black people as raw literary material, and they capitalized on this discovery in the years that preceded the visibility of black writers and the Harlem Renaissance.[32] Thus cultural pluralism at once encompassed white portrayal of African American and other racial/ethnic groups and the self-expression of these groups.

This discovery was under way in the South. The white Poetry Society of Charleston led what would become known as the "Southern Renaissance" in reaction to Mencken's scathing essay debunking southern culture entitled "Sahara of the Bozart" ("Bozart" being a play on the word Beaux-Arts).[33] This group spawned a southern literary movement of which Peterkin was one of the most successful members.

Following three well-received publications, Peterkin wrote *Scarlet Sister Mary* in 1928. In the book the characters speak Gullah, a dialect Peterkin found "not only musical and expressive but filled with wit and wisdom."[34] Peterkin gave her characters a native tongue to speak their stories in their own voice. If language is politics by other means, Gullah endowed Peterkin's characters with a bifurcated identity that was at once American and southern African American.

Peterkin's portrayal of African Americans in *Scarlet Sister Mary* merits particular attention both because it was popular and because it secured the Pulitzer Prize. The novel, which historian Charles Joyner has called a "feminist comedy," focuses on the religion, promiscuity, power, and tenacity of a black woman named Mary Pinesett. The backdrop of the novel is Blue Brook Plantation, a symbol of a passing era in the modern South, where whites are absent. Mary endures abandonment, adultery, and the death of a child; she experiences the rebirth of her belief in God and empowerment by rejecting her true love after years of cruel treatment, but despite her return to the church, she remains loyal to her belief in the power of the conjuring rag. Mary's physical and emotional struggles are universal, and her story is one of reconciliation, contrition, and liberation.[35] *Scarlet Sister Mary*'s popularity in the twenties was due in part to its feminist message.[36] Throughout the story, Mary makes personal choices free from white censure and condemnation, though they are scrutinized by the black community around her. Despite their judgment and the attendant isolation she endures, Mary faces the obstacles life sends her with courage and self-determination. This is a powerful image of a woman defining herself, a feminist message that in the 1920s appealed to a broad audience despite Mary's race. On one hand, Mary is black, and her promiscuity can be understood as reinforcing the image of the black Jezebel. On the other hand, Mary knows her behavior is unacceptable to the black community, and this offers an alternative image of Mary as a woman liberated from restraints, whether religious or community driven, who lives as she deems fit. *Scarlet Sister Mary* is still in print with over a million copies sold worldwide.[37]

The critical reception of *Scarlet Sister Mary* was mixed. Novelist Robert Herrick critiqued Mary as a strong woman who "in her fecundity, kindness, health and happiness . . . embodies many essential qualities of all strong women."[38] But Mary's promiscuity led other early critics to label Peterkin's work notorious. Peterkin reacted by observing that "when I began writing negro sketches I did not dream they'd be regarded as such radical things, or that I'd meet such harsh criticism as has been given me."[39] Still, the world Peterkin depicts reflects universal practices found in both the black and white communities around her, a reality that transcended class, race and gender mores.[40]

Many African Americans seemed to like the book. *Time Magazine* raved, "Negro intelligentisiacs agree with whites—the Authoress Peterkin writes accurately, vividly of the Gullah Negroes."[41] W. E. B. Du Bois and Langston Hughes responded favorably to her work. Pleased by their reception, Peterkin wrote, "I am glad to have approval from Negroes. . . . [T]hey seem to understand my intentions better than whites."[42] Du Bois praised Peterkin, writing, "She is a Southern white woman, but she has the eye and the ear to see beauty and know truth."[43]

Although Hughes liked her work, he recounted an odd experience he had vis-à-vis Peterkin. In 1931, after meeting Peterkin in New York, he accepted an invitation to visit Lang Syne. "I did go to call on a white lady one day on an enormous plantation in South Carolina," wrote Hughes in his autobiography. "The lady was the writer Julia Peterkin, whom I had met at literary gatherings in New York." When Hughes arrived at Lang Syne, he was greeted by a man on the porch of the main house who stared at him "in unfriendly surprise" and said Peterkin was not at home. "As we drove away," recalled Hughes, "I looked back to see the man staring at me openmouthed."[44] Such poor hospitality no doubt played a part in Hughes's 1938 comedic parody of *Scarlet Sister Mary* entitled *Scarlet Sister Barry.*[45]

African Americans in South Carolina also approved of the work. A newspaper article commented on the review Esther Mazyck offered the Louise Fordham Holmes Literary and Art Club of Charleston of Peterkin's *Black April* in 1928. Mazyck described Peterkin's work as a "most sympathetic interpretation of a white southerner's conception of the lowly negro."[46]

Numerous critiques of Peterkin's persona, position, intent, and prejudice address the tensions, both in her characters and in Peterkin herself, that appear in her fiction as a whole. Some recent scholars have charged that Peterkin's depiction of black culture presents a fictitious, thus an inaccurate, portrait of black life and reifies her status as a white plantation mistress spinning fiction from the Big House. Scholar Elizabeth Robeson claims that at the end of her career "Peterkin regressed as a writer, turning back toward pastoralism, to eulogize the vanishing world that had paradoxically eviscerated and sustained her."[47] Historian Charles Joyner differentiates her *conscious* art from folk art, claiming that Peterkin's work embodies her individual vision and values, not the "visions and values of the folk themselves."[48] Nghana tamu Lewis contends that "both the technique and principle of Peterkin's fiction informs our understanding of her politics as a modernist, not realist, in orientation."[49]

Peterkin's own perspective on truth and her writing challenges recent interpretations of her work. When asked about the truth of her stories, Peterkin responded:

> We surely must realize the importance of our right to say what seems to us to be the truth without fear of molestations. Not because what we say matters to anyone but ourselves, but because when we fail to speak what we do believe is true—or substitute for what we think is true with words which we think are not true—then inevitably we lose whatever perception of truth we may have achieved. And surely a persistent will to discover the truth is our only means of ever finding out any particle of what it is.[50]

Naturally, Peterkin did not see her work in the same light as her critics. "The books I write," she noted, "are nothing but an effort to record what some of

the black people I know say and think about other black lives. . . . I know well
the people about whom I write."[51]

Despite the alleged pathos, conflict, and contradictions scholars find in Peterkin's art, it is important to recognize the broader, sociocultural implications that
her work presented to a nation caught in the throes of change. Regardless of the
vein in which Peterkin is observed, through Mary she presented a new narrative on race and feminism that had the potential to alter the consciousness of a
wide national and international audience. Peterkin unveiled a woman's world of
trials and tribulations that evoked sympathy, reflection, and compassion from
those who chose to look into it. More importantly, Mary struggles but survives,
manifesting human qualities that resonated among readers regardless of their
color. She is unique and complicated, a woman who makes choices that throw
her against the winds of acceptability, choices that liberate her. The humanity
of Peterkin's characters in *Scarlet Sister Mary* presents an alternative portrayal
of African Americans to whites in an era when lynching, black illiteracy, and
racial segregation were visible signs of South Carolina's lack of progress, a state
slow to embrace change, and in Peterkin's opinion "willing for everyone to go
to hell in his own way."[52]

Where Peterkin created a conscious art that crafted a unique portrait of black
life, Wil Lou Gray used social science to forge a new conception of black potential. Unlike Peterkin, Gray never married and chose a career as a professional
educator. In 1914 she served as supervisor of rural schools in Laurens County,
and by 1919, she had become supervisor of adult schools for the state, a position
she held until 1947. During this period, South Carolina vied with Louisiana as
the state with the highest adult illiteracy rates in the nation, and Gray dedicated
her career to eradicating this problem. Her job with the state commenced at the
end of World War I when professionalization and standardization of education
and the advent of state control over volunteer work were reshaping the field of
education. During the twenties, service on the national boards of the National
Education Association, the General Federation of Women's Clubs, and the
American Association of Adult Education and an enduring relationship with
colleagues at Columbia University enhanced Gray's professional reputation and
helped garner publicity for her programs.

By the early thirties, academics at teaching universities across the nation were
producing scholarship related to adult education. In 1932, Columbia University,
Vassar, the University of Michigan, and Ohio State received funds from the
American Association of Adult Education to conduct research in adult education. Formed in 1926, the American Association of Adult Education served two
purposes: to disseminate information on developments in the field through its

publication, the *Journal of Adult Education*, and to fund research and scholarship. The organization's main goal, however, was to "supply a medium of exchange for teachers and administrators actually in contact with adults," and by the early thirties, the association had established direct contact with more than five hundred local, state, national, and international organizations.[53] Gray served as a member of the executive board of the association in 1931 and that same year organized an experiment, with the assistance of scholars from the University of Chicago and Yale, to assess the impact of environment on the learning capacity of adult illiterates.[54]

Gray was well known across the nation for her work with adult learners and her signature opportunity schools. "She is one of the most outstanding women in the South. . . . [H]er contribution even to adult education is not only state wide but nationwide. Indeed, she has much to contribute even to China and India and every country of the world facing the dire dilemma of illiteracy," wrote Mabel Carney, a professor at Teachers College, Columbia University.[55] Her opportunity school, a four-week summer school that taught basic literacy skills to illiterate adults, began in 1921 at the Daughters of the American Revolution camp in Tamassee, South Carolina. This experimental four-week camp for adult women was funded entirely by Gray, her church, club patrons and a "barrel of flour" donated by her brother Dial, a salesman for the Red Baron flour company.[56] From this humble start, she expanded the school in subsequent years to include men and black students and used her position as state supervisor of adult education to bolster public support, especially tax support, for her programs. Gray advocated tax-supported adult education, but the South Carolina General Assembly was less inclined to supply the money, leaving Gray dependent on charity and volunteers to conduct adult summer schools each year. For the most part, funding for these opportunity schools was a blend of state money and contributions from "college authorities, church societies, patriotic organizations, civic clubs, textile officials, . . . public spirited citizens," and, in Gray's words, "faith."[57]

Between 1921 and 1946, numerous state colleges—Lander, Erskine, Anderson, and Clemson—hosted opportunity schools and enrollment doubled each year. Gray solicited volunteer teachers from across the state to serve as faculty, and in 1925 at Erskine College, Strom Thurmond conducted an agricultural class for Gray. "In working with so many underprivileged students," he claimed, "we set a high standard for community service and individual excellence."[58] Years later, Thurmond and Gray parted ways when he became a Dixiecrat, and a black confidante of Gray's claimed, "I don't think old Strom would have ever got into Miss Gray's house," because she realized in her final years "she never really did like him."[59] By 1930, the opportunity school was considered an important agent of adult elementary education by both private and public groups in the state. Gray claimed that "mill owners, land owners, and others for whom students had worked both before and after attending the school" noticed the "wholesome, stimulating effect on young men and women" who attended the summer program.

The first opportunity school for black students was held in 1931 at the Seneca Institute in Seneca, South Carolina.[60] In the summer of 1930, Gray submitted an application to the American Association of Adult Education for a subsidy of $5,000 to conduct an educational experiment at her summer opportunity school and received the money from the Carnegie Corporation. William Gray, director of research in reading in the University of Chicago's Department of Education, and J. Warren Tilton, a psychologist from Yale, directed the testing of the students and used materials designed by Edward L. Thorndike, a psychologist at Teachers College. The purpose of the study was to discern the learning capacity of black and white adults with varied levels of education when taught in a "favorable" environment.[61] The goal of the study aimed to prove the effectiveness of adult elementary education on illiterate adults and provide a model for other states. Gray used the study to promote her belief that the "lack of popular education is an expensive and increasing liability which can and which should be turned into rich assets." She wanted all citizens of South Carolina, black and white, to receive tax-supported literacy education as needed, an unpopular and controversial idea at the time. Gray understood that the white state government, already not eager to support literacy education for white adults, was even more unwilling to pay for such education for black adults, and she hoped that her study would justify such spending.[62]

From July 23 to August 22, a combined summer school was held at Clemson College and the Seneca Institute. The $5,000 grant covered the salaries of William Gray and Tilton ($2,000) and the scholarships, twenty dollars each, for fifty black and fifty white participants ($2,000). Private donors paid the tuition for five additional participants. The remaining money paid for materials and testing supplies. Morse Cartwright of the American Association for Adult Education asked that the grant be made as an allocation against the Adult Education Experimental Fund (that contained $16,000 of grant money from the Carnegie Corporation in 1930–31), because "South Carolina's program seems to be the outstanding state demonstration in the campaign against adult illiteracy."[63] Teachers were paid $100, and board was provided by the state.[64] To accommodate the racial demands of the region, the "colored Baptists" loaned the Seneca site to Gray for the black students' housing.[65]

Of the 288 pupils who attended, only the Carnegie-funded students were tested, and these students ranged in age from fourteen to seventy. The school day lasted from 7:30 a.m. to 11:00 p.m. with free time for exercise and chapel incorporated into the schedule. Gray noted that the first week was hard for many of the black students because they were older and struggled with eyestrain or poorly adjusted eyeglasses.[66] Out-of-class time was also different for the black students. Because some of them worked as cooks, many participated in cooking classes that focused on every aspect of the meal from cost analysis to nutritional value. Also, the black students led their own vespers. Here they sang spirituals "as only the colored race can," according to Gray, and recited from newspapers and current events. Owing to a lack of equipment at the Seneca site, moving pictures were absent in the curriculum provided the black students. However, a local theater manager invited them to attend on Saturdays, where many students saw a "talkie" for the first time.[67] A local paper reported the event, observing that "the Richardson theatre gave them a special show and invited the entire school as their guests. All accepted except some members of the Holiness church, these thought this kind of entertainment a sin, so they refused the invitation. It was an interesting study in psychology to hear the reaction of those who had never seen, or heard, a play given on the screen."[68]

Verbal and nonverbal tests were given to the Clemson and Seneca experimental groups during the month-long session to determine the IQ of each student. According to the first chapter of the Seneca study report, published after the experiment was completed, numerous educational research questions were addressed that considered the impact of gender, age, income, previous schooling, and occupation on the intelligence and learning capacity of illiterate adults. These factors explained in part the differences between the black and white students' intelligence test scores. Although the study was clearly designed to determine whether or not race affected educational capacity, as written none of the research questions addressed race. The conspicuous absence of race in the research questions is interesting, because the two experimental groups of equal size were differentiated by race. It is possible that Gray purposely did not include questions about race in order to neutralize potential controversy about the study locally. It is not until the end of the report that Gray debunks the myth of racial difference in mental capacity, concluding that there is "little difference between the learning ability of whites and Negroes."[69]

The average age of the fifty-five students at Seneca was thirty-eight with an average seven months of previous schooling.[70] The black students were approximately thirteen years older than their white counterparts. The average wage of the twenty-six black students reporting salaries was $1.50 per week; among those who worked, there were farmers, cooks, mechanics, laundresses, and one midwife. A local paper reported, "One man who is attending the school has 15 children but quit his job just to learn to read and write. Another earning $10.00 each week as a cook quit his job to learn to read and write."[71] None of the Seneca students worked in the mills, yet thirty of the students came from Oconee County where the study took place, an Upstate cotton and textile center. In contrast, two-thirds of the white students at Clemson worked in the textile industry and earned an average salary of $9.04 per week.[72] Half of the Seneca participants were orphans; twenty-seven came from homes where there were ten to seventeen children; and the participants had an average of three children. The Seneca group read the same materials and took the same tests and measurements as their Clemson counterparts.[73]

The next year, the *Peabody Journal of Education* reviewed the study as a "quantitative treatment of the results of short course schools for adults," describing it as "a bit of definitive evidence in a field marked by many and diverse opinions."[74] Eight years later, Gray summarized the 1931 summer experiment: "In 1931 . . . the Carnegie Corporation of New York City gave the school 5000k to finance an experiment to determine the learning ability of adult illiterates under favorable conditions. The findings of those four work-filled weeks were published in a book and sent all over this country and several foreign ones. We still have a feeling of pride when we see this book and remember the service we were able to render."[75]

It is important to consider the curriculum used to educate the students at Seneca in relation to the findings of the experiment. All of the reading and writing material used at the Seneca site was racially and class biased, with everything from advertisements to etiquette lessons reflecting a white, upper-middle-class lifestyle. For example, Seneca student Katy Smith wrote in her class scrapbook that "an attractive table makes the meal more appealing" above a picture of a table set for a wealthy individual. The caption beneath the picture read "The dark beauty of Ebony and the clearness of Crystal are graciously combined in this setting for a formal luncheon. The Millefleur cutting on the square base tumbler is matched on the crystal service plate. The embroidered organdie cloth is Florentine."[76] It is unlikely that any of the students at either Seneca or Clemson could comprehend, much less find value in, this information. How the black students understood and retained the teaching materials used by the instructors at Seneca probably influenced the outcome of the tests administered during the term.

Despite the biased curriculum, the commencement exercises at Seneca were racially sensitive and reflected the interests of the black students. At the final program, a group of students presented to the audience a booklet called "The Story of My Race," and they sang a "farewell group of spirituals" at the conclusion of the program. "Every one," claimed Gray, "left the Seneca Institute with a feeling of satisfaction."[77] Olema Wiggins, a student at Seneca, wrote to Gray after the summer program ended that "I have found no one so intensely interested in us as a race as you. All I can say will not express my gratitude to you for the interest you have in us."[78] Additionally, the overall health of the Seneca students changed while in residence at the summer school. The local paper reported, "The pupils were given a medical examination at the beginning of school at which time each was weighed. On weighing the same pupils at the end of the month a gain of 11 pounds was noted."[79]

Gray's 1931 study scientifically demonstrated that race alone did not determine an adult illiterate's ability to learn. This result proved the power of democracy in education, where equal opportunity meant equal potential for all people. With her scientific analysis as backing, Gray turned every argument against funding black as well as adult education on its head and made the state's illiteracy liabilities, both black and white, a point of national discussion. Numerous journals published her findings, disseminating this idea to a wide professional audience. Like Peterkin through art, Gray crafted a new conception of black potential through science.

The following year Gray attempted to secure funds for another study but was refused on the grounds that "the activities of the [Carnegie] Corporation" had to be "sharply curtailed."[80] For the next five years, she continued to seek support, urging the governor, private clubs, and local philanthropists to fund adult education for both races, using her study to bolster her call for tax-supported opportunity schools. In 1936 governor Olin Johnston wrote to Gray, "Now is the logical time to begin our renewed efforts for the eradication of this menace to our State's welfare. Looked at from every angle, illiteracy is expensive. . . . [W]e still have 36,000 white and 156,000 colored illiterates who, themselves, in 1930 admitted they could not write their names."[81] With the establishment of New Deal agencies like the National Youth Administration, her work to promote black education found new support. In 1936 and 1937 Gray held opportunity summer schools specifically for black illiterate adults at Vorhees Junior College in Denmark, South Carolina. The curriculum at these camps focused on African heritage, health education, home repair, and domestic training. John Groves, a student at Vorhees in 1936, wrote, "We have made fans about the colored people we have talked about," and Frankie Walker wrote, "I am going to do all I can to teach someone else the things that I have learned." As a sign of support, Modjeska Simkins visited the site.[82] In recognition of her service to the black race, South Carolina State College in Orangeburg awarded Gray a certificate of merit, a loving cup, and flowers at the seventh annual conference on adult education in April 1949.[83]

"It would be hard to say which is the more interesting or distinguished character, Wil Lou Gray, great humanitarian, or Julia Peterkin, brilliant novelist," exclaimed Eunice Ford Stackhouse, a mutual friend of the two.[84] The lives and work of these two important women add to the picture of southern race relations in the years before the New Deal. Peterkin's portrayal of black life in *Scarlet Sister Mary* and Gray's scientific study on the learning ability of black and white adults affirmed in different ways that people, regardless of color, are human beings. Through the printed word, their perspectives reached thousands of readers beyond South Carolina.

Furthermore, *Scarlet Sister Mary* and the Seneca study bear on the question of southern progress in the years before the New Deal. Connecting the histories of Peterkin and Gray reveals the mechanics of progress in a region limited by tradition and defined by social inertia. These projects and their women architects initiated a shift in perception that must be considered a stepping-stone in the path of regional progress. *Scarlet Sister Mary* and the Seneca study demonstrate how Peterkin and Gray, when viewed collectively with other southern writers, activists, and educators, made small ripples, albeit intellectually, that led to the sweeping social changes implemented through policy in the fifties. In 1940, Peterkin recognized her role in this process and claimed, "I think that perhaps what we call progress is merely change and that progress is the ability to adjust oneself to change."[85] Ultimately, Peterkin and Gray used their work to at once adjust to change and forge a new direction in the mindset of their region.

NOTES

1. For a recent interpretation of Gray, see DaMaris Ayres, *Let My People Learn* (Greenwood, S.C.: Attic Press, 1988). For recent interpretations of Peterkin, see Katherine Millar Williams, *A Devil and a Good Woman, Too: The Lives of Julia Peterkin* (Athens: University of Georgia Press, 1997), Thomas Landess, *Julia Peterkin* (Boston: Twayne, 1976), Frank Durham, ed., *The Collected Short Stories of Julia Peterkin* (Columbia: University of South Carolina Press, 1970), Elizabeth Robeson, "The Ambiguity of Julia Peterkin," *Journal of Southern History* 61, no. 4 (1995): 762–86, Harold Dean Thompson, "Minerva Finds a Voice: The Early Career of Julia Peterkin" (PhD diss., Vanderbilt University, 1987), Nghana tamu Lewis, "Politics from the Pedestal: Modernity, Cultural Intervention, and the Myth of Southern Womanhood, 1920–1945" (PhD diss., University of Illinois at Urbana-Champaign, 2001), and William Gray, Wil Lou Gray, and J. W. Tilton, *The Opportunity Schools of South Carolina: An Experimental Study* (New York: American Association for Adult Education, 1932).

2. Julia Peterkin, "One Southern View-Point," *North American Review* 244, no. 2 (1937): 389–98.

3. For a history of the eugenics movement in the South, see Edward J. Larson, *Sex, Race, and Science: Eugenics in the Deep South* (Baltimore, Md.: Johns Hopkins University Press, 1995).

4. Peterkin meant struggle as a universal, ongoing process of change in the world ("What and Why I Have Written," unpublished sketch, folder 28–613–7, Julia Mood Peterkin Papers, South Carolina Historical Society, Charleston [hereinafter cited as JMPP-SCHS]).

5. Julia Peterkin and Doris Ulmann, *Roll, Jordan, Roll* (New York: Robert O. Ballou, 1933), 16.

6. 1924–25 superintendent of adult schools annual report outline, box 24, Wil Lou Gray Papers, South Caroliniana Library, University of South Carolina, Columbia (hereinafter cited as WLGP-SCL).

7. For movie scripts as cultural texts, see Larry May, *The Big Tomorrow: Hollywood and the Politics of the American Way* (Chicago: University of Chicago Press, 2000), and for "print-capitalism" as a means of conceptually linking people by way of media so readers across regions become capable of understanding each other and thus forge a common discourse, see Benedict Anderson, *Imagined Communities: Reflections on the Origin and Spread of Nationalism* (New York: Verso, 1981).

8. See Patricia Sullivan, *Days of Hope: Race and Democracy in the New Deal Era* (Chapel Hill: University of North Carolina Press, 1996), and Jacquelyn Dowd Hall, "The Long Civil Rights Movement and the Political Uses of the Past," *Journal of American History* 91, no. 4 (2005): 1233–63.

9. Harriet Blackwell, *A Candle for All Time* (Richmond, Va.: Dietz Press, 1959), 6.

10. Phillip Stone, archivist, Wofford College, Spartanburg, S.C., April 23, 2007, to author; Mrs. M. Dial Williams, "Father and Mother of Julia Peterkin Recalled by One Who Knew Them," *Spartanburg Herald Journal*, clipping dated 1934, private collection of Anne Neely, Asheboro, N.C.

11. Landess, *Julia Peterkin*, 17.

12. Barbara Esther Outlaw, "Prize-Winning Biography of the Late Julius Alfred Mood," *Sumter Daily Item*, undated clipping, private collection of Anne Neely, Asheboro, N.C.; Irene Elliott, Wil Lou Gray, and Marguerite Tolbert, *Distinguished Women of Laurens County* (Columbia, S.C.: R. L. Bryan, 1972), 105.

13. See Robeson, "The Ambiguity of Julia Peterkin."

14. Julia Mood Peterkin, "What I Believe: Living Philosophies," *Forum* 84, no. 1 (1930): 48.

15. "What and Why I Have Written," JMPP-SCHS.

16. Meade, "Julia Peterkin."

17. Peterkin to William Watts Ball, May 30, 1932, box 20, William Watts Ball Papers, Manuscripts Department, William R. Perkins Library, Duke University, Durham, N.C. (hereinafter cited as WWWBP-WRPL). See Williams, *A Devil and a Good Woman, Too*, for analysis of the relationship between Peterkin and her father.

18. Handwritten account of Sarah Louise Dial Gray by her sister, Emma Dial, box 31, WLGP-SCL.

19. Wil Lou Gray Ogden, interview by author, Whiteville, N.C., October 1995; Marigene Miller, interview by author, Columbia, S.C., June 21, 1996.

20. Blackwell, *A Candle for All Time*, 82.

21. Ibid., 119.

22. JMPP-SCHC; Columbia College Alumnae Office, telephone interview by author, November 12, 2007.

23. Eric Posselt, ed., *On Parade, Caricatures by Eva Hermann: Contributions of Prominent Authors* (New York: Coward McCann, 1929), 114.

24. Peterkin, "What I Believe," 48.

25. Julia Mood Peterkin, "Seeing Things," *American Magazine*, January 1927, 27.

26. Anne Neely, interview by author, Asheboro, N.C., September 23, 2007.

27. Ibid., 20.

28. Medora Fields Perkerson, "Julia Peterkin, Author and Farmer," *Atlanta (Ga.) Journal Sunday Magazine*, April 28, 1940.

29. http://www.sc.edu/library/socar/uscs/1995/durham95.html (accessed April 15, 2005). See Williams, *A Devil and a Good Woman, Too*, for details regarding this period in Peterkin's life.

30. Box 14, Frank Durham Papers, South Caroliniana Library, University of South Carolina, Columbia (hereinafter cited as FDP-SCL).

31. Skip Gates, "Of Negroes Old and New," *Transition*, no. 46 (1974), 45.

32. Ibid.

33. H. L. Mencken, "The Sahara of the Bozart," in *Prejudices: Second Series* (New York: Knopf, 1920), 136–54.

34. Lewis, "Politics from the Pedestal," 41; Posselt, *On Parade*, 117.

35. Julia Mood Peterkin, *Scarlet Sister Mary* (New York: Bobbs-Merrill, 1928).

36. Kristin Schar, "Twentieth-Century American Best Sellers," http://www3.isrl.uiuc.edu/~unsworth/courses/enlt226m/lis590ab/search.cgi?title=Scarlet+Sister+Mary (accessed February 2, 2007).

37. Ibid.

38. Robert Herrick, *New Republic*, December 26, 1928, 172.

39. Peterkin to Ball, March 10, 1925, box 14, FDP-SCL.

40. About the poor white community, a peer wrote, "They know nothing to do and have nothing to think of except breed like rabbits" (Mrs. M. B. Hall to Wil Lou Gray, February 5, 1935, WLGP-SCL).

41. "Peterkin Folk," *Time*, April 11, 1932, http://www.time.com/time/magazine/printout/0,8816,743550,00.html (accessed August 22, 2006).

42. Landess, *Julia Peterkin*, 25.

43. Qtd. in ibid., 25.

44. Langston Hughes, *I Wonder as I Wander*, vol. 14 of *The Collected Works of Langston Hughes* (Columbia: University of Missouri Press, 2002), 77–78.

45. See Joseph McLaren, *Langston Hughes, Folk Dramatist in the Protest Tradition, 1921–1943* (Westport, Conn.: Greenwood Press, 1997).

46. *Columbia Palmetto Leader*, May 26, 1928, 5.

47. Robeson, "The Ambiguity of Julia Peterkin," 770.

48. Charles Joyner, "South Carolina as Folk Culture," keynote address, Sixtieth Annual Meeting of the University South Caroliniana Society, 1996, http://www.sc.edu/library/socar/uscs/1996/addr96.htm (accessed June 5, 2006).

49. Nghana tamu Lewis, "The Rhetoric of Mobility, the Politics of Consciousness: Julia Mood Peterkin and the Case of a White Black Writer," *African American Review* 38, no. 4 (2004): 590.

50. Peterkin, "What I Believe," 52.

51. Posselt, *On Parade*, 118.

52. Peterkin to Ball, May 30, 1932, box 14, FDP-SCL. Original in WWWBP-WRPL.

53. Morse A. Cartwright, "Research Projects and Methods in Educational Sociology," *Journal of Educational Sociology* 5, no. 8 (1932): 514.

54. Luther L. Bernard, "Culture and Environment: The Continuity of Nature and Culture," pt. 2, *Social Forces* 9, no. 1 (1930): 48; Cartwright, "Research Projects and Methods in Educational Sociology," 514.

55. Mabel Carney to Frank Bachman, December 11, 1925, WLGP-SCL.

56. Ayres, *Let My People Learn*, 110.

57. Wil Lou Gray, "South Carolina's Program for Belated Learners," *Journal of the Association of University Women* 23, no. 3 (1930): 84; Gray to Dr. J. B. Nash, April 21, 1930, WLGP-SCL.

58. Senator Strom Thurmond, press release, September 8, 1995.

59. Evelyn Branch, interview by author, Columbia, S.C., August 23, 1995.

60. *Sixty-third Annual Report of the State Superintendent of Education of the State of South Carolina* (Columbia, S.C.: State Department of Education, 1931), 76–87.

61. Gray, Gray, and Tilton, *The Opportunity Schools of South Carolina*, 19.

62. Ibid., 87.

63. Morse Cartwright to Frederick P. Keppel, January 21, 1931, Carnegie Corporation Collection, Rare Books and Manuscripts Library, Columbia University, New York, N.Y. (hereinafter cited as CCNY).

64. Grant application, "Training Illiterates to Read," CCNY.

65. Box 3, WLGP-SCL. See *Sixty-third Annual Report of the State Superintendent of Education of the State of South Carolina*, 76–87.

66. Gray, Gray, and Tilton, *The Opportunity Schools of South Carolina*, 32.

67. Ibid., 89.

68. Carrie McCully Patrick, "Negro School to Close at Seneca," *The State*, n.d., in scrapbooks of the Wil Lou Gray Opportunity School, 1923–49, Office of the Superintendent, Wil Lou Gray Opportunity School, West Columbia, S.C. (hereinafter cited as WLGOS).

69. "The Beginning of the Opportunity School as written by Dr. Wil Lou Gray in 1923," in George M. Smith, *Documents on the Early Beginnings of the SC Opportunity School and Land Acquisition of Vacated Army Air Base in West Columbia* (1999), scrapbooks of the Wil Lou Gray Opportunity School, 1923–49, WLGOS; Gray, Gray, and Tilton, *The Opportunity Schools of South Carolina*, 32.

70. 288 students attended the summer camp, almost double the experimental number. See box 3, WLGP-SCL.

71. Untitled clipping dated July 27, 1931, in scrapbooks of the Wil Lou Gray Opportunity School, 1923–49, WLGOS.

72. Box 2, folder 137, WLG-SCL.

73. *Sixty-third Annual Report of the State Superintendent of Education of the State of South Carolina*, 76–87.

74. *Peabody Journal of Education*, November 1932, 188.

75. Box 4, folder 267, WLGP-SCL.

76. Box 24, WLGP-SCL.

77. Gray, Gray, and Tilton, *The Opportunity Schools of South Carolina*, 90.

78. Olema Wiggins to Gray, August 19, 1931, box 3, WLGP-SCL.

79. Untitled clipping dated September 1931, in scrapbooks of the Wil Lou Gray Opportunity School, 1923–49, WLGOS.

80. Keppel to Gray, January 11, 1932, CCNY.

81. Olin Johnston to Gray, December 17, 1936, box 4, folder 217, WLGP-SCL.

82. Box 4, folder 214, WLGP-SCL.

83. Program, Seventh Annual Conference on Adult Education and the Negro, South Carolina State College, Orangeburg, S.C., April 6–9, 1949, Archive and History Center, Miller F. Whittaker Library, South Carolina State University, Orangeburg, S.C.

84. Eunice Ford Stackhouse, "Julia Mood Peterkin", commencement address to the Opportunity School, Columbia, S.C., n.d., JMPP-SCHS.

85. Perkerson, "Julia Peterkin, Author and Farmer."

Dr. Hilla Sheriff

Caught between Science and the State at the South Carolina Midwife Training Institutes

PATRICIA EVRIDGE HILL

Committed to "scientific" models of modern childbirth but restricted by inequities that denied almost half of South Carolina mothers access to hospitals or physicians, black and white medical women created an alternative form of maternal and infant health-care delivery during the middle decades of the twentieth century. Unlike many physicians and public health officials who blamed midwives for high infant and maternal death rates and sought their eradication, Hilla Sheriff (1903–88) recognized that eliminating lay midwives from a segregated South would deny most African American women access to any form of legal medical assistance during and after their deliveries. Sheriff, who headed the state board of health's Division of Maternal and Child Health or supervised its director from World War II until her retirement in 1974, chose instead to focus on improving training for midwives as a temporary measure until African Americans could have access to a better health-care system.

Beginning in the early 1940s, state law required South Carolina lay midwives to attend a summer institute every four years. New midwives attended every summer for four years, then every fourth year. Most counties also required attendance at monthly meetings with a public health nurse. By the middle decades of the twentieth century, an overwhelming majority of South Carolina's midwives were black women who served rural African American families in the southeastern portion of the state. These lay practitioners were required to attend formal two-week midwife training institutes. A handful of white midwives from South Carolina's northwestern counties attended less formal training sessions organized by county public health officers or visiting nurses from the state board of health.

Between 1940 and 1965, Dr. Hilla Sheriff institutionalized and modernized the medical training received by the state's midwives. She enlisted African American nurse midwives Maude E. Callen, Eugenia Broughton, and Eula Harris to design and deliver the bulk of a program that maintained the legitimacy of lay midwives and raised their status among peers and patients. Neither the black nurse midwives who influenced the daily direction of the training institutes nor Sheriff and the other white physicians and public health nurses who offered organizational expertise and state resources considered the institutes an adequate response to the consistently high maternal and infant death rates in South Carolina's Lowcountry counties. Their respect for lay midwives should not obscure their preference for hospital births (or "normal" home births with a physician or nurse midwife in attendance). Caught between the requirements of science and those of the state, South Carolina medical women, led by Hilla Sheriff, chose pragmatism as a short-term strategy. South Carolina's most highly decorated public health official—Sheriff's accolades included the American Public Health Association's Ross Award in 1969, the Order of the Palmetto in 1975, and the Medical University of South Carolina's Distinguished Alumni Award in 1981— is most often associated with the eradication of endemic pellagra, pioneering contraceptive research for the Milbank Memorial Fund, and an examination of toxoplasmosis and other forms of household poisoning. Yet she touched as many lives through a compromised yet workable program to train and license lay midwives.[1]

Historian Johanna Schoen has noted that health and welfare officials throughout the twentieth-century South operated "within a larger political context of deep suspicion toward any services for the poor."[2] In South Carolina, elected officials had a long history of neglecting the health-care needs of African Americans and poor whites. By working together to create what they perceived to be a transitional alternative to integrated health care, Sheriff and the medical women she supervised both improved maternal and child health and nurtured expectations of social change.

Born in Pickens County, South Carolina in 1903, Sheriff remained quite close to her large family throughout her life. The fifth of seven children, she never remembered being steered toward a particular career or directly pressured to live a conventional middle-class life as a wife and mother. Two of Sheriff's sisters taught school. One also married and raised a family; the other remained single. A third sister married, had children, and devoted a great deal of time

DR. HILLA SHERIFF
Courtesy of South Caroliniana Library,
University of South Carolina, Columbia, S.C.

to medical and educational philanthropy, as had her mother. John Washington Sheriff moved his family and the lumber business his father established in the foothills of the Blue Ridge Mountains to Orangeburg near the center of the state when Hilla was a child. Although some of the Sheriff siblings traveled extensively and Hilla spent a year each in Philadelphia, Washington, and Boston seeking first-rate medical training, all seven lived their lives in South Carolina.

Hilla Sheriff called the chickens whose wings she mended in her family's yard her first "patients" and claimed she could not recall a time when she did not want to be a doctor. "When I was small and would play paper dolls, one was always the doctor," Sheriff recounted. She never wavered from her desire to study medicine throughout high school, although her parents considered it a "childish fantasy." According to Sheriff, they thought she would marry before completing her first year of college. But Sheriff finished two years at the College of Charleston and transferred to the Medical College of South Carolina (now the Medical University of South Carolina) midway through a bachelor's degree, fearful that her parents would change their minds about financing her education.[3] Though her parents worried that she was not physically strong enough for a medical course, Sheriff viewed her chosen vocation in the context of a Southern Methodist tradition that emphasized service both to God and to humanity. A handwritten essay entitled "The Choosing of My Career" written after her first year of medical school described a serious illness she had suffered five years earlier while still in high school. At one point during her illness she believed God told her, "You shall be made well if you give your service trying to make others well. Take up your medicine for there are many whom you can help." Yet after medical school, Sheriff adopted the language of science rather than that of a missionary. She did not attend church regularly until well into her sixties. Throughout her career, however, she remained committed to the service ethic that first motivated her to become a doctor.[4]

Since there were no accredited internship opportunities for female physicians in South Carolina when Sheriff received her medical degree in 1926, she accepted an internship at the Hospital of the Women's Medical College of Pennsylvania in Philadelphia. While there, she developed relationships with a close-knit network of women doctors in the northeast that she would maintain for the rest of her long life and that would provide her with connections to national women's medical associations. She then did residencies at the Children's Hospital in Washington, D.C., and New York City's Willard Parker Contagious Disease Hospital. She returned to South Carolina in 1929 and opened a pediatrics practice in Spartanburg where L. Rosa Hirschmann Gantt, a 1901 graduate of the Medical College of South Carolina—one of the first two female graduates in the institution's history—served as a mentor and became a friend. Gantt had married a Spartanburg attorney and practiced there as an eye, ear, nose, and throat specialist for thirty years. Hallie Rigby, who received her medical degree from Johns Hopkins in 1917, maintained a medical and surgical practice with her husband in Spartanburg, and Lonita M. Boggs, who completed medical training at the Medical College of Virginia in 1924, had set up shop in nearby Greenville. Gertrude Ryan Holmes, another graduate of the Medical College of South Carolina, joined this nucleus of Upstate practitioners in 1933. Sheriff moved rapidly from private practice to public health, guided by Gantt's work with the New York–based American Women's Hospitals (AWH), Rigby's interest in family planning, and the poverty of most of her own patients during the Great Depression.[5]

In 1931, as president-elect of the Medical Women's National Association, Rosa Gantt asked AWH, known for its work in alleviating health crises faced by wartime refugees during and after World War I, to address the poor health of economic refugees in the textile South. AWH hired Hilla Sheriff to direct its first American units. Sheriff concentrated the resources of the AWH and the energies of her staff on the eradication of pellagra, the provision of health care for women and their babies, and the promotion of family planning services. She operated the South's first "healthmobile," a trailer pulled by a truck containing an examining room, an area for cooking demonstrations, seating for sixteen, and a staff of three medical professionals. Sheriff demonstrated how to cook vegetables in less water. While Sheriff treated their children, her nurses conducted classes during which mothers were taught to can fruits and vegetables for year-round consumption. Although physicians were unaware until the mid-1930s that insufficient nicotinic acid or niacin caused pellagra, Sheriff and her colleagues understood that increased quantities of fresh vegetables, lean meat, and dairy products prevented it and that brewer's yeast could help treat its victims. Sheriff used AWH funds to provide especially needy families with pressure cookers, which enabled mothers who worked long shifts in area textile mills to prepare dried peas and beans more rapidly. A gospel of nutritional health spread by southern women proved to be remarkably successful among a population that regarded both domesticity and piety as essential female traits and suspected "outside" experts. Observers noted the mountain people's curiosity on seeing "that lady doctor" and her strange vehicle. Even without an upturn in textile fortunes or fatter paychecks for mill workers, pellagra was reduced by one-half in Spartanburg County between 1931 and 1933.[6]

Sheriff institutionalized AWH programs after 1933 when she joined the Spartanburg County Health Department as its assistant director. Four years later, she assumed the directorship. As South Carolina's first female health officer, she stepped up the organization of prenatal clinics and immunization programs. She also secured funding from the Milbank Memorial Fund for contraceptive research and established the first family planning clinic associated with a county health department in the United States. Sheriff's 1935–36 study of the clinic's first 990 patients provided ammunition for a national movement seeking to overturn nineteenth-century statutes banning the dissemination of contraceptive information and devices. Both black and white South Carolina women involved in the study married earlier and exceeded the birth and pregnancy rates of women referred to family planning clinics in New York City and Cincinnati, Ohio. Half of the black women and 42 percent of the whites had serious illnesses that made future pregnancy dangerous, but before seeking clinic advice, the South Carolina women used contraceptives far less frequently (60 percent of whites, 25 percent of blacks) than women in New York (96 percent) and Cincinnati (92 percent). Sheriff studied spermicidal jellies and diaphragms—low-cost products that women could both afford and control. Her program's popularity led to the creation of clinics throughout South Carolina in 1936 that were based on her model. Three years later, South Carolina became the second state—North Carolina was the first—to make birth control a regular part of public health services. By 1940, in large part due to family planning services and campaigns to train midwives, maternal and infant death rates dropped 25 percent. Sheriff's Spartanburg study and family planning clinic legitimized "birth spacing" and convinced many southern medical practitioners to advocate the use of contraceptives when childbearing posed a serious danger.[7]

Despite the successes of her early career and her scientific bent, Sheriff recognized that she could not replicate the paths followed by many women doctors in northeastern cities. Careers in women's medical schools or women's hospitals and clinics were simply not an option without a concentration of medical women and with dispersed, impoverished populations. Similarly, strict adherence to the tenets of "modern" or "scientific" medicine was often impossible in a rural southern context. Through her Depression-era work among isolated mountain families, white mill workers, and black farmers in Spartanburg County, Sheriff developed respect for the South's most marginalized peoples. She recognized that many African American midwives wanted to become nurses but lacked the financial resources required to attend nursing schools far from their homes (South Carolina's nursing schools refused to admit black applicants well into the 1960s). Sheriff was moved by black women's demonstrated concern for their communities. As director of the state board of health's Division of Maternal and Child Health after 1940 (she moved to Columbia to become the assistant director but soon found herself heading the agency when her boss joined the military during World War II), Sheriff devoted unprecedented state resources to standardizing the sporadic programs that had provided midwife training since the 1920s.

The persistence of African American lay midwifery has generated a variety of historical interpretations, just as the "midwife problem" provoked sympathy, support, condemnation, and ridicule from physicians and public health officials. Bruce Bellingham and Mary Pugh Mathis argue that between 1921 and 1929 (the years Sheppard-Towner funds were available), the federal Children's Bureau "both legitimated and perpetuated racial dualism in maternal and child health services" by endorsing midwifery for southern blacks. Further, they assert that midwife training programs established "only enough official control over midwives to induce cooperation with birth registration procedures, but not enough to improve the quality of service provided to parturient black women." Bellingham and Mathis note Children's Bureau officials' ambivalence about their role in perpetuating racial dualism in the 1930s and 40s, but they assert that "these programs continued to serve southern white officials well" and that they were allowed to continue until the introduction of integrated hospital services after the passage of the Civil Rights Act in 1964.[8]

On the other hand, historian Susan L. Smith concludes, "Ironically, state intervention in the previously unregulated practice of midwifery led to the creation of an unexpected cadre of black public health workers." Her analysis of midwife training programs in Mississippi demonstrates that lay practitioners modernized their skills by attending monthly meetings at midwife clubs and participated in public health work advocating prenatal and postnatal care, venereal disease prevention, immunization against typhoid fever, and diphtheria awareness. According to Smith, "Midwives, along with teachers, were the female counterparts to preachers as the most influential people in rural areas."[9]

Nevertheless, they were perceived by many southern health officials such as Edwin R. Watson, associate director of Georgia's Division of Maternal and Child Health as "untrained, superstitious and, all too often, unclean" servants of what Laurie Jean Reid, Florida's child health director, called an "indifferent" population. Watson's view that African American midwives' "false beliefs are fixed ideas and cannot be changed" made it unlikely that his department would invest in improving their medical skills.[10] Dr. George H. Cooper, director of North Carolina's Bureau of Maternity and Infancy, asserted privately that "many of these women are ignorant and dirty" and publicly concluded that "they represent the lowest class of midwives."[11]

In contrast, South Carolina's Hilla Sheriff claimed that the main problem was not with midwives but with impoverished mothers who had no prenatal care or suffered from untreated venereal diseases. She noted that many poor women were unwelcome in the state's underfunded hospitals. "In the smaller hospitals where there are no interns, it is hard on the local physicians. If the cases are poor, there is no way for the doctor or hospital to be reimbursed."[12] Sheriff's conclusions were based on her experience as a county health officer in Spartanburg, South Carolina, during the 1930s. There, she trained midwives and conducted well-baby clinics attended by both black and white mothers.[13] According to Sheriff, the midwife was often called only after hard labor had begun, "and she sometimes encountered complex delivery problems that are touch and go even in hospitals with expert obstetricians in attendance."[14] Instead of blaming midwives for high infant and maternal mortality rates, Sheriff was concerned that without midwives, many mothers would receive even less medical attention. She explained, "Where there aren't midwives, the mothers often just go into labor and holler on the doctor's doorstep. Or someone will take the baby and the placenta to the hospital for the cord tying."[15]

In 1936, Sheriff designed innovative programs for Negro Health Week in Spartanburg, an event organized by African Americans featuring two black physicians from Spartanburg and one from nearby Greenville, ministers, teachers in the county's seventy-six black schools, and lay midwives. Spartanburg's mayor, the city and county school superintendents, and the secretary of the chamber of commerce spoke at the parade that capped off a week of clinics and demonstrations organized by African Americans to improve the health and welfare of their communities.[16] These experiences convinced Sheriff that the ill health of South Carolina blacks was the result of poverty and a lack of access to health care and not to "indifference."

Laura Blackburn, a white registered nurse who worked with South Carolina midwives from 1920 until her death in 1955, told the Health Education Section of the Southern Branch of the American Public Health Association that public health officials working with midwives were "paid to meddle in people's business" and "have to give up our feeling of superiority and our critical attitudes." She added that midwives "taught her kindness, politeness, a philosophy, long patience and what measure of poise I have."[17] With women like Sheriff and Blackburn in charge of maternal and infant health programs in South Carolina, the presence of a talented group of African American nurse midwives in several key county health departments, and a growing number of white public health nurses ready to challenge social mores and serve black communities, South Carolina provided lay midwives with training that went well beyond surveillance goals and focused on the acquisition of significant new skills.

After 1940, two-week institutes were held at the Penn Community Center on St. Helena Island near Beaufort. Sheriff relied heavily on African American midwives Callen and Broughton from neighboring Berkeley County and Harris, who practiced near Augusta, Georgia, to design a program that would effectively disseminate medical knowledge to lay midwives, many of whom did not read or write.

Callen, a graduate of Florida A&M College and the Georgia Infirmary in Savannah, studied care procedures for patients with tuberculosis in St. Louis at the Homer G. Phillips Hospital and trained as a nurse midwife at the Tuskegee Institute in Alabama. Born in Quincy, Florida, in 1900, she arrived in Berkeley County in 1923 as a missionary nurse for the Protestant Episcopal Church under the auspices of the United Thank Offering. Learning that African Americans requiring hospitalization had to attempt a thirty-mile wagon trip to Charleston that required crossing several unbridged tidal creeks, she organized two-week resident institutes for the local midwives who provided most residents' medical care. In 1936, the county health department hired Callen as a public health nurse.[18]

Callen's scientific training and expertise were tested by the conditions she faced in Berkeley County. Seventy percent of the county's approximately twenty-seven thousand residents were African Americans—most of them tenant farmers with an average cash income of less than $100 yearly. Farmhouses were typically five miles from a paved road and almost completely inaccessible when it rained.[19] Since few farm families owned cars, segregated medical facilities in Charleston were out of reach and travel to Berkeley County's public health clinics was only possible when one's health and the weather permitted a considerable walk. Callen understood the importance in this setting of training local midwives who provided care in isolated women's homes. Callen's early programs were adaptations of those designed by Ruth Dodd, a registered nurse who was sent to South Carolina by the Children's Bureau and became the first director of the Bureau of Child Hygiene in 1920. Dodd wrote a set of regulations governing the practice of midwifery and an outline of ten lectures, which became the first course of instruction for South Carolina's lay midwives. With funding from the Sheppard-Towner Act between 1922 and 1929, the Bureau of Child Hygiene hired a midwife supervisor and a nutritionist, and over four thousand midwives registered voluntarily. Attendance at state-sponsored prenatal clinics, a series of lectures on maternal and infant care conducted during the Presbyterian Conference for Colored Women in 1927, and a month-long course in midwifery and nutrition at Voorhees School (now Voorhees College) indicated that lay midwives were eager to learn.[20] Most traveled across several counties in rough wagons, and some walked more than one hundred miles in order to receive formal training.

When Sheppard-Towner funds were discontinued, South Carolina's General Assembly made no appropriations for the Bureau of Child Hygiene. The position of midwife supervisor was discontinued and the training and supervision of lay midwives turned over to county public health nurses. Without a federally funded state agency that focused on the health-care needs of women and children, infant mortality rates and tuberculosis rates rose for the first time since 1915. Maternal mortality reached its highest level in eighteen years.[21]

By 1940, when the state board of health's Division of Maternal and Child Health hired Hilla Sheriff as its assistant director, South Carolina politicians were still unwilling to allocate state funds to health services associated with blacks, but Social Security funds were available to fund midwife training more systematically. Sheriff was named director just over one year later when her boss volunteered for military duty.

Maude Callen persuaded Sheriff to secure Penn Center, originally a school for newly freed slaves, as a site for the institutes because of its symbolic value in the Lowcountry communities served disproportionally by midwives. Training took place in the historic school buildings beneath moss-draped live oaks on a barrier island claimed by black farm families after the Civil War. Participants frequently described the experience as "inspirational."[22]

By the end of the 1940s, midwives spoke fondly of their summer "reunions" at Penn Center. A day began with breakfast at 7:30, followed by chapel. Classes were held from 9:00 until noon and again from 2:00 until 5:00. Laura Blackburn, who directed the program for the Division of Maternal and Child Health, Callen, and selected county public health nurses and nurse midwives constituted the teaching staff and remained on call throughout the institutes, but films were chosen and most activities were designed by peer group leaders. Many midwives were illiterate, so Callen persuaded Sheriff to send a reading and writing teacher to the institutes. As a result, midwives who had refused to obtain state licenses because they lacked the literacy skills to register births with county health departments were "brought into the fold."[23] The experiences of midwives such as Josephine Matthews indicate that the institutes promoted more than the surveillance objectives of state officials, however. Matthews claimed, "One thing that has meant a lot about being a midwife, is it sent me back to school. When I was 74 years old, I got my high school diploma."[24] Unlike earlier midwife training programs that focused exclusively on cleanliness and completing birth registration forms, beginning in the 1940s the South Carolina training institutes included classes in anatomy and childbirth. An anatomically correct mannequin referred to as "Mrs. Chase" became a popular feature. Charley White, a lay midwife and group leader also recalled observing live births. "They would bring in actual delivery cases for us to watch. The whistle would blow to get us up and we'd sit up all night seeing a baby born."[25] Hilla Sheriff called on an extensive network of physicians to provide guest lectures on pediatric and obstetrical topics to both midwives and public health nurses at the institutes. On one of the first of these occasions, Sheriff removed a screen that divided black midwives from white public health nurses, which complicated the question and answer session after the talk, explaining that the doctor was a busy man who had little time for such nonsense.

Training at the institutes included information on family planning or birth spacing as part of a total maternal and child health package and encouraged midwives to refer new mothers to county public health clinics for contraceptive services. The demand for contraceptive devices among African American women was great. According to historian Schoen, "Public health officials found that black patients tended to maintain better contact with clinics than did white patients."[26]

Catherine Greene, a public health nurse who worked with Sheriff in Spartanburg County recalled Sheriff's ability to persuade white nurses to challenge social mores and serve black patients. On one occasion, Sheriff took Greene and the rest of her staff to a Thanksgiving lunch at a black schoolhouse. It was the first time most of the white public health nurses had shared a meal with African Americans. According to Greene, "We felt very much in place because Dr. Sheriff made everyone feel we were doing exactly the right thing. . . . It didn't faze her at all to go into any one of the colored schools."[27] Despite the growth of interracial cooperation in the decades before the civil rights movement, such willingness to associate with African Americans on a more personal level was still highly unusual in the state.

The medical programs designed by Laura Blackburn that were offered during the institutes attracted the attention of the World Health Organization, which asked her to serve as a consultant. Blackburn offered WHO-sponsored in-service and preservice training to both professional and lay groups interested in improving maternal and child health among peoples with little formal education.[28] Mrs. W. G. Colcock, a public health nurse from Upstate South Carolina, recalled that her first lessons to midwives on the Sea Islands failed because "the women were not understanding one word I said. And I couldn't understand them." Blackburn emphasized "understanding the terminology of the people we are trying to help" and, according to Colcock, learned to "talk just like them." Blackburn told white public health nurses selected for the institutes that to be effective they must treat midwives with the dignity and respect they were accustomed to receiving in their own communities. The nurses were chosen in large part for their ability to work with lay midwife group leaders.[29] More than a decade after Blackburn's death, Betty Ficquett, her successor with the Division of Maternal and Child Health, described a lesson during which she compared the appearance and conduct of the modern midwife to that of her predecessor. "I tell them not ever to forget the granny, because if she hadn't been willing and able to learn, they wouldn't be here."[30]

Hilla Sheriff directed the state's lead nutritionist, Julia Brunson, to work with Blackburn on a special publication to be used during the midwife training institutes. Recognizing midwives' powerful influence on mothers' diets, Brunson and Blackburn designed a tool that lay midwives could share with their patients. Brunson recalled, "'They thought Miss Blackburn was really special; they said she had a white face but a black heart!'"[31]

As Hilla Sheriff and Maude Callen predicted, the midwife license became a source of pride. Black women felt a sense of ownership toward the institutes; in their own space, they acquired long sought-after skills of literacy and medical knowledge and received instruction from role models with whom they identified. Sheriff and Callen encouraged the singing of spirituals and Eugenia Broughton wrote a "Birth Certificate Song" to be sung to a familiar tune:

> Whenever you deliver perhaps a baby boy
> Remember he is human, not just a little toy
> His birth should be recorded within ten days or less
> And in years to come you will be blessed.
>
> We know that it's important, a solid standard rule
> He'll need birth registration to enter any school
> To prove he is the right age to marry or to vote
> So be sure his birth date you report.
>
> He'll need it for enlistment or maybe go abroad
> Producing his birth record will prove he's not a fraud
> It'll make him mighty happy if he can really say
> "I'm a native of the U.S.A."
>
> He'll then be eligible to earn an honest wage
> Receive a monthly pension if he can prove his age
> When sixty-five or over, he then will in due time
> Live in comfort, peace and sweet sublime.

CHORUS
Be sure his name, the date, the place are right
If not, in time he'll be in quite a plight
Check and recheck, then have the mother sign
And you will have great peace of mind.[32]

Broughton's popular lyrics reveal black women's vision of full participation in American social, political, and economic life while reinforcing the state's birth registration requirement through a medium familiar to midwives—the work song.

Dr. Hilla Sheriff built a network of female health-care providers that reflected her respect for the work of nonphysicians—public health nurses, nutritionists, teachers, nurse midwives, and lay midwives. Late in her career, she wrote, "I love to hear the Midwives sing their spirituals" and noted that as late as 1972, midwives still provided important services, although to a smaller number of patients. In that year, 169 midwives delivered almost 2,000 babies in South Carolina—about 3.5 percent of the state's total (compared with 1,318 midwives and 14,254 midwife deliveries—nearly 23 percent in 1952). In various speeches this first American woman to receive a master's degree in public health from Harvard University asserted, "I think I learned more about public health from public health nurses than I learned in any other one place."[33]

Hilla Sheriff organized professional and social networks throughout her long life. She corresponded with the two other women in her medical school class and with the friends she made while an intern and resident until and well after her retirement in 1974. She nurtured relationships with female physicians associated with the federal Children's Bureau long after it became apparent that she would remain in South Carolina. She married Dr. George Henry Zerbst, one of her medical school instructors, after exchanging letters and visits for eighteen years. Her skill establishing and maintaining relationships helps to explain how she built a network of health-care providers in South Carolina's most isolated regions. What is surprising is that she chose to do so while doctors across the nation opposed the continuation of traditional practices involving lay healers. In the process, she empowered midwives and removed some of the barriers that prevented black and white practitioners from working together.

The South Carolina Division of Maternal and Child Health's program to train and license lay midwives was an effective partnership between two groups of medical women—white public health officials who provided supplies, funding, and training and African American nurse midwives and peer leaders who contributed their expertise, experience, and cultural awareness. Maternal mortality in South Carolina fell from 540 per 10,000 live births in 1945 to 175 in 1957. The fetal death ratio (the number of still births per 1,000 live births) fell from 47.4 to 27.1 between 1945 and 1957.[34] An interim step in a society historically unwilling to recognize the equality and basic human rights of almost half its population, South Carolina's midwife training institutes continued to operate until the state's medical facilities opened their doors to black patients in the late 1960s.[35]

The commitment of leading public health officials and black nurse midwives to lay midwife training did not mean that either group preferred midwife deliveries to hospital births or to physician-attended births at home. Hilla Sheriff emphasized that the goal of her agency was "to have every woman under medical care as early in pregnancy as possible and to see that she has a safe delivery in an environment that offers the least risk possible to both mother and baby."[36] Maude Callen's recollections of superstitious, illiterate midwives in a public television documentary on Hilla Sheriff make it clear that she viewed midwife training as a significantly limited enterprise. Although filled with compassion, gentle humor, and a deep respect for Sheriff, Callen's anecdotes are not at all nostalgic.[37]

Southern newspapers attributed the persistence of midwives to "patients who can't have their own physicians because of money, travel or other difficulties," but medical practitioners knew that African American women were denied access to most hospitals and that the region was hostile to black physicians who might attend home births.[38] Prior to the construction of new hospitals and public health centers with federal funds after the passage of the Hill-Burton Act in 1946, few South Carolina hospitals served blacks. White doctors rarely delivered babies in black homes owing to racism, preference for other kinds of medical work, and/or the inability of many black families to pay their fees in cash. The Medical College of South Carolina did not accept its first black student until 1965, and the state's accredited hospitals denied black physicians internships until after the Civil Rights Act was passed in 1964. During the postwar decades, the supply of new African American physicians in the South probably did not replace those who retired or died. Charleston physician T. Carr McFall, a civil rights advocate who led the fight to secure Hill-Burton funds for black health care, claimed that in 1951 there were only three African American doctors under fifty in South Carolina.[39] And as late as the mid-1960s, black women who chose to become nurses had to leave the state in order to find a school that would admit them as students.[40]

When Hilla Sheriff resurrected midwife training and established the institutes at Penn Center in the early 1940s, the eradication of Jim Crow appeared quite distant. Amid race-baiting demagogues and popular and legislative resistance to even limited moves toward desegregation, Sheriff and her allies were determined to save more mothers and babies immediately. Even the chairman of the Fair Employment Practices Committee, Mark Ethridge, opened investigations of discriminatory practices in southern defense industries with an attempt to appease segregationists, asserting that "no power in the world—not even... Allied and Axis [armies together]... could now force the Southern white people to the abandonment of the principle of social segregation."[41] In this context, Hilla Sheriff chose to invest in midwife training and African American practitioners including Maude Callen, and civil rights advocates such as Modjeska Simkins accepted a program that provided a level of care deemed unacceptable by most whites. By "encouraging" lay midwifery, Sheriff went against professional norms and her own notions of modernity and "scientific" childbirth. Similarly, by admitting a segregated program for blacks because of its humanitarian qualities, Callen, Simkins, and their contemporaries rejected the position held by Dr. Louis Wright and others among the NAACP's national leadership that only integrated programs were acceptable.[42]

Perhaps their actions can be better understood by noting the existence of what historian Edward Beardsley has called two distinct southern black populations in the postwar decades, "each with its own health history." One was increasingly urban and able to take advantage of new Hill-Burton facilities with segregated wards. This group's rapid conversion to hospital births indicates that black mothers, like their white counterparts, sought out what they were conditioned to consider the "best" care as soon as they had access to physicians, hospitals, or health centers. Those who advocated ameliorist policies that perpetuated racial dualism among a population that could benefit immediately from desegregated health care neglected one southern black population, while the South Carolina medical women who invested in midwives served what Beardsley described as a second southern black population—"who lived almost entirely outside existing health and medical systems and were practically untouched by educational and economic improvements of the civil-rights sixties."[43] Desegregation would not guarantee even basic care to a poor, isolated rural woman unable to travel to any hospital. A trained midwife could.

NOTES

1. Sheriff's accolades included the American Public Health Association's Ross Award in 1969, the Order of the Palmetto in 1975, and the Medical University of South Carolina's Distinguished Alumni Award in 1981.

2. Johanna Schoen, *Choice and Coercion: Birth Control, Sterilization, and Abortion in Public Health and Welfare* (Chapel Hill: University of North Carolina Press, 2005), 9.

3. See "Dr. Sheriff: Health Pioneer," *Spartanburg Herald-Journal*, June 22, 1986, B-1, and Hilla Sheriff as told to Marshall Plyler, "Young Lady, You Had Better Look It Up!" *Update: The Magazine of South Carolina Department of Health and Environmental Control* 4, no. 3 (1974): 3–6.

4. See "The Choosing of My Career," in Sheriff's handwritten composition book, box 5, Hilla Sheriff Papers, South Caroliniana Library, University of South Carolina, Columbia (hereinafter cited as HSP-SCL). General biographical data can be found in box 3, folder 104.

5. For published biographical information on Sheriff, see Patricia Evridge Hill's "Hilla Sheriff (1903–1988)," in *Doctors, Nurses, and Medical Practitioners: A Bio-Bibliographical Sourcebook*, ed. Lois N. Magner (Westport, Conn.: Greenwood Press, 1997), 251–55, and "Hilla Sheriff," in *South Carolina Encyclopedia*, ed. Walter Edgar (Columbia: University of South Carolina Press, 2006), 862–63. On Upstate South Carolina medical women, see Patricia Evridge Hill, "Invisible Labours: Mill Work and Motherhood in the American South," *Social History of Medicine* 9, no. 2 (1996): 235–51.

6. See Patricia Evridge Hill, "Go Tell It on the Mountain: Hilla Sheriff and Public Health in the South Carolina Piedmont, 1929 to 1940," *American Journal of Public Health* 85, no. 4 (1995): 578–84.

7. Hill, "Go Tell It on the Mountain."

8. Bruce Bellingham and Mary Pugh Mathis, "Race, Citizenship, and the Bio-politics of the Maternalist Welfare State: 'Traditional' Midwifery in the American South under the Sheppard-Towner Act, 1921–29," *Social Politics* 1, no. 2 (1994): 158–59, 173. The literature on midwives and the "midwife problem" is extensive. For a beginning, see Frances E. Kobrin, "The American Midwife Controversy: A Crisis of Professionalization," *Bulletin of the History of Medicine* 40, no. 3 (1966): 350–63. Interesting recent publications include Raymond G. DeVries, *Making Midwives Legal: Childbirth, Medicine, and the Law*, 2nd ed. (Columbus: Ohio State University Press, 1996), and Gertrude Jacinta Fraser, *African American Midwifery in the South: Dialogues of Birth, Race, and Memory* (Cambridge, Mass.: Harvard University Press, 1998).

9. Susan L. Smith, *Sick and Tired of Being Sick and Tired: Black Women's Health Activism in America, 1890–1950* (Philadelphia: University of Pennsylvania Press, 1995), 118–19, 127–29, 139–43.

10. Edwin R. Watson, "20 Centuries and No Progress," *The Mother* 2 (October 1941): 14–15; Laurie Jean Reid, qtd. in Bellingham and Mathis, "Race, Citizenship, and the Bio-politics of the Maternalist Welfare State," 173.

11. Qtd. in Schoen, *Choice and Coercion*, 27.

12. "Midwives Never Stop 'Rocking Them Babies,'" *The State*, November 23, 1968.

13. "Health Officers Holding Meets," *Spartanburg Herald*, August 23, 1932.

14. "Those Gentle Hands Are Honored at Last," *The State*, May 17, 1975.

15. "Midwives Never Stop 'Rocking Them Babies.'"

16. Appreciation of Health Week Expressed at Meet," *Spartanburg Herald*, April 4, 1936.

17. "Tribute Paid to Negro Friends in Address to Health Group," *The State*, February 20, 1955.

18. For published biographical information on Callen, see Patricia Evridge Hill, "Maude E. Callen (1900–1990)," in *Doctors, Nurses, and Medical Practitioners*, 49–54.

19. Schoen, *Choice and Coercion*, 48.

20. "History and Development of Services to Mothers and Children in South Carolina, 1878–1929," typescript, box 4, folder 129, HSP-SCL.

21. Ibid.

22. See materials in the topical files on midwives, pediatrics, and the state board of health, box 4, HSP-SCL.

23. See untitled typescript accompanying photographs of midwife training institutes, box 4, folder 121, HSP-SCL.

24. "Those Gentle Hands Are Honored at Last."

25. "I Just Loved That Job of Delivering a Baby," *The State*, November 24, 1968.

26. Schoen, *Choice and Coercion*, 47.

27. "Dr. Sheriff: Health Pioneer," B-1.

28. "Miss Laura Blackburn Dies at Home," *The State*, February 14, 1955.

29. See photos, box 8, HSP-SCL.

30. "Midwives Never Stop 'Rocking Them Babies.'"

31. Qtd. in Kathleen Whitten, "The More I Did, the More I Saw the Need," *State Magazine*, February 16, 1986, 8–11.

32. Box 4, folder 121, HSP-SCL.

33. "Public Health: Career and Cause," typescript of speech delivered to South Carolina Department of Health and Environmental Control retirees and in amended versions to new employees, box 5, n.d., HSP-SCL.

34. Edward H. Beardsley, *A History of Neglect: Health Care for Blacks and Mill Workers in the Twentieth-Century South* (Knoxville: University of Tennessee Press, 1987), 279, 284.

35. "Midwives Still 'Catch' S.C. Babies," *The State*, November 21, 1968.

36. "South Carolina State Board of Health: History, Organization, Services," 1959, box 4, folder 129, HSP-SCL.

37. "Carrying Health to the Country," South Carolina Educational Television, 1988.

38. "SC's Graduate Nurse Midwives Travel into Remotest Nooks and Corners," *The State*, December 30, 1951.

39. Beardsley, *A History of Neglect*, 255–56.

40. John Pruett, "Black Pioneers in Nursing," 8–11, box 4, folder 121, HSP-SCL.

41. Patricia Sullivan, *Days of Hope: Race and Democracy in the New Deal Era* (Chapel Hill: University of North Carolina Press, 1996), 157.

42. Smith, *Sick and Tired of Being Sick and Tired*, 80.

43. Beardsley, *A History of Neglect*, 274.

Julia and Alice Delk

From Rural Life to Welding at the Charleston Navy Yard in World War II

FRITZ P. HAMER

❀ ❀ ❀

During World War II, two sisters from South Carolina, Julia and Alice Delk, were among the thousands of women who transformed the traditionally male world of the Charleston Navy Yard (CNY) "for the duration." At its peak employment period in 1943 and 1944 the facility's workforce had nearly five thousand women on the production line, almost 20 percent of the total employed. War industries around the nation desperately sought workers as the United States expanded and accelerated its war production for the final assault in Europe and the Pacific. In February 1942 the Department of the Navy ordered the Charleston facility and all other navy yards in the nation to recruit women for production jobs. Until Pearl Harbor, a few months before, the production line had been a male bastion, but with the advent of a national emergency, practical concerns suddenly superseded tradition. As they responded to their nation's call, the Delk sisters found themselves in a new environment with responsibilities, challenges, and financial rewards previously unimaginable for women, especially in the South. In interviews later in life, Julia Frances Delk Webb and Alice Delk Ray recalled how working in the navy yard transformed their lives even as women transformed the navy yard.[1]

Julia and Alice Delk grew up in a rural environment in west-central South Carolina. They worked at the CNY from spring 1944 until late 1945. The war ushered in major changes for them and their family, as it did for thousands of others like them. As war began, South Carolina was one of the poorest states in the nation, and opportunities for women who sought employment outside the home were severely limited. War work in jobs previously occupied strictly

JULIA (LEFT) AND ALICE (RIGHT) DELK
Courtesy of Alice Delk Ray, West Columbia, S.C.

by men exposed these women to many challenges and hazards they would not have encountered otherwise. The Delk sisters accepted all of this with a strong sense of adventure and duty and with few complaints. At the end of World War II, Julia and Alice Delk, similar to many women working in war-related industries in South Carolina and throughout the nation, left their jobs for domestic roles with little protest. The war had, however, produced enduring changes in gender roles in American society that were not readily apparent in the war's immediate aftermath.

Until 1942 the largest contingent of female wage earners in South Carolina was employed by the textile industry, the state's second largest employer next to agriculture. In these jobs, concentrated in Upstate centers like Greenville, Spartanburg, and Rock Hill and further south in Columbia, Camden, and Winnsboro, many women were employed as low-level operators on spinning frames and looms and in clerical work. In all cases they were subordinate to male workers and supervisors and were paid less than their male counterparts, even when they performed similar tasks. Only white women were permitted to work in these positions. For African American women there were few opportunities outside of farm work except as domestic workers in white homes—including mill workers' homes—or as custodial workers in the mills. The American Tobacco Factory in Charleston was highly unusual in the state for hiring black women in the industrial sector. Of its work force of about eight hundred more than half were African Americans. Teaching in the public schools was the only professional opportunity open to significant numbers of women, black or white.[2]

In 1941, before the United States entered the war, the only women employed at the CNY were clerical staff. The rest of the growing work force consisted of approximately six thousand men employed in several different departments or shops. Many had long experience in some aspect of shipbuilding as shipfitters, pipe fitters, or in the loft or machine shops. Prospective hires were required to pass a written test; if they passed and were hired, then they would have to complete a strict apprenticeship. One male apprentice remembered that when he began work in 1941 he spent part of his week in the classroom and the rest in the machine shop, learning how to make basic parts under the watchful eye of a veteran machinist. Once the nation was at war and the navy accelerated its shipbuilding program to meet the growing wartime demands, however, these strict training rules were quickly scaled back. One- and two-year apprenticeships were replaced by six- or eight-week courses by the end of the war's first year in an attempt to get more workers on the production lines to build or repair vessels.[3]

The South Carolina women who were hired in the effort to replenish the depleted ranks of navy yard workers were white women. There were more op- portunities in the yard for African Americans as a result of the emergency, but from the fragmentary evidence it appears that these opportunities were open to black men and that few if any black women worked on the production line. The records indicate that the CNY had employed blacks in some of the shops before Pearl Harbor and that, after war began, their numbers increased despite the fact that whites were reluctant to work with them. Following federal instruc- tions, navy officials hired minorities for unskilled and semiskilled positions, in keeping with local "Jim Crow" customs. And they also hired African Americans as custodians. Neither Delk sister remembered working with blacks; the only ones they recalled seeing in their shop were custodial workers. Black women were not hired into clerical positions at the CNY either: Carletta Wright, a black typist, wanted to work at the navy yard. Yet even though she passed the typing test for one of the navy yard offices, scoring over 90 percent, her prospective employers refused to hire her. Efforts to reverse such discriminatory actions failed.[4]

The wartime replacement of male workers with female was a gradual process. In ordering its yards to hire women in the wake of the attack on Pearl Harbor, the navy was not giving up on seeking out men but rather just making it clear that women must also be recruited. Women first entered the production lines in the spring of 1942. Mainly they provided assistance to male workers while they learned basic skills so they could work more independently. By the time the Delk sisters began working in the CNY in the spring of 1944, every shop in the yard had women working in various capacities. In some shops teams of women worked on projects with minimum male supervision. More than two dozen women electricians were praised in 1944 for their fine work on their assign- ments aboard a new vessel known as a landing ship tank (LST). Large numbers of South Carolina women also worked as welders, that vital task in the produc- tion of war machinery that made "Rosie the Riveter" the iconic image of women during World War II. Little is known about the experiences of these workers in South Carolina before they came to the navy yards, but some, if not most, came from backgrounds similar to that of the Delk sisters.[5]

Julia (1920–) and Alice (1926–) were born and reared in the rural town of Hilda in Barnwell County along with an older sister, Margaret, and two younger brothers, Martin and Isaac. Their father died in an automobile accident in the early 1930s, and they were brought up solely by their mother. Neighbors and relatives helped the widow and her family. She found a job in the school cafete- ria through a relative who worked at the local school board. Although the sisters recalled that their mother took various jobs to make ends meet, soon after the attack on Pearl Harbor she found a better paying job in Orangeburg, thirty miles east of Hilda, and moved the younger children there. To supplement the food she purchased, Mrs. Delk had a garden that local farmers plowed for her each year. She grew tomatoes, peanuts, and sweet potatoes along with peas, squash, and okra.

From an early age, the Delk children helped however they could. By age fourteen Julia had her first job, cleaning classrooms and emptying trash cans after school. Alice, the youngest sister, did not begin working until she was fifteen years old. When their mother moved to Orangeburg seeking a better paying job to support her family, Alice decided to quit school to work in a five and dime store wrapping gifts. Her mother did not want Alice to leave school and take this job, but she brought home wages badly needed to supplement the income of her mother who had found work as a seamstress.[6] Alice continued to work in Orangeburg for the next three years.

Julia and her sister Margaret were the first to leave home. They had actually gone to work in the Wilmington, North Carolina, shipyard even before Pearl Harbor. Julia found work in the yard cafeteria working alongside her sister. Sometime in the early spring of 1944 she returned to Orangeburg, leaving Margaret to continue working in Wilmington where she had met a man she later married.

At home in Orangeburg, Julia and Alice Delk began hearing about jobs at the CNY through the local newspaper and the radio that were "begging people to come to Charleston." In March 1944 Julia went to the coastal city to apply for a navy yard job. It took six months before Alice finally convinced her mother to put aside her misgivings and let her youngest daughter go as well.[7] It may have helped that their brother Martin also began working at the CNY and remained there until he was drafted and joined the air force. Their youngest brother, Isaac, remained at home until his brother entered the service and then enlisted in the navy.

The Delk sisters, however, would remain at the CNY for the rest of the war. Soon after their arrival they began training as welders. Although earlier in the war women were usually prepared for their jobs in classes separate from men, by the time the Delk sisters began training the classes had become coed. According to one description of a welding school at the navy yard in November 1943 there were two units, or classrooms, that ran parallel, ten-day courses with a total student body of 450. More than a quarter of the students were women. The classrooms were long halls filled with simulated decks and bulkheads. They were divided into compartments, each with room for thirty student welders at a time. The Delk sisters' class was conducted by a veteran welder, "Pop" Hayes, a man they remembered fondly as "a wonderful instructor," who treated them

like his children. Even so, everyone in the class was expected to do his or her assignments. "Pop" Hayes showed each student how to get the "bead hit," or "weld
spot," and provided each with the metal that he wanted a "bead" run on.

The trainees practiced different welding positions to simulate the various
places in a ship's hull where they would have to work. The most difficult and
dangerous task was to weld joints of metal above one's head. Any part of the
body not protected by a welding visor and an apron could be seriously burned.
Unfortunately for Alice, one time she forgot to snap her top; white-hot sparks
flew through her helmet and burned portions of her skin beneath her clothes.
She quickly ran for the dispensary for treatment while at the same time trying
to remove her smoldering garments. Although mortified by the presence of several young sailors she ignored them as she peeled off her clothes. As she recalled
more than sixty years later, she continued to seek treatment for her burns at the
dispensary for the rest of the time she worked at the yard.[8]

After a six-week course the sisters and their fellow classmates were assigned
jobs in various shops of the yard. Alice and Julia received their first assignments
in the shipfitter shop, tack welding ship parts, particularly for ship bows, before
they were assembled. Such welding needed skilled hands that could make overlapping joints of metal into a solid, tight bond using an electrode heated to
temperatures of several thousand degrees. During the period that the sisters
worked at the navy yard production was concentrated on building LSTs and
another kind of amphibious assault ship called a landing ship medium (LSM).
These specially designed vessels were built to transport troops and equipment
across the oceans to invasion beaches. These vessels became essential to Allied
amphibious landings such as Normandy in June 1944, the Philippines in October 1944, and Iwo Jima in February 1945. An LST was about 350 feet long, while
an LSM was smaller, about 200 feet in length. They had to be built to withstand
heavy seas and hurricane winds, not to mention enemy fire during beach inva-
sions. Thus welders, including Julia and Alice Delk, had to concentrate intently
and do good work even in cramped spaces in the bows of new ships, producing
tight bulkheads essential to the strength of any ship, but especially those built
for war.[9]

The welders' working conditions were made worse by the intense summer
heat of Charleston; temperatures inside these enclosed spaces could reach well
above 120 degrees Fahrenheit. And there were other challenges and dangers.
The gases given off in the welding process were poisonous and often made
welders sick. Although fans were usually provided to dissipate the harmful
gases, ventilation was rarely sufficient to remove all of it. The Delks often worked
without any ventilation in tight areas such as bows, since fans could not fit into

such confined spaces. The sisters recalled that the workers were allowed breaks but did not take them regularly. They were simply too focused on getting their jobs done.[10]

Decades later, the Delk sisters downplayed the seriousness of their hazardous working conditions, though they acknowledged that they had been exposed regularly to toxic fumes. Julia recalled that once, at the sheet metal shop, "I got the worst case of poisoning you've ever seen. I was sick as a dog." Sent to the infirmary for treatment, she was told to drink two to three cartons of cream daily. According to her doctor this would take the poison out of her system. Both her sister Alice and a brother were prescribed the same treatment for poison gas inhalation during their welding careers at the navy yard. For Alice, the result was a permanent case of severe asthma.[11]

The toxic gas produced in the welding process was only one of the health risks the sisters experienced at the navy yard. Once, as Alice was preparing to weld in a confined space, she bumped her head on a protruding bulkhead before putting on her helmet. When she turned around her sister noticed her head was bleeding profusely. An ambulance was called to take her to the infirmary for treatment. Her head was shaved and the wound dressed so that she could return to work in less than a day. On another occasion Alice suffered a more serious injury while assisting a senior welder. As she was moving the heavy welding cord closer to her partner, she accidentally stepped into a ventilation hole. At first she thought she had broken her leg but it proved to be only a severe sprain. Again, there was no time to waste nursing an injury. Despite the pain, as Alice recalled proudly decades later, "I didn't let it stop me."[12]

The personal experiences of the Delk sisters suggest that the navy was not able to meet all the challenges such hazardous working conditions presented despite the fact that it was aware of the dangers and tried to cope with them. The impressions of the sisters are borne out by documents produced by the Women's Bureau of the U.S. Department of Labor, a subagency created by Congress in 1920 to formulate standards and policies to promote the welfare of wage-earning women. During World War II this small organization worked closely with war-industry management to provide the best working environment for thousands of new female employees. After a 1943 survey of thirty-five navy yards and private shipbuilding facilities on the Atlantic, Pacific, and Gulf coasts, the Women's Bureau made several recommendations for improving working conditions for women working in shipyards.[13]

In the preamble to its 1944 report, the Women's Bureau stated that while the national military emergency had made it necessary to employ thousands of novice women in a "tradition of dirt, sweat, and rough and tumble, so thoroughly male," management had rushed to make the new hires "before essential and obvious provision had been made to accommodate" them. Among more than nine major recommendations—ranging from placing women in the positions that best matched their skills and strength to providing special consulting services for female employees at every shipbuilding facility—it included a section recommending a safety program for women workers. Safety standards for war industries had been formulated a year before the Women's Bureau study was published, but the writer observed that it was difficult to educate the huge influx of novice workers (both men and women) at shipbuilding facilities and meet the production goals required by the navy at the same time. Although the report recommended every supervisor take in a sixteen-week safety instruction course, it is apparent that such recommendations were only loosely followed. The report also recommended that as many employees as possible be enrolled in such courses. The Delk sisters do not recall receiving such instruction during their employment, and the written records do not indicate that supervisors at the Charleston facility received formal safety training either. However, the two sisters recalled that inspectors frequently came by their workstations to check on how safety rules were followed. Perhaps this was the best way facilities such as the CNY could maintain safety standards in the fast-paced, constantly changing work environment. Nonetheless, the Women's Bureau study observed, "the greatest hazard in the [shipbuilding] industry is the lack of trained supervisors" in safety instruction.[14]

In spite of the hazards they faced and the accidents they suffered, the Delk sisters had no criticism when they were interviewed about their supervisors during their navy yard experience. They remembered every supervisor—from their welding instructor when they began their tenure at the facility to their work-site bosses—as compassionate and helpful. The Delks reported working with "very good leading men" (a shipbuilding term for "supervisor") once they started on the production line after completing their six weeks of instruction. They recalled that these men were "good" to the female employees and tended to treat them with greater consideration than the male workers when it came to the more difficult jobs. In one of the last major shipbuilding jobs at the navy yard before the war ended, the sisters were assigned to welding assignments for the new destroyer tender *Tidewater*. The largest vessel built at the yard, it required an extensive amount of scaffolding to reach all areas of the hull's exterior. Women welders were assigned to jobs on the interior of the vessel, jobs considered to be relatively safe as workers had more protection and less climbing to do. The Delks worked with many different leading men in small groups of ten and twelve women who were assigned to each, and they did not recall having any problems with any of their supervisors regarding their gender. As far as they were concerned they were always treated correctly—at least in regard to instruction and supervision.[15]

Nevertheless, the Delk sisters did experience discrimination. This was particularly the case when it came to wage scales, although they seemed not to resent it. Even when their skills improved and they assumed tasks originally performed by experienced welders, their pay remained below that of men in similar positions. When Julia passed the test to upgrade from a tack welder to a third-class level she worked with a male welder who had a first-class grade. Even though Julia was given several assignments usually reserved for a first-class welder, she only received the pay that came with a third-class rating. Such inequity was common both in the shipbuilding industry and virtually every other war industry of the time. The Women's Bureau report observed that in its survey of thirty-seven shipbuilding facilities, wage discrimination was a common practice. Even though an August 1942 navy circular letter sent to all navy yards instructed them to award equal pay for equal work, such instructions were usually overlooked. To continue to attract as many men as possible, naval shipbuilding facilities discriminated using indirect methods. For instance, at one unnamed yard, all women, regardless of experience, were hired as "mechanic learners" at fifty-eight cents an hour; yet men, even those with less experience than some of their female colleagues, entered the labor force as "classified laborers" at seventy-four cents an hour. This was just one of numerous cases in which male workers were better paid than their female counterparts. Although equal pay was also endorsed in all U.S. war industries, the reality was that a vast majority of women workers received lower job classifications, regardless of their skill levels, and thus less pay than male counterparts.[16]

The Delk sisters accepted the situation without protest partly because the pay they received was such an improvement over what they had earned in their prewar jobs. Instead of making a few dollars a day as a store clerk in Orangeburg, Alice began at more than $5 per day at the CNY in welding classes and received over $9 a day once she was on the production line. This was true of women workers in general. In 1944–45 the wartime jobs held by women often paid them two or three times what they earned before the war. So to most women workers during World War II who had been employed previously, the improved pay scale relative to prewar levels was a welcome change and a big incentive to work in war industries, even if under harsh conditions and for less pay than their male coworkers.[17]

Another factor in women workers' acceptance of the unequal pay scale was their sense of patriotism. Although scholars have argued that patriotism was not the primary reason most women decided to enter the production lines between 1942 and 1945, it still played a role for many American women. Many female war workers had husbands, fathers, brothers, and friends serving overseas and felt it was their duty to enter the job market in order to produce the war materials needed to help bring home their loved ones. The Delk sisters had two brothers serving in the armed forces during the war. They recalled specifically that they wanted to do their part for the military; when interviewed decades later they emphasized that they were pleased that they had that opportunity in the final year and a half of the war. This was the case with many women war workers in South Carolina, where a duty to aid male relatives during wartime had a history that went back to the American Revolution. Thus fifty-two-year-old Eliza Dewitt began work at the CNY's joiner shop in the fall of 1942 with more than just a better salary in mind. With seven children, including two sons in the army, she wanted to be sure to do her part so they had a better chance of coming home. And when Carrie Moore, a grandmother, took a job in the sail loft, she was driven by a desire to do all she could to help her two grandsons serving in the armed forces.[18]

In addition to these financial, patriotic, and familial incentives for entering the war industries, women—and certainly the Delk sisters—were motivated by a sense of adventure. Participation in war work afforded many women exciting opportunities unlike any they had ever encountered before. Most of the women who joined the workforce in 1942 were young women between the ages of eighteen and thirty-five; many were unattached or away from their spouses and ready and able to take advantage of the opportunities the war offered. One could do one's duty, make money, and—despite all the worries and hardships—have an adventurous life in the process. The Delk sisters emphasized that a patriotic calling and a desire to earn the better pay that working for the navy accorded them were their prime motives, but they also eagerly seized the chance to have experiences they knew would have been impossible before Pearl Harbor. Having grown up in an isolated farming community, they were now able to experience life in a new setting far removed from the rural routine with low wages and limited opportunities. Being able to meet new people and live in an urban area bustling with excitement must have been alluring as well.[19]

It is interesting to note that with all these incentives to sign on for work in war industries, restraints based on traditional assumptions about women's roles, particularly their responsibility for childcare, made it difficult for war industries to find the increasingly large number of workers wartime production demanded. Indeed, the solicitations in newspapers and radio that attracted the Delks to Charleston and drew a huge influx of labor to the coastal city like nothing ever seen before were necessary, in part, because the majority of eligible women in the Charleston area still could not be induced to enter local war industries. In a July 1944 population study of the Charleston area's work force, a survey of women workers in its war industries and other jobs indicated that a large majority of local females did not seek even part-time employment; the proportion of working women in 1944 stood the same as it had four years before. Well into the war the traditional pattern in which most women working outside the home were young and single was still in effect; most local women that were working in the paid labor force were eighteen to twenty-four years old, while the majority of older women had no paid employment. According to the report, few women entered the labor force because so many of them were occupied in caring for children: of the 18,545 mothers in Charleston County who were between eighteen and sixty-four years old and had one or more children under ten, only 3,220, or 17.4 percent, were employed and just 2,020 of these had full-time jobs. In addition, only 39.9 percent of the 27,195 married, widowed, and divorced women between eighteen and sixty-five who had no children under ten were employed. Most of the working mothers in this survey were African American; as was the case nationally, black mothers were found in the workplace in disproportionate numbers in a society that rarely afforded their husbands wages sufficient to fully support their families. On the other hand, of the group of women in the Charleston area most likely to be induced by these incentives—single women—a high proportion were already employed in 1944; the survey indicated that of the 9,325 single women of Charleston, 78.8 percent between eighteen and sixty-four years of age were in the job force. That a large percentage of single women was already employed and that virtually all eligible Charleston males (those classified as between ages sixteen and sixty-five) were as well, it was imperative to recruit more women workers—such as the Delk sisters—from outside the area.[20]

Many prospective women employees—or their families—were put off by the idea of them engaged in occupations considered inappropriate for their sex. When the Delk sisters first told their mother that they would be working at the cny, Mrs. Delk was not at all pleased. As she told her daughters after they announced their plans, "You girls shouldn't be in a place like that. You're not supposed to be doing men's work." Although Mrs. Delk's attitude soon changed once her daughters began bringing home larger paychecks to help with family finances, not all mothers were convinced.[21] The mother of another young navy yard worker, Eva McCartha, demanded that she quit the navy yard after visiting her daughter in Charleston some months after Eva began work in the metallurgy lab. Seeing her daughter dressed in overalls and spotted with grease and oil stains from a shift that just ended, McCartha's mother was appalled and demanded that Eva find a job more suitable for a woman. Like the Delk sisters, however, Eva refused and remained employed at the Charleston facility until the war ended.[22]

Class issues also clearly played a role in women's—and their families'—feelings about their entering war industries. Charleston was hardly an exception to this; the city certainly had its share of socially conscious persons who resisted the idea that wartime necessity legitimized industrial labor for "ladies." Ann Fox, a young worker from Georgia who came to Charleston in 1941, observed decades later that those women who came from the city's elite families felt that it was inappropriate for such women to get involved with dirty, physically demanding work. They preferred to demonstrate their patriotic duty in the war effort as USO and Red Cross volunteers. Fortunately, women like the Delks saw things differently. While such volunteer activities were important to the war effort, they did not solve the problems of labor-starved war industries.[23]

For Julia and Alice Delk and other women already employed before the war, the expanding and unmet need for labor, coupled with the opportunity to earn lucrative salaries, provided incentive to move. By 1943, with the local sources of labor largely exhausted, the CNY and the Charleston Shipbuilding and Drydock Company, its sister shipbuilding neighbor, were so desperate for new employees that they began a major recruiting campaign in other regions of the state and beyond its borders, seeking workers, male and female. By 1944, 46,825 new people had come into Charleston from elsewhere in the state and beyond. Of these, 42.1 percent came from other South Carolina counties and 57.9 percent came from other states and foreign countries.[24]

Not all who were recruited—women or men—were conscientious or honorable workers like the Delk sisters. As desperate recruiters combed the countryside for employees, they attracted the undesirable with the desirable. Worker absenteeism proved to be a major problem that added to the labor woes faced by the CNY and every shipbuilding facility throughout the country. By early 1943 absenteeism had become so serious that the navy yard began a campaign in each of its shops to stamp it out. Malingering and inappropriate behavior were also problems. The navy yard reports indicate that some workers spent their shifts playing cards in isolated sections of ships' hulls, and while supervisors did their best to curtail such activity, it was impossible to keep track of every worker on every shift who knew where the best hiding places were. At times—not often but enough to damage the image of war workers—a few women carried on an illicit trade with male employees in isolated bulkheads and other sections of the naval facility. Pipe fitter Robert Sneed, a leading man on several projects at the navy yard, recalled that he broke up more than a few card games during work shifts that he stumbled on by accident. He also knew that a few of the women employed at the yard were taking on male clients during their shifts rather than working at their assignments as pipe fitter helpers. There were reports of such activities occurring in other shipbuilding facilities. Katherine Archibald, an Oakland, California, shipyard worker, observed that although it was not a common practice, some of her female counterparts tried to use their feminine wiles to gain favor with male workers—these were isolated incidents that gave other female workers a bad reputation with many male workers and led to jealousy on the part of male employees' wives, who raged that most women shipyard workers at the Oakland facility were dishonorable.[25]

Most female employees tried hard to do good work and took pride in their accomplishments while coping with problems at home that were sometimes as challenging as those they faced on the job. Some also had the burden of having to hold down two jobs at the same time. As single women the Delk sisters did not have responsibilities for a husband and children, but married women remained responsible for all the housework, meals, and shopping then expected of housewives. So after a long eight- or nine-hour shift, a married woman often returned to another arduous set of duties at home, cooking meals, cleaning house, and looking after the needs of children. Such double duty was exhausting, making it hard to concentrate, let alone do a competent job, on the production line. Yet in contrast to the British government, the U.S. government did little to help women war workers with their traditional tasks even though it urged them to undertake untraditional tasks during the war. Consequently more than a few women who had households to maintain did not last long on the production lines. The 1944 federal study of employment of men and women in Charleston emphasized that the inability of industries like the local navy yard to recruit more local women owed to the fact that women were responsible for taking care of children.[26]

Even though there were some rudimentary efforts in the nation, including at the CNY, to provide paid child care for mothers working in war production, these efforts were not enough to satisfy the needs. Even if they had been, it is uncertain that mothers would have taken full advantage of this service. Newspaper reports indicate that in Charleston working mothers preferred to have a relative, either their own mother or another relative, care for their children while they were at work. When Catherine Bowen left her home in Waycross, Georgia, to take a job at the navy yard, her sister, already living in Charleston, cared for her child while she did her daily shift. Nonetheless, a nursery opened as early as March 1943 where a trained preschool educator and her helpers cared for young children of working mothers. It served the local communities near the navy yard and was built for workers and their families. To supplement the federal allotment used to create the facility, mothers had to pay fifty cents daily to place their children in the nursery, which was open from 6:30 a.m. to 6:30 p.m.[27]

Despite this help, the dual responsibilities of women female workers also contributed to the yard's retention problems. Statistics on absenteeism and resignations at the Charleston facility indicate that although both men and women failed to show, more women than men went absent. In fall 1943, Lieutenant Commander John S. Patterson, personnel officer of the CNY, reported that the national turnover rate for the shipbuilding industry was 6.8 per 100 men and 8.2 per 100 women. Patterson did not provide specific numbers for the local navy yard, but it appears that the proportions were similar to the national average. The constant need for new employees and the problems generated by those on the payroll that reported late or just never showed for their shift were issues that navy yard management tried to tackle head on before 1944. The Charleston facility's own newsletter, *Produce to Win*, admitted early in 1943 that absenteeism was "one of the principal headaches" there. Nonattendance by some workers caused a serious delay in production schedules, it reported. While the average absenteeism in other war industries (presumably this refers to a national average) was one in forty workers, for the local navy yard it was one in every twelve. The yard launched vigorous initiatives to remedy this problem; it actually began to interview all employees who had missed work whether or not they had medical excuses.[28]

Women workers at the CNY, however, took steps on their own to address these problems with support from yard management. In September 1943 the pipe fitters' shop began a program to reduce absenteeism in its work force. Gladys Hawkins, the shop's personnel representative, instituted a pledge that all of its women employees made stating that they would not take leave unless absolutely necessary. To inaugurate the program, the women of the shop held a rally and wiener roast at the Hawkins home in downtown Charleston. Apparently each employee had her daily presence recorded on the shop's notice board, and absences and tardiness were publicly recorded for everyone to see. By the end of the month absenteeism in the shop was reduced by 150 percent. Hawkins's efforts were rewarded in November 1943 when the navy yard commandant awarded her a $100 bonus. At the ceremony where she received the check, she announced a new, novel incentive for women at the pipe fitter shop. From November 15 to December 15, the two hundred women employees of the shop would conduct a contest against absenteeism of any kind. The female employee that accumulated the most absences at the end of that period would be required to entertain all of the shop's employees with a party at her own expense.[29] The efforts of the pipe fitters' shop and others at the yard had a positive impact on workplace tardiness and turnover according to the yard newsletter. By the end of October 1943 labor turnover had dropped to one of the lowest of any ship-building plant in U.S. Civil Service District 5 and one of the lowest in the nation, according to O. E. Myers, regional director of the district. Myers claimed that turnover at the Charleston facility was not only one of the lowest in the country but in fact much lower than that of other shipbuilding facilities.[30]

Claims such as these may be accurate for fall 1943 and into the winter lo-cally, but the federal reports for later periods, as already indicated, suggest that the measures by management did not take care of the problem throughout the war. People in Charleston, as in the rest of the country, began to believe by late summer of 1944 that the war was nearly over. With the German army having been virtually pushed out of France by mid-August and the Japanese navy and army being steadily forced back to their homeland in the Pacific, many Ameri-cans thought the war would end by Christmas. Thus many expected that war industries would soon be dismantled and the peacetime economy reestablished. Although the Delk sisters do not recall this, newspapers and other documents are replete with concerns about the civilian population becoming less interested in supporting the war.[31]

The Delk sisters, however, continued to do more than their share to support the war effort. They recalled that they took very few days off and that helping to bring the war to an end through their work at the navy yard remained the focus of their daily lives until Germany surrendered. For much of the war they endured a grueling, eighty-mile commute from Orangeburg to Charleston. Six days per week they rode with seven other workers in a private station wagon, leaving at 4:00 a.m. to reach the navy yard by 6:00 a.m. and have breakfast at the cafeteria before beginning their shift at 7:00 a.m. A normal shift was eight hours, but they usually put in an hour of overtime, which meant they could not leave the yard until late afternoon. In addition, the Delks often worked on Sun-days. Their driver did not work Sundays, so that day they had to take a bus.[32]

At the end of the summer of 1944, the doctor told Julia that she either needed to move closer to Charleston or quit because her health was declining. With the daily, four-hour commute on top of the long hours on the job, she could not keep up the pace. From a newspaper ad the sisters found a boardinghouse in downtown Charleston just ten miles from the navy yard. But the Delk sisters' Orangeburg commute was not unusual. Many workers were forced to commute because, until the last year of the war, Charleston lacked sufficient housing to accommodate the thousands of new war workers, such as Carrie Moore, the grandmother who worked in the sail loft, who commuted eighty miles each day to the yard from her home in Pregnall.[33]

Once in Charleston and living at the boardinghouse just a few blocks from the main street, the Delk sisters had a less hectic daily schedule, but they had to adapt to new living arrangements. They shared a room and a single bathroom with two other girls. The boardinghouse served meals, "good homemade food," Monday through Friday, but on weekends the Delks had to find their own fare. Food service establishments in Charleston were often overcrowded on Saturday and Sundays owing to naval and army personnel on leave, and so finding a place to eat could be difficult. As it turned out, the Delks worked most Saturdays, and on those days they picked up meals at the navy yard.[34]

As the war began to wind down, production at the CNY slowed. After Germany's surrender in May 1945, the Delks had a less rigorous work schedule, even though the war in the Pacific was still raging. With fewer assignments, there were more days off, and some fun times along with all the hard work. Sometimes, they would take the bus to Folly Beach together on their days off, enjoying the beach and eating hot dogs they bought from beach vendors. While in Charleston, the sisters each met the men who later became their husbands.

During the summer of 1945 rumors of layoffs began to circulate among the workers. The Delks learned of their own impending layoff when navy yard management sent them a letter informing them that their tenure would conclude by the end of the summer. While the job had been a great opportunity for them in many ways, neither sister was sorry to see their employment come to an end. They were ready to get on with "normal life." For the Delks and countless other Americans this meant marriage and starting a family. Julia married Jewell K. Webb, a navy veteran, at the end of September 1945 and in February 1946 Alice married Charles Ray, another navy veteran. Julia moved to her husband's hometown in Georgia, near Atlanta. Today she lives in Roswell, Georgia, and her daughter Barbara is employed as a lawyer for the federal government. Julia has traveled to England and Normandy to see the places where her husband made his contributions to the war effort. Alice and her husband remained in South Carolina. She has two grown sons, Charles Douglas, an engineer, and Eugene Winston, a veteran who now works for the Veterans Administration. She moved to West Columbia many years ago, and one son lives nearby.[35]

According to the Delk sisters, none of their other female colleagues at the navy yard desired to stay on the job once the war ended. Like Julia and Alice they wanted to focus on family and home. That many "Rosie the Riveters" as well as many returning veterans shared this point of view is clear in the record number of marriages, the ensuing baby boom, and the withdrawal of women, especially young women, from the labor force just after the war. But there is also evidence to suggest that there were other women working in shipyards in the nation, including the CNY, who wanted to remain on the production line. An early, postwar study of women war workers in ten selected war production areas across the nation showed that an average of 75 percent wished to remain in the postwar labor force. At the one southern center in the study, Mobile, Alabama, the proportion of women that wanted to keep working was at least 80 percent. No such surveys exist for Charleston. But Supervisor Robert Sneed of the pipe fitters' shop remembers that though most of his women workers appeared glad to leave once the war ended, some were disappointed and would have stayed if they could. Those women who had been engaged in war production in ship- yards and elsewhere who indicated that they would like to remain employed stated that economic motives were their main reason. It is easy to understand how the women who would be remaining in the job force would prefer the relatively lucrative work on industrial production lines to the gender-specific, lower-paid positions that had been their only options before the war and would be again when it ended.[36]

Whatever the wishes of women war workers, most lost their jobs; there were fewer ships and tanks to be built, and many war industries simply closed down. In addition, women working in other industries found that few of the employ- ers who had sought their labor so vigorously wanted to keep them on in the postwar period. Practical reasons as well as social mores accounted for the re- turn of traditional occupational patterns once the war ended; most GIs coming home expected to get a job or to return to the one they had left when Uncle Sam called them up. Policy makers in government and industry were eager to comply with these wishes, eager for the former soldiers and sailors of the victo- rious armed forces to reenter civilian life as quickly and smoothly as possible. In Charleston former navy yard workers who had left to serve in the war had their jobs waiting for them upon their return. Johnnie Dodds, an electrician before he entered military service, came back to his position at the navy yard and re- mained there for three more decades before retiring. John Moore, a machinist at the navy yard before he joined the armed forces in early 1943, came back to his old job determined that no one would stop him and stayed until he retired in the 1970s.[37]

It is interesting, however, that during the late 1940s and the 1950s, the num- ber of women in the workforce—especially married women with children in school—would increase dramatically. In part they were needed to take the place of younger women—traditionally the mainstay of the female labor force—who were now marrying at an earlier age, were having larger numbers of children, and were preoccupied with bringing up the baby boomers. National work patterns changed permanently after World War II as married women poured into the labor force, propelled both by the desire to live a middle-class lifestyle and by the postwar inflation that increasingly required wives to work outside their homes to achieve it. And despite the postwar glorification of women as full-time homemakers, there was a growing need for women workers in occupationally segregated positions in education and business such as teaching and clerical work. Some of these were former "Rosies" who had learned during the war that women were fully able to do work traditionally reserved for men and in the future would push for new and better opportunities for themselves and their daughters, thereby contributing to the subsequent development of the modern women's rights movement.[38]

Now more than sixty years after World War II, the Delk sisters look back on their lives during the war with pleasure and nostalgia. They were hard times but also exhilarating. The worldwide conflict that had made their venture into the nation's war production necessary and possible had proven to many women— even in a conservative enclave such as South Carolina—that they had abilities that most people, male and female, had not believed they had. Necessity demanded that they come forward and do the work that needed to be done. Thousands of women like the Delk sisters showed the world that they were capable and dedicated. Although many accepted the fact that these opportunities were only "for the duration," the trail that they blazed for three short years would later be followed by their daughters and granddaughters, who would break down traditional gender barriers in the decades ahead. Women have continued to seek equal opportunities in the workplace, not only in the industrial sectors but in managerial and executive positions that their mothers never dreamed of when they entered war production jobs in factories and shipyards across the nation during World War II.

NOTES

1. Julia Frances Delk Webb and Alice Delk Ray, interview by author, October 24, 2006, Columbia, S.C., transcript, the South Carolina State Museum, Columbia (other interviews by the author cited here are on file at the South Caroliniana Library, University of South Carolina, Columbia [hereafter cited as SCL]). On the Department of the Navy order, see Dorothy K. Newman, *Employing Women in Shipyards*, Bulletin of the Women's Bureau, no. 192-6 (Washington, D.C.: Government Printing Office, 1944), 1–2. On the federal government's directive, see Susan Hartmann, *The Home Front and Beyond: American Women in the 1940s* (Boston: Twayne Publishers, 1982), 58–59. For peak employment of women at the CNY, see Fritz Hamer, *Charleston Reborn: A Southern City, Its Navy Yard and World War II* (Charleston: History Press, 2005), 76.

2. In 1940 there were 31,653 women compared to 61,653 men employed in South Carolina's textile industry ("S.C. Department of Labor Annual Report, 1939–1940," *Reports and Resolutions of the General Assembly of South Carolina, 1941*, 2 vols. [Columbia: State Printer, 1941], 1:59); Jacquelyn D. Hall, James Leoudis, Robert Korstad, Mary Murphy, Lu Ann Jones, and Christopher B. Daly, *Like a Family: The Making of a Southern Cotton Mill World* [Chapel Hill: University of North Carolina Press, 1987], 69–72). On black women working in tobacco factories, see Hamer, *Charleston Reborn*, 78. In 1939 and 1940 in South Carolina there were 7,779 white women and 4,614 black women teaching (in all grades) ("S.C. Department of Education Annual Report, 1939–1940," *Reports and Resolutions of the General Assembly of South Carolina, 1941*, 2:186–87, 188–89).

3. "Resurvey of Employment Situation in Charleston Area, S.C.," October 5, 1942, box 19, series 12, War Manpower Commission (WMC), RG 211, National Archives, Southeastern Center, East Point, Ga. (hereinafter cited as NASE); John Moore, interview by author, Summerville, S.C., March 9, 1995.

4. Since Jim Crow laws were on the books of all southern states during the war, government officials, military and civilian, working in these states were rarely willing to break with local laws (Merl E. Reed, "FEPC, the Black Workers and the Southern Shipyards," *South Atlantic Quarterly* 74, no. 4 [1973]: 446–67; Oliver Perry, interview by author, North Charleston, S.C., April 6, 2003).

5. On the first women to work in production at CNY, see *Produce to Win*, September 3, 1943, SCL. On women electricians, see *Produce to Win*, March 26, 1943, SCL, and Hamer, *Charleston Reborn*, 81.

6. Delk sisters, interview by author, October 24, 2006.

7. Ibid.

8. Ibid.; *Produce to Win*, November, 8 1943, SCL; Newman, *Employing Women in Shipyards*, 73–74.

9. Delk sisters, interview by author, October 24, 2006; Hamer, *Charleston Reborn*, 41; *Charleston News and Courier*, December 7, 1943.

10. Delk sisters, interview; Newman, *Employing Women in Shipyards*, 73–74.

11. Delk sisters, interview by author, October 24, 2006.

12. Ibid.

13. Ibid.; Newman, *Employing Women in Shipyards*, 67–69.

14. Delk sisters, interview by author, October 24, 2006; Newman, *Employing Women in Shipyards*, 67–69.

15. Delk sisters, interview by author, October 24, 2006. On the *Tidewater*, see Jim McNeil, *Charleston's Navy Yard: A Picture History* (Charleston, S.C.: Coker Craft Press, 1985), 102, 142–43.

16. Delk sisters, interview by author, October 24, 2006; Hartmann, *The Home Front and Beyond*, 61–62.

17. Delk sisters, interview by author, October 24, 2006; Eva McCartha Hutton, interview by author, Columbia, S.C., June 19, 1991; Sherlock Hutton, interview by author, Columbia, S.C., June 19, 1991; Newman, *Employing Women in Shipyards*, 31–32.

18. Hamer, *Charleston Reborn*, 85; Delk sisters, interview by author, October 24, 2006; Hartmann, *The Home Front and Beyond*, 79. Hartmann acknowledges that some women were inspired to enter war industries for patriotic reasons.

19. Delk sisters, interview by author, October 24, 2006.

20. "Wartime Changes in Population and Family Characteristics, Charleston Congested Production Area," March 1944, box 4, census file, Charleston, Records of President's Committee of Congested Production Areas (RPCCPA), RG 212, NASE.

21. Hartmann, *The Home Front and Beyond*, 77–78; Delk sisters, interview by author, October 24, 2006.

22. Hutton, interview by author, June 19, 1991.

23. Ann Fox, interview by author, Charleston, S.C., February 16, 1996.

24. "Migration Status of Resident Population by Color for Charleston County and City," November 25, 1944, WMC, series 12, box 19, RG 211, NASE.

25. Robert Sneed, interview by author, Mt. Pleasant, S.C., December 6, 1995; Katherine Archibald, *Wartime Shipyards: A Study in Social Disunity* (Berkeley: University of California Press, 1947), 32–33; Hamer, *Charleston Reborn*, 81–82.

26. William L. O'Neill, *A Democracy at War: America's Fight at Home and Abroad in World War II* (New York: Free Press, 1993), 241–43; Hartmann, *The Home Front and Beyond*, 81–84; "Wartime Changes in Population and Family Characteristics," March 1944, box 4, census file, RPCCPA, RG 212, NASE.

27. Hamer, *Charleston Reborn*, 123–24. On national trends in day care use, see Hartmann, *The Home Front and Beyond*, 58, 84–85, and William M. Tuttle Jr., "*Daddy's Gone to War*": *The Second World War in the Lives of America's Children* (New York: Oxford University Press, 1993), 81–88.

28. "Migration Status of Resident Population by Color for Charleston County and City," November 25, 1944, box 19, series 12, WMC, RG 211, NASE; *Produce to Win*, February 12, 1943, SCL; Hamer, *Charleston Reborn*, 67.

29. *Produce to Win*, October 1, 1943, November 23, 1943, and November 19, 1943, SCL.

30. Ibid., October 29, 1943, SCL.

31. *The State*, December 30, 1944; "Migration Status of Resident Population by Color for Charleston County and City," November 25, 1944, box 19, series 12, RG 211, WMC-NASE.

32. Delk sisters, interview by author, October 24, 2006.

33. Hamer, *Charleston Reborn*, 85.

34. Delk sisters, interview by author, October 24, 2006; "Report on Adequacy of Services and Facilities in Charleston, S.C. area," September 15, 1943, box 4, entry 13, RPCCPA, RG 212, NASE.

35. Delk sisters, interview by author, October 24, 2006.

36. Hartmann, *The Home Front and Beyond*, 90–91; Sneed, interview by author, December 6, 1995; *Women Workers in Ten Production Areas and Their Postwar Employment Plans*, Bulletin of the Women's Bureau, no. 209 (Washington, D.C.: Government Printing Office, 1946), 4, 19, 26. These interviews were based on thirteen thousand women who were surveyed between February 1944 and May 1945. The other areas included greater Baltimore, Detroit-Willow Run, Michigan, and Seattle-Tacoma, Washington.

37. Martin Blum, *V Was for Victory: Politics and American Culture During World War II* (New York: Harcourt Brace Jovanovich, 1976), 94–95. Moore, interview by author, March 9, 1995; Johnny Dodd, interview by author, Mt. Pleasant, S.C., December 6, 1995.

38. On women and work in the late 1940s and 1950s, see William H. Chafe, *The Paradox of Change: American Women in the 20th Century* (New York: Oxford University Press, 1991), 159–63.

Louise Smith

The First Lady of Racing

SUZANNE WISE

In its early days, stock car racing was a disorganized and poorly funded sport featuring hard-drinking, hard-driving men who came from the ranks of moonshine runners, farmers, mechanics, and factory workers. In December 1947 Bill France Sr., a race promoter and sometime driver from Daytona Beach, Florida, spearheaded the founding of NASCAR. France ruled the new organization. He brought some order to the chaos by establishing rules and guaranteeing purses, and he controlled the fiery, independent drivers by outlawing those who competed in races not sanctioned by NASCAR. France was also a savvy promoter. One of his strategies to draw bigger crowds was using women drivers, both in women-only "powderpuff" races and in open racing against men.

France's idea of female drivers was not new. Women have participated in auto racing since the sport's earliest days. Their presence has been marginal, however, as they have found it difficult to break through the pervasive cultural perception of women as passive, physically weak, emotionally fragile, and intellectually lacking. They have been denied opportunities in sport for all of these reasons. Post–World War II American society's emphasis on returning to normalcy—which featured marriage and family life in the burgeoning suburbs— did not promote women's participation in athletics. Professional opportunities in sports for women were limited, a notable exception being the Ladies' Professional Golf Association, founded in 1948. Moreover, the opposition to female athletes has been strongest when they have dared to invade the sports that celebrate the traditionally male characteristics of power, strength, and aggression, such as bullfighting and auto racing.

Despite the obstacles, a surprising number of women have persevered and competed successfully in auto racing. Early role models include Englishwoman

the 1st Lady in Racing and the 1999 Inductee into the International Motor Sports Hall of Fame

LOUISE SMITH

From Suzanne Wise's personal collection. Courtesy of Louise Smith.

Dorothy Levitt, who drove for the De Dion Company in open races against men in the first decade of the twentieth century; the legendary Camille du Gast, whose exploits included an eighth-place finish against 274 men in the 1903 Paris-Madrid race; and Kay Petre, whose excellent racing skills at Brooklands in England in the years before World War II convinced many that women were capable of handling large, fast cars.[1]

In the United States, women racers have been tolerated on occasion as gimmicks to sell tickets but, as in Europe, they have never been fully accepted by the male racing establishment. Their reception in stock car racing was no exception. A few women withstood the hostility to make their mark in the sport. Georgians Sara Christian and Ethel Flock Mobley were successful drivers in the 1940s, but the most notable woman racer of the era was Louise Smith (1916–2006).[2] Smith had by far the longest career of her female peers, competing regularly from 1946 to 1956 and winning thirty-eight times. She was a strong, fiercely independent woman who rose from a conventional Southern upbringing to become one of racing's most celebrated female drivers. Motorsports journalist Jason Stein has said of Smith, "There are pioneers who break new ground, and then there's Louise Smith, a woman who took dynamite to conventional thinking."[3]

In 1946 Bill France was looking for a way to boost attendance at a race he was promoting at the newly reopened Greenville-Pickens Speedway near Greenville, South Carolina. He thought that a woman driver might attract attention. Greenville-Pickens track promoter Hickey Nichols suggested Louise Smith, telling France that the crazy lady was the fastest thing on four wheels and had outrun every lawman in the area. Even though she had never even seen a race, twenty-nine-year-old Smith agreed to compete in a ladies' race before the main event. Without a single practice lap and only a five-minute lesson on track rules, she drove a 1939 modified Ford Coupe owned by Nichols around the dirt track, finishing third.[4]

"It was supposed to be the fastest thing in the Carolinas," she recalled. "Well, I flipped it on the Pickens side, turned it on its side, and it flipped back on its wheels. Back then you could keep on racing."[5] No one had thought to tell her that a checkered flag signaled the end of the race, so when it waved Smith kept doing laps. "I wondered where all the cars went and I'm out there just flyin' around that half-mile track. I kept looking out there in the infield and pit area. All of them were sitting out there." Finally somebody remembered that she had been told to stop if she saw a red flag, so they waved it and brought her in. Her wild driving style made for lots of local gambling action: "One a bettin' against the other that I'd win or wreck. They knew how crazy I was," she recalled.[6]

So began the remarkable auto racing career of Louise Smith. The daughter of William and Eva DeVall, she was born July 31, 1916, in Barnesville, Georgia. The family moved to Greenville, South Carolina in search of a better life when she was four years old, and her father got a job in a cotton mill.[7]

"Lou," as she was always affectionately called by her friends and family, got her first taste of racing when she was ten. With the assistance of her older brother Eddie, she "borrowed" her father's Model T Ford. The little girl, who could barely reach the pedals and knew nothing about brakes, roared around the yard, hit the fence, and destroyed the hen house, setting off a cacophony among the very surprised chickens. Smith was appropriately punished by her father, a third-shift textile mill worker who was roused from a sound sleep, but she never forgot the fun and excitement of driving fast.[8]

The family lived on West Washington Street. Smith attended elementary schools in Mauldin, South Carolina, and on Anderson Street in Greenville. She attended Greenville's Parker High but left without graduating. As a teenager she worked at the Judson Mill. Textile plants were the major employers in the South Carolina Upstate at the time, and the textile companies were a dominant economic force in the region. Many children went to work at the mill when they were twelve. Females were usually paid less than males, working twelve hours a day for $12 a week.[9] Smith recalled, "I worked two hours a day at school, came to the mill, and worked twelve hours a day. They would have somebody come in for one hour and take your place while you went to lunch. They learned me to work in the weave room that way."[10] Judson Mill was one of the Greenville-area mills affected by the 1934 general textile strike, in which workers from New England to Alabama participated. Female workers were very active on the picket lines. During a shift change at Judson Mill "several women armed with clubs began bouncing the clubs off the heads of women workers" (i.e., scabs).[11] There is no evidence as to whether Smith, who was then eighteen years old, was working that picket line. Given her feistiness, it is easy to imagine her there.

Brother Eddie had a major influence on his sister's life a second time when he introduced her to his friend Noah Smith in 1935. Noah ran an auto junkyard, Smith's Auto Parts. Eddie, a mechanic, liked Noah because he had lots of cars in various states of disrepair. Perhaps Louise was also excited by the proximity to cars and the tantalizing connection to speed. Louise and Noah married in 1943 after a five-year courtship. She worked for a short time in a California airplane factory while Noah was serving in the Pacific theater during World War II but returned to Greenville before the end of the war.

Automobiles were not readily available during and immediately after World War II, but Noah gave his bride a Ford, which his mechanics souped up for better performance.[12] Smith loved the exhilaration of speed, and soon she was doing some illegal racing on public roads, often accompanied by the wail of a police siren. She recalled outrunning the local lawmen with some regularity.[13] She laughed, "We did it just to have fun. Sometimes they did follow me home and give me a ticket. But to me, even then, it was still fun. I just liked going fast."[14]

Making and transporting moonshine was integral to the economy of the Southern Appalachian foothills and mountains during this time, and many race drivers of the era developed their driving skills outrunning the law while delivering illegal liquor. Smith denied delivering white lightning, although she admitted that many of her friends did. She said, "I might have ridden with them [moonshine runners] but that doesn't mean I was hauling it," and she once told a young reporter, "Honey, I wasn't hauling the liquor; I was drinking it."[15]

The taste of legal racing at Greenville-Pickens Speedway convinced Smith that she had found her calling. As she told the *Baltimore Sun* around 1997, "I was just born to be wild. I tried to be a nurse, a pilot, and a beautician and couldn't make it in any of them. But from the moment I hit the race track, it was exactly what I wanted."[16]

At first she focused on local ladies' competitions. She issued a challenge to any woman driver in the country to go head to head in a match race but apparently had no response, and she competed in several ten-lap powderpuff events at Greenville-Pickens Speedway. Among the entrants were her driving student Barbara Peigler as well as Sara Christian and Mildred Williams of Atlanta and Carrol Landers of Columbia.[17]

At the urging of Bill France she decided to mix it up with the men. Some of the drivers were not overly fond of France because of the small purses at races he promoted, but Smith had the highest regard for him. She always credited him for her passion for racing and for giving her entree into the racing world. She once called him and said, "You sure got me in a mess."[18] France knew that the novelty of a woman driver competing against men was a good way to increase attendance, so he contacted promoters, who paid Smith appearance money.[19]

Soon Smith had a full racing schedule from Florida to Canada and occasionally into the Midwest. She concentrated especially on the Northeast and Canada, where she received more appearance money, usually at least $150 and occasionally as much as $1,000.[20] She said she fared better there because "those boys up there didn't know how to drive like these Southern boys."[21] The $75–$100 winner's purses barely covered expenses, so appearance money was important. She might be on the road for two weeks, racing at tracks from Tampa to New York, and get $500 in appearance fees plus what she won. Sometimes France used Smith to promote his events.[22] She would arrive at the track a day or two early and do everything from giving interviews to local radio stations to nailing posters on telephone poles.[23]

Noah provided his wife with new cars and a mechanic. Smith had adequate equipment but was not as competitive as some of the other drivers. She did not work on her own cars, and a friend recalled that she "kept it well hid if she did" know about auto mechanics.[24] Her cars were usually painted red and cream, and she always used number 94. Driver Buck Baker's crew often pitted for her.[25]

Predictably, most of the male drivers resented a woman competing head to head with them on a regular basis. "For a long time, all the drivers gave me trouble. . . . [T]hey did not want a woman driver out there. They still don't. . . . The men would yell things at me and they tried to wreck me."[26] Asked if the male drivers gave her any breaks, she replied, "Yeah, broken bones. One threw me into a ditch just to put me in my place when I started."[27] Once or twice Bill France had to fill in for her in Modified races he was promoting when the other drivers objected to a woman in the field. However, he always encouraged Smith to continue racing.

A few drivers befriended the audacious young woman. Buddy Shuman showed her how to tap the back bumper of a car that was holding her up and spin it out of the way. She mastered the trick quite well, and the male drivers quit picking on her on the track. "When they found out I wasn't going to take it any more, they acted right different," she said.[28] Driver Joe Weatherly, later a NASCAR Grand National (now Sprint Cup) champion, supported her, once confronting a driver who refused to race if Smith was in the field. As for the protesting driver, Smith said, "I finally put him over the fence."[29]

It wasn't only male drivers who wanted her off the track. Some female fans were jealous because they thought she was seducing their men.[30] However, most fans loved Smith. She was the first woman ever to compete at Pensacola and Mobile and was the big drawing card for the thousands of spectators, according to the *National Speed Sport News*.[31]

Although she was initially a target of widespread animosity, Smith gradually became one of the boys. She proved to be a fearless competitor, not afraid to mix it up with the men on the track and always ready to party and have a good time off it. Her fellow drivers recognized her intrepid nature. Buck Baker observed, "She drove just like I did. She drove to win."[32] Ned Jarrett said, "In racing we said she wasn't afraid to push the button."[33] Frank Mundy recalled that she was very friendly to everyone and understood the unwritten rules of racing, such as giving way when a faster car came up behind her.[34] Fellow drivers called her "the good ol' gal." She was a member of the "Dirty Four": Smith, Curtis Turner, Bill Snowden, and Buck Baker blocked for each other during races and supported each other in the fights that often ensued afterward.[35] Among Smith's good friends were drivers Lee Petty, Curtis Turner, Fireball Roberts, Buddy Shuman, and the Flock brothers. She was perhaps closest to Buck Baker.

Smith played a part in advancing the career of Glenn "Fireball" Roberts. She had a contract to race every Sunday during the summer of 1948 at Jacksonville Speedway in Florida. One week she was not feeling well. Bill Snowden recommended Roberts, a nineteen-year-old University of Florida student and part-time racer as a relief driver. Smith drove twelve laps then turned the car over to Roberts, who went on to a strong finish. They became good friends, and Smith remained close to Roberts's wife, Doris, after the driver's death.[36]

Despite on-track confrontations, at the end of the day the drivers were all comrades in arms. Money was scarce, and they banded together when one of the group needed help, sharing cars, tools, and food. Many slept in their cars to save money, and Smith and several others drove Nash Ambassadors because they were roomy enough for sleeping.

Fighting was a regular part of the track action in the early days of stock car racing, and at five feet nine inches tall and 180 pounds, Smith was not shy about throwing a punch when the occasion warranted it.[37] Once Buck Baker was still strapped in his car after winning a race when several men starting hitting him. Smith was sitting nearby. She grabbed a tire iron and protected Baker until he could climb from his car.[38] "Louise was something else," said Baker. "She was a strong as most men and just as rowdy. Hell, I wouldn't have wanted to fight her."[39] "Buck Baker, Curtis Turner, Jack Smith and myself were probably the worst of the bunch to fuss and fight," Smith admitted.[40]

The stock car racing circuit in the 1940s and 1950s was uninhibited. Fisticuffs were not limited to the speedway; partying sometimes escalated into a brawl. Smith recalled, "A man came over to us one night at a bar and said he was going to throw us out. I said, 'Go ahead, we've been thrown out of bigger and better places than this.'"[41] The only time she was ever arrested for fighting was when she hadn't thrown a punch. A large group of racers were at a restaurant in Summerville, South Carolina. She had just gone to the ladies' room to put on her last clean blouse when she heard lots of noise. She stepped out into the middle of a full-fledged riot. She recalled, "Would you believe about the time I walked out, the law walked in? I was in the wrong place at the wrong time. They had torn that big, nice restaurant up. I mean torn it up." The whole crew was locked up in jail. Smith finally secured their release by pawning her diamond rings. The drivers then caravanned to Martinsville for the next race. Smith said with a laugh, "We all went up the road together, about 10 to 12 race cars. . . . We got up there and there stands Bill [France]. We were late. He was prancin', walkin', and ravin'. He said, 'Where in the hell have you been Louise?' And I said, 'You really don't want to know.'"[42]

Smith competed in Modified, Sportsman, and Grand National races and even tried a Midget race once in Savannah, Georgia, but the open-wheel vehicle was a tight squeeze for someone her size. She liked driving Modifieds the best.[43] She preferred to race on the small dirt ovals, called bullrings, which featured racing on the ragged edge, and all but one of her victories were on dirt. When asked if he thought one could make a good living racing on dirt tracks, driver Tim Flock replied, "Yes, I do, but not for nervous people."[44] Smith's favorite track was Langhorne, and she also liked Mobile and Birmingham. She thought two of the toughest were Hamburg and Myrtle Beach. She raced only a few times at Greenville-Pickens Speedway because she thought the promoters were not helpful to her (i.e., they did not pay her appearance money).[45]

Smith was already considered a veteran competitor in 1949.[46] By 1950 she was a recognized star. Her photograph appeared on the cover of the January 11, 1950, issue of *National Speed Sport News*, a leading national racing weekly, with the caption "Attractive Louise Smith, woman promoter and champion woman Stock [sic] car race driver, who has become famous this past season by her brilliant performances. Louise will be much in the Sport's News [sic] columns come [sic] 1950 season."[47] She was crowned woman driver of the year in 1951.[48]

Smith was the first woman to compete in U.S. Auto Club stock cars, racing with USAC in 1947 in Dayton and Cleveland.[49] She was offered a car for the Indianapolis 500 by the Anderson Company and applied to compete in the 1948 race. Indianapolis Motor Speedway president Wilbur Shaw told reporters he thought Smith could pass the rookie driving test, but the board said no women competitors were allowed on the track.[50] The policy didn't change until 1976, when Janet Guthrie became the first woman to attempt to qualify for the Indianapolis 500.[51]

Smith recalled a race in 1950 in which she overcame the disadvantaged starting position given to women as a career highlight. She had wrecked both her cars, and Bill Rexford, who went on to win the NASCAR Grand National championship that year, offered to let her drive his. She piloted the car to victory on an asphalt track at Buffalo Civic Stadium in Buffalo, New York. Smith said that she was forced to start at the back of the field in Buffalo because she was female, which "of course burned me inside. I won after they had already said women didn't start first up there at that track." As she took the checkered flag, the wheel, hub and all, came off.[52] After the race she was being interviewed by a television reporter and saw herself on the monitor. "It was the first time I'd ever seen a TV, and I was on it," she said.[53]

Smith was known for her aggressive driving style and spectacular crashes. Young fans would ask her, "Mrs. Smith, are you going to wreck today?" More than likely she would flip the car over. She would tell them, "I could race better if I had the wheels on top!"[54] She won her first trophy at Hatfield Speedway in Pennsylvania for joining the upside-down club, in recognition of her propensity to wreck.[55] She drove over, under, or through anything standing in her way. At Mobile she crashed into Fonty Flock and ended up sitting atop her car in the infield lake. At Hamburg she missed the turn and drove through the wooden fence enclosing the track. She kept going, drove back through the fence farther down the track, and continued on her way.[56] At Asheville-Weaverville Speedway she climbed the bank on the outside of the track and drove through an abandoned house. Spectators perched on the roof watching the race had to scatter quickly.[57]

One of her worst wrecks occurred after she got a driving lesson from Curtis Turner. Turner, whom Smith thought was the best driver on the circuit, was a master of the power slide through the turns of dirt tracks. He agreed to teach her the technique. She crouched down next to him while he drove her car several laps around Occoneechee Speedway in Hillsborough, North Carolina. He told her that the most important thing was to keep her foot on the gas and feather the car using the gas and not the brakes. Then he let her drive while he squatted next to her.[58] She was able to execute the maneuver, so she tried it for real in her qualifying run for the Modified race. The first lap she was going more than a hundred miles per hour, and the other drivers were shouting for her to slow down. She recalled, "Well, I got airborne. That car went over the top of a tree and when it came down, it cut four trees down even to the ground. Then it started backflopping, knocking the radiator back over the engine."[59] In her words, "the car was mashed."[60] Her head had been forced through the larger part of the steering wheel, and it took rescuers thirty-six minutes to cut her out with an acetylene torch. A driver asked Buck Baker if he was going to stop and check on her. Baker replied, "Nah, she's dead this time."[61] Against medical advice, Smith insisted on leaving the hospital and returning to the track. The race was stopped and the drivers came over to hug her. Later she posed for pictures beside her demolished car. The horrific wreck earned her the nickname "Lucky Lou."[62]

When her car was out of commission, Smith went looking for someone else's. She had a spectacular wreck driving Buck Baker's car in a women's race at Florida's Tampa Speedway Park in August 1949, crashing through the rails and rolling over five times while dragging seven of the rail posts with her. Landing right side up, she hit a telephone pole, cutting it in half and uprooting the lower half from the ground. When the car finally stopped, she crawled out without a scratch and said, "Just look at that car!" Baker probably said something a little stronger.[63]

Racing could be dangerous for spectators as well as drivers. Smith recalled an incident at a track in eastern South Carolina. A drunk was sitting on the guard-rail of the track, waving the cars by. She and two other cars came together and crashed into the rail, killing the man. The local police charged the three drivers with manslaughter. Fortunately, the case was never prosecuted.[64]

Smith broke many bones over her career, including an ankle that she injured climbing out of her race car window (race car doors are welded shut for safety).[65] Once a doctor asked her why her body was so beaten up. She showed him some racing photographs and he said, "I don't know how you've still living."[66] She said racing was worse than an addiction to gambling. She always returned to the track as quickly as possible after an injury, asserting, "You stay out too long and you lose your nerve." She even competed in one race with a cast on her arm.[67]

Smith's family was not pleased with her racing. There was the very real danger of serious injury. Beyond that, stock car racing was the sport of choice for the southern working class, an escape from tedious, poverty-ridden lives in textile mills and on hardscrabble farms. Racetracks were gathering places where, like their driver heroes, spectators drank, fought, and raised hell.[68] When her mother, Eva, attended a race, Smith always told promoters to put her high in the grandstand, as far from the action as possible. During a race at Bainbridge, Ohio, Smith was involved in a major wreck. Eva stuck her fingers in her ears to block the sound of cars crashing onto her daughter. Said Smith, "My mother hated racing. She was nervous, she was afraid to stay at home, she was afraid to go with me, she was afraid I was going to get hurt." Once a reporter said to Smith's mother that she must be very proud of her daughter. Eva replied, "No I'm not, no I'm not. She ain't got no business out there." Smith's niece Mickie, however, was enthralled with her aunt's racing. When asked what she wanted to be when she grew up, the little girl replied she wanted to be a race driver like her aunt.[69]

Noah, called "No-ey" by his friends, hated his wife's racing lifestyle. He went to one race and she flipped the car. He never went back. Instead, he stayed home and managed what they always called the junkyard, which was open 365 days a year. He was eleven years her senior, but she was the dominant personality in the marriage, so he reluctantly accepted her passion for the sport. She said in 1993, "It [racing] did worry him, especially the knack I had for wreckin'." Her high-risk occupation made it impossible to get insurance. Noah told her, "You'll go out there, get killed and then nobody's got money enough to bury you, plus, if you don't get killed, you might get crippled for life and whose fault is it? It's not your family's fault."[70]

"Do what you want and apologize later" was a recurring theme in Smith's relationship with her husband. Once Noah told her that if she left to go racing in New York she need not bother coming back. She replied that it would take just a minute to put her belongings in the car, and she left for the track. He forgave her when she returned.[71]

The tale of a race at Daytona showcases her indomitable spirit and willingness to defy conventional wifely behavior. The details have changed in various tellings, but the essence of the story is quintessential Louise Smith. While still serving overseas Noah had written to a car dealer in Easley, South Carolina, and asked him to save him a new Ford. When he got home, the Smiths had a new maroon Ford coupe.[72] In her version, the year was 1947, and Smith told Noah she was taking the new family car to Daytona Beach to watch the races, but she hid a specially prepared engine in the trunk and entered the race.[73] According to primary sources it was July 1949, the first time women went head to head against men on the beach in the annual midsummer event.[74] Smith's interest in racing at Daytona that year had already been announced, as the *Greenville News* reported that "Greenville's own Mrs. Louise Smith . . . said she had just about made up her mind to give the Daytona event a whirl."[75] However it happened, this was her first look as a driver at the Daytona Beach and Road Course, which consisted of a section of U.S. A1A going south, a quick turn onto the beach, a straightaway north along the beach, and a turn through the dunes back onto the highway. Smith drew number thirteen for the race and, being superstitious as most drivers are, she tried unsuccessfully to trade it. Her instincts were correct; she was involved in a seven-car pileup in the north turn that crushed the top of her car. Some spectators righted the vehicle and she continued on, finishing twentieth in the twenty-eight-car field.[76]

The wreck badly damaged Smith's car, so she left it with a mechanic in Augusta, Georgia, to be repaired and took the bus home. When she walked into the office, Noah asked her where the car was. She replied, "You know that old thing weren't no good. You just bought a lemon, and it broke down on me in Augusta, and I had to catch a bus back." Without a word Noah spread the local newspaper out on the counter, and there was an article telling the world that Louise Smith had wrecked at Daytona. She didn't know what to do, so she just walked out. "I didn't know if he was going to kill me or what," she said.[77] Noah eventually got over it, realizing that his headstrong wife was determined to race.

Noah sometimes had to enlist help to track her down. One instance concerned an extended postrace celebration. As Smith told it, "Outside of the Langhorne Speedway was a pretty good, nice loungin' place. We all ended up out there, but some of them had sense enough to leave and go on home. Some of us didn't." Several days after the race, Noah called the Philadelphia police, looking for his wife. "We were having the best time and the law came in and wanted to know who was driving that Nash, that race car. Everybody pointed at me. . . . They said, 'You'd better call home. Your husband is worried to death about you.'"[78]

Considering that his wife was constantly in the company of rowdy, partying racers, Noah didn't exhibit undue jealousy, with two exceptions. He had doubts about Bill France Sr. and country singer Marty Robbins, who also competed in NASCAR races. He made his wife cut in half a photo of herself and France that hung in the Smiths' Auto Parts office. Interestingly, she cut herself out of it and rehung the France half on the wall.[79] France, she said, was "a *good-lookin'* man. Ooo-eee."[80]

The marital relationship was at times strained to the breaking point. Noah apparently considered divorce, as Smith once told a reporter, "My old man don't like me to race because it costs him money, but he was getting ready to air me anyway and he figures the undertaker will be cheaper than the lawyer."[81] They lived in different worlds and had separate groups of friends. However, she said fondly, "He wouldn't quit on me. He must've loved me."[82] They were married for forty-eight years, until Noah's death on March 27, 1990.

Smith's last race was probably in 1956 at Kingsbridge Armory Speedrome in the Bronx, New York. She stopped in Greenville to get ready to go to Daytona in February. Reverend Harold B. Slighter, the minister of Tabernacle Baptist Church, was at the junkyard to buy a radio antenna and started talking to Noah, who was drinking heavily. The pastor counseled Noah about his faith and Noah knelt down in prayer and rededicated himself. Reverend Slighter asked Noah about Louise and her faith; he replied that she was leading a wild life as a racer, so there wasn't much hope for her. Noah came into the house and told his wife he had been saved and was going to start going to church. He also said the preacher would like to talk to her before she left for Daytona. The next morning the reverend telephoned and Smith spoke with him. He asked, "Did you ever think about what would happen to you if you was killed in one of them races? You'd go to hell if you've never been saved." She later commented, "And 'course that makes you stop and think, especially when you stay on your top more than you do anywhere else." She asked the preacher to pray for her on the phone. He did and "I got saved on the telephone," she said.[83]

Smith quit racing cold, started going to church, and immersed herself in charitable activities. She put the same passion that she had for racing into her charity work. She and Noah had no children of their own although she was very close to her nieces and nephews. Tom Kirk, founder and director of the Greenville Rescue Mission, told her they needed a children's home and asked her to help raise the needed funds. Smith adopted the home as her special project. She spoke in some 150 churches and spent three and a half months in Hollywood raising $30,000 for what became Miracle Hill Children's Home. She appeared on a number of television programs, including "You Bet Your Life," "Breakfast in Hollywood," "It Could Be You," and "Queen for a Day," where she asked that a truckload of bricks be delivered to Miracle Hill. One of the dormitories at Miracle Hill built with the money she raised is named for her, and she was listed as a Miracle Maker, a donor who has provided perpetual support, at the time of her death. She also helped raise funds to start a Meals on Wheels program and worked with the Shriners.[84]

In 1971 NASCAR invited Smith to Daytona International Speedway, a 2.5-mile superspeedway constructed after she retired from racing. She was amazed at the changes in the sport. She commented on the higher speeds, the improved facilities, and the civility of the sport, noting there wasn't any drinking in the pits.[85] Smith loved some of the changes in racing but not others. She wasn't pleased with the corporate persona of NASCAR and thought it had taken some of the soul from racing. "They're not having nothing except the money. They're giving their whole life and their families' life and not getting nothing for it," she said.[86] Meeting her old racing friends and being close to the action again awakened her love for the sport, and she returned to racing after a fifteen-year absence.

Over the next few years Smith sponsored several drivers, including Bobby Wawak, Rick Newsome, Jeff Handy, Larry Pearson, Dale Jarrett, and Ronnie Thomas, who was NASCAR Rookie of the Year in 1978 with her backing. They all drove a race car with "Louise Smith Special" painted on the side. A friend recalled that her drivers "thought she walked on water." She was generous with the crew members of her race team and took them out for dinner frequently. Once she rented Cloud Nine, a topless club in Charlotte, for the race team she sponsored. Liquor was dispensed in gallon jugs with a pump.[87]

Smith helped her husband at the junkyard but still relished the spotlight. She confided, "I do enjoy the personal appearances."[88] Longtime friend Willis Smith (no relation) found a discarded 1939 Ford flathead engine auto and restored it to look like her original Modified race car, complete with Smith's Auto Parts and number 94 on the side and, with her permission, "Jesus Loves You!" on the hood.[89] She often appeared at charity and racing events with the car.

Eventually Noah sold the junkyard but kept the house. Smith began traveling with the racing community again. She attended all the Winston Cup races in the

Southeast, participating in the parade laps in her 1976 green Monte Carlo with
white interior that she called the green lizard and cheering "her boys" from pit
road.[90] She very much enjoyed the camaraderie with her old racing buddies.
She even had some thoughts about driving again. When she was fifty-four her
hometown track Greenville-Pickens Speedway invited her to compete in a race,
but she reluctantly declined the offer.[91]

For a number of years Smith was also involved in pageant work. For a while
she was a major financial supporter of the Miss Southland beauty contest in
Daytona. She then became the grand patron of the Miss Southern 500 beauty
pageant for twelve years, stepping down shortly before Noah's death. Smith
had evolved from a rowdy stock car racer into a well-respected member of the
community. She cut a rather glamorous figure in her pageant years and did
everything on a larger-than-life scale. She dyed her hair jet black and added a
large hairpiece, giving her a formidable beehive that she called her "trademark
hair." Her dramatic appearance was heightened by blood red lipstick. She always
bought the best of everything, wearing long glittering dresses and multiple diamond rings. She was very generous, passing suitcases full of gowns along to her
friends when she bought new ones. She was crowned "Queen of the Speedway"
at Darlington in 1981 in recognition of her efforts with the pageant.[92]

Smith maintained a museum devoted to her racing career in a small building
in her back yard. It contained trophies, photographs, newspaper clippings, and
other memorabilia, including a certificate, awarded to her at Daytona in 1952,
that read "Presenting the Silver Award to the Champion She-Driver."[93] Many of
her trophies were stolen when her house on Lake Greenwood, South Carolina,
was burglarized and others are at Talladega and Daytona. The items in her museum were auctioned off after her death.

Smith made some wise real estate investments. She owned land and apart-
ments as well as Smith Village on Lake Greenwood, the latter consisting of a
group of trailers that she rented. She also leased a restaurant at the lake. Smith
had invested a significant amount of savings with Carolina Investors, a company
with four offices in the South Carolina Upstate. In 2003 the company, which offered high yield returns on loans to borrowers with a history of credit problems,
closed its doors to investors, not allowing them to withdraw their money. A subsequent investigation by the state and the Securities Exchange Commission sent
six individuals to jail for fraud of hundreds of millions of dollars, and the more
than eight thousand investors, mostly retirees, recovered only about eighteen
cents on the dollar of their money. Her niece Lib Owens observed that Smith
began a gradual physical and mental decline about then.[94]

Late in her life Smith had mobility problems. Drivers of her era competed in street clothes, and her feet were scarred from the hot oil that dripped on them when she raced. Arthritis crippled her hands. She suffered a heart attack and had hip replacement surgery. Independence was everything to Smith, and she hated using a walker or a wheelchair. She was still energized by speed, sometimes driving her age in her 1996 Buick LeSabre. "I can't walk so good anymore, but when I sit in my car, everything is all right," she said.[95] Smith lived near Greenville-Pickens Speedway for sixty-six years, and when she raised the windows during the summer she could hear the roar of the race cars. In 1993, nearly forty years after she retired from competitive driving, she said wistfully, "I have to let the window down. I can't stand to hear them cars. It makes me have heavy feet."[96]

Smith contracted cancer of the esophagus and died on April 15, 2006, at age eighty-nine. Her passing was noted in the national racing press with special articles and reminiscences by many racing journalists. She lived alone and drove her Buick around town until about four months before her death. She guarded her independence to the end; she would take her walker, get in the car, and go to the grocery store. Smith told her niece not to allow a race car to lead the hearse at her funeral. She wanted—and received—a dignified funeral.[97] She is buried at Graceland West Cemetery and Mausoleum in Greenville.

If enduring status in popular culture is a sign of lasting impact, then Louise Smith's place in racing history is secure. She is featured on a T-shirt, and there are diecast cars of her number 94 Modified Ford for sale. She made the late night talk-show circuit, visiting David Letterman in 1999. A television movie of her life with the working title *Queen of Crashes* is in the works. A children's book about her, *Fearless: The Story of Racing Legend Louise Smith* by Barbara Rosenstock, was published in 2010.

The greatest recognition of her place in racing history was her 1999 induction into the International Motorsports Hall of Fame in Talladega, Alabama, the first woman to be so honored. Only two others, Janet Guthrie and Shirley Muldowney, have joined her in the succeeding years. Most fittingly, Wendell Scott, the only African American driver ever to win a race in NASCAR's top division, was inducted into the Hall of Fame the same year as Smith. Like Smith, he faced prejudice during his career. Among his competitors he was barely tolerated by many, met with open hostility by some, and befriended by a few. Scott was also subjected to blatant racism from spectators, whereas Smith was generally a crowd favorite.[98]

Smith asked NASCAR driver Bill Elliott to induct her into the International Motorsports Hall of Fame. Although she was very pleased to be elected, she made it clear that she understood why it took a third nomination to be chosen.

"I have proven to all the sportswriters [who elect the members] that I was a driver. The only thing holding me back was that some of them didn't want a woman in the Hall of Fame. They treated me just like they did on the speedway. They didn't want me in, and I was beginning to think they would never let me in." Then she received a commemorative certificate inscribed "Louis Smith" and a man's ring. She was issued a corrected certificate but kept the ring for fear she might never get another.[99] She said, "Back in my day I was the first to do a lot of things. Back then women weren't supposed to do all those things. Now, this is certainly an honor."[100] The South Carolina General Assembly passed a concurrent resolution congratulating Smith upon her induction into the Hall of Fame, noting that she was a woman "who gave no quarter and took no prisoners during her stock car days" and that "her spirit and pride is [sic] just as strong at age eighty-two as it was fifty years ago."[101]

Smith helped blaze the way for women in a male-dominated sport, succeeding in a tough arena when the prevailing cultural image of a woman was as a homemaker who deferred to her husband. She liked being the center of attention, had a salty tongue and a hearty laugh, and was a master of colorful storytelling. She drove, drank, and fought, and always had a good time.

However, Smith never considered herself a warrior for women's rights. She was simply an independent, strong-willed individual with a passion for racing who happened to be female. She was pleased to see other women competing and was friendly with female drivers during her racing career and beyond, but in her actions she championed her male racing friends. Smith sponsored male rather than female drivers and once publicly criticized driver Janet Guthrie for blocking her friends David Pearson and Richard Petty on pit road.[102] For many years she sponsored beauty contests connected with races, seeing no conflict between her own efforts to succeed as a female race driver and her promotion of women as simply pretty accessories in racing.

Louise Smith the racer is perfectly captured in an apocryphal story told by Tim Flock to a gullible reporter. Commenting on the tough driving conditions on the Beach and Road Course at Daytona, Flock said, "I thought I was going as fast as I could, but here comes this car fixing to pass me, flying. I looked over to see who it was and this woman was putting on lipstick." The woman was Louise Smith.[103]

NOTES

1. John Bullock, *Fast Women: The Drivers Who Changed the Face of Motor Racing* (London: Robson, 2002), 15–20; S. C. H. Davis, *Atalanta: Women as Racing Drivers* (London: Foulis, 1957), 13–30, 45–76.

2. Sara Christian was called a rising star in stock car racing. She finished fifth in a NASCAR Strictly Stock race at Heidelberg Speedway in October 1949, the best finish a woman has ever had in NASCAR's top racing division. A back injury from a crash at Lakewood Speedway the same year ended her career. Ethel Flock Mobley, the sister of drivers Tim, Bob, and Fonty Flock, competed in races primarily in the Southeast. She bested her brothers on the track on several occasions.

3. Jason Stein, "'Good Ol' Gal' Broke Racing Ground for Women," *Wheelbase Communications*, June 18, 2006, 2, http://www.legendsofnascar.com/Louise_Smith.htm (accessed July 21, 2011).

4. Jim McAllister, "Louise Couldn't Stay away from Racetrack," *Greenville News*, December 31, 1972, D-1; Peter Golenbock, *NASCAR Confidential: Stories of the Men and Women Who Made Stock Car Racing Great* (St. Paul, Minn.: Motorbooks International, 2004), 13; Randy Laney, "Louise Smith Dates Back to the Original 'Good Ol' Boys,'" North Carolina Speedway race program, October 21, 1979, 45–46; Deb Williams, "Louise Smith," *American Racing Classics*, January 1993, 89.

5. David Howell, "Louise Smith," pt. 1, *Greenville News-Piedmont*, June 1, 1975, C-6.

6. Williams, "Louise Smith," 89; Audrey Parente and Jack Koblas, "Woman of Speed," *Trackside*, April 28–May 11, 1995, 52.

7. Golenbock, *NASCAR Confidential*, 12.

8. Williams, "Louise Smith," 93; Pat Berman, "'I Love to Go Fast,'" *The State*, February 18, 2001, E-10.

9. John A. Salmond, *The General Textile Strike of 1934: From Maine to Alabama* (Columbia: University of Missouri Press, 2002), 147.

10. Golenbock, *NASCAR Confidential*, 12.

11. Salmond, *The General Textile Strike of 1934*, 166. Thanks to colleague Pam Mitchem for alerting me to the Judson Mill story through her draft of an article on women's baseball and the strike.

12. Golenbock, *NASCAR Confidential*, 13.

13. Bob Moore, "Where Are They Now? Louise Smith," *NASCAR Winston Cup Scene*, July 2003, 32; Bill Holder, "Louise Smith . . . A NASCAR Pioneer," *Stock Car Racing*, February 2000, 105.

14. Moore, "Where Are They Now?" 32; Holder, "Louise Smith," 105.

15. Golenbock, *NASCAR Confidential*, 13; Berman, "'I Love to Go Fast,'" E-10; "'Good Ol' Gal' Raced 'Good Ol' Boys,'" *Evansville (Ind.) Courier*, November 20, 1998, C-4.

16. Stein, "'Good Ol' Gal,'" 2.

17. "Auto Race Is Set," *Greenville News*, June 7, 1949, 9; "South's Leading Women and Men Drivers to Race Here," *Greenville News*, June 10, 1949, 14; "Stock Car Races Slated at Speedway Today," *Greenville News*, June 11, 1949, 8.

18. Golenbock, *NASCAR Confidential*, 15.

19. Moore, "Where Are They Now?" 33.

20. Jerry Bledsoe, *The World's Number One, Flat-Out, All-Time Great, Stock Car Racing Book* (New York: Doubleday, 1975), 100.

21. Debra Wright, "Louise Smith . . . Once a Tough Character at the Tracks," *Laurens County Advertiser*, March 15, 1978, 17.

22. Holder, "Louise Smith," 105.

23. Williams, "Louise Smith," 94.

24. David Watson, NASCAR team car owner, interview by author and Martha Kreszock, Boone, N.C., April 12, 2007.

25. "Louise Smith Is More Than Miss Southern 500 Beauty Pageant Sponsor," *Florence Morning News*, August 31, 1979, C-13.

26. Golenbock, *NASCAR Confidential*, 17.

27. McAllister, "Louise Couldn't Stay away from Racetrack," D-1.

28. Stein, "'Good Ol' Gal,'" C-4; Moore, "Where Are They Now?" 33; Pete Iacobelli, "Go, Granny, Go: 'First Lady of Racing' Louise Smith Finds Home in Hall of Fame," *The State*, December 8, 1998, C-1.

29. Neal Sims, "'Blackballed' Woman Racer Gets HOF Nod," *Birmingham (Ala.) News*, October 22, 1998.

30. Golenbock, *NASCAR Confidential*, 16.

31. "Mrs. Louise Smith, Stock Car Pilot," *National Speed Sport News*, November 2, 1949, 4.

32. Richard Deitsch, "Flashback: Louise Smith, 82, Stock Car Racing Pioneer," http://sports illustrated.cnn.com/siforwomen/issue_two/introducing.

33. Berman, "'I Love to Go Fast,'" E-10.

34. Louise Smith, "Louise Smith Talks about Racing," Firecracker 400 program, July 4, 1977, 141.

35. Berman, "'I Love to Go Fast,'" E-11; Iacobelli, "Go, Granny, Go," C-2; Stein, "'Good Ol' Gal,'" C-4.

36. McAllister, "Louise Couldn't Stay away from Racetrack," D-1; Leslie Timms, "Greenville Lady Achieved Fame as Race Car Driver," *Greenville News*, June 10, 1964, 11; "Louise Smith Is More Than Miss Southern 500 Beauty Pageant Sponsor," C-13.

37. Berman, "'I Love to Go Fast,'" E-10; Bledsoe, *The World's Number One, Flat-Out, All-Time Great, Stock Car Racing Book*, 97.

38. Debra Wright, "If You Raced You Had to Fight," *Laurens County Advertiser*, March 13, 1978, 4; Williams, "Louise Smith," 91.

39. Frank Vehorn, "Buck Eyes Janet," *Greenville Piedmont*, May 27, 1976, 32.

40. Smith, "Louise Smith Talks about Racing," 139.

41. Mike Hembree, "Hall Immortality Awaits Smith," *Greenville News*, April 22, 1999, C-3.

42. Williams, "Louise Smith," 91.

43. Ibid., 93.

44. Kim Chapin, *Fast as White Lightning: The Story of Stock Car Racing*, updated ed. (New York: Three Rivers Press, 1998), 89.

45. Holder, "Louise Smith," 105; David Howell, "Louise Smith," pt. 2, *Greenville News-Piedmont*, June 8, 1975, C-6; Williams, "Louise Smith," 93.

46. Houston Lawing, "Red Byron Defeats Flock in Daytona Beach 160 Miler," *National Speed Sport News*, July 13, 1949, 2.

47. "Attractive Louise Smith," *National Speed Sport News*, January 11, 1950, 1.

48. *NASCAR Yearbook*, 1952, n.p.

49. Holder, "Louise Smith," 105.

50. Moore, "Where Are They Now?" 33; Williams, "Louise Smith," 93.

51. Guthrie was unable to qualify for the Indianapolis 500 in 1976 owing to mechanical problems, but she did compete in the race in 1977 and 1978, making her the first woman to do so.

52. Howell, "Louise Smith," pt. 1, C-6; Wright, "Louise Smith," 17.

53. Mike Hembree, "40 Years Later, Smith's Mind Is Still Racing," *Greenville News*, June 6, 1995, C-6.

54. Golenbock, *NASCAR Confidential*, 18.

55. Bledsoe, *The World's Number One, Flat-Out, All-Time Great, Stock Car Racing Book*, 98.

56. McAllister, "Louise Couldn't Stay away from Racetrack," D-1.

57. Howell, "Louise Smith," pt. 2, C-6; Bledsoe, *The World's Number One, Flat-Out, All-Time Great, Stock Car Racing Book*, 98.

58. Golenbock, *NASCAR Confidential*, 17.

59. "Louise Smith Is More Than Miss Southern 500 Beauty Pageant Sponsor," c-13.

60. Hembree, "40 Years Later, Smith's Mind Is Still Racing," c-6.

61. Stein, "'Good Ol' Gal,'" c-4.

62. Bledsoe, *The World's Number One, Flat-Out, All-Time Great, Stock Car Racing Book*, 99; Gerald Hodges, "A Woman Named 'Lou,'" http://www.racecolumn.com/SPECIALS.htm (accessed July 21, 2011); Williams, "Louise Smith," 92; Ed Sanseverino, *Occoneechee-Orange Speedway, Hillsboro, NC, 1948–1968*, Premier Collector's Edition (n.p.: Speedway Spotlite Publications, n.d.), cover.

63. Photograph caption, *National Speed Sport News*, August 3, 1949, 1.

64. Bledsoe, *The World's Number One, Flat-Out, All-Time Great, Stock Car Racing Book*, 99.

65. Wright, "Louise Smith," 17.

66. Williams, "Louise Smith," 91.

67. Wright, "Louise Smith," 17; Moore, "Where Are They Now?" 34.

68. Pete Daniel, *Lost Revolutions: The South in the 1950s* (Chapel Hill: University of North Carolina Press for the Smithsonian Institution, 2000), 96.

69. Berman, "'I Love to Go Fast,'" e-11; McAllister, "Louise Couldn't Stay away from Racetrack," d-1; Williams, "Louise Smith," 92; Iacobelli, "Go, Granny, Go," c-2.

70. Williams, "Louise Smith," 91.

71. Stein, "'Good Ol' Gal,'" c-4; Williams, "Louise Smith," 90.

72. Moore, "Where Are They Now?" 33.

73. Hodges, "A Woman Named 'Lou.'"

74. "Louise Smith, Clardy Wreck Cars as Red Byron Wins National Race," *Greenville News*, July 11, 1949, 6; "Byron Takes Daytona Race," *Greenville Piedmont*, July 11, 1949, 23; Lawing, "Red Byron Defeats Flock in Daytona Beach 160 Miler," 1; Greg Fielden, "Byron Nabs Daytona with Late Race Pass," *Forty Years of Stock Car Racing*, vol. 1, *The Beginning 1949–1958*, rev. ed. (Surfside Beach, S.C.: Galfield Press, 1992), 11; Greg Fielden, *High Speed at Low Tide* (Surfside Beach, S.C.: Galfield Press, 1993), 109–12.

75. Jack Caudell, "Baker Wins Stock Car Race," *Greenville News*, July 3, 1949, 11.

76. Moore, "Where Are They Now?" 33; Fielden," Byron Nabs Daytona with Late Race Pass," 11; Fielden, *High Speed at Low Tide*, 109–12.

77. "Louise Smith, Clardy Wreck," 6; Moore, "Where Are They Now?" 34; Golenbock, *NASCAR Confidential*, 14–15.

78. Williams, "Louise Smith," 90.

79. Ibid., 90–91.

80. Bledsoe, *The World's Number One, Flat-Out, All-Time Great, Stock Car Racing Book*, 98.

81. McAllister, "Louise Couldn't Stay away from Racetrack," d-1.

82. Berman, "'I Love to Go Fast,'" e11.

83. Bledsoe, *The World's Number One, Flat-Out, All-Time Great, Stock Car Racing Book*, 100–101; Howell, "Louise Smith," pt. 2, c-6; McAllister, "Louise Couldn't Stay away from Racetrack," d-1.

84. Bonnie and Hardy "Peanut" Turman, friends of Louise Smith, interview by author, Dugspur, Va., April 2, 2007; Timms, "Greenville Lady Achieved Fame as Race Car Driver," 11; Bledsoe, *The World's Number One, Flat-Out, All-Time Great, Stock Car Racing Book*, 101; Howell, "Louise Smith," pt. 2, c-6.

85. Howell, "Louise Smith," pt. 2, c-6.

86. Stein, "'Good Ol' Gal,'" c-4.

87. Watson, interview by author and Kreszock, April 12, 2007.

88. Howell, "Louise Smith," pt. 2, c-6.

89. J. B. Day, friend of Louise Smith, telephone interview by author, August 9, 2007; Turman, interview by author, April 2, 2007; Williams, "Louise Smith," 94.

90. Turman, interview by author, April 2, 2007.

91. Howell, "Louise Smith," pt. 2, c-6.

92. Berman, "'I Love to Go Fast,'" E-11; Turman, interview by author, April 2, 2007; Williams, "Louise Smith," 89.

93. Photocopy, private collection of Hardy "Peanut" Turman.

94. Dora "Lib" Owens, niece of Louise Smith, telephone interview by author, April 23, 2007.

95. Berman, "I Love to Go Fast," E-11; Deitsch, "Flashback."

96. Williams, "Louise Smith," 89.

97. Owens, telephone interview by author, April 23, 2007.

98. Wendell Scott, a native of Danville, Virginia, competed in NASCAR from 1952 to 1973, finishing in the top ten 147 times. He won the Grand National race in Jacksonville, Florida, in December 1963. Buck Baker was initially declared the winner, and Scott wasn't awarded the victory until four hours after the race. At Scott's funeral, driver Ned Jarrett noted that Scott had opened not only doors in racing but also hearts and minds.

99. Berman, "I Love to Go Fast," E-10; Golenbock, NASCAR Confidential, 19.

100. Mike Hembree, "Greenville's Smith Bound for Auto Racing's Hall of Fame," Greenville News, October 21, 1998, A-1.

101. South Carolina General Assembly, S. 737, 113th session, 1999–2000, http://www.scstatehouse .gov/sess113_1999-2000/bills/737.htm (accessed July 27, 2011).

102. Deb Williams, "Louise Smith: 'She Was Just a Good Ol' Girl,'" Grand National Scene, October 8, 1987, 20–24.

103. Golenbock, NASCAR Confidential, 18.

Mary Blackwell Baker

Her Quiet Campaign for Labor Justice

CONSTANCE ASHTON MYERS

❀ ❀ ❀

The events that young Mary Ursula Blackwell (1921–95) lived through with her family and in her community in October and November 1933 during the first big textile strike of the New Deal impressed her deeply and propelled her choices in life and work. At the age of twelve, she saw her parents locked out of the Warrenville cotton mill where her father, Franklyn Blackwell, and her mother, Mary Ellen Maddox Blackwell, had worked as mill hands as long as she could remember. Both of her parents, the children of Irish émigrés, had left farming to work for cash in nearby textile plants. Her father, a roping hauler, was charged with bringing the thread into the spinning room for "the spools that go up and down and make the material." Her mother, a spinner, kept the spools full for the process. The oldest of five children, Mary understood more about the family's situation than her siblings, and she surely suffered some of the pangs about an uncertain future that her parents felt. Although the country was in the midst of the Great Depression, it was nevertheless a time of promise because the recently sworn-in president, Franklin D. Roosevelt, and his cabinet had made swift executive decisions and had sent proposed draft legislation to Congress that became known as the New Deal. The new administration purportedly aimed to redress labor's smoldering grievances and at the same time to breathe renewed confidence in industry at the management level. Mary listened to the news on the radio, and this registered with her.[1]

Years later in an interview, she professed her lifelong fascination with news reports, reflecting that a regimen of daily listening as a child had honed her political sensibility. Her parents' nightly political discussions over the evening supper table ignited a fascination with politics. "Every time they read the morning newspaper, that was a source for talking about politics in the evening when

MARY BLACKWELL BAKER
Courtesy of Sarah Johnson.

[her mother] came in from the mill. You see, she didn't get to read the local paper until night. Then lots of times I used to sit in a little rocking chair and listen to them talk about the different candidates and what they thought, and which one they thought would be the best, and what they thought they'd accomplish, and so forth." Such repeated experiences fed an insatiable interest. The events of 1933—what was happening to kinfolk and neighbors and how the government reacted—provided her with indelible memories.[2] Very likely at this point her awareness of injustices endured by farm and industrial families grew, gradually cementing a determination to do something and sparking a lifelong loyalty to politics and the labor movement.

Notions about injustice and political redress, alongside a powerful work ethic and a belief in learning, fueled her zeal for activism. When asked whether or not anything in her early schooling might have contributed to her later union diligence, she remembered a mill lockout—it may also have been the one in 1933—that left workers struggling to feed their families. The union set up warehouses and brought vegetables and foodstuffs in from Columbia. Baker recalled watching people pick up their food. "I remember people marching up the road in support of the union," she said, "and it was dangerous. People were hungry. Many got knocked in the head and got beat up. I can remember seeing them walking along the road, carrying banners saying 'Join the union! Join the union!' I will never forget that. I was just a small child, maybe eight or nine years old, but I can remember it to this day, them walking and singing." The strength of the union during the six-week lockout made a deep impression. "I saw all of this. It inspired me. I thought then anything worth going hungry for, worth marching for, worth getting locked out of a mill [for] is worth having. And when you find a band of people that would stick together like that to improve conditions, you have to admire them."[3] Mary Baker would join a union for the first time in 1949 and move quickly from elected positions within the union to a lifelong career of paid employment with the union.

Born in Aiken County's Horse Creek Valley situated in the shadow of the pre–Civil War and still formidable Graniteville Mill and neighboring mills built later in the nineteenth century, she absorbed the mill town culture so well described in the history *Like a Family: The Making of a Southern Cotton Mill World*.[4] During and after World War I, the mill hands of the valley had enrolled in the United Textile Workers (utw), and union membership among textile workers reached about five thousand in all the South Carolina mills. In 1919, however, valley mill hands were the first to walk out for an eight-hour day in a wave of walkouts. The strike lasted five weeks; two thousand were locked out when they sought to return to work. The strikers won nothing. Another strike in 1921, accompanied by walkouts in North Carolina mills, had limited success in improving wages and hours. But it was the failed strike of the early New Deal and its bitter aftermath that ingrained itself in Mary's memory. On reflection, she understood that mill owners used natural or other distinctions among workers to divide them, and she realized that only by sticking together could these poor, and largely uneducated, people coming in from the country obtain decent wages and hours.

Over the course of her lifelong career, Baker worked with five unions and a biracial organization that steadily plugged away at finding jobs for mill hands and other blue-collar workers and organizing them. Twenty years into her work with trade unions, the late twentieth-century phase of the women's movement began to take shape. Its many victories included federal policies banning gender-based discrimination in employment. Although she agreed with the goals of the women's rights movement, she remained primarily identified with the labor movement and never took advantage of new civil rights legislation that might have moved her forward more quickly into union positions not previously held by women. Rather than create tensions within the local unions she served by demanding a higher position that paid better, she became a tax consultant at night to augment her income. Baker's formidable interpersonal skills undergirded her success, and she remained highly respected in the Horse Creek Valley despite the fact that "the union" had come to be feared and despised. Furthermore, she was active in South Carolina political life for fifty years, acting as a behind-the-scenes functionary in the Democratic Party even though she was considered a "linthead" from the Horse Creek Valley, and worse still, one identified with the trade union movement. It took personal courage on Baker's part to insert herself into the heart of the union movement in an area where the word "union" was anathema and simultaneously to serve a national party whose support for racial equality alienated many white southerners through the years from strict racial segregation to tentative and never-quite-realized integration. In addition, through the whirl of activity that yielded these achievements and that lasted until a few years before her death, she remained an active and revered member of the local Catholic Church. Catholics were rare in Baker's valley and scorned by some. But significantly, the church was also a rare institution willing—even in a blatantly antiunion community—to befriend the union movement.

For the Blackwell family and other residents of Howlandville, South Carolina, in the early 1930s, life was no easy matter. The town could hardly be called a "town." Mary called it "a settlement." Only twenty-five families lived there as she grew to maturity, most having a connection to one or another of the textile mills in the conglomerate called the Graniteville Company. One tiny country store, Irick's, served Howlandville, and there the Blackwell children spent part of their "one buffalo nickel" allowance every week. In the 1930s six cotton mills were located in this part of Aiken County, one each in Graniteville, Bath, Langley, and Warrenville (a quarter of a mile from Howlandville) and two in Clearwater. The towns were located one after another with no farms or pine forests dividing them. Three thousand workers lived in this area, called the Horse Creek Valley, turning out goods valued annually at $8 million.[5]

Most were skilled workers, but they earned 20 percent less than their counterparts in northern mills, with women earning 20 percent less than men. Seeking cheaper labor, northern owners had closed mills in Massachusetts and moved south. Nearly all the workers were white: mill employment in the South was generally closed to African American men except at the most menial level and completely closed to African American women. An act of the legislature proscribed such mill employment in 1915.[6]

Giving the lie to a widely harbored notion that southern mill hands were passive and docile, in 1876 the first major textile strike in the South erupted in the Graniteville mill; additional strikes at other mills were staged in 1902, 1929, and 1932. By the time of Roosevelt's inauguration in 1933, about twelve hundred Horse Creek Valley workers were organized in the United Textile Workers Union (UTW), which was affiliated with the conservative American Federation of Labor (AFL). According to textile historian Bryant Simon, the mill hands of the Horse Creek Valley "stood at the cutting edge of industrial protest," because they walked out in October 1933, igniting a flame that would blaze one year later in the general strike affecting South Carolina plants as well as those in adjoining states.[7]

In the early days of the New Deal, the National Recovery Administration tried to placate a restless labor movement with several benefits, among them the right to organize and a raise in the daily wage. (There was a corresponding hike in the price of manufactured goods.) In July 1933, President Roosevelt approved a cotton textile code, and to announce their cooperation, the mills adopted the Blue Eagle emblem with its slogan "We Do Our Part."[8] Little wonder that mill workers believed themselves protected enough now to react against a recently imposed speedup. In textile parlance, this was called a "stretchout," meaning that each worker was assigned additional spindles to operate over her average of seventy-two in order to increase production.

When management refused to meet with a visiting delegation of workers at the Bath and Langley mills in August, 1933, the UTW called a strike for October 20. Ibra Blackwood, the governor and no friend of labor, sent in highway patrolmen; the UTW in nearby Augusta, Georgia, where mills were already successfully organized, sent reinforcements to help strikers. After rock battles, tear gas, and ensuing injuries and arrests, Blackwood sent in the National Guard. By October 31, five of the six mills had shut down. Moreover, "workers actually sought to publicize the intransigence of mill owners so that the Federal Government would intervene in local affairs," historian Janet Irons noted.[9]

In this explosive atmosphere, a federally appointed textile committee came to town to find a compromise, but all it did was recommend that the "nonviolent" workers return to work the following week with no recrimination. Without the expected federal support, workers returned to the plants on November 6, 1933, only to find the gates shut against them. Mill owners had meanwhile laid off hundreds and fired those affiliated with the UTW, bringing in truckloads of replacement workers from the country, most of them tenant farmers and their families. Similarly, when Spartanburg County mills erupted the following year, owners recruited strikebreakers from mountain families. This time, the Horse Creek valley mills hired three hundred "spare hands" to avoid taking back any strikers. The governor announced that "not a single non-striker was arrested." Evictions from mill housing came next, followed by the blacklist, which eliminated the possibility of working again in the area and thereby sealed the fate of the strikers. The Blue Eagle banner still flew on mill buildings, but it was clear that the mill owners had defeated the union and the government would not force them to live up to "the code."[10] This incendiary news, broadcast on the radio daily along with the nightly kitchen newspaper analyses and the events she observed on her way home from school, was bound to leave an indelible impression on little Mary Blackwell.

Other area struggles also left their mark on the perceptive youngster and all in her community. When it was over in her neighborhood, the tumult moved north to the mills of Spartanburg County, where seven strikers died, and from there over the border into the mills in Gastonia, North Carolina, where the Communist Party had successfully organized mill hands into its National Textile Workers Union (NTWU) in 1928. Not one of these labor actions realized better conditions for the workers, whether led by the relatively conservative AFL's UTW in 1934 or by the Communist Party's NTWU.[11] Sadly, these failures left a tragic imprint on the valley. Union organizers no longer found any receptive workers. In fact, a tale circulated that a UTW organizer had absconded with the dues monies of the signed and paid members before the failed strike of 1933. In the 1970s valley people still talked about the theft, which fed their smoldering disgust with—and fear of—unions.

Valley residents feared reprisals if they even mentioned the union, unless pejoratively. Such wholesale intimidation was possible in large measure because textile mill owners owned the homes in which many workers lived. One club that owners held over the heads of employees who rented in the mill towns was eviction as penalty for cooperating with union organizers who came to town or, worse, for participating in strike activity. An atmosphere of paternalism reigned in the mill villages, and owners acting like benevolent despots sometimes ruled the lives of the families. In fact, one argument they advanced for the growth of the textile mill industry was that it would provide meaningful and paid employment to tenant farmers who suffered unstable prices and low yields on overworked land. Moreover, the owners viewed themselves as providing a valuable social service. They boasted about the churches they built for workers and touted the schools in the mill towns that required attendance. But in reality owners would not aid ministers who gave Sunday morning support to the entry of unions into these closed communities. Furthermore, mills occasionally had a rule whereby a family could not move in unless there were at least three family members ready to work in the mill. Of course, this included children, who in South Carolina mills were expected to work after reaching age fourteen.[12]

Owners also boasted that the housing provided in mill towns, especially those homes built in the 1920s, had indoor toilets, electricity, and running water, amenities without which the Blackwells—who owned their home—had to manage. After Mary's grandfather Carl Maddox came from Ireland, he chose a three-acre lot and built a five-room clapboard house on it. Even after her mother and father married, they lived in that house, and Mary and her four brothers and sisters were all born there. Because the Maddoxes, and then the Blackwells, owned the house, they did not suffer from the threat of eviction and enjoyed a degree of independence from the paternalism and penalties imposed on village families. Despite strikes and lockouts, long hours at the mill, and evening chores at the house, the "home" remained their own. That fact provided a special sense of security, and Mary lived in the house until she married—the house with no bathroom, no running water, and no furnace.

Bringing in kindling wood and coal for the big fireplace and the one grate was a regular chore the Blackwell children took turns doing every evening after supper. Another nightly task was going out to the well on their property to bring in water with which to bathe, launder, and cook the next day. There were the hogs, cows, chickens, and turkeys that had to be fed and watered. For Mary, from whom much was expected as the oldest, there were the four dozen biscuits that had to be made when it was her turn in the morning and subsequently every morning after her mother died. She also did the weekly "shuck-mopping," using a broom handle with holes spaced regularly through one end. Through the holes one would pass new corn shucks, about six per mop, every few weeks, until they were too worn to serve any longer.[13]

Nor did the family own a car. They walked everywhere they had to go—even the children—as there were no school buses in the early 1930s. The tiniest students walked the quarter of a mile to Warrenville Elementary School in rain, sleet, or sunshine. Mary Baker recalled her first car ride. A neighbor a mile up the road had an "A-model Ford." As she made her usual trek home, the neighbors "picked us up and we rode home in the rumble seat. . . . I thought it was tremendous! I didn't have to walk!" Still, she recollected riding "a lot of times in a wagon." A couple of neighbors had horses and wagons "and they'd hook 'em up and then take us riding. They did this for fun. Sometimes my mother on Sundays made a big churn of ice cream, and they'd come over to eat some, and we'd go for a ride."[14]

Despite the long workdays and labor strife, life was not all work. Residents of the mill community attended to their spiritual needs every Sunday morning as well as Sunday and Wednesday evenings in the Warrenville Baptist Church. Church socials offered dining and conviviality. Still, because Baptists disapproved of dancing, Mary had to seek this diversion elsewhere. When she was in her twenties the Big Apple was a popular dance in nightclubs in Columbia but having babies and then raising them left her no time to try to learn it. As for other kinds of dances, the Horse Creek Valley itself provided an opportunity. Twice a year the Blackwell and Baker families participated in the local square dances. Mary recollected that a person could learn the Charleston in the Horse Creek Valley if he or she had a mind to and that she "just picked it up," as others did. "The little medicine shows that came to town always had . . . a Charleston contest." One year Mary took the prize of five dollars.

Recreation opportunities also included swimming in Langley Pond and the Fourth of July barbecue and Christmas Day with its traditional foods and activities. The young Blackwells occasionally attended movies in the evenings at a theater in Warrenville, walking with their dad the mile and a quarter distance to see them. Mary recalled that the long cold walk home often made her wish they had not gone.[15]

After finishing eighth grade in Warrenville as salutatorian of her class, Mary Blackwell moved on to Leavelle-McCampbell High School in Graniteville. There she continued to excel in her studies, sang in the glee club every year, and belonged to the 4-H club. At the graduation ceremony in 1938 she received the American Legion award in addition to being selected for a four-year scholarship to Winthrop College, where she hoped to fulfill her ardent desire to obtain a degree in nursing. However, these events only served to demonstrate to Mary

her plight as a member of a poor and struggling mill family. First, the graduation ceremony took place at an hour when her father worked his night shift
at the Bath Mill, and the mill superintendent would not let him off to see her
graduate with these honors. "I never will forget . . . the president of the Graniteville Company giving me the medal and kissing me on the side of the face. . . .
I was thinking I could shoot the whole [company] because they wouldn't let
my daddy come to my graduation." This rankled deep in her soul. In addition,
Mary's mother had died, and the young graduate knew she would be unable to
fulfill her career aspirations. Her father could not take care of his family without the second income and help with Mary's four younger brothers and sisters.
Family need forced her to decline the college scholarship.[16]

Therefore, high school diploma in hand, in 1938 she went to work for the superintendent of schools in the valley and came home to cook supper, prepare her siblings' clothes for school the next day, and supervise their homework and chores.
After a year of this regimen, her employer obtained for her a job with higher pay
at the nearby Gregg Dye Plant, where she worked for two years. Continuing with
her household duties as "mother" to her siblings as well as wage earner, in her
second year at Gregg Dye she added the responsibilities of marriage.

Born and raised in Gloverville, another of the valley towns, her new spouse,
Frank Baker, also came from a mill-working family. "My husband was truly
against me working," she explained, convinced as he was that "a woman's place
was in the home, rearing a family and taking care of the needs of the husband. . . .
But shortly after I left the company I came to expect my first child." To earn
money for an expanding family, "he picked up little extra jobs besides—he was
a machinist [at] that mill, but he had a little A Model Ford and rigged it up with
a cross-cut saw to cut stove wood—so many neighbors used wood in stoves to
cook with—and he had many customers." But one day in 1946 five years after
(at his behest) she had stopped bringing in wages, Frank had an accident that
would mandate her return to full-time work. Blind in one eye from a childhood
incident, he "misjudged the distance and stuck his hand too far out in the snow
on top of the wood, and he cut [off] three of his fingers." Only his class ring
prevented the fourth from being sheared away at the time as well.[17] The event
appeared to end his career at Bath Mill because his boss discharged him.

Luckily the young couple's creditors understood the problem, had confidence, and waited until they were able to pay before contacting them. Living in
a tiny community where neighborly relations are close and the community can
be like family helped pull them through the crisis. "We lived off $3.00 a week . . .
for almost a year," she said, given that sum weekly by his sister and brother. At
the time, Mary and Frank were building their own home, "a wooden one," and

like other houses in the community, it lacked facilities. Then in 1947, Frank was unexpectedly called back to work in Bath Mill, where he stayed for three years before accepting work across the Savannah River in Augusta, Georgia, at the Augusta Arsenal.[18]

With Frank back at work, and a little money saved from selling eggs, churned butter, and cream, the two of them entered a business venture, opening and operating Baker's Café in Gloverville, a restaurant that catered to the mill workers. Mary essentially managed the restaurant, doing the cooking through the day until Frank finished for the day at Bath Mill. "He'd come in and allow me to go home and help the children with lessons and then he'd close up at night for me. . . . We opened at seven and we closed at eleven . . . with one woman hired to wash the dishes." She smiled as she recalled, "We made some money back then, we sure did." A disagreement over selling beer caused friction and at last forced them to end the venture.[19]

It was a turning point. Leaving this business, Mary Baker took a job in food service and joined a union for the first time, breaking the community tradition established after the bitter times of the 1930s and starting off on a trajectory that continued for the rest of her life. From that day in 1949, she was a "card-carrying member" of a labor union, usually five of them, for the remainder of her working life. "I wouldn't be without a union not as long as I live," she exclaimed years later.[20]

Mary's expertise running the restaurant helped her obtain a job with a food service company. In 1950, the Atomic Energy Commission chose E. I. DuPont de Nemours and Company to design, construct, and manage a site on the Savannah River near Aiken to produce materials to be used in the fabrication of nuclear weapons to support the country's national defense program. Hundreds of construction workers came to build the new Savannah River Plant, as it was known, and Milan Brothers, Inc., obtained the food service contract for the workers. To work for Milan Brothers, she found she would have to join the union, launching her career with labor organizations. Accepting union steward responsibilities right away, she handled complaints and instructed workers on regulations in the food service business; within two months they elected her financial secretary.

From that time forward, she lived a round of consulting with workers in the union and with leaders at different levels, as well as attending week-long labor conventions as an elected delegate. The first one was in Carpenters' Hall, Charleston, when she had been a member for barely a year. She described the experience: "In 1950 I attended my first convention. . . . I thoroughly enjoyed meeting the people from all over the state and hearin' their problems and how they handled them." The only woman from Aiken to attend the convention, the union elected Mary as a delegate every year thereafter, and she never missed a conference.[21] "I never knew how to say 'no,'" she admitted. As a result, a succession of union locals afterward asked her to serve as their financial secretary.

Once du Pont completed construction and began operating the facility in 1956, Milan Brothers left. Mary Baker then obtained work with the Savannah River Atomic Trades Council, engaged at the time in an effort to organize the oil, chemical, and atomic workers at the site. Twice that year the union narrowly lost an election, so as she noted, "We didn't get into the plant." She soon was hired by the Laborers' Local 58 in Aiken to help place workers in the new facility. The Aiken local shared Baker with Augusta's Local 1137, concurrently in need of a person to place workers at the Columbia Nitrogen Corporation's site, under construction in 1956. At almost the same time, she became secretary-treasurer of the Augusta Federation of Trades and, soon after, added the job of assistant to the secretary of the Building Trades Council.[22] An indefatigable worker, Baker assumed tasks for other labor organizations as well. It is interesting to observe that through the 1950s Mary Baker always served in secretarial or book-keeping positions and never as an organizer. That job was reserved for men.[23]

One union of which Baker remained a member through 1990 was the Carpenters, Operating Engineers, and Painters Local 1736, in the International Brotherhood of Electrical Workers (IBEW). She typed reports for the "international representative," an official in the union with whom she forged a solid friendship. "His name was Morton E. Crist and through the years I worked for him and I became [a] real good friend of his and always tried to help him and his wife." Baker described how she cooked meals for him after his wife died and sat in the hospital with him through his own final hours. "He left me a lot of labor magazines. He left me his desk and a clock, which I really appreciated because I didn't expect anything because what I did for him came from the heart. . . . He was a great, great man as far as labor was concerned." Coming in 1950 from Selma, Alabama, a place as difficult as the Horse Creek Valley in which to raise the union question, he had managed to get "the building trades and the Labor Councils started," which he had served as business agent until "he moved up into the international level." Baker remembered that as union steward she often called on him for advice, describing their relationship as the closest one she experienced in her union work.[24]

When Frank Baker died in an automobile accident in 1961 leaving Mary as her own sole support, she promptly added two more unions to her roster, assuming the duties of financial secretary for the Sheet Metal Workers IBEW Local 399 in Charleston and for the Linemen IBEW Local in Columbia. A widow whose children were married and gone, she lived alone. Nothing could slow her pace at this point. Forced to manage her time masterfully, she balanced it among work duties for the union locals, her church, the Democratic Party, and a new home business she assumed—calculating income tax returns for individuals and for businesses. Union duties still included attending state and regional labor conventions as an elected delegate and, occasionally, going to Washington, D.C., to conferences, sent by one or another of the unions.

In 1970, at the height of all these obligations, the forty-nine-year-old Baker suffered a fall that caused her to lose consciousness and required two weeks' hospitalization with several additional weeks of convalescence. Apparently she was out of work too long for her to resume employment in the assortment of part-time positions she had performed for almost ten years. An income shortfall loomed, mandating a search for a new, permanent, and preferably full-time job. On August 7, 1970, "Miss 'Sula" (as she came to be known, a shortening of her middle name Ursula) began to work for the National Urban League, an organization led by African Americans. With enactment of the civil rights legislation of the 1960s, calculated to usher in a new era of lawful interracial cooperation in the South for the first time, the Urban League advanced to the front in hiring a white woman to carry out its role—to "assist minorities and poor white people in finding employment," as Baker described it. She commuted to Columbia for the job until 1972, when she was dispatched to Augusta, Georgia, to manage the office there. She began as secretary and rose to a position not held before in the organization by a woman, that of field representative.[25]

The movement toward equality in the workplace was slow but steady. Not until 1977, the year she gave her oral history interview, did Baker see a woman become a union organizer. Tradition held that only men took the union cards out for signing. "We had twenty-one organizers in the Aiken area . . . but not a woman among 'em. But now, in this equal rights movement, the lady you met here yesterday, she's a member of the team of organizers," Mary pointed out. In fact, she observed that past organizing campaigns had seldom raised issues pertaining to women. "In all the campaigns I've worked on they were dealing directly with men. No women were involved."[26] The growth of the women's movement in the 1970s, however, brought welcome changes that affected her own career. "It has been very exciting, but I think when I was made field representative of this office, that was one great time, because I had never hoped to be field representative. I never ever hoped to be more than a secretary. The first raise I got from secretary to women's recruitment counselor for labor, though, I met my quota: I placed a lot of women. Placed one lady, Judith Judd, at Owen Corporation as a welder and she experienced two good raises in one year." As evidence of the growing effect of the women's movement in the 1970s, Baker received help in her efforts as recruitment counselor from the Aiken chapter of the National Organization for Women (NOW), to whom one of Judd's teachers at Aiken Technical College had appealed. NOW contacted the prospective employer, who talked to Baker before hiring Judd as a welder, an occupation formerly considered "men's work." Before the intervention Judd had been told repeatedly, "Sorry, we just don't think a woman can weld." But Baker encouraged her, saying, "Well, we'll find you somethin'," which she finally did.[27]

As Baker's story reveals, loyalty to the union movement gave permanent direction to her life. Stating emphatically that "the only salvation for a poor man is to join the union," she then added, "I'll tell you something. . . . [I]f it had not been for the unions I don't believe I would have been able to educate my children the way they are. . . . It's people on the negotiating table that help you and I both; that sit for hours and hours negotiating a wage contract, negotiating an agreement. . . . Everybody benefits from [this work] done by a few." Her daughter Nona lived out her mother's ambition of becoming a trained nurse, graduating from nursing school at St. Francis Hospital in Charleston and becoming head night nurse in the training hospital of the Medical College of Georgia in Augusta. Mary Baker seemed contented with Nona's accomplishment. Fifty-six years of age at the time of the interview, Baker believed herself too old to begin nursing study.[28]

Additionally, Baker was committed to two institutions, the Catholic Church and the Democratic Party, which, like her, supported unions. "Miss 'Sula" served as financial secretary to her parish church, Our Lady of Fatima Church in Gloverville, for many years. Raised a Baptist, on marrying Frank Baker, a Roman Catholic, she readily and enthusiastically adopted Catholicism, taking classes in doctrine and bringing up the children in the faith. The Catholic Church officially supported organized labor, and her prior church, even at the critical times, did not, and so there was a natural compatibility between her political beliefs and her new faith. She attended mass regularly and often headed the Women's Club's Altar Society. But her contribution that drew most heavily on her special abilities and served the parish most significantly was maintaining its financial records, a voluntary task. Asked to name the role models most powerful in her life, one of two she chose was a Catholic priest, retired at the time in Aiken. "He was always so kind and considerate. I never will forget one time when Nona was a baby; he came to the house to give me instruction and I had a swollen-out face [due to a bad] tooth. I had not been workin' and it was real tough. So he sent me to the dentist and had that tooth pulled."

In the valley, residents were unsure about and generally unacquainted with Roman Catholicism. Catholics constituted a tiny minority within this textile center in the Deep South and were considered a bit eccentric. Being Catholic did not always mark a person for ostracism in the way that being identified with a textile workers' union had done in the past. Nevertheless, Baker reported, "My daddy and my sister Betty would not speak to me for over a year . . . when I joined the Catholic Church." Before Franklyn Blackwell died, Mary was vindicated because after a severe illness, her father joined the church. This was despite the fact (as she reported it) that, almost like unions, in their neighborhood Catholics were "not popular at all."[29]

One subtle indication of the pervasiveness of Catholicism in her life was Baker's choice of *Lilies of the Field* (United Artists, 1963) as the film that most affected her. The film stars an African American, Sidney Poitier, in his first major role and dramatizes the experiences of the fictional Homer Smith, a handyman passing through the Arizona desert who stops to help five German nuns build a chapel. Smith, a Baptist, finds himself at first building the chapel almost single-handedly and without pay and is resentful but gains an intangible reward. The joy of music gives respite to the sisters and their new coworker between bouts of hard labor, just as it had to the Blackwell family in Depression-era Howland-ville.[30] Reflecting Baker's personal and community life, the film portrays the amicable confluence of Baptist and Catholic. From all her choices, it is easy to discern the principles that guided Mary Baker's life and work: selfless commitment to a higher cause, kindness to those in need, responsible fulfillment of assumed obligations, and neatness in personal presentation. Her life, however, was distinguished by her personal courage, which she displayed in her dedicated work for the much-maligned union movement.

Baker's beloved Democratic Party supported unions even more than the Catholic Church. Actually, the party and the union were "mostly comprised of the same people" in Aiken County. In working for the party, a person at the same time was supporting the union, and union comrades knew this. Nevertheless, many Aiken County residents knew Baker best not as a union worker but as a leader in the party. Never an elected officeholder, she first secured official status in Aiken County Democratic Precinct 41 in Warrenville. Frank Baker's father had been precinct executive committeeman, and when he died, his son took over. "And then when my husband died, I took it over. . . . We had between seven and eight hundred people in the precinct." She maintained the relationships in the party as steadily as she managed her union work. Asked about party divisions over policy, she said that when the party split over positions or had two candidates seeking the seat held by a Republican, she stayed neutral or, as she phrased it, "I'd keep my mouth shut—and then vote my own conviction." Insisting that her political views had not changed over the years, she added, "Really and truly . . . I'm still a Democrat. I'm what you call a doubtful Democrat [which means] that no matter what happens I'll be a Democrat all my lifetime. . . . You find your little pitfalls and you find your little, well, let's say, inequities. You find all that, and more or less you have to pick out the good points. . . . I can be truthful in saying that I don't agree with some of the philosophies. But being a Democrat and coming from a long line of Democrats—I'll still remain one! No matter what, I'll just live with those inequities. After I weigh everything out I still would never leave the party," she maintained. She served it faithfully as secretary for almost twenty years. Asked why she never ran for office, she replied, "I never wanted a political job where somebody dictated my politics to me. I think I do more good bein' on the outside workin'—and workin' as I do in the party—then I'm obligated to nobody." A firm believer in the democratic process that she was, it is no surprise, as an obituary notes, that in her last working years, "Miss 'Sula" was still serving on the board of the bipartisan Aiken County Election Commission.[31]

In 1987 Mary Baker suffered a stroke and remained almost bedridden until her death in 1995. Therefore it was with difficulty that she journeyed to Atlanta to attend the Organized Labor and Workmen's Circle Twenty-First Annual Awards Banquet in the Atlanta Hilton Hotel on June 2, 1990. There the organization, comprising forty unions with seven supporting private corporations, named her, with other honorees of the year, to labor's hall of fame. An awards list with biographies distributed at the dinner reported that she was included in the archives relating to women in labor at two universities. (They overlooked the University of Michigan's Bentley Library, where her oral history resides.) It also mentioned recent recognition by the AFL-CIO of Georgia for her efforts as chair of the Volunteers in Politics Department for Augusta and cited her "forty years of work" with unions.[32]

In addition to serving the union faithfully for years, Mary Baker also pursued a business in her own home, one that kept her awake until after midnight. "In the morning I get up at six," she said in 1977, and pick up a sister "who helps with the housework"; she would then drive over the river to Augusta to her day's work with the Urban League. On returning to the valley after the workday, she retrieved tax papers from income tax clients. However, "a lot of 'em put them in the screen door," thus cutting down on her driving miles, which were "thirty-five thousand last year, for work and for picking up sales tax [records], so, you know, I really have to be gettin' around." She operated her tax-preparation business for twenty years and her clients included service stations, painting companies, housing contractors, and individuals. It was as successful as she desired it to be, given her shortage of time. Preparing taxes filled evenings during the week, never allowing an hour for watching television news reports until eleven.

Still, a person so immured in politics had to remain current. Therefore Baker supplemented television with newspapers, receiving daily the *Aiken Standard*, *The State*, and the *Augusta Chronicle*. "At night," she explained, "whenever I finish whatever work I'm doin', I read the papers before I go to bed. . . . But I gather from the TV news what's goin' on political." This is why she knew well the issues of the women's movement of the 1970s as they buzzed about her, effecting changes in labor relations. "When I go out on the jobs now with a hard hat . . . they give me some strange looks," she claimed, although she admitted she wore her dress and not "britches." "Men are becoming more accustomed to seeing a woman on the job because we have a lot of women that are working as laborers, truck drivers, and so forth. The rest work as electricians, some are sheet metal workers, so, gradually the field's opening more and more." After finding the job for Judith Judd, she could have added welders to the list. In 1977 Baker believed the Equal Rights Amendment (ERA) should be part of the Constitution. Its on-the-job effect, she hoped, would be equal pay for equal work and a concomitant institutionalizing of maternity leave for women workers as well as for men.[33]

Baker explained her resistance to activism, even to activism in support of the women's issues she hoped to see fully realized, in the same way as she described her supportive party role. Had she mounted a soapbox, she would have gotten nowhere. Baker fully understood the socially conservative beliefs of working men and, for at least ten years into the 1970s women's movement, of their wives and mothers as well. Her quiet and conservative manner inspired confidence, and such minor details as wearing a dress with a hard hat no doubt helped. One would never guess her pro-union, pro-ERA, and often antiestablishment stances unless one knew her more than casually. Having to dissimulate has been an integral part of the culture in the South, especially for women who hold views at variance with prevailing ones. To play the role of the southern lady, or at least to act the part of a woman who does not overtly challenge existing power arrangements, has been a sine qua non. Baker had internalized that fact.

There can be no question that within a slowly changing political environment, her steadfastness for the cause of organized labor made possible a moderate growth in union membership in South Carolina despite hostility to the movement, particularly in the textile industry. In time, however, the perpetual search for cheaper labor had led textile companies to shift production almost completely to the Third World, and the mills of the Horse Creek Valley now stand closed. Therefore, Baker's most enduring legacies were forged through her service as union steward, where she was essentially an ombudsman, handling complaints registered by workers and taking their grievances to a higher level, and through her service as a "labor central," finding blue-collar jobs for hundreds, white or African American, who came to her in her job as women's recruitment counselor, field representative, or secretary with numbers of union locals. In these ways she fought her quiet campaigns for justice.[34]

Mary Blackwell Baker attained the stature of legend in the Horse Creek Valley where she lived her entire life and surely earned the tribute at the labor awards banquet in 1990. She died on March 13, 1995, after several years' illness following the stroke. The funeral mass was held at her church three days later, and her burial took place in Calvary Cemetery in Aiken. Her uniqueness lay in defying the pervasive fear that hung like a cloud over her beloved valley, fear of anything that had a supposed taint of "unionism." Mary Baker adopted the union movement first and her church and the Democratic Party second as the causes to which she dedicated her life. Urban League, union, and Democratic Party colleagues held her in highest regard. And more personally, so did her tax clients who returned to her year after year, as well as her church parishioners in Our Lady of Fatima.

NOTES

1. Mary Blackwell Baker, interview by author, University of Michigan, Ann Arbor, July 27, 1977, 2–7 passim, 22. The present essay is based on Mary's Baker's relation of her life story during this six-hour interview conducted for the Twentieth-Century Trade Union Woman: Vehicle for Social Change Oral History Project. The original tapes and transcription reside in the Bentley Library of the University of Michigan, Ann Arbor.

2. Ibid., 10–11.

3. Ibid., 46–49.

4. Jacquelyn Dowd Hall, James Leloudis, Robert Korstad, et al., *Like a Family: The Making of a Southern Cotton Mill World* (Chapel Hill: University of North Carolina Press, 1987).

5. Bryant Simon, *A Fabric of Defeat: The Politics of South Carolina Millhands, 1910–1948* (Chapel Hill: University of North Carolina Press), 97.

6. Stephen L. Shapiro, "The Growth of the Cotton Textile Industry in South Carolina, 1919–1930" (PhD diss., University of South Carolina, 1972), 106, 121–24, 159. On the role of African Americans in the southern textile industry, see Marjorie A. Potwin, *Cotton Mill People of the Piedmont: A Study in Social Change* (New York: Columbia University, 1937), 58–60, and Allen H. Stokes, "Black and White Labor and the Development of the Southern Textile Industry, 1800–1920" (PhD diss., University of South Carolina, 1977), 180, 203, 264–66.

7. Thomas E. Terrill, "'No Union for Me': Southern Textile Workers and Organized Labor," in *The Meaning of South Carolina History: Essays in Honor of George C. Rogers, Jr.*, ed. David R. Chesnutt and Clyde N. Wilson (Columbia: University of South Carolina Press, 1991), 202–3; Simon, *A Fabric of Defeat*, 97; Jack Irby Hayes, "South Carolina and the New Deal, 1932–1938" (PhD diss., University

of South Carolina, 1972), 311–28; Shapiro, "The Growth of the Cotton Textile Industry in South Carolina," 109–110. For the view that women rayon workers in East Tennessee were in the vanguard of the southern labor movement on account of their strike in 1929, see Jacquelyn Hall, "Disorderly Women: Gender and Labor Militancy in the Appalachian South," *Journal of American History* 73, no. 2 (1986): 380.

8. On the National Recovery Administration, see Studs Terkel, *Hard Times: An Oral History of the Great Depression* (New York: Avon Books, 1970), esp. 287 and 391.

9. Janet Irons, "Testing the New Deal" (PhD diss., Duke University, 1988), 340–42; Simon, *A Fabric of Defeat*, 98–99.

10. See Hayes, "South Carolina and the New Deal," 329–49, and Simon, *A Fabric of Defeat*, 98–100, for detailed narratives of the strike and lockout.

11. Bert Cochran, *Labor and Communism: The Conflict That Shaped American Unions* (Princeton, N.J.: Princeton University, 1977), 34, 38, 75.

12. On paternalism, see Walter Edgar, *South Carolina: A History* (Columbia: University of South Carolina Press, 1998), 504, 506. On mill owners' attempted control of churches and schools in textile mill towns, see Mary Frederickson, "'I know which side I'm on': Southern Women in the Labor Movement in the Twentieth Century," in *Women, Work and Protest: A Century of Women's Labor History*, ed. Ruth Milkman (Boston: Routledge and Kegan Paul, 1985), 156–80, esp. 161–62.

13. On mill women, see Leslie Woodcock Tentler, "The Married Woman Worker," in *Wage-Earning Women: Industrial Work and Family Life in the United States, 1900–1930* (New York: Oxford University Press, 1979), esp. 149–65, and Victoria Byerly, *Hard Times Cotton Mill Girls: Personal Histories of Womanhood and Poverty in the South* (Ithaca, N.Y.: Cornell University Press, 1986).

14. Baker, interview by author, July 27, 1977, 55–56.

15. Ibid., 51–56, 99–100.

16. Gwen Corinth, in the *Augusta (Ga.) Chronicle*, March 28, 1990 (clipping sent to the author by Sarah B. Johnson, daughter of Mary Baker); Baker, interview by author, July 27, 1977, 43–44.

17. Baker, interview by author, July 27, 1977, 67–70.

18. Ibid., 75–78. For mutuality in mill towns, see Hall, Leloudis, Korstad, et al., *Like a Family*, 114–80.

19. Baker, interview by author, July 27, 1977, 82–85.

20. Ibid., 63, 114.

21. "Savannah River Site History Highlights," http://www.srs.gov/general/about/history1.htm (accessed July 21, 2011); Baker, interview by author, July 27, 1977, 63, 111–14.

22. Baker, interview by author, July 27, 1977, 114–17.

23. On traditional views of women as outsiders in trade unions, see Alice Kessler Harris, "Problems of Coalition-Building: Women and Trade Unions in the 1920s," in *Women, Work and Protest*, 110–38, and Alice Kessler Harris, *Out to Work: A History of Wage-Earning Women in the United States* (New York: Oxford University Press, 1982), 158–59, 269.

24. Baker, interview by author, July 27, 1977, 107–8, 130.

25. Ibid., 64–65; Jimmy Johnson, grandson of Baker, telephone conversation with author, December 19, 2008.

26. Ibid., 105.

27. Ibid., 138–40.

28. Ibid., 140–41.

29. Ibid., 113.

30. Ibid., 141–44.

31. Ibid., 61–3, 95–6, 110–11, 128–29; *The State*, March 15, 1995.

32. "Hall of Fame Honorees: Mary Baker," award list for the dinner and list of sponsoring unions and corporations (sent to the author by Sarah B. Johnson in December 2008); Louise Ford, sister of Mary Baker, telephone conversation with the author, December 12, 2008.

33. Baker, interview by author, July 27, 1977, 94–96, 105–6, 123–24.

34. On the persisting fear of South Carolina textile workers, see Terrill, "'No Union for Me,'" 208. For obituaries, see the *Aiken Standard*, March 14, 1995, and *The State*, March 15, 1995. Conversations with former Horse Creek Valley neighbors Sheila and Dennis Drennan provided the author with an impressionistic overview of Mary Baker's life (Sheila and Dennis Drennan, conversation with the author, December 31, 2008, and January 14, 2009, Columbia, S.C.).

Susan Dart Butler and Ethel Martin Bolden

South Carolina's Pioneer African American Librarians

GEORGETTE MAYO

South Carolina's pioneer librarians Susan Dart Butler (1888–1959) and Ethel Bolden (1918–2002) were crucial to the formation of public branches and school libraries for African Americans in South Carolina during the height of Jim Crow segregation as well as during its collapse in the 1960s. Butler fulfilled a community need when she opened her father's school library as a reading room. Her efforts eventually garnered the attention of the Rosenwald Foundation and were instrumental in obtaining branch libraries for all Charleston citizens as well as in establishing the Dart Hall reading room as a Charleston Free Library (CFL) branch for use by African Americans. Several decades later, Ethel Martin Bolden created libraries in black elementary and middle schools in Columbia, South Carolina's capital city. Bolden broke through the Jim Crow barriers by becoming the first African American librarian to integrate a previously all-white high school in 1968. Butler's and Bolden's work as librarians extended and enhanced the role of education in schools and homes. In conjunction with the work of teachers, African American librarians were vital to the endeavors of "uplifting the race," as they facilitated the educational process and counteracted the high rate of illiteracy prevalent especially among blacks in South Carolina.

As clubwomen and civic volunteers, Butler and Bolden stood at the forefront of societal change for race relations in their communities. Butler focused on efforts that would directly benefit the black community through the Charleston Branch of the NAACP and the South Carolina Federation of Women's Clubs.[1]

Butler was president of both the Phyllis Wheatley Literary and Social Club and the Modern Priscillas, which led to her association with the Charleston Interracial Committee. This organization garnered support from elite whites for making her reading room a branch of the newly formed CFL. Yet despite her alliances, she still had to endure and defy racism in the formation of a library for black Charlestonians. Bolden was unable to join the NAACP because of her job in the public schools. But like Butler, she too participated in interracial efforts to improve race relations, serving on the South Carolina Council on Human Relations and the Community Relations Council. The mission of Butler and Bolden was the same: to provide library services to African Americans in Charleston and Columbia. Bolden implicitly understood the connection they shared when, as a library science graduate student in the 1950s, she chose to write about Butler to fulfill a requirement for graduation to research an African American pioneer librarian. Her thesis on Susan Dart Butler's life has endured as the definitive source of information on Butler for over fifty years.

Susan Dart Butler, an educated, articulate, accomplished entrepreneur and proud African American personified W. E. B. Du Bois's vision of "the talented tenth," a minority of elite, educated blacks, missionaries of culture who influenced and strengthened the masses in their race.[2] She was no stranger to leadership owing to the African American men and women of stature who surrounded her in Charleston, most notably her father. The Reverend John Lewis Dart was pastor of the Morris Street Baptist Church and Shiloh Baptist Church. In 1894, Dart established the Charleston Normal and Industrial School as a solution to the overcrowded conditions of the city's black public schools. Starting out as a three-room building on Kracke Street, the school soon expanded to a three-building complex located on the corner of Bogard and Kracke Streets. Her mother, Julia Pierre Dart, taught classes in domestic science, bookkeeping, and typewriting.[3]

John Dart's resolve was to capitalize on his opportunities as a community leader while doing whatever he could to improve his people.[4] In a 1888 speech given to Avery Institute alumni entitled "Political Liberty," Dart stressed that "in order to rise in the social and civil scale, and to secure our political rights and civil liberties, let us get our education, wealth, true moral and religious training, respecting and confiding in one another, and thereby proving before the world that we are worthy and deserve all that we demand."[5] The same year brought the birth of the Darts' first child. Named for her grandmother, Susan Fenwick, a free person of color who purchased her future husband's freedom before the Civil War, Susan Elizabeth Dart grew up nurtured by a philosophy of social

SUSAN DART BUTLER

Courtesy of the Avery Research Center for African American

History and Culture, College of Charleston, Charleston, S.C.

ETHEL BOLDEN
Courtesy of the Bolden Family.

responsibility that stressed the need to uplift her race for the good of her com-munity.[6] Susan Dart's upbringing created a foundation of endurance for life as a black Charlestonian: a member of the majority population deemed second-class citizens by the minority of financially and politically powerful whites.[7]

Susan, nicknamed Susie, attended several private schools, including the Av-ery Institute, before traveling with her mother to live in Washington, D.C., be-ginning in 1896 to care for a relative. She returned at the turn of the century to live in Charleston for several years before leaving again to attend normal teacher training at Atlanta University from 1904 to 1907.[8] Dart then relocated to Boston, Massachusetts, in 1908 to attend McDowell Millinery School. There she met and eventually married Nathaniel Lowe Butler, a Boston native, whose parents James and Fanny Butler were also descendants of free people of color.[9] Butler was a self-employed building contractor and real estate agent living with his older sister Charlotte McKinzie and her family.[10] In a telling letter to her father written in 1912, Susan expressed a desire to remain in Boston because as a part-time milliner she had sold several hats, but she had not earned enough to depend solely on the profession. Yet Nathaniel was also having a difficult time making a living in his hometown, and Susan suggested to her father that he could benefit from Nathaniel's assistance at the school back home in Charleston.

Moving back to Charleston in 1913, the couple settled at 112 Bogard Street (across the street from Dart Hall) with her family, which included her sister Anna and brother John Jr. At her mother's insistence, Susan resumed her mil-linery career. As the first African American milliner in Charleston, Butler em-ployed four women to assist in her small but thriving business. Her husband assisted John Dart with school repairs and briefly partnered with her brother William in a realty company before becoming its sole owner. In 1918 Butler gave birth to her son and only child, Nathaniel Jr.

Susan's concern with her father's failing health was an additional reason to remain in Charleston. Dart retired from the active pastorate of Shiloh Bap-tist and in 1913 sold his printing press, which published the *Southern Reporter* newspaper. In 1911 the Charleston City School Board assumed operation of his school, which ultimately became known as Burke Industrial High School.[11] Two years after Dart passed away, the former school evolved into Dart Hall, a cultural center in the community that held lectures, concerts, plays, and social meetings.

Despite Susan's professional teacher training, Julia Dart instead encouraged her to use her trade skill as an independent businesswoman. This was prob-ably because African Americans could not educate their own in the city's black public schools. Her friends, Mamie Garvin Fields and Septima Clark, taught in the rural locations of James Island and Johns Island, the only public school positions available to black teachers in the area. The only option before 1920 for black teachers who wanted to remain in the city was to establish or partner in smaller private or one-room schoolhouses.[12] In 1918 Butler gave up her millinery shop and reestablished her father's kindergarten program. Located at Dart Hall, it was called the Dart Grammar and Primary School.[13] As principal, she hired three teachers including a recent graduate from Atlanta University and lifelong friend, Albertha Johnston Murray.

The plight of black teachers led Butler to join the NAACP's fight for their employment in the city. In 1917, Susan Dart Butler became the highest-ranking female in the Charleston branch of the NAACP. As treasurer, Butler joined the ranks of the community's most prominent black male leaders, Edwin Augustus Harleston, president, Dr. William H. Johnson, vice president, and Harleston's cousin, undertaker Richard H. Mickey, secretary. The newly established branch fought for the employment of black seamstresses at the clothing factory located at the Charleston Navy Yard and for trained black teachers to instruct their own race in the city's schools.[14] After a successful petition campaign was presented to the legislature in Columbia, the school board relented and began employing black teachers in Charleston's African American public schools on September 1, 1920.[15]

Butler, still teaching, next turned her attention to the need for library services for her community. Nationally the establishment of public libraries for African Americans was one of the most difficult challenges in the entire program of American library service and a crucial, though often underlooked, component in the struggle to improve education for African Americans. The denial of service stemmed from the old attitude that "give a Negro a book and you spoil a good plough hand," in addition to a lack of funds for supporting two separate library systems and no librarian leadership to advocate an inclusive system.[16] Eric Moon, former editor of *Library Journal*, terms the racial segregation of libraries the "Silent Subject."[17] The nonexistence or inadequacy of library collections and services for minorities and inequities faced by minority librarians were often undiscussed or unrecognized.[18]

The first noted public library in the Jim Crow South that admitted blacks was the Louisville Free Public Library's Western Colored Branch in 1908.[19] Prior to 1931 there were no public libraries or reading rooms available for general use to the Charleston community, black or white. The Charleston Library Society, founded in 1748, was open to whites that could afford membership. The Charleston Museum held a notable collection of children's books, but it was also closed to blacks.[20]

An alternative for African American children was to use their school and church libraries, though this was problematic, as most school libraries were small, only accessible during regular hours, and closed during the summer. There were sporadic attempts to establish private libraries. Affluent free blacks formed literary organizations in their pursuit of intellectual enrichment. The Bonneau Library Society, named after the well-known Charleston black educator Thomas S. Bonneau, was organized in 1830 and became one of the first noted libraries in the country for African Americans.[21] Charles H. Holloway, a Methodist preacher, was chairman of the society, which ceased operation in 1846. The Clionian Debating Society, founded in 1847, the Library Society, and the Amateur Literary and Fraternal Association each held libraries for their members.[22]

Close to a century later, the creation of a library for all Charlestonians, black and white, became a key mission for the Charleston Interracial Committee, a branch of the Commission on Interracial Cooperation. The group of "public-spirited women" included Susie Butler, her mother, Julia, and Clelia P. McGowan, an elite and influential white clubwoman and the city's first alderwoman, who attempted to convince the citizens of Charleston of the great need for a public library.[23] Serving as executive director of the committee McGowan made a concerted effort to acquire and distribute traveling libraries for rural schools throughout South Carolina.[24] The director of the Charleston Museum, Laura Bragg, also provided traveling libraries to black schools beginning in 1928 and supported the creation of a public library.[25] McGowan's colleague, Louisa Smythe Stoney of Medway Plantation, chaired the Committee on Colored Work at the Coming Street YWCA and provided books and magazines for their small library.[26] Butler later acknowledged these women for their donations of books to her reading room.[27]

Butler came into librarianship by happenstance when an Avery Institute high school student requested a poetry book that the school library did not carry and a quiet place in which to read. John Dart maintained a well-stocked library for his school and personal enjoyment. As Butler later wrote, she knew the young girl's situation was not an isolated incident. In 1926 Butler chaired a Charleston subcommittee of the commission that surveyed the quantity and condition of books found in local black schools, churches, and civic organizations such as the YWCA and YMCA. The report highlighted what was already suspected; a dismal number of books were found in poor condition. The survey provided tangible proof of the need for a library. In her pursuit to "serve a need," Butler, along with her husband and other family members, decided to renovate her father's printing shop and turn it into a library.[28] The community helped raise money through social functions; Avery students, for example, gave a spiritual concert. Dart Hall's reading room officially opened in the fall of 1927. The room contained two tables, twelve chairs, and built-in bookshelves. In addition to teaching her kindergarten class in the mornings, Butler staffed the reading room from 5 to 8 p.m. on Mondays, Wednesdays, and Fridays.

Attending a Commission on Interracial Cooperation conference in Atlanta, McGowan became inspired by the news of the Rosenwald Fund's interest in establishing public library service for blacks. Julius Rosenwald, the affluent president of Sears, Roebuck and Company, had created a philanthropic fund to support the improvement of educational and service institutions that benefited African Americans.[29]

The major turning point in establishing a Charleston public library happened in 1929 when Rosenwald Foundation representatives visited Butler's reading room. Edwin Embree, president of the Rosenwald Fund, Clark Foreman, director of studies, and William Harrell were impressed with Butler's initiative in creating a library in her community that contained a varied selection of books. Their interest spurred negotiations to establish a public library in Charleston that would incorporate Dart Hall as the library for blacks.[30]

Writing in her unpublished memoir, Clelia McGowan claimed that because of her connection with an influential friend on the Rosenwald board, she "obtained the first, and most liberal grant in the Library Program of that organization. Their offer, $2.00 for $1.00 from Charleston County was not to be resisted."[31] Funding was for the maximum of $80,000 over a five-year period, not to exceed $20,000 in any one year, and library trustees were morally obligated to extend their support after the Rosenwald Fund had ceased to participate. The funds were granted with the stipulation that "the library shall give service to both whites and blacks with equal opportunities to both and with facilities adapted to the needs of each group," intending ultimately to establish countywide library service with two central buildings: one for each race.[32] The Charleston Museum was designated as the temporary main white branch, with Laura Bragg appointed head librarian.[33] The Dart Hall reading room was deemed the "colored branch."

The county delegation initially declined to fund a public library, prompting community leaders to launch a petition drive to gain its attention.[34] The treasurer of Charleston County subsequently subsidized the $10,000 appropriated by the state legislature in the Charleston County Supply Bill. The Carnegie Foundation contributed $20,000 for the purchase of books.[35]

Susan Dart Butler's name was noticeably absent from the official reports of the creation of what would become CFL. McGowan was appointed head of the

Negro Branch Committee, on the libraries' board of trustees as a Dart Hall library representative. Butler lacked a voice on the library board; she could only
speak through McGowan.

One year after Charleston was ranked as the leading city in the country with
a significant black population that offered no public library services available
to them, the CFL opened to all citizens, with purportedly equal yet separate opportunities for both races, on January 1, 1931. Whites could immediately visit
the temporary location at the museum.[36] Three years later, in 1934, the board
of trustees purchased the Ficken residence at Montague Street and Rutledge
Avenue as the new white central branch. This library opened in 1935.

In contrast, black Charlestonians had to wait over seven months for the official opening of the "central Negro branch" because Dart Hall's reading room
was being expanded. Dart Hall Library Branch opened on July 26, 1931, with
Julia Macbeth as designated librarian and Butler and Mary Sparks listed as as-
sistants. A formal opening occurred several days later, which included a program of speeches and a guided tour of the library and Dart Hall facility. The
original single small reading room had been expanded to three rooms measur-
ing approximately twelve hundred square feet containing thirty-six hundred
books.[37] The branch was open forty-six hours a week and closed on Sundays;
in contrast the main white branch was open seventy hours including Sundays.
During the first year of operation, Dart Hall had a registration of 1,001 patrons
with circulation of 6,603 books.[38]

At the outset, Butler consented to free usage of Dart Hall in exchange for
building repairs until a permanent building could be secured.[39] Initially library
trustees did not consider Dart Hall a suitable site. They made a request for
building funds from the Phelps-Stokes Foundation in the fall of 1930 but did
not follow up on it.[40] In lieu of paying Butler for use of the facility, the CFL board
agreed to provide the necessary furniture and equipment.[41] The Dart family ultimately agreed to rent three large rooms for library services to CFL for a dollar
a year. Finally the Charleston County Council officially purchased the building
as a branch library in December 1952 for $9,000, paid in installments.[42]

Although Butler received positive recognition within her community, she
and the library staff were sharply criticized by a consulting librarian/represen-
tative commissioned by the CFL Board of Trustees. Upon the opening of the
CFL, Tommie Dora Barker, the Rosenwald Fund southern regional field agent,
implored the library trustees to hire Helen Virginia Stelle, a librarian from Florida's Tampa Free Library, for a temporary assignment from January to December 1932 to reorganize the entire CFL system.[43]

Stelle individually evaluated the entire CFL staff at the end of her six-month
assignment.[44] Notably the majority of white personnel were untrained as li-

brarians. But Stelle's most scathing evaluation was of the Dart Hall library and its employees. She found the branch in "a deplorable condition . . . with inaccurate records and files in confusion."[45] Steele deemed the head librarian, Julia Macbeth, incompetent and impersonal with patrons and urged her dismissal after her one year of service was up.[46] She concluded Butler would make "a capable librarian" after the proper training, but she would only be good at keeping simple records because "the technical side of library work will always be too complicated for her to master." Remarkably, Stelle further commented that "her chief qualifications for library work are: Dignity and self-respect; interest in Library and community; sympathetic understanding of her race, and the ability to work with the Head Librarian in the right spirit."[47] Admittedly naive about the cataloging of books, Butler wrote that "when books came in I was at a loss to know what to do with them. I visited libraries in Atlanta, West Virginia, Durham, Tuskegee, Washington and the Charleston Library Society on King Street. The books were shelved alphabetically. Later with the help of two young women who were college juniors at home for the summer, we classified them as fiction and non-fiction."[48] Consequently, there were no systematic records of Dart Hall's book and patron registration files at the main library, which led to extensive confusion. Commencing in 1933, a separate county collection for Dart was established in addition to a union registration file, thus uniting the county library system and establishing Dart Hall as a CFL branch.[49] All cataloging work was now performed at the main branch.

Stelle proposed to the CFL trustees that Butler enroll in a summer library-training course at Hampton Institute with pay.[50] Upon her return, Butler assumed the head librarian position in charge of the Dart Hall branch and service to black schools. Perry Seabrook served as her assistant. Unfortunately, the training Butler received at Hampton did not result in a library science degree.[51] Butler's lack of degree should not signify that she was not a dedicated library professional. As historian Stephanie Shaw asserts, one could easily get the impression that many African American female professionals were not deeply committed to advancing themselves in education and degrees.[52] The dilemma for Butler and later Ethel Bolden was that South Carolina did not have an accredited library science school open to blacks. Thus obtaining a degree meant leaving the state. For Butler, who worked full time and had family obligations and heavily committed clubwoman duties, leaving the state to attend school for an extended period of time was not feasible. She did what she could to add to her professional credentials, including holding officer positions in the South Carolina State Library Group, later known as the Palmetto Library Association, from its founding in 1938.[53]

From the inception of the CFL, it was stated that the acquisition of books "shall represent the thought of the world irrespective of prejudice or personal bias. Rejection of books shall in no way be because of the opinions they express, but rather the inadequacy of treatment, or, in the case of belles lettres, of poor literary quality."[54] Yet when it came to the selection of books for Dart Hall library, the main library acted on Virginia Stelle's recommendation to enlarge the collection with an emphasis on "very simple" children's books for circulation.[55] This directive was initially prescribed by the Rosenwald Foundation, as elementary county students (ranging from ages eight to twenty-one) were perceived as possessing limited reading abilities.[56] Butler contested this practice by encouraging her young patrons to read books that would challenge them. If a child selected a book that was too easy for him or her, Butler would return the book to the shelf, telling the child to "pick something harder to read."[57]

Library administrators and officials also neglected or refused to acknowledge the socioeconomic range and status of Dart Hall's patrons. While a campaign against illiteracy aimed at borrowers who used the Dart Branch was much needed, forgotten were Butler's middle-class friends and fellow intellectuals who expected and requested well-written literature and books authored by and about African Americans.[58] Butler also faced difficulties ordering books of substance for her adult readers. Stelle rejected her 1932 book request, *South Carolina During Reconstruction* due to its high price.[59] In the same year, the Phyllis Wheatley Literary and Social Club wrote in its annual report:

> Many of our members had complained that books we would enjoy reading, especially late books and books by Negro authors, could not be had at our public library. We brought this to the attention of our librarian who was one of our members. We were advised to bring in titles and authors of such books as we wanted and a request would be made for them. We did so and many of the late books, best sellers, books of the highest order were made available through our library not only for us but the general public.[60]

Regardless of Stelle's interference, Butler found a way to satisfy her patron's requests even if in a limited way. Former clubwoman and teacher Lois Simms noted Butler did not receive financial assistance for the purchase of books from her fellow club members.[61] Butler had to rely on the main branch to order within reason or purchase the books herself, which proved to be a challenge. In a 1947 report of the Charleston Committee on Interracial Cooperation, Dart Hall library was cited for the limited quantity of books by and about African Americans and the virtual absence of black periodicals and magazines.[62] The board also allowed donations, meaning the acquisition of older secondhand books. Butler received books from Lend a Hand Club, of Boston, Massachusetts.[63] One way Butler supplemented the lack of adequate books was by developing the library's vertical files, which were known to contain good reference materials pertaining to African Americans.[64]

A means of extending the reach of the library was the county library truck, which became operational in the late summer of 1931. It contained a small collection of books made available to black county residents under the Jeanes teacher's supervision. Segregation, however, meant that one side of the truck carried books for black children and the other side for white children.[65] Mamie Garvin Fields, Butler's close friend and fellow South Carolina Federation of Colored Women's club "sister," tells an informative story in her biography, *Lemon Swamp and Other Places: A Carolina Memoir*, regarding "*segregated*" books:

> The County Library truck used to come around with colored and white stacks—in other words, a stack of old books and a stack of new. Looking in at the cargo as time went by, I watched how the "new" white books would move over to become colored and make room for the next white books the county bought. What made it so bad, a Negro woman was instrumental in starting that same County Library— and had the very first branch. I mean *the* County Library, not the County Library for colored people. Charleston had no public library for any color until Susie Dart Butler, my sister in the Modern Priscilla, opened one in Dart's Hall. You can read in the papers she left how, with Mrs. McGowan of the Interracial Committee, they got the first money for a library from the Rosenwald and Carnegie people, on the condition of providing facilities for black and white. Susie Butler was able to open the branch in Dart's Hall right away, because her father had his own library there and had let people in the community use it. They organized the white branch downtown after Susie's. So what happened when you got to it? Our children read from the bookmobile what the other children were through with. Black people were the first and still last.[66]

Despite the numerous obstacles the segregated status of the library posed, Butler and her staff made the best of the situation.[67]

Programs for children included tours of the library facilities, during which they were provided lessons on how to use the card catalogs, and weekly story hours. Periodically Dart Hall hosted book week programs inviting high school students from Burke, Avery, 4-Mile School, and the Shaw Center to review international folk tales and stories.[68] During the summer months the Children's Department scheduled reading games at the completion of which children would receive a reading diploma.[69] The monthly book review held in conjunction with neighboring schools gave parents the opportunity to witness their child making a presentation in critiquing a book. The reviews were held in the evenings, enabling them to attend after work.[70]

Butler's mission to provide African American patrons access to books and information in their community was so important to her that she was willing to tolerate the indignities and patronizing remarks she suffered from whites to succeed in it.[71] She received affirmation from the civic and social organizations she created or collaborated with. Butler's proudest achievements were her students' accomplishments. Like a proud mother she took pleasure in seeing her children develop into adults. Butler poignantly affirmed, "They grew up in this library. They graduated from high school, finished college and returned home with B.S. and M.A. degrees. One even had a Ph.D. But when they are here they still remember and come to the Dart Hall Library."[72]

Susan Dart Butler retired from the Dart Hall Library in May 1957 after twenty-six years of service. Shortly thereafter, the City Federation of Women's Clubs and the Charleston Chapter of the Links Inc. honored Butler as their Woman of the Year. One year later Ethel Martin Bolden, a graduate student from Atlanta University library school, interviewed Butler regarding her life and work in establishing Dart Hall Library. Bolden's endeavor was fortuitous for future researchers and scholars interested in the efforts of Susan Dart Butler, Charleston's pioneer librarian. Butler passed away on June 4, 1959 at the age of seventy-one.

In 1960, the CFL integrated their main branch on Marion Square without pressure or interference from local government and without fanfare.[73] Nine years after Butler's death, the Charleston County Council dedicated the newly built John L. Dart Branch Library in honor of her father at 1067 King Street. The library that began as a small reading room, later known as Dart Hall Library, the "colored" branch of the CFL, is still in existence as part of the Charleston County Library system providing service to all people.

Whereas Susan Dart Butler came into librarianship to serve a community need, Ethel Martin Bolden went into the field to fulfill her lifelong ambition to become a school librarian. Her passion motivated Bolden to create libraries in Columbia's African American schools during the Jim Crow era. As an agent for social change Bolden helped desegregate Columbia by becoming the head librarian in the formerly all-white Dreher High School in 1968. Bolden was proactive and worked behind the scenes to make Columbia's integration process a peaceful transition. Like her predecessor, she too had her own set of obstacles to bear.

Ethel Evangeline Veronica Martin was one of four children and the only girl born to Thomas Jerry and Ethel Veronica Martin on December 14, 1918. Her early years were spent in Charleston, South Carolina, surrounded by educators. Her mother and both grandmothers, all of whom were teachers, stressed the value of education and strong religious beliefs. The Martin family's beliefs belonged in part to an African American creed that education and devout faith were imperative for advancement in a racially hostile southern society.[74]

Martin's youth was spent in constant transition owing to family loss. Orphaned by age six, Martin was first reared by her paternal grandmother, Sara Martin, an educator at St. Simons Episcopal Mission in Peak, South Carolina. After the death of her grandmother, Ethel and her younger brother went to live with her great-aunt Dora Dillard, a seamstress in Columbia. Both women had a lasting influence on Martin. Her grandmother exposed her to books and Paul Lawrence Dunbar's poetry. Growing up in her great aunt's interracial neighborhood of Edgewood near downtown Columbia provided Martin with a belief that blacks and whites could live and interact in a peaceable manner.

Martin graduated from the all-black Booker T. Washington High School in 1936 and continued her education at her ancestral alma mater, Barber Scotia Junior College in Concord, North Carolina. Working at her first job under the tutelage of librarian Robbie Goodloe, Martin became enamored with the library environment and set her sights on joining the profession. Her older brother Thomas, a teacher at Voorhees Normal and Industrial School in Denmark, South Carolina, contributed part of her college tuition. She paid the rest of the tuition with money she earned through her library work in conjunction with a scholarship sponsored by the National Youth Administration, one of Franklin D. Roosevelt's New Deal programs.[75]

Martin then matriculated at Johnson C. Smith College in Charlotte, North Carolina, graduating in 1940 with a bachelor of arts in English. When she returned to Columbia to teach fourth grade at Waverly Elementary School she soon realized teaching was not her true vocation. Remembering her work experience at Barber Scotia, Martin resolved to one day become a librarian.

In 1941 she married her high school sweetheart, Charles Frank Bolden, but they had to keep the marriage secret as female schoolteachers in South Carolina were prohibited from getting married.[76] Their newlywed phase would be interrupted by Charles Bolden's draft induction into the army during World War II.

As the new Mrs. Bolden continued to instruct her fourth grade class, John Whiteman, a school administrator, expressed interest in creating a library at Waverly. This prospect gave her the incentive to take library courses at Allen College and Benedict College or wherever she could obtain them.[77]

Because of her Barber Scotia experience, Bolden knew more about the library environment than most of her peers. She established the first elementary school library in the district's black public schools and eventually served in the double capacity as a part-time teacher and part-time librarian at Waverly. According to

Bolden, Waverly was considered not only the most advanced school for blacks but also the best elementary school in Columbia.[78]

Waverly was one of the few black schools in the state to have a library. In 1935, Lucy Hampton Bostick, secretary of the state library board, issued a report entitled "School Libraries in South Carolina" documenting the disparity in libraries between white and black schools. The state supported 1,600 white elementary schools of which 930 schools had libraries. In comparison, of 2,259 black elementary schools, only 165 had libraries. Bostick notes the figures for black schools would have been lower if it had not been for the financial assistance received from the Rosenwald Fund.[79]

Six years later little had changed. Segregation meant that a minuscule amount of funding was allotted to black school libraries. The district supplied the mandatory books from their reading list but obtaining additional books was the responsibility of the librarian. Bolden and the Waverly administration found other ways to obtain books. The parent-teacher association generously supported the effort, paying for the school's first major book order.[80]

The Julius Rosenwald Fund in collaboration with the R. L. Bryan Book Company published and sold "history libraries." The book sets, which were offered between 1928 and 1948, consisted of fourteen to fifty books. The Rosenwald Fund provided book sets to libraries on a matching basis, with the fund providing one-third of the cost and the South Carolina Department of Education and the local community dividing the remainder of the cost. Waverly Elementary collected enough funds to purchase three library sets. Bolden favored the history books as they illustrated black history at a time when it was difficult to find such materials.[81] Even though the Waverly school staff was eager to acquire books for their students, they opposed the common practice of taking in rejects from the white schools because they considered the practice degrading. Bolden remembers when the Waverly principal was sent several pieces of used furniture from a white school that he stopped the delivery truck in the yard, saying, "Take it back!" They never received any more rejects after that.[82]

When her husband returned from the war, Bolden took time off to have a family. Son Charles Frank Bolden Jr. was born in 1946 and Warren Maurice in 1950. Between pregnancies, Bolden did substitute work as a librarian at Carver Elementary and later at C. A. Johnson High School. Working part time afforded her the opportunity to take more library classes at Allen, Benedict and South Carolina State.

While at C. A. Johnson, Bolden felt pressure from the school's principal, C. J. Johnson, to become qualified as a librarian because he did not want to be confronted by the Southern Association of Secondary Schools and Colleges for not having certified personnel. Although Johnson also urged other faculty members to become certified in their respective fields, Bolden took the directive personally. Viewing it as an opportunity to pursue her dream, she seriously started to consider her options to obtain a library science degree.[83]

Bolden's sole choice was Georgia's Atlanta University because it was the closest accredited library school that accepted African Americans.[84] Though she had already taken library courses at local colleges, none had an accredited program. The University of South Carolina had an accredited library program, but it was not open to African Americans. Attending Atlanta University meant Bolden would have to attend summer semester classes lasting eight weeks for five consecutive summers or remain there for the two-year duration until her coursework was completed. At first, her husband questioned both options, as he would be primarily responsible for the children, who were both under the age of seven. After obtaining assurances of assistance from his sister and a babysitter, Charles Bolden felt he could safely manage the situation. With her husband's support and blessings, Bolden relocated to Atlanta to officially enroll as a full-time graduate student in the School of Library Service in the fall of 1953.

Naively, Bolden thought her school schedule would afford her the opportunity to come home on weekends, but she soon realized the coursework was too rigorous for her to leave on a frequent basis. Instead her family traveled to Atlanta to visit her. Son Warren reflected that their father, a high school sports coach, kept them busy during the school year with practice and with swimming at Drew Park during the summer, which helped with their missing their mother.[85]

Bolden returned to Columbia in 1955, after completing her course work, to write her seminal thesis on pioneer librarian Susan Dart Butler. Bolden later admitted that she came home too soon; it took three years to complete her thesis because she became distracted with family, work, and civic obligations. Virginia Lacey Jones, the library school dean, was also Bolden's advisor. Also considered a pioneer librarian, Jones was the second African American to garner a doctoral degree in librarianship from the University of Chicago in 1945.[86] Bolden remembers Jones urging her, "You know, Mrs. Butler isn't getting any younger. . . . [Y]ou need to finish."[87] Bolden completed her interviews with Butler and finished her thesis only months before Butler passed away in 1959. Bolden returned to the Waverly School upon obtaining her master's degree and shortly thereafter transferred to the newly built black W. A. Perry Junior High School, serving as its head librarian for eleven years.

In the eventful year of 1968, civil rights leader Dr. Martin Luther King Jr. was assassinated in Memphis, Tennessee, and riots erupted in major cities in response to his needless death. Locally, as South Carolina witnessed the student unrest that resulted in the Orangeburg Massacre, the state's dual school system began to be dismantled.[88]

Bolden seized the opportunity to move on with her W. A. Perry students to the previously all-white Dreher High School. Principal Arlie W. Whittinghill invited Bolden to Dreher for an interview. Bolden told Perry's principal, C. W. Fields, about the interview, and he did not understand why she would want to interview elsewhere given that she already had a job.[89] That fact did not deter her, and she resigned from Perry Middle School. Whittinghill hired Bolden as head librarian and Francena Robinson, a fellow African American, to serve as a guidance counselor. Son Warren noted that "the transition was historic, but accepted. . . . Dreher never played up the event."[90]

Noticeably, Dreher initially did not hire any African Americans for classroom teaching positions. Bolden thought the administration probably felt librarians had less influence on the students than teachers. But she believed that librarians actually made more of an impact on students because they worked with them on an individual basis. She firmly believed that librarians were teachers.[91]

As an advocate of free access, Bolden insisted that school librarians should not deem themselves the sole owners of the books. Implementing the practice she utilized in her previous schools, Bolden granted everyone access, even permitting students to check out reference books and other learning aides. She believed it was more important for a student to use these materials at home than for them to be secured in the library. She observed even with the liberal access there were few thefts or incidents of materials not being returned.[92]

On the surface Bolden's appointment to serve as Dreher's head librarian appeared to be pacificatory, designed to smooth the transition to integrated schools. However, at times she felt underlying tensions from both races. Ever cognizant of her professional and black middle-class status in the Columbia community, Bolden was diplomatic yet firm in her relationships with whites and blacks so as not to alienate anyone. Several of her former coworkers deemed her a traitor who deserted her race to take up with white people. However, Bolden felt an obligation to dispel prevalent racial attitudes among her white colleagues and parents who believed integration would bring inferior teachers and students. Deeming herself a good librarian, Bolden asserted that "if they wanted the best, they got the best."[93] Prior to Dreher, Bolden had been a role model for African American children, and she resolved to prove to whites that she could be an effective role model for their children as well.

Bolden also noticed that people felt more comfortable approaching the white library assistant, as many had a difficult time accepting her lead position. When a book vendor would visit, the assistant would cordially chat before alerting them she was not the person who made the decisions. Bolden remarked, "And you could see them say 'No way,' 'this can't be.'"[94] Taking these injustices in stride was part of her resolution to establish herself as a competent African American professional.

In addition to her work at Dreher, Bolden taught evening classes in cataloging during her summer vacations at Allen, Benedict, South Carolina State, and Columbia and became active in the Palmetto State Teachers Association, the South Carolina African American teachers organization. Eventually she became the chair of the school and college librarians section.[95] The section served as a liaison between the various departments within the Palmetto Education Association, but there was no cooperation with the South Carolina Library Association, the white librarian organization and subdivision of the white South Carolina Education Association. Bolden credited the Palmetto Education Association's librarians group for providing a professional forum for leadership and for its recognition of black librarians in South Carolina.[96]

Bolden challenged whites she encountered in her work environment and various professional and civic organizations with her presence and voice, thus forcing them to reconsider interracial interactions. She joined the South Carolina Library Association when it opened its membership to African Americans in 1967. Bolden would never forget the reaction she received after making a comment at her first integrated meeting:

> And when I said it, a white librarian looked at another white librarian and said, "Did you hear what she said?" And that struck me as being something that . . . am I not supposed to have an idea? Am I not supposed to say anything? And it really hurt. But after that I became verbal. I got over that. Here I am and I'm supposed to just sit here. I'm not supposed to have an idea, and if I have one it's supposed to be something unique or something different. A black person with a thought? That's the way it struck me. Now it might not have been intended to be that . . . but you know how all of us have our things.[97]

Because of Bolden's vocalism at meetings, Kitty Daniels, a fellow school librarian, told her, "Ethel, you're the voice in the wilderness[,] . . . the voice crying in the wilderness."

Bolden integrated numerous institutional and civic organizations as she became the first and sometimes sole African American member to serve on various boards during the 1950s and 1960s. Similar to Susan Dart Butler, Bolden believed that service to mankind could be rendered not just through one's profession but also through volunteering in educational, civic, and religious organizations.[98] She was inspired by associations that promoted social change and enlisted as a "closet" member of Columbia's branch of the NAACP during the 1950s

and 1960s when South Carolina teachers and state employees were prohibited
from belonging to the organization. Bolden was one of numerous professionals who secretly donated their dues to Rosena Benson and whose jobs would
have been in jeopardy if they had been found out. A self-employed seamstress
in Columbia, Benson turned the monies over to the local branch.[99] A feeling
of helplessness prevailed among teachers during the separate-but-equal days of
the 1950s. Black teachers were paid a meager salary, less than half of the salary
of whites. Elaborating, Ethel's brother, Thomas Martin, explains, "We didn't feel
we could fight . . . fighting was a thing which wasn't in vogue. So maybe that's
why we devoted our energy to teaching and made sure the students had a better
future than we did."[100] Yet many teachers and school professionals fought back
in their own way by channeling their energies into programs and organizations
they hoped would facilitate civil rights and social change.

The South Carolina Council on Human Relations (SCCHR) evolved from the
South Carolina Committee on Interracial Cooperation that Susan Dart Butler
had been affiliated with. Established in 1954, the SCCHR was a private, biracial
and interfaith council that actively pursued the desegregation of schools, libraries, and places of employment, along with handling issues related to voter
registration and participation, health care, housing, and poverty.[101] According
to Bolden, the organization engaged in extensive work for social change and
eased the tension of integration within the state.[102] Attracted to its mission of
encouraging communication between the races, Bolden volunteered her time
working as the organization's secretary in the early 1970s. Years of struggling for
funding to operate took its toll, and the council dissolved in 1975.

She also joined the Community Relations Council, an organization that was
initially designed as a peacekeeping strategy. Lester Bates, Columbia's mayor,
spearheaded a covert plan in attempts to avert the violent racial unrest and riot-
ing that prevailed throughout the Southeast prior to 1963. Bolden was among
the one hundred black and white business and civic leaders learning how "to
overcome the discomfort of sitting down and talking together."[103] Bolden affirmed, "Columbia was quietly integrated and it wasn't by accident; people were
working together for peaceful integration."[104] The council is now called the
Greater Columbia Community Council.

Bolden retired from school librarianship at Dreher High School in 1982 but
not from public service. She remained involved in community organizations
and libraries. During her lifetime she served on over thirty civic, corporate,
and church boards and committees. Because she was focused solely on school
librarianship, Bolden had objected when she had been required to take a course
in public libraries while attending Atlanta University. But that course ultimately

aided Bolden when she became a board trustee and secretary for the Richland County Public Library (RCPL) in 1977. Having taken the course, she had a better understanding of how public libraries functioned, and she was able to keep the administrators honest and focused on their mission.[105] Prior to her board position, Bolden worked as a library consultant for a federally funded outreach program that served children who were unable to visit the library.[106] During her fifteen-year tenure Bolden oversaw relocation plans for three branches and new construction plans for the main branch in downtown Columbia in 1993.[107]

Bolden was also in constant demand as a motivational speaker; she fondly spoke to youth at public and private schools about the virtues of reading, African American history, obtaining an education, and about her sons, one of whom (Charles) had become a NASA astronaut.

Receiving numerous awards for her civil rights involvement and volunteerism, Bolden more than proved her worthiness as a competent professional and role model for all of Columbia's citizens. In May 2002, Bolden's lifetime achievements were acknowledged with the Order of the Palmetto, the state's highest award. She passed away five months later on October 20.

Bolden is remembered today for her numerous accomplishments: establishing libraries when there were few in African American schools, breaking racial barriers in social and civic organizations, and working for peace in a segregated southern city. Most of all, Ethel Martin Bolden should be remembered as one who opened doors when others were fearful to do so, one who voiced her opinions against the status quo, and one who prevailed to allow others to enter and keep the doors open for human equality.

Susan Dart Butler and Ethel Martin Bolden were far from victims, even though they lived in a racist society. They and many others succeeded in establishing public and school libraries despite the imposed obstacles of segregation and unequal services. While they would have preferred better conditions, they did the best with what they had and did not retreat when faced with opposition. Instead they mobilized their self-determination through education and faith, accompanied by a good measure of dignity and diplomacy to command excellence in their professions and civic work. Their lives and dedicated missions helped pave the foundation for countless African American library professionals.

NOTES

1. For scholarship pertaining to African American pioneer librarians and activism in regional and national women's clubs and on the South Carolina State Interracial Committee, see Cheryl Knott Malone, "Quiet Pioneers: Black Women Public Librarians in the Segregated South," *Vitae*

Scholasticae 19, no. 1 (2000): 69–86, Suzanne Hildenbrand, "Library Feminism and Library Women's History: Activism and Scholarship, Equity and Culture," *Libraries and Culture* 35, no. 1 (2000) 51–65, Joan Marie Johnson, *Southern Ladies, New Women: Race, Region, and Clubwomen in South Carolina, 1890–1930* (Gainesville: University Press of Florida, 2004), and Deborah Gray White, *Too Heavy a Load: Black Women in Defense of Themselves, 1894–1994* (New York: Norton, 2000).

2. W. E. B. Du Bois, "The Talented Tenth," in *The Negro Problem: A Series of Articles by Representative Negroes of To-day* (New York: James Pott and Company, 1903), 31–75.

3. "Announcement of the Charleston Normal and Industrial Institute, 1904–1905," box 1, John L. Dart Papers (hereinafter cited as JLDP), Avery Research Center for African American History and Culture, College of Charleston, Charleston, S.C. (hereinafter cited as ARC).

4. A. B. Caldwell, ed. *History of the American Negro: South Carolina Edition* (Atlanta, Ga.: A. B. Caldwell Publishing, 1919), 211–12.

5. "The Alumni of Avery, Twelfth Annual Reunion of the Association at the Institute," July 5, 1888, *Charleston World*.

6. Deed of transfer, September 29, 1849, box 1, JLDP-ARC.

7. For an account of the socialization of African American women professionals in the Jim Crow era, see Stephanie J. Shaw, *What a Woman Ought To Be and To Do: Black Professional Women Workers during the Jim Crow Era* (Chicago: University of Chicago Press, 1996). For Charleston's racial dynamics, see Edmund L. Drago, *Charleston's Avery Center*, ed. W. Marvin Dulaney (Charleston, S.C.: History Press, 2006), and Walter B. Hill, "Family, Life, and Work Culture: Black Charleston, South Carolina 1880 to 1910" (PhD diss., University of Maryland, 1989).

8. *Catalog of Atlanta University 1890–1891 thru 1909–1910* (Atlanta: Constitution Book Office Print, 1910).

9. 1900 U.S. federal census, Boston ward 8, Suffolk, Mass., roll T623_679, page 1B, enumeration district 1272.

10. 1910 U.S. federal census, Revere, Suffolk, Massachusetts, roll T624_626, page 7A, enumeration district 1681, image 1110.

11. Ibid., 11.

12. Drago, *Charleston's Avery Center*, 127.

13. "The Dart Grammar and Primary School," broadside, box 1, folder 18, Albertha Johnston Murray Papers, ARC.

14. Richard H. Mickey to Marvin J. Taylor, May 10, 1917, box 3, folder 5, Edmund L. Drago Collection, ARC.

15. Edmund L. Drago, "The Origins of Burke High School and Black Public Education in Charleston: An Historical Perspective," 1987, box 15, folder 5, Robert Rosen Papers, ARC.

16. Annie L. McPheeters, *Library Service in Black and White: Some Personal Recollections, 1921–1980* (Metuchen, N.J.: Scarecrow Press, 1988), 1.

17. Kenneth F. Kister, *Eric Moon: The Life and Library Times* (Jefferson, N.C.: McFarland, 2002), 256.

18. Ibid., 256.

19. Malone, "Quiet Pioneers"; Cheryl Knott Malone, "Accommodating Access: 'Colored' Carnegie Libraries, 1905–1925" (PhD diss., University of Texas at Austin, 1996).

20. Louise Anderson Allen, *A Bluestocking in Charleston: The Life and Career of Laura Bragg* (Columbia: University of South Carolina Press, 2001).

21. Lillie Walker, "Black Librarians in South Carolina," in *The Black Librarian in the Southeast:*

Reminiscences, Activities, Challenges, ed. Annette L. Phinazee (Durham: North Carolina Central University, 1976), 87–102.

22. Bernard E. Powers Jr., *Black Charlestonians: A Social History, 1822–1885* (Fayetteville: University of Arkansas Press, 1994).

23. Mary Emily Riley, "The History of the Charleston Free Library" (MA thesis, University of South Carolina, 1950), 2.

24. "Minutes of Meeting of State Interracial Committee, November 18, 1926, Columbia S.C.," Commission on Interracial Cooperation Papers, 1919–44, series 7, reel 53, Robert W. Woodruff Library, Atlanta University Center, Atlanta, Ga.

25. 1931 Annual Report, box 1, (CFL) Papers, special collections, Charleston County Public Library, S.C. (hereinafter cited as CCPL).

26. "Semi-Annual Report of Work at the Coming Street Branch YWCA," November 1922, YWCA of Greater Charleston Papers, box 1, folder 9, ARC.

27. Susan Dart Butler, "Making a Way to Start a Library," Susan Dart Vertical File, John L. Dart Branch Library, Charleston, S.C.

28. Shaw, *What a Woman Ought To Be and To Do*, 138.

29. Edwin R. Embree and Julia Waxman, *Investment in People: The Story of the Julius Rosenwald Fund* (New York: Harper and Brothers, 1949).

30. For Butler's perspective, see "Dart Hall Library for Negroes Was Started," and for Laura Bragg's account see Allen, *A Bluestocking in Charleston*, 124–25.

31. Unpublished memoir, box 2, Clelia Peronneau Mathewes McGowan Family Papers, South Carolina Historical Society, Charleston, 42.

32. Clark Foreman to Charles B. Foelsch, November 17 and November 20, 1930, box 1, CFL Papers, CCPL.

33. CFL trustee minutes, February 27, 1931, 30, CFL Papers, CCPL.

34. Margaret Mosimann, "History of the Charleston Free Library," CFL 1950–1954 Vertical File, CCPL.

35. Foelsch to CFL trustees, December 13, 1932, CFL Papers, CCPL.

36. "Keeping Negroes in the Dark: The Cities That Once Denied Public Library Services to Blacks," *Journal of Blacks in Higher Education* 13 (Autumn 1996): 30.

37. "Pioneer Librarian Retires as Head of Dart Hall Branch," *Post and Courier*, May 19, 1957.

38. The main white branch noted a registration of 3,992 patrons with circulation of 65,508 (1931 Annual Report, CFL Papers, CCPL).

39. CFL trustee minutes, February 27, 1931, 30 CFL Papers, CCPL.

40. CFL trustee minutes, November 2, 1930, CFL Papers, CCPL; Suzanna W. O'Donnell, "Equal Opportunities for Both: Julius Rosenwald, Jim Crow and the Charleston Free Library's Record of Service to Blacks, 1931 to 1960" (MS thesis, University of North Carolina at Chapel Hill, 2000), 21.

41. An auditor recommended the purchase of a fire insurance policy to cover fixtures and stock of books (1931 Annual Report, CFL Papers, CCPL).

42. "Pioneer Librarian Retires as Head of Dart Hall Branch."

43. Parmellee Cheves, South Carolina state library field agent, succeeded Helen Virginia Stelle, becoming the director of the CFL (1931 Annual Report, CFL Papers, CCPL).

44. CFL trustee minutes, January 19, 1932, 46, CCPL.

45. Bolden states Julia McBeth served only one year as librarian, resigning on account of ill health ("Susan Dart Butler: Pioneer Librarian" [MS thesis, Atlanta University, 1959]).

46. Stelle, memorandum to the board of trustees of the Charleston Free Library, June 1932, CFL Papers, CCPL; Stelle, "Report of the Organization of the Charleston Free Library, January 1st thru June 30th, 1932," 7, CFL Papers, CCPL.

47. Stelle, "Report of the Organization of the Charleston Free Library," 3, CFL Papers, CCPL.

48. Butler, "Making a Way to Start a Library," Susan Dart Vertical File, John L. Dart Branch Library, Charleston, S.C.

49. Cheves to Agnes D. Crawford, March 24, 1936, CFL Papers, CCPL.

50. S. L. Smith, "The Passing of the Hampton Library School," *Journal of Negro Education* 9, no. 1 (1940): 51–58.

51. Walker, "Black Librarians in South Carolina," 94.

52. Shaw, *What a Woman Ought To Be and To Do*, 143.

53. Rossie B. Caldwell, "South Carolina State Library Group," in *The Black Librarianship Handbook*, 2nd ed., ed. E. J. Josey and Marva L. DeLoach (Lanham, Md.: Scarecrow Press, 2000) 69–74.

54. "The Charleston Free Library," *Charleston News and Courier*, November 13, 1930.

55. Stelle, "Report of the Organization of the Charleston Free Library," 9, CFL Papers, CCPL.

56. Embree and Waxman, *Investment in People*, 60.

57. Cynthia McCotty-Smith, interview by author, Charleston, S.C., January 10, 2008.

58. For Dart Library's campaign against illiteracy, see "The Dart Hall Branch of the Charleston Free Library, a Wonderful Asset to This City; It Is Daily Becoming a Strong Factor in the Suppression of Illiteracy," CFL Papers, CCPL.

59. Unsigned letter to Susan D. Butler, May 27, 1932, CFL Papers, CCPL.

60. "A History—by Administrations—of the Phyllis Wheatley Literary and Social Club," compiled by Jeanette Keeble Cox, Phyllis Wheatley Literary and Social Club Papers, ARC.

61. Lois Simms, telephone interview by author, August 15, 2007.

62. Charleston Welfare Council, "Charleston Looks at Its Services for Negroes: Report on Recreation Sub-committee Report," May 1947, D-7, Charleston County Vertical Files, ARC.

63. CFL trustee Minutes, December 21, 1931, 43, CFL Papers, CCPL.

64. Wilmot Fraser Jr., interview by author, Charleston, S.C., January 11, 2008.

65. 1931 Annual Report, CFL Papers, CCPL.

66. Mamie Garvin Fields with Karen Fields, *Lemon Swamp and Other Places: A Carolina Memoir* (New York: Free Press, 1983), 209.

67. Riley, "The History of the Charleston Free Library," 22.

68. "BookWeek Program," *Charleston Post and Courier*, n.d.

69. "Reading Diplomas Awarded," *Charleston News and Courier*, August 9, 1956.

70. "Dart Hall Library Marks Anniversary," *Charleston Evening Post*, May 9, 1951.

71. Jack McCray, "Dart Library Project Yields Old Treasure," *Charleston Post and Courier*, July 21, 2002.

72. Butler, "Making a Way to Start a Library," Susan Dart Vertical File, John L. Dart Branch Library, Charleston, S.C.

73. "Integrated County Library," *Charleston Post and Courier*, December 24, 1960.

74. For ways education and faith served as the foundation in the African American family, see Glenda Gilmore, *Gender and Jim Crow: Women and the Politics of White Supremacy in North Carolina, 1896–1920* (Chapel Hill: University of North Carolina Press, 1996), 26.

75. Ethel Martin Bolden, interviews by author, Columbia, S.C., June 29, 2001, and April 19, 2002, transcript, box 1, Ethel Bolden Papers, South Caroliniana Library, University of South Carolina, Co-

lumbia (hereinafter cited as EBP-SCL). For an extensive biography on Bolden, see Georgette Mayo, "'A Voice in the Wilderness': Ethel Evangeline Martin Bolden, Pioneer Librarian" (MA thesis, University of South Carolina, Columbia, 2005).

76. Darwin McBeth Walton, *Overcoming Challenges: The Life of Charles F. Bolden, Jr.* (Austin, Tex.: Steck-Vaughn Company, 2000), 20

77. Ethel Martin Bolden, interview by Robert V. Williams, Columbia, S.C., June 9, 1999, transcript, EBP-SCL).

78. Ibid., 5, 8.

79. Lucy Hampton Bostick, "School Libraries in South Carolina," *Peabody Journal of Education* 12, no. 6 (1935): 308–9.

80. Bolden, interview by Williams, June 9, 1999, 8–9, EBP-SCL.

81. Embree and Waxman, *Investment in People*; Dan Lee, "From Segregation to Integration: Library Services for Blacks in South Carolina, 1923–1962," in *Untold Stories: Civil Rights, Libraries, and Black Librarianship*, ed. John Mark Tucker (Champaign: Graduate School of Library and Information Science, University of Illinois at Urbana-Champaign, 1998), 99.

82. Bolden, interview by Williams, June 9, 1999, 12, EBP-SCL.

83. Ibid.

84. Juan Williams and Dwayne Ashley, *I'll Find a Way or Make One: A Tribute to Historically Black Colleges and Universities* (New York: HarperCollins, 2004), 329.

85. Bolden, interview by Williams, June 9, 1999, 13, EBP-SCL; Warren Bolden Sr., interview by author, Columbia, S.C., December 8, 2004.

86. Casper LeRoy Jordan, "The Multifaceted Career of Virginia Lacy Jones," in *The Black Librarian in America Revisited*, ed. E. J. Josey (Metuchen, N.J.: Scarecrow Press, 1994), 75–83.

87. Bolden, interview by Williams, June 9, 1999, 15, EBP-SCL.

88. Jack Bass and Jack Nelson, *The Orangeburg Massacre* (Macon, Ga.: Mercer University Press, 2002); Cleveland Sellers Jr. and Robert Terrell, *The River of No Return: The Autobiography of a Black Militant and the Life and Death of SNCC* (Jackson: University Press of Mississippi, 1990).

89. Bolden, interview by Williams, June 9, 1999, 25, EBP-SCL.

90. Warren Bolden, interview by author, December 8, 2004.

91. Bolden, interview by Williams, June 9, 1999, 26, EBP-SCL.

92. Ibid.

93. Ibid., 25–26.

94. Ibid., 26.

95. Later known as the Palmetto Education Assoication, or PEA; see Caldwell, "South Carolina State Library Group," 69–74.

96. Bolden, interview by Williams, June 9, 1999, 23, EBP-SCL.

97. Ibid., 21, EBP-SCL.

98. Bolden, "Susan Dart Butler," 10.

99. "Thomas S. Martin: We Did the Job," *Columbia Record*, May 27, 1985, B-1–B-4.

100. Ibid., B-4.

101. South Carolina Council on Human Relations, *A Handbook for Local Councils on Human Relations: 1968*, Records of the South Carolina Council on Human Relations, SCL.

102. Warren Bolden, interview by author, December 8, 2004.

103. "'Secret' Plan Helped Keep the Peace," *The State*, A-6, February 1, 1994.

104. Ibid.

105. Bolden, interview by Williams, June 9, 1999, 14, EBP-SCL; "An Oral History Interview with Ethel M. Bolden," October 26, 1999 (Columbia, S.C.: Richland County Public Library Film and Sound Dept., 1999).

106. Richland County Public Library, "RCPL Recognizes Ethel Martin Bolden—A Pioneer Librarian," May 8, 2002, http://www.richland.lib.sc.us/news/rcpl-recognizes-ethel-martin-bolden-pioneer-librarian (accessed July 25, 2011).

107. Ibid.

Harriet Simons

Women, Race, Politics, and the League of Women Voters of South Carolina

JENNIFER E. BLACK

Harriet Porcher Stoney Simons (1896–1971) of Charleston was a key figure in the development of the League of Women Voters (LWV) in South Carolina after World War II. A white woman from an elite background and a moderately progressive leader in a conservative state, Simons stood out among South Carolina women of her race and class. Like many of them, Simons worked to improve her city and state. However, her positions on controversial issues relating to gender and race placed her at the forefront of change in an often resistant atmosphere. Simons's activities in the late 1940s and in the 1950s, many of them as a leader of the LWV, demonstrated the obstacles to as well as the importance of women's work in public life in South Carolina and the South during those years.

Harriet Porcher Stoney was born in Charleston on November 6, 1896, the descendant of a long line of prominent Charlestonians. Her parents were Samuel Gaillard Stoney and Louisa Cheves Smythe Stoney. She was educated in Charleston except for a short spell at a boarding school in Philadelphia. As a teenager she worked for her father. "My first job was as secretary-stenographer-chauffeur for my Father who was then President of West Point Rice Mill. I got paid for being his secretary, but no salary for my duties as chauffeur," she later recalled. "It was excitement and reward enough in those days for a girl of 19 to get her hands on a model T. Ford. I particularly liked the chauffeuring part of my job and through it I learned my way around this county."[1] This vision of Harriet Simons as one of the first women behind the wheel in the city of Charleston is consistent with her image and personality. According to her daughter, Harriet

HARRIET SIMONS
Courtesy of Harriet Simons Williams.

Simons Williams, she was highly visible within the community and had a reputation for being headstrong and a force to be reckoned with.[2]

Harriet Stoney married architect Albert Simons of Charleston on December 1, 1917, and had three children, Albert, Serena, and Harriet. For several years
during the 1920s she attended courses at the College of Charleston as a "special
student." She also worked intermittently as a secretary for her husband's architectural firm and as a laboratory technician at the Medical College of South
Carolina.[3]

Plagued by severe hay fever and seasonal allergies from the mid-1930s onward, Simons left Charleston each year by August 15 to escape the ragweed and
was unable to return until after the November frost. By 1940 she had developed
asthma and began to suffer serious attacks.[4] In spite of these health problems,
which often left her bedridden, Simons was involved in a vast number of voluntary societies in Charleston in the 1930s and 1940s. Simons and her husband
embraced civic work because of the sense of duty they felt toward the city where
they spent most of their lives. According to her autobiographical writings, Simons "started at a tender age feeling responsible for the city of Charleston and
its welfare."[5] Simons's major interests, encouraged first by her work in various
church groups and then by her service as an officer of the Junior League and
president of the Craft School Parent-Teachers Association, lay in "governmental, health and welfare activities."[6]

Many of the organizations in which Simons participated focused on wom-
en's welfare. After 1937 Simons helped start a privately sponsored birth control
clinic in Charleston and served as the first president of its lay group. Simons's
daughter recalls that Simons made contact with two women from the North
who had worked with the well-known birth control advocate Margaret Sanger
in New York. The women and their husbands were clients of Albert Simons's
architectural firm and had hired the firm to renovate old homes they purchased
in Charleston.[7] The clinics were set up to serve black and white women, and
there is evidence to suggest that the majority of the women who used them
were black.

Simons's achievement in getting such a clinic started during the 1930s was
remarkable given the level of resistance throughout the United States at that
time to the dissemination of contraceptive advice, though there were other
women's organizations and women doctors in South Carolina in the 1930s who
were working to improve women's health through birth control. The popularity of family planning services initiated by Dr. Hilla Sheriff for white and black
women in the Spartanburg area led to the creation of clinics throughout the

state in 1936. And in March 1939, South Carolina made birth control part of its official public health services, the second state, after North Carolina, to do so. This was part of a campaign to cut down on the state's exceptionally high maternal and infant mortality rates. The support for birth control programs by South Carolina women and state public health leaders at this time contrasted sharply to the situation in Connecticut, where Catholics were numerous and influential and where the state supreme court ruled against the use of contraceptives even when it was required by a patient's condition.[8] Well after the 1930s, working with other women in the community, Simons continued to promote access to birth control as a means of aiding women, black and white, in the city of Charleston. She is on record as a supporter of a 1954 plan to place the clinic at the Medical College of South Carolina.[9]

During the Great Depression, Simons led the Charleston Women's Relief Committee and was elected to serve as chair of the women's division of the Unemployment Relief Commission. In 1937 she was on the board of the Charleston Mental Hygiene Clinic. During World War II Simons served on the executive board of the Charleston Red Cross and chaired the Home Nursing Committee. Simons also worked in civilian defense and was vice president of the Civic Union, a "good government" group that focused on improving conditions in Charleston during the war by bringing together representatives from the city's numerous civic organizations.[10]

From 1946 to 1947, as part of her service on the Welfare Council of Charleston, Simons chaired the Urban League Survey Committee. The survey examined conditions for blacks in Charleston, including housing and education. By 1951 she had become a member of the Southern Regional Council, a progressive organization dedicated to social and economic change and improved race relations in the South.[11]

In 1948 Simons ran unsuccessfully for a position on the city council. During her campaign she did not downplay her interest in interracial work but instead drew attention to it: in one campaign speech she stated, "I have tried to do my share of work for all members of the community, regardless of creed or color. All people who live in Charleston are citizens of our city and it is my firm belief that many of the difficult problems which confront us can be solved by understanding and cooperation."[12]

Though she was not elected to the city council, Simons's contributions to her community did not go unnoticed or unappreciated. The same year that she lost the election, a group of representatives from Charleston organizations selected her from a list of ten nominees to receive the honor of 1948 Woman of the Year.[13] Years later Simons said she believed that running the Unemployment Relief

Committee, helping to found the birth control clinic, and completing the Urban League survey were among her most important achievements, along with helping to revive the League of Women Voters in South Carolina.[14]

Both the national LWV and the League of Women Voters of South Carolina (LWVSC) were founded in 1920 by former suffragists when the Nineteenth Amendment was approaching ratification and were intended to educate voters, especially newly enfranchised women, about sound policy. By 1932 the membership, leadership, and finances of the original LWVSC had dwindled to the point that it was dissolved. Simons played a key role in its revival in South Carolina after World War II. The first provisional local league groups were set up in Charleston and Columbia in 1947. Simons helped found the Charleston league over which she presided from 1947 until 1951. She then led in the formation of the state league, serving as state president until 1955.[15] During these crucial years of growth and development, Simons gave advice to new and existing local chapters and traveled around the state advising groups interested in starting local leagues in their area.[16]

In the 1950s the LWVSC faced three potentially explosive issues: the potential for school desegregation that led to the 1952 school amendment, the question of membership of black women in the league in South Carolina, and the campaign for jury service for women. The ways in which the women of the LWVSC dealt with these issues demonstrated how southern women who were members of a national organization at times pushed boundaries as they worked for reform in the face of local and regional obstacles.

The LWVSC was just finding its feet as the U.S. Supreme Court began considering the constitutionality of separate schools for black and white children. Tensions rose in South Carolina even before the *Brown v. Board of Education* decision was announced in 1954. Political leaders in South Carolina, fearing that the Supreme Court would no longer permit the system of separate but clearly unequal schools that existed all over the South and their state, attempted to preempt desegregation of the state's schools by several methods. Governor James F. Byrnes mounted a massive school equalization program supported by a three-cent sales tax and appointed a committee led by Senator Marion Gressette to study the implementation of a "separate but equal" school system.[17] In January 1952 Byrnes officially recommended that the South Carolina General Assembly submit a resolution to repeal article 6, section 5, of South Carolina's constitution, in effect removing the provision for free public education in the state constitution. The bill to support this resolution, introduced by Senator Gressette, passed in the state senate in February and won a two-thirds majority in the house. On February 19 the bill was ratified in a joint session of the state legislature. It was then submitted to the people in a referendum in the general election in October 1952.[18]

The majority of legislators agreed that the removal of the public school provision from the state constitution provided the best means of delaying action if the Supreme Court declared segregation in education unconstitutional. However, there were some in South Carolina who did not agree with this measure and who were willing to speak out against it. Historian David Blick has argued that the faction of white racial moderates who were opposed to the amendment was more interested in education than in the "politics of color" that dominated the state. Members of this faction included women's groups, teachers' organizations, and some legislators.[19]

The YWCA opposed the move on the grounds of the detrimental effects it would have on public education, a decision its leader Laura Smith Ebaugh was quick to communicate to LWVSC president Simons.[20] The South Carolina Education Association also opposed the amendment. The measure provided no alternative to the current system of education nor any solution to the inevitable difficulties if the courts ruled that the South Carolina system did not meet federal requirements.[21]

Although a number of groups came out against the Byrnes amendment, few whites in South Carolina welcomed the prospect of integration. Even moderates and liberals who saw integration as inevitable were unable to imagine it being achieved in the state without threatening the quality of public education for white children.[22] Simons explained the feeling in South Carolina as she saw it: "There is a sense among the thoughtful people in South Carolina that integration is inevitable, but complete dismay is felt by everyone in the coastal plain as to the possibility of early integration. The uppermost thought in South Carolina is that enforced early integration of the schools would so set back white education in South Carolina it would be a serious blow to literacy in the state." According to Simons, many white South Carolinians believed that black children were so far behind in education that mixing the races would make it very difficult for white children to learn.[23]

In May 1952, at its annual state convention, the LWVSC formed a committee to study the school issue and make recommendations based on that study.[24] Later that month, on the morning of May 26, 1952, the members of the committee gathered at the statehouse in Columbia for a conference with Governor Byrnes.[25] The meeting clarified Byrnes's aims in supporting the removal of the public education clause from the constitution and his intentions concerning the fate of the public school system if the amendment passed. Byrnes told the women that "no change in the present school system will result from the passage of the amendment unless the Legislature takes action. Removal of this clause from the constitution makes the control of schools in the state subject to the wishes of the people through their representatives."[26]

When the committee members asked Governor Byrnes why he was proposing the amendment at that time, he responded, "In the event of a Supreme Court decision to do away with the state's right to provide separate but equal facilities for children of the white and colored races, the people of South Carolina could take such action as they deem necessary."[27] The women emerged from their encounter with Byrnes unsatisfied.[28] To Simons it seemed that the governor and others supporting the school amendment were far more interested in avoiding pressure from the Supreme Court to desegregate than they were in the fate of the schools.[29]

This meeting with the governor was a crucial indicator of the future direction of the league in South Carolina. Taking up such a controversial issue was fraught with danger, and the organization's willingness even to study the amendment indicated its relatively liberal stance in a conservative state. But, aware of these risks, Simons urged caution: "The subject is too important and delicate for any of the local leagues to go off on half cocked, and I think the board must consider very carefully what is the wisest thing to do. . . . In any case I feel very strongly that we must do nothing in the League without a great deal of study, and that no consensus should be taken until we feel our members understand all the implications."[30]

As the women in the local chapters embarked on "three and one half months of careful study of the amendment," they found themselves thrust into the racial politics that dominated the state at the time.[31] As historian Cherisse Jones-Branch has asserted, many members of United Church Women who were also confronting this issue were "struggling to overcome their traditional upbringing in conservative, racially segregated communities" in the wake of their realization that continued segregation in schools would perpetuate the cycle of prejudice among whites.[32] It is difficult to tell whether the women of the LWVSC embarked on their study of the school amendment with trepidation or enthusiasm. However, their activities certainly did not go unnoticed: members were labeled race traitors and radicals and harassed for taking even these cautious steps that questioned the policies of the white men leading the state in the fight against integration.

Members of the Columbia LWV were particularly vulnerable to opposition given the level of tension in the state capital. In a report to the state and national boards, the Columbia league claimed that, owing to their location, it was not surprising that "the repercussions . . . were more violent."[33] The Columbia league wanted to host a series of fifteen-minute radio slots giving both sides of the debate that would culminate in a public meeting prior to the November election. But their attempts to secure speakers were blocked. Meanwhile, their opponents bought several fifteen-minute radio slots that they filled with speakers such as Lieutenant Governor George Bell Timmerman Jr. whom the LWV had hoped to use in its own radio slots. The league pressed on with plans for the public meeting, only to find that newspapers that were usually supportive refused to give any space to announcements about the meeting. League members then realized, as stated in Columbia's report, "how completely we were being boycotted."[34]

At the public meeting, Senator Marion Gressette took the opportunity to attack the LWVSC. Instead of debating the issue at hand, Gressette accused the organization of colluding with the NAACP. According to the league report, "Senator Gressette gave a speech that was emotional, rabble-rousing, racial. He first bawled out the League, saying that we based our stand on distrust of the legislature, then he ranted furiously against the NAACP, and then he successfully linked us together. It was appalling. . . . Gressette did not answer one question, but used every opportunity to scream about the end of segregation." Members of the league subsequently were harassed by telephone calls from opponents asking them why they were collaborating with the NAACP and working to end segregation.[35]

League leaders were frustrated and felt that they had failed: they were unable to get equal radio time, to maintain the support of the press, or to get their point across. In their own words they had been "thoroughly bombarded with racist propaganda through every channel," when race, they felt, was "not even the issue."[36]

Meanwhile, local LWVSC chapters around the state were determining the "stand" that the organization would take on the amendment. A poll of local league members on the school amendment revealed that of those members who expressed an opinion, 177 opposed the amendment and only 12 were in favor of it.[37] The largest leagues provided detailed reports on the numbers of women voting for and against the amendment and those abstaining. Most indicate that a majority of the women present at meetings where the membership was polled voted against the amendment. On October 8, 1952, the state board passed a resolution opposing the school amendment "as the result of careful consideration of the reaction reports sent in by the local Leagues." This position was communicated to the public via the press, broadcast on the radio, and printed in LWVSC literature used in the November election.[38]

In spite of the efforts of the LWVSC and other groups to protect public education, on November 4, 1952, the people of South Carolina voted in favor of the school amendment. The general assembly ratified it in March 1954, just two months before the *Brown* decision. Historian David Blick later described the amendment as a final "ultimatum" to the Supreme Court in the face of the impending decision on school segregation. Despite the amendment, however, the public schools did not close in South Carolina, although other states, including Virginia, did try to circumvent the *Brown* decision later in the 1950s by closing schools.[39]

In July 1954, as the nation responded to the *Brown* decision and the national LWV sought to determine its position on the decision, the organization brought southern league leaders including Harriet Simons to Atlanta to discuss and formulate a policy for the difficult years ahead. Soon after the LWVSC had failed in its efforts against the school amendment, the president of the national LWV, Percy Maxim Lee, had sent a letter to the Columbia president congratulating the league on its efforts, stating, "The wonder of it is that so often the amateur in politics, the plain citizen, does actually win out over the skilled and experienced political operator. I'm sure you will eventually meet with this success. Certainly, it is learning the hard way, but I can imagine no more practical method of gaining political experience than this one you have just come through!"[40] Yet despite this supportive letter, the overwhelming conclusion of the 1954 Atlanta meeting was that members must "maintain the integrity" of the LWV by avoiding controversy. State leagues were advised that "to keep the temperature from getting too high might be a better job for the League than to back the public schools."[41]

National LWV leaders recognized the challenges facing the southern leagues and advised survival over risk taking: "At the moment it is very inflammatory to try to preserve the public schools and the League should concentrate on the usual things the League does, and work and think and study a lot and keep quiet. One of the roles of leadership is to follow behind and try to interpret in a better light."[42] Simons and the women of the South Carolina LWV had showed more courage than the national organization when it came to desegregation and had been prepared to take risks the national body did not encourage.

Standing in striking contrast to the cautiousness of the national LWV, the LWVSC's engagement with this issue reflects its willingness to stand by its principles and the views of its members. Simons later observed that the experience of studying and reaching a consensus on the matter had strengthened the state league, that it had developed a stronger profile in South Carolina owing to its refusal to give in on an emotional and controversial issue. She believed that the LWVSC had "earned respect by its adherence to principle and by its refusal to be stampeded by emotion."[43] David Blick has observed that the school issue had given the women in the LWV the opportunity to face major politicians such as Gressette "head on."[44] Gressette tried to use the race element of the debate to taint the league's reputation, but the LWVSC would not be intimidated.

As the events of 1952 forced the league to confront the issue of segregation in education, segregation within the league itself was also under scrutiny. The national LWV prohibited discrimination on the grounds of race; however, by 1954, only six of the eleven southern leagues had any black members and black membership for the South stood at less than one hundred women and no LWV chapters in the Deep South had black members. The LWVSC's response to black women joining the organization constitutes another example of it taking a different approach than the national organization. Whereas with respect to the school amendment, the national league had urged more caution than the LWVSC had displayed, in considering the memberships of black women, the LWVSC was more cautious and took an approach calculated to ensure its survival in the state in which it was operating. And Harriet Simons played a central role in the debate over black membership in the Charleston league.

The black women who had joined the organization were well-educated, middle-class women, often graduates of black colleges in the South.[45] The first person to raise the issue in South Carolina was Maude Thomas Veal, a schoolteacher who moved to Charleston from Cincinnati in 1948 when her husband became pastor of the largest black congregation in Charleston, the Emanuel AME Church. Veal had been involved in the LWV before coming to Charleston, and in 1951, she approached the Charleston chapter with the intention of joining. Aware that her skin color might present a problem to league leaders, Veal did not indicate her race when submitting her written application. However, Veal decided that she would have to inform the leader of the group that she was black before she attended any meetings. She called Simons and told her that they had met previously at a fundraising event at Cannon Street Hospital. Simons had been one of the only white people in attendance. On realizing the full facts of Veal's membership application, Simons went to visit Veal at her home.[46]

As Veal listened politely, Simons outlined the potential disruption her membership could cause for the Charleston LWV. Simons stated that it was not that the league members would object but that the local community might. Important financial backing from local businesses could be lost, she argued.[47] Veal recalled that she did not hear from Simons again for some time—and then only after Veal had complained to the national board. Thereafter, said Veal, she attended meetings and discussion groups "without incident." She also reported that when she was asked by the Charleston LWV board to form a separate black unit she refused and encouraged other black women to do likewise.[48]

There is evidence to suggest, however, that Veal was not as successful at integrating the LWV as her version of the story suggests and that a separate black unit *was* the solution used by the Charleston league—despite Veal's resistance and the national LWV's discouragement of such an approach. In a report to the regional conference of the LWV in July 1954, South Carolina was listed as having one local league with twelve to eighteen black members.[49] LWVSC records indicate that this small group of women who chose to join the LWV in Charleston faced limits to their participation within the organization. Black members were allowed to attend general meetings, which were usually held at prestigious hotels but only after refreshments or meals had already been served.[50]

Despite her initial resistance to Veal joining the white league, Simons did try to accommodate her and other black women who wished to affiliate. She attempted to find locations for general meetings where integrated gatherings were permitted, such as the medical school.[51] When the chapter broke into smaller unit groups for study and discussion, the black women met at Dart Hall, the library for blacks in Charleston. Unit meetings generally took place in members' homes, and the use of Dart Hall as a meeting location was a solution to a potentially difficult problem—many white women did not want to have black women attend meetings in their homes. Simons took her daughter Harriet to the Dart Hall unit meetings "so there would be more than just one white person there." Other white members of the Charleston LWV who attended these meetings included Anne King Gregorie and Flora Belle Surles.[52]

Simons and her colleagues eventually decided to invite a small group of black women to join—some of whom ultimately comprised the twelve to eighteen black women who attended the separate unit meetings. Simons gave a rather condescending speech about black membership in Charleston before the LWV regional conference in 1954, claiming, "After two months of deliberation, they [the Charleston league] invited a dozen or so outstanding Negro women to join. It will never be easy and no one of the women has contributed a great deal because their political education is so far behind. When interested they work awfully hard."[53] Simons may have doubted the ability of black women to make a contribution to the organization in part because African American women had been afforded scant opportunities to vote or be involved in South Carolina politics. However she did not exclude all black women from the LWV on these grounds, and she acted to ensure the survival of this historically white woman's organization while making it accessible to a small group of "outstanding" black women in the early 1950s. Simons's primary goal was ensuring that the LWVSC as a group survived so that it might continue to serve its purpose of educating and informing citizens of the state.[54]

Simons and the Charleston board were influenced in their decision to allow black members to join the LWVSC largely by the reactions of male contributors and newspaper editors. In a letter to the president of the LWV in Gainesville, Florida, Simons explained that league members asked newspaper editors if "they would give us unfavorable publicity in event of our taking in the negroes [sic], and they said no." True to their word, and despite the negative publicity the Columbia LWV received for its role in the school amendment, newspapers did not comment on the integration of the league, perhaps because the meetings were not completely integrated. Simons was also concerned that male financial supporters might abandon the organization, but she received assurances that "they thought no group needed political education more badly [than African American women], and that they were proud to know us."[55] Simons even pointed out that some male supporters did not think that the league should accept Veal, who was not from Charleston, without accepting "old line Charleston Negro women."[56]

The fact that Simons and the board of the Charleston LWV consulted the press and "several leaders in the community" before making the decision about admitting black women showed that they thought it prudent to ensure they had local support before implementing what was a national policy of their organization.[57] It is interesting to note, however, that South Carolina was in the lead among southern state leagues when it came to integration and proud of it. Caroline Toms, who served as president of the Charleston chapter from 1955 to 1957 and as LWVSC president from 1957 to 1960 recalled that "we were very proud of being the first Deep South League to have Negro members."[58]

Overall, the response of Simons and the rest of the Charleston board to the membership request of a black woman was cautious and pragmatic and, for the time, progressive.[59] It is probably no accident that it was in Charleston that the issue was first confronted. Though in one of the most conservative areas of the state, Charleston was also home to a significant group of the kind of educated, civic-minded black women that Simons and others were prepared to work with. Working together in an organization was not the same thing, however, as meeting together: attitudes toward integrated meetings were still conservative. Toms recalled that when some white members withdrew their membership as a result of black women being admitted to the LWV it was "not, they said, because they disapproved in principle but because they just couldn't face such a drastic and unfamiliar experience."[60]

The importance of place to the organizing of women along racial lines was magnified in the South. When leagues began to accommodate requests for black membership the question of where to hold the meetings—in this case in private homes or at hotels, restaurants, libraries and so forth—was particularly problematic. Historian Christina Greene has noted that calls for black membership "transformed white women's homes into semipublic arenas of racial contestation, collapsing rigid boundaries between public and private spaces."[61] It is significant that in Charleston, the part of South Carolina with the least residential segregation, black membership met with the most success, although interracial meetings inside white women's homes were still taboo for many. An assessment of the way white southern LWV leaders, including Simons, handled the matter of black membership and the response of the LWV membership and the local community illustrates the careful balancing act necessitated by time and place.

Simons served as president of the LWVSC until 1955. Thereafter her ability to serve in leadership positions was limited because of her poor health. Throughout the 1950s her health problems escalated, exacerbated by the prescription of cortisone for her asthma, which had terrible side effects. Simons had to go to the Johns Hopkins Medical Center in Baltimore, Maryland, to be weaned from the drug, and her daughter recalls that she never fully recovered from this episode. If she had, she may have gone on to serve on the national board of the LWV.[62]

In spite of her ill health, Simons continued to be as active as possible in the LWVSC, and in the late 1950s she often served in an advisory role. Her knowledge and experience was particularly valuable when the LWVSC began a campaign to secure the right of women to serve on juries.

In the 1950s, South Carolina, Mississippi, and Alabama were the only remaining states that did not allow women to serve on state juries.[63] In 1957, following the suggestion of a member of the national board, Simons and other South Carolina league members launched a campaign for an amendment to the state constitution that would remove this barrier to full citizenship for women.[64] South Carolina's recalcitrance on this issue was highlighted when South Carolina women were granted the right to serve on federal juries by the 1957 Civil Rights Act. This eliminated the requirement that federal jury lists had to be drawn from lists of citizens who were allowed to serve on state juries, but in South Carolina women continued to be excluded.[65] The opposition to jury duty for women was couched in familiar paternalistic terms. In the language of protection of white womanhood, male politicians tried to convince the South Carolina public that there were many dangers involved in allowing women to serve on juries.

The arguments used by South Carolina opponents of women's jury service during this controversy bore a striking resemblance to those used in the South against woman suffrage decades earlier and also anticipated future arguments used by opponents of the proposed Equal Rights Amendment in the late 1970s and early 1980s. Antisuffragists had argued that women's participation in politics would upset the home, that women did not want to vote, and that woman suffrage would undermine essential traditions and practices regarding race as well as gender. Most opponents of the ERA also wished to maintain the status quo and insisted that that the ERA would usher in unwanted changes including unisex bathrooms, military combat roles for women, and homosexual marriage.[66]

The LWVSC's jury service campaign relied on the support of allies attained over the years through the networking of leaders like Simons. By 1960 representatives from the LWVSC were working with various women's organizations such as the Federation of Women's Clubs, the Business and Professional Woman's Clubs, and the American Association of University Women.[67] They also approached women outside these organizations, including farm women. The league worked with other women's organizations and civic groups in conducting a hearing before the House of Representatives Judiciary Committee in 1959.[68]

Allies also included leagues in other southern states. Simons and other members came to rely on communication with those leagues who were currently dealing with the issue or who had recently done so. Mississippi and South Carolina shared a "common goal" in their attack on the exclusion of women from jury service, as the cover of the March 1958 *South Carolina Voter* proclaimed on its front cover.[69] Following the lead of their LWV counterparts in Mississippi, the South Carolina league produced a successful pamphlet entitled "Well Honestly."[70]

As on other issues, LWVSC members saw their main role in the jury service movement as educational. They planned a series of speeches and a media campaign using newspapers, radio, and television. In order to reach women around the state the league urged women to leave copies of "Well Honestly" in doctors' and dentists' offices and libraries and to send them to "civic minded men."[71]

The campaign for jury service for women had support from a number of legislators, officials, and newspaper editors. The LWVSC could rely on the help of a supportive female legislator from Columbia, Martha Thomas Fitzgerald, who introduced legislation on jury service for women throughout the 1950s. There were also male legislators who supported the LWVSC and its efforts.[72] In December 1957, Walker E. Anderson, representative for Darlington County, wrote to Caroline Toms that "as you probably know, a few of us tried to and did support this program during the past year while the Legislature was in session but to no avail."[73] In addition, in July 1958 it was reported that all the candidates for governor supported the idea of women serving on juries. Ernest Hollings, who would go on to win the election, offered special assurances that he would continue to assist the LWVSC.[74]

Despite this support, the LWVSC faced strong opposition from many other

South Carolina leaders. The LWVSC divided the arguments of their opponents into four main points: an article in the October 1957 issue of the league's publication, the *South Carolina Voter*, proclaimed, "There's the washroom argument, the one about the woman's place at home, that statement that courtroom testimony might be unfit for you to hear, and lastly, the real clincher . . . women are too emotional."[75] Governor Timmerman was among the critics of female jury service. In 1958 he said that he believed compulsory jury service would damage women's child-rearing abilities.[76] As during the woman suffrage movement, opponents used race to argue against the proposed change in women's political participation. Senator Francis Jones of Lexington said that he did not want to "expose my wife and your wife to having to argue with a male Negro or a Negro woman as to the outcome of a verdict." Jones also stated that if black women were permitted the right to serve on juries it would lead to more of them registering to vote.[77]

In a further development of the race argument, Senator T. Allen Legare of Charleston voiced his opinion that in order to accommodate men and women of both races at least two new restrooms would need to be built in courthouses. Senator Julius Ness of Bamberg agreed: "South Carolina would be in the position of having white mothers and Negro mothers sitting on the same jury and using the same rest room but their children couldn't go to school together."[78] In response to the level of concern being raised in the senate about racial mixing and restrooms, Toms wrote to the national LWV president: "We thought we'd picked a nice safe subject, too, but now jury service for women seems to be riddled through with racial involvements. We find we must pick our way with care."[79]

The LWVSC used the "Well Honestly" pamphlet to refute their opponents' arguments. In it they explained that women with small children would be exempt from service, and therefore the risk to the quality of child rearing in the state would be minimal. As for restrooms in courthouses, the pamphlet did not mention race, but stated that, if the problem could be solved in forty-five other states, it could be solved in South Carolina. Courthouses already provided for female employees and witnesses. Furthermore, to answer fears about women hearing "sordid" testimony, the pamphlet argued that women already heard such testimony in their roles as witnesses, social workers, and lawyers, and that in cases where girls and women were involved it would be good to have women present. The pamphlet also pointed out that women should not be prevented from taking their share of responsibility in law enforcement, as they were important business owners and operators and consumers.[80]

"Well Honestly" was widely distributed, including to every member of the South Carolina legislature. It did not directly confront race arguments, but it did confront quite directly the idea that it was appropriate and acceptable to restrict the rights and duties of women who were citizens of the state. Repeatedly they expressed "surprise" at the resistance to extending to women this basic right now exercised by women across most of the nation. For example, this statement from Caroline Toms of Charleston appeared in a Spartanburg newspaper: "Many women will be surprised and puzzled by such an excessive reaction to what seems to them a reasonable request. Women of South Carolina are not asking for any special privilege. We are offering to share with men an obligation of citizenship in free countries for which we think we are qualified." Toms went on to argue that equality in education, voting, tax paying, professions, business, and government were all reasons to allow women to serve on juries. She concluded her rebuke with the question: "Isn't justice as much the concern of women as of men?"[81]

Simons at this point was working mainly behind the scenes; she wrote a letter to a judge who had said that women should be excused from jury service on the grounds that they were responsible for taking care of homes and children. Her letter suggests that just as the LWVSC did not address the race issue directly, it also sidestepped rather than argue against the idea that women should be assumed to be busy with domestic duties. She did, however, reject the idea that women were sheltered creatures. She wrote:

> True the young women busy with babies and "broiling size" children will not be able to absent themselves from their homes, but by the time a woman is forty she has some freedom and not being always professionally occupied she is willing to serve her state as a juror. We also feel that life has involved us heavily in much of its grimness and ruggedness, that we are not easily subject to shock, we don't go in for Victorian vapors and do not expect to be treated like tender flowers.

Simons then explained that women already were professionals or assisted their husbands in business and paid taxes. Finally, she reminded the judge that women raised both sons and daughters and that the former would be allowed to participate in South Carolina politics while the latter might "still be relegated to the class of over-protected, unused, taxed but not recognized 'electors'!"[82] Simons fiercely defended the women of South Carolina and their desire to serve on juries. However, it was a reflection of Simons's moderate progressiveness that the woman whose rights she defended seemed to be a combination of the traditional—the mother of tomorrow's citizens—and the modern—the owner of a business.

In the early 1960s, the LWVSC decided to retreat on the issue of women's jury service, as there appeared to be no hope of getting a bill passed and the public was apathetic. Not until 1967, as a new feminist movement was emerging across the nation, did South Carolina women finally gain the right to serve on state juries. That the state so belatedly granted this fundamental right of citizens indicated the level of opposition to full participation by women in civic affairs.

The story of Harriet Simons and the LWVSC during the early years of the organization's rejuvenation following World War II provides insight into the challenges faced by women seeking to take part in the politics and welfare of South Carolina. In the mid-twentieth century—as in other eras in the state's history—reactionary elements within state and regional politics made progress difficult for women and for African Americans. Many of the campaigns and issues with which Simons and the LWVSC became involved demonstrate that gender and race were often tied together quite deliberately by politicians attempting to maintain the status quo. Accordingly, many white women, even those considered to be progressive, sought to expand the boundaries of their own participation in public life by carefully cultivating support without creating additional opposition, and they thereby slowly made advances. Seeking progress for themselves and their state, reform-minded women such as Harriet Simons achieved much but had much to overcome.

Simons was aware of the boundaries to the participation of women in public life and pragmatically and gradually expanded them while working for civic improvement as well as to secure access to birth control and jury service for South Carolina women. She was able to use her status and experience in public life to influence women and men around her and to withstand and confront the hostility that her more controversial actions aroused. Her reform efforts were not always successful, but her achievements included the establishment and growth of the League of Women Voters in South Carolina and successful leadership of this important organization during periods of crisis. For the rest of the twentieth century and into the twenty-first, the LWVSC would continue to be a force for progress in the state.

NOTES

1. Speech, 1948, series 26, box 72, folder 13, Harriet Porcher Stoney Simons papers, 1916–71, South Carolina Historical Society, Charleston (hereinafter cited as HPSSP-SCHS).

2. Harriet Simons Williams, interview by author, Charleston, S.C., March 9, 2005.

3. Biographical outlines 1, 2, 3, and 4, series 26, box 71, folder 3, HPSSP-SCHS; speech, 1948, series 26, box 72, folder 13, HPSSP-SCHS; Williams, interview by author, March 9, 2005; author to Williams, July 28, 2005; Williams to author, July 28, 2005.

4. Author to Williams, July 28, 2005; Williams to author, July 28, 2005.

5. Biographical outline 4, series 26, box 71, folder 3, HPSSP-SCHS.

6. Ibid.

7. Williams, interview by author, March 9, 2005; biographical outline 4, series 26, box 71, folder 3, HPSSP-SCHS. Sanger is regarded as the most important figure in the movement for birth control in the United States at a time when it was illegal even to distribute information on birth control through the mail. She played a major role in pressing for the invention of new methods of contraception. See Ellen Chesler, *Woman of Valor: Margaret Sanger and the Birth Control Movement in America* (New York: Simon and Schuster, 1992).

8. Birth control was prescribed "to mothers for whom it is medically indicated" by doctors at maternal and child health clinics in every county. Some scholars have stated that southern states were receptive to birth control programs because they saw it as a means to curb their black populations, but in South Carolina the birth control program coincided with efforts to save babies, black and white, by improving medical services (by, for example, training midwives). See Patricia Evridge Hill's essay in this volume. Also see "Birth Control: South Carolina Uses It for Public Health," *Life*, May 6, 1940, 64–68; Patricia Evridge Hill, "Go Tell It on the Mountain: Hilla Sheriff and Public Health in the South Carolina Piedmont, 1929 to 1940," *American Journal of Public Health* 85, no. 4 (1995): 578–84. On ideas about birth control in this era, see John D'Emilio and Estelle B. Freedman, *Intimate Matters: A History of Sexuality in America* (New York: Harper and Row, 1988), esp. 247, 248.

9. Williams, interview by author, March 9, 2005; biographical outline 4, series 26, box 71, folder 3, HPSSP-SCHS; Mrs. Frederick E. Kredel to Kenneth M. Lynch, president, Medical College of South Carolina, March 27, 1952, series 26, box 72, folder 1, HPSSP-SCHS; report on the future of the clinic sponsored by the Maternal Welfare Bureau, December 16, 1954, series 26, box 72, folder 1, HPSSP-SCHS.

10. Speech, 1948, series 26, box 72, folder 13, HPSSP-SCHS; "'Working Together': To the *News and Courier*," clipping, *Charleston News and Courier*, February 12, c. 1941–43, series 26, box 72, folder 5, HPSSP-SCHS.

11. Speech, 1948, series 26, box 72, folder 13, HPSSP-SCHS; biographical outline 3, series 26, box 71, folder 3, HPSSP-SCHS.

12. Speech, 1948, series 26, box 72, folder 13, HPSSP-SCHS; biographical outline 3, series 26, box 71, folder 3, HPSSP-SCHS.

13. Biographical outlines 1, 2, 3, and 4, series 26, box 71, folder 3, HPSSP-SCHS.

14. Mary Bryan, *Proud Heritage: A History of the League of Women Voters of South Carolina* (Columbia: League of Women Voters of South Carolina, 1978), 31–32.

15. Bryan, *Proud Heritage*, 21; biographical outlines 2, 3, and 4, series 26, box 71, folder 3, HPSSP-SCHS.

16. Bryan, *Proud Heritage*, 81.

17. Marcia Synnott, "Desegregation in South Carolina, 1950–1963: Sometime "Between 'Now' and 'Never,'" in *Looking South: Chapters in the Story of An American Region*, ed. Winfred B. Moore Jr. and Joseph F. Tripp (New York: Greenwood Press, 1989), 53; Tony Badger, "From Defiance to Moderation: South Carolina Governors and Racial Change," unpublished paper, 5; Walter Edgar, *South Carolina: A History* (Columbia: University of South Carolina Press, 1998), 522–23.

18. David G. Blick, "Beyond 'The Politics of Color': Opposition to South Carolina's 1952 Constitutional Amendment to Abolish the Public School System," *Proceedings of the South Carolina Historical Association* (Columbia: South Carolina Historical Association, 1995), 23.

19. Ibid., 20–21.

20. Ibid., 27.

21. Memorandum from Mrs. Martin D. Young to local and state program resource chairmen, July 28, 1952, program files, box 21, human resources, education, school amendment, 1951–54, League of Women Voters of South Carolina Papers, South Carolina Political Collections, University of South Carolina Libraries, University of South Carolina, Columbia (hereinafter cited as LWVSCP-SCPC).

22. John G. Sproat, "'Firm Flexibility': Perspectives on Desegregation in South Carolina," in *New Perspectives on Race and Slavery in America*, ed. Robert H. Abzug and Stephen E. Maizlish (Lexington: University Press of Kentucky, 1986), 165; Badger, "From Defiance to Moderation," 14.

23. Minutes, meeting of LWV presidents of southern states, Atlanta, Ga., July 27–28, 1954, series 26, box 75, folder 16, HPSSP-SCHS.

24. Bryan, *Proud Heritage*, 34; Simons to W. H. Nicolson Jr., June 21, 1952, program files, box 21, human resources, education, school amendment, 1951–54, LWVSCP-SCPC.

25. Simons to Mrs. J. O. Erwin, May 21, 1952, program files, box 21, human resources, education, school amendment, 1951–54, LWVSCP-SCPC.

26. Report on conference with Governor James F. Byrnes, May 26, 1952, program files, box 21, human resources, education, school amendment, 1951–54, LWVSCP-SCPC.

27. Ibid.

28. Blick, "Beyond 'The Politics of Color,'" 27.

29. Mrs. Albert Simons to Mrs. Martin D. Young, May 30, 1952, program files, box 21, human resources, education, school amendment, 1951–54, LWVSCP-SCPC.

30. Ibid.

31. Bryan, *Proud Heritage*, 35.

32. Cherisse R. Jones, "'How Shall I Sing the Lord's Song?' United Church Women Confront Racial Issues in South Carolina, 1940s–1960s," in *Throwing Off the Cloak of Privilege: White Southern Women Activists in the Civil Rights Era*, ed. Gail S. Murray (Gainesville: University Press of Florida, 2004), 139.

33. Report, South Carolina public school amendment vote, November 4, 1952, administrative records, box 1, general, 1950–60, League of Women Voters of Columbia/Richland County Papers, SCPC (hereinafter cited as LWVCP-SCPC).

34. Ibid.

35. Ibid.; Blick, "Beyond 'The Politics of Color,'" 29.

36. Report, South Carolina Public School Amendment vote, November 4, 1952, administrative records, box 1, general, 1950–60, LWVCP-SCPC.

37. Bryan, *Proud Heritage*, 35.

38. Memorandum, Cain Haley to league members, April 1, 1953, administrative records, box 15, local leagues, Greenville, general, 1947–59, LWVSCP-SCPC; "Women Voters Oppose Schools Amendment," *The State*, October 9, 1952, program files, box 21, human resources, education, school amendment, 1951–54, LWVSCP-SCPC; radio broadcast, October 22, 1952, program files, box 1, Constitution, state, 1952–55, League of Women Voters of Spartanburg Papers, SCPC (hereinafter cited as LWVSP-SCPC); "Why the League of Women Voters Opposes the Proposed Constitutional Amendment to Remove State Responsibility for a System of Free Public Schools," series 26, box 75, folder 16, HPSSP-SCHS.

39. Blick, "Beyond 'The Politics of Color,'" 29–30; Matthew D. Lassiter, *The Silent Majority: Suburban Politics in the Sunbelt South* (Princeton, N.J.: Princeton University Press, 2006), 29, 81.

40. Mrs. Lee to Mrs. Yaghjian, December 3, 1952, administrative records, box 1, correspondence, general, 1949–60, LWVCP-SCPC.

41. Minutes, meeting of LWV presidents of southern states, Atlanta, Ga., July 27–28, 1954, series 26, box 75, folder 16, HPSSP-SCHS.

42. Ibid.

43. Bryan, *Proud Heritage*, 36.

44. Blick, "Beyond 'The Politics of Color,'" 30.

45. Young, *In the Public Interest*, 172.

46. Millicent Ellison Brown, "Civil Rights Activism in Charleston, South Carolina, 1940–1970" (PhD diss., Florida State University, 1997), 259–64.

47. Brown, "Civil Rights Activism in Charleston, South Carolina," 259–64; minutes, meeting of LWV presidents of southern states, Atlanta, Ga., July 27–28, 1954, series 26, box 75, folder 16, HPSSP-SCHS; Bryan, *Proud Heritage*, 44; Williams, interview by author, March 9, 2005.

48. Brown, "Civil Rights Activism in Charleston, South Carolina," 262–63.

49. Minutes, meeting of LWV presidents of southern states, Atlanta, Ga., July 27–28, 1954, series 26, box 75, folder 16, HPSSP-SCHS.

50. Simons to Mrs. P. R. McIntosh, December 14, 1954, administrative records, box 1, general, 1954, LWVSCP-SCPC.

51. Williams, interview by author, March 9, 2005.

52. Ibid. Anne King Gregorie and Flora Belle Surles lived together in Charleston and were both active members of the LWV in Charleston. Gregorie was the first woman to receive a doctorate in history from USC and helped to found the Charleston branch of the American Association of University Women. Surles wrote a book about Gregorie (*Anne King Gregorie* [Columbia, S.C.: R. L. Bryan, 1968]).

53. Minutes, meeting of LWV presidents of southern states, Atlanta, Ga., July 27–28, 1954, series 26, box 75, folder 16, HPSSP-SCHS.

54. Williams, interview by author, March 9, 2005.

55. Simons to Mrs. P. R. McIntosh, December 14, 1954, administrative records, box 1, general, 1954, LWVSCP-SCPC.

56. Ibid.

57. Minutes, meeting of LWV presidents of southern states, Atlanta, Ga., July 27–28, 1954, series 26, box 75, folder 16, HPSSP-SCHS.

58. Bryan, *Proud Heritage*, 47, 44.

59. Williams, interview by author, March 9, 2005; Bryan, *Proud Heritage*, 44.

60. Bryan, *Proud Heritage*, 44.

61. Christina Greene, *Our Separate Ways: Women and the Black Freedom Movement in Durham, North Carolina* (Chapel Hill: University of North Carolina Press, 2005), 51.

62. Williams, interview by author, March 9, 2005; Williams to author, July 28, 2005.

63. Sarah Leverette, "Celebrating Our Past, Charting Our Future," September 10, 1990, 2, administrative records, box 3, folder, league history, Columbia, LWVCP-SCPC.

64. Bryan, *Proud Heritage*, 45.

65. Ibid., 48.

66. James O. Farmer Jr., "Eulalie Salley and Emma Dunovant: A Complementary Pair of Suffragists," in *South Carolina Women: Their Lives and Times*, vol. 2, ed. Marjorie Spruill, Valinda W. Littlefield, and Joan Marie Johnson (Athens: University of Georgia Press, 2010), 144–65; Amy Thompson McCandless, "Anita Pollitzer: A South Carolina Advocate for Equal Rights," in *South Carolina Women*, 166–89; Elna C. Green, *Southern Strategies: Southern Women and the Woman Suffrage Question* (Chapel Hill: University of North Carolina Press, 1997), 80, 84–85; Marjorie

Spruill Wheeler, *New Women of the New South: The Leaders of the Woman Suffrage Movement in the Southern States* (New York: Oxford University Press, 1993). On the 1970s, see Marjorie Julian Spruill, "Victoria Eslinger, Keller Bumgardner Barron, Mary Heriot, Tootsie Holland, and Pat Callair: Champions of Women's Rights in South Carolina," in this volume.

67. Meeting, February 20, 1958, administrative records, box 3, meetings, board, minutes, 1957–58, LWVCP-SCPC; meeting, January 19, 1959, administrative records, box 3, meetings, general, 1955–59, LWVCP-SCPC; meeting, February 18, 1960, administrative records, box 3, meetings, board, minutes, 1959–60, LWVCP-SCPC.

68. Meeting, February 20, 1958, administrative records, box 3, meetings, board, minutes, 1957–58, LWVCP-SCPC; meeting, January 19, 1959, administrative records, box 3, meetings, general, 1955–59, LWVCP-SCPC; meeting, February 18, 1960, administrative records, box 3, meetings, board, minutes, 1959–60, LWVCP-SCPC.

69. Meeting, March 21, 1957, administrative records, box 3, meetings, board, minutes, 1957–58, LWVCP-SCPC; "South Carolina, Mississippi—a Common Goal," *The South Carolina Voter*, March 1958, 1, 3.

70. Bryan, *Proud Heritage*, 48–49; meeting, December 12, 1957, administrative records, box 3, meetings, board, minutes, 1957–58, LWVCP-SCPC.

71. Meeting, February 18, 1960, administrative records, box 3, meetings, board, minutes, 1959–60, LWVCP-SCPC; "League of Women Voters of South Carolina: Jury Service Workshop," November 13, 1958, program files, box 2, judiciary, jury service for women, 1957–58, LWVSP-SCPC.

72. Bryan, *Proud Heritage*, 47; Mrs. C. Smith Toms to Mrs. J. M. H. Fitzgerald, May 26, 1957, box 46, folder 274, Martha Thomas Fitzgerald Papers, 1895–1981, Louise Pettus Archives and Special Collections, Dacus Library, Winthrop University, Rock Hill, S.C. (hereinafter cited as MTFP-LPASC).

73. Walker E. Anderson to Mrs. C. Smith Toms, December 17, 1957, box 46, folder 274, MTFP-LPASC.

74. Mrs. C. Smith Toms to state board members and league presidents, July 1, 1958, administrative records, box 13, local leagues, general, 1954–62, LWVSCP-SCPC.

75. *South Carolina Voter*, October 1957, 1.

76. "On Jury Service: Women Voters Disappointed at Timmerman's Statement," *The State*, February 22, 1958.

77. "By State Senate: Women Jurors Resolution Shuttled Back to Oblivion," *The State*, April 4, 1958.

78. "From the Spartanburg Papers," April 4, 1958, program files, box 2, judiciary, jury service for women, 1957–58, LWVSP-SCPC; "By State Senate."

79. Mrs. C. Smith Toms to Mrs. Errol Horner, January 13, 1958, administrative files, box 1, general, 1958–59, LWVSCP-SCPC.

80. "Well Honestly—a Few Words in Answer to Critics of the Idea That Jury Service Is for All Citizens in South Carolina," box 46, folder 277, MTFP-LPASC.

81. "From the Spartanburg Papers," April 5, 1958, program files, box 2, judiciary, jury service for women, 1957–58, LWVSP-SCPC.

82. Mrs. Albert Simons to the Honorable C. C. Wyche, January 17, 1959, series 26, box 74, folder 2, HPSSP-SCHS.

Alice Buck Norwood
Spearman Wright

A Civil Rights Activist

MARCIA G. SYNNOTT

❀ ❀ ❀

Alice Buck Norwood Spearman Wright (1902–89), executive director of the biracial South Carolina Council on Human Relations (SCCHR) from 1954 to 1967, was one of the few white women in her state deeply committed to advancing civil rights for African Americans. She was a liberal voice within the council, a moderate group that, under her influence, began to work more directly to end segregation. Marion Allen Wright, president of the South Carolina division of the Southern Regional Council (SRC) after World War II and then SRC itself in the 1950s, described Spearman as the only member to speak forthrightly, though "soft voiced and emotional," for integration and against sending black students out of state to segregated regional universities.[1] Perpetually networking, she reached out through the SCCHR to give African Americans "the confidence that they could win."[2] Spearman forged many connections between blacks and whites in the state, as well as aided in bringing together local activists with national leaders. Particularly effective at nurturing relationships with African Americans without personally alienating whites, she was able to mentor college students, communicate the council's position to politicians, and nudge some businessmen into complying peacefully with the desegregation of their own stores or establishments.

Spearman's progressive beliefs and interpersonal skills evolved as she matured. She had been schooled in the class and gender assumptions of white southern ladies by her mother, a great-granddaughter of one of the state's largest slave owners. But Spearman's innate curiosity led her to question the confines of her privileged childhood in Marion, South Carolina. She later described her personal evolution: "I might say that my early childhood was so sheltered, that it developed in me, a determination to see what was across the fence. And so I have always had a desire for new experiences. I have also been determined that I was going to know people of all walks of life. I'm happy to say that my father's attitudes were very, very democratic, and he too felt that way."[3] By becoming "a questioning rebel," Spearman began to break free of her "cultural conditioning," a process that accelerated when she participated in the student YWCA at Converse College in Spartanburg, South Carolina.[4]

The YWCA prepared her for personal and social activism in ways that anticipated the influence that the women's movement had on young women in the 1960s and 1970s.[5] At Converse, Spearman served on the interracial committee of the student YWCA and evolved into a liberal Baptist who believed segregation contravened the New Testament. A member of the YWCA's Student-Industrial Commission, whose members were equally represented by Converse students and young women employed in Spartanburg textile mills, Spearman was one of twelve college women in the South selected by the YWCA's national board to participate in "a student-in-industry" summer experiment in Atlanta. The ninety-five-pound, five-foot-five-and-a-half-inch Spearman turned sacks inside out on the eleven-hour day shift at the Fulton Bag and Cotton Mill. Student government association president her senior year, she earned a bachelor of arts degree in history and literature in 1923.[6]

In 1926, Spearman headed to New York City to attend the resident YWCA National Training School and to earn a master's degree in religious education at Columbia Teachers College. She then worked for the Germantown, Pennsylvania, YWCA.[7] Inspired by that experience to broaden her horizons internationally, she traveled around the world from 1930 to 1932. En route, she attended the fifth All-India Woman's Conference on educational and social reform in Lahore, where she felt "a real awakening" after meeting "women of intelligence & influence from all over India."[8]

Returning home to Depression-era South Carolina, she found her father dead and family assets sharply reduced. Through both family prominence and her own ambition, Spearman was appointed the state's first woman relief director in Marion County. She also helped set up relief for workers who took part in the United Textile Workers of America strike in September 1934. Later she was made the state supervisor of education for federal programs in adult and worker education.[9] These work experiences pushed Spearman to become a "dyed-in-the-wool socialist," and she positioned herself somewhat left of the

ALICE BUCK NORWOOD SPEARMAN WRIGHT
Courtesy of South Caroliniana Library,
University of South Carolina, Columbia, S.C.

center within the New Deal. Thus, she united her liberal feminist views on women's capabilities with a socialist feminist perspective about the ways class, gender, and racial divisions sustained the white male power structure.[10]

In November 1935, she married Eugene H. Spearman Sr., whom she had met when he was working for the South Carolina State Employment Service and the federal rural rehabilitation program. She moved to his dairy and tree farm in Newberry, renamed Algene Acres. After she gave birth to their son, Eugene H. Spearman Jr., on January 14, 1937, her husband "took maternity leave" so that she could continue to direct the teachers of the school for workers' education, because the Employment Act of 1932 barred both spouses from being federal employees. She contributed to their marital partnership both with her earned income and by helping her husband write political speeches for his two success-ful campaigns for supervisor of Newberry County, a position roughly equiva-lent to the chair of county council. At that time, Newberry was a highly union-ized town with three cotton mills, and both Spearmans were sympathetic to the living conditions of mill workers and their children.[11]

Often overwhelmed by family responsibilities—her husband's heart attack, her son's rheumatic fever, and her semi-invalid mother coming to live in their rustic and drafty house—Spearman found release by immersing herself in pro-gressive causes. She joined the South Carolina Committee on Interracial Co-operation and later its successor, the South Carolina division of the SRC.[12] In 1951 financial need forced Spearman to relinquish her part-time work for the council to become full-time executive secretary of the South Carolina Federa-tion of Women's Clubs in Columbia and associate editor of the South Caro-lina *Clubwoman*. She wanted members to discuss substantive, even controver-sial, topics at their meetings—for example, the status of women and the Equal Rights Amendment, civil rights for blacks, Mexicans, American Indians, and others, the United Nations charter of universal rights, and economic and so-cial conflicts dividing capitalists and laborers.[13] Instead, they avoided discussing these issues, especially racial segregation, preferring to talk about their children and grandchildren and favorite recipes. Not only was Spearman bored stiff by the typical concerns of clubwomen but she complained that they "were very inconsiderate" in calling her "any time of the day or night."[14]

In October 1954, her statewide contacts and years of volunteer and part-time work made her the successful candidate for the new salaried position of execu-tive director of the South Carolina division of the SRC, paid through a large grant to the council from the Ford Foundation's Fund for the Republic. One of Spearman's major goals as executive director of the division, renamed the South Carolina Council on Human Relations in January 1955, was to convince black and white South Carolinians that they should participate in the decision-making process concerning desegregation even at the risk of challenging the white power structure. Many African Americans were inhibited by poverty and lack of education from speaking out, but many whites had simply insulated themselves from human relations issues. When she tried to encourage civic, educational, professional, and religious organizations to openly discuss the Supreme Court's May 17, 1954, *Brown v. Board of Education* decision declaring segregated public schools unconstitutional, she encountered silence, which turned to sharp opposition after the court's May 1955 implementation decree.[15]

Sometimes working eighteen or more hours a day, Spearman balanced an ardent commitment to improving race relations with a pragmatic respect for southern manners. She dressed like a lady and frequently signed herself "Mrs. Eugene H. Spearman." Her success as executive director was due, said Rose Rubin, wife of Hyman S. Rubin Sr., a former Columbia city councilman and state senator, to her "sharp intellect and a quiet, very ladylike manner," which gained her the acceptance that "a louder" person would not have had. By the time Spearman retired after thirteen years, on September 1, 1967, her tenure was the longest of any state council executive director, man or woman.[16]

A month after becoming executive director, Spearman had to deal with repercussions of an event that deeply alienated the white clubwomen she was trying to recruit to the council. At the center of the controversy were federal district Judge J. Waties Waring, his twice-divorced second wife, and SRC president Marion A. Wright's tribute to the judge at a testimonial dinner sponsored by the South Carolina Conference of NAACP Branches. White South Carolinians socially ostracized Judge Waring after he struck down the all-white primary in 1947 and 1948 and then divorced his first wife to marry Elizabeth Avery Mills Hoffman, a winter resident from Connecticut. Most egregious of all to many white South Carolinians was Judge Waring's dissent in *Briggs v. Elliott* (1951) from the majority opinion upholding public school segregation in Clarendon County, a dissent that was unanimously adopted by the Supreme Court in the *Brown* decision. Elizabeth Waring further inflamed white Charlestonians by publicly condemning their racial attitudes. Harassed by obscene telephone calls, hate mail, and broken windows, Waring retired in 1952 and moved with his wife to New York City. On November 6, 1954, they returned to Charleston for the testimonial dinner attended by NAACP special counsel Thurgood Marshall.[17] Alice Spearman, who registered guests, was distressed to hear that many whites felt the dinner honoring Judge Waring was an affront. The dinner outraged some of the same women Spearman was courting for the council—moderate white clubwomen like Harriet Porcher Stoney Simons, president of the South Carolina League of Women Voters, and her friend Charleston novelist Josephine Pinckney.[18]

The emotional response of Simons and Pinckney reflected a growing white resistance to any changes in the racial status quo in South Carolina. In reaction to the Supreme Court's decree that public school desegregation should be implemented "with all deliberate speed," most white South Carolinians grew more vociferous in their opposition to desegregation. By August 1955, fifty-two "influential and highly respected" persons posted a resolution in the newspaper calling on the general assembly to interpose state sovereignty to maintain segregated schools. The emboldened Citizens' Councils of America, States Rights League of South Carolina, and Ku Klux Klan of America made tension and fear palpable.[19] From 1955 to 1957, South Carolina launched a massive resistance campaign. On the recommendation of Senator L. Marion Gressette's Special Segregation Committee, voters approved the repeal of the state's compulsory school attendance law. Legislators also passed an administrative act that would cut off funds to any school that admitted a pupil under a court-ordered transfer. Another act of the general assembly would close South Carolina State College if a court-ordered admission of a black student to one of the five state-supported white colleges forced that white school's closing. An additional law barred NAACP members from local, county, and state government jobs. Spearman decried these laws, which she argued inhibited the latent decency in many South Carolinians.[20] As cautiously moderate voices were silenced, the SCCHR's membership precipitously declined from around five hundred to one hundred.[21]

The SCCHR also faced declining financial support from the regional organization and internal problems. When, in 1957, the SCCHR was informed by the SRC that it must assume greater independence as an affiliate, its board of directors raised dues and sent Spearman on one of her many fund-raising trips to Philadelphia and New York.[22] With staff input, she and the executive committee put together the council's July 12, 1957, request for financial aid from the SRC. In it, she contended that although "most of the positive forces in South Carolina today are frozen assets and respond slowly to thawing processes," she believed that whites would respond to "a positive appeal to pride in raising standards of living for all people." The SCCHR requested $8,000 of its projected $13,200 budget from the SRC. Both Spearman and associate director James Thomas McCain, an African American professor and dean at Morris College in Sumter, were to be paid $5,000 each; the part-time secretary would receive $1,200.[23] But after SRC executive director Harold C. Fleming reduced its grant to $5,000, the SCCHR, which could afford to pay only one director, concluded that "a white person could possibly work alone more effectively than a Negro." The council again offered Spearman the executive directorship, and McCain was informed "regretfully" that it could no longer pay his salary. Hired as field secretary by the Congress on Racial Equality (CORE) for its drive into the South, McCain organized student sit-ins and voter registration drives and formed groups on black campuses.[24]

Despite these problems, with a statewide membership of about seven hundred, the SCCHR was "the only organization strategically set-up for" coordinating activities within and between black and white groups. Partly because of Spearman's tireless efforts, almost thirty groups—various chapters of the SCCHR, the YWCA (of Columbia, Greenville, Aiken, and Charleston), the United Church Women of South Carolina, and other religious organizations and social agencies—were working biracially.[25]

Serving as executive director had its hazards. Spearman moved her office four times after whites complained to building owners about the council or its biracial staff. Anonymous telephone calls asked repeatedly whether her office was the NAACP. A white man so intimidated a part-time black bookkeeper that she decided not to return. Another young white man struck Spearman on the head when she was alone in the office. Earl M. Middleton, an African American owner of an Orangeburg real estate business and a council officer, found Spearman on the floor bleeding from her head and face. Though the police came, she never mentioned the attack in her oral histories.[26] Perhaps this was because she knew that other South Carolinians were in similar danger. A friend of the SCCHR, Septima Poinsette Clark of Charleston was one of more than two hundred black teachers dismissed or forced to resign from their positions. Other whites also suffered. Spearman was shocked when the Ku Klux Klan dynamited the Gaffney home of Claudia Thomas Sanders, in November 1957, because of the statement she contributed to *Moderate Approach to Race Relations*, a pamphlet compiled by five Protestant ministers.[27]

Spearman's persistence—and acceptance of personal risks—began to be rewarded with the 1958 election of Ernest F. (Fritz) Hollings to the governorship. He was not, she emphasized, one of the plantation paternalists.[28] The emergence of energized black South Carolinians also buoyed the council. The catalyst was a change of leadership in the South Carolina Conference of NAACP Branches in the person of I. DeQuincey Newman, a United Methodist minister in Spartanburg and NAACP state field secretary, who was elected state conference president and later served as its activist field director. In February 1959, the state NAACP executive committee decided to push public school desegregation in Clarendon County and asked Spearman to help prepare the survey forms to screen potential applicants to white schools.[29]

Spearman's success in building bridges came in part from her ability to collaborate effectively with African Americans from many different organizations, including the NAACP and the Southern Christian Leadership Conference (SCLC). Spearman "was just wild about" Ella Josephine Baker, whom she got to know while serving on a South Carolina interorganizational steering committee for the SCLC's semiannual regional conference held at Columbia's Township Auditorium in 1959. Baker was then SCLC's acting executive director and the only woman administrative staff member. For two months Spearman and three volunteers developed a comprehensive mailing list from black membership rolls, including churches, burial societies, and the Prince Hall Masons. Spearman later recalled she had become "a complete walking encyclopedia of *any* organization, grass roots and all."[30]

The SCLC statewide arrangements committee promoted the 1959 conference so that not only was it "perhaps the most representative gathering of Negroes ever involved in such a program in South Carolina" but also, according to Spearman, it rose above the rivalry between the two-year-old SCLC and the well-established South Carolina State Conference of the NAACP. After Martin Luther King Jr. made a powerful address, SRC president James McBride Dabbs urged blacks to register and vote for justice.[31]

Spearman was also among the two thousand people listening to baseball star Jackie Robinson's address at Greenville's municipal auditorium during the eighteenth annual meeting of the South Carolina State Conference of the NAACP in October 1959. Spearman then marched in an Emancipation Day Proclamation Prayer Pilgrimage to the Greenville Municipal Airport that CORE field secretary James McCain organized because its manager had threatened to arrest Robinson and the group that came to pick him up for refusing to leave the main waiting room. Spearman had to decline the invitation to be a platform guest and to speak to the crowd, because the SCCHR chairman and executive committee warned her that negative press coverage would discourage white membership. On January 1, 1960, state police, a motorcycle escort provided by Greenville's mayor, and a state patrol dispatched by Governor Hollings protected the orderly and dignified demonstrators, who were greeted by more than three hundred whites at the airport, where they joined in a brief song and prayer service. It was Spearman's impression that this was the first time any southern state had protected demonstrators. The Greenville Airport then desegregated its waiting rooms.[32]

Another positive development occurred in 1959 when South Carolina, despite being the last state to do so, formed an advisory committee to the U.S. Civil Rights Commission. Spearman assisted the U.S. Civil Rights Commission staff in finding qualified black and white South Carolinians, who represented a range

of views, including segregationist, to serve on the seven-member advisory committee. One of its important functions was to hear complaints of discrimination
and police brutality against African Americans. Spearman was appointed to the
advisory committee in 1965.[33]

Imprinting her personality and talents on the SCCHR, Spearman had earned
the trust of African Americans. In March 1960, Paul M. Rilling, then SRC director of field services, complimented South Carolina as "the only state where
I have noted a state council playing a definite role in the power structure of
Negro organizations." Because "the Council seems to have the complete trust
and loyalty of Negroes in S.C., reaching into top leadership," Spearman "sits in
on most meetings of Negro agencies and the Council finds itself appealed to by
one Negro group against the other from time to time." Rilling praised Spearman's indefatigable efforts in carrying the SCCHR's message around the state, the
fruitful contacts she established with the Federation of Colored Women's Clubs,
the interesting meetings she held that often attracted as many as 750 persons,
and her detailed quarterly reports. Rilling also recognized that, although Spearman achieved limited success in organization building, state council executive
directors had a "very frustrating job, many disappointments and defeats." They
had to hold onto white people who feared to take a stand while assisting black
organizations and avoiding political positions that might compromise tax-
exempt status.[34]

By keeping the "lines of communication open" and sowing a "few seeds of
good will" over the years, the SCCHR indirectly assisted moderates as they began
to battle for public opinion. Appealing "to the traditional virtues of courtesy and
decency in trying to solve the state's racial problems," the council positioned
itself, writes historian Paul S. Lofton Jr., a former Wofford College student, as
"the most important of the negotiators."[35] Prompted by the February 1960 sit-ins
by four African American students from North Carolina A&T in Greensboro,
Spearman urged whites to lend their support to "the first effective demands by
Negroes for social change; change in their status as consumers, citizens and
persons."[36] However, during the March 6, 1960, executive board's open meeting the sit-in resolution caused an explosion, and the group "split along racial
lines," reported Paul Rilling. Perhaps because of Spearman's persuasive powers,
"a statement of understanding and endorsement" for the sit-ins emerged from
the executive board's closed session.[37]

The 1960 sit-in movement affected many South Carolina communities, but
it caused particular problems during February and March in Rock Hill, Sumter,
Charleston, Orangeburg, and Columbia. The first four cities experienced more
turbulence than Columbia, where Governor Ernest Hollings's determination to

maintain law and order restrained the sit-in movement.[38] The Orangeburg Student Movement Association, led by Thomas Gaither, head of the NAACP chapter at Claflin College, launched a demonstration on March 15 that coincided with similar demonstrations in Rock Hill and Columbia. Over one thousand Claflin and South Carolina State College students were hosed and gassed by the police. More than 500 were arrested, 350 of whom were put in a temporary stockade for chickens and supplies. In forty-five-degree Fahrenheit weather, they sang "God Bless America" and the "Star-Spangled Banner." Of the 388 charged with "breach of the peace," 341 were convicted. Though ultimately the U.S. Supreme Court reversed the student convictions, demonstrations and racial tensions persisted. In an effort "to locate a leak in the dike of white resistance," Spearman and Fred M. Reese, SCCHR chairman, interviewed several leading businessmen in Orangeburg.[39]

After the Student Nonviolent Coordinating Committee (SNCC) issued a South-wide call for students to join demonstrations in Rock Hill in February 1961, civil rights activism intensified in South Carolina. Those sentenced to pay a fine of $100 or serve thirty days incarceration chose to serve out their sentences, thereby strengthening SNCC's "jail, no bail" policy. "Many SNCC staff and Ella Baker subsequently marked Rock Hill as the true beginning of the organization," observed Mary King, "because of the way it blended SNCC people with a local movement."[40]

After Baker spoke at an SCCHR workshop for college students held at Allen University on February 5, Spearman drove her to Rock Hill so she could attend the SNCC students' trial. Baker had faith, she wrote Spearman, "that in the long haul nothing can beat the combination of deep conviction and a willingness to work for that which you believe."[41] For her part, Spearman admired "the sacrificial effort being made in behalf of a better America" by CORE field secretary Thomas Gaither and the other imprisoned demonstrators and offered to send reading material.[42]

In May 1961, another civil rights confrontation occurred in Rock Hill with the arrival from Washington, D.C., of CORE-sponsored Freedom Riders on buses bound for New Orleans for the seventh anniversary of *Brown*. When John Lewis, a future Georgia congressman, stated his legal right to enter the whites' waiting room he was knocked down, but he did not press charges because of his commitment to nonviolence. In Alabama, however, attacks on the Freedom Riders made national and international headlines when Ku Klux Klansmen firebombed a Greyhound bus. "Happily, little violence has occurred in South Carolina in the wake of the freedom rides," Spearman observed, because the state's power structure restrained white thugs.[43]

The white leadership's political and economic pragmatism was demonstrated by Charles E. Daniel's July 1, 1961, Watermelon Festival speech in Hampton. Daniel, chairman of one of the largest construction firms in the South and a member of the South Carolina Development Board, expressed the consensus views of a group of Greenville business and civic leaders that the state would economically benefit by fulfilling its "obligation to increase the productivity of our Negro citizens, to provide them with good jobs at good wages and to continue to assure them of fair treatment." Spearman considered Daniel's forthright speech to be "the most significant public statement made in South Carolina since the 1954 Supreme Court decision on public school segregation" and had the SCCHR distribute excerpts.[44]

Spearman developed a knack for writing friendly letters to political and business leaders. In a letter to Governor Hollings, she personally pledged "to work constructively with you behind the scenes at any level where dedicated footwork may be needed" and enclosed SCCHR brochures.[45] The council also followed up on Hollings's January 10, 1962, address to the general assembly, in which he proposed a pilot program for industrial and technical training. The council had a vital role to play, Spearman emphasized, in motivating black leaders to seek openings for black youth in state technical education centers. Hollings and leading businessmen understood they needed to offer a share of seats to blacks, who were close to 35 percent of South Carolina's population of 2.4 million. Though no black students were admitted to the first technical education center opened in Greenville in September 1962, fourteen enrolled in them a year later.[46]

The council also worked to desegregate the state's white colleges and universities, in part through its support of the South Carolina Student Council on Human Relations. Established in 1960 as a pioneering initiative of the SCCHR, it expanded statewide the outreach of an earlier Columbia-based student intercollegiate group. Advised by Elizabeth Cowan Ledeen, the student council provided a critical forum through a pilot project that ran from December 1960 to June 1962. Some 280 students from seven black and thirteen white higher educational institutions participated in at least one student council program, conference, or workshop.[47] Ledeen invited civil rights activists from other states, for example, Sandra Cason (Casey) Hayden and Constance Curry, director of the U.S. National Student Association's Southern Project, to share their views. Led by student government officers, campus newspaper editors, and religious organization presidents, the members of the biracial student council served as a conduit for communicating information to their own campuses and supported African American Harvey Gantt's attempt to desegregate Clemson Agricultural College (now Clemson University).[48] In 1962 Governor Hollings had begun to meet informally with business leaders and with Clemson administrators and quietly communicated with J. Arthur Brown, president of the South Carolina Conference of the NAACP, about finding a qualified black applicant. Christopher Gantt, a rigger mechanic at the Charleston Navy Yard, agreed that his twenty-year-old son, Harvey Bernard Gantt, then attending Iowa State University, could be an applicant. Since Clemson would not admit him without a court case, Gantt filed a lawsuit through attorney Matthew J. Perry in July 1962.[49] Demonstrating "a new sense of urgency and historic involvement," the student council invited Harvey Gantt to meet with members at the Penn Center on St. Helena Island in December 1962. They discussed the role of students in "the crisis of the South" and aimed to make, noted Ledeen, "friendship and genuine acceptance a natural and normal part of 'The Clemson Story.'"[50]

In admitting Harvey Gantt peacefully under federal court order, on January 28, 1963, South Carolinians heeded the advice of Governor Hollings's January 9 farewell address: "South Carolina is running out of courts" and the general assembly should accept its responsibilities to maintain "law and order" and to "move on with dignity."[51] On his inauguration day, Governor Donald S. Russell held a biracial barbecue buffet and then effectively implemented a campus security plan at Clemson.[52]

Proud of those Clemson students who welcomed Gantt, Spearman was also encouraged by student council leaders at the University of South Carolina who were preparing for that university's desegregation. Their initiative in supporting integration made a striking contrast to white students in the 1950s, who Spearman remembered as "the most provincial, narrow-minded things I ever talked to in my life."[53] Student leaders thoughtfully discussed "the positive and negative factors in the Clemson situation" at their spring conference, and planned with Ledeen and university chaplains to hold a preenrollment conference with "the Negro students seeking admission." After a one-day hearing, the federal district judge ordered Columbia resident Henrie Monteith, denied admission because "she was a Negro," admitted to the university as a transfer student from the College of Notre Dame in Baltimore. The university also decided to admit Robert G. Anderson Jr. of Greenville as a transfer student from Clark College in Atlanta and James L. Solomon, a teacher at Morris College, as a graduate student in mathematics. The integration of the university on September 11 was uneventful.[54]

During the years of initial desegregation, Spearman mentored both African American and white students associated with the SCCHR Student Council. For University of South Carolina students Dan T. Carter, Charles Joyner, and M. Hayes Mizell, the biracial student council, office meetings, and weekend seminars at the Penn Center with Spearman and Ledeen were defining events in their lives. Carter remembered Spearman as "irrepressible," though dressed like a lady with hat and white gloves, "nattering" or chatting with men and women in the power structure, a tactic she used to prevent them from saying "no" to her liberal point of view.[55]

In South Carolina's conservative though generally law-abiding climate, Spearman and Ledeen offered critical guidance to moderate college students, those who did not feel comfortable in joining SNCC or Students for a Democratic Society, groups they considered too radical. To help broaden their small-town provincialism, Ledeen took University of South Carolina and Winthrop College students to Atlanta in November 1964 to the Southern Student Organizing Committee's planning conference for a southern student human rights movement. In 1965 Spearman and fifteen students from South Carolina colleges attended "Challenge '65," a civil rights symposium at Wake Forest College. Moderate students, black and white, found a friend in Spearman, who was, noted Kenneth Dean, a former executive director of the Mississippi Council on Human Relations, "the mother to a lot of young college people about race, politics, and progressive reform."[56]

As Spearman touched the lives of college students, her own life changed with her husband's death from lung cancer in June 1962.[57] She kept herself busy with the never-ending work of executive director. In 1962 and 1963, the SCCHR, the SCCHR Student Council, and the local Columbia Council on Human Relations assisted lunch counter and restaurant desegregation. Members went to boycotted lunch counters to keep them open and desegregated until other whites patronized them again. At the telephoned request of the Columbia city manager's office, the SCCHR launched Operation Grapevine, which asked its own members and other organizations to buy at complying businesses, chiefly variety stores and movie theaters that had lost white customers.[58] In large measure, desegregation in Columbia was a smooth process because of the influence of citizens' committees selected by the city council and informal biracial luncheon meetings at the University of South Carolina.[59] With the desegregation of Columbia's restaurants, the SCCHR held its first integrated banquet in November 1963, at the Downtowner Motor Inn.[60] In December, Spearman wrote Mayor Lester Bates she had "been heartened at reports that you, the City Council and prominent Columbians are working to achieve an open city for Columbia."[61] Despite the lack of employment opportunities, both black and white citizens could take pride that *Look* magazine bestowed on Columbia the 1964 All-America City Award for its racial progress. Columbia was also praised in *Newsweek* in May 1965 for having "liberated itself from the plague of doctrinal apartheid."[62]

School desegregation in South Carolina also occurred slowly, though largely without violence. "The Charleston public schools quietly and peacefully desegregated," Spearman reported, when, on September 3, 1963, eleven black students entered four previously all-white District 20 public schools. The *News and Courier* called it a "decision for disaster," and white parents began to apply for the general assembly's recently authorized tuition grants.[63] While segregationists could not close public schools, they succeeded that September in having the State Forestry Commission close all state parks—twenty-two for whites and six for blacks. Spearman spoke on behalf of their reopening, in Cheraw, site of the state's first park. By the summer of 1964, some of the state parks reopened on a restricted basis—to picnicking, but not to camping or swimming; full desegregation followed in 1965.[64]

Once desegregation was becoming a reality, Spearman directed her energies to addressing the causes of economic inequality. During the last four years of Spearman's executive directorship, one of the SCCHR's major initiatives addressed the lack of job skills training among the disadvantaged and the problems of rural poverty. From February 1963 to December 1969, the council cosponsored the Rural Advancement Program/Project (RAP), a statewide program planned by its Economics and Employment Committee and CORE. RAP was launched with a Field Foundation grant and a financial contribution from the National Sharecroppers Fund that paid the $6,000 salary of its full-time field representative and director, Leonidas S. James, an African American rural sociologist and psychologist. Spearman praised James's work as a pioneering endeavor to elevate economic and social conditions of low-income families in rural areas, in particular African Americans, by improving their training, job opportunities, and contacts.[65]

The SCCHR and the SRC focused on the possible emergency situations that could arise from the passage of the 1964 Civil Rights Act and the 1965 Voting Rights Act. SRC's Operation Opportunity, a short-term program to assist southern communities preparing for the desegregation of public accommodations, targeted Charleston, Columbia, Greenville, and Spartanburg.[66] The SCCHR developed a comprehensive list of those to invite to two Penn Center conferences to discuss Title 6 of the Civil Rights Act. In April 1965, SCCHR staff and representatives from SCLC, CORE, and the NAACP brought together 250 federal, state, and local representatives from thirty-eight counties, many of them parents, interested in hearing about the procedure for applying to white schools.[67] The council also "was the only non-governmental state-wide agency invited to participate" in a conference of state and federal agencies on the 1964 Economic Opportunity Act.[68] When in 1965 South Carolina counties failed to meet the Office of Economic Opportunity's (OEO) initial deadline for Head Start proposals because of the governor's insistence that they operate through South Carolina's senators, Spearman and the council worked around the clock to help some thirty counties meet the final deadline. By 1966, over 18,000 South Carolina preschoolers were in Head Start, a signature program of the Great Society.[69]

Spearman also helped shepherd the student council project, named SPEED-UP (Student Program for Educational and Economic Development for Underprivileged People), from initial concept through implementation in the summer of 1966. Supported by an OEO demonstration grant of $137,454 to the SCCHR, about 110 students from twenty-three South Carolina colleges began working in SPEED-UP teams in twenty-eight neighborhood centers in thirteen counties. More than two thousand children took classes with college student tutors in basic English, mathematics, drama, art, sewing, and African American history, and even more participated in afternoon recreational and cultural activities. However, SPEED-UP did not survive after the federal antipoverty program budget was cut.[70]

Spearman's wide experience with African American civil rights organizations culminated in her introducing Martin Luther King Jr. Sunday, May 8, 1966, to a statewide mass meeting, cosponsored by the South Carolina Voter Education Project, the Williamsburg Voters League, and CORE, in Kingstree, one of the state's most racially troubled towns. A *State* newspaper editorial denounced King for being one of the "professional racists in reverse" and was distressed at the appearance on the platform of "several South Carolinians (native or adopted) who ostensibly have been working for the betterment of what they term 'human relations.'" Not until 2000 would South Carolina make Martin Luther King's birthday an optional state holiday for state employees in conjunction with Confederate Memorial Day, May 10.[71]

The years 1965 and 1966 were the high watermark of the SCCHR's effectiveness under Spearman's leadership. More than any other individual, she nurtured the council, much like the flowers in her garden, and brought to fruition the human relations skills that existed among progressive middle-class white and black South Carolinians. But so great was the drain on her energy that Spearman "was just burned out" and decided to retire on September 1, 1967. As of July 31, the council's membership numbered 1,335; the Columbia chapter had the largest number of members at 263 among the 118 communities.[72]

As Spearman's successor, the council hired Paul W. Matthias, a twenty-nine-year-old white Methodist minister. His $10,000 salary was more than the salary the executive committee had promised but had not fully paid to Spearman. Elected to an honorary life membership on the board, she bid good-bye at the 1967 annual meeting.[73] Spearman had lived up to her description in Converse College's 1923 senior class yearbook as "one of those persons who seem ten people in one." She was a white woman civil rights pioneer; the "sparkplug" of the SCCHR; a seeker of religious and philosophical truths; a progressive and feminist "southern lady"; and a builder of bridges and consensus across generations, races, and classes.[74] Spearman had, moreover, a remarkable "will to persevere" that enabled her to develop among people holding "disparate views" a genuine "community of concern."[75] Firmly committed to New Deal and Great Society programs assisting the disadvantaged, Spearman championed human rights for all people. She received some long-deserved recognition in 1964 when Morris College conferred on her an honorary doctorate in the humanities. At its 1972 annual meeting, the Columbia YWCA saluted her and African American civil rights activist Modjeska Monteith Simkins "for their contributions to the State of South Carolina toward the elimination of racism." They were "'two who overcame' many of the barriers of racism and who overcame the limitations of the role society seeks to assign women."[76]

In March 1970 Spearman married widower Marion Wright, with whom she had forged an enduring comradeship during the civil rights movement. They lived at his rustic Topknot, in Linville Falls, North Carolina. Both were honored with the Frank Porter Graham Civil Liberties Award, he in 1969 and she in 1973.[77] After Marion Wright died in February 1983, she returned to Columbia. On March 12, 1989, her eighty-seventh birthday, Alice Spearman Wright died at the South Carolina Episcopal Home at Still Hopes. She requested that memorials be made to the Oliver Gospel Mission.[78]

NOTES

1. Marion Allan Wright, oral history, n.d., 15–16, Marion Allen Wright Papers, 1936–82, South Caroliniana Library, University of South Carolina, Columbia (hereinafter cited as SCL).

2. Alice Spearman Wright, interview by author, Linville Falls, N.C., July 11, 1983.

3. Alice Spearman Wright, interview by Ann Y. Evans, Rock Hill, S.C., July 3, 1981, in *Women Leaders in South Carolina: An Oral History*, ed. Ronald J. Chepesiuk, Ann Y. Evans, and Thomas S. Morgan (Rock Hill, S.C.: Winthrop College Archives and Special Collections, 1984), 42; Wright, interviews by author, July 10 and 11, 1983.

4. Jacquelyn Dowd Hall, biographical sketch of Alice Spearman Wright, Southern Oral History Program, Manuscripts Department, Southern Historical Collection, Wilson Library, University of North Carolina, Chapel Hill (hereinafter cited as SOHP-SHC); Alice Spearman Wright, interview by Jacquelyn Dowd Hall, Linville Falls, N.C., February 28, 1976, transcript, 39, 40, SOHP-SHC.

5. Marion W. Roydhouse, "Bridging Chasms: Community and the Southern YWCA," in *Visible Women: New Essays on American Activism*, ed. Nancy A. Hewitt and Suzanne Lebsock (Urbana: University of Illinois Press, 1993), 274; Susan Lynn, *Progressive Women in Conservative Times: Racial Justice, Peace, and Feminism, 1945 to the 1960s* (New Brunswick, N.J.: Rutgers University Press, 1992), 17–24, 28, 35.

6. Wright, interview by Evans, July 3, 1981, 43–46, 50–51; Wright, interview by Hall, February 28, 1976, 53–69, SOHP-SHC; Roydhouse, "Bridging Chasms," in *Visible Women*, 270–95.

7. Wright, interview by Hall, August 8, 1976, 1–6, SOHP-SHC.

8. Alice Norwood to Mrs. S. W. Norwood, January 21, 1931, Alice Norwood Spearman Wright Papers, SCL (hereinafter cited as ANSWP-SCL); notes for speech, "Asia As I Saw It," n.d., ANSWP-SCL.

9. Wright, interview by Hall, August 8, 1976, 26–39, SOHP-SHC.

10. Eugene H. Spearman Jr., telephone conversation with author, September 20, 1990; Josephine Donovan, *Feminist Theory: The Intellectual Traditions of American Feminism*, rev. ed. (New York: Continuum, 1992), 62–76, 82–85, 90.

11. Eugene H. Spearman, interview by author, September 26, 1990, SCL; Wright, interview by Hall, August 8, 1976, 36, SOHP-SHC. Eugene H. Spearman Sr. died June 4, 1962. Eugene H. Spearman Jr. died December 20, 1994.

12. Alice N. Spearman to J. M. Dabbs, August 22, 1947, and January 26, 1948, box 1, South Carolina Council of Human Relations Records, 1934–76, SCL (hereinafter cited as SCCHRR-SCL).

13. Mrs. Eugene H. Spearman to Mrs. White, February 18, 1953, South Carolina Federation of Women's Clubs folder, ANSWP-SCL; Margaret W. Macaulay, memorandum to chairmen, June 4, 1951, South Carolina Federation of Women's Clubs folder, ANSWP-SCL; report of the Publications Committee, c. October 1954, South Carolina Federation of Women's Clubs folder, ANSWP-SCL. It was unlikely that other white clubwomen would have attended the South-wide "Youth and Racial Unity through Educational Opportunity" conference hosted by Allen University in December 1953, at which Mary McLeod Bethune gave the final address and summary (South Carolina Federation of Women's Clubs folder, ANSWP-SCL).

14. Wright, interview by author, July 11, 1983; Wright, interview by Hall, August 8, 1976, 98, 99, SOHP-SHC.

15. Marcia G. Synnott, "Crusaders and Clubwomen: Alice Norwood Spearman Wright and Her Women's Network," in *Throwing Off the Cloak of Privilege: White Southern Women Activists in the Civil Rights Era*, ed. Gail S. Murray (Gainesville: University Press of Florida, 2004), 54, 49–76.

16. Rose Rubin, interview by Hyman Rubin III, Columbia, S.C., July 22, 1991; Alice N. Spearman, report of the executive director, April 1955, series 4, reel 146, 1378–84, Southern Regional Council Papers, 1944–1968 (hereinafter cited as SRCP).

17. Marcia G. Synnott, "Alice Norwood Spearman Wright: Civil Rights Apostle to South Carolinians," in *Beyond Image and Convention: Explorations in Southern Women's History*, ed. Janet L. Coryell, Martha H. Swain, Sandra Gioia Treadway, and Elizabeth Hayes Turner (Columbia: University of Missouri Press, 1998), 193–97, 184–207; Tinsley E. Yarbrough, *A Passion for Justice: J. Waties Waring and Civil Rights* (New York: Oxford University Press, 1987), 12, 16–22, 127–212, 226–29.

18. Mrs. Eugene H. Spearman to Mrs. Albert Simons, January 10, 1955, February 3, 1955, and March 10, 1956, box 1, SCCHRR-SCL; Harriet P. Simons to Mrs. Eugene H. Spearman, April 3, 1955, and June 25, 1955, box 1, SCCHRR-SCL; Josephine Pinckney to Alice N. Spearman, August 30, 1955, box 1, SCCHRR-SCL.

19. Alice N. Spearman, report of the executive director, August 1955, series 4, reel 146, 1398, SRCP; *Columbia Record*, August 22, 1955.

20. Howard H. Quint, *Profile in Black and White: A Frank Portrait of South Carolina* (Washington, D.C.: Public Affairs Press, 1958), 92–116; Wright, interview by author, July 10, 1983.

21. Alice N. Spearman to Rebecca Reid, June 6, 1955, box 1, SCCHRR-SCL.

22. Minutes, board of directors meeting, January 30, 1957, box 8, no. 243, SCCHRR-SCL; Alice N. Spearman, report, May 1957, box 9, no. 278, SCCHRR-SCL.

23. South Carolina Council to the SRC, request for financial aid, July 12, 1957, series 4, reel 146, 943, 944, 942–51, SRCP; Alice N. Spearman to George S. Mitchell, August 8, 1955, series 4, reel 146, 270, SRCP.

24. Minutes, SCCHR executive committee meeting, August 4, 1957, box 8, no. 257, SCCHRR-SCL; August Meier and Elliott Rudwick, *CORE: A Study in the Civil Rights Movement, 1942–1968* (New York: Oxford University Press, 1973), 89–90.

25. South Carolina Council to SRC, request for financial aid, July 12, 1957, series 4, reel 146, 946, 943, SRCP.

26. Wright, interviews by author, July 10 and 11, 1983; Wright, interview by Hall, August 8, 1976, 83–84, SOHP-SHC; Earl Middleton and Joy Barnes, conversation with author, Charleston, S.C., April 8, 2000; Earl Middleton, conversation with author, Columbia, S.C., April 27, 2000.

27. Peter F. Lau, *Democracy Rising: South Carolina and the Fight for Black Equality Since 1865* (Lexington: University Press of Kentucky, 2006), 202–3, 208–9, 220–21; Timothy B. Tyson, "Dynamite and 'The Silent South': A Story from the Second Reconstruction in South Carolina," in *Jumpin' Jim Crow: Southern Politics from Civil War to Civil Rights*, ed. Jane Dailey, Glenda Elizabeth Gilmore, and Bryant Simon (Princeton, N.J.: Princeton University Press, 2000), 275–97; Alice N. Spearman, report, July 1957, box 9, no. 278, SCCHRR-SCL; Alice N. Spearman, quarterly report, October–December 1957, box 9, no. 279, SCCHRR-SCL.

28. Jack Bass and Walter De Vries, *The Transformation of Southern Politics: Social Change and Political Consequence since 1945* (New York: New American Library, 1976), 258; Wright, interview by author, July 10, 1983.

29. Alice N. Spearman, quarterly report, December 1958–February 1959, box 9, no. 279, SCCHRR-SCL; Alice N. Spearman to the Rev. I. DeQuincey Newman, March 18, 1959, box 2, SCCHRR-SCL.

30. Wright, interview by Hall, August 8, 1976, 79, 78, SOHP-SHC; Alice N. Spearman, quarterly report, June–August 1959, box 9, no. 279, SCCHRR-SCL.

31. Alice N. Spearman, quarterly report, September–November 1959, box 9, no. 279, SCCHRR-SCL; James McBride Dabbs, address, "Quit You Like Men," October 1, 1959, box 36, SCCHRR-SCL.

32. Alice N. Spearman, quarterly reports, September–November 1959 and December 1959–February 1960, box 9, no. 279, SCCHRR-SCL; Wright, interview by Hall, August 8, 1976, 80–82, SOHP-SHC.

33. Alice N. Spearman, quarterly report, March–May 1959, box 9, no. 279, SCCHRR-SCL.

34. Paul Rilling, telephone interview by author, September 7, 1997; Paul Rilling, interoffice memorandum to Harold Fleming and Paul Anthony, March 10, 1960, series 4, reel 146, 436–38, SRCP; Paul Rilling to Alice N. Spearman, January 18, 1961, series 4, reel 147, 742, SRCP.

35. Paul S. Lofton Jr., "Calm and Exemplary: Desegregation in Columbia, South Carolina," in *Southern Businessmen and Desegregation*, ed. Elizabeth Jacoway and David R. Colburn (Baton Rouge: Louisiana State University Press, 1982), 72.

36. Alice N. Spearman, quarterly report, June–August 1960, box 9, no. 280, SCCHRR-SCL.

37. Paul Rilling, interoffice memorandum to Harold Fleming, March 10, 1960, SCCHRR-SCL; minutes, executive board meeting, March 6, 1960, box 8, no. 243, SCCHRR-SCL; "Human Relations Council Defends Sit-In Students," *The State*, March 7, 1960.

38. Lofton, "Calm and Exemplary," 75; Martin Oppenheimer, *The Sit-In Movement of 1960* (Brooklyn, N.Y.: Carlson, 1989), 152–57; Ernest F. Hollings, interview by author, Columbia, S.C., July 8, 1980, transcript, South Carolina Political Collections, University of South Carolina Libraries, University of South Carolina, Columbia (hereinafter cited as SCPC).

39. Oppenheimer, *The Sit-In Movement of 1960*, 146–52, 168–73; William C. Hine, "Civil Rights and Campus Wrongs: South Carolina State College Students Protest, 1955–1968," *South Carolina Historical Magazine* 97, no. 4 (1996): 322–24; Thomas Gaither, "Orangeburg: Behind the Carolina Stockade," *Sit-Ins: The Student Report* (New York: CORE, 1960), n.p.; Alice N. Spearman, quarterly report, September–November 1963, box 9, no. 281, SCCHRR-SCL.

40. Alice N. Spearman to Paul Rilling, February 9, 1961, and February 20, 1961, series 4, reel 147, 745, 747, 748, SRCP; Alice N. Spearman, quarterly report, December 1960–February 1961, box 9, no. 280, SCCHRR-SCL; Mary King, *Freedom Song: A Personal Story of the 1960s Civil Rights Movement* (New York: William Morrow, 1987), 316.

41. Ella J. Baker to Elizabeth Ledeen, February 9, 1961, and Baker to Alice Ann [sic] Spearman, February 9, 1961, box 2, SCCHRR-SCL.

42. Alice N. Spearman to Thomas Gaither, February 17, 1961, and Gaither to Spearman, February 23, 1961, box 2, SCCHRR-SCL.

43. David Halberstam, *The Children* (New York: Fawcett, 1999), 249–50, 255–67; Taylor Branch, *Parting the Waters: America in the King Years, 1954–1963* (New York: Simon and Schuster, 1988), 415–20; Alice N. Spearman, quarterly report, March–May 1961, box 9, no. 280, SCCHRR-SCL.

44. Walter Edgar, *South Carolina: A History* (Columbia: University of South Carolina Press, 1998), 537–38; Charles E. Daniel, qtd. in George McMillan, "Integration with Dignity: The Inside Story of How South Carolina Kept the Peace," *Saturday Evening Post*, March 16, 1963, 16–17; Alice N. Spearman to Paul Rilling, August 7, 1961, enclosing Mont Morton, "Negro Productivity Hike Is Held Vital," *The State*, July 2, 1961, series 4, reel 147, 780–81, SRCP.

45. Hollings, interview by author, July 8, 1980, SCPC; Alice N. Spearman to Ernest F. Hollings, October 11, 1962, and Betty Bargmann to Alice N. Spearman, October 18, 1962, box 19, no. 551, Ernest F. Hollings Papers, 1943–2009, SCPC (hereinafter cited as EFHP-SCPC).

46. John F. Potts, H. V. Manning, J. A. Bacoats to A. L. Wiggins, January 30, 1962, box 2, SCCHRR-SCL; Alice N. Spearman to Mrs. E. L. McPherson, May 18, 1963, box 3, SCCHRR-SCL; Alice N. Spearman, quarterly report, March–May 1962, box 9, no. 280, SCCHRR-SCL; South Carolina's technical education centers, September 28, 1962, series 4, reel 146, 1252, SRCP; Maxie Myron Cox Jr., "1963—the Year of Decision: Desegregation in South Carolina" (PhD diss., University of South Carolina, 1996), 139.

47. Elizabeth C. Ledeen, curriculum vitae, box 9, no. 277, SCCHRR-SCL, Mrs. T. J. Ledeen, "Highlights: Insights Gained From Recent Events," in Spearman, quarterly report, December 1960–February 1961, box 9, no. 280, SCCHRR-SCL; Mrs. T. J. Ledeen, report in Spearman, quarterly report, March–May 1961, box 9, no. 280, SCCHRR-SCL; Elizabeth C. Ledeen, "The Situation in the Colleges in South Carolina, c. fall 1960, box 10, SCCHRR-SCL; Elizabeth C. Ledeen, "The Purpose of the Student Program of the South Carolina Council on Human Relations," c. December 1960, box 10, SCCHRR-SCL; Elizabeth C. Ledeen, "Student Program of the S.C. Council on Human Relations," January 9, 1961, box 10, SCCHRR-SCL; Elizabeth C. Ledeen, "Evaluation of the Student Program, 1961–62, box 10, SCCHRR-SCL.

48. Student workshop, December 3, 1961, series 4, reel 146, 1236–37, SRCP; Constance Curry to Libby Ledeen, November 7, 1961, and Elizabeth C. Ledeen to Sandra Cason Hayden, December 18, 1961, box 2, SCCHRR-SCL; Ledeen to Hayden, November 25, 1961, and Ledeen to Curry, December 5, 1961, box 10, SCCHRR-SCL.

49. Hollings, interview by author, July 8, 1980, SCPC; Cox, "1963—The Year of Decision," 14–143; Edmund L. Drago, *Initiative, Paternalism, and Race Relations: Charleston's Avery Normal Institute* (Athens: University of Georgia Press, 1990), 276–77; Harvey Bernard Gantt, interview by author, Charlotte, N.C., July 14, 1980, SCL; Orville Vernon Burton, "Dining with Harvey Gantt: Myths and Realities of 'Integration with Dignity,'" in *Matthew J. Perry: The Man, His Times, and His Legacy*, ed. W. Lewis Burke and Belinda F. Gergel (Columbia: University of South Carolina Press, 2004), 183–220.

50. Minutes, board of directors meeting, February 12, 1962, box 9, no. 244, SCCHRR-SCL; Alice

N. Spearman, Elizabeth C. Ledeen, and Charlotte A. Hickman, quarterly report, March–May 1962, box 9, no. 280, SCCHRR-SCL; Alice N. Spearman, Elizabeth C. Ledeen, and Charlotte A. Hickman, quarterly report, September–November 1962, box 9, no. 281, SCCHRR-SCL; Elizabeth C. Ledeen, "Report of the South Carolina Student Council of Human Relations Conference, Penn Center," December 7–9, 1962, in Alice N. Spearman, quarterly report, December 1962–February 1963, box 9, no. 282, SCCHRR-SCL; "The Quotes of the Year: An Interpretive Report from the S.C. Student Council on Human Relations," box 3, SCCHRR-SCL.

51. *Gantt v. Clemson Agricultural College of South Carolina*, 320 F. 2d 611 (1963); Hollings, qtd. in McMillan, "Integration with Dignity," 20; Marcia G. Synnott, "Desegregation in South Carolina, 1950–1963: Sometime 'Between "Now" and "Never,"'" in *Looking South: Chapters in the Story of An American Region*, ed. Winfred B. Moore, Jr. and Joseph F. Tripp (Westport, Conn.: Greenwood Press, 1989), 58–61.

52. Donald S. Russell, interview by author and Herbert J. Hartsook, Spartanburg, S.C., July 6, 1992, transcript, SCPC.

53. Wright, interview by author, July 11, 1983.

54. Elizabeth C. Ledeen, report of program director, March–May 1963, box 9, no. 290, SCCHRR-SCL; Thomas F. Jones, interview by author, Cambridge, Massachusetts, July 29, 1980, SCL; Henry H. Lesesne, *A History of the University of South Carolina, 1940–2000* (Columbia: University of South Carolina Press, 2001), 138–50.

55. Dan Carter, "Returning to South Carolina," South Carolina Historical Association, Charleston, S.C., March 2, 2002; Dan Carter, "Coming Home: Why I Came Back to South Carolina," keynote address, University of South Caroliniana Society, Columbia, April 27, 2002, http://www.sc.edu/library/socar/uscs/2003/carter03.html (accessed July 26, 2011); Charles Joyner, "The Southern Historian in the Modern World," in *Proceedings of the South Carolina Historical Association* (Columbia, S.C., *South Carolina Historical Association*, 1995): 6–7.

56. Elizabeth C. Ledeen, reports of program director, September–November 1964 and March–May 1965, box 9, no. 289, SCCHRR-SCL; Kenneth Dean and Leslie Dunbar, notes of interview by author, Atlanta, Ga., November 11, 1994.

57. Spearman, interview by author, September 26, 1990.

58. Alice N. Spearman, quarterly report, December 1963–February 1964, box 9, no. 281, SCCHRR-SCL; Fred M. Reese Jr., interview by author, Columbia, S.C., December 13, 1994, SCL; Lofton, "Calm and Exemplary," 73–74, 77–78; John Hammond Moore, *Columbia and Richland County: A South Carolina Community, 1740–1990* (Columbia: University of South Carolina Press, 1993), 423–25.

59. Miles Richards, *A History of the Columbia Luncheon Club*, ed. Sarah McCrory (Columbia, S.C.: Columbia Luncheon Club, 2005), 8–16, 22–23; Cox, "1963—the Year of Decision," ix–xxvi, 352–91; Alice N. Spearman to the Honorable Lester Bates, September 5, 1962, box 3, SCCHRR-SCL.

60. Alice N. Spearman, quarterly reports, September–November 1963 and September–November 1964, box 9, no. 281, SCCHRR-SCL; Lofton, "Calm and Exemplary," 79.

61. Alice N. Spearman to the Honorable Lester Bates, December 3, 1963, box 3, SCCHRR-SCL.

62. Lofton, "Calm and Exemplary," 81 and n. 22; Moore, *Columbia and Richland County*, 426.

63. Cox, "1963—the Year of Decision," 180–88, 144–258; Spearman, quarterly report, September–November 1963, box 9, no. 281 SCCHRR-SCL.

64. *Brown v. South Carolina Forestry Commission et al.* 226 F. Supp. 646 (1963); Cox, "1963—the Year of Decision," 269–345; Alice N. Spearman, report on visit to Marion, Conway, Myrtle Beach, Cheraw, Darlington, and Sumter, S.C., September 20, 1963, box 3, SCCHRR-SCL; "Cheraw Park Hearing," *Cheraw Chronicle*, September 19, 1963, 1.

65. L. S. James, "Summary of the Conference for Rural South Carolinians, Penn Center, Frog-more, S.C., February 13–15, 1963," in Alice N. Spearman, quarterly report, December 1962–February 1963, SCCHRR-SCL; Alice N. Spearman, quarterly report, March–May 1963, box 9, no. 281; Alice N. Spearman to Fay Bennett, executive secretary, National Sharecroppers Fund, January 23, 1963, box 3, SCCHRR-SCL.

66. Louis L. Mitchell Jr., "Operation Opportunity—Summary Report," April 30, 1964, series 15, reel 216, 590–93, SRCP.

67. Minutes, board of directors meeting, March 20, 1965, box 8, no. 246, SCCHRR-SCL; Alice N. Spearman, quarterly report, March–May 1965, box 9, no. 281, SCCHRR-SCL; 1964–66 program pro-spectus of the South Carolina Council on Human Relations, series 4, reel 147, 905–6, SRCP.

68. Alice N. Spearman, quarterly report, June–August 1964, box 9, no. 281, SCCHRR-SCL.

69. Wright, interview by author, July 11, 1983; summary facts, 1965 summer Head Start Projects, SCCHRR-SCL; Robert E. Woodward, "South Carolina Council on Human Relations, Inc. Purpose—Programs—Projects," box 24, SCCHRR-SCL; summary report, South Carolina Council on Human Relations, 1965, box 8, no. 241, SCCHRR-SCL; Alice N. Spearman, quarterly report, March–May 1965, and quarterly report, December 1966–February 1967, box 9, no. 281, SCCHRR-SCL.

70. Jack Bass, "South Carolinian Doesn't Pussy-Foot About Life" and "Progress Continues in Human Relations," *Charlotte (N.C.) Observer*, January 3, 1967, A-8; Alice N. Spearman, quarterly reports, March–May 1966, June–August 1966, and September–November 1966, box 9, no. 281, SCCHRR-SCL; report 1, South Carolina Council on Human Relations, 1966–1967, box 8, no. 241, SCCHRR-SCL; Elizabeth C. Ledeen, report of program director, March–May 1966, and reports of extension director, June–August 1966 and June–August 1967, box 9, no. 289, SCCHRR-SCL; Wright, interview by author, July 11, 1983.

71. "Trouble-Making King," editorial, *The State*, May 10, 1966, A-12; Allison Askins, "Sunday, May 8, 1966, the Kingstree Visit: Martin Luther King, Jr. Left an Impact on a Quiet South Carolina Town," *The State*, January 16, 2000, E-1, E-4.

72. Wright, interview by Hall, August 8, 1976, 92, SOHP-SHC; Spearman, quarterly report, June–August 1966, box 9, no. 281, SCCHRR-SCL; membership report by towns, July 31, 1967, and finance report, August 1967, series 4, reel 156, 767–68, SRCP.

73. Bill Wesson Jr. to Alice Spearman, September 2, 1967, box 4, no. 109, SCCHRR-SCL; *SCCHR Review*, October 1967 and December 1967, series 4, reel 156, 884–85, 888–91, SRCP.

74. Alice Buck Norwood, *Y's and Other Y's*, vol. 26 (Spartanburg, S.C.: senior class of Converse College, 1923), 66; Quint, *Profile in Black and White*, 169.

75. Reese, interview by author, December 13, 1994.

76. Alice N. Spearman, quarterly report, March–May 1964, box 9, no. 281, SCCHRR-SCL; 1972 annual meeting of the Columbia YWCA, salute to Modjeska Monteith Simkins and Alice Spearman Wright, box 44, SCCHRR-SCL.

77. Spearman, interview by author, September 26, 1990; Alice N. Spearman Wright, speech, "People on the March," Chapel Hill, N.C., October 20, 1973, ANSWP-SCL.

78. "Alice N. Wright, Worked to Better Human Relations," *The State*, March 13, 1989; statement and motion by Representative Tim Rogers "relative to Mrs. Alice Spearman Wright, a prominent South Carolina citizen," March 15, 1989, *Journal of the House of Representatives of the State of South Carolina*, http://scstatehouse.gov/sess108_1989-1990/hj89/19890315.htm (accessed July 25, 2011). The Oliver Gospel Mission in Columbia, S.C., provides assistance to homeless men.

Modjeska Monteith Simkins

I Cannot Be Bought and Will Not Be Sold

CHERISSE JONES-BRANCH

Mary Modjeska Monteith Simkins (1889–1992) was a leader, an activist, and a visionary. She was part of a cadre of African American leaders in South Carolina in the twentieth century who called the state to task as they pursued civil and political rights for all of its citizens. Her particular activism was part of an impetus to improve the political, educational, and physical lives of African Americans at a time when local and state governments resisted such attempts at every turn.

In turn-of-the-century America, blacks confronted what historian Rayford Logan termed the "nadir" in race relations. African Americans had little hope of receiving equal treatment and as the century began faced the great challenge of defeating rampant and pervasive racism. In the late nineteenth century, virtually all access to the political arena had been wrested from South Carolina's black citizens as the Democratic Party established its dominance and marginalized the Republican Party. Moreover, black South Carolinians' civil rights were dealt a major blow in the Constitution of 1895, which legalized segregation and racial discrimination in virtually every aspect of life.

Born during this grim era in Columbia, South Carolina, on December 5, 1899, Mary Modjeska Monteith was the oldest daughter of Henry Clarence and Rachel Hull Monteith. Her mother had been educated at the Howard Free School, the first school in South Carolina to provide secondary education for African Americans. She was an educator until she married Henry Monteith. Henry was an artisan who had worked at industrial sites throughout the South and a member of the predominantly black Bricklayers and Plasterers Union 5 in Columbia, an affiliate of the International Bricklayers Union.[1]

MODJESKA MONTEITH SIMKINS

Courtesy of South Carolina Political Collection,
University of South Carolina Libraries,
University of South Carolina, Columbia, S.C.

Henry's racial heritage reflected a common exploitative kind of relationship between black women and white men that dated back to the days of slavery. He was the offspring of a prosperous white attorney, Walter Monteith, and his domestic servant Mary Dobbins, a former slave.[2] Mary had been hired by the Monteith family as a nursemaid for their children. She gave birth to Henry in 1870.

Henry and Rachel Monteith's family was fairly prosperous and economically independent, allowing them to enjoy a middle-class lifestyle that was atypical for black families of the time. The fact that the family was not dependent on whites for their economic well-being did not sit well with many whites in Columbia. But, as their daughter later recalled, Henry was a fearless man. At a time when a black man could be lynched for the slightest infraction of the law or custom whether real or imagined, he refused to be intimidated. On one occasion when he was "backing a chimney," a white man came in and showed him a finger that had been cut off of a black man. Henry Monteith however, would not be moved; he "offered to fight" the man "with his trowel and hammer." The man did not bother him again.[3]

Because their mother was an educator, the Monteith children were literate, unusual for black children in early twentieth-century South Carolina. Rachel Hull Monteith and her sisters encouraged reading among their children. Modjeska recalled that her mother's sisters, who were also teachers, sent them Hans Christian Andersen's fairy tales, including *The Little Match Girl*, Gene Stratton-Porter's *A Girl of the Limberlost*, and Bible stories. The children were expected to excel academically and were given the best private education available to blacks in South Carolina at that time. Modjeska later recalled that, growing up in a rural area, she and her siblings attended a Sunday school where most of the other black children and adults could not read. Because of the demands of tenant farm life, most black children attended school for only three months of the year. Modjeska was first formally educated at a private grade school at Benedict College in Columbia.[4]

Founded in 1870 as the Benedict Institute and affiliated with the Baptist Church, the Benedict College of Simkins's time offered one of the finest educations for blacks from around the state and the nation. At the time most of the faculty were white missionaries from the North who were committed to providing quality education for recently freed African Americans and their children. While at Benedict Mary Modjeska Monteith chose to stop using her first name. She remained there until she earned an bachelor of arts in 1921. Upon graduating, Modjeska followed in her mother's footsteps by becoming a teacher, first at Benedict and then at Booker T. Washington, a prominent black school in

Columbia, where she taught mathematics. She later did postgraduate work at Columbia University, the University of Michigan, Morehouse University, and Michigan State University.[5]

Modjeska Monteith remained at Booker T. Washington School until she married Andrew Whitfield Simkins of Edgefield, South Carolina, in 1929. School policy did not allow married women to continue working.[6] Andrew, who had previously been married three times, was a widower with five children. He did not expect his career-minded wife to care for his children and hired a housekeeper so she could pursue other opportunities.

Andrew Simkins, sixteen years older than Modjeska, possessed skills and attitudes that she found particularly admirable. He was a prosperous businessman, who owned real estate and operated a gas station in Columbia. Unlike many husbands of the time he encouraged and supported her career goals.[7]

Modjeska Simkins soon emerged as one member of a generation of young black leaders who challenged the nation to live up to its democratic ideals, particularly in the wake of World War I. In the 1920s, she joined the Columbia branch of the NAACP, which had been organized in February 1917. It was her mother's influence that motivated her to join the organization. Both of Simkins's parents were politically active. Rachel Monteith had participated in the Niagara movement, the forerunner of the NAACP, and subscribed to its publication.[8] After the founding of the NAACP, she also subscribed to its magazine, *The Crisis*. Simkins's mother and sisters were instrumental in the founding of the Columbia branch of the NAACP.

Although she was busy at school and lived in the country, Simkins believed that it was her duty as the oldest child to become involved in the NAACP. Because there were no youth chapters at the time, Simkins, who accompanied her mother to meetings, was often the youngest person in attendance. But her age posed no serious obstacles. Because she was so well read and informed about the political and civil rights issues of the day, older members not only listened to her but often deferred to her insights.[9]

In the 1930s, Simkins went to work for the South Carolina Tuberculosis Association (SCTA). This was her first job since her marriage. Her supportive husband interceded on her behalf when he heard about the position. He contacted his good friend Robert Shaw Wilkinson, the president of the Colored Normal Industrial, Agricultural, and Mechanical College in Orangeburg, South Carolina, and asked him to recommend Modjeska for the job.[10]

The association was looking for someone to teach health instruction to teachers as part of a statewide program. After taking the job, Simkins was sent for training to the University of Michigan in Ypsilanti, known for its public health initiatives. Upon returning to South Carolina, Simkins was appointed the director of Negro work for the South Carolina Tuberculosis Association. She was charged with the responsibility of raising funds and awareness about the disease.

This was not an easy task for several reasons. Raising funds meant acquiring contributions from South Carolina's most impoverished citizens in the financial abyss of the Depression years.[11] Blacks were excluded from the association's board, and, as was often the case, segregated programs for blacks within organizations meant having white overseers. Simkins and other blacks who worked with her in the association were merely advisory to the board. African Americans were rarely present at annual meetings. If they happened to attend the meeting, they were relegated to the corners of the room and the margins of the organization.

Such treatment infuriated Simkins. Her travels around the state revealed astonishing poverty in rural areas. Many rural blacks were sharecroppers or tenant farmers whose living conditions were little better than those of their enslaved ancestors and in some cases worse. Inadequate access to health care meant that poor rural blacks were particularly susceptible to tuberculosis. When the association met to discuss the illness, they acknowledged its pervasiveness among South Carolina blacks and even brought in experts for advice. Still they failed to invite black representatives to attend these meetings.[12]

Clearly, Simkins's relationship with the scta and its leaders was contentious. Although Simkins focused on treating tuberculosis among blacks, she alienated her boss by also highlighting such problems as poor infant and maternal health and venereal disease. Discussions about venereal disease in particular did not sit well with her boss, who thought that blacks caught it by "sinning." Simkins sought to move away from such antiquated and counterproductive thinking and to focus instead on lessening the devastating impact of tuberculosis on black communities. To this end, she created a newsletter that she disseminated among rural blacks in South Carolina to keep them informed about the latest procedures in combating tuberculosis. Ever aware of the poor education of many of her constituents but not wanting to insult their intelligence, Simkins was very careful to write the letter in the terms most accessible to them. She produced the newsletter by herself, which she first called the *News* and then the *Newsreel*, writing, typing, and copying it for distribution. These skills she developed served her well in later years when she became associated with the newspaper *The Lighthouse and Informer* in the 1950s.[13]

Simkins spent eleven years working with the scta and received a commendation for raising $42,000 through the sale of Negro Christmas Seals to benefit blacks with tuberculosis. She was also instrumental in creating tuberculin clinics before she left the organization in 1942.[14]

While working for the SCTA, Simkins also undertook other endeavors. In 1935, the introduction in the U.S. Congress of an antilynching bill encouraged African Americans in South Carolina to create the State Negro Citizens Committee under the direction of Simkins and Robert W. Mance of Columbia, a clinician with the SCTA. This committee sent telegrams to President Franklin Delano Roosevelt urging him to support the proposed legislation. The committee was also concerned about racial discrimination in New Deal programs. For example, Simkins, Mance, and other black leaders realized that work-relief programs under the WPA relegated blacks solely to labor-intensive employment.[15] The State Negro Citizens Committee mounted intense pressure to force New Deal program officials to hire educated blacks in white-collar positions. Their efforts resulted in blacks being employed as teachers, health-care professionals, and writers for the state history project.[16] Among Simkins's other projects during the Depression years was her work with the health department, from which she obtained literature and film slides to show rural blacks who were uninformed about proper health care. She was also able to procure cottonseed meal to use for the prevention of pellagra when yeast supplies ran short.[17] According to Simkins, yeast was used to feed rural blacks and others who were so malnourished that they developed pellagra.[18]

Simkins also continued to participate in the NAACP while working for the SCTA. The white leadership of the SCTA found her activism on behalf of the NAACP too subversive and told her to give up her membership in the organization. She particularly angered her supervisor, Chauncey McDonald, who opposed the NAACP because it threatened to change the racial status quo in South Carolina. When Simkins refused to sever her association with the NAACP, SCTA officials contrived ways to eliminate her position with the SCTA. In 1942, the board of directors decided that, owing to budgetary constraints, they would retain only the black public health nurse. The SCTA budget for the fiscal year 1942–43 included two months salary for Simkins but, by the time the board met again, this too had been eliminated. Simkins was thus removed from her post with the organization.[19]

This dismissal, however, only strengthened Simkins's resolve to improve conditions for black South Carolinians through the NAACP. By 1942, she had been active in the organization for decades. In the NAACP, however, she encountered gender bias. For instance, back in 1939, members of the Cheraw, South Carolina, NAACP led by Levi G. Bird met with members of Columbia NAACP executive board at Benedict College to encourage an alliance that resulted in the founding of a state organization. Simkins—a member of the branch's executive committee and the chair of the program committee—attended.[20] Although many of the participants at this meeting were women, only two, Simkins and Maggie B. Robinson, were selected as officers. Even then the two were given roles traditionally assigned to women in patriarchal, male-dominated organizations. Simkins served as corresponding secretary in early 1941 and was elected state secretary in June 1941. By 1942, she was also head of the publicity committee, a role for which her time with the scta had prepared her well.

Simkins was involved in virtually all aspects of the South Carolina conference of the NAACP from the time of its inception in 1939. She played a key role in one of the organization's main battles, to equalize teachers' salaries statewide. As a former teacher, Simkins was well aware of the differences in salaries among black and white teachers in the Columbia school system. She recalled the time she went to cash her check at a local bank and observed white teachers passing their checks through the teller's window and getting back twice the pay that Simkins and other black teachers received. South Carolina NAACP attorney Harold Boulware and NAACP counsel Thurgood Marshall initiated a lawsuit to equalize teachers' salaries. The plaintiff in the first suit was Viola Duvall, a teacher in the Charleston school district, whose case succeeded in 1944.[21] The South Carolina NAACP then brought a suit against the Columbia city schools in the 1944 case of *Thompson v. Columbia School System*; black teachers won this case in 1945. All the while, Simkins was at the forefront of the teachers' fight in Columbia.[22] She helped raise funds for the lawsuit and also organized black teachers and publicized their activities in local black newspapers.[23] Furthermore, because accommodations for black out-of-town visitors were few and segregated, several of the NAACP lawyers, including Thurgood Marshall, chief counsel for the organization, stayed at the Simkinses' home.[24]

Membership in the NAACP in the 1940s was a dangerous business for black state employees. The teacher equalization victory did not come without a price for many black teachers in Columbia who feared—in many cases accurately—that testifying against the state of South Carolina would cost them their jobs. In response, the state conference formed a new, parallel organization in 1944, the South Carolina Citizens' Committee—essentially the same organization but with a different name. The committee had the same officers as the state and local chapters of the NAACP. Simkins, who was elected reporter, was its only female officer.[25]

In addition to equalizing teachers' salaries, the state conference focused on restoring African Americans' voting rights. Among the injustices black South Carolinians faced was the inability to vote in primary elections, which, in a one-party state, were all-important. In the late nineteenth century, fearful of the political strength blacks had amassed in the state during Reconstruction, Governor "Pitchfork" Ben Tillman and South Carolina's Constitutional Convention of 1895 used every measure imaginable to eradicate black suffrage and secure the hegemony of the Democratic Party in the state. Even before the constitutional convention, a grandfather clause was used to limit political access: it stated that a black person could vote if he could prove that his grandfather had voted for Wade Hampton for governor in 1876. Ironically, according to Simkins, it was entirely possible that her white paternal grandfather had voted for Governor Hampton.[26] After the Constitution of 1895 went into effect in South Carolina, the Republican vote dropped precipitously from fifteen to twenty thousand ballots to less than five thousand. To add insult to injury the statewide primary instituted in 1896 replaced the state convention that had formerly nominated Democratic candidates for office. In due time, African Americans were excluded from Democratic primaries and were only able to vote in general elections, which were virtually meaningless.[27]

Despite black South Carolinians' long association with the Republican Party, factionalism and the national Republican Party's adoption of "lily-white" Republicanism—an effort to woo white voters by limiting the role of blacks in the party—led to a decline of Republican strength in the state. Even as they were excluded from the franchise by the Democratic Party, African Americans increasingly found that Republican Party leaders paid them scant attention. Indeed, Republicans often imitated Democrats in their calls for white supremacy in politics. As the century progressed, the number of black Republicans in South Carolina continued to decline. By 1944 there were barely five hundred.[28]

In this same year, the Texas Supreme Court ruled in *Smith v. Allwright* that blacks could not be prohibited from voting in the Texas Democratic primary. The immediate reaction among white Democratic leaders in South Carolina was a resolution declaring that "this party shall continue, as it is now, a party of and for white Democrats only, and that no Negro shall be admitted to membership in our party."[29] To counteract statutes dealing with primary elections, South Carolina's state legislature converted the Democratic Party into a private fraternal organization that was legally immune to federal judicial interference. The national press dubbed this the "South Carolina Plan."[30]

Simkins recalled that she and others pleaded with members of the all-white Democratic Party to be allowed entry, only to be told that it was a private club. In May 1944, the Progressive Democratic Party (PDP) was founded in Columbia, South Carolina, by Osceola McKaine, a civil rights activist, and by John McCray, editor of the *Lighthouse and Informer*, a black newspaper, to counteract black exclusion from the state Democratic Party. The PDP, which was open to all regardless of race, provided a necessary forum for African Americans in South Carolina to cultivate their increasing political activism.[31] Three months after its founding, the PDP claimed forty-five thousand members in forty-four of the state's forty-six counties.[32] Black political leaders wasted little time in using the power of the PDP to change the political destiny of black South Carolinians. From 1944 to 1947, PDP members encouraged black South Carolinians to register to vote and even joined forces with the NAACP in a suit against the all-white state Democratic Party.[33]

Although Simkins remained a member of the Republican Party until 1952, she also had a close relationship with PDP founders McCray and McKaine. She planned the organization's conventions and wrote its statements and resolutions.[34] The PDP held its first convention in late May 1944 to elect delegates for the national Democratic convention in Chicago. Their goal was to contest the seating of the "regular" delegates and to support Roosevelt's reelection. Their efforts in Chicago failed. But their bold stand against racial exclusion from South Carolina politics embarrassed the state's white power structure by further exposing the hypocrisy of the American political system.[35]

Relentless canvassing among black leaders and the realization that the battle for access to the political arena would be a long one eventually led black leaders and the NAACP to bring suit against the South Carolina Democratic Party. Simkins was once again deeply entrenched in South Carolina voting cases. In the first case, *Elmore v. Rice*, she not only was active in the court proceedings but also attended courtroom sessions in Columbia and Washington, D.C.[36]

In 1946, George Elmore went to the voting precinct office in Columbia and presented himself for the purpose of voting to John I. Rice, chairman of the Richland County Democratic Executive Committee for South Carolina. Rice refused to allow Elmore to vote, stating that "no Negroes were permitted to vote in the Democratic Primary."[37] The following year, a black citizens' committee from Richland County, backed by the NAACP, sued to participate in the state's Democratic primary.[38] *Elmore v. Rice* was tried before district court judge J. Waties Waring, who in 1947 determined that blacks could not be excluded from the primary and that the South Carolina Democratic Party could not operate as a "private club" and restrict its membership as it pleased. He also added in passing that "it is time for South Carolina to rejoin the Union."[39]

Unfortunately, this did not deter Democratic leaders in South Carolina in their determination to limit black voting rights. In May 1948, the Democratic State Convention adopted a new set of rules designed to discourage black voters. They required all would-be voters to sign an oath declaring themselves in favor of "separation of the races" and "states' rights" and opposed to the "proposed Federal so-called F.E.P.C. [Federal Employment Practices Commission] law," which would ban racial discrimination in federal positions.[40]

Some white Democrats opposed this move, however. The Greenville County Democratic Executive Committee broke with the state organization and repudiated the registration oath by allowing blacks to register. Richland and Marlboro counties followed suit.[41] Waring dealt the white primary its deathblow in July 1948 with his decision in *Brown v. Baskin*, which threw out the registration oath. He further threatened to jail anyone who attempted to keep blacks from voting. Significantly, the U.S. Supreme Court refused to review either of Waring's decisions. The following month, large numbers of African Americans voted in South Carolina's Democratic primary. Without question, the *Brown v. Baskin* ruling was a major step toward ensuring full African American political participation, restoring rights blacks had been denied in the state since the post–Civil War era.[42]

Simkins became secretary of the South Carolina State Conference of the NAACP at its annual state conference in 1948. In this position, she traveled throughout South Carolina talking to various groups and gaining a clearer sense of the problems black South Carolinians faced. When Thurgood Marshall took his case to federal court in *Elmore v. Rice*, he asked her to sit behind him by the rail that separated the lawyers from observers, as he recognized the value of Simkins's travels and the experiences of the people she had met along the way. She was more knowledgeable than he was about what had occurred in the state, and so she was able to advise Marshall during the in-court proceedings.[43] Simkins also gave direct assistance to George Elmore. When he found himself in financial distress and facing foreclosure on his home, Simkins gave him a personal loan and a job managing one of her husband's businesses.[44]

Simkins later observed that compared to states such as Mississippi and Alabama, there was very little violence in South Carolina as blacks attempted to vote. However, she did not consider whites in South Carolina to be any better than whites in the other states. In her view the difference was that, because of judges like Waring, South Carolina whites knew black South Carolinians had the power of the federal court behind them.[45] In the wake of these victories in the federal courts, blacks were no longer afraid to push for access to South Carolina's political arena.

Although African Americans had won the right to vote in South Carolina, they faced an even greater challenge in overturning the racist practices associated with the well-established Jim Crow system. Simkins often traveled to black communities around the state to advance the NAACP's agenda. In 1947, for example, she gave a speech at a meeting of the Sumter NAACP, during which she urged African Americans to "put up an all out fight against discrimination," positing that "discrimination and segregation are the most poisonous [aspects] of American life."[46] To those who had never voted before she distributed literature with instructions on what to do at the polls. Although blacks in South Carolina exercised their newly acquired power of the ballot, this right did not come without a price. Afterward, many feared retaliation and were afraid to leave their homes.[47]

Significantly, Simkins turned to black women as a force for gaining the franchise in South Carolina, knowing that unlike black men they were not required to pay a poll tax in order to vote. A flyer Simkins wrote entitled "Simple Facts About Registration" proclaimed that "since WOMEN ARE NOT REQUIRED TO PAY POLL TAX, THOUSANDS OF THEM, no matter how poor, can qualify to vote if they can READ and WRITE. WOMEN should REGISTER and VOTE in large numbers. WORK for this!"[48]

In 1948, the Republican Party, whose chair in Richland County was Simkins, not only encouraged African Americans to vote but also gave instructions on how to do so. Before the November 1948 election, she, along with other Republican Party members instructed voters to select the state chairman, J. Bates Gerald of Charleston, as a candidate for the U.S. Senate over the Democratic incumbent, Burnet R. Maybank. According to Simkins, "When a voter drops the Gerald ticket into the box, he also votes for Thomas E. Dewey, because the Dewey presidential electors are printed on the Gerald ticket." It is very likely that GOP leaders suspected possible ballot tampering, because they forewarned voters to check polling places to ensure that Gerald or Dewey ballots were on display. If they discovered a problem, they were to report the discrepancy to Republican Party officials.[49]

Simkins's days with the Republican Party were numbered, however. As an active member of the Republican Party, Simkins witnessed the rise of the PDP and the inroads blacks made into the state Democratic Party after they had been given access to the direct primary. She also saw the mass exodus of South Carolina whites to the Dixiecrat and Republican Parties after black participation in the Democratic Party increased and President Harry Truman issued his civil rights report in 1948. Dealing with these new, white Republican Party members who joined the GOP because they could not accept the president's mandate on civil rights in America was for Simkins the straw that broke the camel's back. During the 1952 election, she dramatically terminated her affiliation with the South Carolina Republican Party at a meeting at the Jefferson Hotel in Columbia. In what was a characteristic tirade against racial discrimination and the failure of the democratic system, Simkins recalled that, when white members "talked some things that I didn't like to hear I gave them a little piece of my mind and walked out and slammed the French door. And that's the last I've been in the Republican meetings." She voted for the Democratic candidate for president, Adlai Stevenson.[50]

In the late 1940s and early 1950s, Simkins continued her activism on behalf of black political access and also became increasingly involved in working for improved educational opportunities. One of the most important cases for her and the NAACP began in predominantly black, rural Clarendon County in 1947, when black parents requested buses to transport their children to school. There were 8,906 children in the county's school system of which 6,531 were African American.[51] White students had thirty buses available to transport them to school. Black students had none. In some cases they had to walk nine miles each way in order to attend school. Black parents, encouraged by Joseph A. DeLaine, an AME minister and schoolteacher, petitioned the school board to provide buses for their children. When they approached the chairman of the school board, R. W. Elliott, they were told, "We ain't got no money to buy a bus for your nigger children." One of the parents filed suit in 1948. According to *Plessy v. Ferguson* in 1896, which provided for "separate but equal" facilities, black schools should have been provided with buses. Unfortunately, the case was thrown out on a technicality.[52] Levi Pearson, who had had filed the suit, found that his credit had been cut off at all of the county's white-owned stores in retribution.

In this important case Simkins's participation was evident at many junctures. She was instrumental in helping Pearson secure funds as he tried to make a living on his farm. She also worked with DeLaine, who was president of one of the NAACP branches in Clarendon County and wrote the declaration that appeared in the case of *Briggs v. Elliott* in 1950.[53] Initially this case was heard in a special, three-judge court in South Carolina. Among the judges was J. Waties Waring, the sole dissenting voice in the case that became part of *Brown v. Board of Education* in 1954. African Americans achieved a significant victory when the Supreme Court unanimously ruled that "separate but equal" was unconstitutional on May 17, 1954. But the battle was far from over. Black leaders still had a long fight ahead of them to desegregate the state's school system. The state's white leaders, in an uproar over the decision, were bound and determined to make this transition as difficult as possible.

Once again, Modjeska Simkins played an integral role in the struggle. She and other black leaders realized that blacks faced retribution for attempting to place their children in formerly all-white schools. White citizens' councils sprang up around the state and exerted economic pressure to keep blacks in segregated facilities. These organizations, largely centered in Orangeburg and Clarendon counties, resorted to withholding credit from blacks, making it difficult for them to earn a living and limiting where they could spend their money when they had it. Simkins recalled that black South Carolinians reacted in kind to this economic terrorism. In Orangeburg blacks either refused to patronize such businesses—for example, a Sunbeam bread franchise—or else pitted businesses against one another. Blacks were encouraged, for example, to buy from the Piggly Wiggly grocery store but not from its competitor Winn Dixie, thus running the latter out of business. According to Simkins, blacks also targeted such businesses as the Ford Motor Company and Prudential Life Insurance.[54]

Simkins was also instrumental in helping blacks in Elloree and Orangeburg County and in Clarendon County who lost their homes and farms after banks refused to extend them credit or called in their mortgages early. In this Simkins had an unusual resource, the black-owned and black-operated Victory Savings Bank of Columbia of which her brother Henry Dobbins Monteith was president and where she had been employed since 1955. She made use of this resource to help black victims of economic retaliation to secure much-needed financial assistance.[55] Simkins contacted friends, churches, and other institutions in northern states, and secured donations that were then deposited into a savings account at Victory Savings Bank. A letter was even placed in *Jet* magazine to solicit donations. Adam Clayton Powell, the pastor of Abyssinian Baptist Church in Harlem, New York, and the first black congressman from that state, saw the letter and invited Simkins to speak to his congregation. Her visit resulted in large amounts of aid pouring in to South Carolina.[56]

This money and the bank helped relieve blacks of economic pressure by allowing them to secure loans to save their property and livelihoods.[57] According to Simkins, such loans were particularly necessary in Elloree where many blacks were tenant farmers. At times black tenant farmers received help that was not strictly monetary. On one occasion, when blacks could not obtain fertilizer, they awoke the next morning to find a fertilizer truck had been sent to town for their use.

In the years after the *Brown* decision, Simkins remained a member of the NAACP, but in 1957 she was dropped from her post as secretary. The reasons are unclear, but it appears from existing sources that she was dropped because of alleged association with Communist organizations. Being accused of having Communist affiliations was a commonly used scare tactic during the Cold War years. Many organizations, including the NAACP, were frightened into purging members whose sensibilities were deemed too left-leaning. Simkins had worked with the National Adult Advisory Board of the Southern Negro Youth Congress, the Southern Conference for Human Welfare, and the Southern Conference Educational Fund. All of these organizations had been charged with having connections to the Communist Party and were often under the surveillance of the House Un-American Activities Committee (HUAC).[58] She was also friends with historian Herbert Aptheker, a noted Communist during the McCarthy era who was visited by Communist Party officials into the 1980s. NAACP leaders in South Carolina were also concerned about their association with Simkins because she had appeared with singer and activist Paul Robeson at a rally for Benjamin J. Davis, a convicted black Communist Party leader. Although she was never personally visited by HUAC officials, the committee had a file on her activities that dated back to the 1940s.[59]

Simkins insisted, however that these charges of guilt by association were unjust. She proclaimed "I am not, and have never been a communist. Sure I signed some petitions. I'm against transgressions of civil liberties."[60] After being purged from the ranks of the South Carolina NAACP's leadership in 1956, Simkins returned to full-time employment in public relations at Victory Savings Bank. But she continued to work with and through other organizations to improve the lives of black Carolinians in the 1950s and 1960s.[61]

In the 1950s Simkins continued her activism as a member of numerous organizations in Columbia and around the state. One such organization was the Richland County Citizens Committee (RCCC). Founded in 1944 and chartered in 1956 as a direct offshoot of the South Carolina Citizens Committee, the RCCC led the fight to integrate public schools, parks, and city buses. It also fought against urban renewal that threatened black home ownership and sought an end to police brutality, an atrocity that overwhelming affected African Americans.[62]

The activities of the RCCC were not limited to Richland County, however. Because Simkins had so many contacts as a result of her time as secretary of the NAACP and her membership in other organizations, she and the RCCC were influential in movements that affected the entire state. The organization was instrumental in the integration of the South Carolina Mental Hospital and participated in the sit-ins in the 1960s. For seven years, the RCCC also had a black radio station that was able to run independently of public funding, leaving the organization free from local censorship.

Simkins had a weekly radio program on the station entitled "I Woke Up This Morning with My Mind Set on Freedom" in addition to serving as director of publicity and public relations for the RCCC from 1956 to 1988.[63] In her radio broadcasts, which lasted from 1964 to 1980, Simkins had no qualms about challenging the white establishment's treatment of African Americans. Nor did she have a problem with lambasting complacent blacks. For example, in preparation for an election in 1966, Simkins appealed to children to get their parents and others to register to vote. She argued that they should "be ashamed" if their parents did "not register[,]. . . be ashamed if they do not vote." Simkins also attacked African Americans directly when she referred to unregistered adults as "those lazy ones who do not vote" and those "disinterested ones that just do not bother at all."[64]

Modjeska Simkins continued to campaign for myriad causes for African Americans and other dispossessed people into the 1970s and beyond. In the 1960s she ran unsuccessfully for the Columbia City Council and the South Carolina State House of Representatives. Simkins also lent her support to causes unlikely to attract African Americans at the time. In the late 1970s, for example, she was one of the first to advocate preserving the environment when she spoke out against the Savannah River Site, wondering "how some folks think they breathe different air than the rest of us." Being an environmentalist was merely an expansion of Simkins's lifelong political activism.

When the women's rights movement developed in South Carolina in the 1970s, Modjeska Simkins was not among its leaders, but she did support many of its goals. During the June 1977 state conference in South Carolina that was a part of the congressionally mandated International Women's Year (IWY) program, she was a key participant. At an opening session celebrating black and white women of the state uniting for a better future for women, she was honored for her role in "breaking barriers" and introduced as a "civil rights activist and businesswoman who is still respected and feared by elected officials." When participants elected delegates to represent the state at the National Women's Conference in Houston, Texas—the culmination of this series of IWY conferences intended to involve American women in developing guidelines for federal policies affecting women—Simkins was elected. Of the 172 people nominated, only one received more votes, despite the fact that conservatives battling feminists over the selection of delegates and resolutions to be carried forward to the Houston conference distributed what Simkins called a "communist smear sheet" on her.[65]

Simkins supported many of the feminist causes to which the conservatives objected, including the proposed Equal Rights Amendment, whose ratification was then hotly debated in the state and the nation. Interviewed at the Houston conference, Simkins stated, "I think it would be a sad day, I mean a sad thing in this country that's calling for human rights all over the world if they can't give rights to their women." She said that she had long been concerned about discrimination against women and that as a black woman she had "been doubly victimized." She mentioned in particular the lack of representation of women in state and national government and the denial of leadership positions to women in many organizations, including churches, and insisted that women must "try to crash these barriers that have been set up." She wanted to see "more positive action against rape" and action on behalf of poor women such as those living in Appalachia and working in cane fields and textile mills.[66] In later years—even at the age of eighty-seven—she was part of a delegation of South Carolina women that went to Washington, D.C., to participate in the 1986 March for Women's Lives.[67]

Simkins's support for women's rights was part of her support for human rights. She called herself "a people's activist." She was a member of numerous organizations that were committed to community and political activism in the 1970s and 1980s, and she used whatever means were at her disposal to highlight the problems that poor and black South Carolinians faced.[68] Not only was Simkins assertive in her opinions and observations about the unjust and impoverished conditions throughout the state but she was also adamant about the ballot being the most effective means to bring change to those who were dispossessed.

When Modjeska Simkins died in 1992, many recalled that she often said, "I cannot be bought and I will not be sold." She lived her life with integrity. From her earliest years as a member of the Columbia NAACP until her bid for political office in that city, Modjeska Simkins was a force to be reckoned with for blacks and whites, Democrats and Republicans. As local and national political and civil rights leaders gathered in Columbia for her funeral, they remembered a woman who "always told it like it was." As they celebrated her life, they hailed her as "one of the world icons of the civil rights movement."[69] Clearly, no truer words have been spoken.

NOTES

1. Barbara Woods Aba-Mecha, "Black Woman Activist in Twentieth-Century South Carolina: Modjeska Monteith Simkins" (PhD diss., Emory University, 1978), 46.

2. Barbara A. Woods, "Modjeska Simkins and the South Carolina Conference of the NAACP, 1939–1957," in *Women in the Civil Rights Movement: Trailblazers and Torchbearers, 1941–1965*, ed. Vicki L. Crawford (Bloomington: Indiana University Press, 1990), 101.

3. Modjeska Simkins, interview with Jacquelyn Dowd Hall, July 28–31, 1976, reel 1, 9, Modjeska Simkins Papers, South Carolina Political Collections, University of South Carolina Libraries, University of South Carolina, Columbia (hereinafter cited as MSP-SCPC).

4. Ibid., reel 1, 15.

5. Modjeska Simkins, interview by Ann Y. Evans, Rock Hill, S.C., July 3, 1981, in *Women Leaders in South Carolina: An Oral History*, ed. Ronald J. Chepesuik, Ann Y. Evans, and Thomas S. Morgan (Rock Hill, S.C.: Winthrop College Archives and Special Collections, 1984), 54; Bettye Collier-Thomas, *Sisters in the Struggle: African American Women in the Civil Rights–Black Power Movement* (New York: New York University Press, 2001), 101.

6. Simkins, interview by Hall, July 28–31, 1976, reel 1, 33, MSP-SCPC.

7. Crawford, *Women in the Civil Rights Movement*, 104.

8. Simkins, interview by Evans, July 3, 1981, 55.

9. Simkins, interview by Hall, July 28–31, 1976, reel 1, 24, MSP-SCPC.

10. Woods Aba-Mecha, "Black Woman Activist in Twentieth-Century South Carolina," 90. His wife was Marion Birnie Wilkinson, a Charleston native and leader of the South Carolina Federation of Colored Women's Clubs.

11. Simkins, interview by Hall, July 28–31, 1976, reel 1, 35, MSP-SCPC; Crawford, *Women in the Civil Rights Movement*, 104.

12. Simkins, interview by Hall, July 28–31, 1976, reel 1, 35–36, MSP-SCPC.

13. Woods Aba-Mecha, "Black Woman Activist in Twentieth-Century South Carolina," 114.

14. Simkins, interview by Evans, July 3, 1981, 61.

15. Jack Irby Hayes Jr., *South Carolina and the New Deal* (Columbia: University of South Carolina Press, 2001), 168.

16. Hayes, *South Carolina and the New Deal*, 169.

17. Pellagra is a disease caused by niacin and protein deficiencies in the diet. The most common symptoms are dermatitis and gastrointestinal and central nervous system disorders.

18. Simkins, interview by Hall, July 28–31, 1976, reel 1, 46, MSP-SCPC.

19. Woods Aba-Mecha, "Black Woman Activist in Twentieth-Century South Carolina," 128–29.

20. Crawford, *Women in the Civil Rights Movement*, 106. Another source states that the first state meeting was held on November 10, 1939 (Edwin D. Hoffman, "The Genesis of the Modern Movement for Equal Rights in South Carolina, 1930–1939," *Journal of Negro History* 44, no. 4 [1959]: 368).

21. Collier-Thomas, *Sisters in the Struggle*, 101.

22. Simkins, interview by Evans, July 3, 1981, 61.

23. Crawford, *Women in the Civil Rights Movement*, 107.

24. Ibid., 108; Simkins, interview by Evans, July 3, 1981, 62.

25. Crawford, *Women in the Civil Rights Movement*, 108; Simkins, interview by Hall, July 28–31, 1976, reel 1, 87, MSP-SCPC.

26. Simkins, interview by Evans, July 3, 1981, 63.

27. Ernest McPherson Lander Jr., *A History of South Carolina, 1865–1960* (Chapel Hill: University of North Carolina Press, 1960), 42; Bryant Simon, "Race Reactions: African American Organizing, Liberalism, and White Working-Class Politics in Postwar South Carolina," in *Jumpin' Jim Crow: Southern Politics from Civil War to Civil Rights*, ed. Jane Dailey, Glenda Elizabeth Gilmore, and Bryant Simon (Princeton, N.J.: Princeton University Press, 2000), 241; Ralph J. Bunche, *The Political Status of the Negro in the Age of FDR* (Chicago: University of Chicago Press, 1973), 239.

28. Hanes Walton Jr., *Black Republicans: The Politics of the Black and Tans* (Metuchen, N.J.: Scarecrow Press, 1975), 115; George Brown Tindall, *The Emergence of the New South, 1913–1945* (Baton Rouge: Louisiana State University Press, 1967), 168.

29. "Confusion in South Carolina," *Southern Frontier* 5, no. 6 (1944): 1. This resolution was passed during the state convention.

30. Miles S. Richards, "Osceola E. McKaine and the Struggle for Black Civil Rights, 1917–1946" (PhD diss., University of South Carolina, 1994), 166.

31. Explanation of the plan for "Beating the Primary," April 2, 1944, reel 1, John H. McCray Papers, 1929–89, South Caroliniana Library, University of South Carolina, Columbia (hereinafter cited as JMP-SCL).

32. Kari Frederickson, "'Dual Actions, One for Each Race': The Campaign against the Dixiecrats in South Carolina, 1948–1950," *International Social Science Review*, 72, nos. 1 and 2 (1997): 15; Edmund L. Drago, *Initiative, Paternalism, and Race Relations: Charleston's Avery Normal Institute* (Athens: University of Georgia Press, 1990), 238.

33. Frederickson, "'Dual Actions, One for Each Race,'" 15.

34. Woods Aba-Mecha, "Black Woman Activist in Twentieth-Century South Carolina," 204; Simkins, interview by Hall, July 28–31, 1976, reel 1, 48, MSP-SCPC.

35. Walter Edgar, *South Carolina: A History* (Columbia: University of South Carolina Press, 1998), 519; *A Monthly Summary of Events and Trends in Race Relations* 1, no. 5 (1943): 10; 1, no. 8 (1944): 7; 2, no. 11 (1945): 320, 349; 4, no. 5 (1943); Drago, *Initiative, Paternalism, and Race Relations*, 23.

36. Crawford, *Women in the Civil Rights Movement*, 108.

37. Part 4, reel 10, Voting Rights Campaign, 1916–1950, National Association for the Advancement of Colored People Records, Library of Congress, Washington, D.C. (hereinafter cited as NAACPR-LOC).

38. Lander, *A History of South Carolina*, 169, 195.

39. "Courts Define the Right to Vote," *New South* 4, no. 2 (1949): 2.

40. Howard H. Quint, *Profile in Black and White: A Frank Portrait of South Carolina* (Washington, D.C.: Public Affairs Press, 1958), 5.

41. "The White Primary," *New South* 3, nos. 6 and 7 (1948): 15.

42. Part 4, reel 9, Voting Rights Campaign, 1916–1950, NAACPR-LOC; Edgar, *South Carolina*, 519; David W. Southern, "Beyond Jim Crow Liberalism: Judge Waring's Fight against Segregation in South Carolina, 1942–1952," *Journal of Negro History* 66, no. 3 (1981): 214.

43. Alice Stovall, secretary to Thurgood Marshall, to Mrs. A. W. Simkins, April 13, 1949, part 4, reel 9, Voting Rights Campaign, 1916–1950, NAACPR-LOC.

44. Woods Aba-Mecha, "Black Woman Activist in Twentieth-Century South Carolina," 207; "South Carolina Urges Drive for Vote," October 14, 1948, part 4, reel 11, Voting Rights Campaign, 1916–1950, NAACPR-LOC.

45. Simkins, interview by Evans, July 3, 1981, 65.

46. Minutes, Sumter NAACP meeting, November 23, 1947, Sumter NAACP Records, SCL.

47. Aba-Mecha, "Black Woman Activist in Twentieth-Century South Carolina," 209.

48. "Simple Facts About Registration," reel 7, JMP-SCL; Bunche, *The Political Status of the Negro in the Age of FDR*, 336.

49. "Republicans Tell Voters How to Recognize Ballot," *The Lighthouse and Informer* 12, no. 30 (1948): 1.

50. Simkins, interview by Hall, July 28–31, 1976, 48, MSP-SCPC.

51. Edgar, *South Carolina*, 521–22.

52. Ibid, 522.

53. Crawford, *Women in the Civil Rights Movement*, 109.

54. Simkins, interview by Evans, July 3, 1981, 66.

55. The Victory Savings Bank had been black owned and operated since 1921.

56. Simkins, interview by Hall, July 28–31, 1976, 77, MSP-SCPC. She even received funds from a farmer in Quito, Ecuador.

57. Ibid., 67; Crawford, *Women in the Civil Rights Movement*, 112–13; Woods Aba-Mecha, "Black Woman Activist in Twentieth-Century South Carolina," 240.

58. Crawford, *Women in the Civil Rights Movement*, 115.

59. Ibid., 115; "Information from the Files of the Committee on Un-American Activities, U.S. House of Representatives: Subject: Modjeska Simkins," July 13, 1965, box 1, folder 1, Modjeska Simkins Papers, Louise Pettus Archives and Special Collections, Dacus Library, Winthrop University, Rock Hill, S.C. (hereinafter cited as LPASC).

60. "Remembering Modjeska," *Point*, January 1995, reel 1, MSP-SCPC.

61. Biographical sketch of Modjeska Simkins, reel 1, MSP-SCPC.

62. Simkins, interview by Evans, July 3, 1981, 67, 68.

63. RCCC broadcast, March 22, 1967, reel 11, MSP-SCPC.

64. "We Appeal to Boys and Girls," September 28, 1966, reel 11, MSP-SCPC.

65. Lessie M. Reynolds and Maryneal Jones, *The South Carolina Woman: Heritage to Horizons* (n.p.: South Carolina International Women's Year Committee, 1977); Marianna W. Davis, interview by Constance Ashton Myers, November 20, 1977, South Carolina International Women's Year Conference, 1976–2003, Constance Ashton Myers Collection, SCL.

66. Davis, interview by Myers, November 20, 1977.

67. Nancy Moore to Marjorie Spruill, July 2008.

68. "Remembering Modjeska," *Point*, January 1995, reel 1, MSP-SCPC, reel 1. She was also a member of the United Citizens Party, which was formed in 1969 in South Carolina because the state Democratic Party refused to nominate blacks for political offices. Simkins was later named honorary lifetime president of the organization.

69. "Simkins' Spirit Lives, Mourners Say," *The State*, April 10, 1992, A-1.

Septima Poinsette Clark

The Evolution of an Educational Stateswoman

KATHERINE MELLEN CHARRON

❀ ❀ ❀

Septima Clark (1898–1987) is most frequently remembered for her role in developing the Citizenship Schools, an adult education program that began on Johns Island, South Carolina, in 1957 and spread throughout the South after the Southern Christian Leadership Conference (SCLC) adopted it in 1961. In these civil rights era classes, thousands of disfranchised African Americans learned to read and write so they might register to vote. Beyond that, students gained a better understanding of skills that ranged from managing a bank account and paying taxes to establishing local voting leagues and lobbying for improved municipal services. Linking the power of the ballot to concrete strategies for individual and communal empowerment, the Citizenship Schools provided a crucial, if underappreciated, tool for mobilizing local communities.[1] Yet to evaluate Clark's contribution to the African American freedom struggle—within the Palmetto State and beyond—by focusing solely on this program is to obscure both its historical significance and hers. Drawing on four decades of experience, Clark adapted an organizing tradition forged by earlier generations of black women activist educators, one premised on addressing a wide range of community needs, to meet the demands of the modern civil rights movement, thus contributing greatly to its success.[2]

Education was never a politically neutral issue in the Jim Crow South. Throughout the twentieth century, black and white South Carolinians were embattled over education precisely because they understood its centrality in either upholding or challenging the racial, economic, and social status quo. Septima Clark participated in these battles on several fronts, including the classroom, the community, the state legislature, and the courts. Her experiences illustrate how southern black women activist educators laid a foundation that made the civil rights movement possible. They also remind us that both African American militancy and the response of white officials changed over time. Clark gleaned valuable insights from victories and failures in each stage of the struggle, and she applied these in pursuit of racial, economic, and social justice.

Born in Charleston, on May 3, 1898, Septima Earthaline Poinsette inherited a world shaped as African Americans gained and lost political power in the post–Civil War years. Freedom for most black South Carolinians, including her slave-born father, had arrived only three decades earlier, and the Lowcountry, with its black majority population, had served as an epicenter of black political activism. Former slaves and their allies prioritized education in the mighty effort to institutionalize their newfound liberty.[3] The African American men who won seats in the state legislature established a free, state-supported school system; at the grassroots, a determination to secure an education by any means necessary took root.[4] Yet Septima Poinsette also spent her girlhood traversing a terrain scarred by the hatefulness of white supremacy. White elite Democrats, united by a passionate conviction that black political power was illegitimate and committed to regaining control over the state's black agricultural labor force, led the counterrevolution that ultimately owed its victory to violence. Seizing control of the state government in 1876, they did not succeed completely until 1895 when, overriding the objections of six black delegates, members of the state constitutional convention wrote a new constitution that disfranchised thousands of poor South Carolinians, both black and white.[5]

Inevitably, black education remained secure only as long as African Americans retained a vestige of political power in state government. As one white state school official explained in 1911, "The objections to negro education arise chiefly from the feeling that it unfits the negro for the place he must fill in the state . . . and that the so-called educated negro too often becomes a loafer or a political agitator."[6] In practice, this hostility translated into miserly spending on facilities and equipment for black schools and on the salaries of those who taught within them. Overcrowded, dilapidated classrooms that lacked basic supplies with high teacher-to-pupil ratios and shorter terms became the norm. By 1916, South Carolina spent 9.4 times more money educating its white pupils. As late as 1949–1950, it spent 2.1 times more on whites.[7]

Such realities presented problems for Poinsette's parents, Peter and Victoria, who remained committed to educating their children. In 1903 Septima Poinsette began attending Shaw Memorial School, a public school. She later claimed that one hundred black first graders sat on bleachers in what was called the "ABC gallery" and that the white teachers spent most of their time escorting students to the bathroom outdoors. "We didn't learn too much," she recalled.

SEPTIMA POINSETTE CLARK

Courtesy of the Avery Research Center for
African American History and Culture,
College of Charleston, Charleston, S.C.

Worse, she observed, these white teachers "didn't like for black children to speak to them in the streets. I guess they didn't want other people to know they were teaching blacks."[8] In the Charleston of Poinsette's girlhood, the white women who benefited from the city fathers' refusal to hire black teachers also played a role reinforcing white ideas of black inferiority.

At a time when the financially pressed family "zealously hoarded coupons" to exchange as birthday and holiday gifts, Peter and Victoria Poinsette used their meager funds to send their children to black-run private schools whenever possible. Their second daughter passed the second and third grades under the tutelage of two black women who taught in their home. Such instruction circumvented the inadequacies of black public schools controlled by whites. Smaller teacher-to-pupil ratios in the private schools meant more attention devoted to each child and longer terms allowed children to make greater progress academically. Moreover, for teachers the lack of white oversight—especially pertaining to curriculum matters—provided the freedom to include lessons on black history and achievement. African American private school teachers also offered nonacademic lessons in culture and manners as a way to cultivate an overall commitment to excellence in their students. In this way, they attempted to produce leaders for the future and to bequeath a legacy of pride to subsequent generations.[9]

After the opening of the Charleston Colored Industrial School, later renamed Burke High School, Septima Poinsette returned to public school and completed grades four through eight. For decades Burke was the lone public institution in the entire county where black students could obtain more than an elementary education. Remarkably, Poinsette could have begun her career when she finished the eighth grade because her graduating certificate qualified her to teach. Her mother refused to consider it. "You must get some more education," Victoria Poinsette insisted. "You'll go to Avery next year."[10]

Founded in 1865 and sponsored by the northern-based American Missionary Association, the Avery Normal Institute in Charleston cast a shining light onto an otherwise dismal educational landscape. For Septima Poinsette, Avery represented an academic "paradise." Its liberal arts curriculum appealed to the scholar in her, and she relished perusing the books in its library. She participated in many extracurricular activities as well, including singing in the glee club and playing for the girls' basketball team. She also joined the King's Daughters, a group established to aid the less fortunate; her work through this organization complemented the lessons in community service that Poinsette learned at home and at church.[11] The school was less than a social paradise, however. If Poinsette's friends ignored the class and caste distinctions that divided Charleston's

African American community, their families did not. "I was considered beneath a lot of the students since my mother was a washerwoman and my father had been a slave," she noted, "and so I couldn't go to any of the parties that were given by the parents of my classmates."[12]

As a teacher training institute for black South Carolinians, Avery was unsurpassed. The school's pedagogical approach reflected broader educational trends in the Progressive Era, particularly the importance of "learning by doing" and the close relationship between the curriculum and life experiences. The fact that there were no jobs available for black teachers in Charleston's public schools meant that Avery graduates who wanted to stay in the Lowcountry had to teach in the rural county system. There, they had to adapt current educational theories to stark realities: most rural African Americans lived in perpetual debt, working for white landlords as tenant farmers, sharecroppers, and cotton pickers. Still, Septima Poinsette's instructors taught their students that black women had a special role to play as moral agents who shouldered the responsibility of promoting self-help and self-sufficiency in rural hinterlands.[13]

After receiving her licentiate of instruction in 1916, an eighteen-year-old Poinsette secured a job on Johns Island, an isolated sea island off the coast of Charleston. Like many African American teachers, she embraced a strong commitment to the community in which she taught. "I felt I was in a position as the school teacher," Poinsette averred, "to help them in some small way at least toward achieving a better life." This is what sustained her. "I was not discouraged," she added, "despite the sea of faces that confronted me everyday that I walked into our crude and uncomfortable classroom."[14]

As long as white South Carolinians proved indifferent to conditions in black rural schools, black teachers operated with a considerable degree of autonomy. On one hand, this created daily hardships. The young Poinsette and another teacher met 132 students in a building that had mud-filled cracks in the walls, shuttered windows that kept the wind out but darkened the room, a fireplace that spread its heat unevenly, and makeshift homemade benches for pupils. The only equipment supplied by the district trustees included a bucket and dipper for water, one table, one chair, and an ax in lieu of firewood.[15] On the other hand, the two women had considerable leeway in devising ways of coping with these problems.

Circumstances in rural black schools required educators to hone their improvisational skills and combine them with flexibility and creativity. In the absence of textbooks, Septima Poinsette encouraged her children to tell stories of their everyday lives, which she then incorporated into reading and spelling lessons. When she secured a few dog-eared books from the local school trustees, Poinsette had her students compose a story based on the illustrations. "You can't say 'Get a book and open it,'" she realized. Instead, you had to ask, "Look at this picture. Does it look like people are living here?" Smoke rising from a house with a chimney, for example, signaled the affirmative. "This is the way you build up your story," she asserted. "*Your* creative ability is the thing that you need to pull out of these children *their* creative ability."[16]

Black educators also labored to reach beyond the schoolhouse into the homes of students because their training had emphasized the necessity of forging relationships with parents. Rural educators, especially, knew that improving the quality of life meant instilling the desire to learn in both children *and* adults, and that, as Rose Butler Browne put it, "a good teacher meets her learners where they are."[17] To this end, teachers sacrificed afternoon, evening, and weekend hours. Septima Poinsette spent two days a week after school helping women who wanted to learn to sew. Other afternoons, as she walked back to the house where she boarded, she stopped "to help" her neighbors "drop seed in their garden." On Saturdays, she visited with them again.[18] Such informal activities dissolved the boundaries between the school and the home. The first task was to put at ease people who, in many cases, harbored unpleasant memories of the classroom or failed to appreciate how education might benefit their children. It took time.

Rural communities likewise took pride in "our teacher" and expected her to aid them in the business of daily life, such as by writing letters, filling out mail order forms, and figuring crop prices and wages. In the course of fulfilling these duties, Septima Poinsette began to reevaluate Johns Islanders. Initially, she had judged them as a people "who led listless, indifferent lives." From Charleston, the young teacher had brought preconceived biases based in the difference between urban and rural living. When a group of men who had formed a black fraternal organization sought her help in speechwriting, however, she began to change her mind. At first Poinsette and her coteacher wrote the speeches and read them to the men, who then memorized them. Before long, though, the men wanted to write their own speeches. Poinsette discerned that the men's desire to improve themselves enhanced the success of this informal adult education effort. They learned faster as they applied themselves to a specific and personally relevant goal.[19] By assisting such groups, Poinsette promoted the development of lay leadership in the community.

More broadly, the young Septima Poinsette helped others to imagine a different world by teaching people how to help themselves. Throughout the bleakest years of segregation, she and other black activist educators painstakingly built a social service and educational infrastructure that linked theories of racial uplift to practical needs of local communities. If success was uneven, the experience of rural teaching conditioned their sensibilities to the interdependence of short-run survival strategies and long-term change. By her own testimony, teaching and living on Johns Island prompted Poinsette to start thinking about "getting things done."[20]

She soon applied this lesson to more explicit political action. Following World War I, Poinsette accepted a job at Avery, moved back home, and joined the Charleston NAACP in its campaign to press the city government to hire black teachers and principals for its segregated public schools.[21] White school board officials argued that the impetus for the change came from the black professional classes and that the majority of working-class black parents believed their children would benefit more from white teachers. To prove them wrong, Poinsette led her sixth-grade students through the city's neighborhoods collecting signatures that NAACP leaders then submitted to members of the state general assembly. The campaign accomplished several things. First, the attempt to procure the desired change through legislative action raised the black community's awareness of their right "to participate in matters of public concern."[22] Second, taking the fight to the state legislature taught disfranchised black South Carolinians that they could reenter politics as lobbyists, if not as voters. The proposed legislation to force Charleston to hire black teachers never came to a vote because city officials acquiesced. In Poinsette's first organized political experience, activism worked. Moreover, she had chosen an issue that offered her a chance to advocate on behalf of black children *and* to expand personal and professional options for black women. She would follow that pattern throughout her life.

The ensuing decade taught Septima Poinsette a cruel lesson in the ways of men. Nerie (pronounced Nee-rye) David Clark, a sailor from Hickory, North Carolina, first caught the young teacher's eye one night at the segregated USO club where she was serving as a hostess. Despite her mother's disapproval, Poinsette married him in the spring of 1920. Septima Clark later explained her reasoning: "Since I had never fallen in love before, I had a feeling that this was my chance. This was my life, so I went ahead with it."[23] Often away with the navy, Nerie Clark visited his wife when he could. In March 1921, she gave birth to a daughter but, twenty-three days later, the baby died. Disconsolate, Clark left Charleston and eventually moved north with her husband, settling in Dayton, Ohio. The couple welcomed a healthy son in February 1925 and named him for his father. But while she lay in the hospital, Clark "learned that my husband had been divorced from one woman and was virtually living with another right there in Dayton."[24] Within four months, she and the infant Nerie Jr. had moved to Hickory to live with her in-laws. That December, Septima Clark was called back to Dayton as her husband lay dying of kidney failure. She escorted his body home and assumed the role of grieving widow.

Clark never remarried. In time, she developed a rationale for her decision. Aside from the trauma of Nerie Sr.'s infidelity, she worried over how a new man would treat her son. "I never felt as if another man would take the other man's child, and I didn't want him shunted aside by anybody," she maintained. When she returned to Johns Island to teach in 1927, however, poor local health conditions forced her to send Nerie Jr. to live full time with his paternal grandparents. Over the years, Clark also came to assign a high value to the freedom to make her own life decisions, claiming that she "never could take a lot of foolishness off a man." This became especially clear to her during the heyday of the civil rights movement, when she either resided far from home or when fund-raising demanded constant travel. "I don't think I would have been able [to do] very much," Clark asserted. "I'm very sure a man wouldn't have put up with it."[25]

In 1929, Septima Clark seized an opportunity to relocate to Columbia. With this move, she became part of a much larger network of influential black men and women who led attempts to dismantle segregation and to insist on integration on equitable terms. As she observed, living in the urban state capital "strengthened my determination to make my own life count . . . in the struggle to aid the underprivileged" and "gave me excellent training in procedures that could be used effectively in the struggle."[26] The Depression contributed to a decline in membership in the state chapters of the NAACP and its political inertia in the mid-1930s. Yet during these years Clark gained important training in woman-centered organizations including the Palmetto State Teachers Association and the South Carolina Federation of Colored Women's Clubs.

In Columbia Septima Clark first taught third graders at the Booker T. Washington School, which served students in grades one through eleven. Her colleagues in Richland County District no. 1 embraced the same educational ethos as rural teachers. The less-than-ideal conditions of the physical plant and the lack of equipment at Booker T., for example, forced the faculty to improvise pedagogically. Teachers were also encouraged to "know the parents, and the only way you could know them was to visit."[27] The biggest difference that urban teachers encountered was greater supervision of their work, though usually from African American school administrators. "From the beginning," Clark recalled, "teaching in Columbia opened my eyes. In the first years there . . . I'm sure I learned more than I taught." Her principal, Cornell A. Johnson, convened weekly meetings with his staff that emphasized pedagogical planning and methodology as well as professional development. Though some faculty "grumbled" about having to stay after school two days a week, Clark felt Johnson's sessions were beneficial. "They really prepared me for the teacher's examination I had to take later on," she claimed.[28] Nor could Clark have failed to notice the impressive credentials of her colleagues. All of the black elementary school teachers in Richland County District no. 1 held first-grade teaching certificates, which required two years of normal or college training. In an environment that promoted professional development, Clark made the decision to complete her undergraduate education and to pursue a master's degree, which she eventually obtained from the Hampton Institute. Every teacher at Septima Clark's new school also belonged to the Palmetto State Teachers Association (PSTA), and she joined that group as well.[29]

Retaining black control of black education underlay the mission of the PSTA, which had been established in 1900. By the early 1920s, its leaders had developed a program that would define the association's agenda for the next thirty years. Their primary goal was to make South Carolina's separate education equal in terms of school funding and facilities, teacher preparation and pay, and the length of the school year. Power within the PSTA had always been concentrated in the hands of a few, mostly men, who filled prestigious administrative positions in the state's public schools and private colleges.[30] Women comprised the majority of rank-and-file members, however, and represented 80 percent of the state's black teaching force by 1932. When Septima Clark added her name to its rolls in the early 1930s, PSTA leaders oversaw one of the most influential black professional groups in the state. Membership had increased seven times in the past decade. By 1940, PSTA enrollment would double again, and thirty-eight counties would count 100 percent of their teachers as members.[31]

For thousands of black teachers in South Carolina, participation in the PSTA offered instruction in organizing and fighting the battle to equalize educational opportunity. Particularly notable were the legal and legislative committees of county chapters that acted as watchdogs, as one member put it. Their job was "to study proposed school legislation and conduct conferences on them," "to plan a program of action," "to facilitate their passage if we indorse them or to insure their deport if we do not," and "to propose legislation and work for [its] passage."[32] Membership in the PSTA inspired Septima Clark. Attending the annual PSTA conventions during the interwar years, she realized "we teachers had a visible demonstration of our importance, of what we already were; it didn't take much to imagine what we might be in the life of our state." A broader perspective informed Clark's sense of the impact these women could make. Surveying her PSTA colleagues, she saw many in the crowd who, like herself, devoted their spare time to civic improvement. As she asserted, "More important to me than the teacher-training programs and even the teaching itself, as far as my own development was concerned[,] . . . were the opportunities I had in Columbia to participate in civic activities."[33] Clark's vision of political possibility in the interwar years took the potential power of both teachers and clubwomen into account.

Marion Birnie Wilkinson, the wife of the president of South Carolina State, the state's black public college, and Celia Dial Saxon, a history teacher at Booker T. Washington, were among the women who founded the South Carolina Federation of Colored Women's Clubs (SCFCWC) in a Columbia church in 1909. Their goals, as stated in the organization's constitution, included promoting the "education of colored women," working "for the social, moral, economic, and religious welfare of women and children," and securing and enforcing "civil and political rights for our group." The SCFCWC specifically targeted teachers in its recruiting efforts. Clark was attracted to the program from the beginning.[34]

Becoming a clubwoman taught Septima Clark how to work within a network of women for more systematic improvements. African American women activists who aimed to advance health conditions for black South Carolinians, for example, depended upon the state's teaching force to reach local communities. In 1931 Modjeska Simkins became a field worker for the South Carolina Tuberculosis Association, charged with the duty of raising child health awareness through education. She approached South Carolina's teachers first, addressing them at state and county educational meetings and PTA gatherings. Next, Simkins organized a two-day institute in the summer teacher training sessions at South Carolina State. As community liaisons and community leaders, teachers played pivotal roles in getting the message to parents and other adults.[35] Black clubwomen also crossed the color line to work with white clubwomen as they sought to capitalize on social welfare opportunities underwritten by the state. Finally, involvement with the SCFCWC schooled Septima Clark in becoming an effective community leader. "*Real leadership*," clubwoman Etta B. Rowe asserted, "does not mean standing at the head of an organization—real leadership is that technique . . . that induces others to work and perform in a like manner."[36] Clark came to believe that better living conditions, better schools, better health facilities, and respect for black womanhood could only materialize with concerted and collective effort.

Engaging in a flurry of educational and civic service also convinced Clark of the need to participate in a more systematic program of adult education, which brought her into contact with white educator Wil Lou Gray, one of South Carolina's most dynamic women. As the state supervisor of adult education, Gray embraced an educational philosophy and organizing sensibility that resembled the uplift efforts of black teachers and clubwomen like Septima Clark.

Adult classroom instruction focused on surmounting mundane problems that students confronted, from the relationship between better work habits and increased wages to health education and domestic science, to becoming "better informed" citizens. By the 1930s, Gray oversaw schools for adults in every county of the state and had institutionalized the Opportunity School, a summer program for both white and black South Carolinians that she had originally created for white textile workers in 1921.[37]

On March 25, 1935, Septima Clark began teaching in Gray's Richland County adult school program. She met her class at Booker T. Washington three evenings a week for nine weeks. Her fourteen students ranged in age from seventeen to sixty-five, and the majority were at the fourth-grade level. Two could not read at all, and Clark reported that she taught them to sign their names, "fill out money orders," and to read "simple directions," and the "names of occupation[s]." With regard to improving "community ideals and attitudes," Clark stated that "health standards" had been "built up from Social Science" instruction, and "worthy citizens" had been "developed from understanding the laws through discussions." When asked what might be done to improve the work, Clark took a cue from what she had learned from her former principal Cornell Johnson. "Have group meetings for adult teachers twice a month to improve methods of presentation of the work," she advised.[38]

Clark later observed that Gray was an important influence on her. Specifically, Gray relied on two distinct pedagogical methods to teach adult learners that Clark found compelling. The first was giving each pupil a piece of cardboard on which to trace their names until they learned how to write. The second was the compilation of a booklet full of information on South Carolina, such as population figures or crop acreages, to teach reading. Gray's reader reflected the ongoing concern with fashioning a curriculum relevant to students' lived experience, but there was a more practical purpose as well. Teachers used Gray's booklet in lieu of traditional elementary primers that she recognized embarrassed grown men and women.[39]

Clark also characterized Gray as racially progressive for the era. "I think when she came over to the place where we were . . . she had just as much of a good feeling about the blacks as she did the whites, but they were segregated."[40] Wil Lou Gray's program provided no overt challenge to the social and political status quo. Yet teaching reading and writing to black adults helped Septima Clark to realize that her students would never feel like full citizens without literacy. Coupled with her participation in the PSTA and the SCFCWC, Clark's activism during the interwar years reflected a practical response to specific problems that black children and black adults confronted.

By the time Clark left Columbia to return to Charleston in 1947, however, the PSTA had abdicated whatever leadership it might have offered black South Carolinians in the emerging postwar civil rights struggle. Teacher activism of the 1940s—not the lack of it—split the PSTA into two factions. There were "young Turks" who advocated launching a direct attack on educational inequalities by filing court suits with the help of the NAACP, on the one hand, and cautious leaders who were determined to preserve their hard-won standing with white officials, on the other. Though hardly a "young Turk," Septima Clark characterized her participation in Columbia's 1945 teacher salary equalization case as her first "radical" act, "the first time I had worked *against* people directing the system for which I was working." Many of her colleagues, she noted, opposed court action out of a fear of failing a more rigid examination for teacher certification to equalize their salaries.[41]

Their fear was not unfounded. Before any suit had been filed, W. Brantley Harvey Sr. assured his colleagues in the state senate that "we intend to get around the matter of equalizing teacher salaries on the basis of our plan to re-certify Negro teachers."[42] In the wake of the NAACP's victory, as Harvey had predicted, white supremacists in South Carolina mandated recertification for the state's entire teaching corps and tied salaries to teachers' scores on the National Teachers' Examination. At the same time, they provided funds for white teachers to secure the additional training that would enhance their performance on the test but offered no assistance for African Americans. From the mid-1940s onward, increased white surveillance of black educators replaced decades of white indifference. In this new environment, black teachers secretly supported the NAACP, but the majority refused to risk their livelihood by agitating for civil rights. Septima Clark adopted the view that her individual courage strengthened her entire community. "I felt that in reality I was working for the accomplishment of something that ultimately would be good for everyone, and I worked not only with an easy conscience but with inspiration and enthusiasm."[43]

At forty-nine, Clark returned to the Lowcountry with considerably more personal confidence and familiarity with political affairs. She resumed her civic participation with vigor and, except for her work with the NAACP, her activism continued to express itself in women-centered organizations, including the local chapter of the National Council of Negro Women and the segregated branch of the YWCA. Clark's most controversial act in this period of her life was befriending federal judge J. Waties Waring, a white Charlestonian blueblood, and his wife, Elizabeth. Waring's 1947 ruling that South Carolina must "rejoin the union" and allow its black citizens to register and vote in the Democratic primary sent shock waves throughout the state and made him a pariah among those determined to thwart civil rights progress.[44] Elizabeth Waring entered the fray in 1950 when she gave an incendiary speech at Charleston's black YWCA attacking white segregationists. White Y women had pressured their African American counterparts to rescind Waring's invitation to speak, brandishing as leverage the possible appointment of a black woman to their board. As chairwoman of the black Y's Committee on Management, Septima Clark refused their request. On the night of Waring's talk, she took precautions against possible retribution from the Ku Klux Klan by stationing black men around the room and near the lights.[45] Black Charlestonians generally approved of the Warings' civil rights stance. Still, as the stakes rose, most weighed the personal and professional costs of association with the iconoclastic couple and kept their distance.

That she risked alienation indicates how much her relationship with the Warings meant to Septima Clark. This represented her first genuine interracial friendship; the couple became the first whites with whom she socialized and shared meals. The Warings served as important political mentors as well, and their counsel helped crystallize Clark's sense of what kind of civil rights work to pursue: complete integration. Not all black Charlestonians agreed. At school, Clark's colleagues complained that her actions legitimated segregationists' claims that "the real reason blacks wanted integration was to socialize with whites."[46] In the civic arena, where Clark labored to abolish segregated auxiliaries in various community organizations, she encountered opposition from both white and black women. For black women, the chief problem was forfeiting control of their finances and their programs for token representation on a white-dominated board. Thus, by adopting an uncompromising stand for full integration in the early 1950s, Septima Clark distanced herself from the civic-minded black women whose value system she shared and with whom she had worked intimately for years.

In addition, attempts to wield the power of the ballot exposed the divisions within Charleston's black community. This became especially apparent in the 1951 mayoral race, when African Americans split over whether to support the incumbent William Morrison or state senator Oliver T. Wallace. Septima Clark attributed Morrison's victory to the fact that he "gave away more money" in key black wards, which implied that some black leaders aimed to profit by selling black votes in return for future favors.[47] A year later, despite a community-wide registration effort to add nearly thirteen thousand African Americans to the voting rolls, an unsuccessful bid by three prominent black Charlestonians to gain seats in the state house of representatives underscored how much voter confusion handicapped the newly enfranchised. In this instance, failure alerted Septima Clark to the need for a new kind of voter education. Less than satisfactory progress on several other fronts—including attempts to secure a new school for black children and to get the school board to desegregate Charleston's schools in the wake of *Brown v. Board of Education*—led Clark to conclude that most of Charleston's black leaders were either too timid or lacked the vision and skills to achieve results.

Seeking a more useful course of action, Clark attended a workshop on integration at the Highlander Folk School (HFS) in the summer of 1954. She found its approach a welcome change. The school based its pedagogical philosophy on cooperative problem solving. Director Myles Horton and his staff began with the assumption that "oppressed people know the answers to their own problems" and developed workshops geared toward discovering answers contained within the "experience and imagination of the group."[48] The school strove to make the American democratic ideal a reality by equipping students to improve conditions where they lived. In this sense, its philosophy was not altogether different from that which infused Septima Clark's activist educational world. Yet the HFS concept of leadership emphasized the importance of ordinary people— not just the educated—taking part in the decision-making process and assuming the responsibility of getting their neighbors involved. HFS broadened Clark's thinking about who exactly could serve as a leader. By the end of 1954, she had become the main conduit for Highlander's efforts in the Lowcountry. The next summer she worked at the school part time.

In 1956, Clark's interests collided with the attempts of white supremacists in South Carolina to quell African American activism. That March, Governor George Bell Timmerman Jr. signed into law a bill that barred city, county, and state employees from belonging to the NAACP. With the blessing of the state board of education, local school boards added a page to their annual job applications mandating that all teachers list their organizational affiliations. Septima Clark refused to conceal her NAACP membership on the questionnaire. Consequently, the school board voted not to renew her teaching contract. Clark knew full well why she lost her job. "I had been completely outspoken in my talks and participation," she conceded, "though I was mindful of the fact that as a teacher in the public schools I would be vulnerable to criticism." Disavowing concern, she asserted "I was trying to do what I felt was my duty; I was trying then as I had tried through the years before and have been trying in the years since to contribute something to the advancement of our southern community by helping elevate the lives of a large segment of it."[49] Unemployed, Clark joined the HFS staff full time.

The initial request for an adult education program designed to promote voter registration had come from Johns Island community leader Esau Jenkins whom

Clark had recruited to go to HFS in 1954. Returning home, Jenkins ran for a seat on the school board and lost by a slim margin. The experience convinced him of the need to increase the number of black registered voters on Johns Island. Back at HFS in 1955, Jenkins announced, "I need a school. I need somebody to help me, tell me how I can get a school going to teach my people."[50] Septima Clark answered his request.

In designing the Citizenship School program, Clark brought forty years of practice as an African American educator and civic organizer to the task. Literacy training, she believed, was the key to success. Myles Horton disagreed. According to Clark, he thought that if an HFS staff member explained the laws to people and prepared them specifically for the voter registration test, they would be ready to make the trip to the registrar's office. Experience teaching adult literacy classes and familiarity with the shortcomings of past voter registration campaigns led Clark to a different conclusion. If the school could make the people more self-sufficient it would enhance their self-confidence to the point where they could assume the risks of civil rights agitation in their communities.[51] Translating practical literacy into political literacy, Clark linked individual and communal resources to a vision of citizenship that would guarantee that the newly enfranchised made informed decisions and took effective action after leaving the voting booth.

Equally significant, Clark devised a radical adult education program that appeared nonthreatening because it looked like what black women teachers had been doing in the Jim Crow South for decades. Few moderate white South Carolinians would have seen teaching semiliterate black adults to read and write as anything less than a worthy activity—as long as it did not interfere with the demands of planters and landowners for whom they worked. The first Citizenship School, which opened on Johns Island in January 1957, ran two nights a week for two months in the agricultural off-season.

Septima Clark's cousin, Bernice Robinson, a beautician less vulnerable to white economic reprisals, served as the first teacher. Beyond using their new literacy skills to obtain a voter registration certificate, most of the adult students told Robinson they wanted to use them to read the newspaper, their Bibles, and letters coming from their children far away as well as to fill out catalog and mail order forms. Drawing on her teaching for Wil Lou Gray, Septima Clark suggested to Robinson that each student receive a piece of cardboard with their name written on it so they could trace the letters until they learned how to write. Like Gray, Clark also compiled a special reading booklet for students. Because Clark viewed a large part of achieving citizenship as acquiring the information that citizens needed, materials in the booklet stressed the importance of law and procedure. Its most critical lesson was not altogether different from Gray's primer; to be "heard" by community officials, citizens had to speak their language.[52] But whereas Gray's "citizenship education" had uncritically celebrated South Carolina and aimed to inculcate respect for existing political institutions, Clark's curriculum connected learning directly to social change through political action. As she pointed out, "We need to think about taxes, social welfare programs, labor management relations, schools and old age pensions. These affect our daily lives and are definitely tied to the vote."[53]

Within a year, demands for similar classes reached HFS from neighboring Sea Islands and Charleston. This forced Clark and Horton to formalize pedagogical procedures so that the program could be applied to other locations. The two agreed that all classes would be taught by African Americans who came from the local community. Well-meaning whites, Horton conceded, would have trouble breaking the habit of controlling discussions, and black adult students needed to dismantle any internalized belief that "white was right." As for teacher qualifications, "those who could read well aloud and write legibly," Clark confirmed, "that was our standard."[54] Prospective teachers were required to attend a five-day training workshop at Highlander and to return at a later date for a weekend follow-up session. At home, Citizenship School teachers had to conduct research. They had to know the location and hours of the voter registration office, the names of local elected officials, and when elections were held. They also had to know what health services were available in the community, and the location of the nearest Social Security and welfare offices. By 1961, when state repression—including the arrest of a teetotaling Septima Clark for allegedly possessing liquor in a dry county—forced HFS to bequeath the program to the Southern Christian Leadership Conference (SCLC), its pedagogy and methodology had been firmly established.

Septima Clark joined Dorothy Cotton and Andrew Young in the Citizenship Education Program (CEP) division of SCLC and, together, they conducted teacher training sessions once a month at the Dorchester Center in Liberty County, Georgia. Over the years, the trio adapted the curriculum around what people said they wanted to learn and to new developments in the movement. For instance, they instituted a training session entitled "New Trends in Politics," which described how political machines and policy-making bodies worked as well as how CEP graduates could leverage that knowledge as advocates for civil rights, social security, or farm and labor legislation. The CEP's genius lay both in its flexibility and its specificity. By 1963, classes extended across the southern Black Belt from east Texas to the Virginia Tidewater.[55]

Typically, in the CEP, women outnumbered men—which is why Septima

Clark believed that "training in citizenship education helped women to realize their worth in society."[56] Education had long been perceived by the broader
society as "women's work," yet the Citizenship Schools also provided a space
for women to exercise decision-making autonomy. For example, during a meeting in Montgomery, Alabama, in January 1961, three women and one man volunteered to establish classes. On hearing what was expected of them, Clark
reported, one woman "made it clear that this would be her program and there
would be no dictation." In other words, she would brook no orders from above.
Such autonomy produced quick results. By April of that year, five teachers instructed a total of 235 students in Montgomery.[57]

Becoming Citizenship School teachers changed grassroots women's self-
perceptions and establishing local classes allowed them to articulate what these
changes meant. Following their teacher training sessions, Fannie Puckett, Mary
Dowdy, and Mattie Shaw wrote Septima Clark a letter in which they outlined
their organizing classes in their community in Fayette County, Tennessee. "We
as Freedom Fighter[s] with all the oppsitation [sic] we have meat [sic]," they
concluded, "will fight until the Battle is fought and the victory is won."[58] Puckett,
Dowdy, and Shaw pledged themselves to the struggle and redefined themselves
in the space created by that commitment. In the process of canvassing their
communities, teaching classes, and sustaining their programs, these formerly
disfranchised and semiliterate women became "Freedom Fighters."

Aside from the one week a month that she devoted to training teachers, Clark
spent most of her time traveling to places where CEP graduates had requested
help, reminding local planners beforehand that "my idea is to work with the
teachers and not be concerned about big meetings."[59] She did, however, confer with community members in crisis situations. During all of SCLC's major
campaigns, "Septima met with women in the churches to explain what was
going on," Andrew Young confirmed, "and it was far less threatening for her
to do [so] than say, for me to do it, or even for Martin Luther King to do it."[60]
As Clark knew from a lifetime of teaching and civic organizing, women spoke
more frankly among other women and were able to get things done in their
community as a result.

Respect for and recognition of black women's "behind-the-scenes" activities,
however, amounted to another matter entirely. SCLC welcomed women's contributions as long as they remained invisible. Years later, from a post–women's
movement perspective, Clark characterized "the way the men looked at the
women" as "one of the weaknesses of the civil rights movement."[61] Within SCLC,
she added, black women "were never able to put ourselves on the agenda to
speak to the group." If they had, SCLC's tactical and financial decisions might

have been different, particularly with regard to the crippling reallocation of scarce resources to northern and urban campaigns in the mid-1960s.[62] Nevertheless, the CEP became the forum in which Septima Clark transferred both the philosophy and the know-how of an earlier cohort of black women teachers to a new generation of civic organizers. As such, the ongoing activism of women who passed through the CEP in the 1960s must be understood as reflecting an enduring educational and political culture forged by southern black women. Like those before them, Citizenship School teachers and students used their training to expand the goals of the movement beyond voter registration to tackle employment, health care, and public education issues in their local communities.

Clark retired from SCLC in 1970, but she hardly stopped working. Back in Charleston, she focused on the issues that had always commanded her attention. In 1974, Clark won election to the same school board that had fired her eighteen years earlier. As the lone African American board member, she proved a fierce advocate for providing citizenship education to students. She believed that teaching youth "how change comes about" and helping them "to develop their own thinking and not accept unjust things but . . . change them" was critical.[63] Behind the scenes, Clark worked to get scholarships for black youth. According to the local superintendent, "Few in the community, other than the donor or recipient, are aware of this great human service since she never seeks praise or publicity."[64] Nor did Clark limit her service to the school board. After five children died in five separate house fires, she joined Charleston clubwomen to raise money to build a day care center and to hire a qualified teacher for it.[65] As a member of the Advisory Council for the Aging, Clark voiced her concern for the elderly who lived alone. Then she made a series of calls and composed a list of volunteers willing to phone older people to check on them regularly.

Toward the end of her life, Septima Clark began to receive widespread recognition for her achievements. The National Education Association recognized her with its Race Relations Award in 1976. The College of Charleston bestowed an honorary doctorate of humane letters in 1978. President Jimmy Carter granted a Living Legacy Award in 1979, and South Carolina conferred the Order of the Palmetto, its highest honor for civilians, in 1982.[66] Looking back, Clark asserted that if she had the chance to retrace her steps, "I'd do the same things over and over again." Where others bemoaned social and political chaos, she saw an opportunity for new ideas to emerge. "I have a great belief in the fact that whenever there is chaos, it creates wonderful thinking. I consider chaos a gift and this has come during my old age."[67]

Septima Clark's gift to the modern civil rights movement was education. Yet her evolution as an educational stateswoman did not proceed in a straight trajectory. There were twists and turns, detours and failures. She assumed personal risks and paid personal costs. Still, the significance of what Clark achieved lies in the choices she made as she formulated a response to these setbacks. She remained a learner as she matured and, with increasing confidence, found ways to apply her accumulated wisdom to benefit her community. Septima Clark passed away on December 15, 1987, at the Sea Island Health Care Center on Johns Island, the local health facility established by graduates of the Citizenship Schools.

NOTES

1. See, for example, Adam Fairclough, *To Redeem the Soul of America: The Southern Christian Leadership Conference and Martin Luther King Jr.* (Athens: University of Georgia Press, 1987).

2. For scholarship that emphasizes the "long civil rights movement" and how women's biographies challenge the movement's traditional chronology, see Jacquelyn Dowd Hall, "The Long Civil Rights Movement and the Political Uses of the Past," *Journal of American History* 91, no. 4 (2005): 1233–64, Kathryn L. Nasstrom, "Beginnings and Endings: Life Stories and the Periodization of the Civil Rights Movement," *Journal of American History* 86, no. 2 (1999): 700–11, and Christina Greene, *Our Separate Ways: Women and the Black Freedom Movement in Durham, North Carolina* (Chapel Hill: University of North Carolina Press, 2005).

3. On Reconstruction in the South Carolina Lowcountry, see Thomas Holt, *Black over White: Negro Political Leadership in the South during Reconstruction* (Chicago: University of Illinois Press, 1977), Wilbert L. Jenkins, *Seizing the Day: African Americans in Post–Civil War Charleston* (Bloomington: Indiana University Press, 1998), and Bernard E. Powers Jr., *Black Charlestonians: A Social History, 1822–1885* (Fayetteville: University of Arkansas Press, 1994).

4. See Heather Andrea Williams, *Self-Taught: African American Education in Slavery and Freedom* (Chapel Hill: University of North Carolina Press, 2005).

5. See Stephen Kantrowitz, *Ben Tillman and the Reconstruction of White Supremacy* (Chapel Hill: University of North Carolina Press, 2000).

6. W. K. Tate, "Statement of the Rural School Problem in South Carolina, 1910–1911," box 5, folder 106, Southern Education Board Papers, Southern Historical Collection, Manuscripts Department, Wilson Library, University of North Carolina, Chapel Hill (hereinafter cited as SHC).

7. See *Forty-ninth Annual Report of the State Superintendent of Education of the State of South Carolina, 1916–1917* (Columbia, S.C.: Gonzales and Bryan State Printers, 1917), 9; *Eighty-second Annual Report of the State Superintendent of the State of South Carolina, 1949–1950* (Columbia, S.C.: Joint Committee on Printing, General Assembly of South Carolina, 1950), 232.

8. See Septima Poinsette Clark, *Ready from Within: Septima Clark and the Civil Rights Movement*, ed. Cynthia Stokes Brown (Navarro, Calif: Wild Tree Press, 1986), 98, 99, and Septima Poinsette Clark, interview by Jacqueline Dowd Hall, Charleston, S.C., July 25, 1976, transcript, Southern Oral History Project, SHC (hereinafter cited as SOHP-SHC).

9. See Septima Poinsette Clark with LeGette Blythe, *Echo in My Soul* (New York: Dutton, 1962), 20, and *Ready from Within*, 98–99.

10. Qtd. in Clark, *Echo in My Soul*, 22. On Burke, see John Meffert, Sherman Pyatt, and the Avery

Research Center, *Black America Series: Charleston, South Carolina* (Charleston: Arcadia Publishing, 2000), 50.

11. See Clark, *Echo in My Soul*, 24, and Edmund L. Drago, *Initiative, Paternalism, and Race Relations: Charleston's Avery Normal Institute* (Athens: University of Georgia Press, 1990), esp. chaps. 3 and 4.

12. Septima Poinsette Clark, interview by Sue Thrasher, New Market, Tenn., June 20, 1981, transcript, Highlander Education and Research Center, New Market, Tenn. (hereinafter cited as HERC.]

13. See Drago, *Initiative, Paternalism, and Race Relations*, 82–83. For an account of black women educators and racial uplift efforts in this era, see, for example, Glenda Elizabeth Gilmore, *Gender and Jim Crow: Women and the Politics of White Supremacy in North Carolina, 1890–1920* (Chapel Hill: University of North Carolina Press, 1996).

14. Clark, *Echo in My Soul*, 75, 53.

15. Ibid., 36–39.

16. Clark, *Ready From Within*, 106–7, emphasis added.

17. Rose Butler Browne and James W. English, *Love My Children: An Autobiography* (New York: Meredith Press, 1969), 239. See also 136.

18. Clark, *Ready from Within*, 109.

19. Clark, *Echo in My Soul*, 52. See also 54. The phrase "our teacher" is Dorothy Redus Robinson's; see *The Bell Rings at Four: A Black Teacher's Chronicle of Change* (Austin, Tex.: Madrona Press, 1978), 16–17.

20. Septima Poinsette Clark, interview by Peter Wood, Charleston, S.C., February 3, 1981, transcript, Avery Research Center for African American History and Culture, College of Charleston, Charleston, S.C. (hereinafter cited as ARC).

21. Clark, *Echo in My Soul*, 60–61; *Ready from Within*, 110. For in-depth analysis of this campaign, see Michael Fultz, "Charleston, 1919–1920: The Final Battle in the Emergence of the South's Urban African American Teaching Corps," *Journal of Urban History* 27, no. 5 (2001): 633–49, and Katherine Mellen Charron, *Freedom's Teacher: The Life of Septima Poinsette Clark* (Chapel Hill: University of North Carolina Press, 2009), chap. 3.

22. This observation was made by the editor of the local black-owned newspaper. See "An Objection Cured," clipping, *Charleston Messenger*, n.d., box 62, folder 9, Edwin Augustus Harleston Papers, South Carolina Historical Society, Charleston.

23. Clark, *Ready from Within*, 112. See also Mellen Charron, *Freedom's Teacher*, 105–15.

24. Clark, *Ready from Within*, 113.

25. Clark, interview by Hall, July 25, 1976, SOHP-SHC.

26. Clark, *Echo in My Soul*, 77. There are a number of excellent studies on the civil rights movement in South Carolina and its local leaders. See Barbara Woods Aba-Mecha, "Black Woman Activist in Twentieth-Century South Carolina: Modjeska Monteith Simkins" (PhD diss., Emory University, 1978), Miles S. Richards, "Osceola E. McKaine and the Struggle for Black Civil Rights, 1917–1946" (PhD diss., University of South Carolina, 1994), and Wim Roefs, "Leading the Civil Rights Vanguard in South Carolina: John McCray and the *Lighthouse and Informer*, 1939–1954," in *Time Longer Than Rope: A Century of African American Activism*, ed. Charles M. Payne and Adam Green (New York: New York University Press, 2003), 462–91.

27. Fannie Phelps Adams, interview by author, Columbia S.C., April 16, 2002. On conditions at Booker T. Washington School in this era, see Janet Scott Leake, "Survey of the Negro Public Schools of Columbia, South Carolina" (MA thesis, Winthrop College, 1932), 50–51, 54.

28. Clark, *Echo in My Soul*, 76.

29. On certificates and PSTA membership, see Leake, "Survey of the Negro Schools of Columbia, South Carolina," 54–55, 57. See also Clark, *Echo in My Soul*, 86.

30. See John F. Potts Sr., *A History of the Palmetto Educational Association* (Washington, D.C.: National Education Association, 1978), 31–58.

31. Ibid., 54–58. On the black female teaching force in 1932, see *Sixty-fourth Annual Report of the State Superintendent of Education of the State of South Carolina, 1931–1932* (Columbia, S.C.: Joint Committee on Printing, General Assembly of South Carolina, 1932), 28.

32. See "Constitution of the Charleston County Education Association," n.d., folder 19, Albertha Johnson Murray Collection, 1889–1982, ARC.

33. Clark, *Echo in My Soul*, 79, 76.

34. See *South Carolina Federation of Colored Women's Clubs, 1909–1949*, 6–7, 9, copy at the South Caroliniana Library, University of South Carolina, Columbia (hereinafter cited as SCL), and Clark, *Echo in My Soul*, 78–79.

35. Woods Aba-Mecha, "Black Woman Activist in Twentieth-Century South Carolina," 103–6.

36. Etta B. Rowe, "Our Heritage," 5, box 4, folder 2, Ethelyn Parker Collection, ARC, emphasis in original.

37. On Gray's pedagogy, see "Information Sheet: Why an Opportunity School?" n.d., box 3, folder 145, Wil Lou Gray Papers, SCL (hereinafter cited as WLGP-SCL). See also Leon Fink, "Teaching the People: Wil Lou Gray and the Siren of Educational Opportunity," in *Progressive Intellectuals and the Dilemmas of Democratic Commitment* (Cambridge, Mass.: Harvard University Press, 1997), 242–74.

38. Septima Poinsette Clark, "Annual Report of the Booker T. Washington Adult School," March 25–May 24, 1935, box 3, folder 201, WLGP-SCL.

39. Clark, *Echo in My Soul*, 148–49.

40. Clark, interview by Hall, July 25, 1976, SOHP-SHC.

41. Clark, *Echo in My Soul*, 81, 82, emphasis in original. See also Potts, *A History of the Palmetto Educational Association*, chap. 8.

42. Qtd. in John Henry McCray, "Address before Barnwell County Teachers' Association," 8, March 30, 1946, John Henry McCray Papers, reel 14, Sterling Memorial Library, Yale University, New Haven, Conn.

43. Clark, *Echo in My Soul*, 82. For a more in-depth analysis of the teacher salary equalization campaigns in South Carolina, see Mellen Charron, *Freedom's Teacher*, chap. 5.

44. On the Warings, see Tinsley E. Yarbrough, *A Passion for Justice: J. Waties Waring and Civil Rights* (New York: Oxford University Press, 1987), esp. 64–70.

45. Clark, *Ready from Within*, 24–26; Clark, *Echo in My Soul*, 95–100.

46. Clark, *Ready from Within*, 28. See also Katherine Mellen Charron, "We've Come a Long Way: Septima Clark, the Warings, and the Changing Civil Rights Movement," in *Groundwork: Local Black Freedom Movements in America*, ed. Jeanne Theoharris and Komozi Woodard (New York: New York University Press, 2005), 116–39.

47. Septima Poinsette Clark to the Warings, August 2, 1951, box 9, folder 223, Judge Julius Waties Waring Papers, Mooreland-Spingarn Research Center, Howard University, Washington, D.C.

48. Qtd. in Aldon Morris, *Origins of the Civil Rights Movement: Black Communities Organizing for Change* (New York: Free Press, 1984), 142. See also Frank Adams with Myles Horton, *Unearthing Seeds of Fire: The Highlander Idea* (Winston-Salem, N.C.: John F. Blair, 1975), and John M. Glenn, *Highlander: No Ordinary School, 1932–1962* (Lexington: University Press of Kentucky, 1988).

49. Clark, *Echo in My Soul*, 114; "Timmerman Signs NAACP Employe [*sic*] Bill," *Charleston News and Courier*, March 18, 1956, A-1.

50. Qtd. in Bernice Robinson, interview by Sue Thrasher and Elliot Wigginton, New Market, Tenn., November 9, 1980, transcript, HERC. See also Carl Tjerandsen, *Education for Citizenship: A Foundation's Experience* (Santa Cruz, Calif: Emil Schwarzhaupt Foundation, 1980), 152–53.

51. Clark, *Ready from Within*, 51–53.

52. See "My Reading Booklet," box 38, folder 13, Highlander Research and Education Center Papers, State Historical Society of Wisconsin, Madison (hereinafter cited as HRECP-SHSW). On cardboard tracing see Clark, *Echo in My Soul*, 147–48.

53. Septima Poinsette Clark to Myles Horton, September 24, 1963, box 9, folder 12, HRECP-SHSW.

54. Clark, interview by Wood, February 3, 1981. See also Morris, *Origins of the Civil Rights Movement*, 153.

55. Dorothy Cotton, "Citizenship School Report," November 1963, series 3, box 153, folder 19, Southern Christian Leadership Conference Papers, King Center, Atlanta, Ga.; Jack O'Dell, "Report on Voter Registration Work," February 15–September 1, 1962, 2–3, box 6, folder 42, Septima Poinsette Clark Papers, ARC (hereinafter cited as SPCP-ARC); Taylor Branch, *Parting the Waters: America in the King Years, 1954–1963* (New York: Simon and Schuster, 1988), 478–82.

56. Qtd. in Grace Jordan McFadden, "Septima P. Clark and the Struggle for Human Rights," in *Women in the Civil Rights Movement: Torchbearers and Trailblazers, 1941–1965*, ed. Vicki L. Crawford, Jacqueline Anne Rouse, and Barbara Woods (Bloomington: Indiana University Press, 1993), 94.

57. Septima Clark, "Memo of Meeting with MIA," January 23, 1961, 2, box 38, folder 13, and "Progress Report, Highlander Folk School," April 26, 1961, box 38, folder 2, HRECP-SHSW.

58. Mrs. Mary E. Dowdy, Mrs. Mattie Shaw, and Mrs. Fannie Puckett to Septima Poinsette Clark, n.d., box 38, folder 8, HRECP-SHSW.

59. See Septima Poinsette Clark to L. Francis Griffin, December 11, 1961, box 3, folder 86, SPCP-ARC.

60. Andrew Young, interview by author, Atlanta, Ga., January 29, 2002.

61. Clark, *Ready from Within*, 79.

62. Clark, interview with Hall, SOHP-SHC. On sexism within SCLC, see Clark, *Ready from Within*, 77–79, and Barbara Ransby, *Ella Baker and the Black Freedom Movement: A Radical Democratic Vision* (Chapel Hill: University of North Carolina Press, 2003), esp. chaps. 4, 6, and 8. See also Kathryn L. Nasstrom's argument regarding men and women's ability to define movement goals and objectives in "Francis Freeborn Pauley: Using Autobiography to Interpret a White Woman's Activist Identity," in *Throwing Off the Cloak of Privilege: White Southern Women Activists in the Civil Rights Era*, ed. Gail S. Murray (Jacksonville: University Press of Florida, 2004), 77–100, esp. 96.

63. Clark, interview by Thrasher, June 20, 1981.

64. Alton Crews to Keith Davis, November 3, 1976, box 5, folder 21, SPCP-ARC.

65. Septima Poinsette Clark, interview by Joan Mack, March 18, 1987, SPCP-ARC.

66. Clark, *Ready from Within*, 120; "Funeral Services for the Late Septima Earthaline Poinsette Clark," SPCP-ARC.

67. Clark, *Ready from Within*, 124–25.

Mary Elizabeth Massey

A Founder of Women's History in the South

CONSTANCE ASHTON MYERS

❀ ❀ ❀

When Mary Elizabeth Massey (1915–1974) arrived at the Rock Hill bus station one late summer day in 1950 to begin a long teaching career at Winthrop College, "the South Carolina State College for Women," administrators could not know that they had invited to their small campus a future powerhouse in her field and a real innovator in scholarship. In her dissertation for the University of North Carolina and in books written while on the faculty at Winthrop, Massey became one of the first historians in the South to tackle social and women's history.[1]

Massey knew, however, what awaited her as far as her new social environment was concerned. This young southern woman had her first college experience pursuing a bachelor's degree at a small institution, Hendrix College, founded by and affiliated with the Methodist Church. It was an idyllic school in Conway, Arkansas, a town remarkably similar to Rock Hill. She had been quite a success at Hendrix by the time of her graduation in 1937. Campaigning in the 1936 election for senior class president (which she won), she declared confidently that she was "big enough to fill the office," a reference to her considerable ability and size.[2] In the college yearbook she was not only named the campus "politician" but was said to be "headed for the governorship." Moreover, she served as president of her sorority for two years and was elected as third "best all-'round woman." All of these tributes point to a certain social astuteness that would serve her well. Hendrix was and would remain proud of Massey. In 1969 she received its Distinguished Alumna award, the very first awarded by the college.[3]

On that day she arrived in Rock Hill, Massey had already accumulated two years of administrative experience plus six years of postsecondary level teaching, two in a junior college in Red Springs, North Carolina, two in a four-year college in the "sleepy town" of Chestertown, Maryland, on the Chester River near Chesapeake Bay, as well as another two—master's degree in hand—back at Hendrix, her alma mater.[4] If it were not for the discrimination that women scholars endured during the first half of the twentieth century in their efforts to enter university teaching, one might conclude only that she sought familiar situations in which to live and work. But that would be to overlook another factor that may have influenced her decisions: the scarcity of opportunities for women as college professors may have led her to Rock Hill and Winthrop. She recognized the limitations, did not complain, and apparently felt comfortable in an environment similar to that of her past experiences.

In 1915 Mary Elizabeth Massey was born in tiny Morrilton, Arkansas, a rural settlement whose population almost one hundred years later still numbered only 6,551. There she went to school and grew into a young woman. It marked her. She remained—and said as much in conversation—a "country girl," contentedly living and working apart from an urban environment. Both Morrilton and Conway, so formative in her early life, were within fifty miles of Little Rock but safely out of its penumbra. Five exhilarating years in graduate school in the university community of Chapel Hill, North Carolina, learning, teaching, researching, and hobnobbing with established as well as budding scholars in her chosen field, the history of the Confederacy, opened wide the eyes of this country girl. She had a glimpse of the possibilities in the world of advanced academics and professional associations; she formed friendships and enlisted loyalties renewed at annual historical association conferences, alliances she respected the rest of her life. But Mary Lib (as her familiars called her) found comfort in the place she called home for the next twenty-four years: the friendly, nearly rural, railroad, textile manufacturing, and agricultural exchange town of Rock Hill in York County, South Carolina.[5]

Though also in a small town, Winthrop College was neither coeducational nor church affiliated, as was Hendrix. It was a state school established through the persistence of a South Carolina politician from Edgefield County, Benjamin Ryan Tillman, who rose to the position of governor and then senator. Winthrop first opened in Columbia in 1886. Later, Rock Hill won a competition for the college's permanent site.[6]

To head the new school, a tentative board of trustees selected Columbia's superintendent of schools, Tennessean David Bancroft Johnson. The school's seed money came from the Peabody Fund in Massachusetts after Johnson made a personal appeal to Robert Charles Winthrop, chairman of the fund's board.

MARY ELIZABETH MASSEY
Louise Pettus Archives, Dacus Library,
Winthrop University, Rock Hill, S.C.

This was the beginning of the "Winthrop Training School," its purpose being to educate young women for teaching the youth of South Carolina. Tillman had been prescient in the matter of future state needs: his venture was indeed successful. By 1970, 34 percent of the state's teachers were Winthrop graduates.[7]

Rock Hill expanded as new industries and retail establishments opened, and its population grew alongside that of Winthrop. Tillman remained the school's guiding hand through the last thirty years of his life. To counter fears that "emancipated women" might emerge from its halls, he delivered speeches assuring state citizens that the school would never be "the cause for unsexing women" but rather would "teach girls to be good wives and mothers." He served on the board of trustees from 1891 until his death in 1918.[8]

Despite Tillman's reassurances, Winthrop women did their bit for the woman suffrage movement in the state, marching through town armed with banners demanding "Votes for S.C. Women." Rock Hill had mature suffrage leaders, as well, in the persons of Mrs. Alexander Long, wife of the president of a chain of textile mills, and Hazel Huey, widow of political figure Thomas Huey. In 1974 interviews, both Hazel Huey and Marguerite Tolbert, a former Winthrop teacher, remembered a sizeable meeting in Rock Hill at which national leader Anna Howard Shaw addressed a full auditorium and subsequently moved over to Winthrop College to give a talk—at the invitation of President Johnson.[9] After woman suffrage became law, to the chagrin of most state legislators, the school's president invited Columbia University in New York to send "an excellent teacher" down to Rock Hill to help prepare groups of South Carolina teachers to lead seminars in voting for the women of the state.[10]

When Massey arrived, Winthrop had already been wracked by several controversies, one of which had to do with unequal pay scales for men and women professors. Two women professors had asked for equality in pay, and both were fired at the insistence of the trustees, an act that brought censure from the American Association of University Women and the American Association of University Professors. School officials excused the dismissals by arguing that the two were "radically-minded" and were teaching "advanced social theories far ahead of the traditions of our true southern women." Whatever the actual reason, the firings put the school on "probationary status" and there it remained, until the 1950s, when a number of graduates sought to have the probation lifted, claiming that their Winthrop diplomas were scorned by graduate schools and prospective employers.[11]

Still in force when Massey arrived, the probation did not end until 1955.[12] There is no indication, however, that women teachers enjoyed raises in their salaries that secured the desired "equality." As scholar Joan Hoff has pointed out, it was only after the passing of the Equal Pay Act (1963) and the Civil Rights Act (1964) that women began to be accorded juridical equality with men. The United States Constitution offered women no explicit protection against discrimination.[13]

A brief time before Massey arrived, the school held the first officially sanctioned dance. Certain church groups had linked the activity with smoking and denounced card playing as "sinful," but a canvassing of the parents revealed they approved of dancing, and so the school held regularly scheduled dances that grew to be high points in the school year. The bans on card playing were removed in 1942. Smoking rooms appeared on campus. Radios, formerly prohibited, could be heard from the dormitories, to the dismay of some faculty members. And in 1955, five years into Massey's tenure on campus, the school discarded its traditional uniforms of navy blue and white, adopted when the doors first opened in 1905. Tillman had desired that the school offer training to young white women of modest means. He and the trustees regarded the uniforms as equalizers, obscuring background differences. But by 1950 students already wore shorts and short skirts anyway, shunning the uniforms except for classes and Sundays. On Sundays navy blue dresses were de rigueur, especially the first Sunday of the school year when, led by the president and his wife, students lined up as they had done since the school's beginning and walked two by two in procession to their respective churches. This was the impressive "Blue Line," a part of the Winthrop tradition that Rock Hill inhabitants loved. Another relic of Winthrop's past was May Day, a romantic and ritualistic celebration on the campus, steeped in pre-Raphaelite imagery: young women in flowing white dresses, a May pole, and the singing of the school anthem and nineteenth century refrains. The college was not unique in this. Such observances took place annually on many other southern women's college campuses from the 1890s through the 1950s. It too had its demise at Winthrop during Mary Elizabeth's time there.[14]

Winthrop would continue to face controversial issues including the possible future admission of male students. In the same year that uniforms were voted out, the school considered for the first time the matter of coeducation. Evidently men entered classes in the 1960s, because one male student sued for his degree but was denied it because of Winthrop's charter as "a college for women." In 1969, a mature man did receive a master's degree in teaching. By 1995, the one hundredth anniversary of Winthrop's move to Rock Hill, the student body was 31 percent male.[15]

From 1950 through the 1960s, the institution went through wrenching self-evaluations. Events in the United States forced those affected to think through the goals of a school purportedly for young women of modest means. The Supreme Court had reached the decision that separate education cannot be equal education in *Brown v. Board of Education* (1954). Winthrop desegregated, and Cynthia Claire Roddey, a young African American native of Rock Hill, entered the school in 1964, finishing with a "master of arts in teaching" in 1967. Rock Hill was the site of one of the state's most important civil rights protests. In 1961, a group of young African American men calling themselves "the Friendship Nine" staged sit-ins in Woolworth's and McCrory's lunch counters to protest segregation, becoming the first sit-in demonstrators to go to jail. Meanwhile, some of the town's churches, the Roman Catholic Church in the lead, settled the issue for themselves by integrating peacefully.[16] During Mary Elizabeth Massey's last years on campus, then, she taught a diverse student body of males and females, African Americans and whites, as well as a growing number of international students.

Massey also witnessed astonishing changes in gender roles in society generally as well as on campus. In the fifties and through much of the sixties a domestic ideal held sway through the entire nation. Veterans of World War II and the Korean conflict returned home to pursue higher education funded by provisions of the "GI Bill of Rights"; they married, purchased homes financed through GI Bill guarantees, and settled down to raise families. Many American women embraced these changes, wholeheartedly welcoming domestic roles after years of conflict and the absence of boyfriends and husbands. Aware of this social climate, Massey had planned her personal affairs carefully, leaving the way clear for a professional life by opting not to marry.[17]

Countering these prevalent views, Simone de Beauvoir's *The Second Sex*, which appeared in English translation in 1953, and Betty Friedan's 1963 *The Feminine Mystique* reverberated in American society.[18] Women paid attention to these bold calls for their self-assertion, especially to Friedan, who proclaimed that domestic partnerships with prescribed sex roles could never be so fulfilling for women in a vibrant technological world as their complete participation in the society outside the home. Keenly aware of movements swirling about her, Massey pondered the matter and addressed the issue indirectly in the research for her third book, *Bonnet Brigades*, written for Allan Nevins's series The Impact of the Civil War.[19]

In fact, woman's successful ability to cope with whatever challenges the wartime environment presented served as one theme in Massey's three books. A second thematic, a lasting consequence of the first, was woman's developing self-confidence to act forcefully outside the private, domestic sphere. Massey herself became a living monument to the principle she elaborated through her careful, methodological research.

Through the general tumult that characterized this era, Mary Elizabeth

Massey was making her way, securing her place on the faculty, astutely refusing to engage in rivalries and petty gossip or to infringe on other faculty members' perceived prerogatives, and avoiding campus political movements. She evaded alienating those in power on campus, on the board of trustees, and in professional historians' associations. All the while, she steadily showed what a woman could accomplish in a chosen field, even one considered a masculine prerogative.[20] Planning intelligently and carefully to preserve her good standing, Massey quietly moved ahead without openly affiliating herself with feminism, despite a personal interest in the advancement of feminist goals, as revealed in cautious comments made publicly and privately.[21]

Massey made her way as a teacher prudently, earning praise from students. As recalled by one mid-1960s freshman, she spoke "eloquently, brilliantly, using no notes, and was very fair in grading but intolerant of those who came unprepared." Massey impressed another young woman who served as her assistant for a time by announcing on the first day of class, "No matter what you may have heard about history—that it is all names, facts, and dates—remember the actors are all people like you, who get up in the morning, drink coffee, get dressed, go to work, come home, and play with the kids." Jean Wells, who would return to Winthrop decades later to take up a position as a reference librarian, changed her major from English to history, so taken was she by this opening statement.[22] New history students remembered another opening quip: "South Carolinians are like the Chinese. They eat a lot of rice and worship their ancestors."[23]

A third student, who worked as her assistant during Massey's final years on campus, remembered that she was gracious and courteous but noted that she "had an edge to her and did not suffer fools gladly." She "had a good opinion of herself and was not going to step aside for anybody."[24] By now she enjoyed a professional reputation for solid achievement and was aware of her standing regionally and even nationally. A history faculty colleague who taught at Winthrop for two years just after finishing his doctorate, John Hammond Moore, remembered Massey's dynamism: she displayed a sense of humor, and one could hear her hearty laugh all the way down the hall. Confirming the student assistant's description, Moore recollected that she did not take second place to anyone on campus.[25] In fact, she stayed on a first-name basis, not common for faculty at most institutions, with successive Winthrop presidents, one of whom, Charles Davis, had been a graduate student with her at the University of North Carolina.

Invited often to present lectures on other campuses by her many associates in the professional history associations, Massey invariably impressed her audiences of faculties and students. Francis Butler Simkins, a historian of the South (and a South Carolinian) teaching at a small school in Virginia, wrote Massey informally, after a 1959 lecture at Longwood College, observing that all "were delighted and amazed by the combination of good looks, good clothes, an interesting exposition of a phase of history and a female bold enough to speak out in a Southern accent." Simkins added: "The only Southern females they know are delicate and almost had rather go in a whore house as shout learnedly from a stage. . . . Your researches were most original, the most original we have heard."[26]

Massey's students remembered her for assisting them beyond the campus walls after their graduation. Friendly letters explaining usage in their own classrooms of her teaching and research techniques abound in the Massey Papers in the Pettus Archives at Winthrop, as do letters thanking her for a variety of thoughtful gestures. One young woman believed Massey helped her gain admission to the Duke University graduate school.[27] Another remembered that Massey had called her back to Rock Hill to fill a teaching position in history when she lost her job in Florida after the school she was teaching in closed. Such deeds brought actions in kind. Two years later, for instance, the former student nominated Massey for membership in the prestigious South Caroliniana Society on the campus of the University of South Carolina.[28]

Sometimes former students poured out their trials and grievances to Massey in long letters, especially those who had entered the world of elementary through high school teaching. They solicited advice on relationships with school principals, with students' parents, with students themselves, and townspeople. One relayed graphically her experiences teaching a class of thirty in a recently integrated school in Greenville, South Carolina, "when five or six cannot read, get bored and cause trouble." She continued, "The Negro world and the white world are galaxies apart," and felt herself attacked for being white.[29] Massey responded to her former students' queries sympathetically but without the detailed advice she could give were she in greater proximity to them. To her credit, she handled racial problems that arose in her classes with aplomb, and her letters reveal no racist ideology whatever—although her former graduate school classmates at North Carolina sent her letters voicing the racism common among southern whites at the time.[30] Such letters stopped coming as teachers, students, and entire campuses gradually accommodated themselves to new realities.

One political viewpoint that she did not mind expressing (although in muted tones) concerned women's position in the society of her day. She tiptoed around smarting questions such as equal treatment on the job and eschewed the term "feminism" until after she faced heart surgery two years before her death. In June 1972 she gave the commencement address at Winthrop, centering her remarks on the life of Eliza Frances Andrews of Washington, Georgia, who saw her father, a judge, lose his wealth in the Civil War. At twenty-one, Andrews entered the public sphere as a writer, working for periodicals and publishing two texts in botany that furnished the royalties that supported her for the rest of her life. Elected to an international society for literature and science, she dared become a Fabian socialist, and was listed in *Who's Who in America* from 1897 to 1931. This is the kind of woman Massey admired. In recounting Andrews's life story, she underlined feminist Betty Friedan's ideas, clearly desiring to hold it forth as exemplary.

However, she preceded and ended her biography of Andrews with statements delineating a personal philosophy. "We have always had aspirations which often have to be modified because of unforeseen developments," she told her audience. According to Massey how much a person is able to adapt has much to do with success or failure. "The individual is more responsible for the course of her life than circumstances of the time," she admonished, thus reaffirming one tenet of the American belief system that is contested in every generation. Massey used the example of Eliza Andrews to demonstrate the level of success a woman might attain. She maintained that such successful lives as her subject's, if well publicized, would promote the progress of women toward full emancipation more certainly than feminist parades and other public demonstrations.[31] Throughout her career, as a professor and participant in history professional associations from 1950 until 1974, Mary Elizabeth intoned this creed. She did so right before her final illness when she gave the presidential address to the Southern Historical Association (SHA) in 1972, recounting the life of another independent, ambitious Georgia woman during and after the Civil War.

Yet Massey never openly asked the most obvious question about her own life: why, when she published more, and more successfully, than some of her male classmates, fellow students of Fletcher M. Green at North Carolina, was she not offered a professorship in Civil War history at a major university where she could have her own graduate students writing under her direction, release time for research, small research seminars, and so on? These classmates, with whom she corresponded, taught at research universities including Emory, Tulane, the University of Houston, the state universities of Florida, Georgia, Kentucky, Louisiana, Maryland, and more. However, A. Elizabeth Taylor (also a Green student, later earning her doctorate at Vanderbilt) and the few other women who had completed advanced studies found themselves similarly quarantined in less prestigious state universities or women's colleges. For example, Taylor, who contributed significantly to the literature on the woman suffrage movement, remained through her entire career at Texas State Woman's College in Denton, Texas.

Offers from both Tulane and Emory to teach summer courses did not attract

Massey; she preferred to do undistracted research through the summer months. She did receive full-time teaching offers, but they came from other women's colleges, including Longwood College and Georgia State Woman's College in Milledgeville. This was despite the support of male colleagues. "They could do no better in the academic world than to get you," wrote Rembert Patrick, who had recommended her to fill a post at the University of South Florida. Patrick also wrote to the president of Winthrop to remind him that "Mary Elizabeth is the crown jewel you have" there, apologizing to him for having recommended her for a $25,000 a year professorship at North Carolina (which she was not offered).[32] Massey drew a salary in the mid-1960s of little over half that sum.[33] "I think your College does not properly appreciate your gifts!" exclaimed Allan Nevins.[34] Still, on receiving the second of her three volumes, Winthrop's president wrote to her, praising her writing ability and adding that "we have so few people who can do as well and it would be a shame to waste talent making out class schedules, fooling with small budgets and sitting in meetings. " To his credit he gave her release time to produce the next, and last, volume.[35]

Massey had direct evidence that a partial answer to her failure to win a professorship at a major university was sexism. She received a note from Rembert Patrick in 1966 in which he reported to her that Fletcher Green had confided in Patrick that he "was all for getting Massey to North Carolina, but the powers of history thought . . . women should be limited to assistant professorships and temporary appointments."[36]

Yet despite this evidence, Mary Elizabeth protested that she had not felt discrimination because of sex. She had addressed the problem when she was a graduate student, remarking to Green that she knew she was entering a field dominated by men: "I just told him bluntly that 'I've heard you don't welcome women.'" "It's not that we don't welcome them," Green replied. "It's just that we don't do anything for them." The old boys' networks prevalent on campuses held the view that women were too frail for PhD work or, at best, poor investments because they would marry and leave academe. Mary Elizabeth did, however, enjoy a teaching assistantship while she wrote her dissertation.[37] Proving them wrong, Massey finished her degree and eventually was named distinguished professor in 1965 at Winthrop, where she remained whether by choice or not.

Massey also achieved success in the SHA. Her movement upward in its echelons paralleled her rise on the campus at Winthrop. She never missed the November conventions, purchasing a fresh wardrobe annually for the event and fitting committee work for the association into her crowded schedule.[38] One attraction was likely the presence of a fellow graduate student from the University of North Carolina who held a central and powerful office, that of secretary-treasurer, for most of her years in the organization. His name was Bennett C. Wall. The two probably enjoyed an intimate relationship, either beginning sometime in her three years as doctoral student at North Carolina or developing within "the Southern," as the SHA is called by its members, at the annual meetings. For nearly thirteen years, Wall was "between marriages." We cannot know what Massey hoped for in the relationship, but with his help, she moved from chairing the membership, program and nominations committees (1955–65) to serving on the executive council (1959–61) and, at last, to assuming the presidency of the association (1972). Likely she would have attained what she sought without Wall's aid, so strong was her drive for success, her political acumen, and her talent. But his office gave them untold hours together in this political avocation. Letters over the years from his several campuses—Emory, Kentucky, and Tulane—evidence a genuine devotion to her but also to the management of the association. It was a tripartite affair involving "the Southern," with annual trysts in its bosom. Pleading "I love, love, love, love love you" and repeatedly signing "yours eternally" or "my love always" in his letters, he often spoke of their secret affair and his love for her.[39]

However, in 1968 a "surprise" came for Mary Elizabeth, one she may have anticipated. She received a letter from Hugh Lefler, one of her teachers from her graduate school years, announcing Ben Wall's marriage to Neva Armstrong, his SHA secretary. The letter, written on Tulane letterhead stationery, was found among Massey's papers; it had been completely wadded, then straightened out and pressed, probably with an iron. Evidently Massey was so bitter on learning that Ben had wed Neva (whom she knew) that her first reaction had been to destroy the letter.[40] Professional that she was, she saved the letter, and the cooperation with Wall for work within the SHA continued unabated. She was to move ahead in it until she reached the top.

As historian Barbara Bellows found, however, Massey did not have the company of many other women in her professional life. Women constituted only 6 percent of the membership in the SHA in 1970. Still, the organization had two female presidents, both teachers in women's colleges, before Massey attained that post, more than the American Historical Association (AHA), which by 1980 had chosen only one woman as president in its 104-year history, and the Mississippi Valley Historical Association (later the Organization of American Historians), which had brought only two women to its presidency in fifty years.[41]

Despite the dearth of female colleagues, much camaraderie enlivened the annual meetings, where of course men predominated, and Mary Elizabeth socialized and partied with former classmates, many who were Fletcher M. Green students. She made her membership in this professional association a substitute for the big university, from which she was essentially shut out owing to her sex. To fit in, she threw aside the reticence associated with stereotypical ladylike behavior and exchanged risqué jokes. Additionally, she endured—without raising objections—condescending remarks made in a half-jesting manner against women's foibles, real and imagined. For instance, Rembert Patrick did not hold back from using locker-room stereotypes in writing to her. The fact that she was "considered by all the men as one of the regular guys and not some effeminate creature around whom men couldn't swear or tell dirty jokes" clearly gratified her, or at least she was willing to put up with it to share collegial relationships with leading men in the SHA.[42]

However, in December 1969, several female historians in the far larger AHA at its annual convention in Washington, D.C., called a meeting in the basement of the Shoreham Hotel to air the problems of slow promotions, withholding of tenure, pay inequity, and the like. This first meeting, presided over by Bernice Carroll of the University of Illinois and addressed by Gerda Lerner of Sarah Lawrence College, began a movement that acted as a magnet drawing more women into paying memberships in the three associations. By 1971, "caucuses" had formed in all of them; these united within two years to become the Coordinating Committee for Women in the Historical Profession, which published a newsletter and arranged meetings to be held at the annual conventions.

Mary Elizabeth resisted supporting any social movement with activist implications. "Women's lib I'm not," she wrote Ben Wall in 1971 in correspondence about a forthcoming meeting of the SHA, "but I would like to have one woman committee chairman. I think I will ask Elizabeth Taylor to chair [one] . . . since she has worked on woman suffrage, she should be acceptable to 'the girls.'"[43] Massey simply did not want to make waves within the association, even though there exists ample evidence that she held strong feminist convictions; it was a question of style—and method—rather than substance.

Nor did she wish to risk alienating Ben Wall, who resisted the new women's caucuses. "I want you and need you in Louisville," he wrote her two months before the annual meeting in 1971. "It is very definite that the Women's Liberation group is going to move in on us with a bunch of high-powered requests and resolutions. After you have seen Mrs. Carroll from the University of Illinois you will understand why men are opposed to liberating women." He ended his letter by labeling those in sympathy "kooks of all descriptions."[44]

Wall predicted correctly; a women's caucus in the SHA met to organize formally in 1970. Two months before the convention, Mollie Davis of West Georgia College, a caucus organizer, wrote Massey's colleague Taylor urging her to attend the meeting, as she was one of the few older, published women scholars and could perhaps provide a bit of respectable luster to the group dubbed "lefties" by the men. On receiving the plea, however, Taylor informed Massey that although the SHA might have to support the caucus resolutions passed in other associations "to have peace," she did not believe in equal rights for women based on anything other than "qualifications." She had attended a women's panel at the AHA annual convention and agreed with Ben Wall that they seemed "a bunch of kookies," some of whom "wouldn't know a piece of scholarly work if they saw one." Nevertheless, A. Elizabeth Taylor showed up at almost every women's caucus meeting as well as the breakfasts that organizers arranged in subsequent years, cooperating with the young activists and supporting the measures they presented.[45] The caucus in the SHA evolved into the Southern Association for Women Historians (SAWH), Davis serving as its first president. According to Taylor, Massey herself joined in 1972.[46]

A word should be said about the women who joined this new body. A majority of them derived from the educated middle classes, with parents who were either professionals or had enjoyed some college training, and most enlistees had a southern upbringing. Distinct from the society surrounding them, they tended not to embrace the traditional southern viewpoint on the place of women (or African Americans) in society. All had earned a bachelor's degree, and almost all had proceeded beyond the master's to earn a doctorate in history, a fact that in itself was a departure from the southern ladyhood model. There is little doubt that such immersion in the liberal arts has a humanizing, even liberating, effect on an individual, especially if she has already veered from a prescribed path, and it serves as a mandate to engage in critical thought that gives rise to the will to transcend narrow regional or group ideologies. The higher educational process itself, then, in combination with personal experiences with sexist remarks many encountered in dealing with men in the professional hierarchy during educational careers and in the job market, made women historians receptive to the notion of a caucus wherein they might share concerns, work together for their own advancement *as women*, and promote the emerging field of women's history.

As it transpired, at its meeting in Houston in November 1971, the SHA chose Mary Elizabeth Massey as its president for the coming year. Interviewed on a number of questions including her approach to sex discrimination in the profession, she said she had always assumed "that if her work were comparable to work done by male professors she wouldn't have to worry. And she hasn't," said the *Houston Post* reporter. Continuing in the same vein, as newly elected president she said she wanted to find out what women in "the women's lib group" were unhappy about and try to correct it.[47] She was treading very gingerly on this unknown turf.

However, just as the perceived threat of African American colleagues and students in southern schools and colleges did not lead to the collapse of those institutions, the threat of a women's movement within the professional associations, once realized, did not bring radical changes. The colleges and the associations remained more or less the same, and what change did take place came in good time and decorously. Massey, however loath initially to embrace the term "feminism," contributed to this evolution but in her own style and as a scholar. Her friend Taylor disclosed that Massey feared SAWH members might "do something [which would] embarrass her as a woman and as SHA president." Had she not been ill, Taylor insisted, she would have become active and "would have told the men off because she knew how to do it, in a way that they would laugh about but not forget."

The third woman president of the SHA in its history, she presented the keynote address at the November 1972 meeting in Hollywood-by-the-Sea, Florida, a most improbable place for a convergence of scholars, with the ocean lapping outside and white beaches luring conventioneers. She entitled it "The Making of a Feminist." In the essay Massey evaluated the life of another Georgia woman of privilege, Ella Gertrude Clanton Thomas. Coming into poverty as a result of war privations and her husband's improvidence and poor judgment, Thomas was forced to scramble for survival. Finally, having pulled successfully through the worst woes, this Civil War and Reconstruction-era woman was emboldened to act publicly to make her voice heard in women's organizations and for woman suffrage and to serve as a leader in her state for the movement.[48]

One reviewer has called the presidential address Mary Elizabeth's most important work. Making public the details of Thomas's life, Massey played "a part in overturning many time honored concepts," according to Barbara Bellows. A spirited presentation, it "was no usual presidential address, filled with meaningless platitudes, large statements, and boring detail," Samuel Proctor wrote to Massey two weeks later.[49]

Gertrude Thomas's story bore a resemblance to Massey's own life. Thomas encountered obstacles in Old South Georgia similar to those encountered by Massey in World War II and midcentury American society. The male-dominated culture erected impediments against female decision making and achievement in a multiplicity of areas. Choosing to research and reveal the details of this life before her professional associates, Massey made public her own embrace of the goals of the feminist movement, despite a personal rejection of social activism. In the presidential address, as if she knew she was revealing the sentiments that guided her own life, she said of her subject: "Although Mrs. Thomas always respected specific regional conventions and traditions, she never permitted either to shackle her mind and spirit. Realizing that change is necessary to progress, she supported those changes she believed to be in the best interest of society, always relying on reason rather than emotion and persuasive discussion rather than agitation to achieve her purpose." Before her untimely death Massey also undertook the editing of the Thomas diary for publication. As it developed, however, her presidential address in 1972 culminated her career in her beloved "Southern."[50]

Massey's success in the SHA was due in large measure to her scholarship. With a tremendous gift for rhetorical flow—even though protracted by the historian's careful referencing—Mary Elizabeth sailed to the top in her field, the history of the Confederacy. "You can write rings around me. It is so ego-deflating," complained one of her former fellow graduate students from North Carolina.[51] Her three volumes reflect her rigorous scholarship, yet at times they read like novels. The compelling narratives that her research uncovered and her instinctive awareness of story line made readers want to learn what would befall the characters. Writing concisely, clearly, and in an easy-to-read style, Massey told good stories. She found the same techniques useful in all three studies, from the first, published in 1952, through the last, published in 1966.

"Shortages and Substitutes on the Confederate Homefront" (her dissertation) became her first book, with a title change to reflect an interest she had in the World War II home front: *Ersatz in the Confederacy.*[52] By 1952 the term "ersatz" had passed out of usage, which led to questions about her choice of title. One client in a bookstore reportedly commented, "[Ersatz] was a general I never heard of." A professor in Mississippi, reviewing the book in one of the history journals, poked fun at the word by using it several times in a petulant, negative review that conceded, however, that "it is a substantial effort and has been done with commendable thoroughness." So successful was the volume that within a month of publication in 1952 it was a University of South Carolina Press best seller. Forty years later, editors of the Southern Classics series at the press chose it for inclusion, the principal editor John Sproat claiming in 2007 that "it has been one of our best titles."[53]

The work not only is a study of southern ingenuity in the Civil War but also shows how total war touched every life. Massey draws on the standard outlines of the war, referencing the Union blockade, the single-crop economy, reliance on imports, and so on, all of which resulted in a general poverty that outlasted the conflict and defined the South through much of the next century. That is not, however, what distinguishes her scholarship. What makes it unique is that she focuses on civilians rather than political and military leaders, and as the title suggests, she seeks to link her World War II generation with that of the Civil War. With men away at war, the search for substitutes for food, textiles, and other unavailable commodities fell largely to southern women. Men made the political decisions that affected supplies, and women were left to deal with the consequences. Therefore women are the protagonists in the study. With this approach, Massey was veering away from the traditional and writing in the new field of social history. In addition, *Ersatz* touches on themes that would be taken up in the field of women's history.

Scholars in Confederate history at the time agreed her work was thorough, logical, and well presented, although there was disagreement about its originality. Frank Vandiver thought the work a fine introduction to a fresh area of inquiry. Bell Irvin Wiley, her old confidant from graduate school days, on the other hand, saw the data unearthed by Massey as "already familiar," but he gave her credit for "rounding out the story and enriching the detail." An Arkansas newspaper paid homage to the native daughter with an editorial about her book entitled "Ersatz Coffee." The writer quoted Massey's lists of varieties of grains, nuts, and vegetables used in experimenting with coffee substitutes— they "tasted horrible"—with no comment on the volume's readability or value as innovative history.[54]

Following publication, the history profession took note of her abilities; she began to receive books for review from the journals as well as invitations to appear on panels. Her entire life centered on her teaching, research, and professional association activities. She did fit into her scarce time a copious correspondence with family, fellow historians—especially those who were Fletcher Green's students when she was—and Ben Wall, even after his marriage. Over summers, she traveled at her own expense to research libraries to lay the groundwork for the publication of her next book. Ten years later she published *Refugee Life in the Confederacy*, almost a sequel to *Ersatz*.

In *Refugee Life*, Massey drew closer to the new field of women's history; women tended to lead families out of the way of invaders into havens of presumed safety, either voluntarily or by acts of expulsion. Lee, Beauregard, Sherman, and other generals banished populations in their paths. Inevitable clashes took place between those who fled and those in the areas where they sought refuge, often bringing social classes into close and equal proximity for the first time.

Refugee Life garnered praise as her best book—"the most thoroughly researched." She had used letters and diaries from 131 manuscript collections. In fact, one reviewer thought she might have done too much research. Gerald M.

Capers claimed that the book examined "every conceivable aspect of the subject," but few, he ventured, would read it from cover to cover.[55]

In his introduction to the 2001 edition of the work, George C. Rable generally agrees with Capers's review, adding a comment repeated by other reviewers of her work over the years, namely, that Massey displayed a lack of interpretive insight. Massey had written first under the tutelage of Fletcher M. Green, a follower of the German school of historiography, who believed analysis and theory should be avoided in favor of gathering the data and presenting it readably and objectively. Most important is Massey's conclusion, in which she sketched in a final comment: "Tens of thousands of unprepared, unguided, and undisciplined Southerners voluntarily displaced themselves and floundered around the contracting Confederacy for months and years, but they paid a high price for the privilege."[56]

While Mary Elizabeth was revising the volume for publication, she was teaching six days a week and was chair of the faculty in history. In addition, she had just been invited by historian Allan Nevins to write a book for a series on the impact of the Civil War for the Centennial Commission. She was the only woman among the fifteen historians invited.[57]

At the same time, she was preparing to participate in the seventh national assembly of the Civil War Centennial Commission on a panel entitled "The Confederate Homefront" along with her fellow Fletcher M. Green alumni, Patrick and Wiley. This was one of the busiest periods of her life and may have been her most productive."[58]

Green's former students thrust another burden on her in 1961. With Green on the verge of retirement, his alumni believed a festschrift to be in order to honor this "master teacher" who guided so many embryonic and soon-to-be prolific Civil War specialists. Arthur S. Link and her old friend Rembert Patrick, editors of the project, encouraged Massey to contribute an essay for the volume, to be published shortly before the November 1965 SHA meeting. At the event, a party would be held in celebration. Once again she was the sole female contributor, this time out of seventeen writers. Her study consisted of an exhaustive essay covering twentieth-century scholarship on the Confederacy and the home front, incorporating major theses, often strikingly contrasting ones, offered by scholars of the Civil War as to the causes and consequences of the conflict.[59] Link wrote to all the contributors that Massey's own contribution to the project was "such a model of lucidity and good coverage—in short, of what we have in mind—that I have asked her to have it mimeographed and sent to each of you."[60]

Massey carved out her most enduring legacy in the book commissioned by Nevins, *Bonnet Brigades* (1966), in which she purported "to show how the Civil

War affected American women." Editor Nevins glowed, "A thrill of pride and pleasure ran through the [Huntington] Library yesterday when I exhibited *Bonnet Brigades* just received." He described it as "one of the most original contributions we have had to the literature of the Civil War." Explaining its purpose, Massey affirmed that it "is meant to be an account of the impact of the war on women, not of women on the war. I trust it is."[61]

The paradox is that the study actually made an original contribution to the literature because Massey shows through extensive use of diaries, memoirs, letters, and other documents that women did in fact help determine the outcome of the war, that is, had an *impact* on it. Refusing the status of "victim," women north and south reacted innovatively to events. Southern women especially determined the outcome of numerous crises produced by wartime shortages, family deaths, invasion by hostile armies, and destruction (or theft) of homes, crops, livestock, and other property.

Two new theses come from the pages of *Bonnet Brigades* that have changed the way historians write about the Civil War. First, as a major focus, Massey affirms that the Civil War brought women forward in a revolutionary manner and "not in a slow, evolutionary one." It "provided a springboard from which they leaped beyond the circumscribed 'woman's sphere' into that heretofore reserved for men," telescoping fifty years into four. Opportunities opened for them "to do new kinds of work, some of which were called into being by the war itself." In the process, they developed new images of themselves and their capacities. They became more self-reliant, more independent, more ready to engage in reform.[62] It was no wonder that the immediate postwar years saw the explosion of women's voluntary associations of every sort from patriotic groups, to missionary societies, to temperance societies, to woman suffrage organizations, because women, still shut out of careers in business and public life yet newly self-confident, were determined to play a meaningful social role. Subsequent historians picked up Massey's thesis and developed it further. For example, women, permitted to enter nursing during wartime (despite qualms about maintaining "respectability"), were sent home after war's end. Most female employment was terminated in an effort to restore traditional social structures and, with them, traditional gender roles. The energy and will to act in the public sphere were to remain, however, and both were to pour into social action through voluntary associations. However, women teachers, initially expected to step down at war's end and return the field to men, were unable to do so due to extreme financial need; families swallowed their pride as wives and daughters opened schools.[63]

Massey's second, more tentative, thesis inspired greater controversy. It was, nevertheless, picked up by subsequent historians who found further documentary evidence to substantiate it. At the onset of the war, women of the South showed extraordinary patriotism. Without hesitation, they sent sons and husbands off to war to defend their "way of life." They sacrificed, found substitutes where the blockade shut off accustomed commodities, managed entire households financially all through the general decline, until at last weariness set in and letters encouraging menfolk to come home and shoulder the burdens—to desert, in short—began to arrive in encampments. Historian Drew Gilpin Faust has pointed out that as the war wore on, conditions undermined the traditional southern "deal" in which women accepted submission and restrictions on personal liberties in exchange for male courtly deference and male responsibility for management of family properties as well as all political decision making. However, at war's outset, women left at home were forced to assume male responsibilities, often in the worst of wartime circumstances. Faust agreed with Massey: the experience empowered southern women in that it made clear their own capabilities. But Faust also underlined a premise that Massey only suggested: morale sank to such a level that, as Faust phrased it, "it may well have been because of its women that the South lost the Civil War," as by 1865 women had "deserted the ranks." They ended up both challenging the objective of the war and undermining its ideological foundations; they did not want the Confederate effort to survive any longer.[64]

Since Massey's publications, writing about the Civil War has changed irrevocably. In her introduction to a 1994 republication of *Bonnet Brigades*, Joan Berlin comments that "recent work on gender and the Civil War has echoed many of Massey's contentions about women while raising new ones." Nevertheless, once again a "lack of probing analysis" emerges as a principal criticism of her work, always followed by acknowledgment of its high quality and valuable contribution to the growing literature on the subject. Berlin aptly notes that in her work Massey's ideology tends to be implicit.[65]

Centering her life on her profession and eschewing family in favor of profession, Mary Elizabeth Massey feverishly wrote articles, ten in all, numerous book reviews for the scholarly journals, and three painstakingly researched volumes. She made herself available for lectures to share the fruits of her researches and conclusions and submitted gracefully to a gender discrimination that kept her in a small woman's (but later coeducational) college. Rents from an Arkansas farm supplemented her salary; her archived papers contain correspondence about upkeep of buildings, depositing of rent moneys, and such matters.[66] A serious altercation between Massey and her father dating from years earlier, about which no details are known because Massey destroyed the letters in which they were confided, permanently estranged them, but she maintained close contact with the rest of her nuclear family. Her mother Corinne, two brothers, Charles and John, and one sister Sarah Massey O'Donnell carried on a warm and regular correspondence with her.[67]

In the wake of her series of successes, in August 1972 Massey underwent heart surgery in the Presbyterian Hospital of Charlotte, North Carolina, and recovery was so slow she could not be present at the start of classes in the fall.[68] Two months earlier she had given the commencement address at Winthrop College. In an alarmingly short time after the surgery, Mary Elizabeth mustered the strength to give the presidential address at the SHA meeting in Florida. Although she resumed her teaching in the spring of 1973, she never fully recovered. Brother Charles Massey, an administrator with the National Foundation for the March of Dimes in its New York headquarters, used his influence to arrange for her admission to Duke University Hospital in Durham when she might need it. There she died on December 24, 1974, of heart and kidney failure.

Aware of her serious condition and dedicated professional that Massey was, she had called on close friend A. Elizabeth Taylor to find someone who could teach her new class at Winthrop in the history of women in the spring 1975 semester. Mollie Davis agreed to do it, making the thirty-minute drive over to Rock Hill from her home in Charlotte, North Carolina, through the semester, fulfilling one of Massey's last wishes.[69] The networking among women historians facilitated by the SAWH, created in 1972 from the caucus in the SHA, had made the arrangement possible and assured Mary Lib at this sad time that her work would go on. Paradoxically, by 1980 Winthrop had filled the faculty position by employing a young male scholar with an Emory doctorate, Arnold Shankman, who researched and published in the history of American women.

The Rock Hill newspaper announced a memorial service at a local funeral home, saying the family would receive friends "at 513 Charlotte Avenue," Mary Elizabeth's residence. No mention appeared of a church service or any kind of religious rite.[70] At the time of her death, she had completed an essay about Mary Todd Lincoln, brought to the topic by a scholarly concern with the history of women's education in the South. It had been read for her at a meeting of the National Historical Society in September 1974.[71] Left unfinished was her editing of the Ella Gertrude Clanton Thomas diary.

Mary Elizabeth Massey left her mark on several state and national historical institutions. She belonged to the South Carolina Commission on Archives and History (1962–63), the Advisory Council of the National Civil War Centennial Committee (1961–65), the South Carolina Civil War Centennial Commission

(1961–65), and the South Carolina Tri-Centennial Commission (1968–71). At the time of her death she was serving on the board of advisors of the National Historical Society.[72] She cherished above all her membership in and activities for the Southern Historical Association.

Massey's students at Winthrop College remember her as a woman of brilliance, wit, and inspiration. Colleagues at Winthrop and in the many professional organizations likewise knew her as a woman of considerable accomplishment in a time when few women reached such a high level of achievement in university life and scholarship. She is and will be most remembered for her significant contributions to Clio, the muse of history, in her three volumes, all of which advanced themes in women's history that spurred later scholars to continue along the paths she cleared, but especially in her third, *Bonnet Brigades: Women in the Civil War*.

NOTES

1. Frederick Heath, "Mary Elizabeth Massey," in "The Three Women Presidents of the Southern Historical Association: Ella Lonn, Kathryn Abby Hanna, and Mary Elizabeth Massey," *Southern Studies: An Interdisciplinary Journal of the South*, 20, no. 2 (1981): 121.

2. Heath, "Mary Elizabeth Massey," 121. For a history of Hendrix College, see www.hendrix.edu and Harold Russell, ed., *Hendrix College Troubadour 1937: A Year Book* (Conway, Ark.: Student Body of Hendrix College, 1937), passim, Mary Elizabeth Massey Papers, Louise Pettus Archives and Special Collections, Winthrop University, Rock Hill, S.C. (hereinafter cited as MEMP-LPASC).

3. *Hendrix College Troubadour 1937*, MEMP-LPASC; James E. Major to Mary Elizabeth Massey, April 17, 1964, and Fletcher M. Green to Mary Elizabeth Massey, July 21, 1967, MEMP-LPASC; Heath, "Mary Elizabeth Massey," 116.

4. On Chestertown, Maryland, see travel section, *Washington Post*, July 30, 2000: "After dark, it's almost comatose." For Washington College, see www.washcoll.edu. Flora Macdonald Junior College was in Red Springs, N.C., but it no longer exists; see Heath, "Mary Elizabeth Massey," 116–17.

5. Louise Pettus, conversation with author, Rock Hill, S.C., August 6, 2007. Pettus became student assistant to Mary Elizabeth Massey, newly arrived on the Winthrop campus, and later taught history herself at Winthrop. For a short description of industrial growth in York County, see Walter Edgar, *South Carolina: A History* (Columbia: University of South Carolina, 1998), 427, and Ron Chepesiuk, *Rock Hill, South Carolina* (Charleston, S.C.: Arcadia Publishing, 2001), 71–106 passim.

6. Peggy Diane Neal, "Benjamin Ryan Tillman: His Role in the Founding and Early History of Winthrop College" (senior honors thesis, Winthrop College, November 19, 1970). Massey inspired this study and then read and critiqued the manuscript. See also Edgar, *South Carolina*, 437.

7. Neal, "Benjamin Ryan Tillman," 2–4; Ron Chepesiuk and Magdalena Chepesiuk, *Winthrop University: History and Traditions, 1886–1945* (Charleston, S.C.: Arcadia Publishing, 2000), 9–11; E. Thomas Crowson, *The Winthrop Story, 1886–1960* (Baltimore, Md.: Gateway Press, 1987), 548.

8. Neal, "Benjamin Ryan Tillman," 4–5, 17. One such speech, delivered in 1894, is cited by Chepesiuk and Chepesiuk, *Winthrop University*, 23.

9. Hazel Thompson Huey, interview by author, Rock Hill, S.C., May 21, 1974, South Caroliniana

Library, University of South Carolina, Columbia (hereinafter cited as SCL); Marguerite Tolbert, interview by author, Columbia, S.C., June 14, 1974, Southern Oral History Program, Southern Historical Collection, Manuscripts Department, Wilson Library, University of North Carolina, Chapel Hill (hereinafter cited as SOHP-SHC).

10. Tolbert, interview by author, June 14, 1974, SOHP-SHC.

11. Crowson, *The Winthrop Story*, 557–58; "Statement with Reference to Winthrop Made by the Hon. Edgar A. Brown [Barnwell]," March 15, 1944, 3, Martha Bee Anderson Papers, March 1944–June 1970, SCL.

12. Tolbert, interview by author, June 14, 1974, SOHP-SHC.

13. Joan Hoff, *Law, Gender, and Injustice: A Legal History of U.S. Women* (New York: New York University, 1991), 3, 6. The urgently felt need for an equal rights amendment arose from the facts as presented by Hoff.

14. Crowson, *The Winthrop Story*, 485–86, 491–95; Chepesiuk and Chepesiuk, *Winthrop University*, 13, 113; Sheila Drennan, conversation with author, Columbia, S.C., August 1, 2007. Drennan studied history under Massey at Winthrop in the mid-1960s.

15. Edgar, *South Carolina*, 572; Chepesiuk and Chepesiuk, *Winthrop University*, 81–89 passim.

16. Chepesiuk, *Rock Hill*, 91, 94, 98. Crowson showed that the college was not without incident (*The Winthrop Story*, 487).

17. Emma Perkins to Mary Elizabeth Massey, September 13, 1969, MEMP-LPA.

18. Betty Friedan, *The Feminine Mystique* (New York: Norton, 1963).

19. Simone de Beauvoir, *The Second Sex* (London: Jonathan Cape, 1953); Friedan, *The Feminine Mystique*.

20. Artist Georgia O'Keeffe believed she advanced women's rights more through her professional success than activists did (O'Keeffe, interview by author, Abiquiu, N.M., April 27, 1980). Massey voiced essentially the same view.

21. Heath, "Mary Elizabeth Massey," 119–20; Barbara Bellows, introduction, *Ersatz in the Confederacy: Shortages and Substitutes on the Southern Homefront* (Columbia: University of South Carolina, 1990), xvi; Massey, interview, *Houston (Tex.) Post*, November 19, 1971, B-5.

22. Sheila Drennan, interview by author, August 3, 2007; Jean Wells, conversation with author, Rock Hill, S.C., August 7, 2007.

23. *Houston (Tex.) Post*, B-5.

24. Chuck de Young, telephone conversation with author, August 29, 2007.

25. John Hammond Moore, telephone conversation with author, August 24, 2007. Moore dedicated his first book to Mary Elizabeth Massey. It was published in 1974, the year of her death.

26. Francis Butler Simkins to Mary Elizabeth Massey, April 25, 1959, MEMP-LPASC.

27. There are numerous letters from former students thanking her and often asking advice in box 3, MEMP-LPASC.

28. Mary Elizabeth Massey to Louise Pettus, January 23, 1966, and Les Inabinett to Mary Elizabeth Massey, April 19, 1968, MEMP-LPASC; Pettus, conversation with author, August 6, 2007.

29. Kaye Masters to Mary Elizabeth Massey, May 7, 1969, MEMP-LPASC.

30. Hugh Lefler to Mary Elizabeth Massey, May 7, 1955, Malcolm Macmillan to Mary Elizabeth Massey, October 8, 1958, and Ben Wall to Mary Elizabeth Massey, July 15, 1968, MEMP-LPASC.

31. Commencement address, Winthrop College, 1972, folder 132, MEMP-LPASC.

32. Rembert Patrick to Mary Elizabeth Massey, January 23, 1966, Patrick to Charles S. Davis, president, Winthrop College, December 17, 1966, Ben Wall to Mary Elizabeth Massey, April 15, 1968, Jack [illegible] to Mary Elizabeth Massey, October 2, 1972, MEMP-LPASC.

33. Teaching contract, dated May 17, 1965: "Dr. Mary Elizabeth Massey. Title: Professor for 1965–66. $13,500. Sign by May 24," box 3, MEMP-LPASC.

34. Allan Nevins to Mary Elizabeth Massey, September 27, 1962, MEMP-LPASC.

35. Charles S. Davis to Mary Elizabeth Massey, May 28, 1964, MEMP-LPASC.

36. Rembert Patrick to Mary Elizabeth Massey, December 10, 1966, MEMP-LPASC.

37. Qtd. in *Houston (Tex.) Post*, B-5. See also Heath, "Mary Elizabeth Massey," 119, and Bellows, introduction, xii.

38. Heath, "Mary Elizabeth Massey," 119.

39. See various letters from Ben Wall to Mary Elizabeth Massey through 1950s and 1960s, esp. September 8, 1964, December 15, 1964, December 4, 1965, and November 17, 1966, MEMP-LPASC.

40. Hugh Lefler to Mary Elizabeth Massey, September 7, 1968, MEMP-LPASC.

41. Bellows, introduction, xiii; Heath, "Mary Elizabeth Massey," 101.

42. Rembert Patrick to Mary Elizabeth Massey, August 9 and November 16, 1964, and Ben Wall to Mary Elizabeth Massey, October 27, 1966, MEMP-LPASC; Anne Firor Scott, "On Seeing and Not Seeing: A Case of Historical Invisibility," *Journal of American History* 71, no. 1 (1984): 7–21, esp. 8.

43. Mary Elizabeth Massey to Ben Wall, January 28, 1971, MEMP-LPASC.

44. Ben Wall to Mary Elizabeth Massey, September 1, 1970, MEMP-LPASC. See also Bernice Carroll, "Women's Consciousness and Professionalism," *CCWHP Newsletter*, June 1973.

45. Mollie Davis to Elizabeth Taylor, September 28, 1971, and Taylor to Mary Elizabeth Massey, October 16, 1971, MEMP-LPASC. I also recall her presence at most of these meetings, which I likewise attended.

46. Mollie Davis to Elizabeth Taylor, September 28, 1971, and Taylor to Mary Elizabeth Massey, October 16, 1971, MEMP-LPASC. Taylor's comments regarding Massey's fears about possible actions of the women's caucus are in *Clio's Southern Sisters: Interviews with Leaders of the Southern Association for Women Historians* (Columbia: University of Missouri, 2004), 27–28. I also recall her relaying Massey's concerns at the meetings.

47. *Houston (Tex.) Post*, B-5.

48. Mary Elizabeth Massey, "The Making of a Feminist," *Journal of Southern History* 39, no. 1 (1973): 3–22.

49. Heath, "Mary Elizabeth Massey," 117; Bellows, introduction, xvii; Samuel Proctor to Mary Elizabeth Massey, December 1, 1972, MEMP-LPASC.

50. Mary Elizabeth Massey to Mrs. F. B. Despeaux, April 7, 1968, and Mary Elizabeth Massey to Mrs. Thad W. Sparks, June 18, 1968, MEMP-LPASC. Both of these letters laid the groundwork for gaining access to the Thomas diary.

51. Rembert Patrick to Mary Elizabeth Massey, June 6, 1964, MEMP-LPASC; Heath, "Mary Elizabeth Massey," 117.

52. Mary Elizabeth Massey, "Shortages and Substitutes on the Confederate Homefront" (PhD diss., University of North Carolina, Chapel Hill, 1947; Massey, *Ersatz in the Confederacy* (Columbia: University of South Carolina Press, 1952).

53. John K. Bettersworth, review of *Ersatz in the Confederacy*, by Mary Elizabeth Massey, *Mississippi Valley Historical Review* 39, no. 4 (1953): 767–768; Bellows, introduction, xi; John Sproat, telephone conversation with author, May 25, 2007.

54. Frank Vandiver, review of *Ersatz in the Confederacy*, *Journal of Southern History* 19, no. 2 (1953): 248–49; Bell Irvin Wiley, review of *Ersatz in the Confederacy*, *American Historical Review* 58, no. 3 (1953): 718; "Ersatz Coffee," *Arkansas Gazette*, February 7, 1954.

55. Heath, "Mary Elizabeth Massey"; Gerald M. Capers, review of *Refugee Life in the Confederacy*, *Journal of Southern History* 31, no. 2 (1965): 217.

56. Mary Elizabeth Massey, *Refugee Life in the Confederacy* (Baton Rouge: Louisiana State University Press, 1964), 282; Bellows, introduction, xii; George C. Rable, introduction, *Refugee Life in the Confederacy* (Baton Rouge: Louisiana State University Press, 2001), xvi.

57. Bellows, introduction, xvii; Allan Nevins to Mary Elizabeth Massey, October 18, 1962, and William B. Hesseltine to Mary Elizabeth Massey, November 19, 1962, MEMP-LPASC.

58. Allan Nevins to Mary Elizabeth Massey, June 17, 1964, MEMP-LPASC.

59. Mary Elizabeth Massey, "The Confederate States of America: The Homefront," in *Writing Southern History: Essays in Historiography in Honor of Fletcher M. Green*, ed. Arthur S. Link and Rembert W. Patrick (Baton Rouge: Louisiana State University Press, 1965), 249–72; William C. Binkley, review of *Writing Southern History: Essays in Historiography in Honor of Fletcher M. Green*, *Journal of Southern History* 33, no. 3 (1966): 370. Louis Harlan's review praised Massey's piece as written "with her usual verve and human interest but without bias" (*Agricultural History* 42, no. 2 [1968]: 153).

60. Arthur S. Link to contributors, October 1, 1962, MEMP-LPASC.

61. Allan Nevins to Mary Elizabeth Massey, July 20, 1966, MEMP-LPASC; Mary Elizabeth Massey, preface, *Bonnet Brigades: Women in the Civil War* (New York: Knopf, 1966), xi. Francis B. Simkins and James W. Patton had published a volume about women of the Confederacy three decades earlier (*The Women of the Confederacy* [Richmond: Garrett and Massie, 1936]).

62. Massey, *Bonnet Brigades*, 367; Anne Firor Scott, review of *Bonnet Brigades*, *Journal of Southern History* 33, no. 2 (1967): 410.

63. See Cheryl A. Wells, "Battle Time: Gender, Modernity, and Confederate Hospitals," *Journal of Social History* 35, no. 2 (2001): 409–28, Drew Gilpin Faust, "Altars of Sacrifice: Confederate Women and the Narratives of War," *Journal of American History* 76, no. 4 (1990), 1210–28, and Drew Gilpin Faust, *Mothers of Invention: Women of the Slaveholding South in the American Civil War* (Chapel Hill: University of North Carolina Press, 1996). Massey had spoken in *Ersatz* of "mothers of invention," Faust's title. The term, she explained, applied to "all the people, and the citizens proved that they could manage even though the blockade and the invading armies squeezed them like an anaconda" (*Ersatz in the Confederacy* [University of South Carolina Press, 1993], 98). See also Jean E. Friedman, *The Enclosed Garden: Women and Community in the Evangelical South, 1830–1900* (Chapel Hill: University of North Carolina Press, 1985), 104–5.

64. Faust, "Altars of Sacrifice," 228. She expands on this thesis in *Mothers of Invention*. See also George C. Rable, *Civil Wars: Women and the Crisis of Southern Nationalism* (Urbana: University of Illinois Press, 1989). Rable shows the despair and near loss of religious faith that afflicted southern women in the chapter titled "From Exaltation to Despair" (202–20).

65. Joan Berlin, introduction, *Women in the Civil War* (Lincoln: University of Nebraska Press, 1994), xiv–xv and n. 4. See also Scott, review of *Bonnet Brigades*, 411.

66. Marvin E. Burgess to Mary Elizabeth Massey, October 30, 1969, J. M. Reynolds, First State Bank, Morrilton, to Mary Elizabeth Massey, November 4, 1969, and Mary Elizabeth Massey to Burgess, November 7, 1971, MEMP-LPASC.

67. Corinne Massey to Mary Elizabeth Massey, September 5, 1966, MEMP-LPASC.

68. Sanford W. Higginbotham to Mary Elizabeth Massey, August 14 and 23, 1972, Bell Irvin Wiley to Mary Elizabeth Massey, August 29, 1972, Allen Going to Mary Elizabeth Massey, September 17, 1972, and Fletcher M. Green to Mary Elizabeth Massey, December 3, 1972, MEMP-LPASC.

69. Charles L. Massey to Dr. George W. Brumley, Duke Medical Center, Durham, N.C., August 27, 1973, MEMP-LPASC; Davis, conversation with author, March 25, 2011.

70. *Rock Hill Evening Standard*, December 26, 1974, SCL.

71. Ross A. Webb, obituary, "Recent Deaths," *American Historical Review* 80, no. 4 (1975), 1087–88; Thomas S. Morgan, obituary, *Journal of Southern History* 41, no. 2 (1975) 292–93.

72. Morgan, obituary.

Polly Woodham

The Many Roles of Rural Women

MELISSA WALKER

If you ask Polly Hill Woodham (1930–) to describe how she spent her adult years, she says she was a farmwife. Yet an outsider listening to Polly's oral history account might think her involvement in the farm seemed minimal. She was not born to farm life but came to it as a result of marrying into a farming family. The privileged eldest granddaughter of a Spartanburg, South Carolina, textile mill owner, Polly grew up in town. While attending Converse College, she met Willis Woodham, a Lowcountry farm boy who attended Wofford College, the men's institution across town. Polly married him immediately after her graduation. Willis worked the family farm in Lee County, South Carolina, but the Woodhams lived in the town of Bishopville most of the time. Here, for several years after her marriage, Polly focused on her roles as wife and mother. When her youngest son entered kindergarten, she taught elementary school. Later she started a private riding academy and horse-breeding operation. Not until her fifties, when she embarked on a career as a volunteer activist in the 1970s farm protest movements, did farm-related activities come to take center stage in her daily life. Then she became distanced from the farm again. By her sixties, she had parlayed a part-time job selling Lady Love cosmetics into a full-time job running a distribution center for Lady Love and then into her own retail business specializing in women's clothing and accessories.

Indeed Polly's life looks much different than the lives of an earlier generation of South Carolina farm women. Take, for example, her husband's distant relative Mary Skinner.[1] Also the wife of a landowning Lee County cotton farmer, Skinner never held an off-farm job. The daughter of another landowning farmer, she lived on the land worked by her husband and his sharecroppers. She spent her days rearing her eight children, sewing the family wardrobe, working the

POLLY WOODHAM

Courtesy of Converse College
Communications Office.

garden, preserving food, and caring for livestock. She made butter and gathered eggs that she sold or bartered for household necessities and luxuries. She supervised the work of her children and her African American domestic servants and farmworkers. The farm was both the location and the source of Mary Skinner's work, the center of her daily life. By contrast, Polly Woodham seems detached from the farm.[2]

It is precisely her relative distance from the farm that makes Polly Woodham's life so instructive regarding the ways that South Carolina agriculture changed in the twentieth century and how those changes reshaped the roles of farm women. Most scholarship on southern farm women examines the pre–World War II period.[3] By shifting the focus to the second half of the twentieth century, we gain new insight into the complex ways that twentieth-century changes in the agricultural economy transformed the daily lives of southern farm women, their place in the family economy, and their public roles. Woodham's experiences mirrored those of many women in her generation of landowning white farm women. For example, by midcentury, the sons of landowning farmers often attended college where they met and married young women who did not have farming backgrounds. Young farm-born women also attended college in record numbers and sometimes married farmers. This new generation of farmwives, more educated than most of the farm women of a younger generation, faced the challenges of farm life with a new and different set of skills. They forged new roles on and off the farm.

World War II sparked a revolution in agricultural productivity that transformed rural life and brought industrial agriculture—the application of industrial notions of specialization, mechanization, efficiency, and economies of scale to the farming enterprise—to the South at last. Several factors contributed to this revolution. The first was mechanization, a process that made it possible to work many more acres of land with fewer workers. The introduction of improved varieties of crops and animals, made possible largely by advances in genetics, also fueled increased productivity. Finally, new chemicals eliminated weeds and insect pests that destroyed crops and fertilized the land, making it fruitful.[4] In the years during and after World War II, southern farmers bought tractors, mechanical cotton pickers, and combines, used DDT to eliminate the boll weevil and other pests, and applied new herbicides to eliminate the need to chop cotton by hand. All these changes led to dramatic increases in production. In the 1950s and 1960s, many southern farmers also diversified, giving up cotton for new strains of grains and livestock that were more profitable.[5] The shift to machinery and new crops meant there was less need for sharecroppers, a group whose numbers had been declining since the late 1930s. Between 1940 and 1960,

about half a million sharecroppers left the land.[6] Government agricultural policies, including a complex system of acreage allotments for certain crops, encouraged the consolidation of landholdings and thus contributed to the shift
to large-scale commercial farming. By the 1970s, fewer southerners worked the
land, but most of those that were left operated larger and more complex farms
than farmers of their parents' generation.[7]

Like many other landholding farmers, the Woodhams changed their farming
practices in the postwar period. They invested in new equipment and began to
borrow increasing amounts of operating capital each spring so that they could
purchase hybrid seed, fertilizers, and pesticides. In most years throughout the
1960s and early 1970s, the cotton crop profited enough to pay off the operating loans and service the debt on capital investments. Still, in years when bad
weather decimated crops or cotton prices fell below the cost of production,
operating debt was sometimes refinanced and carried over to subsequent years.
In short, farming became much riskier during their lifetime, and like many
farmers, they watched their indebtedness grow.

In order to understand the lives of women in this changing economy, it is
important to know something about how farm families understood the family
economy and the place of women in it. Farmers, like all workers, seek to "make
a living." Today we associate making a living with earning a cash income, and
we tend to think of the farmer's living as the money he or she receives from selling livestock and cash crops. That understanding to some degree describes the
market-oriented, specialized commercial agriculture that we usually see today,
but early in the century most farm families combined subsistence and market-
oriented economic activities in ways that were calculated to meet their own
goals of independence, well-being, and family persistence on the land.[8]

As a result, early twentieth-century farmers did not equate making a living
with simply earning money. Rather, they understood the family economy in
broader and more complex terms. The family economy included everything
the farm family did to support itself, such as raising livestock and crops to sell
and providing the family's subsistence. Raising a garden was part of the family
economy. So was caring for a milk cow. Canning and drying foods for the winter
was part of the family economy. All three of these activities fell within the pur-
view of farm women. Even cutting back on expenses was an economic act. For
every dollar that a farmwife saved by making instead of buying her daughters'
dresses or her husband's shirts, another dollar was available to buy seed corn,
purchase a mule, or pay real estate taxes. Farm women also earned money. They
sold butter and eggs, using the income to buy schoolbooks or the staple foods
they could not produce at home or to pay mortgages, real estate taxes, and col-

lege tuition for the children. Many even worked in the fields, comprising an essential part of the labor force that produced farm commodities for the market. In other words, the work of men *and* women proved essential to the survival of the farm family *and* the survival of the farm.[9]

The transformation of the Southern farm economy in the twentieth century changed women's place in the family economy and the types of work they performed. As southerners increasingly turned to specialized commercial agriculture, farm women's subsistence and petty commodity production became less important. Still farm women remained central to the family economy, shifting their efforts to working in the commercial farming operation or, like Polly Woodham, to taking off-farm jobs that contributed to the family economy in different ways. This biographical essay uses Polly's life as a lens through which to view the impact of a changing farm economy on southern farm women and their responses to that change.

In the summer of 1930, Margaret Law Hill and Gabe Hill embarked on a "mad dash" down winding mountain roads to their hometown of Spartanburg from the family cabin at Lake Summit, thirty miles away in North Carolina. Margaret's labor pains had started, and she was determined to deliver her firstborn in Mary Black Hospital. The couple arrived in plenty of time: Polly Margaret Hill, named for her maternal grandmother and her mother, greeted the world in the textile mill town where her grandfather was a respected community leader.[10]

Polly was born into an illustrious Upstate family. Her maternal great-grandfather, Thomas Hart Law, a former Confederate chaplain, pastored Spartanburg's First Presbyterian Church, religious home to many of the city's movers and shakers. Thomas's wife, Anna Adger Law, came from one of Charleston's merchant families. Thomas and Anna's daughter and Polly's great-aunt, Margaret Law, graduated from Converse College, a liberal arts women's college established by Spartanburg city leaders in 1889. She went on to study art with William Merritt Chase and Robert Henri at the Art Students League in New York City. Later she studied in Paris, taught at Bryn Mawr College, and became the art supervisor for Baltimore City Schools as well as a noted social realist painter. When Polly was a child, Margaret returned to Spartanburg where she taught art in local schools and became a leader in the effort to develop a local art museum.[11]

Margaret Law's brother and Polly's grandfather, John Adger Law, inherited commercial instincts from his mother's family. After graduating from Wofford College, John A. Law clerked for the Spartanburg Savings Bank before becoming president of Central National Bank in Spartanburg, a position he held for thirty years. John A. Law married Pearl "Polly" Sibley, a Converse student. Polly Sibley Law's father was a textile mill owner in Augusta, so perhaps his influence helped John A. Law get his start in cotton manufacturing. In 1900, Law began seeking investors for his Saxon Mills Company. He opened his first mill on Spartanburg's west side in 1903 and later opened another mill in the nearby town of Chesnee. He ran the mills until they were sold in 1945. Law and fellow mill owner Walter S. Montgomery formed Manufacturers Power Company (later known as Blue Ridge Power Company) to build two hydroelectric dams on the Green River just over the border in North Carolina. The power generated by these dams helped supply reliable and inexpensive power to local mills. Known as a visionary business leader, Law was among the first mill owners in South Carolina's Upstate to apply the principles of Progressive Era welfare capitalism to managing his mills, both in an effort to improve worker productivity and to discourage attempts at unionization. He encouraged improved education for his workers by participating in the work-study program run by Textile Industrial Institute (TII, now Spartanburg Methodist College), founded in 1911. TII sought to use a liberal arts curriculum "to transform textile workers into stable, productive citizens." To support themselves while they attended school, workers alternated weeks in the classroom at TII with weeks working in the mills. Law's company was one of the first to allow workers to participate in TII's work-study program. In 1916, Saxon Mills employed a community director to help deal with worker concerns. This position essentially combined the functions of a social worker with some modern human resource responsibilities. The director, Marjorie Potwin, was educated at University of Chicago and earned a PhD from Columbia University. Beginning in 1920, Saxon Mills offered company life and health insurance plans to its workers. The same year, Law created a vacation camp for workers—a lodge and tent space—on the shores of Lake Summit, one of the lakes created by his dam project and home to his own family vacation compound. Law established a system of vacation leave for mill workers. Recognized far beyond the local area for his leadership, Law served as the president of the American Cotton Manufacturers Association in 1917.[12]

Polly grew up surrounded by members of her illustrious family. Her father Gabe Hill worked as a bookkeeper for Saxon Mill, and the Hills lived in Saxon mill village, in a house around the corner from her grandparents and near most of her first cousins. John Adger Law was a conservative man who did not believe in paying extravagant wages, not even to his sons and son-in-law who assisted him in managing the mills. Polly's father supplemented his income with a "moonlight job" officiating football games. He began with local high school and college games, but in later years, he also officiated major games, including the Sugar Bowl and the Orange Bowl. Thanks to regular attendance at football games, Polly grew up sharing her dad's love of all things athletic. "He was a very loving person," she said of her father. Her mother was also a "loving mother" and a quiet community servant who "did so much good that nobody ever knew about. I'd have my friends tell me that when somebody in their family died, she came and instead of going to the funeral, she kept all the grandchildren so the rest of the family could go to the funeral. You know, just those little quiet things like that."[13] Polly's family provided her with inspiring role models: career women, entrepreneurial risk takers, prominent civic leaders, and quiet community servants. She would draw from all these examples as she carved out her adult niche in the world.

Polly recalled her childhood as a happy one, surrounded by a lively jumble of cousins. She remembered that the entire family "always went to Granny's for dinner on Sunday. . . . [I]n later years, she had to have a hearing aid, and we could always tell when we got too loud, because she would reach up and turn her hearing aid off so she didn't have to hear us." Five of Pearl Sibley Law's children, their spouses, and the eleven grandchildren were usually in attendance for these weekly gatherings. Polly remembered her grandfather as a distant presence. The grandchildren called him Demi, a nickname that she believed derived from John Adger Law's childhood nickname of Demijohn. "Demi was not a large part of our family," she explained. "When I was young, I can remember it was almost like the family members . . . were trying to keep me from bothering him. In other words, it was like children bothered him. That was the impression that I got. I can remember one Sunday when he came in, we were all there for dinner, and I ran and jumped up in his arms, and I can remember everybody saying, 'No, come here.'" In spite of his perceived aloofness, Polly adored her grandfather. "I remember him being very loving and gentle with me."[14]

Polly credited her grandfather with introducing her to horseback riding, one of the most satisfying activities of her life. "I have pictures of myself as a very very small child up in front of my grandfather on the horse because he loved to ride. . . . In fact, I think I inherited my love of horses and the outdoors from him." Her parents bought Polly her first pony when she was five, and she spent many happy hours on horseback for the rest of her childhood. "When I was about fourteen, he [Demi] got me a nice horse that I could ride at horse shows and things." Her grandfather also kept a horse for Polly's friends to ride when they visited her. The horses were stabled behind Law's large house in the mill village. After school, "in the afternoons, I would come home and ride. You know, if I had somebody to ride with, I would ride with them. Jimmy and Donny Fowler [two neighbor children][,] . . . they liked to ride so we rode a lot of horseback." She rode with cousins, with neighborhood children who also owned horses, and, most often, alone. In fact, memories of time spent with her horses dominated Polly's childhood recollections, and she learned to enjoy spending time alone at an early age.[15]

Although she grew up in the mill village, Polly did not recall playing with mill workers' children very often. All of the Law children attended Pine Street Elementary School in downtown Spartanburg instead of the elementary school in Saxon Mill Village. At Pine Street, their classmates included the children of other Spartanburg mill owners as well the offspring of Spartanburg's professional class. Many of these same children summered at family compounds near that of the Laws on Lake Summit. The Montgomery children, the children of John Law's partner in Manufacturers Power Company, "were almost like family. Because we lived right there together. We were together all the time in the summer." Still, her early childhood years were sheltered ones. She explained, "Mother was protective, so I didn't venture far from home until I was a little bit older."[16]

Polly's idyllic childhood came to an abrupt end when she was fourteen. That year, her grandfather left her grandmother to marry Marjorie Potwin, the community director at Saxon Mills. "I loved him [Demi] very much, but he hurt our family very badly when he divorced Granny. And that was just unheard of at the time." Bitter at John Law's betrayal, Polly's mother would not permit Polly or her siblings to talk to their grandfather. Polly never saw her beloved Demi again after her fourteenth year. "Everybody seemed to love Demi. . . . I think that's why it . . . was such a blow to everybody when he took up with Miss Potwin. I'm sure everybody in the mill knew it before we did, especially with someone in a prominent position like him." The next few years were hard ones for Polly and her mother. "She was going through so much anguish at that time that we just kind of drifted apart. We never had any bad feelings, but . . . I didn't understand what was going on, and she couldn't tell me. . . . She was very insecure about a lot of things" because she had been hurt so much.[17]

Polly consoled herself by spending time with her horses and with her high school and college social activities. Polly attended Converse College, the same Spartanburg institution attended by her grandmother, her mother, and her aunts. A psychology major, Polly was not a serious student. "I think when I was at Converse, I was too dumb to know what I had," she laughingly recalled years later. "I think when I was in school I wasn't focused. I loved being in the dorm. I enjoyed the athletic department, I think, probably more than I did most of my classes. I swam on the swim team, and I played field hockey." She also continued her horseback riding and gave riding lessons to children in the community during her college years. One of Polly's favorite teachers was Professor Gibson, a physical education teacher who taught modern dance. "She was a neat lady," Polly recalled. Clearly, Polly preferred vigorous physical activity to sedentary scholarly pursuits, but she maintained an acceptable academic record, graduating from Converse in 1951.[18]

To some extent, Polly's lack of focus in college seemed to come from her varied interests. She explained, "I had five [children], and I had one who knew what she wanted to do when she was in grade school. My son knew what he wanted to do when he was in college. I still don't know what I want to do when I grow up."[19]

After Polly and Willis married, Willis, like most young men during those Korean War years, was drafted into the army. He served stateside for just over a year, while Polly lived in Spartanburg with her parents. The couple's first child, daughter Martha, was born during this time. In 1952 when his father became ill, Willis obtained a hardship discharge to go home and run the farm.[20] He and Polly rented an apartment in Bishopville and set about raising a family and building a life in a new community. Daughters Susan, Mary, and Kathy soon followed big sister Martha. Four years after Kathy's birth, son Will was born.[21]

Lee County was and is a predominantly rural county in the Lowcountry of South Carolina. Situated on a coastal plain about fifty miles from the coast, Lee County boasts a fertile sandy loam that fostered cotton and tobacco production. The majority of the county's population was African American, and most of them were landless farmers.[22] The land that Willis worked there had been in his family since before the Civil War. When the young Woodhams took over the eight-hundred-acre farm, nineteen sharecropping families assisted with working the land. Willis Woodham described those years in the 1950s as "the last ages of sharecroppers." The croppers used mules to work the cotton and tobacco crops, but within about ten years, many of the sharecroppers had died or left the land, and the Woodhams began to purchase the equipment they needed to mechanize their cotton operation. Because it was so labor intensive, the Woodhams continued to use sharecroppers to raise tobacco until the late 1960s.[23]

Soon after their arrival in Bishopville, the couple constructed their own house on the farm. They did most of the work themselves, with the help of family, farmworkers, and friends. Polly marveled, "I did most all of the painting myself, and that was a lot of fun with two little tiny children." As the family expanded, they outgrew their little farmhouse, however, and by the time Will was four, they had moved to a larger house with some acreage on the edge of Bishopville, near schools and the amenities of town life. Willis Woodham drove to the farm each day. The practice of moving farm families to town so that children could be close to schools was fairly common among white farm families in rural South Carolina at the mid-twentieth century.[24]

The fact that she did not live on the farm, coupled with her town upbringing, distanced Polly from day-to-day agricultural work. She enjoyed the assistance of an African American domestic worker named Marie, and she admitted that this made her more privileged than some farmwives. Even so, Polly saw herself as central to the family economy through her work in food production and preservation. Instead of engaging in the petty commodity production and fieldwork that occupied farm women of an earlier generation, she spent the early years of her marriage caring for five children and her home, tending a large garden, preserving food, and occasionally assisting her husband by fetching equipment parts or other supplies for the farm. The garden occupied many hours of Polly's time from spring to fall, and she insisted that the children work in the garden with her, provoking vigorous complaints from her children even after they were grown. "We filled three freezers every summer. Two for us and . . . my sister-in-law . . . and I would fill Willis's mother's freezer. . . . We did a lot of freezing, a lot of canning. I put up jelly. . . . Canned a lot of peaches and tomatoes and string beans."[25]

When son Will was four years old, an unexpected opportunity came Polly's way. In 1966, the Woodhams had joined a number of other leading citizens of Lee County in founding a private academy, Robert E. Lee Academy in Bishopville. Initially offering only elementary grades, Lee Academy was organized for the "purpose of providing the best possible education for students in a wholesome and religious atmosphere."[26] The younger Woodham children attended Lee Academy from its inception, but eldest daughter Martha was already in high school and finished her education at the public school in Bishopville. As Polly tells the story, "The headmaster came to me and said, 'We have a challenge. We need an English teacher. Could you teach sixth grade English?' And like an idiot, I said, 'Sure, I can do that.'" She laughed at her own naïveté. Polly enrolled Will in kindergarten at Lee Academy. Each morning, she would drop the children off at school and head to her own classroom. Marie, her domestic worker, picked Will up from school at lunchtime, and Polly brought the other children home with her in the afternoon. Polly often felt overwhelmed by the demands of teaching. "I would go to school and teach all morning and come home and cry all afternoon and study all night. I stayed about a week ahead of the children," Polly recalled. "I loved teaching because I just thoroughly enjoyed the children. But that was really a hard time in my life." Juggling her family responsibilities with the hours of preparation required by teaching was always a difficult balancing act. "It just became more and more difficult and so I stopped teaching" after three years.[27]

Polly's absence from the paid labor force was short lived, however. On the farm, she had continued to ride horses regularly, and she introduced her children to the joys of horseback riding as soon as they were old enough to sit a saddle. Shortly after she left teaching, a friend asked if Polly would give riding lessons to her children. Polly recalled, "I said 'yes,' and before I knew it, I had about ten students." She quickly expanded the riding school, buying horses and taking children to horse shows. She even began a small horse-breeding operation. "That was a wonderful time in my life because I loved the horses and I loved the children," she said. Polly explained that her riding academy paid the private school tuition and, later, college tuition for her children. In short, Polly's income supplemented the farm income, allowing the family to enjoy many elements of a middle-class lifestyle, including a college education for each of their children. She said, "We educated all five of them in the very best schools."[28]

After about ten years, however, Polly decided to close her riding academy. As she put it, the schedule of lessons and the demands of caring for the horses tied Polly to her house and stable. She explained, "It was hard on Willis, you know, for me not to be available to help him, to go get tractor parts, and things." By the last third of the twentieth century, mechanization had replaced sharecroppers on the Woodham farm, but Willis still needed farm labor, particularly a person who was available to run errands so that he did not have to leave the fields at peak times. Polly felt increasing pressure to fill that gap for him.

During the early 1970s, many farmers like the Woodhams enjoyed a short-lived agricultural boom fueled by tax policies that encouraged agricultural investment, the ready availability of government-backed loans at below market interest rates, high inflation that allowed borrowers to pay back debts with inflated dollars, President Nixon's Soviet grain deal, and a strong demand for U.S. agricultural exports (fueled in part by a weak dollar). Farmers met the increased demand by ratcheting up production. Many purchased additional land and equipment, but they did so largely by taking on debt. For a brief time, profits soared. As a result, land values also climbed to new heights, increasing landowners' collateral and in turn encouraging farmers to borrow ever larger amounts of money. Thanks to rising debt levels, even as their equity increased, many farmers experienced cash flow problems. Agricultural experts—who, in the words of economist Barry J. Barnett, simultaneously played "the roles of coach, cheerleader, and fan"—encouraged this rapid expansion. Between 1970 and 1973, net farm income doubled. Many southern farmers briefly prospered, but prosperity proved illusory.[29]

By the end of the decade, the boom began to slip away for now highly lever-
aged farmers. Increased production had resulted in lower commodity prices.
Foreign nations recovered from the droughts and other natural disasters that
had temporarily increased the demand for American products. President Jimmy
Carter's grain embargo, part of the American response to the Soviet invasion
of Afghanistan, hit American farmers hard. Adding to the crisis, in the late
1970s and early 1980s, the Federal Reserve tried to curb inflation by raising
interest rates, a particular hardship for farmers who depended on annual operating loans. An appreciating dollar reduced foreign demand for American
agricultural products. Land values plummeted as commodity prices dropped
and interest rates rose. Between 1980 and 1987, the value of net farm assets
declined 30 percent. Lenders would not refinance farm loans. Because many
overextended farmers could not meet their debt payments, agricultural banks
failed.[30]

By the mid-1970s, the Woodhams and many other American farmers found
themselves engulfed by this maelstrom of rising costs and falling prices. Overextended and no longer able to borrow operating funds from traditional lenders,
in 1977, the Woodhams turned to the Farmers Home Administration (FMHA)
for a loan. This agency, originally called the Resettlement Administration, was
established in 1935 and made loans and grants to farm families stricken by the
Great Depression. Over the years the agency was renamed (more than once),
and it evolved and expanded. By the 1970s, it was known as the "lender of last
resort" for struggling farmers, providing credit and credit counseling for the
heavily indebted.[31] An FMHA loan got the Woodhams through the 1977 growing
season, but cotton prices continued to fall. The Woodhams found themselves
unable to pay off their loan at the end of the year. Polly explained that she went
with her husband to meet with the FMHA official after the 1977 growing season.
At that meeting, the official encouraged the couple to borrow more money the
following year and to use their increasingly valuable land as collateral. Polly
said, "They said, 'Well, now this year, you can borrow this much.' And I said,
'Wait a minute.' We hadn't paid last year's yet. 'We're not borrowing until we can
pay that back.' Well, the land had appreciated, and we could get this much more.
And like Willis said, they talked us into taking more than there was any way we
could ever pay back. I mean, if everything had been perfect, if prices had been
good, we still could not have paid it back."

Polly's decision to join her husband in meeting with FMHA officials signaled
her sense that she was an integral part of the family economy. So did her willingness to cosign the note that mortgaged the Woodham's family home, in addition
to their land, in exchange for another farm operating loan. Polly said, "A friend

of mine whose husband is a tremendous hog farmer said when they asked her to sign to include the house on the mortgage, she said she wasn't going to do it. But I said I'd do it. You know, I wanted to help him as much as I can [to keep our land] and so I signed the mortgage." If Polly ever regretted that decision, she did not say so.[32]

Still, farm commodity prices continued to plunge and operating costs escalated. Polly Woodham's stories about this time demonstrate a sophisticated understanding of the obstacles faced by modern commercial farmers. She explained that

> if you cannot make a profit, you cannot stay in business. And there was no way that we could make a profit. I think that one year, . . . we got as much for our cotton as Willis's great-grandfather had during the War Between the States. And I think that what the general public does not understand—think about a really big tractor. $150,000 for the tractor. . . . The general public will pay that much for a house, and that will be a once in a lifetime investment for them. But for a farmer, he's going to have to replace it in ten years.[33]

Soon the Woodhams found themselves on the brink of foreclosure, unable to meet their interest payments, much less pay off their loans.

The Woodhams were devastated by their financial reverses. Willis Woodham said, "I hated to even admit it." Polly said, "It was very demoralizing. And you know, I think the farmwife feels their pain because she feels her husband's pain, and she feels her own, too. . . . It would hurt my heart to see him so despondent." However, the financial difficulties they faced had one happy result. Polly and her husband joined other farmers in protesting their situation. "But one thing we did that I have been very proud of and that I will always be proud of," she said, is that "we joined the farm strike and drove a tractor in Washington."[34]

Like many farmers in the late twentieth century, the Woodhams were part of a new generation of farmers who did not passively watch their farming dreams disintegrate. Educated and politically savvy, they joined the ranks of farmers who lobbied for government action to staunch the flow of red ink onto the pages of the nation's farm ledgers. Some lobbied Congress to act on behalf of struggling farmers through the channels of traditional farm organizations like the American Farm Bureau Federation. Others, including the Woodhams, took a more activist approach through new organizations. They joined the American Agriculture Movement (AAM). AAM was formed in 1977 after Congress failed to revise farm programs in a way that would have guaranteed farmers subsidized commodity prices that met the cost of production. Beginning with a small group of Colorado farmers who proposed a farmers' strike, the AAM quickly developed a national network of farmers who were not content to quietly lobby congressmen for assistance. AAM members used dramatic public protests and the mass media to draw attention to their plight. AAM farmers announced that they would go on strike on December 14, 1977, if several conditions were not met. Farmers drove their tractors to nearly every state capital on December 10; these processions became known as tractorcades. The spectacle drew intense media attention, and AAM members went on radio and television talk shows to educate the public about the plight of American farmers. On January 18, 1978, when Congress reconvened, fifty thousand farmers greeted returning legislators with public demonstrations. Another AAM-organized march drew thirty thousand farmers to Washington in March of the same year. Congress responded to the pressure by passing some temporary farm relief measures in the 1978 session, but AAM activists were not satisfied with half measures. They organized another demonstration, this one a national tractorcade scheduled for February 5, 1979.[35] The Woodhams joined the farmers who converged on the nation's capital that day. As we talked, they proudly shared photographs showing Willis sitting atop his tractor on the National Mall.

Polly also became active in an organization called Women Involved in Farm Economics (WIFE). WIFE was organized in December 1976 by a group of Nebraska farm women. WIFE engaged in a range of activities designed to educate lawmakers and the general public about the importance of farmer contributions to the economy and the problems that they faced.[36] Polly was one of many women who played a central role in late twentieth-century farm organizing and advocacy. Polly explained that joining WIFE "was one of the things that I think that really helped me and made me feel so much better [about their financial plight]." In the process of working with WIFE, she learned that "we were not the only ones with problems. You know, . . . we would see our friends who seemed to be doing all right. But we hadn't looked in their books. But these guys who were in Washington, and the farm women who were up there with them, were not ashamed to say, 'These are my books. Everything is in red ink.' [WIFE members] wore red, you know, to signify that our husbands were operating in the red."

Polly represented South Carolina at national WIFE meetings. She said, "[We did] everything promotional that we could think of, everything educational that we could think of. . . . I went to Washington and testified before the House Ag Committee and the Senate Ag Committee." She described her work with WIFE as a series of learning experiences in which she stretched herself and continually took on new challenges. "I really enjoyed being up there even though I felt very much anger. I really enjoyed . . . being able to talk" to lawmakers about the problems facing farmers.[37]

In WIFE meetings and the halls of Congress, Polly Woodham gained a greater understanding of the complexities of the political process and the difficulties of changing federal farm policy. She described her growing disillusionment with lawmakers who seemed indifferent to the suffering of farm families:

It made me angry that, the first time I went . . . into the Senate gallery. . . , there were two senators . . . sitting and talking and the other two were standing up talking at each other. You know how that is. "My learned colleague this, my learned colleague that." You know I thought that I was going to hear them say, "You know this country really does need agriculture" or something. But do you know what they were talking about? Which school had the number one football team in the nation. I nearly came unglued. . . . I was so angry that when they asked me if I would testify I said, "Yes." . . . I started talking, and you know the green light's on while you talk and then the orange one means you have one minute left and then the red one comes on and you have to stop. Well, I let some of my time go by, and they said something to me. And I said, "Well, you know, my mother taught me that it was rude to talk when somebody else was talking." Talking among themselves, you know, they weren't listening to what I was saying. And we were losing our way of life, our opportunity to make a living. We were losing land that William's grandfather, his great-grandfather had farmed. It was fourth-generation land that we were losing, and they cared no more about that than I cared about talking about that football.[38]

The activist efforts of WIFE and AAM members garnered a great deal of media attention but little immediate congressional action. The farm crisis slowly faded in the last half of the 1980s as the Federal Reserve eased interest rates and the federal government made massive increases in direct payments to farmers. The 1985 Farm Bill provided some debt relief and bankruptcy protection to small farmers, but for many southerners, federal programs provided too little relief too late. Thousands more left agriculture during the 1990s.

Through protracted negotiations with FMHA, the Woodhams managed to hang on to their land throughout the 1980s and 1990s, but they were never able to get out of debt. Neither was Willis able to obtain operating loans large enough to allow him to farm at his previous level; bit by bit, his operation grew smaller. By the mid-1980s, cash flow was so tight that Polly began selling Lady Love cosmetics to friends and neighbors as a means of supplementing the couple's income. Apparently she was successful enough with her direct sales to catch the attention of company executives in Asheville, North Carolina. "They called me and asked me if I'd come up here [to Asheville] and run their distribution center," she explained. "And we discussed it and decided it might be a good thing to do because things were so bad on the farm. At least we'd have some income. And if things didn't work out on the farm, Willis could come up here and get a job." Intending the Asheville job to be a short-term arrangement, Polly rented an apartment and began her new job. Most weekends, she commuted four hours home to the farm.

In spite of the difficulties of maintaining a commuter marriage, Polly loved her work. She also had an opportunity to renew her relationship with her parents and particularly to come to a new understanding of the pain that her grandparents' divorce had inflicted on her mother. Asheville was just over an hour away from Spartanburg where the Hills still resided, so Polly often spent at least one night a week with her parents. "It was wonderful because it gave me five more years with Daddy and Mama and then five more years with Mama [after her father died]. . . . It gave me the chance to really get to know her a lot better."[39]

After a few years, Lady Love Cosmetics closed owing to financial problems, and Polly went to work for one of the company vice presidents who started her own cosmetics line. Meanwhile, Willis had taken a job with the U.S. Postal Service. He worked as a rural mail carrier in Bishopville. The extra income from both of the Woodhams' off-farm jobs enabled them to make payments to FMHA and thus cling to the family land. Accepting that Polly would probably work and live in Asheville until her retirement, she and Willis purchased a condominium there in the late 1980s.

Perhaps Polly inherited her grandfather's entrepreneurial bent, but she seemed drawn to being her own boss. In the early 1990s, she began doing occasional color analysis sessions and makeovers at an Asheville women's retail shop. Soon the proprietor had offered her space in the corner of the store to begin selling some cosmetics and accessories. When the owner of the shop sold out, Polly opened her own retail shop in Asheville's upscale Biltmore Village Shopping Center. She sold handmade jewelry and scarves as well as cosmetics and women's apparel. In one of our oral history interviews, Polly spent more than twenty minutes talking about the details of running her retail store. "It was like playing dress-up!" she exclaimed. She discussed the hours she spent agonizing over what merchandise to buy for the shop. She commented on the importance of developing good relationships with her customers. Polly specialized in helping older women dress in stylish and flattering ways. She explained, "I had a lot of customers who were older women because I was an older woman. But I don't think like an older woman or dress like an older woman, and I helped them develop a style. Fashions come and go, but style sticks." The retail shop proved the perfect fit for the last stage of Polly Woodham's career, bringing together her interest in fashion, her love for working independently, and her zest for new challenges. "The Lord has blessed me with a happy heart," she told me. "I liked everything I ever did. I loved being a momma. I loved being a teacher. I loved my riding school. But I *really* loved that shop," she said.[40]

Willis Woodham suffered a stroke in 1999, forcing him to retire from the Postal Service. The couple made the wrenching decision to sell the family land and their Bishopville home in order to pay off their debts. Willis moved to Asheville, and Polly closed her retail store in order to aid in his recovery. She nonetheless continued to work part-time in a friend's retail shop and in a church-run thrift shop for several years. She also became an active community volunteer and served on the Converse College alumnae board. When asked whether she missed life on the farm, Polly replied, "No, I don't. I don't miss the garden. We enjoy planting things around here, but I don't miss all that work. I definitely do not miss seeing Willis so despondent, you know, over how things are." She paused and pondered a minute more.

I guess you always look back and miss the past to some extent. And I do miss being able to have all my children with me. I told Willis the other night, his mama always wanted us all around her and I know why now. [Laughs.] Around us growing and giving us grandbabies. And you know, that way of life is a wonderful wonderful way to raise children. It was a wonderful way to rear a family; it just wasn't a very good way to make a living.[41]

Polly Woodham's life story offers new insights into the complex ways that twentieth century changes in South Carolina's agricultural economy transformed the daily lives of the state's farm women, their place in the family economy, and their public roles. Early in their marriage, the gender division of labor in the Woodham family more closely resembled the middle-class suburban model promulgated by 1950s advice literature than that of the traditional farm family. Even so, Polly saw herself as central to the family economy through her work in food production and preservation. As financial pressures mounted, however, Polly took on new roles in the family economy. Her off-farm work was crucial to the family's ability to maintain a middle-class lifestyle and educate their children while continuing to work the land. In addition, the Woodhams' experience demonstrates the central role that women played in late twentieth-century farm organizing and advocacy. Sometimes better educated than their husbands and always more free from the daily demands of farmwork, farm women were at the forefront of the 1980s fight to save the family farm.

In short, Polly's flexibility—her ability to adapt to a rapidly changing farm economy—enabled the Woodhams to weather economic hardships and provided Polly with a satisfying life. She believed that her versatility and her strong

Christian faith allowed her to accept change with equanimity. Polly journeyed a long way from her privileged beginnings as a mill owner's granddaughter, but she traveled that distance with a "happy heart."

NOTES

1. Mrs. Skinner's first name is unknown.

2. See Mrs. Skinner's daughters' description of her life in Melissa Walker, ed., *Country Women Cope with Hard Times* (Columbia: University of South Carolina Press, 2004), 160–88.

3. See Jacqueline Jones, *Labor of Love, Labor of Sorrow: Black Women, Work, and the Family, from Slavery to the Present* (New York: Vintage, 1985), chap. 3, Rebecca Sharpless, *Fertile Ground, Narrow Choices: Women On Texas Cotton Farms, 1900–1940* (Chapel Hill: University of North Carolina Press, 1999), Melissa Walker, *All We Knew Was to Farm: Rural Women in the Upcountry South, 1919–1941* (Baltimore, Md.: Johns Hopkins University Press, 2000), and Lu Ann Jones, *"Mama Learned Us to Work": Farm Women in the New South* (Chapel Hill: University of North Carolina Press, 2002).

4. Deborah Fitzgerald, *Every Farm a Factory: The Industrial Ideal in American Agriculture* (New Haven, Conn.: Yale University Press, 2003); David B. Danbom, *Born in the Country: A History of Rural America* (Baltimore, Md.: Johns Hopkins University Press, 1995), 234–37.

5. Bruce L. Gardner, *American Agriculture in the Twentieth Century: How It Flourished and What It Cost* (Cambridge, Mass.: Harvard University Press, 2002), 16–17.

6. Gavin Wright, *Old South, New South: Revolutions in the Southern Economy Since the Civil War* (Baton Rouge: Louisiana State University Press, 1986), 248; Danbom, *Born in the Country*, 238; Jacqueline Jones, *Labor of Love, Labor of Sorrow*, 260–62.

7. For accounts of the structural changes in southern agriculture in the post–World War II period, see Pete Daniel, *Breaking the Land: The Transformation of Cotton, Tobacco, and Rice Cultures since 1880* (Urbana: University of Illinois Press, 1980), Pete Daniel, *Standing at the Crossroads: Southern Life in the Twentieth Century* (New York: Hill and Wang, 1986), Jack Temple Kirby, *Rural Worlds Lost: The American South, 1920–1960* (Baton Rouge: Louisiana State University Press, 1987), and R. Douglas Hurt, ed., *The Rural South since World War II* (Baton Rouge: Louisiana State University Press, 1998).

8. For more on the shift to capitalist agriculture and the ways this shift effected a corresponding shift in the gender division of labor, see Allan Kulikoff, "The Transition to Capitalism in Rural America," *William and Mary Quarterly* 46, no. 1 (1989): 120–44, Alan Kulikoff, "Households and Markets: Toward a New Synthesis of American Agrarian History," *William and Mary Quarterly* 50, no. 2 (1993): 342–55, and Nancy Grey Osterud, "Gender and the Transition to Capitalism in Rural America," *Agricultural History* 67, no. 2 (1993): 14–29.

9. For more on the work of Southern farm women and their role in the family economy, see Sharpless, *Fertile Ground, Narrow Choices*, Walker, *All We Knew Was to Farm*, Jacqueline Jones, *Labor of Love, Labor of Sorrow*, esp. chap. 3, and Sally McMillen, "No Easy Time: Rural Southern Women, 1940–1990," in *The Rural South since World War II*, 59–94.

10. Polly Hill Woodham, interview by author, Asheville, N.C., August 15, 2005.

11. "Margaret Law, Artist, Dies in North Carolina," *Spartanburg Journal*, August 2, 1956, 2; William Law Watkins, "My Aunt Margaret, the Painter," *Carologue* 13, no. 2, 3, 31; Zan Schuweiler Daab, *Margaret Law: Painter of Southern Life* (Spartanburg, S.C.: Spartanburg County Museum of Art, 1999).

12. "John A. Law, Textile Pioneer, Dies Monday," *Spartanburg Herald*, December 20, 1949, 1; Carolyn Law, interview by Betsy Wakefield Teter and Don Bramblett, in *Textile Town*, ed. Betsy Wakefield Teter (Spartanburg, S.C.: Hub City Writers Project, 2002), 64–65; Woodham, interview by author, August 16, 2005; "Saxon Is Lovely Textile Center," *Spartanburg Herald*, June 14, 1934, 1; Norman Powers, "Power from the Hills: John Law's Lake Campaign," in *Textile Town*, 131–32; Katherine Cann, "The Gift of Literacy: Camak's Textile Industrial Institute," in *Textile Town*, 130–31; Marjorie A. Potwin, *Cotton Mill People of the Piedmont: A Study in Social Change* (New York: AMS Press, 1968, 137–39, 152, 129–30; "Our Heritage: Saxon," *Spartanburg Herald*, August 22, 1982, 1.

13. Woodham, interview by author, August 16, 2005.

14. Ibid.

15. Ibid.

16. Ibid.

17. Ibid.; Alice Hatcher Henderson, "Marjorie Potwin: Shaping a Brave New World in Saxon," in *Textile Town*, 138–40.

18. Woodham, interview by author, August 16, 2005; "Converse College Claims Three Generations of Law-Hill Family," *Spartanburg Herald*, May 25, 1951, 12.

19. Woodham, interview by author, August 16, 2005.

20. Willis and Polly Woodham, interview by author, Asheville, N.C., April 30, 2002.

21. Woodham, interview by author, August 16, 2005.

22. A. W. Dick, et al., *Lee County: Economic and Social Conditions* (Columbia: University of South Carolina, 1925), 14–25, 33–35, 44–45; Lee County Bicentennial Committee, *Lee County, South Carolina: A Bicentennial Look at Its Land, People, Heritage, and Future* (n.p.: Reeves Brothers, 1976).

23. Woodhams, interview by author, April 30, 2002.

24. Mary Hipp McCutcheon, conversation with author, Spartanburg, S.C., March 7, 2006; Carolyn McCall, conversation with author, Spartanburg, S.C., April 4, 2006.

25. Woodhams, interview by author, April 30, 2002; Woodham, interview by author, August 16, 2005.

26. Robert E. Lee Academy, http://releeacademy.org/student%20Handbook.htm (accessed June 19, 2006). The focus of my interview with Polly Woodham was her activism on behalf of farm families, and she and I did not discuss her reasons for participating in the founding of Lee Academy at any length. Many of the private schools founded in the South in the 1950s were measures intended to circumvent school desegregation, but I have no way of knowing whether that was the case with Lee Academy or whether resistance to desegregation motivated the Woodhams.

27. Woodham, interview by author, August 16, 2005; Woodhams, interview by author, April 30, 2002.

28. Woodham, interview by author, August 16, 2005; Woodhams, interview by author, April 30, 2002.

29. Barry J. Barnett, "The U.S. Farm Financial Crisis of the 1980s," in *Fighting for the Farm: Rural America Transformed*, ed. Jane Adams (Philadelphia: University of Pennsylvania Press, 2003), 160–71, quote on 166.

30. Ibid., 167–68.

31. U.S. Department of Agriculture, "A Brief History of the Farmers Home Administration" (Washington, D.C.: Government Printing Office, 1989), http://www.rurdev.usda.gov/rd/70th/History%20of%20Farmers%20Home.pdf (accessed July 11, 2006).

32. Woodhams, interview by author, April 30, 2002.

33. Ibid.

34. Ibid.

35. American Agriculture Movement, "History of the American Agriculture Movement," http://www.aaminc.org/history.htm (accessed July 7, 2006).

36. "Women Involved in Farm Economics website, http://www.wifeline.com (accessed July 7, 2006).

37. Woodhams, interview by author, April 30, 2002.

38. Ibid.

39. Woodham, interview by author, August 16, 2005.

40. Ibid.

41. Woodhams, interview by author, April 30, 2002.

Mary Jane Manigault

A Basket Maker's Legacy

KATE PORTER YOUNG

Since its arrival in the Carolina Lowcountry in the late seventeenth century, coiled basketry has evolved from its humble origins as an implement of rice processing introduced by African agriculturalists to an American art known throughout the world. For fifty years, Mary Jane Manigault (1913–2010) was a leader in developing baskets as an art form and gaining recognition for the tradition as part of America's national heritage. Her life history is a vivid portrayal of the lives of the African American women who, as entrepreneurs and artists, played a vital role in the regional economy and culture and, as pioneers and farmers, created and sustained communities of their own making.[1]

By the time Manigault was born in 1913, her parents had already settled their farm in the newly established community of Hamlin Beach. African Americans, newly emancipated, had forged this community out of wilderness on land they gained from the Hamlin family after the Civil War. The Hamlins, like other planters along the South Carolina coast, yielded to freedmen's demands for land in exchange for labor in their cotton fields.[2]

In Christ Church Parish lying just across the Cooper River north of Charleston, seven black communities were established from land freedmen and freedwomen gained from local plantations: Four Mile, Six Mile, Seven Mile, Ten Mile (named for miles distant from Charleston), Snowden, Phillip, and Hamlin Beach. Manigault's family was one of a dozen that settled the community's two-hundred-acre tract of virgin forest and marshland located next to Hamlin Sound just behind the Isle of Palms.[3]

In a 1978 interview, Arthur, Manigault's husband, vividly recalled stories his grandmother, Patsy Manigault, told of pioneering and settling the community during the late 1800s. Patsy, born on the west coast of Africa, lived on the nearby

MARY JANE MANIGAULT
Courtesy of Greg Day.

plantation of Boone Hall during the Civil War. After the war she moved to Hamlin Plantation and lived on the "street" (slave quarters) with her son and his wife while they worked to pay for the land and garner the resources needed to establish their own farm in Hamlin Beach. Arthur proudly recounted the difficulties his family had faced:

> My Old People been through something. They was some tough people, I tell you. When my Old People first come this side off the plantation, all this land you see wasn't nothing but jibland one time back—just woods and the biggest kind of snake and alligator. Sha, you could hunt deer and all back here. They clear all this land with nothing but axes and mules. It taken them years and years fo' do that. They first house was right next to the sound da da on a little island under some cedar trees right next to the sound. They lived in a "board and brush house"—that's what my mama call it—just something to keep them out of the wind and the rain. Then too they didn't live out there too long 'cause a storm come and carry that house, mash um up.

The family continued to face natural disasters but showed great resilience. As Arthur recalled, "The next house they build was right up there where the paved road end next to the creek. Well, sir, around 1911 another storm come. I was a three-weeks-old baby then. My mother taken me in her arms and run for higher ground. That house got washed clean out. So my daddy gather up the board from that house, cut some more, round up a bunch of fellas and go to building the next house way back here in the corner of our land right next to Hamlin's fields da da" (he was pointing to land that could be seen from the Manigaults' porch). As time passed, and with a great deal of hard work, his family was able to produce a substantial crop. "By the time I had sense enough to know myself, my family was farming people just as much as the white folks," Arthur recalled. "We raise rice and cotton and all the thing we eat. That was some good eating back then."

Most families like Arthur's made their living raising diverse food crops— okra, tomatoes, beans, squashes, melons, millet, rice, collards, and so forth— and a few acres of cotton, which continued to be a valuable cash crop until the 1920s and 1930s. Arthur's father also fished with a crew of boys from Hamlin Beach and sold his catch to white families in Mount Pleasant and on Sullivan's Island and the Isle of Palms.

Taking advantage of their proximity to Charleston, the people of Christ Church Parish had for centuries been the primary producers of foodstuffs— vegetables, seafood, poultry products, pigs—for urban residents as well as suppliers of other products for local businesses and manufacturers.[4] The vigorous entrepreneurial activities of African Americans from Christ Church Parish earned them the nickname in downtown Charleston as the people from "Hungry Neck." The older marketing women remembered other black entrepreneurs from Charleston, and Johns, James, and Wadmalaw islands teasing them: "Ya'll sho must be hungry on your side. You always be over here in Charleston hunting money."

Among the products they sold in Charleston were utilitarian household baskets, commonly referred to as "Mount Pleasant" baskets, named after the nearest large town. In the early twentieth century people in Mount Pleasant started making "show baskets" to sell to tourists and retailers in Charleston. According to historian Dale Rosengarten, they adapted traditional forms and invented new ones, ending up with "a large repertory of functional shapes—bread trays, table mats, flower and fruit baskets, shopping bags, hat box baskets, pocketbooks, church collection baskets, missionary bags, clothes hampers, sewing, crochet and knitting baskets, spittoon baskets, wall pockets, picnic baskets, thermos bottles or wine coolers, ring trays, cord baskets, cake baskets, can baskets, waste paper baskets, and platters in the shape of small fanners." These African-style coiled baskets were made of rushes, sweet grass, and pine gathered in nearby marshes and forests. The coils were bound together with narrow strips of palm leaves inserted in the coil after a space had been made with a sharpened spoon handle or traditionally a thin animal bone (like a rib).[5]

In 1916 the baskets caught the attention of a prominent Charleston merchant named Clarence W. Legerton, who established the first wholesale trade in Mount Pleasant baskets. With the importation of European baskets disrupted by World War I, Legerton sought out Manigault's father, Solomon Coakley, to arrange purchases of large quantities of baskets from producers in Hamlin and surrounding settlements.[6] Coakley was the leader of the Praise House, a community institution that had functioned as a religious and judicial governing body for centuries. All conflicts and wrongdoing were addressed by the Praise House leader, and elders decided appropriate punishments and restitutions.[7] Every two weeks, Legerton would visit "Unc Sam," as everyone in the community called him, and place an order for one to two hundred baskets of specified sizes and shapes. Solomon would then divide up the orders among families in Hamlin Beach and surrounding communities.[8]

Women and children sat on porches sewing baskets late into the night after working in their fields or in the cotton fields of nearby plantations. Basket makers earned varying prices for each piece depending on its size and complexity. Table mats brought ten to fifteen cents, while baskets with sides and lids brought twenty-five to fifty cents. In an afternoon or evening of sewing, a woman could make a couple of mats or a lidded basket. In comparison, wages in plantation fields in the 1920s and 1930s ranged from seventy-five cents to two dollars a day.

Manigault's earliest memories were of sewing baskets. By the time she reached school age, she could make mats and simple baskets well enough to be included in the family basket production. Her job was to make two mats every afternoon after school. These mats—flat round or oval pieces six to nine inches in diameter—were used as the foundation for more complicated baskets made by Manigault's kinswomen.

In Manigault's family everyone contributed to the household economy by working on the family farm or the neighboring plantations, by fishing, or by making baskets. Like most children of her generation, Manigault left school at the age of ten or eleven to "help out the family." Besides sewing baskets, she helped her mother, aunts, and cousins care for their children, and she worked in cotton fields owned by large landholders.

Manigault remembered plantation labor as "hard work," "working out," and "working for nothing." "That cotton is an awful thing to pick," she said. "You clean the row and the next day, the cotton bolls opened up and it's all right there again. All bunk up, working in the hot sun all day for nothing." Worse still was the way the workers were treated and cheated. She said, "The bosses keep behind you, watch you close all the time—'Come on, bring that row up! You falling behind!' They talk to you just like that. And you get paid two dollars for a hundred pounds. They cheat you too—weigh it and say that it was only eighty pounds. One day I come home for lunch, left my hoe in the field, left everything right there. I ain't never picked or hoed a row of cotton since. Made up my mind right there."

That day was the turning point for Manigault. While her sisters continued working in the fields, Manigault decided to take her chances in Charleston. During the week, she lived in the city with her aunt Bess. Early on Monday mornings, before day break, she would walk to the highway and catch a ride to the ferry landing in Mount Pleasant for the trip to Charleston. She worked in a peanut factory and helped her aunt sell the vegetables and flowers that she purchased from small farmers in Christ Church Parish, including Manigault's family. Through these activities and the experience of living in the port city of Charleston she met people from other parts of the coast as well as tourists and visitors from all over the world. "I never was no shame-face person, you know. I talk to anybody. I meet people from all over."

Manigault was eighteen the year she moved to Charleston. It was 1933 and the height of the Great Depression—"Hoover times" everybody called it—and money and jobs were scarce. The boll weevil had been ravaging cotton fields for more than a decade. The severe decline in production was economically devastating to large and small farmers alike. Cotton had been the one cash crop on which families with a few acres of rich black coastal soil could depend.

In this tough economic climate sewing and selling baskets and producing foodstuffs for local markets were essential to the livelihood of African American families in the Charleston area. Women like Aunt Bess prided themselves on their abilities as entrepreneurs, business women, and producers of goods on which Charlestonians depended. As Irene Foreman, an entrepreneur and farmer during the 1920s and 1930s, put it: "You could make some money back then—all of ten and twenty dollars in a day—'cause that [city market] used to been the only place for people to buy their vegetables. Even the stores come right to us to get the things wholesale. I used to love to go down there and sell. I had some nice vegetables, nice long collards. Used to make good money selling."[9]

Edna Rouse, a well-known basket maker in the 1960s and 1970s, spent her younger years as a farmer and entrepreneur selling vegetables and flowers in Charleston. She described the weekly routine she and her husband followed back then:

> Me and my husband work the garden equal. We both gather and shell bean. On Monday we gather. On Tuesday we go to the market. On Wednesday we gather and go again on Thursday. Sometime we stay home and just get everything ready for Saturday. We hire some of these children around here to help us shell beans. We go to the market together. I would sell in the retail, and he would sell in the wholesale. I sell to the housewife all the shelled beans and things like that in small quantities. He would sell by the bushel to the store owners.

Rouse also recalled growing and selling flowers, recollecting she made "more money off flowers than anything else." She did not sell flowers on the street, however, but "had a contract with a floral place on King Street." She also sold "benne," sesame seeds cultivated in Africa that were introduced to the Low-country by enslaved Africans.[10] "Well, we used to grow that too," she recalled. "It grow on a stalk. You shake the seed off the stalk and fan them in a fanner [basket]. I sold them by the quart to a lady who run the slave market. I had a contract with her too. She pay me $2.50 or $3.00 a jar for all the benne I give her."[11] Resourceful and energetic, Rouse put together a living by a variety of means. She worked as a domestic for a while but said that "buying and selling—that's me." "Mostly I been selling my vegetables and basket. If I just got two baskets, I'll come down here and sell them myself, and that will be the money I have. I can get my money with my own two hand. Then I know they ain't no cheating going on."

It was from women like Aunt Bess, Irene Foreman, Edna Rouse, and Edna's mother, Betsy Johnson, that Manigault learned "how to be somebody" and make her way in the larger world. Craving independence as a girl she had no intention of marrying. "You know when I was young, I had a plenty of offer to marry, but I didn't have no mind fo' married," she recalled. "I wanted to see a few things, get out on my own, see what I could do for myself."

Arthur Manigault, however, was determined to win her hand in marriage. "Oh, she was the prettiest girl on this beach. I mean to marry she, nobody but she," he remembered. He tried for years to win Manigault's affections, even though their families never gave their formal approval for the couple to "court." Manigault remembered their romance as an "on and off thing. We go together for a while, then I'd run him. We gone back and forth like that for five years. One time I quit him cause I heard his family didn't want me, wanted him to marry another girl he been seeing. So I told him he should go by what his parents say. I didn't care whether he married me or not. I had plenty of suitors. On Sunday evening, my porch be full. No, we never did court the right way—my father never give permission for that."

The reason for his refusal was that Arthur's parents had not followed the customary protocol of presenting a signed "courting letter" to Manigault's parents. The purpose of the "courting letter" was to ensure that any children born during courtships, which often went on for many years before marriage, would be recognized by the father and his family and that material support for the child would be their responsibility. Without the formality of a "courting letter," Arthur's claim on Manigault was tenuous at best.[12]

Much to Arthur's chagrin, Manigault continued accepting suitors on her porch on Sunday afternoons. One Sunday Arthur hid in the bushes and shot a gun up in the air to scare off his competition. Manigault described the incident years later: "This same man here been so fool—it was Sunday afternoon and I sitting on the porch with this one boy, talking just as nice as that and BOOM— BOOM—BOOM. A gun da shoot in the bush across the road. He scare that poor boy to death. That boy never come back. And you know he still won't admit that thing."

While Manigault was living in Charleston, Arthur worked his main job as the water works manager on Isle of Palms and did side jobs for island residents as well. During this time, he was supporting his aging parents and saving money to buy a car. "I was the first person on the beach to have a car. I used to meet Mary Jane at the bridge in Mount Pleasant fo' take her home after she come from the city."

Arthur was also saving to be able to build Manigault a "Marriage House." Courting letter or not, Arthur began construction on the house—a simple two-

room structure with a "hall" or parlor, a bedroom and a loft in the gabled roof
where children usually slept. This traditional architectural form allowed wings
to be added to the house as the family grew and needed more space. The kitchen
shed was attached at the back. The house was proof of Arthur's intentions to
marry Manigault despite their parents' objections. He spent one year working
two jobs to save the money needed to buy the materials for the house, another
year building the house on weekends, and a third year raising the money for his
half of the wedding expenses.

The wedding preparations reflected the community's ideal of marriage equality. The families of both husband and wife were considered vital to formation
and maintenance of the marriage household. Meanwhile, Manigault moved
back to her parents' home, cared for their two children, and began her own
preparations for marriage. As she recalled, many family and friends helped her
prepare: "I had a lot of people help me with the wedding expense. I got more gift
and thing than I know what to do with. A lady I work for paid for the cake. She
bring that cake over in a bushel basket, it was so big. My mother was in charge of
choosing the person who would cut my cake and his mother choose the person
to cut his own. We had a crowd of people to that wedding. I had a nice wedding.
People stay and party til day clean [dawn]."

Manigault and Arthur married in 1945 in the midst of a postwar society that
was rapidly changing. Between 1950 and 1970 the white population of Charleston County increased by 42 percent, from 96,402 to 142,414.[13] Employment opportunities created by the Charleston Navy Yard, paper mills, chemical plants,
the expanding port of Charleston, and the medical school and hospital complex attracted new and more affluent residents. Newcomers meant increased
demand for services and commodities, including foodstuffs, which in turn
lured national grocery stores and commercial fishing outfits with big, expensive
trawlers and chains to the coast.

Large-scale agriculture had shifted from cotton production—already depressed by the boll weevil and competition from other world markets—to truck
farming. Commercial farmers began growing tomatoes, cucumbers, green
beans, and soybeans, or ceased production altogether. Entrepreneurs from Atlanta and other financial centers bought sizeable tracts of fertile Lowcountry
land and established agribusinesses, supplying vegetables for local markets and
metropolitan areas along the eastern seaboard.[14]

In wholesale vegetable markets, black farmers now competed with white
growers and often got paid less for their produce. Arthur witnessed the treatment his father and other African Americans received in Charleston. "Just like
Hamlin right over there be growing his big load of bean and take um wholesale

by the van load . . . and we grow ours over here in this field—maybe we take fifty bushels," he recalled. "But, man, you couldn't tell the difference in those bean. Our bean was good as theirs, sometime better." Yet as the buyer inspected each farmer's beans, and offered a price, his assessment changed depending on the color of the farmer. As Arthur described it, "He come along and dig he hand down into the bean, then he look around, say, 'Who bean is this?' and the white man speak up and say, 'I think they worth about ten dollars [a bushel].' Say the same thing to the colored farmer and the farmer would ask his price of ten dollars. And the man would say, 'No, I don't believe I can give you that price for these beans here.' Claim they was rusty. The colored farmer would only get eight dollars or six dollars for his bushel."

During the 1950s and 1960s, restrictive measures were introduced by the City of Charleston and its health department to stop vendors from selling vegetables and fish in the streets and local markets. According to older marketing women, a system of licenses, fees, and fines was imposed on street vendors. The health department deemed the sale of fish by local black fishermen in the street and in the Charleston market a health hazard.

For Manigault and her elder kinswomen the changes were devastating, robbing them of their economic independence.[15] Manigault felt this loss keenly for both herself and the black community as a whole. "I don't know why they tried to cut all that out," she said. "That's a way for we black people to make a living. The way we black people go is trying to do things for ourselves. But seem like when you try to do something, they try to stop you. We always doing something fo' hunt money. You got something you raise, something you make, you can make some money selling." It was also foolish in that it deprived whites of goods that they clearly wanted. As Manigault put it, she was "doing them a favor bringing fresh, nice things to sell. And white people buy it too. Now they say the fish and things stink up the city all that kind of junk."

"Black people is some wise people. We know how to do most anything," she said. "We ain't had much schooling, but we learn good from mother wit. Don't you know that we build up this whole countryside. They might a had some white man over them, but it was we black people who know how to do them thing."

Manigault viewed this as part of a pattern of calculated assault by whites on black autonomy, meant to make black people dependent and compel them to take the worst jobs. "I tell you this is a time here. They got it fix so you can't help yourself. They just want you to sit home and collect that same little [welfare] check or else work out in they field or clean up their hog mess." But this was not going to work on her, she said. "Not me! I only work out one time in my life— when I was a young girl trying to help out my parents."[16]

Displacement from independent entrepreneurial activities undermined
women's power and status, especially in their marriages. While the ideal in
community and family institutions was equality between the sexes, with "all
two at the head [of the household]," the fact that men usually made higher
wages, working primarily in the expanding construction industry, created tension between husbands and wives and was the cause of much marital conflict.
Women often commented that they would not let their husbands "rule" them
just because they contributed more to the household income. Women viewed
their own work "for the family" and their monetary contributions as equally
important and thus as giving them the right to equal decision-making power in
the household. When men made decisions without consulting with their wives,
they were accused by wives and the community of "going over the wife's head."
Younger women coming of age in the 1950s and 1960s found few opportunities for regular employment other than domestic work. One place that did hire
black women was the medical university complex, consisting of five hospitals.
Competition for jobs such as nursing assistant and kitchen or janitorial worker
was stiff; the jobs were usually filled by applicants with previous experience or
with high school diplomas.

In response to the scarcity of employment and educational opportunities,
black women in greater numbers than men joined the millions of African
Americans who left the South for northern cities. Between 1950 and 1960, 13,581
women and 11,192 men out of an aggregate population of 70,000 migrated out
of Charleston County. African American women were part of a massive exodus
in which 35 percent of the black population left the area—at the same time that
there was a 47 percent increase in the white population.[17]

The Manigaults were not among them, however. From the 1950s until 1970,
Arthur continued to work on the Isle of Palms. Although he was responsible for
the waterworks on the island and supervised a maintenance crew, the salary he
received was not enough to meet his family's needs. So, in addition to sewing
baskets for her father to sell for Mr. Legerton, Manigault once again worked in
the fields—this time picking vegetables instead of cotton. "I had to work hard
to raise my children, I tell you."

In 1954, through her father's connections, Manigault was fortunate to get a
managerial job at Boone Hall Plantation. She was made foreman in charge of
work crews for the truck farm, flower gardens, and grounds that attracted thousands of tourists each year. She worked there for eight years, bringing her older
sons to help her while her nieces cared for her younger daughters. It was a job
she really liked. "That place used to been beautiful when I work over there . . .
and we all get along as good as that," she recalled. "The white children working

there just as hard as the colored. And the man in charge was a nice man." After he left, however, things changed. "The next man come—he wasn't nothing but a pile of liquor and insulting talk. Come pay day, he start talking junk. 'You come to me for money. I already pay you the other day and now you trying to trick me.' Well, that was the last for me. I come out that field, bring my children, and never been back."

By the time Manigault quit working at Boone Hall in the early 1960s, all five of her children were old enough to work and contribute to the household income, and the expanding family continued to live in close proximity. Her three sons, like many of the Manigault men of their age, had learned carpentry and plumbing by working for a local construction company and with Arthur on the Isle of Palms. The Manigault men followed in the community tradition of building their own houses upon marriage and settling on "family land." Manigault Corner occupies the twenty acres that Patsy Manigault and her son Thomas and his wife purchased from O. D. Hamlin, land that they cleared and settled in the late 1800s.

Ancestral lands like these are called "family lands" and in the coastal African American tradition are held in common by all descendants. Any family member growing up on the land has the right to claim a house spot, though it is most often men who exercise this claim. Just like Arthur had, men needed land in order to build the "marriage house," the traditional prerequisite for marriage. Community membership and residence is to this day based entirely on rights to land secured through kin connections, primarily through patrilineage of males. A woman usually moves to her husband's land when she marries. By 1970 a hundred people lived in a dozen households surrounding a central clearing in Manigault Corner. Similar family estates—Jackson Town, Johnson Hill, Coakleyville—reflected the tight kin-based settlement pattern.

For the Manigault children and other young men and women who chose to stay at home despite the appeal of higher wages and wider opportunities in northern cities, the family estate and the nexus of kin provided security and the basis of many domestic and economic activities, including basket making. When women were not working for wages, they gathered in each other's yards to sew baskets while minding children and attending to other household tasks. Older children sat at the knees of their mothers and aunts, learning how to make baskets just as children had for generations.

From these kin cooperatives new family businesses emerged in the 1960s and 1970s to take advantage of a burgeoning local market—tourism. Each year thousands of tourists traveled the main coastal highway, Highway 17, which passes through several black settlements to the north of Mount Pleasant. Women who lived on property along the highway set up stands in front of their homes. Women from nearby communities also began building stands on highway easements, gaining access through relatives or local white landowners.

In 1962, Manigault set up her own basket stand in the Seven Mile community on an easement bordering her cousin's family land. At that time, over seventy basket stands, each representing kin cooperatives totaling approximately five hundred women, lined Highway 17 for miles.[18] The road had become the new marketplace, catering to growing numbers of tourists who flocked each year to Charleston, the nearby beaches of Sullivan's Island, Isle of Palms, Folly, and Kiawah, and south to resorts in Georgia and Florida.

"My children were grown by then, so I could take a chance. I like to sew. It settles my mind." Yet Manigault had been following her "good mind" and taking chances all her life, beginning at age eighteen when she walked out of plantation fields to become an entrepreneur in Charleston and then an artist, teacher, and visionary leader.

After Manigault started her highway basket stand business, she was soon leading the way toward a renaissance in basket innovation and design. The new forms and techniques she created influenced other basket makers, as they saw how successful Manigault was in attracting a clientele interested in baskets primarily as artistic expression. She became known for her daring executions of baskets as large as two feet in diameter and height. Most basket makers of her generation would not even attempt such a feat because of the physical stamina and craftsmanship required to maintain tight, uniform coils bound together with the delicate strips of palm leaf. Manigault pushed her artistic edge even further with executions of curved basket walls flowing out from a base then back in again and with corrugations of thirty-degree angled rows forming what is called an "in and out" basket.

Manigault recognized that this was an art form through which one could express one's creativity and that it required great skill and patience. "A lot of people don't understand about craft," she explained, "what a special thing that is. People put themselves in the things they make with their hands. When you sew baskets, you just concentrate on that one thing. You have to have long patience. You can't be a nervous somebody and make good baskets. You have to sit in one place and really get into what you are doing. You can't have your mind running on all kinds of different things. You got to have a settled mind."

Besides her virtuosity, another quality that made Manigault a leader was her deep respect for the baskets as a "gift handed down from the ancestors," and her desire to teach this knowledge about Afro-Carolinian traditions to the public. At the center of her repertory were basket forms handed down for centuries, in particular the rice fanner, a "work basket" used to winnow rice that was inspired by African rice technology.

In the mid-1970s, Manigault shifted her basket-making business from Highway 17 to the Charleston Market. There she enjoyed more contact with tourists and folk art connoisseurs, who sought her out and became regular customers and collectors of her work. She eagerly shared her vision, her wisdom, and her knowledge of the basket-making tradition. "It don't take nothing off you to talk to people now," she said. "Those same people will come back again or send their friends. I try to give them an understanding about what goes into these baskets and they history and all. Then they appreciate them more."

Manigault's commitment to teaching the public about the Lowcountry basket-making tradition eventually took her to Washington, D.C. She had heard about the Smithsonian Institution from basket makers who attended the Folklife Festival held in the nation's capital on the National Mall each summer during the early 1970s. Manigault wanted to secure national recognition for Lowcountry baskets, a desire she shared with scholars she met when they were doing research in South Carolina. When I was an undergraduate anthropology student in the early 1970s, I, along with Greg Day, a fellow student, met Manigault at her highway basket stand on a fieldtrip. In 1971 the Smithsonian provided a small grant to us to document the techniques of basket making, fishing, and rice cultivation practiced in Hamlin, Seven Mile, Six Mile, Four Mile, Phillips, and other black communities in the area and to collect examples of African-inspired material culture for the Division of Western and Ethnic Culture History.[19] Manigault's baskets and her knowledge of the tradition were the centerpieces of this collection. Since that time Manigault's baskets have been acquired and exhibited by many museums, including the Santa Fe Folk Art Museum, the William Mathers Anthropology Museum at Indiana University, the Cleveland Museum of Art, the American Museum of Natural History, and the McKissick Museum at University of South Carolina. In 1984, Manigault was awarded a National Heritage Fellowship by the National Endowment for the Arts in recognition of "a lifetime of excellence in a local tradition that reaches a really high level of artistry."[20]

The basket-making tradition has been the subject of several major exhibitions over the past twenty-five years. In 1984, Charleston's Gibbes Museum of Art mounted a one-woman exhibit of Mary Jackson's baskets. That same year Dale Rosengarten began to record oral histories and conduct archival research for McKissick Museum's Lowcountry basket project, which resulted in the 1986 exhibition *Row Upon Row: Sea Grass Baskets of the South Carolina Lowcountry.* A fanner basket made by Manigault dominates the cover of the *Row upon Row* catalog, and her work was featured in the show. Manigault Corner achieved an even higher profile in the 2008 exhibition *Grass Roots: African Origins of an American Art*, cocurated by Dale Rosengarten and Enid Schildkrout for the Museum for African Art in New York. A gallery of photographs taken by Greg Day in the early 1970s provided a panoramic view of what Mount Pleasant looked like before the onslaught of massive development transformed the landscape—a process accelerated by Hurricane Hugo in 1989. Baskets from Manigault and her kinswomen are displayed in the photographs alongside other examples of the best of the tradition. When *Grass Roots* opened at the Gibbes Museum of Art in Charleston, South Carolina, in September 2008, generations of basket makers whose images and handiwork were on exhibit came to celebrate the momentous occasion. *Grass Roots* has been exhibited at museums across the country, including the Smithsonian in the nation's capital.

This vibrant artistic culture has prevailed owing both to choice and necessity. With their own resources, skills, and collective efforts, Lowcountry black communities forged a life grounded in African-inspired traditions and secured a place in American society of their own making.[21] As Theodore Rosengarten states in the introduction to *Grass Roots*, "Coastal African Americans have made choices about how they should live at every step along the way, and what they have learned about relating to others has given them the confidence to project their culture onto the world stage."[22]

At the age of ninety-seven, Manigault was still sewing baskets, a practice that was as much a part of her life as breathing the salt air that blows in off Hamlin Sound, although she rarely left Manigault Corner and had passed on the family business to her sons, daughters, and grandchildren. Mary Habersham, Manigault's eldest daughter, has a basket stand on Highway 17 and travels to regional craft shows with the help of her daughter, Karen, and her son-in-law, Corey Alston. Manigault's daughter-in-law Marie, her son Arthur Manigault Jr., and his wife Shirley, also sew baskets and carry on the family business. She passed away on November 8, 2010.

NOTES

1. I am grateful to Dale Rosengarten for urging me to write this essay. Her guidance in shaping and revising the article for publication was invaluable. Dale's scholarship, publications, and exhibitions on Lowcountry baskets and their African origins provide a crucial framework for understanding the historical and contemporary significance of this distinctive African-inspired tradition. Many thanks also to Theodore Rosengarten for his guidance and suggestions during the final phases of writing this chapter.

2. See Peter H. Wood, *Black Majority* (New York: Norton, 1974), and George Brown Tindall, *South Carolina Negroes, 1877–1900* (Columbia: University of South Carolina Press, 1959), 92–123.

3. Much of the information in this article is based on formal and informal interviews I conducted, conversations I had, and observations recorded in my research field notes from the period 1971–78.

4. Wood, *Black Majority*; Tindall, *South Carolina Negroes.*

5. Dale Rosengarten, *Row upon Row: Sea Grass Baskets of the South Carolina Lowcountry* (Columbia: McKissick Museum, University of South Carolina, 1994), 12–13.

6. Ibid., 33–34.

7. Thomas J. Woofter, *Black Yeomanry: Life on St. Helena Island* (New York: Henry Holt, 1930), 46, 236–38.

8. Rosengarten, *Row upon Row*, 33–36; Dale Rosengarten "Missions and Markets: Sea Island Basketry and the Sweetgrass Revolution," in *Grass Roots: African Origins of an American Art*, ed. Dale Rosengarten, Theodore Rosengarten, and Enid Schildkrout (New York: Museum for African Art, 2008), 133–36.

9. Kay Young Day (Kate Porter Young), "'My Family Is Me': Women's Kin Networks and Social Power in a Black Sea Island Community" (PhD diss., Rutgers University, 1986), 20–25.

10. "Benne" is the Gullah word for sesame seed. "Gullah" refers to the culture and creole language spoken on the coast of South Carolina and Georgia. This particular creole, or mixture of languages, consists of African languages, English, French, Spanish, and Portuguese.

11. The slave market in Charleston is now a museum. During the antebellum period, it was where slaves were brought to be sold.

12. Woofter, *Black Yeomanry.*

13. Calculated from 1950, 1960, and 1970 U.S. federal census data for Charleston County, S.C.

14. Chalmers S. Murray, *This Our Land* (Columbia, S.C.: R. L. Bryan, 1949), 222–25.

15. With the displacement of women's family-based production by large-scale agriculture and industrialization in many regions, women's economic independence and their social status has declined. See Ester Boserup, *Women's Role in Economic Development* (New York: St. Martin's Press, 1977), 176–79.

16. Young, "'My Family Is Me,'" 40.

17. Calculated from U.S. census data, 1950, 1960 and 1970.

18. Rosengarten, *Row upon Row*, 42.

19. We conducted fieldwork and documented these African technologies for the Division of Ethnic and Western Culture History of the Smithsonian Institute for fifteen months, from June 1972 to September 1973. During this time Manigault's sponsorship allowed us to meet and work with many basket makers in Hamlin and nearby communities, and we worked with them on a number of projects over the next six years.

20. J. Lorand Matory, "Islands Are Not Isolated: Reconsidering the Roots of Distinctiveness," in *Grass Roots*, 234.

21. Matory, "Islands Are Not Isolated," 232.

22. Theodore Rosengarten, introduction, *Grass Roots*, 17.

Dolly Hamby

The Rise of Two-Party Politics
in South Carolina

JOHN W. WHITE

❀ ❀ ❀

When Lottie "Dolly" Hamby (1918–2001) was born, South Carolina was an agrarian state with a political system dominated by rural elites. Democratic primaries were the only competitive elections and restrictive voting laws limited political participation. This one-party system was maintained by a combination of Jim Crow laws and corrupt registration practices that severely limited the voting rights of African American and poor white men. Women could not vote at all until 1920, when they were enfranchised by federal amendment, and after that these same restrictions kept many of them from voting as well.

In the three decades after World War II, however, major economic and social changes led to significant changes in South Carolina politics. The state experienced unprecedented industrial expansion, striking changes in laws and customs in regard to race, and the emergence of the Cold War economy—all of which led to the birth of a competitive two-party political system for the first time in nearly a century.

Dolly Hamby not only lived through this transformative period in South Carolina history but helped to bring about this profound shift in the politics of the state. As one of the founders of a small public relations firm established in Columbia, South Carolina, in 1951, she was in a unique position to influence the evolution of two-party politics in the state. The firm, known as Bradley, Graham and Hamby and operated by Hamby together with Jane Bradley and Cora Graham, was a crucial engine of change. Throughout the 1950s and 1960s this modest agency was a major conduit for marketing political alternatives to voters throughout the state. Hamby was the partner with the most influence over the agency's political accounts.

The foundation for Hamby's understanding of South Carolina's political terrain was established during her childhood. Her mother, Lottie Hamby, was a graduate of Richmond College in Virginia and later taught French at Greenville Women's College in South Carolina. Dolly's father, Theodotus Capers Hamby, was a civil engineer and a graduate of North Carolina State University. When Dolly was six years old, her mother died and her father moved in with Hamby's maternal grandparents, who helped to rear their granddaughter. From their home at 532 Harden Street in Columbia, Hamby acquired the love of politics she shared with her beloved grandfather, a Baptist minister and loyal southern Democrat. In 1928, to her grandfather's delight, ten-year-old Hamby paraded around town with a homemade "Al Smith for President" sign on her bicycle. "That was my introduction to politics," she later claimed.[1]

When Hamby was sixteen she was admitted to the University of South Carolina. As a University of South Carolina student she was active in student organizations and a member of Delta Delta Delta sorority. She graduated in 1938 with a bachelor's degree in French. Two years later she returned and completed a year of course work toward a master's degree, also in French. It appeared that Hamby would follow a career path similar to that of her mother. However, becoming an educator never appealed to her. "I signed up for four education classes to please my grandmother," she remembered. Luckily she found an appealing alternative, her friendship with Bradley and Graham helping her launch a career in advertising.[2]

Hamby met Cora Graham at the University of South Carolina. She had known Jane Bradley before that. After graduation, Graham took a job working for Jane Cox Oliver at Cox Advertising and Bradley soon followed. Hamby did not join the advertising world until later. During World War II she worked for South Carolina Health and Welfare Services before taking a job conducting research at the University of South Carolina. After Graham and Bradley convinced Oliver that Hamby's research skills could be a valuable asset, Hamby also joined Cox Advertising. The agency, however, had a difficult time maintaining a solid financial footing. In January 1951, having not received the customary Christmas bonus, Graham left the agency. Hamby, who later shared a home with Graham, was also frustrated and was set to return to work at the University of South Carolina when a Cox Advertising client suggested that Graham start her own agency with Hamby. Soon thereafter, Bradley, Graham, and Hamby each contributed $2500 toward the establishment of their own public relations company, and the firm was born.[3]

The founders were determined to be successful in their male-dominated profession. Initially they sought industrial clients: though desperate to drum up business, Bradley, Graham, and Hamby were careful to avoid contracts that

DOLLY HAMBY

Courtesy of South Carolina Political Collections,
University of South Carolina Libraries,
University of South Carolina, Columbia, S.C.

might pigeonhole them as an agency for "women only." Hamby later recalled, "We never would take a women's dress account, or anything that was typically for women. That would have just been ruination, I believe." Instead, the firm signed contracts with companies like Kline Iron and Steel, WIS Radio in Columbia, and the University of South Carolina Press. During the firm's first year of operation, the three women had a difficult time cultivating clients—but they were resourceful and persistent. For instance, Hamby sought membership in Columbia's Palmetto Club, believing it would provide a good meeting place to bring potential clients. When she was denied because of the club's "men-only" policy, she did not give up and eventually convinced it to grant her a membership. Despite small victories such as this the agency did not cement its reputation in South Carolina until it was hired to conduct the marketing for the Dwight D. Eisenhower campaign in South Carolina during the presidential election of 1952.[4]

To say that the Eisenhower campaign in South Carolina was an unusual one for the state would be an understatement. Many of the former general's most ardent supporters were well-known members of the state Democratic Party. Fearing that backing a GOP candidate would jeopardize their standing in their party, they felt compelled to channel their support through an organization independent of the Republican Party. Thus Eisenhower's campaign in South Carolina was mostly conducted under the auspices of a grassroots political group, South Carolinians for Eisenhower. Moreover, the Democrats who dominated South Carolina politics made sure that Eisenhower's name appeared on the ballot as an "independent" candidate as well as the candidate of the GOP.[5]

In addition, South Carolina Democrats who supported Eisenhower convinced their party at its state convention to adopt a resolution stating that Democrats who voted for an "independent" would not lose standing in the party. There was moderate opposition from Democratic loyalists, but most white Democrats supported the resolution. They knew that Eisenhower had strong support from white South Carolinians and that many of them were disaffected with the national Democratic Party owing to President Harry Truman's recent support for the civil rights of African Americans. And they were eager to avoid having dissident Democrats change their official party affiliation because of national political developments.

Eisenhower's support was especially strong in the Lowcountry, where Mount Pleasant Mayor Francis Coleman, former Charleston Mayor Thomas Stoney, and L. Mendel Rivers, congressman from the First Congressional District, all campaigned for him as members of South Carolinians for Eisenhower. South

Carolina Democrats for Eisenhower even enjoyed the backing of Governor
James F. Byrnes.[6]

Despite this support, Hamby recognized that the firm faced an uphill battle.
Even the most zealous South Carolina detractors of the national Democratic
Party were apprehensive about backing a Republican. Indeed, that in 1952 South
Carolina remained a one-party state with an entrenched Democratic majority
ensured that Adlai Stevenson's campaign staff in South Carolina was more experienced and better financed than that of his opponent. During the presidential campaign in 1948 and in the primary election for the U.S. Senate in 1950,
there had been initial stirrings of the factional schisms and popular discontent
that would later develop within the Democratic Party, but those cracks had not
widened enough to create room for two-party competition. Even Eisenhower's
supporters tended to think of South Carolinians for Eisenhower as little more
than a temporary organization. Thus, their commitment to fundraising and
volunteer service was unpredictable. In other words, when they were hired,
Bradley, Graham, and Hamby had no idea if they would receive the support
necessary to operate a successful campaign.[7]

Aware of these challenges, Hamby went to work to enhance the groundswell
of popular support that had secured more than fifty thousand signatures to
place Eisenhower on the ballot as an independent. Stevenson was popular with
African Americans and textile workers in South Carolina's Upstate, but, in the
Black Belt, white voter disenchantment with the Democratic nominee was palpable. Taking the pulse of the state, U.S. senator Burnet R. Maybank concluded
that "the political situation in South Carolina is bad for the Democrats. . . .
The people are very bitter about the Civil Rights Program, the Supreme Court
opinions, etc." Congressman L. Mendel Rivers confided to Georgia congressman E. E. Cox that "in my locality people are frenzied. Just about everybody
who is anybody is supporting Eisenhower. It is very possible that I will have to
make a strong statement on his behalf before the election."[8]

In this uncertain atmosphere Bradley, Graham, and Hamby had their first experience working for a political campaign. The Eisenhower campaign's choice
of a female-owned firm no doubt seemed unusual to many at the time, but
the effectiveness of the firm was apparent from the start. Hamby, in particular,
displayed a knack for crafting simple political slogans and advertisements that
resonated with South Carolina voters. She was able to take advantage of the
existing political schisms and attract white Democratic voters to the independent movement without the polling or focus groups that South Carolinians for
Eisenhower could ill afford.[9]

Hamby had little experience and no training in operating a political campaign, but she used the election as an opportunity to indulge her love of politics and make use of her keen understanding of South Carolina's political system. Following Hamby's directions, the independent Eisenhower campaign underscored the fact that voting for the former general would cause Democrats "no loss of face in their party standing or in any way affect their party loyalty on a state basis." Hamby recommended that "except for buttons, ribbons, and car stickers, no material from National Republican Headquarters should be used" in the campaign. Instead, she insisted that it was "imperative that the voters know that this is a movement of *all* people, that it is an independent group with no political aspirations of its own and no affiliation with any party."[10]

In addition, Bradley, Graham, and Hamby argued that exploiting voters' disgust with the highly unpopular Truman administration would be the most effective way to oppose Stevenson, as many within the Democratic Party viewed Stevenson positively as "a man of integrity" very different from Truman. Issues involving Truman-era "graft, corruption, socialism, secrecy in government, inefficiency, government by crony, big government" and "bureaucracy should be hit again and again," the agency advised. Bradley, Graham, and Hamby recommended that the publicity committee of South Carolinians for Eisenhower urge the campaign to undermine Stevenson's image by "innuendo in ads, making it clear that only a complete change, not a 'refreshing,' can clear up the present rottenness in government."[11]

In her first political contest, Hamby proved to be adept at one of the thorniest tasks confronting conservative southern Democrats who favored Republican candidates: appealing to whites alienated by national Democratic support for civil rights without appearing to be political extremists or reactionaries. Eisenhower's supporters, especially Governor Byrnes, feared that a divisive election might help forge a new political alliance between white moderates and African American voters. To attract racial conservatives without alienating white moderate voters, Hamby recommended that the campaign be very cautious in making references to racial controversies. Essentially, the agency recommended that the independent Eisenhower group campaign on its conservative philosophy without defining how that philosophy would be incorporated into the day-to-day operations of the executive branch. For example, one radio commercial produced by the agency pointed out that "one of Eisenhower's views that's most important to South Carolina is his position on . . . States' Rights," but it never declared how Eisenhower would change existing policies if elected.[12]

The Eisenhower campaign relied heavily on carefully crafted language proposed by Bradley, Graham, and Hamby. Rather than engage in the kind of blatant race-baiting that had typified Strom Thurmond's Dixiecrat campaign in

1948, the campaign pioneered the use of "catchwords" that would later become mainstays of the Republican Party in the South. South Carolinians for Eisenhower consistently attacked corruption, bureaucracy, and "big government," knowing that, despite the lack of specific references to African Americans, most white South Carolinians would draw a connection between these terms and their resentment of the federal government's entitlement programs and civil rights legislation. For example, in a radio program produced by Bradley, Graham, and Hamby, the organization proclaimed:

> We believe that extravagant Federal spending, high taxes, inflation, and the many Federal "handouts" hiding under the name of welfare and leading us down the dead end road of socialism and ruin. . . . WE BELIEVE that a workable foreign policy, a strong defense program, and a sound domestic program can be achieved . . . and TAXES reduced . . . by eliminating the many "hog troughs" in our present bureaucracy. . . . WE BELIEVE that all sovereign states should be free to handle local problems locally and to govern themselves according to the expressed wishes of the people in each state.[13]

Hamby's agency developed this strategy and slogans and also found ways for South Carolinians for Eisenhower to get this message across to potential voters. Byrnes, Rivers, and other prominent Eisenhower supporters furnished the campaign with its tenor and credibility, but it was Bradley, Graham, and Hamby that, by organizing radio broadcasts of important speeches and blanketing the state with print advertisements, provided the infrastructure through which the campaign made its appeal to traditionally Democratic voters.[14]

In the end, Eisenhower earned 165,000 votes in South Carolina, but Stevenson carried the state with over 170,000 votes. Loyal Democratic voters in the Midlands and Upstate regions of the state voted two to one in favor of Stevenson. The votes of white textile workers and the strong support of African American voters helped the Stevenson-Sparkman ticket win one of its few victories. Though Stevenson made almost no official effort to reach out to black voters in South Carolina, African Americans were more comfortable with the Democratic candidate than they were with the more conservative Eisenhower. To black voters, the former general's promises to respect states' rights and his overtures to southern political leaders like Rivers and Byrnes were evidence that the Republican would be more inclined to roll back gains in civil rights than his Democratic opponent.[15]

In South Carolina black voters were more likely to support Strom Thurmond's Dixiecrat campaign in 1948 than to vote for Eisenhower in 1952. In an election postmortem, Governor Byrnes estimated that about fifty-nine thousand black voters had cast their ballots for Stevenson. For the first time since the 1870s, African American votes proved to be the deciding factor in a presidential election in South Carolina. Less than 2 percent of the popular vote separated the two candidates, and, much to the chagrin of segregationist whites, even limited enfranchisement of African Americans played a crucial role in the outcome,[16]

For Hamby, however, the election's result demonstrated that the strategy employed by South Carolinians for Eisenhower was an effective approach with which to capitalize on white anxiety, especially in the state's Black Belt region. It also demonstrated that overcoming Democratic advantages in South Carolina would be difficult. Eisenhower overwhelmingly carried those areas where fears of widespread racial change were strongest. South Carolina's First Congressional District, comprised of the Lowcountry and parts of the Pee Dee regions, provided the most support for the independent ballot, casting over 65 percent of its vote for Eisenhower. The Republican also won the Second Congressional District, which included the area around Columbia, with 60 percent of the combined independent and GOP vote, and the Sixth Congressional District, with 50.29 percent. Eisenhower supporters tended to be white, working-class voters who were not employed in the textile industry and who lived near large African American communities.[17]

Owing in part to Hamby's work to portray South Carolinians for Eisenhower as an acceptable option for disenchanted white Democrats, the Republicans were able to surpass the ballot totals garnered by Strom Thurmond during his contentious 1950 primary contest with Olin Johnston—an election in which Thurmond unsuccessfully attempted to utilize white anxiety to unseat the popular liberal senator. Eisenhower was especially successful in increasing support among white professionals in Charleston and Richland Counties, surpassing Thurmond's totals. It is especially noteworthy that Hamby had crafted a successful political vocabulary that criticized the erosion of white privilege without alienating professional workers who were put off by crass race-baiting. Political correspondent Raymond Moley concluded that Stevenson's total vote from white South Carolinians was a scant 114,000. Byrnes argued that white South Carolinians jumped on the Eisenhower bandwagon because they feared the "socialistic policies" adopted by the Truman administration.[18]

Although Eisenhower failed to carry South Carolina in 1952, the campaign's strong showing contributed to Bradley, Graham, and Hamby's reputation across the state as a potent advocate for politicians as well as businesses. More importantly, it filled the firm's coffers with the capital to secure the financial stability of the firm at least for the near future. Its owners were able to secure a plethora of new customers and to expand their client base among the state's political

leaders. In the next round of elections, the agency not only managed Strom
Thurmond's successful write-in campaign for one of the state's seats in the U.S.
Senate, but it also directed Lieutenant Governor George Bell Timmerman Jr.'s
efforts to win the gubernatorial primary against Columbia mayor Lester Bates.
In both elections the firm relied on lessons it had learned during the Eisen-
hower contest.

In Thurmond's case Hamby demonstrated considerable initiative and political savvy. As soon as she heard rumors of his candidacy she contacted the
former governor, emphasizing that as a write-in candidate he would need the
services of an experienced public relations firm. Thurmond and Hamby had
a difficult task: Thurmond had decided to run for a vacancy created by the
sudden death of Senator Burnet Maybank, but he was not the official nominee
of the Democratic Party. Due to the short period of time between Maybank's
death and the general election, the party's executive council had decided to
forgo a primary election and simply name state senator Edgar Brown as the
party's nominee for the U.S. Senate. The move created a major public controversy and was widely denounced by the press and the public. Thurmond and
many of his former constituents were outraged by the undemocratic "appointment" of Brown.[19]

Since he was not on the ballot, Thurmond's campaign would be quite different from his previous senate campaign of 1950 when he attempted to unseat
Senator Olin Johnston. Hamby recognized that this time, with an unexpected
opportunity, a hastily constructed campaign, a short time frame, and lack of
support from the Democratic establishment, Thurmond would have to rely on
untraditional tactics. In an early phone conversation with Hamby, Thurmond
admitted that a write-in campaign against a powerful state Democrat like Brown
was a long shot. He told her, "I don't have anything. I don't have any headquarters, I don't have any money, I don't have anything." Undeterred, Hamby assured
Thurmond that the agency would come up with a plan to win the election.
"We'll get you a headquarters," she said, "and then we can talk after that."[20]

Hamby and her colleagues quickly convinced the manager of the Columbia
Hotel to reserve the entire mezzanine for Thurmond's campaign headquarters.
They then began developing a strategy to pay for the election. Hamby later recalled: "When it came to the money, I said, 'Strom, get about three to five people
whom you know from every county up here for a meeting.' We figured that we
would need $350,000 for the campaign. . . . And I worked it out on a percent-
age basis of population, how much each county should contribute, and gave it
to Strom." Hamby expected the candidate to implement the strategy. Instead,
Thurmond insisted that Hamby sell the idea to his supporters. Her efforts were
fruitful, and in a short time the campaign was up and running.[21]

Hamby also proved to be astute at exploiting the special circumstances of the write-in election. The voters had to be educated on how and why to support the write-in candidate. "We knew we had a big job ahead of us," she later recalled, "not the least of which was to teach people how to vote for a write-in candidate rather than the hand-picked candidate of the Democratic Party. We had to show how to do this on paper ballots as well as on voting machines." The agency flooded the state with billboard, print, and radio advertisements urging voters to "Use your right to write in," and to "Be a pencil totin' Democrat." The firm went so far as to have stools made for each of the state's voting machines so that even the shortest voters could reach the space for writing in a candidate's name. Unlike in his unsuccessful campaign in 1950, Hamby insisted that Thurmond avoid getting bogged down in a single-issue campaign. And the agency sought to capitalize on voter anger over "cronyism" in the Democratic Party. It successfully branded Thurmond as a conservative reformer with an independent streak who was unlikely to kowtow to the wishes of Democratic Party bosses in Congress. After the election, Thurmond credited Hamby for being the one most responsible for ensuring that his message reached the majority of the state's voters. "You keenly analyzed the advertising needs of the campaign," he wrote, "systematically and efficiently laid the groundwork for the most effective presentation possible, and spent long hours carefully implementing the program."[22]

The firm's role in the Timmerman election was less complicated. White South Carolinians were in an uproar over the Supreme Court's decision in *Brown v. Board of Education* but still hoped for a legal remedy that protected both segregation and public education. As in 1952, Hamby sought to capitalize on white anxiety without branding her agency's candidate an extremist and eschewed blatant race-baiting at a time when such tactics were common in many other southern states. The agency promoted Timmerman as the candidate most likely to find a lawful solution to the burgeoning racial crisis that peacefully preserved the existing racial hierarchy. They hailed Timmerman as a moderate candidate in the vein of his predecessor, James Byrnes, but took covert action to be sure that racial anxieties benefited their candidate. When *Ebony*, a national African American publication, endorsed Lester Bates, Bradley, Graham, and Hamby used the endorsement to disparage the Columbia mayor. Hamby recalled, "That was all we needed. . . . We just passed [the magazine] around." This subtle strategy worked, and Bates was unable to garner significant support from white voters.[23]

Both of Bradley, Graham, and Hamby's clients were victorious in 1954. Moreover, both Timmerman and Thurmond easily defeated their opponents. Timmerman collected over 60 percent of the primary vote and Thurmond became the first candidate in the history of the U.S. Senate to mount a successful write-in campaign. Hamby again demonstrated a knack for capitalizing on existing tensions within the Democratic Party. She contributed to the demise of South Carolina's single-party system by highlighting these divisions and providing a basic vocabulary with which to channel South Carolina voters' disillusionment with the national Democratic Party. Within a decade the factions that had rejected Brown and Bates in the elections of 1954 became a core constituency for the emergent Republican Party in South Carolina.[24]

After its successes in 1954 the agency's services were sought after by a number of well-known candidates. Between 1954 and 1960, Bradley, Graham, and Hamby managed the public relations aspects of several successful political campaigns. Notably, the agency represented Lieutenant Governor Ernest "Fritz" Hollings in his bid to succeed Timmerman as the state's governor in 1958. Hollings borrowed heavily from Timmerman's 1954 tactics and attempted to sell his candidacy based on his position as a "moderate" though committed segregationist. As an experienced candidate and an important cog in the Democratic machine in South Carolina, Hollings was less reliant on Bradley, Graham, and Hamby to get his message to potential voters. Nonetheless, the agency was the main conduit for the distribution of Hollings's campaign ads and radio commercials. For example, it created and disseminated advertisements praising Hollings for being appointed by Byrnes to "help present South Carolina's position in the Clarendon County segregation case before the United States Supreme Court." Hollings easily won the contest and became the state's next governor.[25]

During the presidential election of 1960 the agency was hired to promote the candidacy of Richard Nixon in South Carolina. This time the agency worked for both the national Republican campaign and the independent organization Democrats for Nixon and Lodge. Again Bradley, Graham, and Hamby exploited the ever-deepening cracks in the façade of Democratic Party unity. To appeal to the largest possible voter bloc, advertisements created by the agency tended to take up different, yet complementary, issues that appealed to South Carolina's conservative white voters. For example, in a film produced for Democrats for Nixon and Lodge by Bradley, Graham, and Hamby, state representative Albert Watson declared that Nixon's opponent, John F. Kennedy, was "100 per cent against the South," and that, under a Kennedy administration, farmers would have to seek permits for "practically every acre they planted." It also quoted Thurmond's opinion that the national Democratic Party platform was a "road map for economic collapse" and "racial amalgamation."[26]

In many ways the film (along with Hamby's other work) was a precursor to strategies later employed by Republicans in South Carolina. Years before Thurmond's chief strategist Harry Dent, Lee Atwater, and other Republican leaders crafted the party's "southern strategy," Hamby constructed the basic roadmap for electoral victory in the South. She understood that appeals to anxious whites would garner a large number of votes, but she also recognized that the support of more moderate white voters was crucial to overcoming Democratic loyalties in South Carolina. Therefore, the film emphasized themes that would attract white professionals and merchants who were concerned about heavy-handed federal policies but unwilling to jeopardize their own self-interests to fight an unwinnable conflict over Jim Crow. Hamby realized that many middle-class white South Carolinians were uncomfortable with federal interventions in local racial arrangements but were equally concerned about the potential for the politics of "massive resistance" to incite public unrest. She recognized much earlier than most political strategists that by attacking the "abuses" of federal power in general rather than focusing solely on race, her clients could attract voters who were put off by what they viewed as post-*Brown* demagoguery.[27]

Hamby also pioneered in reaching out to conservative women. In one commercial, Mrs. R. E. Lipscomb, the women's chair of South Carolina Democrats for Nixon, insisted:

South Carolina women are deeply concerned over whether we will have war or peace. . . . We do not want our sons in foxholes in foreign lands . . . or, for that matter, in any so called "peace corps" scattered over the world among strange people and foreign influence and morals.

We want as president a man who is firm[,] . . . a man who will not give an inch when he is fighting for what is right.

We admired the way Vice President Nixon, on his visit to Moscow . . . shook his finger in Khrushchev's face and boldly challenged the vulgar untruths of the heathen dictator. We do not want a man to lead us who would apologize to this barbarian. . . .

We do not want a president who is too young, too impetuous, or who acts before he thinks in a world where just one mistake might set off an atomic war. We do not want a man who was handed his first million when he was just 21 years old. He couldn't possibly understand the problems of the working man or the farmer.[28]

Like Eisenhower, Nixon lost the state in a close election, but unlike Ike, he was listed on the ballot as a Republican. In 1960, many white voters remained angry at Eisenhower's decision to use force to desegregate Central High School in Little Rock, Arkansas in 1957 and were reluctant to trust another Republican who promised to respect "states' rights." Nevertheless, Nixon became the first Republican to win the majority of South Carolina's white votes while running as a member of the GOP. He thus provided evidence to many South Carolinians that the Democrats were losing their hold on the Palmetto State.

As with the Eisenhower campaign, the Nixon campaign directed by Bradley, Graham, and Hamby provided the blueprint for a successful Republican campaign in a number of Black Belt counties. One year after orchestrating Nixon's strong showing in South Carolina, the agency utilized similar tactics to elect a Republican to the state legislature for the first time in the modern era. In a special election to fill a vacated seat in the South Carolina House of Representatives, Bradley, Graham, and Hamby represented a Columbia attorney, Charles E. Boineau Jr., a Republican, in his bid to represent Richland County in the state legislature. Like most of the state's newest Republican converts, Boineau had formally joined the party during the 1960 campaign but had not supported the Democratic nominee in a presidential election since 1944. The election was especially challenging for the agency in that both he and his opponent, Joe Berry, a Democrat, held similar political views. Both men were avowed conservatives who believed in segregation. The biggest difference between them was their party affiliation. Even though the election was for a state office, Boineau was able to win by a landslide simply by campaigning against the national Democratic Party. Boineau condemned the Kennedy administration for "telling us whom we should hire" and attacked federal "control" of education. His economic conservatism, his subtle criticisms of desegregation, and his carefully constructed defense of white rights projected the idea that Boineau believed in white privilege but was averse to race-baiting.[29]

In many ways, the Boineau campaign was the most important of Hamby's career in that it was the most in line with Hamby's own personal ideology. Like Boineau, she was conservative but disinclined to support the kind of violent segregationists that seemed to dominate politics in Mississippi and Alabama. Moreover, Hamby did not want to utilize the harsh racial language of many recalcitrant southern segregationists (George Wallace in Alabama and William J. Simmons in Mississippi, for example) in campaigns managed by her agency. Boineau's victory in a solidly Democratic state was evidence of the groundswell of popular support for an alternative political option in the South Carolina Midlands. Moreover, it demonstrated that the campaign tactics that Bradley, Graham, and Hamby had utilized for nearly a decade could help some candidates achieve success with South Carolina's white electorate. Over the course of the next decade Hamby worked for both Democrats and Republicans, but, regardless of party affiliation, her most successful political clients all followed a path similar to Boineau and ran campaigns reflective of the 1952 Eisenhower campaign.[30]

During the election Boineau employed "states' rights" rhetoric while avoiding racist demagoguery. In a half-hour television commercial produced by Bradley, Graham, and Hamby for wis in Columbia, Boineau's campaign manager, Drake Edens, interviewed a number of "regular" South Carolinians about the upcoming election. In the advertisement, one woman claimed that she was voting for Boineau because "the Republican Party is now the home of conservatism" and the "defender of states' rights." Another commended Boineau for speaking out against "socialism in Washington" and proclaimed that she was now "ready to join him and start fighting in my own backyard." Others praised Boineau for his criticism of the welfare state and for his commitment to education.[31]

Hamby worked with Edens to craft Republican campaign tactics in the early 1960s. Together they revived Thurmond's criticisms of single-party cronyism to condemn the "un-democratic" nature of state politics under its one-party system. Under their direction, the campaign bombarded Richland County with propaganda declaring Boineau a "true conservative" and they reinforced the notion that the Democratic Party was a bastion of corruption—hell-bent on centralizing governmental power in Washington, D.C. After the election, Boineau wrote to thank the agency: "The luckiest day of our lives," he wrote, was the day that he and "'4 naïve & dedicated amateurs' came calling."[32]

After the success with Boineau the agency presided over several Republican campaigns in 1962 and 1964. Not all of them followed Hamby's now proven formula for success, and, largely as a result, none of the candidates were elected. In 1962 the firm represented Republicans William Workman, Bob Chapman, and Floyd Spence in the general election. Each candidate was opposed by an entrenched Democrat with more experience, but each hoped to secure an "upset" by capitalizing on voter angst over the wave of desegregation that had swept across the peripheral South in the late 1950s and early 1960s. Like most new members of the GOP in South Carolina the candidates felt that white anxiety would hasten a shift in political allegiances. Chapman, for example, declared that "the Republican Party is now . . . the defender of States' Rights," and warned about the dangers of "Negro rule."[33]

The most serious candidates were Workman, who was a well-known journalist, and Spence, who had made a much-publicized switch to the Republican Party after supporting Democrats for Nixon and Lodge in 1960. Workman challenged the state's senior senator, Olin Johnston, and Spence ran against fellow racial conservative Albert Watson, who represented the Second Congressional District in the U.S. House of Representatives.[34] During the election neither Workman nor Spence heeded Hamby's advice to avoid running a campaign that could leave them open to being labeled as extremists. She warned the candidates

that although racial politics would energize a sizable portion of the electorate, the lingering strength of loyal New Deal Democrats in the state (including
roughly seventy to ninety thousand registered African American voters) would
undermine both campaigns unless the candidates broadened their appeal beyond opposition to integration. But both candidates ran single-issue campaigns
that focused on the issue of segregation alone, and each paid a price for ignoring
Hamby's advice. Workman lost to the entrenched Johnston, and Spence was
defeated by Watson. Hamby found this extremely frustrating. She remained
critical of Workman and his campaign for the remainder of her life.[35]

Although Hamby was disappointed with the outcome of the 1962 elections,
GOP leaders were overjoyed that both Workman and Spence earned over 40 percent of the popular vote. Republicans were accustomed to losing by much wider
margins. GOP leaders were pleased enough that they hired Bradley, Graham,
and Hamby to conduct the public relations for Barry Goldwater's presidential
campaign in South Carolina in 1964.[36]

Owing to his unquestioned credentials as an anticommunist and committed
conservative as well as his opposition to the Civil Rights Act of 1964, the Republican had widespread support among white voters in the South. As a politician
who managed to garner white southern support without George Wallace-style
appeals to virulent racists, he was a perfect candidate for Hamby. Goldwater offered a legalistic argument for the preservation of "states' rights" with which white
professionals were more comfortable. Hamby made sure that South Carolina
voters were familiar with the Arizona senator's brand of conservatism. On election day he carried the state with almost 60 percent of the popular vote. Hamby's
friend and former client Strom Thurmond was delighted with the results. In a
letter to Hamby, he gave her much of the credit: "In the Goldwater Campaign
you again performed magnificently, and as a result, we scored effectively in South
Carolina with better than 59 per cent of the vote, even in the face of a large block
vote [of African Americans]." Goldwater's victory, combined with Thurmond's
official conversion to the Republican Party in 1964, gave GOP activists confidence that a political breakthrough would occur in the very near future.[37]

Some observers as the time, including Maurice Bessinger, Floyd Spence, and
Albert Watson, concluded that Goldwater's victory owed to his opposition to
desegregation by federal mandate—that such opposition on the part of a candidate was enough to win an election in South Carolina. Hamby had a more nuanced understanding of her client's success in South Carolina. She recognized
that the willingness of South Carolinians to vote for a national Republican was
not confirmation that they would change party affiliation on the local level.
Moreover, she appreciated that without a comprehensive strategy that empha-

sized more than racial anxiety, Republican candidates stood little chance of un-
seating entrenched southern Democrats. In a 1965 speech to the Republican
Women of Augusta, Georgia, Hamby declared: "The thoughts which I'll present
somewhat at random tonight have been collected after many campaigns. . . .
First and most important is the fact that voters will not be sold on extremism."
She also proposed that candidates for political office should follow basic themes
and remember that "EVERY REGISTERED VOTER is a prospect." Using Spence as
her prime example, Hamby reminded her audience that a winning campaign
needed "50.1% of the people 50.1% of the time," and she encouraged them not to
"write off any group" and not to "blame any loss on any specific group."[38]

In 1966 Bradley, Graham, and Hamby created advertisements for the
GO-Party Bandwagon but its two most renowned political clients were Democrats who, unlike her unsuccessful clients of 1962, Republicans Workman and
Spence, were more amenable to Hamby's strategy. Indeed she and her partners
were unwilling to endure the same frustrations that had hindered their success
four years earlier and so would only work with clients who were willing to heed
their advice. The agency represented Robert McNair in the gubernatorial contest in 1966 and Cyril Busbee in the race for state superintendent of education.
Although both candidates were Democrats, their campaigns were similar in
tone to Eisenhower's 1952 campaign in South Carolina and Boineau's in 1961.
While the GOP ran campaigns focused almost entirely on white resentment of
the national civil rights movement, Hamby crafted advertisements that presented her clients as moderate, steady leaders. In both cases, Hamby's strategy
proved successful.[39]

Though the GOP had grown vigorously during the early years of the 1960s,
Hamby's predictions proved to be true, and Republican progress stalled after
the 1966 elections. Republicans won twenty-five seats in the state legislature but
lost seventeen of them two years later. As Hamby had warned, the increased
number of black voters and disenchantment among white moderates with the
hardcore race-baiting utilized by GOP candidates led to a reversal in the party's
fortunes in 1968.[40]

As Republicans floundered, the firm again represented a well-known Democrat when it was hired to represent Hollings in his reelection campaign for the
U.S. Senate. As with fellow Democrats Busbee and McNair, Hollings succeeded
as the GOP languished at the polls: each was victorious despite the fact that
they all supported compliance with federal desegregation standards. Hamby
recognized that the road to electoral success was becoming more difficult for
Democrats in statewide elections, but she had also witnessed firsthand the key
weaknesses of the GOP in South Carolina. In order to take advantage of Repub-

lican limitations, she again recommended that candidates appeal to the state's conservative values without falling victim to charges of fanaticism that had typified the politics of segregation in other southern states. For example, Hamby concluded that in order for McNair to offset voter anger over national Democratic support for civil rights legislation, he should remind voters that he was a member of the party of "[John C.] Calhoun, [James F.] Byrnes, Olin Johnston, and Mendel Rivers."[41]

Hollings, for example, used Bradley, Graham, and Hamby advertisements to highlight the fact that he was "dedicated to South Carolina" and not to the national Democratic Party. Like Hamby, Hollings knew that a large number of whites were considering a move to the Republican Party but also recognized that South Carolina voters regarded in-state Democrats as very different from "liberal" members of the national party.[42]

It is no coincidence that, in many ways, Hollings's campaign resembled Hamby's most successful campaigns from the previous decade and a half. She urged the former governor to underscore his political conservatism by emphasizing key subject areas like "law and order," the war in Vietnam, "textiles," support for agriculture, religion, and patronage, and opposition to "big government" and tax increases. She then assembled several quotations from Hollings's public appearances to use in print advertisements. These highlighted the fact that Hollings was "not in the pocket of *any* presidential candidate or any president—of any organized group or party" and that he was opposed to "kooks and peaceniks who would have us stop the bombing NOW and leave our boys at the mercy of the Communists."[43]

Bradley, Graham, and Hamby had developed a strategy that was demonstrably effective, but in 1970 the agency took a significant risk that provided even more evidence of the value of that strategy. Owing mainly to Thurmond's influence, the Republican Party of South Carolina selected Bradley, Graham, and Hamby to direct public relations efforts for its candidate, Albert Watson, who was attempting to become the first Republican to be elected governor of the state in the century. Although Watson had participated in a number of race-baiting campaigns in the early 1960s, Hamby was certain that, with the right strategy, Watson could achieve a majority vote in the general election. He was a member of the South Carolina House of Representatives and a well-known conservative who had officially left the Democratic Party in 1964 after being stripped of his seniority for supporting Goldwater in the presidential election. Moreover, he was a close ally of Thurmond and was considered more charismatic than his Democratic challenger, Lieutenant Governor John West.[44]

Deep-seated political divisions and uncertain party loyalties made the outcome of the election difficult to predict. South Carolina had supported Nixon in the presidential election of 1968 but had also given a significant number of votes to the independent, segregationist candidate George Wallace. As the gubernatorial election commenced, Watson was convinced that a combination of Nixon and Wallace voters would end the Democratic control of the governor's office that had been unbroken since Reconstruction. Much to Hamby's chagrin, however, throughout the campaign Watson not only denounced federal desegregation policy but engaged in a blatant race-baiting against his Democratic opponent. Like Workman and Spence in 1962, the candidate ignored Hamby's cardinal rule and did not temper his language with nuanced criticisms of racial change. Rather he denounced "forced integration" and spoke about race almost exclusively during the final months of the election, frequently wearing a white tie to symbolize his support for white supremacy and utilizing Wallace-like rhetoric that reminded voters of his hardcore segregationist views. As Hamby had feared, this strategy allowed West to label Watson a single-issue candidate with little to offer "law-abiding" South Carolinians.[45]

West, like Hamby, understood that a combination of African American voters and white moderates could offset Watson's strong support among whites in the state's Black Belt. West and his supporters hoped that white voters would recognize that the state's Democratic leadership had made the inevitable more palatable and refused to allow Watson's race-baiting to alter the state's commitment to conservative, measured change. Moreover, West urged voters to ignore outrageous Republican promises, such as a pledge to save the very limited form of school desegregation known as "freedom of choice," that Watson was incapable of keeping.[46]

The political differences between Watson and West were encapsulated in their attitudes toward busing and the effect of Watson's campaign against it. Shortly after declaring his candidacy Watson spoke at an antibusing rally in Lamar. On February 22, 1970, he and twenty-five hundred white protesters called on Darlington County to resist any further federal pressure to integrate its public school system through the use of busing. Watson appealed to the county's white population to resist forced busing to the bitter end and to use every means at its disposal to forestall federal pressure for meaningful change. His actions, which were contrary to Hamby's advice, contributed to a later protest turning violent when a mob of angry whites overturned two school buses that had carried black children to a newly desegregated school. The incident brought national attention to the debate over busing in South Carolina. Yet, despite widespread criticism for stirring up white emotions and contrary to the advice he received from Hamby, Watson's campaign did not desist from courting further controversy.

Several months later the principal of A. C. Flora High School near Columbia, the mayor of nearby Forest Acres, the Columbia Police Department, and Governor McNair accused Watson campaign aides of instigating a racial fight at the high school so that Watson could exploit the issue for political purposes. The two violent eruptions were enough to convince some white moderates that Watson's inflammatory style would lead to widespread racial unrest, bring unwanted attention to South Carolina, and generate unwelcome, negative publicity. In the wake of the Orangeburg Massacre two years earlier—an incident in which three peaceful protesters were killed and twenty-eight were injured at a protest over a segregated bowling ally—many white South Carolinians were unwilling to risk further violence and worried that Watson simply did not have the temperament required for a post–Jim Crow governor.[47]

Watson won an overwhelming majority of the white vote, but West was able to win with 52 percent of the total vote. Less than half of West's votes came from white voters. The election demonstrated for the first time that the Voting Rights Act of 1965 had brought undeniable change to South Carolina's statewide elections. As Hamby had predicted four years earlier, alienating even the smallest voting bloc could sway an election. Some Republicans, such as Arthur Ravenel of Charleston, agreed with Hamby and argued even before the election that the state's GOP could not overcome its Democratic opponents consistently unless it abandoned its blatant racism. Moreover, Ravenel, Hamby, and others called on the Republican Party to reach out to black voters. Like Hamby, Ravenel concluded that the GOP could not win while campaigning to only 65 percent of the registered voters. Even if African Americans refused to vote Republican, Hamby and Ravenel agreed that that a more diverse campaign strategy would help sell the GOP as a moderate political party and offset the kind of charges that had doomed Watson in the gubernatorial race.[48]

At this point, Hamby helped Thurmond see the importance of altering his own strategy in regard to race. Although Thurmond was arguably the most popular political leader in the state, Hamby cautioned that, without a serious alteration in election strategy, he or his Republican allies could face a similar fate to Watson's. She claimed that the ability of the West campaign to label Watson as a "racist" "REALLY hurt!" She encouraged him to adopt a more moderate political position and abandon last-ditch efforts to preserve or restore segregation. It is well known that Thurmond made a dramatic shift in policy and tone at this point in his career; he apparently took Hamby's advice seriously. Thurmond, unlike Watson, recognized that a new political reality had settled over South Carolina. Whether he was motivated by his own political ambitions or the belief that it would help his state, Thurmond followed Hamby's advice and quickly adapted. Almost immediately he hired African American staffers and began openly campaigning to black voters. Likewise, the South Carolina Republican Party softened its rhetoric regarding racial politics. Arguably, this made possible the election of James B. Edwards, the state's first modern GOP governor, in 1974.[49]

For most of her life Dolly Hamby's activities and interests focused on Bradley, Graham, and Hamby. She was deeply committed to its success. It meant something to her as a woman: she took pride in being successful in a field in which most of her competitors were male. She knew that she and her colleagues had little room for error: indeed they had to perform at a much higher level than the men. In a 1972 interview she claimed to work fifteen to sixteen hours per day. "We couldn't just be as good as or better than our male competitors," she claimed, "but so much better that they couldn't just ignore us." Don Fowler, a longtime leader of the Democratic Party in South Carolina and the nation, recalls that many of those competitors envied her success as a political consultant, in some cases resenting that they were bested by a woman. Hamby was a warm and dignified person, Fowler recalled, and had "a real presence" about her— that when you were around her you clearly sensed that you were with someone of great capability and importance. She was recognized for her pioneering work in her field and was the first South Carolinian to be listed in *Foremost Women in Communications in America*.[50]

Hamby did have a life beyond the firm, however. For much of her life she lived in a home she shared with Graham. Hamby enjoyed gardening and playing the piano. She was also an athlete, known as an outstanding tennis player who competed in local and regional tournaments. She was active in her community, a member of the public relations committee for the Richland County Chapter of the Mental Health Association, a member of the Richland County Cancer Society, and of the Greater Columbia Chamber of Commerce. She died in 2001.[51]

The story of Dolly Hamby and her role in the transformation of South Carolina politics is largely unknown. At a time when women were a rarity as candidates in either party, she had a lasting impact on the politics and history of the state as she shepherded clients through the dynamic intersections of race and politics in South Carolina. As an advisor to some of the most influential South Carolina politicians of her era, however, she influenced the development of modern party politics, including the politics of race. Her warning to Thurmond that the politics of massive resistance had run their course in South Carolina may have been the most prophetic and influential political advice the long-serving senator ever received.

Hamby occasionally gave speeches but generally preferred that her candidates, and not their political consultant, be in the limelight. Despite her lifelong fascination with politics, she liked working behind the scenes and never publicized her own political beliefs. Don Fowler recalls that keeping her political preferences to herself was essential for a consultant who hoped to work for candidates from both parties but that she was clearly conservative at heart. Indeed, he guessed that in her later years she most likely voted for the Republicans.[52]

Born before women were even allowed to vote, Hamby lived to see profound changes, changes she helped bring about. Her success as a political consultant paved the way for women in business and politics in South Carolina and the strategies that she helped devise became the foundation of a competitive two-party system in the state.

NOTES

1. Lottie "Dolly" Hamby, interview by John Duffy, October 5, 1999, transcript, Oral History Project, South Carolina Political Collections, University of South Carolina Libraries, University of South Carolina, Columbia (hereinafter cited as SCPC).

2. Ibid.

3. Ibid.; Lottie "Dolly" Hamby, 1949 resume, Lottie D. Hamby Papers, 1946–2001, SCPC (hereinafter cited as LDHP-SCPC); "Their Ads are 'So Logical,'" Charlotte (N.C.) Observer, May 26, 1965.

4. "Their Ads are 'So Logical,'" Charlotte (N.C.) Observer, May 26, 1965.

5. Gregory Sampson, "The Rise of the 'New' Republican Party in South Carolina, 1948–1974: A Case Study of Political Change in a Deep South State" (PhD diss., University of North Carolina, 1984), 217–36; Charleston News and Courier, January 30, 1952, 2.

6. For evidence of the grassroots campaign in South Carolina, see Burnet R. Maybank to Wright Morrow, Democratic National Committee, Texas, January 11, 1952, Burnet R. Maybank Senatorial Papers, 1941–54, special collections, College of Charleston Library, Charleston, S.C. (hereinafter cited as BRMSP-COFC), H. Sanford Howie Jr. to James F. Byrnes, July 11, 1952, BRMSP-COFC; Paul Quattlebaum to James Lee Platt, Myrtle Beach News, March 15, 1952, Paul Quattlebaum Papers, Strom Thurmond Institute, special collections, Clemson University, Clemson, S.C.; Alice T. Beckett, secretary of the Colleton County Citizens Grass Roots Crusade, to L. Mendel Rivers, April 21, 1952, and L. Mendel Rivers to Alice T. Beckett, April 23, 1952, L. Mendel Rivers Papers, South Carolina Historical Society, Charleston (hereinafter cited as LMRP-SCHS).

7. Sampson, "The Rise of the 'New' Republican Party in South Carolina," 217–36. For factions in the South Carolina Democratic Party, see Kari Frederickson, The Dixiecrat Revolt and the End of the Solid South, 1932–1968 (Chapel Hill: University of North Carolina Press, 2001), Howard Quint, Profile in Black and White: A Frank Portrait of South Carolina (Washington D.C.: Public Affairs Press, 1958), and Frank E. Jordan, The Primary State: A History of the Democratic Party in South Carolina, 1876–1962 (Columbia: R. L. Bryan, 1968).

8. Burnet R. Maybank to Wright Morrow, Democratic National Committee, Texas, January 11, 1952, box 50, BRMSP-COFC; L. Mendel Rivers to E. E. Cox, October 22, 1952, LMRP-SCHS.

9. Hamby, interview by John Duffy, October 5, 1999, SCPC.

10. "Recommendations to Publicity Committee, South Carolinians for Eisenhower," Dwight Eisenhower file, South Carolinians for Eisenhower, 1952, LDHP-SCPC.

11. Ibid.

12. Ibid.; untitled radio transcript, Dwight Eisenhower file, South Carolinians for Eisenhower, 1952, LDHP-SCPC.

13. "Recommendations to Publicity Committee, South Carolinians for Eisenhower," Dwight Eisenhower file, South Carolinians for Eisenhower, 1952, LDHP-SCPC; untitled radio transcript, Dwight Eisenhower file, South Carolinians for Eisenhower, 1952, LDHP-SCPC.

14. *Greenville News*, October 26, 1952, 1; *Charleston News and Courier*, October 26, 1952, A-1; *Charleston News and Courier*, October 26, 1952, A-4; L. Mendel Rivers to Robert L. Scott, November 4, 1952, LMRP-SCHS; *Hampton Guardian*, n.d., LMRC-SPCOFC; *Jasper Record*, October 29, 1952.

15. Raymond Moley, "A Political Perspective," *Newsweek*, December 15, 1952, 108; "Byrnes, Ike, and the South," *Newsweek*, December 15, 1952, 31. These totals include the ballots cast in both the Republican and independent columns. In the election the ballot totals were not combined. Had Eisenhower collected more total votes than Stevenson but collected less ballots on the independent ticket, he still would have lost the state (*Charleston News and Courier*, November 11, 1952, A-1; Sampson, "The Rise of the 'New' Republican Party in South Carolina," 230–32).

16. Sampson, "The Rise of the 'New' Republican Party in South Carolina."

17. Ibid.

18. Ibid.

19. Jack Bass and Marilyn W. Thompson, *Strom: The Complicated Personal and Political Life of Strom Thurmond* (New York: Public Affairs Press, 2005) 155–82.

20. Hamby, interview by John Duffy, October 5, 1999, SCPC.

21. Ibid.

22. Ibid.; Strom Thurmond to Dolly Hamby, December 2, 1954, LDHP-SCPC.

23. Hamby, interview by John Duffy, October 5, 1999, SCPC.

24. Quint, *Profile in Black and White*, 128–129; Numan V. Bartley, *The Rise of Massive Resistance: Race and Politics in the South During the 1950's* (Baton Rouge: Louisiana State University Press, 1969), 70–71; Doyle W. Boggs, "A Different Brand of Education: Strom Thurmond Goes to the Senate, 1954," *Proceedings of the South Carolina Historical Association* (1984): 77–85.

25. Ernest Hollings file, general, 1958, LDHP-SCPC; *Southern School News*, January 1958, 12; John Sproat, "'Firm Flexibility': Perspectives on Desegregation in South Carolina," in *New Perspectives on Race and Slavery in America: Essays in Honor of Kenneth M. Stampp*, ed. Robert H. Abzug and Stephen E. Maizlish (Lexington: University Press of Kentucky, 1986), 164–84.

26. Script, untitled film, South Carolina Democrats for Nixon and Lodge, 1960, Richard Milhous Nixon file, LDHP-SCPC; Taylor Branch, *Pillar of Fire: America in the King Years, 1963–65* (New York: Simon and Schuster, 1998), 242.

27. Script, untitled film, South Carolina Democrats for Nixon and Lodge campaign, 1960, Richard Milhous Nixon file, LDHP-SCPC.

28. Ibid.

29. Ibid.

30. Ibid.

31. Charles Boineau, television transcript, broadcast August 3, 1961, Charles Boineau file, 1961, LDHP-SCPC.

32. Charles Boineau to Dolly Hamby, August 14, 1961, Charles Boineau file, 1961, LDHP-SCPC.

33. Floyd Spence file, LDHP-SCPC; Robert Chapman file, 1962, LDHP-SCPC; Hamby, interview

by John Duffy, October 5, 1999, SCPC; *The State*, January 28, 1962; "Bob Chapman Believes," 1962 campaign pamphlet, Robert Chapman file, 1962, LDHP-SCPC.

34. Hamby, interview by John Duffy, October 5, 1999, SCPC; "Words for Spence Rally," scrapbooks, folder 2, LDHP-SCPC; Russell Merritt, "The Senatorial Election of 1962 and the Rise of Two-Party Politics in South Carolina," *South Carolina Historical Magazine* 98, no. 2 (1997): 281–301; Billy B. Hathorn, "The Changing Politics of Race: Congressman Albert William Watson and the S.C. Republican Party, 1965–1970," *South Carolina Historical Magazine* 89, no. 4 (1988): 227–41; Sampson, "The Rise of the 'New' Republican Party in South Carolina," 274–343; Donald L. Fowler, *Presidential Voting in South Carolina, 1948–1964* (Columbia: Bureau of Governmental Research and Service, University of South Carolina, 1966), 99–127; Bruce H. Kalk, *The Origins of the Southern Strategy: Two-Party Competition in South Carolina, 1950–1972* (Lanham, Md., Lexington Books, 2001), 25–54.

35. Barry Goldwater file, general, 1964, LDHP-SCPC.

36. Merritt, "The Senatorial Election of 1962 and the Rise of Two-Party Politics in South Carolina"; Hathorn, "The Changing Politics of Race"; Sampson, "The Rise of the 'New' Republican Party in South Carolina," 274–343; Fowler, *Presidential Voting in South Carolina, 1948–1964*, 99–127; Kalk, *The Origins of the Southern Strategy*, 25–54.

37. Strom Thurmond to Dolly Hamby, November 25, 1964, Strom Thurmond file, correspondence, 1954–86, LDHP-SCPC; Kalk, *The Origins of the Southern Strategy*, 62–65; Sampson, "The Rise of the 'New' Republican Party in South Carolina," 310–16. For more on Goldwater, see Rick Perlstein, *Before the Storm: Barry Goldwater and the Unmaking of the American Consensus* (New York: Hill and Wang, 2001), Jeremy D. Mayer, "LBJ Fights the White Backlash: The Racial Politics of the 1964 Presidential Campaign," *Prologue: Quarterly of the National Archives and Records Administration*, vol. 33, no. 1 (2001): 7–19, and Bernard Cosman, *Five States for Goldwater: Continuity and Change in Southern Presidential Voting Patterns* (University: University of Alabama Press, 1966).

38. Untitled speech, Republican Women of Augusta, Ga., 1965, LDHP-SCPC.

39. Kalk, *Origins of the Southern Strategy*, 55–78; Ernest F. Hollings file, general, 1968, Cyril B. Busbee file, 1966, and Robert McNair file, general, 1966, LDHP-SCPC. For a sampling of candidates' views on federal desegregation standards, see *Southern Education Report*, November 1967, 15–17.

40. Jack Bass and Walter De Vries, *The Transformation of Southern Politics: Social Change and Political Consequences since 1945* (Athens: University of Georgia Press, 1995), 254–55; Randy Sanders, *Mighty Peculiar Elections: The New South Gubernatorial Campaigns of 1970 and the Changing Politics of Race* (Gainesville: University Press of Florida, 2002), 113–45.

41. Kalk, *Origins of the Southern Strategy*, 55–78; Ernest F. Hollings file, general, 1968; Cyril B. Busbee file, 1966, and Robert McNair file, general, 1966, LDHP-SCPC.

42. Ernest F. Hollings file, general, 1968; Anthony Badger, "From Defiance to Moderation: South Carolina Governors and Racial Change," in *The Citadel Conference on the Civil Rights Movement in South Carolina* (Charleston: The Citadel and Columbia Cooper Educational Films, 2003).

43. Ernest F. Hollings file, general, 1968, folder 3, LDHP-SCPC; Hamby, interview by John Duffy, October 5, 1999, SCPC.

44. Sanders, *Mighty Peculiar Elections*, 113–45; Hathorn, "The Changing Politics of Race," 227–41.

45. Hathorn, "The Changing Politics of Race," 227–41.

46. Ibid.

47. Ibid.

48. Ibid.

49. "Race Memo Prodded Thurmond," *The State*, October 3, 2004.

50. Donald L. Fowler, telephone interview by Marjorie J. Spruill, March 9, 2011.

51. Hamby, interview by John Duffy, October 5, 1999, SCPC; "Their Ads are 'So Logical'"; "Women Own Successful Advertising, PR Firm," *The State*, November 9, 1972, D-1.

52. Fowler, interview by Spruill.

Harriet Keyserling

Political Trailblazer

PAGE PUTNAM MILLER

❀ ❀ ❀

Harriet Hirschfeld Keyserling (1922–2010) entered politics in 1974 at the age of fifty-two when rural South Carolina was beginning to offer more opportunities to women. Keyserling's life experiences reflect this trend and reveal the transformation of a timid homemaker into a major player in the South Carolina legislature, where she worked tenaciously for the enhancement of education, protection of the environment, promotion of the arts, and improvement of women's status. One of her special gifts was an astute ability to understand how institutions worked and then to fashion methods of operating within the system to achieve her goals. Her innate facility with written language combined with her skill in analyzing issues served her well as a legislator as she pursued policies that reflected her visions of more efficient government and a more just society.

While Keyserling claimed the small town of Beaufort, South Carolina, as her home for almost sixty years, her roots in New York City provided her with a special vantage point for understanding the South and the role of southern women. Born in 1922 into a middle-class Jewish family, Harriet Hirschfeld Keyserling was surrounded in her youth by musicians, artists, and lively political conversations. Her parents were immigrants from Latvia and Lithuania who came as youngsters to America and worked diligently to take advantage of the rich array of opportunities available in their new country. Her father, Isador Hirschfeld, overcame great obstacles to become a prominent dentist and a president of the American Academy of Periodontia. Pauline Steinberg, Harriet's mother, delivered milk from her sister's dairy farm in New Jersey to pay for her tuition at Barnard College, from which she graduated in 1908. Although Pauline's goal was to teach biology or mathematics, the only teaching job she could find was teaching shorthand. But when she was young, her spunk and determination led to a number of adventures; one of the most exceptional was selling canoes in Venice. And it was through canoeing that she met Isador. They married when she was thirty-two years old and soon had two children, Lennie and Harriet.[1]

Keyserling recalls growing up in a household both comfortable and stimulating. The family's apartment, a penthouse with a garden, was located near Central Park and afforded ample opportunities for the outdoor activities that the family enjoyed. Keyserling can rarely remember a time when someone was not staying with them—a relative, a struggling artist or musician, or refugees from Hitler's Europe, primarily dentists. Home life tended to be more interesting for her than the public school for seven thousand girls that she attended. Keyserling claims to have been a mediocre student who spent her time pining for attention from boys.[2]

While politics were often discussed around the dining room table, Keyserling's parents were not political activists. Yet their Jewish faith instilled in them a strong sense of social justice. Keyserling attended the Free Synagogue but felt more attuned to the discussion of ethics than to Bible stories. Her liberal parents did not encourage dogma or blind loyalty to any group.[3]

Although only 5 percent of women in the United States at this time graduated from college, there was never a question whether or not Keyserling would follow in her mother's footsteps and attend college. She received a bachelor of arts with honors in economics in 1943 from Barnard College, Columbia University's college for women. During two summers, she participated in work camps cosponsored by Harvard's American Friends Service Committee and International Student Service and gained new insights that complemented her academic study of industrial relations.

While a college student she renewed a friendship with Herbert Keyserling, a family friend who was at the time pursuing his medical studies and was a resident at a New York hospital. Harriet's family had visited Herbert's family home in Beaufort, South Carolina, a decade earlier, and the Keyserlings often visited New York. In 1942 Herbert and Harriet became reacquainted as adults. World War II, however, interrupted their courtship when Herbert became a battalion surgeon stationed in the South Pacific. They married in 1944.

Prior to their marriage, Keyserling worked in management for the Eagle Pencil Company and at the time of her engagement had just been offered a promotion. In reminiscing about her early adulthood, she noted that middle- and upper-class women of her generation were expected to follow the established pattern of marrying, raising children, and going where one's husband went. Regarding the couple's place of residence, Keyserling said, "It didn't even occur

HARRIET KEYSERLING

Photograph by Paul Keyserling.

Courtesy of Harriet Keyserling.

to me to say 'I have a good job, and I want to go somewhere where I can get another one.'" While her mother anticipated the culture shock she would experience in moving to Beaufort and suggested that Herbert might want to study dentistry and enter into practice with his father-in-law in New York, that was never an option for Herbert. Like her mother-in-law before her, Harriet moved as a bride to a social environment that was dramatically different from that in which she had grown up. [4]

South Carolina, where Herbert's family had established roots, became Harriet's home. Herbert Keyserling's father, William, had moved to Beaufort from Lithuania in 1888. After learning English and gaining business skills as an apprentice, he eventually became the president of a large farming and mercantile business. When William decided at the age of thirty-eight to marry, he chose a New Yorker who was a friend of Harriet's mother.

Unlike the Beaufort of today, Beaufort in 1944 had a population of only thirty-five hundred with few cultural organizations or institutions. Being used to the diversity and stimulation of a large city, Keyserling found the town "one dimensional," defined by a basically provincial, conservative, and Protestant culture. Since Herbert was just beginning to establish his medical practice, the twenty-two-year-old Harriet decided the best course of action was to remain as invisible as possible. Topics such as politics, race relations, and states' rights, about which she often thought, were just too controversial to discuss even with the circle of women with whom she initially became acquainted. [5]

Keyserling's feelings of being an "outsider" were soon subsumed into a hectic schedule, however. Herbert had a solo medical practice that demanded long hours away from home, and thus responsibility for raising four children—two of them twins—and managing the house fell to her. She also handled the bookkeeping for the medical practice. Keyserling still managed to carve out time for playing the piano and tennis and participating in the public arena as a volunteer leader in countless organizations.

Late in life Keyserling observed that the lifestyle that she enjoyed in which she had time "to play and volunteer" rested on a very special person, Maybelle Mack, her full-time helper who cleaned, cooked, and helped care for the children. Keyserling drew on her New York connections in hiring Mack. As a young woman Mack, along with many other southern blacks, left the South Carolina Sea Islands and moved to New York. Mack worked for a three-generation Jewish family who lived close to where Keyserling grew up. When Keyserling learned that Mack was moving to Beaufort to care for her ailing mother, Keyserling said, "I was lucky enough to get to her before anyone else." Mack, who had learned wonderful, old Russian-Jewish recipes while in New York, treated the Keyserling family to the most marvelous meals.[6]

Keyserling, who was always on the lookout for people with whom she could discuss the arts, politics, and the issues of the day, brought interesting assortments of people of different backgrounds to her home for dinner parties made possible by Mack's cooking and willingness to work late. These informal gatherings were at first a setting in which Keyserling could discuss controversial issues that she had learned to avoid in Beaufort. Later, when Keyserling became a volunteer in numerous cultural and civic organizations, the dinner parties enabled her network to meet and hatch new strategies. As Keyserling reflected on these years, she noted how different her world was from that of her daughters, who do not have the luxury of full-time help and who struggle to manage jobs and children and consequently have little time for volunteer work. Keyserling noted that many organizations, such as the League of Women Voters (LWV) and Planned Parenthood, that, in the past, depended on young women to be their foot soldiers, now have to draw from a shrinking pool of volunteers.[7]

Raising four children and assisting her husband with his medical practice consumed Keyserling's initial years in Beaufort. Once she had some discretionary time, she worked to bring more cultural opportunities to the small town. Later she became involved in public policy issues. Thus for many years prior to her decision in 1974 to seek her first elected office as a member of the county council, civic engagement was a central factor in Keyserling's life.

Beaufort in the 1940s seemed culturally barren to Keyserling, having grown up in a city and family that were immersed in the world of the arts. But Keyserling soon changed that and became a guiding force in bringing concerts, a dance troupe, art exhibits, and foreign films to Beaufort. The formation of the Beaufort Concert Association, which brought first-class musicians to Beaufort, was one of her first efforts. This achievement was soon to be followed by Keyserling's championing the Byrne Miller Dance Theater, the Beaufort Art Collection that focused on acquiring and exhibiting South Carolina artists, and the Beaufort Foreign Film Series. In all of these initiatives she served both on the front line as the president of the organization and in the rear guard as one of the workers selling tickets and making arrangements for special events.[8]

Keyserling eventually became involved in politics as well. The two most prominent examples of Keyserling's civic engagement in the political sphere were a voter registration project and the subsequent founding of the Beaufort chapter of the League of Women Voters. As the 1972 presidential election approached, it became clear that people were having a difficult time registering to vote. Because the registrar's office had limited hours, Beaufort County residents often had to take time off from work to register. Keyserling was part of a group that successfully lobbied to make registration more accessible. This work led to the formation of the county chapter of the LWV, which has as one of its primary goals improvement of the elective process. Keyserling was one of those who contacted the league in Columbia to seek assistance in getting a Beaufort chapter started, but when the group asked Keyserling to be the first president, she declined because a trip to Afghanistan would keep her away during the initial organizing period.[9]

As an active member of Beaufort's fledgling chapter of the LWV, Keyserling chose to "observe" county council meetings as her assignment. She was amazed to discover just how much the decisions made by county government impacted her life. She discovered that the council dealt not only with taxes but funding and setting policies for local schools, roads, and law enforcement.

Keyserling recalled a prolonged discussion at one council meeting, after which the council voted to fund a big Christmas party for all county employees including road workers and office managers. It was at that moment that it occurred to Keyserling that a woman's perspective was missing on the council. If a woman had been a part of the discussion, Keyserling thought, she would have suggested that a large turkey for each family would be more appreciated by most of the employees than a party. But more importantly, Keyserling was dismayed that the county council was not focusing more on economic development so as to create good jobs and was not adequately funding the newly integrated public schools. Furthermore, she foresaw that since Beaufort was experiencing a spurt of growth, zoning and land-use planning needed to be strengthened to ensure a better balance of economic, social, and environmental factors in development.[10]

On a summer evening in 1974, while having dinner with friends, Keyserling raised the question of whether it would make a difference to have a woman's voice on county council. George McMillan, a resident of St. Helena Island and a widely published freelance journalist, responded by challenging her to run for a seat. Keyserling remembers how McMillan flattered her with compliments about her skills and insights. Before she knew it, word had circulated around the small town that Keyserling would be a candidate. It all happened so fast that Keyserling did not have time to retreat; however, she had considerable concerns about her shyness, her reluctance to speak in public, and her lack of knowledge about county government. Yet as George McMillan observed, Keyserling's children were grown, her husband worked long hours as doctor, and she had gone about as far as she could go with volunteer organizations. She was at a crossroads in her life. With an empty nest, Keyserling at the age of fifty-two was ready for a challenge that offered possibilities for influencing public policy in the county that would tap her unrealized capabilities.[11]

As one of seven candidates running for three at-large seats on the Beaufort County Council, Keyserling stood out as the only woman. Yet, in analyzing her situation, Keyserling concluded that "Watergate had soured people on politicians, and I think in that climate a woman who was a community worker and not a politician had an advantage."[12] Keyserling reaped considerable support from all the women with whom she had worked for thirty years in volunteer organizations. They knew her as a person who shared their hopes for the community and who was a smart, shrewd, dependable worker who would deliver on her commitments.

Keyserling's entry into politics coincided with the national spotlight focusing on women's issues. In 1964 Congress had passed legislation barring discrimination in hiring on the basis on sex. This was followed two years later with the founding of the National Organization for Women (NOW). Then, in 1970, to mark the fiftieth anniversary of the ratification of woman suffrage, there were countless events celebrating women's rights and contributions. By 1974, when Keyserling sought support for her bid for a seat on the county council, women were the foot soldiers in her campaign. Women who wanted a woman's perspective on the council introduced Keyserling to neighbors, handed out flyers, and worked the telephones.

It was not just the women's movement that worked in Keyserling's favor but also the civil rights movement. As her friend George McMillan examined her chances for winning, he noted that she had fortunately chosen a time when there was in Beaufort County a "well-organized group of restless blacks, looking for change, organized and ready to support change at the ballot." What particularly helped Keyserling with the rural black community was the fact that Herbert, her husband, had delivered most of the babies born on outlying St. Helena Island. These families and many of the now-grown babies turned out at the polls in strong support for Keyserling.[13]

Another group that supported Keyserling consisted of citizens who had recently relocated from the North. The 1960s migration of retirees from colder climates to the South produced economic growth in the Sun Belt and brought new blood to her area. By the mid-1970s, Beaufort County's Hilton Head Island had become a premier retirement community. Many of the Hilton Head voters found Keyserling, with her northern accent and Ivy League diploma, an appealing candidate. As the author of a regular column in the *Hilton Head Magazine* on cultural events in Beaufort and owing to her participation in meetings of the

Hilton Head branch of Planned Parenthood, Keyserling enjoyed significant name recognition in the southern part of the county.

The combination of Keyserling's network of women volunteers and supporters among blacks and retirees gave her not only a seat on the county council but the distinction of receiving more votes than any of her opponents. She was also the first woman ever elected to the county council in Beaufort County. And this was accomplished without the backing of the usual political establishment that seemed to be caught totally off guard by the genuine excitement for her candidacy. McMillan, a keen observer of the South, wrote that Keyserling's victory marked a landmark in southern politics, for she created an "entirely new, and by South Carolina standards, a revolutionary constituency."[14]

Keyserling's presence on the county council did change the organization's mode of operation. After getting over the awkward issue of how to address her—"Lady" or "Mrs. Keyserling"—the council members soon got down to routine business. But, as Keyserling observed, the men were "conscious, even self-conscious, about the presence of a woman." Keyserling also realized that when she took the floor she "often sounded strident or combative," but that did not reflect her feelings. Keyserling credits an article from a public management magazine given to her by Jim Zumwalt, the county manager, with helping her to understand her situation. This article emphasized that when women move into traditionally male roles, there is a time of discomfort, but that with time and practice, a readjustment of roles takes place. And this indeed was the case.[15]

Keyserling brought to her council work a commitment to consultation. Soon after becoming a council member, Keyserling formed a "kitchen cabinet" to meet regularly around her dining room table to help her understand the issues. Not being an extrovert, Keyserling was very comfortable with the role of listener and she actively sought the advice of others. She was most troubled by the suspicion and different agendas that existed between upscale Hilton Head in the southern part of the county and the poorer areas north of the Broad River that included St. Helena Island and the rural areas north of Beaufort. She brought together in her "kitchen cabinet" individuals from both sides of the Broad River to try to seek greater understanding of the complexity of issues.

Keyserling did not avoid controversy, even at the beginning of her political career. One of her early assignments on the council was to make a recommendation for a public art project that would be funded by a grant from the South Carolina Arts Commission. This led Keyserling to spearhead an initiative to commission a sculpture of a bust of Robert Smalls, a former slave who returned to Beaufort and became a political leader after the Civil War. The bust, which stands in front of the Beaufort Tabernacle Baptist Church where Smalls worshiped, has a special significance in that it marked the first time a governmental body in South Carolina had honored a former slave. And as Keyserling pointed out, Smalls was not just any slave; he was a slave who captured a Confederate ship and turned it over to the Union navy.[16]

Funding of libraries was another county council issue to which Keyserling brought her skills of leadership and consultation. She began by evaluating a request from the University of South Carolina for $300,000 to enlarge the library on its Beaufort campus. However, she learned that the Technical College of the Lowcountry in Beaufort was planning to build a new library, and the Beaufort County Public Library had projected a need for $500,000. Keyserling's housewifely instincts of trying to get the most out of the family budget kicked in, and she began to wonder if the county could afford the luxury of "triplication," especially when there were so many other pressing needs.[17]

After some preliminary meetings with the heads of the three libraries, Keyserling created a blue-ribbon committee chaired by the dean of the library school at the University of North Carolina to supervise a study on how the libraries could work together. The individual institutions, however, resisted the cost-saving recommendations. Keyserling had her first experience with a bureaucratic turf battle in which independence and control issues trumped money-saving strategies. But all was not lost. The three libraries created a consortium to share information and agreed that one library card could be used at any of the three. Keyserling had successfully negotiated a compromise and in the process had gained experience in how to navigate political waters. She also had to reverse her preconception that, in political deliberations, men would be "more open, more frank, more to the point, more efficient than women." Instead she discovered that she had to interpret for others what some men really meant when they spoke and to convince others that she really meant what she said.[18]

Keyserling was able to put her cost-saving strategies to work when the county council decided that it needed a logo for stationery and signage and planned to pay a $5,000 commission to an artist to design it. Recalling her experiences with volunteer groups, Keyserling suggested a contest with a prize of $100. A commercial artist, who had recently moved to Hilton Head, submitted a design at the urging of his daughter that for the last thirty years has been the county's distinctive logo, featuring a large house, spreading oak tree, shrimp boat, and fish.

One of Keyserling's chief disappointments on the county council came when she was unable to persuade her fellow commissioners to develop a countywide land-use policy. In the heart of the South Carolina Lowcountry, Beaufort County was growing swiftly as new residents, particularly retirees, were discovering the beauty of the area's live oaks, marshes, tidal creeks, and islands. Keyserling proposed that the county council hire a specialist in rapid growth in coastal areas to prepare a report to aid them in strengthening zoning and managing growth. The expert Keyserling had in mind was well known and respected by many on the council. She assumed her motion would be easily passed. However, the council defeated it. In recounting lessons learned, Keyserling put near the top of her list the need to confer beforehand with all your supporters and be sure you have a majority before calling for the vote.[19]

Keyserling was completing her two-year term on the county council in 1976 when a new and unexpected opportunity presented itself. Jim Moss, who had represented the area around Beaufort in the state legislature for three terms, decided not to run for reelection. He approached Keyserling, urged her to run, and even offered to be her campaign manager. It was flattering that Moss saw her as the best person to succeed him. Yet what enticed Keyserling the most about the possibility of being in the state legislature was the realization—gained from her county council experiences—that many changes had to occur at the state level before the county could implement new policies. Furthermore, she knew that women were grossly underrepresented in South Carolina state government.

Working in the state legislature in Columbia would require spending time away from home, and Keyserling felt that she needed to confer with her family about whether or not to run. Her husband and their four children were all in favor. Herbert said, "It's your turn to do your thing," reminding her that he "was out every night for years delivering babies." He provided assistance at every level, even helping to fold and stamp mailings. Her oldest son, Billy, at this point working as a legislative aide on Capitol Hill in Washington, felt it was a great idea and helped develop a strategy for organizing her campaign. Her daughter Judy, at the time the marketing director of the Washington Ballet, and her other daughter, Beth, a psychotherapist, both offered words of encouragement in frequent telephone calls. Her son, Paul, a cinematographer, supplied wonderful pictures.[20]

With strong support from her family and from the winning coalition she had put together, Keyserling proceeded to run for the state legislature. Yet the campaign was not easy. Because she was shy, making door-to-door calls and speaking in public did not come naturally. Since she hated to ask people for money, it was a blessing when an able person came forward to accept the role of treasurer of the campaign. Her ads in the Beaufort *Gazette* laid out her platform: promotion of better education, more jobs, more efficient government, and protection of the environment. She used a number of slogans: "Thirty years of public service"; "A full-time worker for Beaufort"; "If she wins . . . we all win."[21]

Keyserling's opponent in the Democratic primary was George O'Kelley, who had the support of the Democratic Party establishment. It was disappointing to her to find old friends actively supporting O'Kelley. The primary race was extremely close with Keyserling winning by about two hundred votes. O'Kelley decided to contest Keyserling's victory legally on the grounds that both her name and his had been omitted from the ballots in a small precinct with fewer than two hundred people. The review of the election results by the county executive committee and the state Democratic Party upheld Keyserling's victory. Yet to have the victory contested in this way was also a troubling experience. Jim Moss observed some years later that Keyserling found the voting controversy so disturbing because she had not yet acquired toughness, what he called a "political shell." Through this event her "political shell" began to form, however. Following the primary Keyserling went on to win the general election with 60 percent of the votes against the Republican candidate.[22]

An analysis of the voting, particularly in the Democratic primary, brought home to Keyserling that southern good manners, including a reluctance to state a personal political position, had affected her polling and made her think she had more support than she did. She won only one white-majority precinct. Keyserling understood this as a message that she needed to work harder at finding ways to communicate to her constituents who she really was so they would not be taken in by her opponent's labeling of her as a northern liberal who supported abortion and gun control. While she did hold a pro-choice position and worked for the control of guns, these two issues represented a small part of her legislative work.

Seeking to communicate more effectively with her constituents, Keyserling wisely played to her strength, which was writing. After making arrangements with the editors of various local newspapers she began to publish persuasive, insightful columns. Once in the legislature, she found that on matters that made her angry it was much better to write than to speak. While other Beaufort area members of the legislature also had the opportunity to write columns, only Keyserling consistently pursued this strategy as a means of keeping in touch with her district. The columns had an added advantage in that their preparation required Keyserling to undertake a thorough examination of the issues, which invariably paid off later. Her goal was to present all sides of an issue and then explain her own position, letting people know that she approached decision making from an informed perspective.

The state house of representatives that Keyserling joined in 1977 was a formidable place for a female legislator. There were 124 members. The large majority of them were white male Democrats. There were also about a dozen Republicans, twelve blacks, and only ten women. The Democrats were still in power. But in 1974, South Carolina elected its first Republican governor since the Reconstruction era. During the 1970s, South Carolina continued to take gradual steps toward desegregation while standing firm against the Equal Rights Amendment (ERA) designed to ensure women all the legal rights of men. Yet opposition to the ERA did not prevent the election of some women to the state legislature.

When Keyserling arrived in Columbia in 1977, Nancy Stevenson, a Democrat from Charleston who had been elected two years earlier, took Keyserling under her wing and suggested that she join her in staying at the Wade Hampton Hotel across the street from the state house. Stevenson and Keyserling had much in common. Both had family ties in New York City and had attended college in the North; both represented a coastal constituency and shared a commitment to improving education. Stevenson and Keyserling often had dinner together after a hectic legislative day. Most of the men had their own informal political social groups composed only of men. Keyserling surmised that this was because in those days men felt uncomfortable inviting a woman and then letting her pay for her own meal. Stevenson's career skyrocketed in 1979 when she was elected lieutenant governor, becoming the first woman in South Carolina to hold a statewide office.[23]

Keyserling later acknowledged that she was initially very naïve about the legislative process. In orientation workshops for new legislators, she learned how to introduce a bill, but she admitted feeling more like a constituent than a member of the legislature. Finding allies was something Keyserling did well, however, and she quickly found a group with whom she could work. The political tensions in those days were not between the parties but between the Upstate and Lowcountry, the urban and rural, and the reform minded and the traditionalist.[24]

The legislators to whom Keyserling gravitated were, as she remembers, "bright, progressive, funny, and very energetic," and mostly freshmen. Since all the subgroups in the legislature adopted names, they called themselves the "Crazy Caucus." If there was one issue that bound the group together, Keyserling said, it was the defense of the public interest against special interests. Their major opponents were a group that called themselves the "Fat and Uglies," an ambitious group of young conservatives who lunched together each Thursday on a lobbyist's expense account.

There were several other stalwarts of the Crazy Caucus besides Keyserling who were women. Jean Toal of Columbia was at the time a young lawyer known for her grasp of legislative procedures and ability to analyze pending bills. When Toal became chair of the House Rules Committee, she became the first woman in South Carolina to hold a leadership position in the House. Later, she had the even greater distinction of being named the chief justice of the Supreme Court of South Carolina. Another member of the group was Ginger Crocker of Laurens, whose special contribution to the caucus was her ability to round up the votes needed. Having been active in Democratic politics in the state since her college days, Crocker served as the caucus whip. Two other women who met regularly with the Crazy Caucus were not legislators but staffers, Inez Tenenbaum, a director of research for a house committee who later became the state superintendent of education and then the Democratic nominee for the U.S. Senate, and Elizabeth Crum, the director of the House Judiciary Committee. Keyserling described her own role in the Crazy Caucus as "doing research, developing position papers, printing up persuasive material and working the floor to explain our position." It was this careful attention to building a persuasive case that, during her sixteen years in the state legislature, won her the respect of her colleagues. Only two years after she entered the legislature she was invited to be a member of the prestigious Judiciary Committee, the first nonlawyer to serve on that body.[25]

One of the most troubling aspects of the political climate for Keyserling was the slapping of backs and paying off of favors among the "good ol' boys," conservative politicians who faithfully protected special interests. Keyserling's approach to legislation was issue oriented with an eye to sifting through all the evidence to try to determine the long-term consequences. She was disturbed by oversimplification and appeals to emotionalism and pressed for rigorous research. A feature article on Keyserling in the State Magazine in 1987 noted that "lobbyists are still unlikely to round her up at cocktail time." Keyserling surmised that they realized that she approached the legislative game from a different angle. But she considered her approach as an asset. She had a strong aversion to political "horse trading" and cronyism that required support of a friend at the expense of a principle. Keyserling believed that South Carolina legislators were particularly susceptible to the giving and taking of favors. Her theory was that, because South Carolina had a five-month legislative session, one of the longest of any state, and because the pay was so low, it was more difficult for South Carolina wage earners to give up the time necessary to serve in the legislature. Thus many members began to depend on free meals and entertainment from lobbyists to supplement their stipends. By 1990, when Keyserling had served for thirteen years in the house, the FBI's Operation Lost Trust investigated vote selling among members of the South Carolina state legislature and implicated a number of members of the Fat and Uglies Caucus; several were eventually sent to jail.[26]

One of the chief legislative tactics used by the Fat and Uglies was the filibuster.

It is not surprising that Keyserling considered one of the major achievements of her legislative career the adoption of a house rule to limit the filibuster. As long as opponents could protect special interests and block reform legislation with the filibuster, there was little hope that any issue on her progressive agenda could be passed. Time and again Keyserling observed that opponents who knew they did not have enough votes to defeat a measure would use the filibuster to prevent the bill from coming to a vote. While noting that the filibuster could be a valid instrument of democracy if not abused, Keyserling soon concluded that in the South Carolina House, it was "handcuffing" the majority. The campaign to change the house rules for debate in order to curtail filibusters grew out of a deep feeling of despair among the members of the Crazy Caucus. They had concluded that "the House was completely crippled by the filibusters, and we just couldn't get any decent legislation through." Some were so discouraged that they had considered not running for reelection.[27]

As usual, however, Keyserling approached the problem not by complaining but by documenting the problem, keeping a diary of how much time the house spent in filibusters. This research revealed that legislators spent about a third of their time sitting and doing nothing during filibusters designed to prevent bills from coming to a vote. She circulated her diary among house members and made a case for changing the house rules. The first year that Keyserling began work on the filibuster issue, one-third of the legislators supported her efforts. The next year there was a majority in favor of limiting the filibuster, still short of the required two-thirds. The following year, 1982, Keyserling took her arguments for a change of house rules to the press and numerous favorable editorials helped her cause. After five years, Keyserling's campaign to get a bill passed that reformed rules for house debate finally succeeded, the result of remarkable determination and persistence against formidable opponents. In 1983 the *Greenville News* named Keyserling legislator of the year for her work on nuclear waste and filibusters. Keyserling particularly valued this recognition for, as she wrote, "I was being cited by those—staff and press—who understood the issues better than anyone and who had no personal stake in making the selection."[28]

Making government more efficient and representing the issues of the consumer had been part of Keyserling's campaign platform. The first bill that she introduced, entitled "Writing of Contracts in Laymen's Language," reflected these themes. Keyserling often struggled with the wording in insurance policies and lease contracts and wished that there were a requirement that these documents be written clearly in common, everyday words. Once in a position where she might do something about this, she learned that a number of other states had such legislation. Legislative counsel assisted her in developing a similar bill.

Although she had thought this to be a noncontroversial issue, opposition from the financial and business communities surfaced. Keyserling had to make some compromises but the bill finally passed.

Promoting better education, protecting the environment, and supporting the arts were also core issues about which Keyserling cared deeply and on which she concentrated much of her energies during her sixteen years in the state legislature. During her first term she served on the Education Committee and the subcommittee that worked to equalize funding for education by distributing state funds to the neediest districts. South Carolina at this time had more high school dropouts and a higher rate of illiteracy than any other state. Two months into her first term, in her first speech on the house floor, Keyserling spoke on the education finance bill, saying, "I strongly believe that the people will agree to spend more on education IF they have the opportunity to be involved on the grassroots level, IF they can help set priorities on using their resources, IF they can be shown that the added money is producing better schools and IF they are regularly given information about what is happening in their schools." She focused on the part of the bill that resonated with her League of Women Voters experience of advocating accountability and offering citizens a meaningful way to participate in decision making.[29]

In 1979 the coalition to improve education gained a big boost when Richard Riley of Greenville was elected governor. Keyserling became one of his strong allies in working on a cluster of education bills: raising standards for teachers, expanding early childhood programs, and providing significant increases for education funding. By the early 1980s the whole country was involved in a debate over the nation's inadequate educational system. South Carolina, which ranked fiftieth in the nation in per pupil spending, was in the greatest need of reform. Riley's comprehensive educational package, designed as an investment in the future to improve the economic growth of the state by providing a prepared work force, faced strong opposition, primarily on the issue of funding. When Riley finished preparing the South Carolina Education Improvement Act and began searching for cosponsors, Keyserling was among the few house members to step forward. Riley later recalled: "Not one of the twenty-one early supporters were in a leadership position. We had to organize a new leadership." Keyserling was a part of the emerging leadership.[30]

Keyserling joined a hard-working team of house members who took the message of educational reform to the public, holding forums in districts across the state. Within the legislature they had to be ready to counter all the new tactical maneuvers thrown their way. With public opinion on their side, the five weeks of debate on the bill were crucial for gaining the needed votes. Keyserling's task was to assign sections of the massive bill to various colleagues who would be responsible for explaining and answering questions on the house floor as those sections came up for a vote. Each day the balcony of the House chamber filled with supporters, and the drama mounted as more compromises were negotiated and more business leaders became supporters of the bill. Keyserling remembered that passage of the bill in the house came at 2:00 a.m. following hectic days of deliberations. In the end, the senate passed the Educational Improvement Act with relatively little debate; the real battleground had been in the house, where Keyserling's role was so important. Noted South Carolina historian Walter Edgar credits these education bills as being the most important pieces of education legislation ever passed in South Carolina.[31] The new law also put South Carolina in the spotlight as being, for a short time at least, in the forefront of educational reform. Governor Riley did not forget his early supporters. He appointed Keyserling to education commissions and included her in special seminars and panels. She had become a seasoned and forceful legislator whose work, often behind the scenes, made the difference between a bill's victory and defeat.

When Keyserling began working on education policy, there were already a number of people committed to strengthening the state's educational opportunities. When she first approached the protection of the environment, however, she was operating alone. Her work on the environment focused on the disposal of much of the nation's nuclear waste in South Carolina. Keyserling was unaware of the size of the problem until 1979 when she received an anonymous letter accompanied by a *Charlotte Observer* article reporting that South Carolina was allowing more low-level nuclear waste to be buried in the state than regulations allowed. It required incredible perseverance on Keyserling's part to discover what was really happening.

There were several formidable challenges in working on the nuclear waste issue. South Carolina has a long history with military installations and with the making of weapons. Developed in the 1950s, the Savannah River Site (SRS), which comprised 310 square miles outside of Aiken, had been a major component in the manufacturing of nuclear bombs. Located in a poor part of the state, SRS is a large employer and has had strong, vocal representation in Columbia and Washington. By the 1980s, SRS had shifted its focus from making weapons to becoming a center for the handling of nuclear waste. Keyserling had to frame the issue carefully so that she did not appear to be opposed to the military or to nuclear weapons.

Keyserling's major strategy was to educate people about this practice that was taking place out of the spotlight. The basic danger, Keyserling explained, was the unknown quality and quantity of radioactive materials that could be emitted into the air, water, and food. There was considerable evidence that tiny specks of radioactive materials could cause cancer or birth defects. Keyserling queried Chem-Nuclear, the private disposal company that had the contract to bury low-level waste, and learned that the only official definition of "low level" was that it was not "high level." When Chem-Nuclear began its work in South Carolina, it dumped truckloads of clothes, tools, and parts of machines that had been used in nuclear plants and medical and research facilities into unlined holes. Eighty-five percent of the low-level waste in the country was coming to SRS. South Carolina was also taking in about 30 percent of the high-level defense waste, known to be dangerous for several hundred thousand years. In addition, a number of influential South Carolina leaders were lobbying the federal government to make the state a depository of high-level commercial waste in the form of spent fuel rods from the nation's nuclear power plants. Meanwhile, many other states were passing legislation prohibiting any nuclear waste from passing through or being buried in their states. Keyserling asked the question that many did not want to hear: "Why should we bear all the risks to health and safety while the other states enjoy the benefits of nuclear technology without sharing the risks?"[32]

Timing, Keyserling noted time and again, is everything in politics. And her campaign against South Carolina's nuclear waste policy was helped immeasurably by two nuclear-related disasters: Three Mile Island and Chernobyl. The economic benefits, particularly that the waste disposal projects provided jobs, remained a sticking point. Yet Keyserling insisted that this had to be weighed against all the risk factors. When legislative strategies failed, Keyserling became a lead plaintiff along with environmental groups in suing the governor and the legislature for using unconstitutional tactics in support of nuclear waste–dumping policies. However, the state supreme court ruled against them.

Keyserling was undeterred, however. She stepped back, regrouped and devised a new strategy. At the time, the Department of Energy in Washington was looking to South Carolina as the "temporary storage" site for the nation's commercial nuclear waste. From past experience, Keyserling knew that other states might, under extreme pressure, create a disposal site, but as long as South Carolina seemed willing to accept the nation's nuclear waste, they would be happy to avoid creating dumps in their own backyards. Thus Keyserling introduced a nonbinding resolution that she framed as a "states' rights issue," wording that, as she knew, strongly resonated in South Carolina. The resolution required that, before the federal government could make South Carolina a central storage center, the legislature and the governor would have to approve the measure.

She took her "states' rights" case to the people through articles in the press. A *Greenville News* editorial gave Keyserling a strong endorsement: "That the Keyserling Resolution passed with practically no fanfare is a tribute to the Beaufort lawmaker who has withstood untold pressure from the pronuclear lobby but who in the end prevailed because she listened to all sides and earned the respect of even her opponents."[33]

During her career, Keyserling introduced and shepherded through the legislative process half a dozen successful nuclear-related bills dealing with all aspects of the problem. One of them, the Southeastern Interstate Low-Level Waste Compact, sought to share with other states the responsibility for disposing of nuclear waste, while others sought to prohibit accepting nuclear waste from foreign countries and to push for adequate study and consultation on a variety of nuclear-related issues.

It was during the nuclear waste battles that Keyserling had what she called her first real "flutter of power." Former governor Robert McNair, whose law firm represented several nuclear-related industries, called and asked if she would come to his office for a cup of coffee. Usually Keyserling would oblige such a request, but it was raining and she was expecting one of her bills to come before a committee for discussion. When she declined, he came over in the rain to her office. She had entered the political arena to improve education and protect the environment. She worked best behind the scenes and had never sought the limelight. But she had gained what her legislative colleague in the "Crazy Caucus," Bob Sheheen, called "power derived from knowledge" rather than power gained from position.[34]

Keyserling also gained distinction in the legislature for her work on the arts. She recalled that when first elected, she had never thought that she would be able to promote the arts because South Carolina was such a poor state and there was always pressure to finance more pressing needs. However, as she observed, it was "serendipity that put her in the right place at the right time to become a chief advocate for the arts."[35]

Keyserling's journey to becoming a sponsor of arts legislation began with her appointment by Speaker of the House Rex Carter in 1978 to an arts task force of the National Conference of State Legislatures (NCSL). She was given the opportunity to participate in this newly formed group because her interest in the arts was well known and perhaps because she was already serving on the Energy Committee and no additional travel money would be required. Keyserling remembered the early task force meetings as being more "show and tell," as various members described innovative arts programs in their states. And she observed that this task force, later elevated to a full committee, had a disproportionately large number of women and Jewish members. Thus she felt especially at home among the group. During one of the task force meetings that happened to be in Charleston, the group had a chance to meet with Gian Carlo Menotti, then the artistic director of Charleston's Spoleto Festival, and to hear from city officials about the economic benefits of the festival. They learned how Spoleto had given a major boost to Charleston's cultural tourism and in turn had helped to create jobs and revitalize the city.[36]

After two years of serving on the NCSL Arts Committee and gathering background material, Keyserling suggested to Governor Riley that the state create a task force on the arts. Riley agreed, appointed Keyserling as chair, and charged her with selecting twenty-four members to serve with her. Keyserling shrewdly picked both key legislators whom she wanted to educate on the broader impact of the arts and representatives of major agencies with a potential to include arts in their programs. During its five years of existence, under Keyserling's leadership, the South Carolina Task Force on the Arts made remarkable progress. The committee strengthened the role of the South Carolina Arts Commission, fostered collaboration between public and private arts programs, expanded arts education in the schools, promoted the establishment of a film office to entice the film industry to come to South Carolina, and created financial support for the arts from the accommodation, or "bed," tax. While Keyserling had never been known for "bringing home the bacon" to her district in the form of money for special projects, the accommodation tax was a boon for Beaufort County. As Keyserling pointed out, in 1995, the mostly out-of-state visitors to Beaufort County paid over $3 million in bed taxes that went to help the area's cultural programs.[37]

When the task force evolved into the Joint Legislative Committee on Cultural Affairs, Keyserling became the chairman with Senator John Land as the vice chairman. With committee chair status came a staff aide and greater clout. The committee conducted research on the economic impact of cultural industry in South Carolina and introduced legislation on an array of cultural issues. The committee sought, for example, to pass legislation that would establish a South Carolina folk heritage award and that would encourage the preservation of historic buildings through local option property tax incentives.

Keyserling knew they were making headway when a member of the South Carolina Arts Commission reported to her that during one of the NCSL meetings in New York, she had overheard a person on the elevator say: "Have you heard about the arts in South Carolina? They're really way ahead of everyone." Despite a growing national reputation and notable achievements, in 1996, after Keyserling had left the legislature, a new governor and a new legislature defunded the Joint Legislative Committee on Cultural Affairs. Keyserling was disappointed but consoled herself with the knowledge that the much stronger South Carolina Arts Commission and a vibrant grassroots constituency could carry on without the legislative committee.[38]

In recognition for her contributions to the arts in South Carolina, in 1981 Keyserling was awarded the Elizabeth O'Neill Verner Award, South Carolina's most prestigious arts award. Named after the Charleston artist known for her watercolors of the Lowcountry, the Verner Award recognizes outstanding achievements in the arts. Keyserling was praised as "an aggressive initiator and proponent of private and public activities to further the arts in South Carolina." The nomination form for her award listed her many contributions, from her early days in Beaufort as an organizer of the Beaufort Concert Association, the Byrne Miller Dance Theatre, the Beaufort Art Collection and the Beaufort Foreign Film Series to her later legislative work as cochair of the Governor's Task Force on the Arts and stressed that "her leadership in the arts has been specific, effective and constant."[39]

At the awards ceremony, held at the state house, Keyserling remarked that this special occasion had brought the relationship of the arts in her life full circle. Growing up in New York City in a family devoted to the arts, music, artists, and art had surrounded her. When she moved to South Carolina she sought out kindred spirits, who worked with her to bring new cultural opportunities to Beaufort. She concluded by saying: "I wish my parents were here to see that even though I chose a country road over the city streets, I still managed to follow in their footsteps." A few years later, in 1988, the Joint Legislative Committee on Cultural Affairs, chaired by Keyserling, won the award. This was a tribute not only to the whole committee but to Keyserling's leadership in particular.[40]

Just as Keyserling had not initially envisioned herself as a leader of the arts in the state legislature, neither had she imagined herself as a proponent of women's issues. But again her experiences with the NCSL influenced her thinking and course of action. She was serving on the NCSL energy committee and the arts task force when she was unexpectedly nominated to its thirty-four-member executive committee, a first for South Carolina. In her modest fashion, Keyserling attributed her appointment to the need for geographic and gender representation. But clearly her grasp of issues and political savvy impressed the nominating committee. Once Keyserling was among this "inside" group, which included only one other woman, she became a link between the executive committee and the Women's Legislative Network, an organization of women legislators, and subsequently became the cochair of the network.

Keyserling's positions on the NCSL Executive Committee and on the Women's Legislative Network opened a whole new world of opportunities. Not only was there travel with special delegations to foreign countries but there was also a chance to attend conferences designed to expand women's participation in government. She saw a new generation of women who had come to power not, as she had, through volunteer experience and participation in the LWV but through professional careers; these were tough, articulate women who, as Keyserling observed, "understood the need for power, sought it, and gained it."[41]

As cochair of the Women's Legislative Network of the National Conference of State Legislatures, Keyserling served on a planning committee for the ten-year anniversary of the Center for American Women in Politics, which had been founded in 1971 at Rutgers University. The culminating conference had a major impact on Keyserling. There were informative talks, motivational speeches, and workshops to provide instruction on how, for example, to make a state women's legislative caucus effective. Keyserling recalls that she left the meeting with an enhanced commitment to women's issues, which she interpreted as including all public policy issues, for every policy has an impact on a woman's world.[42]

Beginning in South Carolina with small informal gatherings of women, Keyserling then helped to sponsor statewide women's luncheons with nationally recognized speakers. From this evolved the Women's Legislative Caucus, which Keyserling helped to form during her last year in the legislature. Since it was a bipartisan group, the only issue they could all agree on was sponsoring a bill to mandate the inclusion of mammograms in the insurance policies of state employees. Yet they worked not only on legislation but also on strategies for getting more women appointed to state boards and commissions. Even though the caucus had no meeting room, staff, or funds, it still managed occasionally to have an impact.

In 1992 Keyserling decided not to run for reelection. After her first election, she had faced no real opposition. By the late 1980s, however, there were far more Republicans in the county and they had developed a strong organization. In the 1988 election a statewide probusiness organization targeted Keyserling along with nine other representatives for defeat. The Religious Right, which opposed Keyserling's efforts to retain a program of comprehensive sex education in the schools, actively worked to defeat a Keyserling initiative to create a nonpartisan county school board. This group also attacked her personally: her opponent erected a large billboard that read "Ron Atkinson—One of Us." Keyserling surmised that he may have lost more votes, especially among Jewish, female, and black voters, than he gained with this sign. When a mass mailing attacked Keyserling on dubious grounds, the *Beaufort Gazette* came to her defense and noted that she had been named Legislator of the Year by the South Carolina Wildlife

Federation, the South Carolina School Board Association, the South Carolina Business and Professional Women, and many other organizations, and had received the Rotary Bowl for outstanding service from a group of conservative Beaufort business leaders. Despite these attacks, Keyserling's impressive record secured her position, and she handily won the election.

During the 1990 campaign, Keyserling was again one of several Democrats targeted by the state Republican Party. But her opponent was not very strong. She had a big win, gaining more votes in her district than the Republican governor. Yet when 1992 came, Keyserling was weary from the personal attacks and the inability to accomplish much because of legislative gridlock. Most of her allies from the Crazy Caucus were no longer in the house. She did not feel productive. "The civility was gone and was replaced by a tense, acrimonious, confrontational atmosphere," Keyserling lamented. The stress was also taking its toll on her health. Keyserling began to look for a woman who would be willing to run for her seat. Finding none, she turned to her son Billy, who subsequently served two terms. Keyserling's departure from the political arena gave rise to numerous gatherings to celebrate the accomplishments of her sixteen years in the house.[43]

In retirement Keyserling did not abandon the causes for which she had worked. After returning to live full time in Beaufort in 1992, she provided leadership on a number of fronts. That year the Beaufort County Council decided to create the Target 2010 Committee to address the problem of uncontrolled growth and its impact on the environment, roads, schools, water supply, and sewer lines. The council asked Keyserling to chair the growth management subcommittee. Within a year, the group had produced an impressive report that urged the adoption of a single comprehensive plan. "The failure to do this," Keyserling wrote, "could allow key decisions to be made by developers, without regard to the community's needs, and could result in a haphazard and irreversible reduction of community assets, such as open land and vistas, natural resources, cultural heritage and most important, 'a sense of place' which makes Beaufort County so special." Keyserling then helped to make Beaufort County a leader in pushing for state legislation requiring all counties to develop comprehensive plans and effect stricter zoning requirements.[44]

Subsequently, Keyserling's involvement at the state level in the arts enabled her to be of special service to Beaufort County. A case in point was her role in bringing Charles Wadsworth's chamber music to Beaufort. In 1986 when Keyserling chaired the Joint Legislative Committee on Cultural Affairs, the Spoleto Festival USA, founded ten years earlier, asked her to sit on its board. As a board member she got to meet many of the artists, one of the most memorable being

Wadsworth, who founded and directed the Chamber Music Society of Lincoln Center in New York City. In 1996, when the Beaufort concert series was having difficulty, Keyserling volunteered to call Wadsworth to get his ideas. From this telephone conversation, Wadsworth agreed to bring young musicians to Beaufort for several performances. Keyserling was especially pleased that Beaufort could be a venue for such a special musical treat. Wadsworth's first season in Beaufort led to another season and then another. Thus began a tradition that has continued for over a decade.

As elder stateswoman, Keyserling served on a number of boards, committees and task forces, including the board of the South Carolina Coastal Conservation League and the advisory committees to the Jewish Studies program at the College of Charleston and the State Energy Office. The state Budget and Control Board invited her to be a part of a task force to study the status of women in state government. This was a natural assignment for her because Keyserling had expressed concern that there were so few women in top management positions in the state government.

Keyserling still found that articles and opinion pieces in newspapers provided an effective means for expressing her views. Writing often for the *Beaufort Gazette* as well as *The State* in Columbia, she spoke out on the issues that had consumed her during her years in the legislature: energy, education, arts, and the environment. For example, in June 1995, she relied on her trusted tactic of extensive research to spell out in an article in *The State* the potential problems that could arise from easing environmental regulations on industry. Citing examples of health hazards arising from air pollution and landfill leaks, she built a strong case against looking only at short-term costs and not long-term benefits.

Keyserling was by then an accomplished public speaker and groups from across the state invited her to address their meetings. She was the keynote speaker in March 2005 at the third Pickens-Salley Symposium on Southern Women's History at USC Aiken. Drawing on her own experience, Keyserling said that she had lacked confidence in herself when she first ran for office, but in the political arena she found an "intensity and drive" that she did not know she had. Furthermore, she discussed a change in her views on power, stating: "I had thought of it in negative terms. But there are opportunities to use power for the common good. I want more women to have that power and get involved." She observed that even in 2005 the "good ol' boy" culture still existed in the state legislature in South Carolina and that these men tended to veer away from tackling problems such as the need for better health care that resonate with women.[45]

In May 2006 Keyserling spoke to the Georgetown County League of Women

Voters on the subject "Why is South Carolina So Conservative?" Keyserling
looked at the larger context and remarked that "the old Southern fears are still
alive in the Southern psyche," referring to a legacy of racism, a lost war, and an
aversion to change. She explored the long-term consequences of a poor educational system and the intertwining of religion and politics.[46]

By far the biggest undertaking of Keyserling's retirement years was the writing
of her political autobiography, *Against the Tide: One Woman's Political Struggle*,
published in 1998 by the University of South Carolina Press. In an extremely
candid fashion, she described her entry into politics and then detailed at some
length the major issues and legislative battles in which she participated and the
individuals and groups with whom she worked. The book received outstanding reviews. The *Island Packet* summarized the book as chronicling the experiences of "a New York City Jewish liberal in the 'good ol' boy' realm of Southern
politics." William Starr, writing for *The State*, concluded that the book "offers
an eye-opening course in how state government really works. And it shows us
how one woman not only tried but also succeeded in making a difference in the
state she came to love." Claudia Smith Brinson, in another review in *The State*,
wrote: "While she may tell you in her memoir that she lacked confidence, that
she hated making speeches, she got things done, good things, and she kept plug-
ging until the day she said good-bye in 1992. We owe her a lot for swimming
against the tide." In an unusual move, the *Beaufort Gazette* had two side-by-
side reviews of *Against the Tide*, one by an early colleague from her LWV days,
Lolita Huckaby, and the other by the *Gazette*'s editor, Jim Cato. Huckaby wrote:
"Keyserling has collected her observations about the South Carolina's political
system and colored them with the enthusiasm of being a part of a changing
government that saw improvements in such areas as public education, energy
conservation and recycling, disposal of nuclear waste and South Carolina's role
in that process." Cato praised the book's readability and its value in chronicling
a portion of history that might otherwise be unknown.[47]

Richard Riley, former governor and secretary of education, wrote in the fore-
word to *Against the Tide* that Keyserling "was more given to quiet research,
serious conversations, and careful organization, and less to the smoke-filled-
room politics of much big talk and little listening." He commended her for her
descriptions of "the people and the unique groupings that developed in the legislature." Her observations and reflections, Riley wrote, gave a personal account
of how difficult it is to bring about a new direction.[48]

Keyserling cited a number of reasons for writing her book. She sought to provide a basic instruction manual and encouragement for women contemplating
running for office. "I wrote to tell women they can do it and that we need them."

Additionally she hoped that the book would be a vehicle for acquainting people with the legislative process and explaining how laws get passed. In a private conversation in 2007, Keyserling confessed that one of the strongest motivational factors was her anger that so many of the laws that she had helped get passed were being rolled back by subsequent legislatures. In her frustration at seeing hard fought gains lost, she wanted the public to understand the issues and to appreciate how the passage of laws in Columbia affected their lives.[49]

In the midst of a tight gubernatorial campaign in South Carolina in the summer of 2010, Keyserling decided it was time to assist in marshaling supporters for state senator Vincent Sheheen, whose opponent was state representative Nikki Haley. Keyserling had long advocated for more women in public office; she believed, however, that priorities dear to her heart and those of many women in the state were being threatened by the positions taken by Haley. Using the slogan "Agenda over Gender," Keyserling initiated a bipartisan internet campaign to get one hundred women to sign a letter titled "Women for Sheheen." Working tirelessly at her computer, she initiated a website, emailed, blogged, and compiled a list that even surprised her when it eventually numbered over one thousand.[50]

When the local *Beaufort Gazette* failed to follow the major state newspapers by endorsing Sheheen, Keyserling raised the money for a full-page ad that included the names of hundreds of women, the letter, as well as an excerpt from *The State*'s endorsement of Sheheen. After Haley's narrow victory, Keyserling wrote to the women who had signed her letter: "Remember that the journey is as important as the destination. By staying involved we can model the kind of leadership we want to see."[51]

The following month Keyserling decided to undertake risky surgery to reduce pain and to enable her to stay active in the causes that had been central to her life. At eighty-eight she still had a sharp mind and a passion for public advocacy. She died in the hospital on December 10, 2010, owing to a number of complications that developed following the surgery. Across the state there was an outpouring of sorrow at the loss of this remarkable woman who with great courage had championed education, arts, environmental protection, and economic development.[52]

A quotation that appears at the beginning of *Against the Tide* reveals much about Keyserling's values and about why she chose the paths she did. It is a quotation from Alice Walker: "My activism pays the rent on being alive and being here on the planet. If I weren't active politically, I would feel as if I were sitting back eating at the banquet without washing the dishes or preparing the food." As she incorporated this philosophy into her life through her legislative career, her children observed, she became "a stronger and more contented person." From her initial efforts at "trying to blend in" when she first arrived in Beaufort, Keyserling moved into uncharted waters to discover untapped talents and to pursue goals that were consistent with her family background and upbringing. Although Keyserling was often in the minority, as a woman, a northerner, and a Jew, she had a remarkable way of finding practical and measured responses that relied on her exceptional writing skills, commitment to research, and savvy institutional insights and that together combined to make her a political trailblazer for women.[53]

NOTES

1. Harriet Keyserling, *Against the Tide: One Woman's Political Struggle* (Columbia: University of South Carolina Press, 1998), 4–9.

2. Harriet Keyserling, conversation with author, January 26, 2007.

3. Ibid.

4. Linda Kuntz Logan, "Harriet Keyserling—Lady Legislator," *Latrobe (Penn.) Bulletin*, February 9, 1981.

5. Howard Schneider, "Rep. Harriet Keyserling: The Cotton Dress in an Army of Pinstripes," *The State Magazine*, July 7, 1985, 10.

6. Keyserling, *Against the Tide*, 43.

7. Ibid., 45.

8. "Achievements in the Arts Are Recognized," *The State*, February 18, 1981; Harriet Keyserling, conversation with author, April 30, 2007.

9. Harriet Keyserling, conversation with author, January 26, 2007.

10. Keyserling, *Against the Tide*, 46–47.

11. George McMillan, "A Singular Woman," *McCall's*, March 1980, v-2, v-4.

12. Keyserling, *Against the Tide*, 47.

13. McMillan, "A Singular Woman," v-2, v-4.

14. Ibid.

15. Keyserling, *Against the Tide*, 49.

16. Ibid., 56.

17. Ibid., 57.

18. Ibid., 59.

19. Keyserling, conversation with author, January 26, 2007.

20. Ibid.

21. *Beaufort Gazette*, October 29, 1976, B-3.

22. Schneider, "Rep. Harriet Keyserling," 10.

23. *Against the Tide*, 71.

24. Keyserling, conversation with author, June 1, 2007.

25. Keyserling, *Against the Tide*, 71–82; Keyserling, conversation with author, June 1, 2007.

26. Schneider, "Rep. Harriet Keyserling," 10; Keyserling, *Against the Tide*, 78–79.

27. *Florence Morning News*, September 22, 1998, 3.

28. *Greenville News*, June 19, 1983, 1; Harriet Keyserling to Tom Inman, editor of the *Greenville*

News, June 30, 1983, Harriet Keyserling Papers, South Carolina Political Collections, University of South Carolina Libraries, University of South Carolina, Columbia (hereinafter cited as HKP-SCPC).

29. Keyserling, *Against the Tide*, 132.

30. Ibid., 224.

31. Walter Edgar, *South Carolina: A History* (Columbia: University of South Carolina Press, 1998), 555.

32. Keyserling, *Against the Tide*, 179.

33. *Greenville News*, March 25, 1980.

34. Keyserling, *Against the Tide*, 192, 193.

35. Keyserling, conversation with author, June 1, 2007.

36. Keyserling, *Against the Tide*, 243, 224.

37. Ibid., 288, 289.

38. Ibid., 306.

39. Nomination form for Harriet H. Keyserling for the 1980 Verner Award, HKP-SCPC.

40. Keyserling, *Against the Tide*, 308.

41. Ibid., 255.

42. Keyserling, conversation with author, June 1, 2007.

43. Keyserling, *Against the Tide*, 351.

44. *Beaufort Gazette*, October 24, 1993.

45. *Aiken Standard*, March 27, 2005.

46. *Pawleys Island Coastal Observer*, May 18, 2006.

47. *The State*, October 18, 1998; *The State*, March 13, 1999; *Beaufort Gazette*, September 27, 1998.

48. Keyserling, *Against the Tide*, xii, xiv.

49. "Keyserling Looks Back on Political Personal Growth," *Charleston Post and Courier*, October 25, 1996, E-2–E-3; Keyserling, conversation with author, June 1, 2007.

50. www.womenforsheheen.com.

51. *Beaufort Gazette*, October 31, 2010, A-9; www.womenforsheheen.com.

52. "Pioneering State Lawmaker Keyserling Dies," *The State*, December 12, 2010.

53. Keyserling, *Against the Tide*, xix; Keyserling, conversation with author, June 1, 2007.

Victoria Eslinger, Keller Bumgardner Barron, Mary Heriot, Tootsie Holland, and Pat Callair

Champions of Women's Rights in South Carolina

MARJORIE JULIAN SPRUILL

The modern women's rights movement that began in the 1960s had a tremendous effect on American society. In South Carolina, where traditional views concerning women and their role in society were deeply ingrained, many people were suspicious of feminism and its goals. In the early 1970s, however, a vigorous feminist movement emerged in the Palmetto State. There were women's rights advocates working throughout the state whose efforts greatly enhanced women's lives. This is the story of five Columbia women, Victoria Eslinger (1947–), Keller Bumgardner Barron (1932–), Mary Heriot (1921–), Eunice "Tootsie" Holland (1931–), and Pat Callair (1946–), who were among the most influential champions of women's rights in South Carolina.[1]

This able and determined group, working through the long-established League of Women Voters (LWV), the newly established National Organization for Women (NOW), and other organizations supported a variety of reforms on behalf of women including the proposed Equal Rights Amendment (ERA), a key feminist goal of the 1970s.[2] Heartened by the successes of the civil rights movement and of their own nascent movement, they sought further changes that would benefit South Carolina women of all races and classes. They won considerable support from both women and men. They sought to educate South

PAT CALLAIR, KELLER BARRON, EUNICE "TOOTSIE" HOLLAND
(FRONT), VICTORIA ESLINGER, AND MARY HERIOT
Photo by Clint White.

Carolinians about the need for and the justice of new laws and policies regarding women, yet arguably they produced the most change by insisting that the state adhere to new federal laws brought about by the women's movement at the national level.

This group of Columbia activists varied in age, experience, personal style, and circumstance, as well as in their approaches to reform, but they had in common considerable ability, determination, and courage. In the 1970s—as in the earlier movement to gain the vote—it was not easy to be a champion of women's rights in the South. And in South Carolina, a state profoundly conservative and wary of social change, there were many defenders of tradition who were not at all happy about the massive changes taking place with respect to the role of women.

American society had changed dramatically in the two decades following World War II, but in regard to women there was a significant lag between actual changes in their lives and a consequent adjustment in attitudes and practices. This contributed to a new wave of feminism in the United States often called the "second wave" of the women's movement. The reality was that large numbers of women, including mothers, were entering the job force even as the ideal was still the patriarchal family in which the woman was a wife and mother who worked exclusively in the home. Partly because many Americans viewed women's participation in the work force as temporary or as a means of earning "pin money," women workers faced pay inequities, sex segregation in jobs, and obstacles to advancement to more desirable and better-paying jobs. In the 1950s and well into the 1960s, most universities openly discriminated against women and denied or severely restricted their admission to professional schools. Even those women who managed to attain advanced degrees found it difficult to find jobs outside traditionally female occupations. Despite major antidiscrimination legislation enacted by Congress, including the Equal Pay Act of 1963 that mandated equal pay for equal work, Title VII of the 1964 Civil Rights Act that prohibited gender discrimination by employers, and Title IX of the Higher Education Act of 1972 that required equal treatment of women in educational institutions, South Carolina women looking for employment still confronted discriminatory treatment from employers in state government, colleges, and the private sector.[3]

Women who worked solely in the home were widely regarded—and often regarded themselves—as privileged but also faced problems that policy makers rarely acknowledged or addressed. A 1976 study of the status of homemakers in South Carolina coauthored by Vickie Eslinger noted that "South Carolina

women, particularly those who have chosen to be full-time homemakers, are
not in fact the 'privileged suitors' referred to by the courts." The report indicated
that wives had "no enforceable interest in the family income during marriage"
and "no real protection from physical abuse." Despite the widespread opinion
that husbands were required to support their wives in the instance of divorce—
a relatively new institution in the Palmetto State—the report revealed that divorced women in South Carolina were unlikely to get alimony, that child support was usually insufficient and very difficult to collect, and that wives had no
legal claim on any marital property held in their husbands' names. If a husband
died, his wife's continued financial security depended on his "whim."[4]

Supporters of the modern women's movement saw it as an effort to address
these and other problems women faced. Yet many conservatives viewed the
feminist movement *itself* as the problem, believing that it was not only responsible for the massive movement of women into the paid labor force and other
undesirable trends but that it was also taking away women's traditional rights
and privileges. In fact the name of the organization that conservative women,
led by Illinois Republican Phyllis Schlafly, created to defeat the ERA was "STOP
ERA," "STOP" being an acronym for "Stop Taking Our Privileges." By the mid-
1970s their ad hoc movement had grown into a full-blown campaign against
feminism—a backlash particularly strong among Christian conservatives in the
South.[5]

Increasingly, South Carolina feminists faced not only opposition to the reforms they supported but also personal vilification as advocates of a movement denounced as anti-God, antifamily, unpatriotic if not communist, and
"unladylike"—a powerful insult in the South. Public support for women's rights
brought considerable criticism and in some instances alienation from friends
and family. Some lost jobs or had their jobs threatened, and a few even faced
threats of violence.[6] As was the case during the suffrage movement, many South
Carolinians viewed the women's rights movement as a northern invention that
women of the South—supposedly better treated, indeed worshipped on a pedestal—should reject.[7]

Therefore it took courage for these five South Carolina women to affiliate
themselves with the women's movement and take the lead in confronting injustices faced by women in their state. They were active in the movement in state
and national organizations. Fighting gender discrimination by the state and
the private sector, they sought redress of grievances in the legislature as well
as the courts. And like South Carolina suffragists, who in 1920 had to accept
the right to vote "with the help of Uncle Sam" after their state declined to ratify
the Nineteenth Amendment, South Carolina feminists of the 1970s sometimes

had to win rights for women in their state by demanding the enforcement of federal law.[8]

Though Vickie Eslinger is one of the youngest of this group of five, it is often said that she launched the modern women's rights movement in South Carolina through her legal battle to gain the right to serve as a page in the state senate (the so-called page suit).[9] In the early 1970s, when she was one of the few female students enrolled in the University of South Carolina School of Law, Eslinger was appointed by her state senator to serve as a page—an easy and lucrative job often held by male law students. But she was denied the opportunity on the grounds that she was "a girl." The clerk of the state senate who turned her away famously said, "So sue me." She did, with Laughlin McDonald and Jean Hoefer Toal, one of Columbia's few women lawyers, as her attorneys. A district court judge ruled against her but the case was ultimately resolved in Eslinger's favor in the U.S. Court of Appeals for the Fourth Circuit in 1973. Significantly, Ruth Bader Ginsburg—then a Columbia University Law School professor and later a U.S. Supreme Court Justice—assisted with the case.[10]

The case received enormous coverage in the media and a largely favorable response from the public, especially after a judge hearing the case made a major gaffe. Eslinger was an effective advocate for her cause: though rather radical in her views for South Carolina, she was the daughter of a well-known Columbia lawyer and was as attractive and well spoken as she was intelligent. She was also pragmatic—believing, for instance, that especially in the South it was important for feminists to dress in a feminine manner—and she was skilled at working with others.[11] Though very young she commanded and usually received respect. Yet the judge hearing the page suit not only denied her claim but insulted her from the bench. When Toal presented evidence to refute the state government's argument that the "no women" policy was justified because pages were sometimes required to visit lawmakers in their hotel rooms at night, the judge interrupted Toal to say, "Maybe that's the opportunity your client seeks." Such was the uproar that he called all parties into the court a few days later, issued a grudging apology, and recused himself from the case.[12] In a state where "imputing unchastity to a woman" was punishable by law, this error won a good deal of sympathy for the plaintiff and her cause.[13]

The page suit was neither the beginning nor the end of Eslinger's work for women's rights in her state: as Nancy Moore, another veteran South Carolina feminist recently recalled, "Eslinger knocked down the door, walked through it, and kept knocking down and knocking on doors."[14] In high school Eslinger had been a Young Republican and a "Goldwater Girl." She attended college at the University of Georgia and the University of Dijon in France before transferring to the University of South Carolina (usc) in 1966. But Eslinger often returned to France: her mother was from Marseilles and Barcelona, and she had lived in France and Spain growing up, going back and forth, learning French, Spanish, and Italian. Witnessing the historic student protests in Paris in 1968 was an eye-opening experience.[15]

At usc she soon proved to be a leader intent on changing institutions from within. She was active on and off campus in the civil rights movement, the anti-war movement, and the women's movement. As secretary of coed affairs in the cabinet of Harry L. Walker, usc's first African American student body president, she protested curfews for women students. As president of the student union she held up funding for the intramural program because the university refused to hire women lifeguards. She was active in the Association of Women Students (aws) that planned conferences on feminism and was on the committee that created the university's women's studies program. The same year that she filed the page suit she went to the University of California at Berkeley to attend the second National Conference on Women in the Law and persuaded the organization to hold its next annual meeting at the usc School of Law instead of Harvard University—apparently convincing the organization the conference might do more good in South Carolina. Upon returning home, she mollified an astonished dean by explaining that usc had beaten out Harvard for this honor.[16]

Eslinger's consciousness of women's rights issues grew partly in response to seeing women students suffering from the results of unwanted pregnancies including botched abortions; she heard frequent reports of dead fetuses being found in wastebaskets on campus and had to rush her own roommate to the hospital after she had an illegal abortion. She gained support of the then-president of the university, Tom Jones, to open a "reproductive freedom area" in the Russell House, which housed the student union. From it Eslinger and twenty-four volunteers ran a hotline that offered counseling and information about birth control, adoption, and abortion.[17] Eslinger, brought up both Presbyterian and Catholic, recruited both Protestant and Catholic clergy as counselors. They distributed "Women and Their Bodies" (the booklet first published by a Boston feminist collective in 1970, soon to be famous as *Our Bodies, Ourselves*). They advised students about all their legal options—which were expanding during these years. In 1972 in *Eisenstadt v. Baird*, the Supreme Court ruled that it was legal for doctors to prescribe birth control to unmarried women, and the hotline apprised students of which doctors were willing to do so. Until abortion was available locally after the Supreme Court's 1973 *Roe v. Wade* decision, the hotline aided women who decided to obtain abortions to do so safely and legally by providing information about clinics in New York, which legalized abortion in 1970, the first state to do so.[18] A 1972 editorial in the *USC Gamecock* praised Eslinger and the hotline, noting that USC had one of the few university hotlines in the country despite its being "possibly one of the most sexist institutions around," and stated "there is no way to tell how many pregnant girls have been saved from a back-alley butcher because of it."[19]

Obviously not all South Carolinians were as approving of these efforts to make students aware of new rights regarding birth control and abortion. By 1974, critics of the *Roe* decision had organized the large and well-funded South Carolina Citizens for Life. And abortion was somewhat controversial even within the women's movement. Some South Carolina feminists were uncomfortable with defending abortion rights either because of personal convictions or because they believed that the movement should focus on other less radical goals. They established a chapter of the Women's Equity Action League (WEAL), an organization founded at the national level by NOW members after NOW made the issue of "choice" a priority. In 2010, Eslinger recalled that she received a few letters critical of her pro-choice stance but looking back believed the issue was less divisive in the 1970s than it later became. To her a woman's right to control her own fertility was a fundamental part of feminism.[20] When she was a student, Eslinger became a member of the national board of the Women's National Abortion Action Council and gave speeches in other states in the Southeast on reproductive freedom and women's issues. During one of Phyllis Schlafly's visits to South Carolina, Eslinger debated her on the subject of reproductive rights; afterward Schlafly told her she was not accustomed to her opponents being so "polite." Eslinger's early experiences with the page suit and with the hotline were formative: for the rest of her distinguished career, first as a lawyer for Legal Services and then in private practice, she would continue to defend women's rights to birth control and abortion and fight against discrimination in employment and elsewhere.[21]

In 1972 Eslinger entered the national spotlight when she challenged the South Carolina Democratic Party on the issue of representation of women in its delegation to the Democratic National Convention. In this she teamed up with other South Carolina women, Janet Wedlock and Margaret Young, and two of the nation's most famous feminists, New York congresswoman Bella Abzug and *Ms.* magazine editor Gloria Steinem, who were among the leading Democrats in the newly created, bipartisan organization, the National Women's Political Caucus (NWPC). Eslinger, Wedlock, and Young issued a formal challenge to the state party for failing to adhere to the new national party policy requiring proportionate representation, one designed to ensure the presence of more African Americans, young people, and women. Only nine of the thirty-two delegates were women. Don Fowler, then chair of the state Democratic Party, defended it against this challenge, shrewdly selecting the well-known and respected lawyer Matthew Perry, an African American and a civil rights leader, to handle its case. Eslinger charged that the South Carolina Democratic Party, while recognizing discrimination against blacks and working effectively to overcome past actions, neither recognized nor was working to address party discrimination against women and that her effort to point this out through the challenge had been met with hostility, as indeed it had. Barbara Sylvester of Florence, the state's "National Executive Committee Woman," told the press that "if there's a stronger word than 'totally,' that's how much we are opposed to this special women's effort." She feared it would lead women in South Carolina who were interested in becoming more involved in the Democratic Party to think Democratic women like her were "women's liberationists" rather than "ladies." As the convention approached, the leading candidate for the Democratic nomination, Senator George McGovern, promised to support the South Carolina feminists' challenge, but changed his mind when it appeared that it could cost him the nomination.[22] In that same year Eslinger also helped establish a Columbia chapter of the National Organization for Women (NOW), and when Congress approved the ERA, Eslinger became a strong supporter.

Indeed, all five of these South Carolina women's rights leaders, Vickie Eslinger, Keller Bumgardner Barron, Mary Heriot, Tootsie Holland, and Pat Callair were avid supporters of the ERA which became the centerpiece of the national women's movement in the 1970s as well as the focus of the conflict between feminist and conservative women. In the early 1970s there was strong support for the proposed amendment, which was overwhelmingly approved by Congress with a vote of 354 to 23 in the House of Representatives on October 12, 1971, and 84 to 8 in the Senate on March 22, 1972. The ERA had first been proposed back in 1923, originally advocated by suffrage leader Alice Paul as a "blanket bill" that would do away with all of the remaining legal inequities that American women still faced even after being granted the vote in 1920. If approved by three-fourths of the states, the ERA would render unconstitutional all laws that discriminated "on account of sex." By 1972, as the women's rights movement grew in popularity and influence, the amendment won the support of most women's organizations, national leaders in both parties, and nearly all members of Congress. Both senators from South Carolina, Democrat Ernest Hollings and Republican Strom Thurmond, as well as most members of the state's congressional delegation voted for it, and ERA supporters in the state had good reason to be optimistic.[23]

Certainly the ERA ratification campaign had strong leaders. One of the most visible, Keller Henderson Bumgardner Barron, then Keller Bumgardner, was an experienced and talented organizer, dignified and politically savvy and so-cially and politically prominent. She grew up in Atlanta and was educated at Vanderbilt and Agnes Scott College, from which she graduated in 1953 with a bachelor of arts in history and political science and an elementary teaching certificate. She then moved to South Carolina with her husband, Sherrod L. Bumgardner, and taught elementary school briefly at Arden Elementary School in Eau Claire.[24] She was soon the mother of four even as she gained prominence as an advocate for social justice and good government.[25] Bumgardner served mostly through the LWV, an organization she credits with being the "Holy Grail" that drew her into a wider world of learning and service. She served as Colum-bia LWV president (1963–65) and state LWV president (1967–71) before being ap-pointed to the national board (1971–76). At the time she became involved in ERA advocacy she was serving as the appointee of Governor John West on the State Reorganization Commission (the only woman) and the State Human Affairs Commission. She taught Sunday school at Columbia's First Baptist Church. In 1974 the South Carolina Baptist Convention selected her for the McDowell Award for Distinguished Christian Service, the first woman recipient.[26]

Bumgardner was an advocate of racial justice as well as the advancement of women. At Agnes Scott College she had become involved with the Christian Association, an ecumenical organization that promoted racial harmony and brought white Agnes Scott students together with black students from Atlanta University.[27] She supported the integration of the South Carolina LWV and trea-sured new friendships with African American women, including Ethel Bolden. While president of the South Carolina LWV she made the *New York Times* for the first time when she spoke up at a national LWV convention against a proposal that they delay support for federal fair housing legislation out of consideration for southern sentiments. In the 1970s she served on the Greater Columbia Com-munity Relations Council, on the Board of Governors of the Southern Regional Council, and—from 1977 through 1979—as chair of the South Carolina Com-mittee of the U.S. Commission on Civil Rights.[28]

Bumgardner's conversion to ERA advocate coincided with that of the LWV itself. The LWV, an organization that had grown out of the woman suffrage movement and that promoted voter education and good government, had yet to endorse the ERA at the time she attended its national conference in Atlanta in 1972. But at that conference the LWV underwent a "consciousness-raising experience" when the keynote speaker, national feminist leader Gloria Steinem, asked, "Are you for us or against us?" She challenged them to get on board with the movement, indeed chiding them for listing their leaders on LWV statio-nery by their husbands' names as well as for failing to join the ERA effort. The

LWV and Bumgardner became avid ERA supporters. Together with Barbara Moxon, another well-respected leader and Bumgardner's successor as president of the League of Women Voters of South Carolina (LWVSC), she mobilized this influential organization in support of ratification in her state.[29]

In 1972, like women's rights advocates everywhere, South Carolina ERA supporters were buoyed by the overwhelmingly positive vote in Congress and the fact that states were scrambling to be among the first to ratify. As Barron later recalled, Senator Thurmond provided South Carolina ERA proponents with "a wonderful letter" saying that he supported ratification because he wanted his daughters to have every opportunity that his sons had.[30] Many South Carolina legislators asked to support the amendment were enthusiastic; as Barron recalled, "People were stepping up to do that, they were excited about it, they wanted to do that." In late March shortly after Congress approved the ERA, Carolyn Frederick, a Republican from Greenville, also an Agnes Scott graduate and one of the few women in the South Carolina legislature, introduced the ratification resolution in the state house of representatives, and to the delight of its supporters the ERA was approved unanimously on a voice vote. It was then sent to the state senate, where it passed on second reading. However it was ultimately blocked in the senate and died in the Judiciary Committee, headed by the powerful Marion Gressette, staunch opponent of the women's rights movement.[31] And, having failed to be ratified in the afterglow of congressional approval, the ERA's chances of ratification in Palmetto State were greatly diminished, even more than its advocates could have known at the time.

Phyllis Schlafly and her supporters across the nation proved to be very successful in building a strong, grassroots movement to block the proposed amendment. A seasoned politician from the Republican Party's far right, Schlafly proved to have tremendous skill in organizing and in working with the media and raising doubts about the benefits of the ERA. Its opponents insisted that the ERA would not just correct injustices but would lead to undesirable, even dangerous changes—"throwing out the baby with the bath water." While feminists argued that the whole idea of separate legislation for women and men was based on outdated theories about innate differences in the sexes and buttressed traditional social roles, conservative women and men insisted that divinely inspired differences in the sexes justified the existence of laws that affected the sexes differently, and they defended traditional gender roles as desirable. Opposition to increased federal power also fueled the resistance to the ERA. While ERA supporters were eager for the federal government to give the women's movement the strong support it had given to the civil rights movement, conservatives who had opposed federal action on civil rights now argued against the ERA as another example of unwanted and unwarranted intervention on social issues.[32]

Schlafly and STOP ERA found many supporters in South Carolina, many of them already active in conservative organizations, including Women for Constitutional Government, and in their churches.[33] Among them was Theresa Hicks, who won Schlafly's praise for filing a class action lawsuit against the South Carolina Commission on Women. Hicks objected to the commission using taxpayer funds to promote the ERA, which she charged was a radical measure supported by radical women and not by the majority of South Carolina women.[34] In early March 1975, ERA opponents led by Hicks and Zilla Hinton combined forces to establish a formal, statewide STOP ERA organization.[35] They found an able leader in Irene Neuffer, who opposed the amendment because of her belief in state's rights and her objection to federal efforts to use the law to change attitudes—which she insisted could not be done. Neuffer believed that "the government should stay out of the home as much as possible."[36]

In the legislature, Senator Gressette continued to be a formidable foe of the ERA. Gressette was well known for his opposition to federal action to advance civil rights for African Americans and now similarly warned fellow legislators against the ERA: "It would let the U.S. Congress decide on all domestic matters. South Carolina is providing its own laws, and I don't know of any state anywhere where women are more favored than in South Carolina." His wife Florence Howell Gressette, who often sat with her husband in the senate, was a proud graduate of the state's women's college, Winthrop College, and feared the ERA would force Winthrop to become coeducational. She was active in the campaign against ratification: on one occasion, along with the wife of Marshall B. Williams, another veteran senator, Florence Gressette led ERA opponents who placed homemade cakes on the desks of all members of the legislature.[37] Barron later observed that Florence Gressette "was absolutely determined that Winthrop was not going to go coed. And so he [Senator Gressette] worked so hard to save Winthrop for her."[38] Governor James B. Edwards's wife, Anne, another influential political wife, though not a member of STOP ERA, opposed the ERA and was a great admirer of Schlafly: when Schlafly visited the state, she hosted her.[39]

Norma Russell, a Republican from Lexington, led the opposition to the ERA in the state house of representatives. Speaking with Schlafly at a STOP ERA rally at Columbia Bible College, Russell proclaimed, "I thank God for Phyllis Schlafly" and insisted that the ERA would lead to government interference in private schools, threaten the integrity of single-sex schools, and force women into combat roles. "The purpose of ERA is to build a sex neutral society," she said. "The women's lib ideology is that there is no difference between the sexes." "Women's libbers," she predicted, wanted the amendment to promote their radical goals, and if they succeeded, homosexual marriages as well as abortions could become as common as "tonsillectomies and appendectomies." "Your imagination is not vivid enough to think of all the uses that ERA-ers could find," she insisted. "The ERA will give federal judges and the Supreme Court a blank check on interpreting the law."[40]

As the controversy grew Keller Bumgardner and other ERA supporters in South Carolina faced quite a challenge, yet they managed to build a formidable organization and win considerable support if not an ultimate victory. In January 1973 the South Carolina LWV, working with NOW, announced the creation of a coalition of pro-ERA organizations called the South Carolina Coalition for the ERA under the direction of Bumgardner and Janet Wedlock. The coalition was composed of a diverse array of progressive organizations including among others the American Association of University Professors, the Associated Women Students of the University of South Carolina, the American Civil Liberties Union, Church Women United, the Columbia Urban League, the YWCA, Communication Workers, the Christian Action Council, the NAACP, WEAL, Business and Professional Women, the Home Economics Nurses' Association, the Tenants Organization, and the Winthrop Coalition.[41]

The South Carolina Coalition for the ERA was well run and well funded. Wedlock was paid by NOW and Bumgardner by the LWVSC—her first paid job after having her children. They employed a male assistant, Tim Rogers, a Clemson University student who assisted them in designing their political strategy. Keller Bumgardner Barron recalled that they worked "feverishly" for ratification, conducting extensive research, lobbying legislators, organizing letter-writing campaigns, cultivating the media, and educating the public on the amendment—emphasizing the need for the amendment and defending it against charges of radicalism. They opened a headquarters in the basement of a building on Hampton Street owned by her father-in-law where he and her husband had their dental office. The headquarters remained in this location until Bumgardner's father-in-law, no fan of her work for women's rights, ordered them to vacate his building immediately after seeing his daughter-in-law interviewed in front of the ERA headquarters—and his building—on the evening news. (His other daughter-in-law, Judy Bumgardner, was a leader among ERA opponents.) The South Carolina Coalition for the ERA moved the headquarters to the Chesnut Cottage, running their ratification effort out of the same house where the famous diarist Mary Chesnut had lived near the end of the Civil War and where Jefferson Davis once addressed Columbia citizens from the porch.[42]

In 1973, the ratification bill was again introduced by Carolyn Frederick in the house and in the senate by Dewey Wise of Charleston. Although the Judiciary Committee reported favorably, the house passed a motion to table the ERA. Bumgardner and the South Carolina Coalition for the ERA were left to speculate what created such a change in the house of representatives that had approved ERA 83 to 0 in 1972 and then in 1973 tabled it by a vote of 62 to 44. In the senate the bill was again buried by Gressette's Judiciary Committee.[43] Barron recalled that this loss was very disappointing but "not overwhelming," and the coalition continued its work. In 1974 they sponsored a symposium on the USC campus to educate the public on how the ERA would affect state laws, which featured "one of the most respected authorities on the legislative history of the Equal Rights Amendment," Thomas I. Emerson of Yale School of Law, as their main speaker.[44] 1974 was an election year for the house, and they focused on getting candidates to commit to the ERA, seeking to build support for another attempt at ratification in 1975.[45] Bumgardner reported to the press that ERA forces had secured "pre-election commitments" from close to a majority of the people elected, and Janet Wedlock noted that polls showed a majority of women in the state supported ERA ratification. So in March 1975 ERA proponents were stunned when, after two more years of lobbying and considerable support, including from some of the leading members of the state legislature, a parliamentary maneuver by opponents in the house of representatives succeeded in tabling the bill by a narrow margin while 30 percent of the representatives were absent, many of them supporters who had not yet returned from lunch.[46] Keller Bumgardner Barron later remembered how frustrating it was to lose in that manner: "We won every debate in our own minds because we were putting up the facts. But the facts didn't make any difference; it wasn't going to make any difference. So when the votes came, we lost the votes."[47]

Meanwhile Bumgardner had become increasingly active at the national level. From 1973 through 1976 she served as the national LWV's point person on the ERA, chairing its campaign to ratify the amendment.[48] When the national organization ERAmerica was created to coordinate groups working for ratification of the amendment, she became the LWV's representative and gave speeches across the nation on its behalf. As national leaders searched for the last three states—knowing some of these must come from the South—they recognized the appeal of this woman who was not only extremely talented but, as Barron put it, "spoke 'Southern,' had four little children, [was] married to a Baptist and was in an un-ratified state."[49]

Other South Carolina women kept the fight going in South Carolina. One of them was Mary Heriot who played a major role in bringing the women's rights movement to South Carolina. A native of Pennsylvania, she had been a nurse in the South Pacific during World War II where she met and married Henry Heriot, an army officer from South Carolina. After the war they moved to Columbia, where he completed law school, and then to Greenville, where he opened a law office and Mary earned a degree in economics at Furman—graduating at the top of her class.[50] That top rating did her little good: she later recalled that all of her male classmates got job offers in their fields while all she was able to get at the time was a job as a secretary in an insurance firm. When her three children were in their teens and the family had moved back to Columbia, she began teaching economics at Richland College (now Midlands Technical College) and also earned a master's from USC. After years of working at Midlands Tech—first as a teacher and then as dean of students—she went to work at the State Commission on Aging and became the head of the Department of Research and Grants.[51]

In 1972, disturbed by discrimination against women in employment, including in the state government, and by the underrepresentation of women on the USC Board of Trustees and in other leadership positions in the state, Heriot took action. She teamed up with law student Vickie Eslinger, then much in the spotlight as a result of her page suit, and issued a call for a meeting to organize a Columbia chapter of NOW. In preparation they sent out a letter, inviting people to attend a meeting at the Richland County Library and asking that they pass the letter on to others. Heriot also sent it to every woman employee of the state.[52]

The letter opened with the question: "How do you feel about the following facts?" The fact list began with the statement that "state-supported institutions of higher learning in this state do not have women on their governing boards." In addition, it stated that "a USC professor received a federal grant of money to study discrimination in state employment and did not include women in the study." Also noted was that "out of some ninety state agencies, only three small ones (the Children's Bureau, the State Board of Nursing, and the Library Board) are headed by women." Heriot and Eslinger also included information from the recent census showing that "approximately half of the families living below the poverty line are headed by women" and that "the largest single segment of the poor are women 65 years of age and over." They also noted that the situation regarding women's wages was actually worsening, that "in 1955 the median wage for women workers was 63.9% of the median wage for men," but by "1969 it had fallen to 60.5% and women with college degrees averaged just $249 a year more than men with only eighth grade educations." "If these statistics incense you," the letter concluded, "why not resolve now to do something about them?" It extended an invitation to "join us so that we can speak with a concerted voice" through NOW, "a non-political, non-partisan organization committed to improving social, financial, and political conditions of women . . . and comprised of intelligent, informed, and dedicated people of both sexes, all colors and creeds."[53]

Heriot had expected a small crowd but was delighted at the large turnout. To a reporter for the *USC Gamecock*, Heriot described their goals and their approach. She insisted they knew there was already "an active core of concerned women" that they would be joining to secure their primary goal of passage of the ERA. But she emphasized that the new organization intended to "be active in areas of employment where women are discriminated against, in promotion, wage and hiring practices." Heriot stated that they hoped men would "become involved also" and that they were "not a group of men haters. We want to be part of the mainstream—to participate along with men, not behind them."[54] Heriot was eager to attract support without making enemies for her cause or herself. This former nurse who had worked at the Philadelphia Municipal Hospital for Contagious Disease (before the discovery of antibiotics) treating diphtheria, typhoid, polio, and even leprosy and then volunteered for wartime service was not easily intimidated. Nonetheless, as she later recalled, with tuition to pay for three children, she was more than a little worried when Irene Neuffer, head of South Carolina STOP ERA, published a letter to the editor calling for Heriot to be dismissed from her job with the state government for having criticized its policies. She also remembered that she "had a bit of protection" because governors "Fritz" Hollings, Bob McNair, and John West had been law school classmates and fraternity brothers of her husband. The feminist movement, she noted, had been largely a white, middle-class movement because such women "could better afford the backlash and there was plenty of that."[55]

Mary Heriot later recalled that, as she waited to see who would appear at that first NOW meeting, the first person to walk in the door was Eunice "Tootsie" Holland. Thus began a cherished and productive friendship that would endure for the rest of their lives. Tootsie Holland, though under five feet tall, became one of the towering figures in the South Carolina women's movement. The dignified but determined Heriot did not shy away from controversy but did not relish it. She recalled, "You know we had grown up as ladies and we were supposed to act politely and that sort of thing, and then you have to go out and carry a placard or scream 'WOMEN NOW!'" or "picket your husband's college"; "it was not easy," but it was necessary to "make the public aware of the fact that we were there."[56] The feisty and fun-loving Holland, however, took a mischievous pleasure in defying public opinion; she was amused, for example, when agents of the South Carolina Law Enforcement Division (SLED) began to follow them and monitor their actions as if they were somehow a threat to public safety. Yet she too was shaken when an anonymous caller threatened to kill her beloved Chihuahuas, and after a male critic of the women's movement threatened her in person she began carrying a gun. Both women were blessed, however, with husbands who were feminists and enthusiastically supported the women's movement in the 1970s and for the rest of their long lives. By coincidence, both Henry Heriot and Bruce Holland died in August 2008.[57]

Tootsie Holland was born in Conway, South Carolina, and grew up in Moncks Corner. She was educated at USC, supported by a much older sister who had been unable to afford a college education but was determined that Tootsie would have that chance. After graduating, Tootsie married Bruce Holland, a Citadel graduate, and settled in Columbia. She had hoped to go to USC Law School but was turned down: as she recalled they told her "we already have a woman in the law school." She went into business, managing the local franchise of a temporary office workers agency called "DOT Girls" (Dictaphone Operators Temporary) that employed about fifty women clerical workers. When *The State* newspaper published a photograph of Holland as the vice president of the new NOW chapter, her company demanded that she quit NOW or resign. She resigned from DOT Girls and continued to work for NOW for decades. Holland remembered that she was not the only woman in Columbia who lost her job because of her association with NOW but that she was more fortunate than most because her husband's support made it possible to continue her active involvement without fear.[58]

In the 1970s Tootsie Holland served as regional director of NOW and on its national board as well as taking her turn as president of the Columbia chapter. Together with Mary Heriot, she learned a great deal at NOW conferences and workshops and brought back ideas and tactics valuable to their cause in South Carolina. For instance Holland recalled the "assertiveness training" classes being especially important in helping women overcome decades of training in being deferential. If in fact she had a problem with this before, Tootsie Holland quickly overcame it. She said that NOW had booklets prepared for every need, including instructions on "how to hold a press conference" and how to "find out if your school is discriminating against women teachers and paying men more," adding "ours was of course."[59]

In 1976, building on the coalition developed earlier by Keller Barron and Janet Wedlock, Tootsie Holland and Gemma Arnot, a NOW leader from Spartanburg, organized a new group, ERA-SC, with Holland as executive director. When the American Association of University Women (AAUW) joined, more funding was added to the basic funding provided by NOW. Another great addition from AAUW was Mabel Stoudemire, who was elected president of ERA-SC. Stoudemire was dying of cancer and "wanted to do something that would help women before I pass." These women put together an impressive organization. Holland boasted that at the time they would reach over 250,000 in two days, which given that they contacted people by phone was quite an accomplishment. She said that even Senator Gressette, their archenemy, called them "the best lobbying group . . . that has ever been in South Carolina." The ERA-SC office was staffed by Tootsie's sister, Angella Fifield, who was secretary, Robin Anderson, a volunteer, and Charles Brimmer, a college student and "super 'go-for.'" Carolyn Johnson of Columbia NOW served as treasurer. This coalition worked well because it brought together groups with different agendas and styles. Holland explained, "Each member group was free and encouraged to do its special thing, but they still worked together whenever it was necessary."[60]

Holland recalled proudly, "We had a minister, Diane Moseley, who established People of Faith for the ERA" and every day the legislature was in session "we had a rabbi, a priest, a Baptist minister, a Methodist, whatever, and their wives . . . to greet the senators as they came in." ERA-SC also utilized another approach: it held weekly cocktail parties at the Wade Hampton, the hotel where most of the out-of-town legislators stayed. Holland noted that legislators did not have offices in those days, so the parties provided opportunities to talk to them. Representatives of Business and Professional Women (BPW) organized a morning breakfast for the senators. ERA-SC established a headquarters across the street from the statehouse so it could see who was coming and going. It kept a tight rein on ERA lobbyists, including monitoring what they wore, requiring them to dress in a manner that would not offend the legislators.[61] Heriot recalled, "We never would have gone in there in slacks." Some lobbyists, said Holland, "wore gloves, hats, the whole smash."[62]

Holland recalled that they drew support from some unexpected sources: one day, as they were working at the ERA-SC headquarters, a "beautiful woman walked in," saying "I am a call girl . . . and I want to help." She said that the legislators with whom she kept company talked in front of her like she was a piece of furniture, and she offered to feed the ERA-SC headquarters information, which she did. Someone came up with the idea of letting her help the effort as a "visual aid." During a senate hearing, when one anti-ERA speaker made the inevitable remark that women did not need equal rights since they were privileged and "up on a pedestal," ERA supporters wheeled her in literally on a pedestal in an antebellum gown and in chains with a banner that read "Please Unchain Me from This Pedestal—Pass the ERA." Holland denied having any foreknowledge of this stunt but thought it was hilarious. Whatever effect it had on the legislators, she said, given that it took place the same day that STOP ERA leader Phyllis Schlafly was in town, it did keep the media from focusing on her.[63]

ERA-SC was affiliated with ERAmerica, and Holland was proud to say, it was one of the few state ERA coalitions in the United States that was working without friction between member organizations. Across the nation there were indeed tensions among ERA supporters—understandably frustrated as an ERA victory that had in 1972 seemed inevitable was slipping away. Most of the "unratified states" were in the South and national leaders at times displayed impatience with southern ERA advocates for failing to get the last three states needed for ratification: southern feminists—including Tootsie Holland—got a bit fed up with that attitude on the part of "Yankee women." As she recalled, "In the end we all started to blame one another, and some of the national organizers said, 'You Southern women don't know how to get the thing passed! What's wrong with you?' . . . And we say 'Come down here and see how fast they run *your* ass out of town.'"[64]

Eslinger, Heriot, Holland, and South Carolina's NOW leaders gained a valuable ally when Lutricia "Pat" Callair moved to Columbia. Callair, a South Carolina State graduate, had been an English teacher in Spartanburg, where she married, had two sons, and divorced; she came to USC to get a master's degree in counseling and psychology, which she received in 1977. While pursuing the degree she worked in the university's desegregation center. After getting the degree she was hired as a social work director for the South Carolina Department of Corrections. During part of her time there, she worked with inmates on death row at the state penitentiary on the Broad River. In 1989, she received a master's in social work from USC.

When she moved to Columbia, Callair was already a member of NOW: after years of working with the NAACP and the Congress of Racial Equality (CORE), organizations that she found to be too male dominated, she responded when she saw an ad from NOW organizers in Spartanburg inviting people committed to social justice to become members.[65] Callair and other South Carolina feminist leaders saw the women's rights movement as overlapping with the civil rights movement, as being a part of a larger human rights effort. Callair received criticism from coworkers in the NAACP and CORE for becoming active as a feminist, but she stuck with NOW. Indeed, she became the first statewide NOW leader in South Carolina as well as a member of NOW's national board and was a fervent proponent of the ERA.[66]

Though Callair was one of the few African American women actively involved in the ERA fight or the women's rights movement in South Carolina generally, she and her white coworkers were eager to change that. She recalled that she was "coming into my own as a feminist at a time when African American women who were willing to be actively involved in the feminist movement were at a premium" but that she believed "people of color should be supportive of the women's movement and vice versa." She was also interested in expanding the class base of the South Carolina feminist movement.[67] Looking back she remembered that

> the women I was interested in getting into the organization were working-class women, poor women, and women of color. I felt like those women were the women who were the most challenged by sexism because they were not being paid as much, they were not getting the jobs that men could get, they were not even as well educated and didn't get the same educational opportunities that even white women had. I felt like that base of women was important to our organizing effort in South Carolina. I went looking for women who worked in the Lowcountry of South Carolina who were working in the kitchens in resort hotels, and laundry cleaners, and other occupations of the sort. Those were the types of women I targeted."[68]

The South Carolina ERA coalition put out a pamphlet entitled "The ERA and the Black Community" that insisted that "Black + Female = Double Jeopardy," that black women "were caught in two minority groups which have been discriminated against in our society," and that "we don't get anywhere by comparing the trials of being black to the trials of being a woman. It's enough to recognize that we are a double minority, and that ratification of the Equal Rights Amendment would help us as women, and as black women." It also stated that sex discrimination was not in the Bible, and that President Jimmy Carter was seeking to do through the ERA what President Lyndon Johnson had done for civil rights. And it reminded the reader that the NAACP and the National Association of Colored Women's Clubs supported ratification while anti-ERA groups included the Ku Klux Klan, the John Birch Society, and the Mormon Church.[69]

Pat Callair was much admired by other South Carolina feminists for her leadership abilities, her ability to think on her feet, and her fearlessness. Like Holland she appeared to relish the fight. She debated the skillful and seasoned Phyllis Schlafly in a live radio broadcast—a daunting prospect for anyone. "She killed me!" Callair recalled, laughing. "At that time I thought I knew what I knew and I didn't!" She said she was probably naïve in agreeing to do it but also recalled that not too many feminists in the state were willing to debate Schlafly. However Callair, like Eslinger, was young but brave, and she stepped up to the plate to face Schlafly—as did the more experienced Mary Heriot and Jean Toal, then a legislator and a key ERA proponent.[70]

Callair was known for her use of "feminist theater," particularly a one-woman performance as the former slave, famous abolitionist, and woman's rights advocate Sojourner Truth. Together with Tootsie Holland and another woman named Fran Chester, she owned and operated a feminist bookstore named Sojourner's, then located on the corner of Pickens and Gervais streets in Columbia.

The bookstore, according to a Greenwood, South Carolina, newspaper, tried "to carry at least one copy of all feminist literary works in existence," and it served for a while as an informal headquarters for their women's rights activities.[71] Interestingly, at that time, Vickie Eslinger's law office was upstairs in the same building, and they all worked well together, proud of one another and eager to put their collective talents together to work for the cause.[72]

All of these five women, Eslinger, Barron, Heriot, Holland, and Callair, were involved in an important series of federally funded conferences held in 1977 as part of the International Women's Year (IWY) program. The conferences, mandated by Congress at the behest of the United Nations and American feminist leaders, were designed to help get the women of the nation to participate in formulating policy regarding women's issues and in making recommendations that were to guide Congress and the president. The IWY program was established in 1975 and a supportive Gerald Ford administration appointed a largely feminist National Commission on the Observance of International Women's Year to lead it. That group later created state commissions that planned state IWY conferences open to all where issues would be debated, resolutions adopted, and delegates elected to send on to a culminating National Women's Conference in Houston, Texas, in November 1977.[73] National organizers tapped Benedict College professor Marianna Davis and Richland County councilwoman Candy Waites to head the South Carolina IWY organizing committee, Davis serving as chair, Waites as vice chair, and Keller Bumgardner as one of its members.[74] In advance of the state conferences, IWY leaders commissioned research in every state; Vickie Eslinger and her law partner Lucy Knowles were commissioned to write a report on the status of homemakers in South Carolina—a key point since a primary goal of IWY leaders was ratification of the ERA and opponents in the state insisted ratification would cause South Carolina women to lose advantages, including dower rights peculiar to the state. The report indicated that South Carolina homemakers had more problems than privileges and concluded that "legislative attention to these problems is essential to correct the inequities that affect the lives of nearly all South Carolina women at some time."[75] And Eslinger was chosen to conduct the workshop on Equal Employment Opportunity Law at the South Carolina IWY meeting held in Columbia in June 1977.[76]

The IWY conferences were much resented by Schlafly and ERA opponents who denounced the IWY as a "federally funded festival for frustrated feminists."[77] As the South Carolina IWY meeting began, there was conflict between feminist organizers and socially conservative women that mirrored the struggle taking place at the national level. Conservative leaders urged their followers, many of them active in the opposition to the ERA, to attend the IWY state meetings in large numbers and challenge feminists for the right to speak for American women through the resolutions and delegates to be sent on to Houston. Some of the most vehement South Carolina opponents of the feminist movement, including state senator Norma Russell, George Ann Pennebaker, and Shirley Holcombe, and a number of men, including Oliver "Runt" Willis, attended and sought election as South Carolina delegates to the national conference. At the state IWY conference, unlike in the state legislature, feminists won the day: Russell was elected as one of the state's twenty-two delegates and Pennebaker, Holcombe, and Willis were elected as alternates, but the rest of the delegation consisted of women's rights supporters, including Keller Barron, Tootsie Holland, and Pat Callair.[78]

The National Women's Conference in Houston attracted international publicity: an array of celebrities and dignitaries attended, including former First Ladies Lady Bird Johnson and Betty Ford as well as the current First Lady, Rosalynn Carter, most of the nation's women elected officials, and official observers from all over the world. The predominantly feminist group of delegates adopted a "National Plan of Action" that made recommendations on a wide range of issues encapsulating most of the goals of the modern feminist movement and that, not surprisingly, endorsed ratification of the embattled ERA. Workshops, speeches, and discussions throughout the conference gave participants—including these South Carolina women—opportunities to make contacts, exchange information, and collect ideas to bring back to the state.[79] Tootsie Holland, interviewed in Houston, said she had made valuable contacts and learned much from the workshops that she could use back home.[80] When the IWY Commission produced a film, "A Simple Matter of Justice," to promote ERA, it chose to feature Keller Bumgardner along with three other women from unratified states and the actress Jean Stapleton, at that time playing Edith Bunker, the most famous housewife in America, on the hit television comedy *All in the Family*.[81]

As organizers had hoped, the IWY conference expanded the ranks and mobilized supporters of the women's rights movement. It also mobilized social conservatives: their highly organized campaign to block, gain control of, or protest the IWY conferences in combination with their earlier and ongoing campaigns against the ERA and the *Roe* decision galvanized conservative women and helped them convince many politicians across the nation and in South Carolina that it was more important to please them than the feminists. Schlafly insisted that the National Plan of Action, which had included planks supporting abortion rights and gay rights as well as the ERA, had sealed the fate of the proposed amendment. Across the nation conservatives redoubled their efforts to roll back many of the gains of the women's rights movement. In South Carolina, Senator Norma Russell renewed her criticism of the South Carolina Commission on Women and attempted to get it defunded using the state's "sunset law."[82] South Carolina feminists continued to support the ERA, which was introduced in the state legislature again and again without success until the amendment was officially defeated when the deadline for ratification came and went in 1982.

South Carolina women's rights leaders, including Eslinger, Barron, Heriot, Holland, and Callair, were keenly disappointed that all the time and effort they invested in the ERA had come to naught. Years later Tootsie Holland recalled heading to the beach with a friend and coworker to grieve over the defeat and cope, each in her own way, with their loss. "She cried and I cussed," said Holland.[83] Mary Heriot also remembered shedding tears over the defeat. "That failure to have women's equality affirmed in the Constitution," she said, suggested that the legislators did not "recognize you as a person." It was as if to say that "all men are created equal but that does not include women." She said that South Carolina feminists "never really regrouped after that. . . . Our chapter was so demoralized that we just disintegrated. I cannot begin to describe how we felt when the S.C. senate voted to table it. Maybe that was the worst day of my life."[84]

Looking back at the ERA campaign, Heriot wondered about its cost. "We believed in the ERA," she said, "but we did not anticipate that we would be working on it for such a long time." It meant that "all our other goals went on the back burner." And then, "after the ERA went down . . . we had absolutely nothing to show for all the hours and money spent on it." Holland resented the fact that even after it was clear there was little chance of ratification in South Carolina, national NOW leaders insisted that the ERA be their top priority. "The reason we worked on the ERA [in its last years] is because we were in the capital city and we had to. They made us." Still Heriot and the other South Carolina feminist leaders know that they "got a lot of things right" and accomplished a great deal.[85]

In the years South Carolina women's rights leaders worked for ERA, they were also busy advocating change in areas where their efforts were quite fruitful. Beginning with Eslinger's lawsuit—which put the state on notice that women in the state could and would sue successfully for their rights—South Carolina women did much to "raise the consciousness" of South Carolinians about women and their rights. They recognized from their own experiences, observation, and research, the areas in which changes were needed. And through national women's organizations they learned about laws and programs that had been tried and tested elsewhere. They also brought newly adopted federal laws to the attention of authorities in South Carolina and demanded that they be applied in their state.

Some of their most important achievements related to job discrimination and rape. As Mary Heriot had told the reporter back in 1972 and as she and Tootsie Holland later recalled, one of the South Carolina feminists' primary goals was to bring an end to the widespread discrimination against women in employment. This was where they invested most of their efforts as they began organizing, determined to "get equal rights in employment and to improve the financial status of women." They were aware, Heriot recalled, "of the civil rights act that had passed in 1964 and that we [women] were supposed to have equal rights under the law, but no one in South Carolina paid one bit of attention to it." The newspapers had stopped running separate ads for blacks and whites but continued to carry job ads posted by employment agencies that said "female help wanted." Into that category "all the junky jobs went," while the "male help wanted" listed all the professional jobs.[86]

Together with Margaret Young, president of the state WEAL, Holland confronted the editor of *The State* who, as they remembered it, more or less threw them out of his office.[87] So for the next two months, they gathered evidence. Holland recalled, "every Sunday we would meet, five or six of us, and cut all of the ads out of the newspapers and send them to the Equal Opportunity Office in Atlanta. They were breaking the law, so we sent these in." Soon representatives from the employment agencies that posted the ads invited Heriot and Holland to a dinner and pleaded their case. As Holland recalled, they said: "You know the newspaper makes us do this. We wouldn't break the law, you know, we just really wouldn't do that except that the newspaper makes us do it." In turn Heriot replied, "We have some perfectly wonderful young attorneys that would love to take your case and sue the newspapers for you." About two weeks later, said Heriot, the newspapers issued a statement that "they had gone to a new computer system and would no longer be using that [the gender-specific ads]. So, it wasn't us, of course, it was them" that brought about the changes.[88]

NOW soon joined the South Carolina Commission on Women and other women's organizations in supporting women teachers in Richland County in their campaign to get "equal pay for equal work." The local school district defended paying male teachers more than female teachers on the grounds that the men "had families to raise," ignoring equal pay laws. Holland later recalled that when they asked how single women with families or widows were expected to cope with the lower salaries, they were told "they'll get married, you know." NOW members wrote letters to the Justice Department, so many, said Holland, "that they sent some investigators and scared the school district half to death and they got all that straightened out in a big hurry."[89]

Columbia NOW's first major public confrontation came when they filed petitions with the FCC calling on it to deny renewal of licenses to ten Columbia-area television and radio stations. Their petition, filed November 1, 1972, charged that the stations collectively employed 205 persons and had only 49 women on their staffs, that of these, 41 were "subjected to dead-end, low-paying, traditionally 'female' office and clerical jobs," and that none of the stations employed women in managerial or technical capacities. Columbia feminists gathered this data; then lawyers from NOW's national office flew down, and working with local lawyers Carrington Salley and Pat Hartley, they drew up a formal petition to deny the licenses. Columbia NOW members filed it with the FCC and then unveiled it at a press conference. Holland recalls, "I had gotten a little booklet on how to hold a press conference" which "was a good thing because of course every radio and television station in the area was there." The stations immediately began negotiations. Station managers and their lawyers met with NOW members. As Holland recalled, "an unforgettable statement by one manager was, 'Do you women realize how much money you are costing us?' Needless to say they had no comprehension of the amount of money they had cost women by denying them the right to hold a decent job!" This, said Heriot, "was one of the most important things we did." Suddenly there seemed to be a lot more women in highly visible and better paying roles at these stations. And the Columbia case led the way for feminists in other states to bring about change by threatening "to do another 'Columbia.'" Eslinger, who had been involved in the challenge to their licensing, was then hired by local television and radio stations to give annual feedback on important community issues for a five-year period.[90]

The next year, 1973, NOW, WEAL, and the LWV held a press conference charging the state government with widespread sex discrimination. As the press reported, "Outspoken women representing three statewide women's groups" were particularly critical of Governor John West. They launched "verbal barbs" at him for recent statements saying he was "convinced that there was no sex discrimination in state government" despite a recent USC study of state employees' salary levels that showed that males earned an average of $7,139 a year to $3,771 for female workers and that half of the state employees were women but they received less that one third of the pay. The Columbia NOW chapter led by Vickie Eslinger, its legal advisor, then filed charges with the Equal Employment Opportunity Commission (EEOC) against Governor West and the state employment office for discrimination.[91] In addition, in 1977 Holland filed an individual suit against the personnel division of the state. Holland charged that in 1972 and 1974 she applied to the state government for a job in personnel and was told she met the qualifications but that the agency did not hire women for those particular jobs. When she protested the discriminatory treatment, she said, they "blackballed her." U.S. District Judge Matthew Perry ruled in her favor awarding damages and court costs.[92]

In addition, they invoked federal law in a challenge to the University of South Carolina, demanding compliance with Title IX of the Education Act of 1972, which required ending gender discrimination, including in the controversial area of collegiate athletics. NOW members, working with members of WEAL, an organization that attracted a number of women faculty, met with the USC Board of Trustees. Betty Mandell, a USC professor who was a member of both organizations, presented their case, citing statistics that showed neglect of women's sports. As a result, Holland claimed, an outstanding but underpaid "lady coach" got a sizable raise and "the girls got scholarships." Heriot recalled that they also met with the provost, charging that all students paid the same activities fees while women students got almost nothing for their fees. She debunked the argument being made currently by college football supporters who were furious about Title IX.[93] The feminists' demands that Title IX be enforced supported the efforts of those within the USC athletic program who were advocates for women's athletics. By 1976, four years after Title IX was adopted, USC was providing over $239,000 intended for the use of the female sports—a small fraction of what was spent on men but still progress.[94]

South Carolina women's rights advocates also confronted private businesses and championed individual women who came to them for help. In one instance a woman called to say she was being fired from Woolworth's because she was pregnant. As Holland recalled, when they met with the store manager who said "we don't want our customers to be looking at the woman," Pat Callair demanded that he pick up his phone and call his boss in Atlanta. "This was one of the things we learned to do is do research first so we knew where we were standing. Learn the law . . . before you go in. Learn who his boss is before you go in." The manager made the call with them listening, then gave the woman back her job, and with a raise.[95]

In such cases they employed the assertiveness training tactics learned from NOW. But at times these South Carolina women also employed what might be called a southern feminist version of a "good cop, bad cop routine"—confronting an errant manager with southern femininity and respectability but also a suggestion of radicalism and toughness. Holland recalled with amusement that on one occasion, during a confrontation with the manager of a Sears department store they were picketing, she and Pat Callair went together, with Tootsie wearing "a suit and little bitty heels" and assuming a conciliatory manner and Pat sporting an Afro and a NOW T-shirt and displaying a "kind of aggressive attitude," talking to him in "street language." "We had him coming and going."[96]

In addition to their successful campaign against employment discrimination, South Carolina feminists made major contributions during the 1970s by changing attitudes, laws, and policies concerning rape and by raising awareness about violence against women committed by men they knew—a problem then called "the battered woman" issue. Despite all of the talk about women of the state being protected, in reality violence against women was common. It was also common for people to joke about it and to blame women for inviting assault. In rape cases, the fact that the victims' own reputations suffered and their personal histories were often put on trial deterred many women who had been assaulted from pressing charges. It was difficult to secure convictions: Heriot and Holland recalled that they and other women were particularly distraught and moved to action after a woman pressing charges in a highly publicized rape case went out and shot herself when her assailant was acquitted.[97]

Again South Carolina feminists began by conducting research into rape laws in other states. They proposed new legislation based on Michigan law that included "degrees of rape" to replace the "all or nothing" law of South Carolina that made it so difficult to gain convictions and, they believed, gave assailants a powerful motive to kill their victims. They also proposed that the laws be framed in such a way as to protect male victims of rape. Eslinger, who chaired NOW task forces on rape, lent her legal skills to this effort. In 1974 she testified before the South Carolina legislature on pending legislation regarding rape and criminal sexual conduct.[98]

South Carolina feminists also called for reforming the way that authorities dealt with rape victims, believing that law enforcement officers were often insensitive and insufficiently aggressive about gathering evidence to support prosecution. At that time there was but one physician in Richland and Lexington counties charged with examining rape victims, and he was only available during daytime office hours. Armed with a list of questions from the national NOW office and notebooks to record what he said, a small group of women, including Heriot and Holland, met with the examiner to learn about his practices. He mentioned that he looked for signs of resistance, such as bruises. When one woman asked about detecting bruises on black women, they said he disgusted them by suggesting that African American women were oversexed and not likely to be victims. Holland recalled him saying: "'Now girls, write this down. I want to make real sure you get this right. You can't rape a black woman.' He didn't use the word 'black.'" They marched out; some of the women, including one who was a rape victim herself, were in tears. "That's how hard the meeting with this guy was," Holland said.[99] Heriot, Holland, and the other women present were too shocked to say much to him at the time but, Holland said, they "got him ousted" later.[100]

They also held rallies to draw public attention to these problems, demanding female investigators to handle rape cases and an end to the practice of charging victims for analysis of evidence.[101] They found that many police officers were receptive to their efforts to bring about improved methods of dealing with rape and rape victims. Heriot recalled that often the police had little or no training and did not understand the behavior of victims and were glad to have volunteers who had studied this and could help them. "We changed some things on that. I really think we did."[102] One of their most important achievements was the development of a "rape protocol" based on practices in other states and drawn up by one of the feminists, then a medical student, Mary Anne Sens. Sens secured a meeting with Governor Edwards, who agreed to sign off on it and send it to every hospital and gynecologist in the state.[103]

South Carolina feminists organized rallies and marches to raise awareness about rape in the state and to call for more protection of women. In one case, Mary Heriot led 150 women, including Tootsie's mother who was in a wheelchair, in a march to the statehouse. They carried signs that read "Rape No More," "Against Rape," and "Take Back the Night"—which became a major slogan of the women's movement as feminists realized that fear of assault was in itself a deterrent to women's equal participation in society.[104] On the USC campus, Vickie Eslinger and others pressed the university to provide escort services and better security. Also Holland recalled they ran an article in the USC *Gamecock* on how to protect yourself and what to do if you were raped. Inspired by Susan Brownmiller's book *Against Our Wills*, they tried to educate people that rape was a crime of violence, a political act reinforcing male dominance.[105]

While working to secure reforms, they took matters into their own hands and established "their own rape crisis center" at the bookstore and even took victims into their homes: they let it be known in the city that they were on call, ready and willing to help those in need.[106] In 1975 NOW, working with a number of other organizations, including the YWCA, the Junior League, and the state mental health commission, established the Columbia Rape Crisis Center. Tootsie Holland traveled throughout the state to help establish rape crisis centers and give advice wherever she was invited. Holland conducted sessions with officials at Fort Jackson, who bought the rape protocol manual they had developed for the state.[107]

These South Carolina feminists knew that one of the most important tasks was to educate women themselves. Even while still in law school Eslinger taught South Carolina women about their legal rights and how to seek redress of grievances by giving speeches to women's groups and civic clubs and conducting workshops sponsored by NOW. Women learned about criminal law, marriage law, job discrimination, class action suits, and EEOC guidelines. Together with her law partner, Lucy Knowles, Eslinger also conducted research that helped set the agenda for future reform efforts. In addition to coauthoring the 1976 study on the status of homemakers in South Carolina, in 1979, together with Knowles and Ann L. Furr, Eslinger was retained by the South Carolina Commission on Women to prepare a report entitled "Current South Carolina Laws and Procedures Which Are Sex Biased." The report identified problems regarding criminal law, marriage, separation and divorce, will and intestate succession, labor and employment, and other miscellaneous areas, in each case making recommendations for reforms with which the commission concurred.[108]

Thus the efforts of these South Carolina women brought much needed change to their state—and helped set the stage for more. And they have continued to work for women's rights and social justice.

Victoria Eslinger became one of the most outstanding lawyers in the state, indeed winning national recognition. In 1979 she moved to France, where she practiced law until returning to Columbia in 1983. While in France she married a theoretical physicist who later joined the faculty at USC. They have two daughters.[109] Eslinger entered private practice and continued to handle plaintiff discrimination suits and women's issues. With Ann Furr she founded the South Carolina Women's Law Association in 1991. She has been active in the community, serving on the board of numerous civic organizations, including Planned Parenthood and the South Carolina Campaign to Prevent Teen Pregnancy and as a deacon and elder in the Presbyterian Church. Since the late 1970s she has taught trial advocacy workshops to Harvard law students. Today she is a lawyer with one of the state's most prominent law firms, Nexsen Pruet, where she continues to handle labor and employment cases and business litigation. Fluent in French, Spanish, and Italian she handles international cases as well. Eslinger is a frequent lecturer at South Carolina Bar seminars. In 2004, the USC School of Law honored her with its Compleat Lawyer Platinum Award in recognition of her more than thirty years of practicing law. It is given to USC law graduates who have made "a significant contribution to the legal profession" and exemplify "the highest standard of professional competence, ethics, and integrity."[110]

Barron also went on to have a distinguished career. From February 1979 to her retirement in 1997 she worked as an employee of the state government where she was director of research for the Joint Legislative Committee on Aging in the South Carolina General Assembly. She has also continued to work through an array of organizations devoted to equal rights and social justice. She is still a devoted member of and leader in the LWV and has won many awards for distinguished service to the organization. She is an elder at Columbia's Eastminster Presbyterian Church USA. In 1982 she was awarded the Modjeska Simkins Prize

for Outstanding Work for Social Justice, Civil Rights, and Community Understanding. She was an officer in the Southern Regional Council and in 2004
was honored by selection as one of the organization's "life fellows"—an award
given to a select number of recipients who have worked for racial equality and
unity. Other recipients include Daisy Bates, Joseph Lowery, Benjamin Mays,
and Modjeska Simkins.[111]

Mary Heriot retired in 1985 and lives in Cayce, a Columbia suburb. She and
Tootsie Holland are active in efforts to encourage more women to run for public
office and in a reenergized NOW chapter in Columbia.[112] "We backed off" after
the ERA defeat, recalls Holland. However in recent years they have been working with a "lively group of young people . . . who are very interested in seeing
that NOW starts back." She and Heriot and other NOW veterans, she said, are "so
excited about these new 'kids on the block'" and predicted young women were
really going to need to be organized to defend rights that had been gained in
the 1970s.[113]

After the defeat of the ERA Callair left NOW and in the late 1980s created
an organization called the South Carolina Women's Consortium funded by a
Unitarian nonprofit organization. It was an attempt, she recalled, to keep the
women's movement going and to bring together women and bridge divisions
that had emerged between them. She received training and guidance from the
Grassroots Leadership organization in Charlotte, North Carolina. These efforts
reflected her view that she and other feminists had lost the ERA battle not just
because their opponents had "access to powerful ears" but because they had
failed to maximize their own strength by reaching out more to women who
were not part of their movement, responding to their fears and looking for
common ground. She also believes that in other respects she and her coworkers in the South Carolina women's movement accomplished a great deal and
that they made a great team, together accomplishing what no one could do by
themselves. In 1990, after Callair completed her last degree at USC, she left South
Carolina—the only one of the five who moved away from the state. Her goal
was to study therapy and have her own private practice. She currently lives in
Greensboro, North Carolina where she is executive director of the Leadership
and Empowerment Institute and works with at-risk children and teenagers as a
therapist.[114] She is also an instructor in the Africana Women's Studies Program
at Bennett College.

Clearly these champions of women's rights in 1970s South Carolina have
made a big difference. Their stories are for the most part success stories. Because of the failure to gain ratification of the ERA, many people—historians,
members of the public, even feminists themselves—sometimes fail to recognize

the many victories of the women's rights movement, without which our society would be quite different. South Carolina often lags behind other states on leading indicators of women's status, and many South Carolinians recognize that there are still important issues involving women's status that need improvement. But there has also been considerable progress for women, much of it owed to these five women and those who worked with them on behalf of women's rights in the 1970s. These women, together with many others whose stories need to be told, brought the benefits of the modern women's rights movement to South Carolina.

NOTES

1. I am grateful to these five women for their assistance in providing sources for this article and agreeing to numerous interviews, both with me and with my students in a series of undergraduate seminars on preserving the history of the women's movement in South Carolina. This essay reflects our collective efforts. Sources we have gathered are housed in the South Carolina Women's Rights Collection, South Carolina Political Collections, University of South Carolina Libraries, University of South Carolina, Columbia (hereinafter cited as SCWRC-SCPC). This collection includes oral histories with veterans of the state women's movement and tapes of their class visits (recorded and transcribed by the students) and most of the seminar papers. Other participants in events discussed in this essay who have assisted us with our research include Nancy Moore, Mary Baskin Waters, Constance Ashton Myers, Candy Waites, Marianna Davis, Malissa Barnett, Harriet Keyserling, Diane Moseley, Ellie Setser, Carole Tempel, Sheila Haney, Sarah Leverette, Jean Toal, Matthew Perry, Don Fowler, Sherry Shealy Martschink, and Zilla Hinton as well as USC archivists Herb Hartsook, Mark G. Cooper (director of the moving image research collections), and Nicholas Meriwether and history professor Kent Germany. This paper also benefits from the work of graduate students Laura Foxworth, Kyna Herzinger, Michele Coffey, and the late Johanna "Micki" Blakely.

2. Congress sent the proposed ERA to the states for ratification in March 1972. The ERA stated that "equality of rights under the law shall not be denied or abridged by the United States or any state on account of sex" and that "the Congress shall have the power to enforce by appropriate legislation the provisions of this article." It specified that the amendment would take effect two years after the date of ratification. For the ERA to become part of the U.S. Constitution it had to be ratified by thirty-eight state legislatures by 1979; the deadline was later extended to 1982. On the ERA, see Jane J. Mansbridge, *Why We Lost the ERA* (Chicago: University of Chicago Press, 1986), Donald Critchlow, *Phyllis Schlafly and Grassroots Conservatism: A Woman's Crusade* (Princeton, N.J.: Princeton University Press, 2005), Winifred Wandersee, *On the Move: American Women in the 1970s* (Boston: G. K. Hall, 1988), Sara Evans, *Tidal Wave: How Women Changed America at Century's End* (New York: Free Press, 2003). On another southern state, North Carolina, see Jane Sherron De Hart and Donald Mathews, *Sex, Gender, and the Politics of ERA: A State and the Nation* (New York: Oxford University Press, 1990).

3. On the changing status of women, see Susan M. Hartmann, *The Home Front and Beyond: American Women in the 1940s* (Boston: Twayne, 1982), Susan M. Hartmann, *From Margin to Mainstream: American Women and Politics since 1960* (New York: Knopf, 1989), William Chafe, *The Paradox of Change: American Women in the 20th Century* (New York: Oxford University Press, 1991), Gail Collins, *When Everything Changed* (New York: Penguin, 2008), Ruth Rosen, *The World Split*

Open: How the Modern Women's Movement Changed America (New York: Penguin, 2001), Evans, *Tidal Wave*, and Wandersee, *On the Move*.

4. Victoria L. Eslinger and Lucy M. Knowles, *The Legal Status of Homemakers in South Carolina* (Washington, D.C.: Center for Women Policy Studies, 1977), 28, 29.

5. Critchlow, *Phyllis Schlafly and Grassroots Conservatism*; Marjorie J. Spruill, "Gender and America's Right Turn: The 1977 IWY Conferences and the Polarization of American Politics," in *Rightward Bound: Making America Conservative in the 1970s*, ed. Bruce Schulman and Julian Zelizer (Cambridge, Mass.: Harvard University Press, 2008), 71–89; Carol Felsenthal, *Sweetheart of the Silent Majority: The Biography of Phyllis Schlafly* (Garden City, N.Y.: Doubleday, 1981); Jean Hardesty, *Mobilizing Resentment: Conservative Resurgence from the John Birch Society to the Promise Keepers* (Boston: Beacon, 1999).

6. Mary Heriot to Marjorie Spruill, October 13, 2008; Ellie Setser, Nancy Moore, and Carol Tempel, class visit with Marjorie Spruill's senior seminar, April 5, 2010, transcribed by Elizabeth Layne, SCWRC-SCPC.

7. Marjorie Spruill Wheeler, *New Women of the New South: The Leaders of the Woman Suffrage Movement in the Southern States* (New York: Oxford University Press, 1993).

8. Spruill Wheeler, *New Women of the New South*, 180–181. On the suffrage movement in South Carolina, see James O. Farmer Jr., "Eulalie Salley and Emma Dunovant: A Complementary Pair of Suffragists," in *South Carolina Women: Their Lives and Times*, vol. 2, ed. Marjorie Julian Spruill, Valinda Littlefield, and Joan Marie Johnson (Athens: University of Georgia Press, 2010), 144–65, and Amy Thompson McCandless, "Anita Pollitzer: A South Carolina Advocate for Equal Rights," in *South Carolina Women: Their Lives and Times*, vol. 2, 166–89.

9. Keller Henderson Bumgardner Barron and Eunice "Tootsie" Holland, class visit with Marjorie Spruill's senior seminar, September 2007, transcribed by Alexandra Chapman, SCWRC-SCPC; Annie Boiter-Jolley, "Change from Within: Victoria Eslinger and the South Carolina Women's Movement," December 2007, SCWRC-SCPC.

10. Victoria Eslinger, interview by Annie Boiter-Jolley, Columbia, S.C., November 16, 2007, SCWRC-SCPC; Jean Hoefer Toal, interview by Brooke Mulenex, Columbia, S.C., April 9, 2008, SCWRC-SCPC; Brooke Mulenex, "*Eslinger v. Thomas* and the Triumph in the Courts for Women's Rights," April 2008, SCWRC-SCPC; Ruth Williams Cupp, *Portia Steps Up to the Bar: The First Women Lawyers of South Carolina* (Raleigh, N.C.: Ivy House, 2003), 154, 186–88.

11. Boiter-Jolley, "Change from Within," SCWRC-SCPC; Eslinger, interview by Boiter-Jolley, November 16, 2007, SCWRC-SCPC; Mulenex, "*Eslinger v. Thomas*," SCWRC-SCPC; Toal, interview by Mulenex, April 9, 2008, SCWRC-SCPC; Victoria Eslinger, class visit with Marjorie Spruill's senior seminar, February 8, 2010, transcribed by Tessa Johnson, SCWRC-SCPC.

12. "Page Aspirant Gets Apology," *The State*, April 2, 1971; Toal, interview by Mulenex, April 9, 2008, SCWRC-SCPC; Victoria Eslinger, interview by Brooke Mulenex, March 24, 2008, SCWRC-SCPC.

13. Eslinger, interview by Boiter-Jolley, November 16, 2007, SCWRC-SCPC. Regarding the statute, see Victoria L. Eslinger, Lucy M. Knowles, and Ann L. Furr, *Current South Carolina Laws and Procedures Which Are Sex Biased: A Report for the South Carolina Commission on Women* (Columbia, S.C.: Commission on Women, 1979), 28.

14. Nancy Moore to Marjorie Spruill, April 14, 2009.

15. Boiter-Jolley, "Change from Within," SCWRC-SCPC; Eslinger, interview by Boiter-Jolley, November 16, 2007, SCWRC-SCPC; Mulenex, "*Eslinger v. Thomas*"; Eslinger, interview by Mulenex, March 24, 2008, SCWRC-SCPC; Victoria Eslinger, class visit, February 8, 2010, SCWRC-SCPC.

16. Eslinger, interview by Boiter-Jolley, November 16, 2007, SCWRC-SCPC; Eslinger, interview by

Mulenex, March 24, 2008, SCWRC-SCPC; Eslinger, class visit, February 8, 2010. On the founding of USC's Women's Studies Program, see USC Productions, "A Cup Half Full," 1993, transcribed by Jason Furtick, 2008, SCWRC-SCPC. The original film is in the library of the Women's and Gender Studies Program, USC, Columbia. See also Tifani Gonzalez, "Carolina Women: A Force to Be Reckoned With," April 28, 2008, SCWRC-SCPC.

17. "Nice Girls Are Victims Too" and "Women Wanting Abortions," clippings, n.d., Victoria L. Eslinger Collection, SCPC (hereinafter cited as VEC-SCPC); "Hotline: A Service For Abortion and Health Information," *The State*, April 14, 1978; Cupp, *Portia Steps Up to the Bar*, 187; Eslinger, interview by Boiter-Jolley, November 16, 2007, SCWRC-SCPC.

18. Biographical data sent by Victoria Eslinger to Marjorie Spruill, February 2010; Eslinger, class visit, February 8, 2010, SCWRC-SCPC; Boiter-Jolley, "Change from Within," SCWRC-SCPC; Eslinger, interview by Boiter-Jolley, November 16, 2007, SCWRC-SCPC.

19. "Women's Rights," editorial, *USC Gamecock*, March 15, 1972, VEC-SCPC; Harry L. Walker, "Presidential Comment," clipping, *USC Gamecock*, n.d. (c. 1971–72), VEC-SCPC; biographical data sent by Eslinger to Spruill, February 2010; Boiter-Jolley, "Change from Within," SCWRC-SCPC; Eslinger, interview by Boiter-Jolley, November 16, 2007, SCWRC-SCPC.

20. Eslinger, class visit, February 8, 2010, SCWRC-SCPC; Tessa Johnson, "Rape and Reproductive Rights Reform and the South Carolinian Women's Rights Movement," spring 2010, SCWRC-SCPC. On the division among South Carolina feminists with respect to abortion, see Setser, Moore, and Tempel, class visit, April 5, 2010, SCWRC-SCPC.

21. Biographical data sent by Eslinger to Spruill, February 2010; Boiter-Jolley, "Change from Within," SCWRC-SCPC; Eslinger, interview by Boiter-Jolley, November 16, 2007, SCWRC-SCPC.

22. Elias Petersen, "'Everything, in the End, Is Political': Victoria Eslinger and the Story of the 1972 Democratic Convention and the Feminist Challenge to the South Carolina Delegation," April 2008, SCWRC-SCPC; Eslinger, interview by Elias Peterson, April 21, 2008, SCWRC-SCPC; "In the Matter of the Challenge of the South Carolina Delegations," record of a hearing conducted on June 6, 1972, in Columbia, S.C., VEC-SCPC; Barbara Sylvester, qtd. in "South Carolina Women Embarrassed by Challenge," *The State*, July 11, 1972, A-10.

23. Felsenthal, *Sweetheart of the Silent Majority*; Mansbridge, *Why We Lost the ERA*; Keller Henderson Bumgardner Barron, class visit with Marjorie Spruill's senior seminar, April 9, 2008, transcribed by Bellamy Wenum, SCWRC-SCPC; Keller Henderson Bumgardner Barron, interview by Johanna "Micki" Blakely, Columbia, S.C., 2007, transcribed by Sheila M. Haney, 2009, SCWRC-SCPC.

24. Barron and Holland, class visit, September 2007, SCWRC-SCPC; Keller Barron, interview by Marvin Ira Lare, December 9, 2004, transcript, South Caroliniana Library, University of South Carolina, Columbia (hereinafter cited as SCL).

25. Her children are Sherrod Lewis Bumgardner Jr., George Keller Bumgardner, Margaret Anne Bumgardner DuBose, and Charles Gaither Bumgardner. She married William Brown Barron in 1984.

26. Mary L. Bryan, *Proud Heritage: A History of the League of Women Voters of South Carolina, 1920–1976* (Columbia: S.C.: R. L. Bryan, 1977); biographical data sent by Keller Barron to Marjorie Spruill, spring 2009.

27. Barron, interview by Lare, December 9, 2004, SCL.

28. Barron, interview by Lare, December 9, 2004, SCL; Barron, interview by Blakely, 2007, SCWRC-SCPC. On Ethel Bolden, see the essay by Georgette Mayo in this volume, 154–78.

29. Keller Barron, interview by Marjorie J. Spruill, Columbia, S.C., June 26, 2006, SCWRC-SCPC; Barron and Holland, class visit, September 2007, SCWRC-SCPC.

30. Barron, class visit, April 9, 2008, SCWRC-SCPC.

31. Barron, class visit, April 9, 2008, SCWRC-SCPC; L. Marion Gressette Papers, c. 1920–1984, box 3, SCPC (hereinafter cited as LMGP-SCPC).

32. Spruill, "Gender and America's Right Turn." See pamphlets opposing ERA in Theresa M. Hicks Papers, 1965–2005, SCL (hereinafter cited as TMHP-SCL).

33. For accounts of South Carolina conservatives organizing against the ERA and feminism, see TMHP-SCL, LMGP-SCPC, and Irene Neuffer Papers, 1973–83, SCL (hereinafter cited as INP-SCL).

34. TMHP-SCL; "Anti-ERA Lawsuit Is Ordered to Trial," *The State*, October 28, 1975. On the SCCW, see Meghan McMahon, "The South Carolina Commission on Women: Its Struggles, Efforts, Victories, and Future," December 11, 2007, SCWRC-SCPC; Mary Baskin Waters, interview by Meghan McMahon, Columbia, S.C., November 30, 2007, SCWRC-SCPC, Mary Baskin Waters Collection, SCPC, and Marjorie J. Spruill, "The Conservative Challenge to Feminist Influence on State Commissions on the Status of Women," in *Women and Social Movements of the United States, 1600–2000*, scholar's ed., ed. Kathryn Kish Sklar and Thomas Dublin (Alexandria, Va.: Alexander Street Press, 2009).

35. Organizers of the first meeting also included Bob Slimp, Merlin Fish, Gladys Swindler, and Tresi Powers (STOP-ERA organizational meeting), March 2, 1975, TMHP-SCL.

36. Don Evans, "Dark Clouds Forming: Opponents of the Equal Rights Amendment in South Carolina," April 23, 2008, SCWRC-SCPC; Brandi Horn, "Irene Neuffer," fall 2007, SCWRC-SCPC; *Charlotte Observer*, clipping, n.d., INP-SCL.

37. Douglas Mauldin, "Opponents of ERA Resort to Culinary Art for Cause," *The State*, February 17, 1977; *The State*, March 20, 1977; UPI, "Sen. Gressette Accused of ERA Defeat," *The State*, February 20, 1978; Howard Brutsch, "South Carolina: The Rejection of the ERA," spring 2008, SCWRC-SCPC.

38. Freeman Belser, "Gressette, Lawrence Marion," in *The South Carolina Encyclopedia*, ed. Walter Edgar (Columbia, S.C.: University of South Carolina Press, 2006), 406; Evans, "Dark Clouds Forming," SCWRC-SCPC. On Florence Gressette, see Barron and Holland, class visit, September, 2007, SCWRC-SCPC, Elizabeth Layne, "South Carolina Ladies against the ERA," spring 2010, SCWRC-SCPC, and Barron, interview by Blakely, 2007, SCWRC-SCPC.

39. Layne, "South Carolina Ladies against the ERA," SCWRC-SCPC.

40. *The State*, January 28, 1980; Evans, "Dark Clouds Forming," SCWRC-SCPC; Brad Jovanelly, "South Carolina's Social and Political Hindrances to the ERA," spring 2010, SCWRC-SCPC.

41. Barron, class visit, April 9, 2008, SCWRC-SCPC. Barron was reviewing their strategy as depicted in "The Victory Book," published by the South Carolina Coalition for the ERA in 1974 (South Carolina Coalition for the ERA Papers, 1963–78, SCPC).

42. Barron, interview by Blakely, 2007, SCWRC-SCPC; Bryan, *Proud Heritage*, 77, 78; Barron and Holland, class visit, September 2007, SCWRC-SCPC. On Judy Bumgardner, see TMHP-SCL.

43. Barron, class visit, April 9, 2008, SCWRC-SCPC.

44. Bellamy Wenum, "Dueling Perspectives: The Battle Over the Equal Rights Amendment in South Carolina, 1972–1983," spring 2008, SCWRC-SCPC.

45. Ibid.

46. Jan Stucker, "Stage Set for Round Three in S.C. Battle over ERA," *Columbia Record*, March 1975, B-1; Douglas Mauldin, "ERA Proponents Are Hopeful despite Setbacks," *The State*, March 12, 1975, B-3; *The State*, March 27, 1975 A-1; Jan Stucker, "Toal Considering ERA Alternative," *Columbia Record*, March 27, 1975; "ERA Dies," editorial, *Columbia Record*, March 28, 1975.

47. Barron and Holland, class visit, September 2007, SCWRC-SCPC.

48. Biographical data sent by Barron to Spruill, spring 2009.

49. Barron and Holland, class visit, September 2007, SCWRC-SCPC; Barron, class visit, April 9, 2008, SCWRC-SCPC.

50. Mary Heriot to Marjorie Spruill, October 13, 2008, Henry Green Heriot obituary enclosed; Priscilla Lara, "Herstory: The Beginnings of the Columbia Chapter of NOW," December 2007, SCWRC-SCPC.

51. Mary Heriot was born in Oil City, Pennsylvania. She received a bachelor of arts, a master's, and an RN degree. She served for thirty months in the South Pacific theater (Australia, New Guinea, and Philippine Islands). She has three children, twins Geoffrey Heriot and Gail Heriot Silverman and son Kirk Heriot. For Heriot's personal life, see Mary Heriot and Tootsie Holland, class visit with Marjorie Spruill's senior seminar, March 26, 2008, transcribed by Seamus Welch, SCWRC-SCPC.

52. Karen Burchstead, "Women to Meet to Organize NOW," USC Gamecock, February 21, 1972; "Women's Rights Group Formed: Columbia Chapter of NOW," The State, February 18, 1972; Vickie Eslinger and Mary R. Heriot, "Dear Ms.," February 21, 1972, SCWRC-SCPC; Heriot and Holland, class visit, March 26, 2008, SCWRC-SCPC.

53. Eslinger and Heriot, "Dear Ms.," SCWRC-SCPC.

54. Burchstead, "Women to Meet to Organize NOW"; "Women's Rights Group Formed."

55. Heriot and Holland, class visit, March 26, 2008, SCWRC-SCPC; Heriot to Spruill, October 13, 2008.

56. Heriot and Holland, class visit, March 26, 2008, SCWRC-SCPC.

57. Ibid.; Heriot to Spruill, October 13, 2008.

58. Barron and Holland, class visit, September 2007, SCWRC-SCPC.

59. Ibid.; Heriot and Holland, class visit, March 26, 2008, SCWRC-SCPC; Lara, "Herstory," SCWRC-SCPC.

60. Barron and Holland, class visit, September 2007, SCWRC-SCPC; Heriot and Holland, class visit, March 26, 2008, SCWRC-SCPC; Tootsie Holland to Marjorie Spruill, January 2011.

61. Barron and Heriot, class visit, September 2007, SCWRC-SCPC; Diane Moseley, class visit with Marjorie Spruill's senior seminar, March 22, 2010, transcribed by Shannon Brandon, SCWRC-SCPC.

62. Heriot and Holland, class visit, March 26, 2008, SCWRC-SCPC.

63. Ibid.; "Scenes at the ERA Hearing," The State, March 23, 1977, C-1.

64. Heriot and Holland, class visit, March 26, 2008, SCWRC-SCPC.

65. Lutricia B. "Pat" Callair, telephone interview by Oliver Francis, summer 2008, SCWRC-SCPC; Lutricia B. "Pat" Callair, telephone interview by Marjorie Spruill, May 30, 2009, SCWRC-SCPC; Heriot and Holland, class visit, March 26, 2008, SCWRC-SCPC. The Spartanburg meeting was at the home of NOW leader Anne Hicks. This was the first NOW chapter in South Carolina.

66. Callair, interview by Francis, summer 2008, SCWRC-SCPC; Heriot and Holland class visit, March 26, 2008, SCWRC-SCPC.

67. Callair, interview by Spruill, May 30, 2009, SCWRC-SCPC.

68. Callair, interview by Francis, summer 2008, SCWRC-SCPC.

69. "The ERA and the Black Community," Nancy P. Moore Collection, SCPC.

70. Callair, interview by Spruill, May 30, 2009. A recording of Callair's debate with Schlafly is available in the South Carolina Coalition for the ERA Papers, SCPC.

71. "NOW Member Calls for a Change in S.C. Rape Laws and Attitudes," Greenwood Index-Journal, April 28, 1976, 6. The bookstore and law office were located at 1210 Pickens Street, Columbia.

72. Heriot and Holland, class visit, March 26, 2008, SCWRC-SCPC. Eslinger worked for the local Legal Aid office from 1973 to 1975; she then founded an all-women law firm with Lucy Knowles, which Ann Furr later joined, that handled many suits related to race, age, and sex discrimination.

She was a board member for the National Conference on Women and the Law from 1973 to 1978, served as the South Carolina representative to the Young Lawyers Division of ABA from 1976 to 1979, and was chair of the YLD Equal Opportunity committee. In 1974 she was featured in a bar magazine as one of the most outstanding young women attorneys in the United States (biographical data sent by Eslinger to Spruill, February 2010).

73. Spruill, "Gender and America's Right Turn"; Caroline Bird et al., *The Spirit of Houston, the First National Women's Conference: An Official Report to the President, the Congress, and People of the United States* (Washington, D.C.: Government Printing Office, 1978).

74. Candy Waites, class visit with Marjorie Spruill's senior seminar, March 29, 2010, transcribed by Ashton Parrish, SCWRC-SCPC.

75. Eslinger and Knowles, "*The Legal Status of Homemakers in South Carolina*"; Setser, Moore, and Tempel, class visit, April 5, 2010, SCWRC-SCPC. On opponents and dower rights, see Layne, "South Carolina Ladies against the ERA," SCWRC-SCPC.

76. Boiter-Jolley, "Change from Within," SCWRC-SCPC; Lessie M. Reynolds and Maryneal Jones, *The South Carolina Woman: Heritage to Horizons* (Columbia, S.C.: South Carolina International Women's Year Committee, 1977).

77. Spruill, "Gender and America's Right Turn."

78. Reynolds and Jones, *The South Carolina Woman*. On the conservatives, see Layne, "South Carolina Ladies against the ERA," SCWRC-SCPC, LMGP-SCPC, and TMHP-SCL.

79. Bird et al., *The Spirit of Houston, the First National Women's Conference.*

80. Eunice "Tootsie" Holland, interview by Constance Ashton Myers, Houston, Tex., November 1977, Constance Ashton Myers Collection, SCL.

81. National Commission on the Observance of International Women's Year, "A Simple Matter of Justice," 1977, SCWRC-SCPC; Barron, interview by Spruill, June 26, 2006, SCWRC-SCPC.

82. Spruill, "The Conservative Challenge to Feminist Influence on State Commissions on the Status of Women"; clipping, Papers of the South Carolina Commission on Women, South Carolina Department of Archives and History, Columbia, S.C.

83. Barron and Holland, class visit, September 2007, SCWRC-SCPC.

84. Heriot and Holland, class visit, March 26, 2008, SCWRC-SCPC.

85. Heriot to Spruill, October 13, 2008; Heriot and Holland, class visit, March 26, 2008, SCWRC-SCPC.

86. Heriot and Holland, class visit, March 26, 2008, SCWRC-SCPC.

87. Mary Heriot and Tootsie Holland, "It Changed Our Lives," speech, 2000, SCWRC-SCPC; Lara, "Herstory," SCWRC-SCPC.

88. Heriot and Holland, class visit, March 26, 2008, SCWRC-SCPC; "Announcement," *The State*, August 27, 1973.

89. McMahon, "The South Carolina Commission on Women"; Heriot and Holland, class visit, March 26, 2008, SCWRC-SCPC.

90. Barron and Holland, class visit, September 2007, SCWRC-SCPC; Heriot and Holland, class visit, March 26, 2008, SCWRC-SCPC; clipping, Tootsie Holland scrapbook, SCWRC-SCPC; biographical data sent by Eslinger to Spruill, February 2010.

91. "Sex Bias Charged in Hiring by State," *Charleston News and Courier*, January 12, 1973; "Women Demand Amendment OK," clipping, Tootsie Holland scrapbook, SCWRC-SCPC; Pat Berman, "NOW Files Bias Charges against West," *The State*, September 15, 1973.

92. Heriot and Holland, class visit, March 26, 2008, SCWRC-SCPC; Anne Marshall, "Woman Wins $5,000 in Suit Against State Agency," clipping, n.d., *The State*, SCWRC-SCPC.

93. Heriot and Holland, class visit, March 26, 2008, SCWRC-SCPC.

94. Jason Furtick, "The Struggle and Strides of Women at the University of South Carolina," April 30, 2008, SCWRC-SCPC; *USC Gamecock*, February 10, 1967; Sally Wilson, "Women Athletes Benefit from Scholarships," *USC Gamecock*, September 13, 1976; Sally Wilson, "Former Women's Coaches Criticize Program, *USC Gamecock*, November 22, 1976.

95. Barron and Holland, class visit, September 2007, SCWRC-SCPC; Heriot and Holland, class visit, March 26, 2008, SCWRC-SCPC.

96. Heriot and Holland, class visit, March 26, 2008, SCWRC-SCPC.

97. Barron and Holland, class visit, September 2007, SCWRC-SCPC; Heriot and Holland, class visit, March 26, 2008, SCWRC-SCPC.

98. Heriot and Holland, class visit, March 26, 2008, SCWRC-SCPC; clipping, Tootsie Holland scrapbook, SCWRC-SCPC; Eslinger, class visit, February 8, 2010, SCWRC-SCPC; Johnson, "Rape and Reproductive Rights Reform and the South Carolinian Women's Rights Movement," SCWRC-SCPC; biographical data sent by Eslinger to Spruill, February 2010.

99. Heriot and Holland, class visit, March 26, 2008, SCWRC-SCPC; Lara, "Herstory," SCWRC-SCPC.

100. Heriot and Holland, class visit, March 26, 2008, SCWRC-SCPC.

101. Lara, "Herstory," SCWRC-SCPC; clipping, Tootsie Holland scrapbook, SCWRC-SCPC.

102. Heriot and Holland, class visit, March 26, 2008, SCWRC-SCPC; Heriot and Holland, class visit, February 15, 2010, SCWRC-SCPC.

103. Heriot and Holland, class visit, March 26, 2008, SCWRC-SCPC; Heriot and Holland, class visit, February 15, 2010, SCWRC-SCPC.

104. Johnson, "Rape and Reproductive Rights Reform and the South Carolinian Women's Rights Movement," SCWRC-SCPC; Jackie Brooks, "NOW Rallies Against Rape," clipping, n.d., Tootsie Holland scrapbook, SCWRC-SCPC.

105. Eslinger, interview by Boiter-Jolley, November 16, 2007, SCWRC-SCPC; Lara, "Herstory," SCWRC-SCPC.

106. Barron and Holland, class visit, September 2007, SCWRC-SCPC; Heriot and Holland, class visit, February 15, 2010, SCWRC-SCPC.

107. Heriot and Holland, class visit, March 26, 2008, SCWRC-SCPC.

108. Eslinger, Knowles, and Furr, *Current South Carolina Laws and Procedures Which Are Sex Biased.*

109. Vickie Eslinger and Richard Creswick have two daughters, Caitlin and Alexandra Creswick. Biographical data sent by Eslinger to Spruill, February 2010.

110. Biographical data sent by Eslinger to Spruill, February 2010; Nexsen Pruet website, http://www.spoke.com/info/p7PRyOu/VictoriaEslinger (accessed May 29, 2009).

111. Biographical data sent by Barron to Spruill, spring 2009; Chuck Burris, executive director, Southern Regional Council, to Keller Barron, December 7, 2004, SCWRC-SCPC.

112. Heriot and Holland, class visit, March 26, 2008, SCWRC-SCPC.

113. Barron and Holland, class visit, September 2007, SCWRC-SCPC.

114. Callair, interview by Spruill, May 30, 2009, SCWRC-SCPC; Callair, interview by Francis, summer 2008, SCWRC-SCPC.

Jean Hoefer Toal

The Rise of Women in the Legal Profession

W. LEWIS BURKE AND BAKARI T. SELLERS

On January 28, 1988, an "IT'S A GIRL" sign appeared on one of the ornate granite columns of the Supreme Court building in Columbia, South Carolina. The banner, festooned with pink ribbon, announced the arrival of the first woman on the Supreme Court of South Carolina—Jean Hoefer Toal (1943–)—destined to become the court's first female chief justice as well.[1] On that same day Carol Connor achieved another South Carolina first when she was elected the state's first female circuit judge. The newspapers were full of stories and images of the triumphant Toal. There was one photo of Toal and Connor celebrating together on the balcony of the state house of representatives.[2]

This day of triumph for women lawyers in South Carolina came after considerable striving. The story of Jean Hoefer Toal's election to the supreme court and her later ascension as its first female chief justice includes many elements of the classic American saga of individuals overcoming great obstacles to achieve great things. Her great-grandparents were part of the nineteenth-century European migration to America. The Civil War would be the direct cause of one of her ancestors moving to the state. These and other factors are critical components of her story. But the long, interrelated history of the struggle for civil rights for women and African Americans in the nation and the state provides the main historical narrative within which the arrival of this "girl" on South Carolina's high court is best understood. Only after these two movements brought considerable change to the United States and to South Carolina was Toal's achievement possible.

Jean Toal's climb to the chief justice's chair is remarkable when one considers how restricted women's rights had been in South Carolina throughout much of

JEAN HOEFER TOAL
Photo by Erik Campos. Courtesy of the
South Carolina Judicial Department.

its history. Obviously white women enjoyed many rights and privileges in sharp contrast to African American women in a slave state, yet, in the nineteenth century, white women had limited property rights and essentially no "political" rights. After Reconstruction-era amendments ended slavery and granted black men full rights of citizenship including the right to vote, women—white and black—remained unequal in the eyes of the law and could neither vote nor run for office nor enter contracts, become lawyers or serve on juries.[3]

The twentieth century would bring change, however. The woman suffrage movement was on the rise across the country and had support among South Carolina women, even though it faced its greatest obstacles in the South. African American men were simultaneously experiencing a dramatic decline in their rights. In South Carolina African American men's right to the vote had been wrested away by 1900 through a combination of lying, cheating, stealing, and murder, much of it justified by the perpetrators as necessary for the protection of white women against black male presumption.[4]

The white male leadership's response to woman suffrage reveals this complex relationship between the rights of women and African Americans. Congress had approved the Nineteenth Amendment granting women the right to vote on June 4, 1919, and sent it to the states for ratification, but the South Carolina General Assembly refused to approve it.[5] Many argued that a vote for ratification of the Nineteenth Amendment would have signified approval of the Fifteenth Amendment and the right of the federal government to determine voting rights within the states. On March 7, 1921, nearly seven months after the amendment was ratified by the required number of states, the South Carolina legislature begrudgingly enacted a statute granting women the right to vote in the state.[6] While the right to vote theoretically applied to all women, the Nineteenth Amendment's promise proved to be just as false for black women in South Carolina as the Fifteenth Amendment's had been for black men. When the NAACP organized a group of well-educated black women to register to vote in the state's capital city in 1920, virtually all of them were prevented from doing so and humiliated in the process.[7]

Even for white women, the Nineteenth Amendment did not mean equality before the law. The all-white, all-male legislature of South Carolina immediately exempted women from jury service—making it clear that the federally imposed change in women's status was limited to the vote.[8] When this exemption was challenged in court, the state supreme court drew an analogy between the constitutional rights of women and blacks. The court reasoned that "it has been repeatedly held by the Supreme Court of the United States that the 15th amendment does not confer upon colored men the right of suffrage; it only forbids discrimination."⁹ Therefore, citing the U.S. Supreme Court's decision in *U.S. v. Reese*, the Supreme Court of South Carolina held that the Nineteenth Amendment did not confer on women the right to serve on juries.¹⁰ Consequently, an exemption became a prohibition. South Carolina women did not obtain the right to serve on juries until 1967, two years after passage of the 1965 Voting Rights Act by the U.S. Congress, the legislation that finally assured African Americans the franchise in the South.¹¹

Clearly, the progress of women and African Americans in South Carolina law and politics was related, but their trajectories did not proceed in tandem. Although the majority of African American men were disfranchised, as the twentieth century began one lone black man still sat in the South Carolina legislature, whereas no woman had ever served there.¹² During the first decade of the new century, black lawyers were active in the state; there were over a hundred African American men admitted to the state's bar before the first woman, Miss James Perry, was admitted in 1918.¹³ A black woman, Cassandra E. Maxwell, did not overcome the double handicap until 1940, by which time the number of black male lawyers was beginning to recover from a decline in the 1930s.¹⁴ Furthermore, the state had had a black supreme court justice nearly fifty years before the first woman was admitted to the bar. Jonathan Jasper Wright became the first African American to serve on any state supreme court in the nation's history when he was elected by the South Carolina General Assembly in 1870. A second African American man was elected to the court in 1985.¹⁵ Toal was a candidate in that contest in 1985 but chose to withdraw, allowing Ernest A. Finney to be elected without opposition and become the second African American to sit on the court. While it was quite an anomaly for a white woman to run against a black man for the court, the contest and Toal's withdrawal were indicative of progress in the state, Toal's dedication to civil rights, and her political acumen.

Who was this extraordinary woman? Jean Hoefer was born on August 11, 1943, to Lilla Farrell and Herbert Wellington Hoefer. Her mother was from Atlanta, the daughter of James Edward Farrell, an Irishman who had moved from Boston in the 1920s to start a plumbing business. Herbert Hoefer was born in Columbia, South Carolina. His father Frederick was the child of German immigrants. In fact, Jean Toal's great-grandmother had been born on a ship en route to the United States from Germany in the middle of the nineteenth century. Her great-grandfather Hoefer had arrived in Charleston and worked first as a cobbler before moving to Columbia.¹⁶ Her great-grandfather Frederick Schmidt had come to the country from Germany during the Civil War as a hired substitute for an Ohio man who did not want to be drafted. Schmidt moved to Columbia with the Union army units that occupied the city after the Civil War.[17]

Establishing themselves in Columbia, these families became solid members of the middle class. Frederick Schmidt served on the city council in the late 1890s. Toal's grandfather, Frederick Hoefer, was the manager of a cottonseed oil company and a member of the Columbia City Council.[18] Her father graduated from Clemson College with a degree in engineering and subsequently obtained a master's degree from Cornell. Eventually he would own a sand quarry and continue in the family tradition of being successful in business. Jean's mother was a stay-at-home wife and mother. The family lived in Heathwood, one of the city's more prestigious neighborhoods, and attended St. Joseph's Catholic Church where Jean sang in the choir.[19]

Jean was the oldest of five children. She graduated from the neighborhood high school, Dreher, in 1961. Among family and friends, Jean was known for her talent and toughness. Her sister recalled in an interview in January 1988 that "when it came time to choose sides for teams, the boys demanded that it would take two girls to equal a boy—except for Jean."[20] This ability to command respect, together with her family's values, would play a role in producing a chief justice of South Carolina.

Born during the height of World War II and at the commencement of the modern civil rights movement, Jean Hoefer Toal grew up in a world in transition. During the war, the United States struggled with multiple identities. One identity was a united nation drawn together by idealism and patriotism to defeat the horrors of fascism. Another more shameful aspect of America's identity was the hypocrisy and racism of Jim Crow. The eyes of many were opened as African Americans soldiers were asked to spread "democracy" in Europe while facing oppression and degradation at home. Southern black soldiers saw racism in a new light. One of Jean Toal's heroes, Matthew J. Perry Jr., had a life-changing experience traveling on an army troop train when it stopped in Alabama. As he recalled, he was hungry but was not allowed in the terminal restaurant because of his race. "I and other blacks had to go to a window outside the kitchen. . . . This was nothing strange; I had done this before. I am in uniform, I am in *uniform*. I am a United States soldier. I could look through [the window] and here seated inside . . . [are] these Italian prisoners of war. And of course, the young waitresses were smiling and literally flirting. . . . You have no idea of the feeling of insult that I experienced."[21] Perry returned to South Carolina, attended law school, and became the leading civil rights lawyer in the state's history. Civilian groups also reacted to racism. The NAACP organized on a statewide basis and launched one of its first campaigns: "Double Victory—Democracy at Home

and Abroad."[22] Before the end of the war, the civil rights organization had its
first legal victory in the state when it won a teacher pay equalization case for
black teachers.[23]

Women were also responding to a changing world. Encouraged by a society
and government that was desperate for their labor as men left for war, many
women assumed traditional male roles. Best known of these were the "Rosie the
Riveters" who worked in the defense industries, including Charleston's naval
yard, and enjoyed good wages and a new sense of their own abilities. The legal
profession also saw changes. At least twenty women attended the University of
South Carolina School of Law during the war, and sixteen ultimately became
members of the state's bar. One female graduate of the law school has said that
the enrollment of the women students kept the doors of the law school open
during the war.[24] While these women lawyers did not become activists for wom-
en's rights, many were ahead of their times in other respects.[25] Louise Wideman
and Sarah Leverett held various public service positions, including serving as
workers' compensation commissioners.[26] Many combined careers and families. For example, Doris Camille Hutson married and had three children. She
also has had a very successful career as the first woman on the Texas Court of
Appeals.[27] Sarah Graydon McCrory married and raised five children and then
practiced law for twenty years after her youngest child went to college.[28] Hazel
Collings Poe combined family life with a career, serving as a municipal judge
for many years.

Toal was too young to have been aware of the civil rights activities in the state
during the war or the fact that women were attending law school in increased
numbers. But these people and their actions had sown a fertile field in which a
Jean Toal could and would grow. As she started school, she soon became aware
of the degree to which civil rights lawyers were changing the South. While she
was in elementary school, the U.S. Court of Appeals for the Fourth Circuit declared Columbia's segregated public bus system unconstitutional in *Flemming
v. South Carolina Electric & Gas Company*.[29] Also, the case many consider to be
the most important civil rights case ever brought, *Brown v. Board of Education*,
originated in South Carolina as *Briggs v. Elliott*.[30] As Toal gained an awareness
of these cases, she was influenced by the fact that her family was more open
minded than most southern white families about changing race relations.

This is best illustrated by Jean's father's relationship with Matthew J. Perry.
Despite the fact that Perry brought cases like *Flemming*, Herbert Hoefer hired
the young black lawyer, and they developed a personal relationship.[31] Although
Perry had a private law practice, his major legal endeavors were on behalf of
the NAACP. This meant that he represented student protestors across the state.

While Toal was a high school student, she became involved in a biracial student organization to oppose segregation. As a result she was a witness to a demonstration at the state capitol building that resulted in the arrests of two hundred students.[32] Shortly thereafter she attended the trial of those black students and observed Perry in action in the courtroom. Perry lost that day, but the case was won on appeal and became the landmark First Amendment case of *Edwards v. South Carolina*.[33] Toal was impressed. Her memory of Perry in action in the *Edwards* trial was captured in a short essay she wrote about him. She described him as "an imposing figure—tall, slender, conservatively and impeccably dressed, with a deep, melodious voice. His command of the language was a thing of beauty. His command of the law was complete and powerful."[34] The title of her essay was "A Life Changed."

In 1961 Jean Hoefer entered Agnes Scott College in Atlanta and majored in philosophy. She demonstrated her talent and toughness on the debate team, the judicial council, and the varsity field hockey team. The Phi Beta Kappa student was also drawn to activities off campus. She had opportunities to see Martin Luther King, and she spent her collegiate summers on voter registration drives in South Carolina, Georgia, and Mississippi.[35]

The call of the law and the challenge of racial injustice were major influences on Jean's postcollege choices. Recalling those years, Justice Toal noted that "my personal conviction, my membership in student organizations, and my first-hand witnessing of the civil rights struggle in Columbia and Atlanta inspired me to become a civil rights activist."[36] In 1965, after a family friend encouraged her to attend law school instead of graduate school, she enrolled at the University of South Carolina School of Law.[37] In a class of over two hundred, she was one of only four women. The school had no women of color and only two black male students. Although counseled against the legal profession by those who felt "the profession was not open to women," Jean Hoefer was not deterred.[38] Her good friend and classmate Robert Sheheen later stated that "law school was a different world for her, the women stood out then because there so few of them. But . . . I knew she'd be a successful lawyer."[39]

Toal made many friends and allies in law school. During her second year she married classmate William Thomas Toal. They became quite a team, she as managing editor of the law review and he as editor in chief. The couple developed a close friendship with I. S. Leevy Johnson, the only black student in their class. Johnson credits the Toals with making law school more bearable and at times even enjoyable.[40] Later, their friendship resulted in a law partnership between Bill Toal and Johnson—the first law partnership between a black man and a white man in modern South Carolina history.

As Jean Toal graduated from law school in 1968, the nation and the world
were in turmoil. The Vietnam war was at its height: that summer the Los Angeles *Times* stated that the war's death toll had reached 25,068. The assassinations
of Martin Luther King Jr. and Robert Kennedy threw a pall over the United
States. Riots occurred all across the country, and even the Democratic National
Convention was marred by street violence. And in 1968 three college students
were killed and twenty-eight wounded by shots fired by state highway patrolmen on the campus of South Carolina State College. The shootings have ever
since been known as the Orangeburg Massacre.

But Toal did not become a civil rights lawyer. Instead, she took a job in a
unique place for women in the state, with the prestigious firm of Haynsworth,
Perry, Bryant, Marion, and Johnstone in Greenville, South Carolina. This was
the Haynsworth firm. U.S. circuit judge Clement Haynsworth, later to be nominated for the U.S. Supreme Court, had been a member of the firm.[41] Jean's husband was a law clerk to Judge Haynsworth. With sixteen lawyers, the Greenville
firm was the largest in the state. One of its founding partners was Miss James
Perry, the first woman lawyer in the state. In 1968 the firm was unique not only
because of its distinguished history but also because it had a woman partner,
Jean Galloway Bissel, who had been mentored by Miss Perry.[42] Naturally, Bissel became Toal's mentor. Under Bissel's tutelage she performed many tasks:
research and assistance in drafting documents for the first public stock offering
for Daniel Construction Company; pension and profit-sharing plans for J. P.
Stevens, Alice Mills, Hollingsworth on Wheels, Daniel Construction Company,
and many other corporations; trusts and wills for many individuals and foundations; corporation certifications; and defense work in products liability, workers' compensation, automobile liability, and medical malpractice cases.[43]

At the time Jean Toal joined the Haynsworth firm, only forty women were
licensed to practice law in the state and only ten were in active practice. Since
women were not allowed to serve on South Carolina juries, it is not surprising that only two women lawyers were trying jury cases. Toal recognized very
quickly that she was a rare bird and that she could use this fact to her advantage.[44] She soon found her way to the courtroom. The 1957 Civil Rights Act had
given women the right to sit on federal juries, but not until 1968 did South Carolina allow women on state court juries.[45] This historic milestone created a great
opportunity for Toal. According to Toal, "because so many men had job-related
exemptions and women did not, many juries were female," and male litigators
thus were eager to hire this rare female lawyer to impress their new "feminine
juries."[46] The male litigators also discerned that in Jean Toal they had the makings of a great litigator.

Jean Toal's time with the Haynsworth firm prepared her for the next phase of her career. Toal and her husband returned home to Columbia, where she joined the medium-sized Belser law firm in 1970 and Bill became a law professor. The Belser firm was known primarily for its defense work, but Toal had broader interests. Toal recalled, "I expanded our base to include more plaintiffs' cases, administrative law cases, domestic litigation, and employment cases."[47] By January 1974 she was a partner at the firm. In a 2008 interview, she described her law practice in the mid-1970s: "I was privileged to appear on a frequent basis in all levels of trial and appellate courts in this state, including trials, or appeals before the Magistrates Court, County Court, Probate Court, Master-In-Equity, Circuit Court, Family Court, South Carolina Court of Appeals and South Carolina Supreme Court. . . . I also had considerable administrative law experience in litigation involving environmental matters, federal and state procurement, hospital certificates of need, employment matters and election matters."[48]

But Toal did much more. In response to the changing world, she took on more cutting-edge cases and tried to expand into civil rights areas. One of the most important cases of Toal's early career was that of Victoria Eslinger, a law student who brought a sex discrimination case against the state senate. Eslinger had been appointed by her state senator as a page, a lucrative position much sought after by University of South Carolina law students, who could study between errands. But the clerk of the senate denied her the job because of her sex. Toal recognized that neither law school nor her corporate and defense firm law practice had fully prepared her to handle such a case, and so she called on the Center for Study of Women for the expertise she needed. The center, a joint venture of the law schools at Columbia and Rutgers, was headed by law professor Ruth Bader Ginsberg.[49] Ginsberg, later to become the second woman appointed to the U.S. Supreme Court, was enormously helpful.[50]

Senior U.S. district court judge Robert W. Hemphill initially heard the case. The South Carolina Senate clerk took the position that the duties of pages might require them to come to the senator's hotel rooms on personal errands and that such visits would create an appearance of impropriety. Toal had obtained affidavits from male pages that trips to hotel rooms were only a small part of the job. When Toal tried to present her evidence and arguments on this point, the *Eslinger* case took a disturbing turn. Toal was interrupted by Judge Hemphill who stated, "Maybe that's the opportunity your client seeks." The shocked Toal responded that she thought the remark was unfair to her client and moved on with her argument.[51] But the next day the local newspaper excoriated the judge. The headline read "Impropriety by Judge." Toal's law firm was upset with her, fearing the case had upset a judge before whom they frequently argued cases;

some of the male lawyers protested that they had warned her not to take such a case. But soon she and all the other parties were summoned before Judge Hemphill, who issued a weak apology and recused himself from the case.[52] Despite the assignment of a new judge, Eslinger lost. On appeal, however, the Court of Appeals for the Fourth Circuit reversed the district court and established the right for women to serve as senate pages.[53]

During this time, Toal had other public interest cases. She handled some criminal appeals such as *Downey v. Peyton*, a death penalty case (*State v. Larry Portee*) and a large personal injury case (*Owen Martin v. National Railroad Passenger Corporation AMTRAK*).[54] She also represented the Catawba Indian Tribe in the third largest eastern Indian land claim in the country (*Catawba Indian Tribe v. South Carolina*).[55] These cases reflected Toal's commitment to progressive change through the law. However, *Eslinger v. Thomas* was the highlight of her early legal career and demonstrated Toal's commitment to helping other women in the profession.[56]

When she returned to Columbia, Jean Toal was determined to live a full life as a wife and mother and member of her community as well as a member of the legal profession. During the *Eslinger* case, she gave birth to her first child, a girl. A second daughter was born in the 1980s and both children went to Columbia's public schools. Toal also returned to her home church, St. Joseph's, where she served as a member of the parish council and as a lector.[57] She and her husband also chose to live downtown instead of in the white flight suburbs that had grown up around the capital city during the 1960s. They bought a home in the Shandon area, located near the University of South Carolina campus and just a few blocks from downtown. Jean Toal was one of the founders of the Shandon Neighborhood Council and served from 1972 to 1974 as the organization's first chair. During this same period, she attracted the attention of Governor John West, who appointed her to the newly formed Human Affairs Commission.

Soon political life beckoned. As Toal tested the waters of the political scene in 1974, the currents and cross-currents of state, regional, and national politics were creating both opportunities and dangers. Richard Nixon had been elected and then reelected to the presidency in 1968 and 1972 using the so-called southern strategy, which exploited the fears of white conservatives.[58] South Carolina was represented in Washington by a Republican senator and a Republican congressman. In 1966, Carolyn Frederick had become the first Republican woman ever elected to the South Carolina legislature. In 1970, the first African Americans in the modern era were elected to the state house of representatives, all Democrats.[59] However, in the Republican landslide of 1972, all three new black representatives were defeated while three Republican women and one

Democratic woman were elected to the house.[60] Yet significant changes were forthcoming. The election of 1974 was dramatically altered by litigation brought by civil rights attorney Matthew Perry. In *Stevenson v. West*, the U.S. Supreme Court reversed a lower court order and caused South Carolina to elect its legislature using single-member districts, a decision that would favor candidate Jean Toal.[61]

Aided by the nationwide bipartisan "Win with Women '74" campaign sponsored by the National Women's Political Caucus, which had been founded in 1971, Toal made the decision to run for the state house of representatives.[62] As a woman and a Democrat she would have both advantages and disadvantages. In the newly created house district, she would face a Republican male incumbent, Roger Kirk.[63] But the smaller, single-member districts did offer her an advantage. The district encompassed many downtown neighborhoods where she was already known because of her activities on behalf of the community. With this advantage and her tireless campaigning, she won in November. That fall three Republican women had been returned to the house, along with four Democratic women, including the first African American woman, Juanita Goggins.[64] Also elected was I. S. Leevy Johnson, Toal's law school classmate and friend. Eleven other black men were elected to the legislature as well. The women's movement, the increasing power of black citizens, and single member districts had combined to produce the most diverse legislature in the state's history.

In her first year, Toal was appointed as a member of the Judiciary Committee. She was also the floor leader for the successful fight to pass the Home Rule Act, which gave counties more control over their budgets and other aspects of local government. The fight for this bill was difficult and complex. South Carolina had always been a legislatively controlled state. The new scheme reduced the power of the county senators and representatives, who had previously made most local government decisions.[65]

Toal's interest in the law and in equal legal rights for women led her to become active in supporting the proposed Equal Rights Amendment (ERA) that was, along with the Nineteenth Amendment, the most significant women's rights issue of the twentieth century. The ERA, which banned discrimination on the basis of sex, was first proposed in 1923 by former suffragists who were eager to see ended all remaining legal discrimination against women. The ERA was approved overwhelmingly by the U.S. Congress in 1972 but ultimately fell short of ratification by three states. Even before her election, Jean Toal had been an advocate for the proposed amendment on the grounds that it would make "women first-class citizens."[66] There was strong support for ratification of the ERA in South Carolina but also strong opposition, including from

Marion Gressette, one of the most powerful members of the state legislature. Early in Toal's first term in the legislature, debate on ratification was stifled and then cut off by the bill's opponents using the house rules. While thirty-three legislators were still away for lunch, opponents of the amendment quickly "tabled" approval of the ERA, which meant that it could not be considered again in that session. ERA supporters, including Toal, were, of course, very disappointed. Yet in response to the tactics, Toal calmly responded, "They played it very well. Some of our key people had not gotten back from lunch. We were simply caught short—which is perfectly legal."[67]

After reelection to the house in 1976, Toal was appointed to the Rules Committee and continued to work for the ERA. She introduced another ERA resolution in 1977 and again in 1978 and 1982.[68] She debated with local opponents of the legislation as well as with Phyllis Schlafly, one of the nation's leading anti-ERA figures.[69] However, after ten years, women's efforts across the nation to obtain ratification of the ERA failed, and the period for approval expired. South Carolina was one of fifteen states that failed to ratify the amendment.[70] Toal later observed that "regardless of passage of the ERA, the impact of its debate is evident in the increased opportunities available to women today."[71]

In 1983, Toal was the chief advocate and floor leader as Judy Bridges endeavored to become the first woman family court judge in South Carolina. After she succeeded, Bridges stated that "Jean Toal's energy was boundless, and her ability to persuade and cajole her male colleagues to vote for a woman (who at the time was pregnant) as a family Court Judge turned the tide." Bridges won by a single vote.[72]

Toal eventually chaired the Judiciary Committee in the house. She was the first women to head a standing committee in the general assembly's history and was "generally regarded as an expert on constitutional law and state finances."[73] Dwight Drake, chief political aide to Governor Richard Riley, observed that "if you ask every member up there to list secretly the five leaders in the House, she'd be up there on everyone's list. She's one of the brightest people I've ever come across."[74] Toal's persona, intelligence, and success demanded respect from friends and foes alike. That talent and toughness she had displayed from an early age served her well. When asked about her style, Toal simply said, "I do my homework on the issues and I know each of the other 123 members of the House. I know their names. I've had conversations with them. That's how you get legislation passed."[75] Toal was often criticized for her brashness and her language.[76] However, her ability was never questioned. As one state house observer noted, "Even on one of her bad days, she's one of the best legislators here."[77]

However, her work ethic and her manner would test Toal, the legislature, the press, and the public as they adjusted to a woman in power.

Toal's participation in national Democratic Party politics, particularly with the presidential campaign of Jimmy Carter in 1976, opened up the possibility of appointment to the federal bench.[78] To the surprise of many, however, Toal did not want to be a federal judge; instead, she aspired to a position on the South Carolina supreme court.[79] Her journey to that court would require breaking through a strong "glass ceiling," the newly coined term for barriers to the rise of women to positions of power and leadership that were no less strong for being unofficial and invisible. Judicial offices are elected by the legislature in South Carolina. As a member of the legislature, she knew all the members. However, the vast majority of these voters were men and the legislature had only chosen one female judge before—the family court judge Toal helped elect.

In 1984 Jean Toal began her first campaign for the supreme court. However, the time was not yet right for her. Once again, the aspirations of women and African Americans collided in a way that proved to be significant for Toal, a champion of equal rights for both groups that were battling traditions that had excluded them. Toal was seeking to be the first female justice, but at the same time circuit court judge Ernest Finney was seeking to be the first African American justice since Reconstruction. Circuit court judge A. Lee Chandler was also a candidate. The two nontraditional candidates were not successful, and Chandler won.[80] In 1985, Toal and Finney both tried again. With very strong support from the South Carolina Legislative Black Caucus and other Democratic leadership, Finney emerged as the choice of the legislature. He was senior both in age and experience to Toal and had also been the first African American to serve as a circuit court judge in South Carolina. As John Snow, a Democrat from Williamsburg and chair of the house Agriculture Committee, stated, "I'd like to see a women on the court and would like to see a black. My choice right now is Finney. My next choice would be Toal."[81]

On January 29, 1985, Toal withdrew her name for consideration, thus clearing the way for Finney. Upon her withdrawal Toal said, "Ernest and I represent the dreams and aspirations of many South Carolinians who have previously had only limited opportunities for public service in our state. These factors make it even more difficult for us to be pitted against each other."[82]

In late 1986, Toal again sought a seat on the court. Again she faced a sitting circuit court judge. Based on his connections and his experience, Judge Rodney Peeples appeared to be the front-runner. But for one of the first times in state history, a judicial election was being closely examined by the press and the public. Early in the process, the Judicial Screening Committee failed to recommend Peeples but unanimously found Toal qualified.[83] One newspaper even endorsed her because of her "squeaky-clean" record.[84] Ultimately Peeples's ethical problems forced him to withdraw from the race.[85] In fact, in 1988 Peeples was publicly reprimanded by the Supreme Court for his ethical misconduct.[86]

Toal's election not only shattered the glass ceiling but stood out in many other respects. She was the first justice elected to the court without judicial experience since Representative Lionel K. Legge in 1954; she was more than a decade younger than her fellow members of the bench; and she was a Catholic.[87] She did have at least one thing in common with the rest of the court; all of the other justices had also been members of the South Carolina House of Representatives.

Jean Toal was sworn in on March 17, 1988. The press was full of the news. Her delighted former client, Columbia lawyer Victoria Eslinger, quoted in *The State* newspaper, pointed out how much times had changed in the sixteen years since Toal represented the law student in her case against the state senate; Eslinger noted that she had recently been in a courtroom where the three lawyers, the law clerks, the clerk of court, the court reporter, and the judge had all been women.[88] "The face of the court system in South Carolina," she said, was changing.[89] Toal confided to another reporter, "My prayer at Mass this morning was that I might ultimately prove worthy of this great trust and heavy responsibility."[90] Toal also announced that she hoped "to be known as a strict constructionist of the constitution with a high regard for individual rights."[91]

Three decisions from early in her tenure as an associate justice demonstrated that Toal would be the type of justice she promised. In *South Carolina Department of Mental Health v. State,* Toal wrote for a unanimous court that "it is impermissible . . . to confine children in a mental institution just because an adequate detention facility is unavailable. . . . The practice of committing juveniles to DMH for safekeeping *prior* to adjudication has developed because of the lack of better alternatives. It is the responsibility of the Legislature to designate an appropriate place."[92] In *State v. De La Cruz,* again writing for a unanimous court, she found that the legislature had not violated the state constitution's separation of powers doctrine by imposing a mandatory twenty-five-year drug sentence of which no part could be suspended by a judge.[93] In another case, she demonstrated her judicial sympathy for victims of crimes and found that the testimony of the lingering emotional pain suffered by a rape victim was appropriate evidence to present to a jury.[94] Toal was certainly willing to push the legislature on behalf of confined juveniles. The *De La Cruz* decision shows judicial deference to the legislature, but taken together the two later cases showed her conservative approach to getting tough on crime.

As an associate justice, she was assigned many administrative projects by the chief justice. In 1989–90, Toal was chair and codrafter of the new South Carolina Appellate Court rules, the first major revision in twenty years. She supervised the renovation of the supreme court building, which required her to make budgetary presentations to the legislature. Toal also was chair of two task forces: the juvenile justice task force created by Governor Carroll Campbell and U.S. district court judge Joseph Anderson to study the Juvenile Justice Department and the task force for the adoption of rules of evidence for the state patterned on the federal rules of evidence. The juvenile task force resulted in a report that sought $32 million from the general assembly as "an investment in the future." As a result of the evidence task force, in 1995 South Carolina became the thirty-sixth state to adopt a form of the federal rules of evidence.

Over the last two decades of the twentieth century, public figures were subjected to more intense scrutiny than they had been before. Toal did not escape such attention. While she had benefited from the troubles of circuit court judge Rodney Peeples in her successful run for the court in 1988, she faced a strong challenge to her reelection to the court in 1996 in the person of circuit court judge Tom Ervin of Anderson. Judge Ervin's candidacy was apparently encouraged by Republicans: state newspapers and the AP reported that "Republicans had started a quiet movement to oust Justice Toal."[95] Many conservatives, especially Republicans, had long considered Toal a "liberal."[96] It was true she had been a Democrat, but a doctrinaire liberal she was not. In 1987 when she was running against Peeples, one newspaper interviewed numerous legislators and bar officials about the judicial philosophy of the two candidates, and none seemed to think that Toal would impact the conservative philosophy of the court.[97] In fact, one newspaper reported that Toal was a death penalty proponent like her opponent and more probusiness than her opponent in 1988.[98] Another newspaper stated that the liberal label was "diluted in more reasonable minds by her opposition to abortion, her support of the death penalty, and her fight against pornography."[99] In 1996, the press reported that Toal responded to the "liberal" label by emphasizing her conservative credentials in her testimony before the legislative screening committee.[100]

Yet a Republican challenge was not surprising. In 1988, even after half of the members of the screening committee declared the circuit judge unfit, the Republican chairman of the Judiciary Committee had continued to support Peeples.[101] Despite the issuance of the screening committee's report on Peeples's ethical breach, one newspaper poll found that sixty-two Republican legislators were still favoring him.[102] Since there was a Republican majority in the legislature in 1996, the challenge to Toal was quite threatening. But her record simply did not warrant a challenge based on her judicial philosophy. Some believed there were other motives behind the challenge.

The *Greenville News* quoted a local woman lawyer as saying that "female judges are sometimes held to a different standard than their male counterparts." One reason Toal was attacked was that she sometimes used coarse language. The lawyer asserted that "I have never heard of a male judge being criticized for that."[103] In 1988, one newspaper quoted an anonymous legislator who opposed Toal because "pure and simple, Jean Toal is an abrasive woman. . . . She is very intelligent[,] . . . she fights for what she wants and believes in, and generally she gets it." The newspaper then editorialized: "It's odd that such a characterization is held up as an indictment of Mrs. Toal; such characteristics, when applied to a male legislator, generally are held in high esteem."[104] When the Ervin challenge first arose, *The State*, the major newspaper in South Carolina, opined that his candidacy was simply an attempt by the Republicans to flex their muscles.[105] Certainly prior sitting supreme court justices had been controversial, as a December 22, 1987, *Columbia Record* editorial criticizing Chief Justice Julius "Bubba" Ness noted. However, it had been over a hundred years since a sitting justice had been challenged for reelection.[106]

When the first hearings were held on the qualifications of the two candidates in December 1995, Toal drew praise from the press, but early in the new year it was announced that a second set of hearings would be held on Toal's "temperament."[107] Then a taxpayer group attacked Toal for being "liberal and elitist." The chief complaint was that Toal had been in the three-person majority in a controversial case.[108] The case was a challenge to a state environmental statute that allegedly resulted in a taking of private property without just compensation. Thereafter, it was rumored that the Republican governor, David Beasley, was opposed to her reelection because the court had ruled against his family in a large business dispute.[109] On January 16, 1996, *The State* newspaper labeled the second inquiry into Toal's qualifications "a witch hunt."[110] On the next day, the governor's father accused Toal of having stolen or erased the tape recordings of arguments in his case before the court.[111] Toal's reelection was in doubt. But some rallied to her side. Later, to the surprise of many conservatives, a right-to-life group endorsed her. Though an advocate of women's rights, Toal's Catholicism led her to depart from the majority of feminists on the abortion issue. *The State* pointed to this endorsement as exposing "the silliness of political labels."[112]

When the second round of hearings began, three former chief justices testified, as well as a number of employees or former employees of the court.[113] Five individuals, including the clerk of court and a former court administrator, criticized her for what was generally described as "abusive conduct." Apparently, the witnesses were referring to her language and tone of voice. On the next day of the hearings, after a dozen former and current employees of the court defended Toal, she dramatically apologized to anyone she had "hurt or embarrassed."[114] While some still questioned whether a male justice would have been subject to such scrutiny, others concluded the process had been fair and appropriate.[115] In the end, Toal was found qualified by the screening committee and her opponent withdrew, assuring her reelection.[116]

Recalling these events in a 2000 interview with the *Charleston Post and Courier*, Toal was "philosophical about the process. . . . She says the challenge was as much about politics—Republicans trying to unseat a Democrat—as about salty language and a tough approach to work." But she admitted, "It taught me some good lessons. I learned to be not so hard-charging. I came out of a very tough trial lawyer climate, and I need to learn to soften my approach."[117] Throughout the battle Toal always looked ahead and invariably gave credit for her success to others. One news article said she credited her husband, Bill, for his support in getting through tough times. The reporter noted, "Her voice softens as she speaks of him," and she described Bill as having "a gentle nature and an easy going personality."[118] With a record of achievement, her resilience, and her support network, Toal survived the toughest battle of her career.

It is likely that her gender, personal demeanor, religion, judicial philosophy, and political alliances, as well as the desire for "closer scrutiny," all played a role in this challenge. As her defenders noted, most of Toal's "abrasive and aggressive" traits were considered normal if not positive attributes of male politicians. Yet the major issue was the partisan political divide: Toal correctly identified the challenge as being about party politics. But one cannot easily separate sex from the equation. When she assumed the bench, she said she would be a strict constructionist in her judicial philosophy and she was: one newspaper's examination of the decisions for which she was attacked revealed that she and the court had strictly interpreted acts of the South Carolina legislature.[119] Toal certainly was no activist judge making new law. The fact that she was a female Democrat played into this misunderstanding of her and her positions. This is best illustrated by the surprise of many conservative Republican legislators when Toal was endorsed by the right-to-life organization. They were confounded, and some even moved to reconsider their opposition.[120] The battle over her reelection settled much about Toal's relationship with the legislature, and without question, her ability in the end prevailed.

In February 1999, South Carolina supreme court chief justice Ernest Finney announced he would retire in a year. As news of Finney's decision spread, Toal's ambition to become his successor as chief justice also became public.[121] The press immediately began to ask how tough the road would be for her. However, Republican leaders in the house and senate were quick to praise the court's only female justice. Senator Glenn McConnell, who had chaired the screening committee in 1996, applauded her and said that her standing with the legislature was much improved.[122] Hardly a week later, *The State* newspaper endorsed Toal for chief justice.[123] After that point, Toal seemed to have no critics. She drew endorsement after endorsement and quickly cleared the screening process, with no one to oppose her.[124]

On June 2, 1999, the South Carolina state legislature made history on two fronts as it elected Jean Toal chief justice of the South Carolina supreme court and Judge Kay Hearn chief judge of the South Carolina Court of Appeals.[125] After being sworn in as the state's thirty-first chief justice, Toal noted that she was "the first woman, the first Roman Catholic, the first Richland County lawyer since 1876."[126] James Moore's eye was caught by the editorial in his local newspaper that seemed to capture the meaning of the moment and faxed it to Toal, Finney, and Hearn. The Greenwood newspaper praised retiring Chief Justice Finney, chief justice–elect Toal and chief judge–elect Hearn, noting that though some people might claim that the three judges had gotten their positions because of their race or sex, "That would be wrong. . . . Finney, Toal, and Hearn made their reputations on the bench through ability, hard work, and courage, not on race, gender, social standing, or anything but their administration of the law."[127]

On the eve of Toal's swearing in, newspaper reporter John Monk's column was headlined "Toal Teaches Lessons in Endurance."[128] Monk revealed that his early stories on Rodney Peeples's ethical problems were leaked to him by an intermediary for then Chief Justice Julius "Bubba" Ness. Ness had been Peeples's mentor but had turned on the circuit court judge, accusing him of disloyalty. If these charges had not been leveled against Peeples, it seems highly unlikely that Toal would have been elected to the court in 1988. But the story had an impact, and Toal was elected. She was reelected in 1996 and then elected chief justice without opposition. Monk concluded that while Toal had been lucky against Peeples, the reality was that "when her time came, she was ready."[129]

In 2001 Toal was charged with leaving the scene of a minor automobile accident.[130] Toal pled guilty and admitted having had a drink before the accident. Shortly thereafter, a newspaper headlined the story "A Dent or a Scratch?"[131] The incident turned out to be nothing more than a scratch on her record. Toal was reelected to a full term as chief justice on June 9, 2004, again without opposition. Her term expires on July 31, 2014.[132]

Jean Toal's journey to the South Carolina supreme court came during a time of substantial progress for women in public life. By 1992 South Carolina ranked thirty-sixth in the nation in the number of women in public office. However, ten years later, in 2002, the state had the lowest number of women holding public office among the fifty states.[133] In 2000, there were fifteen women in the state house of representatives and two women in the senate.[134] In the 2007–8 legislative session, there was one female senator and thirteen female representatives.[135] Since 2008 no women have been elected to the state senate. Despite the 2010 election of Nikki Haley, the state's first female governor, South Carolina remains last in the nation in the number of women in office.[136]

While the number of women in public office in South Carolina declined, the numbers of African Americans showed steady progress. In 2000, there were thirty-one black legislators, and in 2008, there were thirty-four.[137] African Americans held eight state judgeships in 2001 and ten in 2008, according to the *South Carolina Bar Lawyers Desk Book*. Less than 6 percent of the South Carolina bar is African American, but one of the thirteen appellate judges is black, and (as of May 2007) seven out of ninety-two circuit and family court judges were black.[138] So at 7.5 percent, the percentage of Africans Americans on the bench exceeds the percentage of blacks on the South Carolina bar.[139]

Unlike in the legislature, the number of women in judgeships has increased in recent years. Three out of thirteen members of the two appellate courts are women.[140] Six out of forty-six circuit court judges are women.[141] Sixteen of the fifty-two family court judges are women.[142] Three women serve on the U.S. District Court for the District of South Carolina and one of the three federal bankruptcy judges in the state is a woman. There has been a net gain of twelve women judges since 2001.[143]

In 2004, Toal was nominated for and ultimately awarded the prestigious Margaret Brent Women Lawyers of Achievement Award by the American Bar Association, selected by the association's Commission on Women in the Profession. Citing Toal as their role model, virtually all of the women judges in South Carolina joined in a letter supporting her nomination. These South Carolina women included a U.S. circuit court judge, two U.S. district court judges, two South Carolina court of appeals judges, three circuit court judges, and thirteen family court judges.[144]

On March 23, 2000, when Jean Hoefer Toal was sworn in as the chief justice of the Supreme Court of South Carolina, a color photograph was taken on the steps of the Supreme Court Building where the handwritten "IT'S A GIRL" sign had been displayed in 1988. In the photograph, Toal is surrounded by a crowd of smiling women dressed in an array of colors, and the chief justice is in her black robe clutching a bouquet of roses—with her right fist thrust into the air.[145] This image must certainly indicate how Toal would like the moment to be remembered. Her words to a reporter after the ceremony also expressed the solidarity with other women Toal felt on that day. As she said "it is an achievement by a lot of women, not just Jean Toal."[146]

Fittingly, senior U.S. district judge Matthew J. Perry said this about Toal: "Her accomplishments provide proof that women are fully capable of achieving everything that anyone else can accomplish. Her life demonstrates that discrimination against women does a disservice not only to women, but to the rest of the world who are deprived of the benefits that can be bestowed by women who are allowed to serve at their full potential."[147] While Toal's judicial record is still in the making, her legacy for women and minorities in the law is one of which she and the state can already be proud.

NOTES

1. Jeff Amberg, "Marking History," *Columbia Record*, January 29, 1988.

2. "Double First for S.C. Courts," Orangeburg *Times and Democrat*, January 28, 1988.

3. South Carolina Constitutional Convention, 1868, *Proceedings of the Constitutional Convention of South Carolina*, vol. 2 (New York: Arno Press, 1968), 838.

4. W. Lewis Burke, "Killing, Cheating, Legislating, and Lying: A History of Voting Rights in South Carolina since the Civil War," South Carolina Law Review 57, no. 4 (2006): 859–87; Marjorie Spruill Wheeler, *New Women of the New South: The Leaders of the Woman Suffrage Movement in the Southern States* (New York: Oxford University Press, 1993).

5. Walter Edgar, *South Carolina: A History* (Columbia: University of South Carolina Press, 1998), 471.

6. "An Act to Confer upon Women the Vote in All Elections," in *Acts of the General Assembly of the State of South Carolina* (Columbia, S.C.: Gonzales and Bryan, State Printers, 1921), 268.

7. Burke, "Killing, Cheating, Legislating, and Lying," 881.

8. "An Act . . . Relating to Persons Exempt from Serving as Jurors by Including Their Female Electors," in *Acts of the General Assembly of the State of South Carolina*, 269.

9. *State v. Mittle*, 120 S.C. 526, 113 S.E. 335 (1922).

10. 92 U.S. 214 (1875).

11. Act No. 494 (1967), *Code of Laws of South Carolina, 1976, Annotated* (Rochester, N.Y.: Lawyer's Co-operative Publishing, 1976), sec. 14-7-850.

12. *Biographical Directory of the South Carolina House of Representatives*, ed. Walter B. Edgar (Columbia: University of South Carolina Press: 1992), 475–76.

13. W. Lewis Burke and William C. Hine, "The South Carolina College Law School: Its Roots, Creation, and Legacy," in *Matthew J. Perry: The Man, His Times and His Legacy*, ed. W. Lewis Burke and Belinda Gergel (Columbia: University of South Carolina Press, 2004), tables 1–3, 40–43. Also see James Lowell Underwood and W. Lewis Burke, *At Freedom's Door: African American Founding*

Fathers and Lawyers in Reconstruction South Carolina (Columbia: University of South Carolina Press, 2000), 127–29.

14. Burke and Hine, "The South Carolina College Law School," table 2, 42.

15. David F. Kern, "Way Clear for Finney to Take Seat on State Supreme Court," *The State*, January 30, 1985.

16. Jean Hoefer Toal, telephone interview by W. Lewis Burke, May 2008. See also *Columbia Directory*, comp. Julian Sleby (Columbia, S.C.: R. W. Gibbs, 1860), 20. The directory lists "G. Hoefer" as a watchmaker, but the family remembers him as a cobbler.

17. Toal, telephone interview by Burke, May 2008.

18. 1910 U.S. federal census, Richland County, S.C., 1920 U.S. federal census, Richland County, S.C., and 1930 U.S. federal census, Richland County, S.C.

19. Rick Brundrett, "Jean Toal Sworn in as Chief Justice," *The State*, March 24, 2000.

20. "Toal Should Now Have Clear Sailing to Court," *The State*, January 22, 1988.

21. Robert J. Moore, "Matthew J. Perry's Preparation," in *Matthew J. Perry*, 61.

22. Peter Lau, *Democracy Rising* (Lexington: University of Kentucky Press, 2006), 128.

23. *Duvall v. School Board*, CA No. 1082 (EDSC 1944). Also see *Thompson v. Gibbes*, 60 F. Supp. 872 (EDSC 1945).

24. Ruth Cupp, *Portia Steps Up to the Bar: The First Women Lawyers of South Carolina* (Raleigh, N.C.: Ivy House, 2003), 67.

25. Ibid., 82.

26. Ibid., 79, 82, 84.

27. Ibid., 89–90.

28. Ibid., 81.

29. 224 F.2d 752 (4th Cir. 1955).

30. 347 U.S. 483 (1954); *Briggs v. Elliott*, 98 F. Supp. 529 (EDSC 1951).

31. Matthew J. Perry to Jean Hoefer Toal, December 10, 2003, book 1, Jean Hoefer Toal Papers (hereinafter cited as JHTP). These papers are the personal property of Chief Justice Toal, but she graciously loaned them to the authors.

32. Jean Hoefer Toal, "A Life Changed," in *Matthew J. Perry*, 152.

33. 372 U.S. 229.

34. Toal, "A Life Changed," 153.

35. Biography, Toal nomination package, book 1, 1, JHTP.

36. Ibid.

37. Ibid., 5.

38. Ibid.

39. Jan Collins Stucker, "The Lady Is a Lawmaker," *The State Magazine*, March 13, 1983.

40. I. S. Leevy Johnson, phone conversation with W. Lewis Burke, June 3, 2008.

41. *Martindale-Hubbell Law Directory*, vol. 2 (Summit, N.J.: Martindale-Hubbell, 1957), 4021; Alfonso A. Narvaez, "Clement Haynsworth Dies at 77; Lost Struggle for High Court Seat," *New York Times*, November 23, 1989.

42. Cupp, *Portia Steps Up to the Bar*, 128. Also see *The Lawyer's List*, 65th ed. (New York: Law List Publishing Company, 1968), 92.

43. Narrative, book 1, 5, JHTP.

44. "Toal Enjoys Busy Pace of the Court," *Shandon Times*, July 21, 1989.

45. Charlan Nemeth, Jeffrey Endicott, and Joel Wachtler, "From the 50's to the 70's: Women in Jury Deliberations," *Sociometry* 39, no. 4 (1976): 293–304.

46. Cupp, *Portia Steps Up to the Bar*, 154.

47. Ibid.

48. Biographical sketch, book 1, 7, JHTP.

49. Stephanie Harvin, "Making History," *Charleston Post and Courier*, February 27, 2000.

50. Jean Hoefer Toal, interview by Brooke Mulenex, April 9, 2008, South Carolina Women's Rights Collection, South Carolina Political Collections, University of South Carolina Libraries, University of South Carolina, Columbia (hereinafter cited as SCWRC-SCPC).

51. "Page Aspirant Gets Apology," *The State*, April 2, 1971.

52. Toal, interview by Mulenex, April 9, 2008, SCWRC-SCPC.

53. Biographical sketch, book 1, 7, JHTP.

54. *Downey v. Peyton*, 452 F.2d 236 (4th Cir. 1971); *State v. Larry Portee*, Fifth Judicial Circuit, general sessions (1980); *Owen Martin v. National Railroad Passenger Corporation AMTRAK*, U.S. District Court District of South Carolina, CA No. 3-86-539-16 (1986).

55. 476 U.S. 498, 106 S. Ct. 2039, 90 L. Ed. 2d 490 (1986); 740 F. 2d 305 (4th Cir. 1984); 718 F.2d 1291 (4th Cir. 1983).

56. 324 F. Supp. 1329 (D.S.C. 1971), 470 F. Supp. 866 (D.S.C. 1972), affirmed, 476 F.2d 225 (1973), reversed.

57. "St. Joseph Parishioner Chosen as Assoc. Justice," *Catholic Banner*, February 4, 1988.

58. See Jack Bass and Walter DeVries, *Transformation of Southern Politics* (Athens: University of Georgia Press, 1995), for a discussion of both the southern strategy as well as the emergence of new Democrats.

59. See 52 *S.C. Legislative Manual* 97, 98, and 100 (1971). I. S. Leevy Johnson, a classmate of Toal's from law school, was one of the three.

60. 54 *S.C. Legislative Manual* 91, 103, 123 and 125 (1973).

61. 413 U.S. 902 (1973).

62. "Toal Joins Washington Meet," *The State*, February 14, 1974.

63. Ibid.

64. 56 *S.C. Legislative Manual* 67, 77, 78, 100, 103 and 106 (1975).

65. Edgar, *South Carolina*, 551. Also see Mary Jane Benston, "Counties' Voting Past Important in Home Rule Decisions—Toal," *The State*, October 29, 1975.

66. "Women Hit, Back Rights Amendment," *The State*, May 18, 1972.

67. "ERA Opponents Kill Measure In House Vote," *The State*, March 27, 1975.

68. "Toal Introduces ERA Resolution," *The State*, March 2, 1977; "ERA Dies in the House," *The State*, April 29, 1982. Also see "ERA Makes a Fresh Start on Road to Ratification," *The State*, July 15, 1982.

69. Betsy Annese, "Pro," *The State*, February 3, 1978; Toal, interview by Mulenex, April 9, 2008, SCWRC-SCPC.

70. Book 1, 11, JHTP.

71. "ERA Needed, Toal Tells Girl Staters," *The State*, June 11, 1976.

72. Diane Schafer Goodstein to ABA Commission on Women in the Profession, December 9, 2003, JHTP.

73. Cupp, *Portia Steps Up to the Bar*, 154.

74. Stucker, "The Lady Is a Lawmaker," 6.

75. Ibid.

76. David F. Kern, "Toal Thinks New Rules Will Prod House," *The State*, December 19, 1982.

77. Stucker, "The Lady Is a Lawmaker," 6.

78. Cupp, *Portia Steps Up to the Bar*, 153.

79. Ibid.

80. 66 *South Carolina Legislative Manual* 238 (1985).

81. *The State*, December 24, 1984.

82. Kern, "Way Clear for Finney to Take Seat on State Supreme Court."

83. John Monk, "Judicial Panelists Divided," *Charlotte (N.C.) Observer*, December 23, 1987.

84. "Rep. Toal Logical Choice for Justice," *Myrtle Beach Sun News*, January 3, 198[8].

85. Cindi Ross, "Peeples Tried to Silence Opponents," *The State*, January 30, 1988.

86. *In the Matter of Peeples*, 297 S.C. 36 (1988).

87. Ibid.

88. Peter O'Boyle III, "Toal Steps Forward Today to Set Landmark Precedent," *The State*, March 17, 1988.

89. Ibid.

90. Dawn Hinshaw, "Toal Dons New Robe for New Role," *The State*, March 18, 1988.

91. Larry Crib, "She Plans to Be More Than Just the First," *Living in South Carolina*, March 1988, 5.

92. 301 S.C. 75, 390 S.E.2d 185 (1990).

93. 302 S.C. 13, 393 S.E.2d 184 (1990).

94. *State v. Alexander*, 303 S.C. 377, 401 S.E.2d 146 (1991).

95. AP, "Panel Researches Toal, Ervin Backgrounds," *Charleston Post and Courier*, January 4, 1996. Democratic representative Tim Rogers asserted that Ervin had admitted in a telephone conversation that he had been encouraged by Republicans to run. Ervin said they had talked, but he denied there was any organized effort by Republicans to defeat Toal ("A Judge's Dilemma," *Anderson Independent-Mail*, September 13, 1995).

96. Maureen Shurr, "Jean Toal Elected to Court," *Columbia Record*, January 27, 1988.

97. Al Dozier, "Peeples, Toal Set Sights on Ness' High Court Seat," *Greenville News*, August 23, 1987.

98. John Monk, "High Court Candidates Both Driven," *Charlotte (N.C.) Observer*, December 6, 1987.

99. "Toal Has the Makings of a Good Court Justice," *Greenville Piedmont*, January 28, 1988.

100. Cindi Ross Scoppe and Lisa Greene, "Toal Stresses Conservative Credentials," *The State*, December 13, 1995.

101. John Monk, "Judicial Panelist Divided," *Charlotte (N.C.) Observer*, December 24, 1987.

102. John Monk, "Judge's Lead Erodes Sharply in Legislature," *Charlotte (N.C.) Observer*, January 10, 1988.

103. Andrea Weigl, "Women Take Charge of Top State Courts," *Greenville News*, February 26, 2000.

104. "Toal Has the Makings of a Good Court Justice."

105. "Let's Keep Politics out of Judicial Re-election Bids," *The State*, September 10, 1995.

106. Robert Tanner, "Judge Describes Pressure to Stay out of Bench Race," *Myrtle Beach Sun Times*, December 12, 1995. The article refers to when sitting justice Samuel McGowan was defeated by Lieutenant Governor Eugene Gary in 1893.

107. Scoppe and Greene, "Toal Stresses Conservative Credentials." Also see "Expanding Influence," *Greenville News*, January 6, 1996.

108. Mark Johnson, "Justice Toal's Opinions Reflect 'Liberal, Elitist Contempt,'" *The State*, January 11, 1996.

109. Sid Gaulden, "Toal Challenge May Be Result of '94 Ruling," *Charleston Post and Courier*, January 12, 1996.

110. "Will Jean Toal's Hearing Become a Witch Hunt?" *The State*, January 16, 1996.

111. Sid Gaulden, "Blank Tape Is Blamed on Toal," *Charleston Post and Courier*, January 17, 1996.

112. Brad Warthen, "Toal Endorsement Exposes Silliness of Political Labels," *The State*, February 7, 1996.

113. Lisa Greene and Cindi Ross Scoppe, "Workers Pour Out Their Tales of Toal," *The State*, January 24, 1996.

114. William Fox, "Justice Toal Apologizes to Detractors," *Greenville News*, January 25, 1996.

115. Robert Tanner, "Toal Victim of Double Standard?" *Charleston Post and Courier*, January 28, 1996; "Toal Hearings Are Fair, but System Needs Changes," *The State*, January 28, 1996.

116. Cindi Ross Scoppe and Lisa Greene, "Screening Panel's Report Lifts Toal," *The State*, February 3, 1996; Gaulden, "Toal Challenge May Be Result of '94 Ruling."

117. Stephanie Harvin, "Making History, Jean Toal Poised to Become Chief Justice," *Charleston Post and Courier*, February 27, 2000.

118. Ibid.

119. Lisa Greene, "Critics See Liberal Slant in Some Rulings by Toal," *The State*, January 17, 1996.

120. Cindi Ross Scoppe, "Toal's Opponent Steps Up Attacks," *The State*, February 2, 1996.

121. Rick Brundrett and John Allard, "Finney, S.C. Judicial 'Giant' Plans to Step Down in 2000," *The State*, February 24, 1999; Rick Brundrett and John Allard, "Toal's Goal: Becoming 1st Female Chief Justice," *The State*, February 24, 1999.

122. Bill Swindell, "Finney Set to Retire Next Year," *Charleston Post and Courier*, February 24, 1999.

123. "Jean Toal Will Make an Excellent Chief Justice," *The State*, March 4, 1999.

124. Rick Brundrett, "Toal Nominated to Lead State Supreme Court," *The State*, May 13, 1999; AP, "Toal Moves Closer to Top Court Post," *Greenville News*, May 5, 1999; "The Bell Toals," *Myrtle Beach Sun News*, April 4, 1999.

125. AP, "Madame Chief Justice," *Sumter Item*, June 3, 1999.

126. Brundrett, "Jean Toal Sworn in as Chief Justice."

127. Fax from Moore to Finney, Toal, and Hearn, June 4, 1999, book 3, JHTP; "Top Courts Get Top Women with History-Making Votes," *Greenwood Index Journal*, June 3, 1999.

128. *The State*, March 22, 2000.

129. Ibid.

130. "Chief Justice Charged with Leaving Scene of Accident," *The State*, May 19, 2001.

131. Clif LeBlanc and Rick Brundrett, "Toal's Car Accident: A Dent or a Scratch?" *The State*, May 27, 2001.

132. *South Carolina Bar Lawyers Desk Book* (Columbia, S.C.: South Carolina Bar, 2007–8), 434.

133. *The Status of Women in the States* (Washington, D.C.: Institute for Women's Policy Research, 2002), app. 4, 84.

134. Aaron Sheinin, "Toal Says Women Leaders Need to Be Developed," *The State*, December 10, 2000.

135. 88 *South Carolina Legislative Manual* 44, 84–141 (2007).

136. Roddie Burris, "S.C. Runoff: Senate a Boys Club Again," *The State*, June 28, 2008.

137. See 81 *South Carolina Legislative Manual* (2000) and 88 *South Carolina Legislative Manual* (2007).

138. *South Carolina Bar Lawyers Desk Book*, 435.

139. South Carolina bar membership data as of June 2, 2008, supplied by the bar to the authors. Only 8,078 out of 12,777 members report their race, with just 5 percent reporting their race as black.

140. *South Carolina Bar Lawyers Desk Book*, 443–45.

141. *2011 South Carolina Legislative Manual*, 361–86.

142. *South Carolina Bar Lawyers Desk Book*, 468–81. One of the women is a Filipino American (475).

143. Aïda Rogers, "The Lady Is a Judge," *Sandlapper*, summer 2001, 12. Rogers noted that there were seventeen women judges in the state. *South Carolina Bar 2011–12 Lawyers Desk Book*, 539. The 2001–2 *South Carolina Bar Lawyers Desk Book* reveals that there were nineteen, including the two federal judges, in 2001.

144. Goodstein to ABA Commission on Women in the Profession, December 9, 2003, JHTP.

145. Brundrett, "Jean Toal Sworn in as Chief Justice."

146. Mark Pratt, "Chief Justice Toal sworn in," *Greenville News*, March 24, 2000.

147. Letter from Matthew J. Perry on behalf of Justice Toal for the Margaret Brent Award, JHTP.

Contributors

JENNIFER E. BLACK is the fundraising coordinator for the Anna Freud Centre, a child mental health charity based in London. She received her master's in 2003 in history from the University of Glasgow and her PhD from the University of Cambridge in 2007. Her MPhil dissertation was on religion and the black family in the Mississippi Valley from 1865 to 1877. Her doctoral research focused on the League of Women Voters in South Carolina from 1947 to 1960.

CAROL SEARS BOTSCH is a professor of political science at the University of South Carolina, Aiken. She received a PhD in political science from the University of South Carolina in 1988 and also holds a master's degree in public administration from the University of North Carolina and a bachelor's degree in sociology from Syracuse University. She was principal author of *African-Americans and the Palmetto State* (1994) and has published a number of articles on women in politics, on African Americans in politics, and on the civic education and political socialization of college students.

W. LEWIS BURKE is a professor at the University of South Carolina School of Law. He is chair of the Department of Clinical Legal Studies and teaches clinics, alternative dispute resolution, trial advocacy, and South Carolina legal history. He is the author and editor of four books. These include *Dawn of Religious Freedom*, coedited book with James L. Underwood; *Matthew J. Perry: The Man, His Times, and His Legacy*, coedited with Belinda Gergel; and *At Freedom's Door: African American Founding Fathers in Reconstruction South Carolina*, coedited with James Lowell Underwood. He is the author of numerous chapters and articles on legal history. Presently, he is working on a book on the history of South Carolina's black lawyers to be published by the University of Georgia Press.

KATHERINE MELLEN CHARRON is an associate professor of history at North Carolina State University. She received a master's degree in Afro-American Studies from the University of Wisconsin, Madison, and a PhD in history from Yale University. Her fields of study include U.S history, African American history, women's history, and southern history. She is the author of the award-winning *Freedom's Teacher*, a biography of Septima Clark, and coeditor of *Recollections of My Slavery Days* by William Henry Singleton.

FRITZ P. HAMER received his bachelor of arts in history from Acadia University, Wolfville, Nova Scotia. He earned his master's in 1982 and his PhD in 1998 in history from the University of South Carolina. He began his museum career in 1982 in Alabama and joined the South Carolina State Museum in 1986, as a curator of history. In 2011 he became the curator of published materials at the South Caroliniana Library at the University of South Carolina. He has published articles and planned exhibitions on a variety of topics, with a particular focus on World War II and South Carolina. These exhibits include "The Palmetto State Goes to War: World War II and South Carolina" and "Operation Overlord: Breaking through the Atlantic Wall, D-day, 6 June 1944." The state museum has a small online exhibit on its website (www.southcarolinastatemuseum.org) on important women in South Carolina history. One of his publications is *Charleston Reborn: A Southern City, its Navy Yard, World War II.*

PATRICIA EVRIDGE HILL received a bachelor of arts in history from Southern Methodist University and a master's and PhD from the University of Texas at Dallas. Currently, she is associate professor of history and department chair at San Jose State University. The University of Texas Press published her monograph *Dallas: The Making of a Modern City* in 1996. Hill's articles on Hilla Sheriff have appeared in the *American Journal of Public Health* and *Social History of Medicine*. After a six-year hiatus to serve as a statewide officer of the California Faculty Association, a union representing more than twenty thousand faculty members on twenty-three California State University campuses, Hill has resumed work on a full-length biography of Hilla Sheriff.

JOAN MARIE JOHNSON teaches women's and southern history at Northeastern Illinois University in Chicago and is the cofounder and codirector of the Newberry Library Seminar on Women and Gender at the Newberry Library in Chicago. She received her PhD in history at the University of California, Los Angeles, in 1997. Johnson is the author of *Southern Women at the Seven Sister Colleges: Feminist Values and Social Activism, 1875–1915*; *Southern Ladies, New Women: Race, Region and Clubwomen in South Carolina, 1898–1930*; and the editor of *Southern Women at Vassar: The Poppenheim Family Letters, 1882–1916*. She has also published numerous articles in women's history. She is writing a book on women philanthropists who funded the women's movement.

CHERISSE JONES-BRANCH, a native of Charleston, South Carolina, received her bachelor of arts and master's in history at the College of Charleston and her doctorate at the Ohio State University. Her publications include "'How Shall I Sing the Lord's Song?': United Church Women Confront Racial Issues in South Carolina, 1940s–1960s," in *Throwing Off the Cloak of Privilege: White Southern Women's Activists in the Civil Rights Era*; "'To Speak When and Where I Can': African American Women's Political Activism in South Carolina in the 1940s and 1950s," published in *South Carolina Historical Magazine*, and "Mary Church Terrell: Revisiting the Politics of Race, Class, and Gender," in *Tennessee Women: Their Lives and Times*. She currently is an associate professor of history at

Arkansas State University in Jonesboro, Arkansas, and is completing her manuscript, "Repairers of the Breach": Black and White Women's Racial Activism in South Carolina, 1940s–1960s," for publication with the University Press of Florida. Her fields of study are women's history and African American history.

VALINDA W. LITTLEFIELD is an associate professor of history and the director of the African American Studies Program at the University of South Carolina. She received her bachelor of arts from North Carolina Central University and her PhD in history from the University of Illinois, Urbana-Champaign. Littlefield is a scholar of the history of women, African Americans, and education, with an emphasis on southern African American women and African American history from 1877 to the present. Her publications include several articles on African American educators and her book on southern African American schoolteachers during the Jim Crow era is forthcoming from the University of Illinois Press.

GEORGETTE MAYO is the archivist at the Avery Research Center for African American History and Culture at the College of Charleston, where she was formerly a project and reference archivist in addition to interim director. In 2005 she graduated from the University of South Carolina joint master's program in library science and public history, with a concentration in archival management. She holds a bachelor of arts degree in African American studies from the same institution. Her entry on Ethel Martin Bolden is included in the *African American National Biography*.

PAGE PUTNAM MILLER grew up in Columbia, South Carolina. She graduated from Mary Baldwin College in 1963, studied in 1964 at Yale Divinity School, and received a PhD in American history from the University of Maryland in 1979. For twenty years she headed the National Coordinating Committee for the Promotion of History, the national advocacy office in Washington, D.C., for the historical and archival professions. She has written extensively on legislative issues and testified frequently before congressional committees on federal information policy, preservation and interpretation of culture resources, and support of the National Archives and the National Endowment for the Humanities. She worked collaboratively with the Organization of American Historians on a women's history landmark project and with the National Park Service on a guide for interpreting women's sites. From 2000 to 2005 she was a visiting distinguished lecturer in the Public History Program at the University of South Carolina in Columbia. She is the author of *A Claim to New Roles*, *Landmarks of American Women's History*, and *Fripp Island: A History*.

CONSTANCE ASHTON MYERS received a master's in American Studies at Claremont Graduate School and her PhD. at the University of South Carolina. Before her retirement in 1986, she taught U.S. history, American intellectual history, women in America, and oral history methodology at California State University, Arizona State University, and the University of South Carolina. Among her publications are a book, *The Prophet's Army: Trotskyists in America, 1928–1941*, and an article, "The United States and the Inter-American Commission on Women: First Twenty-five Years of the Relationship." She is the recipient of several fellowships from the Rockefeller Foundation, the Smithsonian Institution and the National Endowment for the Humanities. For International Women's Year (IWY) in 1977 she served as principal investigator for the oral history record of the South Carolina meeting and the international meeting in Houston. These taped interviews are held by the National Archives. Transcripts of many of the IWY interviews and other oral histories by Myers are housed at the South Caroliniana Library. She was the consultant on numerous oral history projects at the University of Michigan, the University of North Carolina, Columbia University, Arizona State University, and the University of South Carolina. On retiring, she lived in Managua, Nicaragua for five years. Currently, she is a docent for the Columbia Museum of Art.

MARY MAC OGDEN is a graduate of Presbyterian College and received her PhD from the University of South Carolina in 2011. Her research examines the life of Wil Lou Gray of South Carolina.

BAKARI T. SELLERS is a Democratic member of the South Carolina House of Representatives, representing the Ninetieth Congressional District since 2006, when he was first elected at the age of twenty-two. He is currently serving his third term. Sellers is a graduate of Morehouse College and of the University of South Carolina School of Law and an associate with the Strom Law Firm in Columbia.

MARJORIE JULIAN SPRUILL is a professor of history at the University of South Carolina. She received her bachelor of arts from the University of North Carolina, Chapel Hill, a master's from Duke University, and a master's and PhD from the University of Virginia. She is the author of *New Women of the New South: The Leaders of the Woman Suffrage Movement in the Southern States* and the editor of four other books on woman suffrage including *One Woman, One Vote: Rediscovering the Woman Suffrage Movement* (the companion volume to the PBS documentary). She is also coeditor of *Mississippi Women: Their Histories, Their Lives* and *The South in the History of the Nation*. Her work has been supported by the National Endowment for the Humanities, the Radcliffe Institute for Advanced Study, the Woodrow Wilson International Center for Scholars, and the National Humanities Center. Her current work is about the rise of the modern women's rights movement, the rise of a conservative women's movement in opposition, and the impact of these movements on American political culture.

MARCIA G. SYNNOTT earned her bachelor of arts from Radcliffe College in 1961, her master's from Brown University in 1964, and her PhD from the University of Massachusetts in 1974. She is a professor of history emerita at the University of South Carolina, where she taught twentieth-century United States History and the history of American women from 1972 to 2005. Her research concentrates on discrimination and desegregation in higher education. Since the 1980s, she has also been researching South Carolina women who challenged conventional behavior. She is the author of *The Half-Opened Door: Discrimination and Admissions at Harvard, Yale, and Princeton, 1900–1970*, recently republished with a new introduction; "Crusaders and Clubwomen: Alice Norwood Spearman Wright and Her Women's Network," in *Throwing Off the Cloak of Privilege: White Southern Women Activists in the Civil Rights Era*; and "The Evolving Diversity Rationale in University Admissions: From *Regents v. Bakke* to the University of Michigan Cases," in the *Cornell Law Review*.

MELISSA WALKER is George Dean Johnson Jr. professor of history at Converse College. She is the author of *Southern Farmers and Their Stories: Memory and Meaning in Oral History* and *All We Knew Was to Farm: Rural Women in the Upcountry South, 1919–1941*, winner of the Southern Association for Women Historians' Willie Lee Rose Prize. In 2007, she was named the Carnegie Foundation/CASE South Carolina Professor of the Year.

JOHN W. WHITE is the archivist of special collections at the College of Charleston Library. He received his PhD from the University of Florida in 2006. His dissertation is entitled "Managed Compliance: White Resistance and Desegregation in South Carolina, 1950–1970." His publications include "The White Citizens' Councils of Orangeburg County, South Carolina," in *Toward "The Meeting of the Waters": Journeys in the History of the Civil Rights Movement in South Carolina, 1901–2003*, and "Association of Citizens' Councils of South Carolina," for the *Encyclopedia of South Carolina*.

SUZANNE WISE is the curator of the Stock Car Racing Collection at Appalachian State University Library, in Boone, North Carolina. She holds degrees from the University of South Carolina, the University of Kentucky, and Appalachian State University. Her area of scholarship is sports, with a special interest in women in motorsports. She is the author of *Sports Fiction for Adults* and *Social Issues in Contemporary Sport*, as well as a number of articles on auto racing.

KATE PORTER YOUNG has worked with African American and Hispanic women for over four decades. She earned her bachelor of arts in anthropology at Georgia State University in 1972 and her PhD from Rutgers University in 1986. Her academic research and teaching has focused on women, work, and development in the American South, Latin America, and Africa. She has published several articles on her extensive ethnographic work with Lowcountry African American women and families, including "Sisterhood, Kinship, and Marriage in an African American South Carolina Sea Island Community" for the Center for Research on Women at Memphis State University, and "Kinship in a Changing Economy," in *Holding Onto the Land and the Lord: Kinship, Ritual, Land*

Tenure and Social Policy in the Rural South. She founded the Little River Family Resource Center in Durham, North Carolina, serving Hispanic and African American
women and children, which she has directed for the past fifteen years. In 2006, she was
chosen as a Rotary Cultural Ambassador to Venezuela, where she studied Spanish and
Latin American culture and community development. She has also served as a consultant for community-based development projects in San Ramon, Nicaragua. Currently
she is a Peace Corps volunteer working with indigenous women in Uspantan Quiche,
Guatemala.

Index

A. C. Flora High School (Columbia), 21, 340
abortion, 16, 356, 378–79, 423
Abzug, Bella, 379
Adams, David King, Jr., 21, 22
Adams, Fannie Phelps, 6, 17, 25; community activism, 30–31; early life and marriage, 21–22; teaching career, 20, 21–22, 25, 27–28, 30–31
adult education, xiv, xvi, 7, 11–12, 58, 68–74, 240, 245, 249–50, 253–57
African American women, xii, xiv, 3, 4; activism, xiv–xv; clubwomen, xiii–xiv; early voter registration attempts, 172, 206, 253–54, 255, 257, 350, 415; free, xiii; health care, 78, 91; labor, xiii, 4, 97, 105; negative stereotyping, xv, 398; women's rights movement 235, 236, 390–94
African Americans, 3, 7, 91, 98, 200, 316; alleged inferiority, 7, 17; education, 2, 6–7, 17, 35, 167, 241; employment, 9, 316; fictionalized portrayals, 58, 65; health care, 78, 79, 225–26; midwifery, 84–86, 87, 90; violence against, 208, 230, 241, 339, 340; voting, xiv, 11, 229, 230–31, 322, 327, 329, 411, 412. See also public education: African American teachers
Against the Tide (H. H. Keyserling), 369, 370
Agnes Scott College, 16, 381, 382, 415
Aiken County Election Commission, 149
Allen College. *See* Allen University

Allen University, 21, 22, 32n10, 167, 171, 209, 216n13
Allison, Rita, 52–53
Alston, Corey, 320
Amateur Literary and Fraternal Association, 160
American Agriculture Movement (AAM), 299–300, 301
American Association of Adult Education, 68, 70
American Association of University Professors (AAUP), 265
American Association of University Women (AAUW), 192, 265, 388
American Cotton Manufacturers Association, 292
American Farm Bureau Federation, 299
American Historical Association (AHA), 272, 273
American Public Health Association, 79
American Women's Hospitals (AWH), 82
Anderson, James, 28
Anderson, Joseph, 423
Anderson, Robert G., 211
Anderson, Robin, 389
Anderson, Walker E., 192
Anderson College, 69
Andrews, Eliza Frances, 269, 270
Anzilotti, Cara, xiii
Archibald, Katherine, 107
Arnot, Gemma, 388
Atkinson, Ron, 366

Printed in the USA
CPSIA information can be obtained
at www.ICGtesting.com
LVHW030024090124
768326LV00025B/1566